PARADE

The Best

OF
Walter Scott's
PERSONALITY PARADE

From the Fifties through the Nineties

THE SUMMIT PUBLISHING GROUP • ARLINGTON, TEXAS

THE SUMMIT PUBLISHING GROUP

One Arlington Centre

1112 E. Copeland Road, Fifth Floor

Arlington, Texas 76011

95   96   97   98   99   5   4   3   2   1

Printed in the United States

ISBN: 1-56530-150-1

Book design by David Sims

CONTENTS

FOREWORD

Nearly forty years ago—1957 to be precise—I wrote a series of personality profiles for *Parade*, the syndicated Sunday magazine.

In response to these articles, readers asked me to reveal further truths concerning some of the world's most publicized celebrities. They asked, for example, if Katharine Hepburn was living out of wedlock with Spencer Tracy, if General MacArthur hated General Eisenhower, if actress Marilyn Monroe was passed around for lunch in a Hollywood studio, if author Sinclair Lewis was an alcoholic. On and on it went. The questions were startling, as was the readers' hunger for truth.

I then suggested to Jess Gorkin, *Parade*'s editor at the time, that we publish a column devoted to separating fact from fiction, truth from rumor—that we tell, without libeling anyone named, what the readers wanted to know and probably could not find out on their own elsewhere. Jess agreed, and in March 1958, "Walter Scott's Personality Parade" appeared for the first time in *Parade*.

Readers wrote in by the thousands, asking mostly about show business personalities, leaders in government, well-known figures frequently in the public eye—in general, concerning men and women about whom they wanted to learn in full, or at least in part regarding a particular truth.

The "Personality Parade" feature became so popular that it was expanded to a full page. Soon newspapers and magazines throughout the world began copying and in some cases even plagiarizing it. The imitators still exist, but they lack the flavor of the original, largely I suspect because we at *Parade* spend more time, money, and energy chasing down the correct answers to the questions sent us by readers.

We now receive thousands of letters every week, and research and print answers as you will see in the pages ahead, arbitrarily chosen as some of the most interesting, informative, and stimulating from each of the thirty-six-plus years that the column has run as a weekly feature in *Parade*. We've gone from Katharine Hepburn and Spencer Tracy to the likes of O. J. Simpson and Nicole Brown Simpson, Arnold Schwarzenegger and Maria Shriver, and Michael Jackson and Lisa Marie Presley.

We published a "Personality Parade" anthology similar to this one in the early 1970s. But a lot has happened in the two decades since, thanks to a continuing parade of new stars, celebrities, and notables who continue to intrigue us. Another book of this type was long overdue, and I have no doubt you will treasure this volume from start to finish. As you proceed through this book, you will get an incredible taste and feel for the people, events, and trends of each particular era.

Over the years, "Personality Parade" has periodically evolved, mainly in the number of questions and answers and overall text length of each week's column. For the purpose of this book, we have utilized a standard page design that integrates photos and text. In a few places where a particular week's text ran "heavy," we took a few carefully selected liberties in removing a "low-profile" question/answer or two to make room for the photos. We believe we have produced a true kaleidoscope that makes use of nearly one thousand photos, giving you an up-close-and-personal view of how our world has aged and/or changed over the last thirty-six years.

Enjoy.

INTRODUCTION

I thought I knew what I was getting into when I accepted this opportunity to research thirty-six years' worth of the best of "Walter Scott's Personality Parade." Simple, right? Review almost two thousand weeks of selections featuring celebrities, political icons, and events that defined history. Then cull the three hundred most intriguing weeks for inclusion in this book. Put some eyedrops in to get the red out and call it a day. At the very least, it would be a nostalgic venture that would tickle the trivia buff in me.

This undertaking was all that and more. First of all, it was by no means a one-day job. It was much better than that, as I found myself spending several months soaking up all these wonderful pieces of history. From the time I was introduced to my first decade of photocopied *Parade* pages (actually, it started with 1959) to my final review in 1995, I enjoyed a thrilling ride through the last thirty-six years. Each page brought another surprise, making me thankful that I had been asked to be the editor for this fantastic and exciting project.

I was continually intrigued while reading about people and events unknown to me. For example, I kept running into references to the John Birch Society. Although I had occasionally heard of it while growing up, I really didn't know what kind of society it was. Now, upon further research, I do.

My favorite "Personality Parade" questions and answers were about those celebrities and events more familiar to me. For example, do you know why Carol Burnett would rub her finger under her nose or twitch an ear at the end of the *Garry Moore Show*? She did it as a code to let her relatives watching at home know that she was okay. That's one of hundreds of inside tips revealed in this book.

Other readers submitted question after question about political scandals, such as the issue of Princess Grace's absence from President Kennedy's funeral in 1963. Parade soothed our worries by answering that the princess had not snubbed our fallen leader—she simply arrived later to mourn at the president's grave. And did you know that there was a time when the motion picture producer's code forbade scenes of a couple in bed whether married or unmarried, clothed or nude? Then we get the movie *Basic Instinct*, in which Sharon Stone and Michael Douglas performed all those steamy scenes themselves, without the benefit of body doubles. Amazing!

This was the consummate trip down memory lane, and it was a trip that pulled my heartstrings at times. Readers' inquiries pertaining to the JFK assassination swept me back into my seat in a third-grade classroom, where a teacher broke the awful news to me and my classmates. Where were you when you heard of the Kennedy assassination? As the years went by, the pages turning in my hands, I reminisced about my years growing up, vividly recalling the many newsworthy events and people that shaped my childhood and adolescent memories. I fondly think back to the summer of my eighth-grade year, watching history unfold both back here in the United States at Woodstock, and a quarter million miles away, as Neil Armstrong in 1969 became the first human to set foot on the moon.

My review of the chronological unfolding of history as seen through "Personality Parade" unveiled numerous trends. For instance, many questions at a given time pertained to the monumental news events of the era, whether it be Watergate or the war in Vietnam. There was also an abundance of questions about world leaders and idols, such as JFK and Liz Taylor. Also evident through these pages was the American public's inquisitive fascination with material things and famous people's personal lives: "Does so-and-so wear a toupee?" "How much does he really make?" Or, "Will the marriage survive all of those affairs?"

There have been times in my life when I have daydreamed about the glamour of Hollywood or the simplicity of the fifties and early sixties, at times wishing I could return to that era of perceived innocence. After all, the fifties were about poodle skirts and bobby socks, a poofed beehive, and Elvis either swooning on the radio or gyrating on stage. Revolution in all spheres marked most of the sixties, a time of "make love, not war" and a president's assassination. As an adolescent during much of this era, I perceived it as a time of mass confusion and chaos. The seventies watched me step out into the world in a time defined by miniskirts, disco dancing and—please—polyester leisure suits.

The seventies also gave us Watergate and spawned a "we" generation that gave way to the "me" decade of the eighties. By then, Vietnam and Watergate were in the distant past, an actor was in the White House, and "Personality Parade" seemed to turn more of its attention to the entertainment industry. Finally, we arrive at the nineties, a time of politically influenced questions. Readers turned their attention to George Bush and Bill Clinton, instead of Marilyn Monroe and Liz Taylor. However, the one constant through all these turbulent and fascinating times was Jackie Kennedy, elegantly lending a sense of continuity to the years.

As you have probably figured out by now, I fell in love with "Walter Scott's Personality Parade." I returned in my mind to familiar faces, places, and events, and was constantly thrilled by the discovery of new facts and juicy gossip that somehow remains timeless. My personal perceptions of the last thirty-six years were sharpened. I came away with a richer understanding of recent history, documented so well by "Personality Parade." Hopes and dreams of each passing era have been captured here to preserve the public's focus. We can learn more about our history by investigating those people, events, and issues on which we place importance. "Personality Parade" celebrates our voracious and persevering curiosity, a quality I believe the American people will never lack.

—*Joanne Gavin*

1959
1960
1961
1962
1963
1964
1965
1966
1967
1968
1969

Shirley MacLaine

Prince Philip

Dinah Shore

Q *Actress Shirley MacLaine gets $15,000 a film. Yet I understand MGM had to pay $150,000 to get her for Ask Any Girl. Who gets the balance?—S.R., Long Island, N.Y.*

A Producer Hal Wallis, who owns her contract, loans Shirley out to other studios whenever he can—at a suitable profit.

Q *Would you please tell me how old actress Greer Garson is?—H.T., Miami, Fla.*

A Miss Garson is 50.

Q *I understand that Truman Capote is not the original name of the famous writer (Breakfast at Tiffany's). What is?—L.Y., New Orleans, La.*

A Truman Strecklflus Persons.

Q *Is it a fact that the late Robert Donat—a great actor—left his wife not one penny in his $70,000 will?—J.D., Fort Worth, Tex.*

A Yes. Donat stipulated that his money be divided among his three children: Joanna, 27, John, 25, and Brian, 22. Renee

Asherson, who was his second wife, was left nothing.

Q *I'm told Queen Elizabeth's husband, Prince Philip, has the greatest collection of guns in Europe, but that he can't hit the side of a barn. Is it true?—T.R., Newark, N.J.*

A The Prince owns an arsenal of guns—all embossed in gold with the letter "P." He used to be a terrible shot, but after much practice, he's improving.

Q *Is it true that Winston Churchill and the late President Roosevelt could have been murdered at the Casablanca Conference in 1943 because German Intelligence had been tipped off about the conference ahead of time?—P.I., Baton Rouge, La.*

A True. A Spanish agent of German Intelligence tipped off Berlin about the Conference. The Spanish interpreter in Berlin not only translated the message but also the word Casablanca (in Spanish, white house). The result: German Intelligence was led to believe that the Conference was being scheduled for the White House at Washington, D.C.

Q *I've heard a dozen rumors about Robert Cummings' age—and also*

about his special diet to help conceal it. How old is he really?—B.T., Lincoln, Neb.

A The TV comedian is 50.

Q *How do you account for Dinah Shore's tremendous success on TV, when she was such a flop in motion pictures?—F.T., Winchester, Tenn.*

A Dinah is more apt at projecting her own personality than those of fictional characterizations.

Winston Churchill

Marlon Brando

Jim Arness

Charles de Gaulle

Q *Can you tell me why it is that Marlon Brando registers in hotels under the name of Lord Greystoke? Does the name have any special significance?—A.T., Charleston, W. Va.*

A Lord Greystoke is supposedly the real name of Tarzan, the hero in the Tarzan books by Edgar Rice Burroughs. This is one of Brando's favorite fictional characters.

Q *What happened to Dimitri Shepilov, the former Soviet foreign minister who was supposed to be such a hot shot?—F.T., Newark, N.J.*

A Shepilov was exiled in the Malenkov purge to Kirghizia, in central Asia, where he is director of the Institute of Economics. The present Soviet administration currently exiles dissenters instead of shooting them, as happened in the Stalin regime.

Q *Can you tell me if all chiefs of staff of the United States Army must be graduates of West Point?—N.T., Washington, D.C.*

A Gen. George C. Marshall, former chief of staff, did not attend West Point. He is a graduate of the Virginia Military Institute. Most chiefs, however, do come from the Point, but there is no rule on this.

Q *Is it true that Jim Arness is tired of* Gunsmoke *and wants out? I'd like to know so I can settle a bet.—A.O., Tucson, Ariz.*

A Arness wants to leave the *Gunsmoke* TV series because he doesn't own a piece of the program; he is only under salary.

Q *Is it true that Audrey Hepburn turned down the Ingrid Bergman role in* The Inn of the Sixth Happiness *and Cary Grant the Bill Holden role in* The Bridge on the River Kwai?—*W.M., Lansing, Mich.*

A True.

Q *Japan's Prime Minister Nobusuke Kishi recently announced that most of the American troops had left his country. How many American troops still are in Japan?—J.T., Oakland, Calif.*

A About 60,000.

Q *I understand that General de Gaulle has had a law passed in France that requires all radiator ornaments on automobiles to be removed. Is this true; if so, what is the purpose?—L.T., Miami, Fla.*

A It is true. De Gaulle's transport minister says the edict is a safety measure.

Sophia Loren

Q *I read recently where Rome's public prosecutor charged actress Sophia Loren and her film producer-husband Carlo Ponti with bigamy. What exactly does this mean?—S.E., Fort Worth, Tex.*

A Italy recognizes Ponti's church wedding to his first wife, not his Mexican marriage to Miss Loren. If the bigamy charge is substantiated, it would mean exile from Italy for Miss Loren and Ponti for they would be arrested if they tried to return there.

WALTER SCOTT'S

PERSONALITY PARADE®

May 31, 1959

Pamela Churchill and Randolph Churchill

Susan Hayward

Willie Mays

Q *Is Randolph Churchill's ex-wife, Pamela, supposedly one of the great European beauties, marrying into the Rothschild family?—D.I., Detroit, Mich.*

A Pamela Churchill and Leon Lambert, a Belgian cousin of the Rothschilds, are said to be close friends.

Q *Is* The Steve Allen Show *definitely moving to Hollywood?—L.G., Newark, N.J.*

A Yes.

Q *Is it true that the Japanese are experimenting with atom-powered fishing boats?—F.Y., Miami, Fla.*

A Prof. Atsushi Takagi, one of Japan's leading naval architects, says his country will have atom-powered trawlers in 10 years. She has none now.

Q *Why has Susan Hayward's film,* I Want to Live, *been banned in England?—V.O., Fort Worth, Tex.*

A John Trevelyan, secretary of the British Board of Film Censors, has offered the film an "X" censorship certificate, meaning suitable "for adults only," if the execution scenes are deleted. Says Mr.

Trevelyan: "We have never allowed details of an execution, whether by rope, gas or electric chair. We have always felt that taking life by execution is not a fit subject for entertainment."

Q *How tall, how old, how wealthy is dance teacher Arthur Murray?—F.M., Beaumont, Tex.*

A Murray is 5' 10 1/2" tall, was born on April 4, 1895, is a millionaire several times over.

Q *How come Danny Kaye has not had a real money-maker of a picture in years?—D.Y., Baton Rouge, La.*

A He has one coming up in *The Five Pennies.*

Q *Is Jean Simmons married to actor James Stewart?—L.I., New Bedford, Mass.*

A Jean is married to actor Stewart Granger, whose real name is James Stewart. He took a stage name to avoid conflicting with Jimmy Stewart.

Q *Is it true that Willie Mays, who earns $80,000 a year playing for the San Francisco Giants, lives on a small weekly budget?—K.Y., Oakland, Calif.*

A Mays lives on $300 a week. The remainder of his salary goes to investments and taxes.

Q *I have been told that the Jeremiah Milbank family of New York has more money than the Rockefellers and Fords combined. Is this true?—G.U., Flushing, N.Y.*

A The Milbank family controls the least publicized big American fortune. It is estimated at $125,000,000. However, this is considerably less than the combined fortunes of the Rockefellers and Fords.

Q *Is it true that Robert Montgomery and James Cagney own the forthcoming film,* The Admiral Halsey Story?—*L.T., San Diego, Calif.*

James Cagney

A No. However, instead of salaries they will get 75 percent of the net proceeds. United Artists is supplying the production money, approximately $950,000.

Richard Nixon

Dwight Eisenhower

Charles Lindbergh

Q *I've heard that Vice President Nixon frequently shaves as often as three times a day. Is this true?—F.Q., Washington, D.C.*

A Yes, when he has to make public appearances.

Q *I understand that in 1957 comedian Sid Caesar asked to be released from his contract with NBC, guaranteeing him $100,000 a year, even though it had another seven years to run. Why did Caesar do this, and what is he doing now?—D.P., Denver, Colo.*

A Caesar was unhappy at NBC because officials didn't want him to continue his one-hour weekly TV program. They suggested he limit his appearances to four spectaculars a year. Caesar has now signed with CBS for six one-hour comedy specials, plus a United States Steel program scheduled for October 21.

Q *Is it true that Loretta Young's husband recently committed suicide?—M.S., Newark, N.J.*

A Her first husband, Grant Withers, recently took his life. Tom Lewis, her second husband, from whom she is separated, is very much alive.

Q *Can President Eisenhower put any of our atom bombs up for sale?—F.L., Miami, Fla.*

A U.S. atom bombs are for sale for peaceful purposes. One atom bomb 30 inches in diameter can be bought for $500,000, providing the AEC and other government agencies okay the sale.

Q *Arthur Flemming, Secretary of Health, Education and Welfare, predicts that the cost of a college education will go up 33 percent in the next four years. How much has it jumped in the last four?—E.M., Erie, Pa.*

A Approximately 33 percent.

Q *How much, if anything, do baseball players like Stan Musial and Duke Snider get for appearing on those bubble-gum baseball cards?—G.R., Jackson, Miss.*

A Royalties of $125 a year.

Q *Would you settle a bet? Was Charles Lindbergh the first man to fly the Atlantic?—P.S., Fort Wayne, Ind.*

A No. The first were Sir John Alcock and Sir Arthur Brown, who flew from

St. John's, Newfoundland, to Clifden, Ireland, in 1919. Lindbergh was the first to do it alone.

Q *I read that Joan Crawford was broke. Can this be true?—A.N., Fresno, Calif.*

A No. Miss Crawford gets $60,000 a year from the Pepsi-Cola Company and has extensive real estate holdings in Los Angeles.

Joan Crawford

Fabian

Dorothy Dandridge

Charles de Gaulle

Q *I understand that practically every top pop singer has his recordings souped up via various electric gimmicks. Is this true of Elvis Presley, Fabian, and Ricky Nelson?*—G.P., Oakland, Calif.

A Presley, Fabian, and Nelson have been helped considerably by recording engineers. Some of these engineers are so talented they can make even the most miserable voices sound acceptable on a recording.

Q *What connection does Ellen Rice of Houston, Texas, have with Howard Hughes?*—B.L., Fort Worth, Tex.

A She was the first Mrs. Howard Hughes.

Q *Is it true that Bethlehem Steel Corporation pays its president and executives higher salaries and bonuses than any other company in America?*—R.O., Scranton, Pa.

A Bethlehem's president Arthur B. Homer has been the nation's top-paid corporation executive, with $511,249 paid to him last year. Recently a minority group of stockholders filed a lawsuit in Delaware charging Bethlehem with excessive pay for its officials. The lawsuit

was withdrawn when the company announced it would lower its annual compensation to officers.

Q *I've been told that Dorothy Dandridge, Lena Horne, and Harry Belafonte are all married to members of the white race. Can you confirm or deny?*—C.S., Yakima, Wash.

A Confirm.

Q *President Eisenhower is reputedly a millionaire. Is Vice President Nixon one, too?*—L.S., Washington, D.C.

A No. Nixon owns a $75,000 house in Washington, D.C., and is paying off a $50,000 mortgage at 5 percent. He has $10,000 in government bonds, owns no stock and lives on the salary he is paid as Vice President.

Q *I have heard Kathy Grant, who married Bing Crosby, described by four different Hollywood actresses as "calculating." Why is this?*—O.T., Wheeling, W. Va.

A Sounds like sour grapes. Kathy won Bing, and they're just jealous.

Q *Is it on the level that President Charles de Gaulle has refused to let us build rocket bases in France?*—P.E., San Bernardino, Calif.

A Yes. De Gaulle wants exclusive French control of all rocket bases in France.

Q *How come so fine an actor as Cary Grant has never won an Academy Award?*—G.P., Newark, N.J.

A For two reasons: Grant has played in many comedies, which are seldom dramatically memorable; he is not particularly popular with his voting colleagues.

Q *Were Gregory Peck, Frank Sinatra, Marlon Brando, and Montgomery Clift in the service in World War II, or is it true that they were all classified as 4-F, physically disabled?*—M.Y., Miami, Fla.

A All were classified 4-F.

Montgomery Clift

Anthony Eden

Benito Mussolini

Jill St. John

Q *Is it true that Anthony Eden has already been paid $300,000 by an American publisher for 40 percent of his memoirs?*—V.P., Newark, N.J.

A An American magazine has paid that sum for an excerpt from *The Memoirs of Sir Anthony Eden,* which Houghton, Mifflin will publish next year.

Q *I understand that Loretta Young is a descendant of the great Mormon leader Brigham Young. I understand that Rhonda Fleming and Laraine Day are also Mormons. Is Loretta one, too?*—K.P., Provo, Utah.

A Miss Young is a Roman Catholic, Miss Day and Miss Fleming are of the Mormon faith.

Q *I've been told that since his marriage to Elizabeth Taylor, Eddie Fisher cannot find a major sponsor on television. Is this on the level?*—C.R., Boston, Mass.

A Many agents say it is substantially true at the moment but that the situation will change. Fisher's TV program last year was not the highest-rated show on the air, and it is difficult to tell whether sponsors are shy of him for that reason or because of his marriage to Miss Taylor and

its effect on the public.

Q *Can you tell me who now occupies the lovely Roman villa Mussolini once bought for his mistress, Clara Petacci?*—H.S., Columbus, Ohio.

A The villa has been turned into one of Rome's most fashionable and expensive restaurants.

Q *Can it be true that stage producer Leland Hayward plans to divorce his wife and marry Pamela Churchill, ex-wife of Randolph Churchill?*—L.G., Jamaica, N.Y.

A Long Island society is buzzing with the rumor, but all three parties concerned deny comment at this point.

Q *One of the greatest manhunts has been for Adolf Eichmann, the Nazi in charge of the Gestapo's Jewish department. He was the man who supervised the extermination of 6 million European Jews. He changed his identity after the war and disappeared. Has anyone traced him?*—E.O., Fort Worth, Tex.

A The Israeli radio station in Tel Aviv recently announced that Eichmann is now working as an oil company

employee in the Persian Gulf sheikdom of Kuwait.

Q *What is the real name of Jill St. John, who is engaged to marry Lance Reventlow, an heir to the Woolworth millions?*—L.S., Washington, D.C.

A Jill Oppenheim.

Q *Have Herbert Marshall, Cole Porter, and sports announcer Bill Stern each had one leg amputated?*—E.F., Buffalo, N.Y.

A Yes.

Q *I've heard a rumor that too much swimming has caused Esther Williams to lose her hair and that she now wears a wig. True or false?*—B.P., Erie, Pa.

A False.

Esther Williams

WALTER SCOTT'S

PERSONALITY PARADE®

December 13, 1959

Marx Brothers

Lucille Ball and Desi Arnaz

David Garroway

Q *Does Groucho Marx use writers on his quiz program,* You Bet Your Life?—*C.P., Oakland, Calif.*

A Yes, but Howard Harris and Hy Freedman are not listed as writers. They are called members of the "program staff."

Q *Since the days of Al Capone up until the present, there have been more than 900 gang murders in Chicago. Can you reveal how many of these gunmen have been caught and convicted?—L.S., Peoria, Ill.*

A Many have been caught, only 17 convicted according to Cook County criminal records.

Q *Almost every day I read of a new Air Force plane crash. How many accidents has the U.S. Air Force had, say, since 1950?—W.P., Harrisburg, Pa.*

A Accidents since 1950 have cost the U.S. Air Force as of this writing, 7,062 planes and 3,471 pilots, largest losses of any country except Russia.

Q *Has Fidel Castro ever been married?—S.L., Miami, Fla.*

A Castro was married to Mirta Diaz Balart in 1948. She is the mother of his son, Fidel Jr. Mrs. Castro divorced the Cuban revolutionary after he had served a prison term for his unsuccessful revolt of 1953.

Q *I understand the Lucille Ball-Desi Arnaz marriage is not a happy one. Is a divorce imminent?—F.M., Fort Worth, Tex.*

A This marriage is experiencing many stresses, many strains, may eventually come apart when and if Lucy and Desi can liquidate their extensive TV holdings.

Q *I understand that actor Jackie Coogan is broke today after earning $7,000,000 as a child star. What happened?—D.P., Denver, Colo.*

A Coogan earned $7,000,000 as a child star. Later he sued for his share of his earnings, had to settle for $200,000. After legal fees and expenses, he ended up with $30,000. As a result the California legislature has passed a law making it mandatory for a share of the earnings of each child star to be deposited in the court's custody.

Q *The* Today *TV program featuring David Garroway—is it true that* Today *is video-taped yesterday?—V.R., Boston, Mass.*

A Much of it is.

Q *There is a very famous anecdote involving Oscar Levant and his first wife, Barbara Smith. Can you print it?—S.N., Washington, D.C.*

A Oscar's first wife was Barbara Smith, a musical comedy star who married Arthur Loew the theater magnate. Shortly after Mr. and Mrs. Loew returned from their honeymoon, Levant phoned his ex-wife at two in the morning. "How dare you wake me up at this hour!" his former wife stormed. Oscar said, "But I have a very important question." She said, "Yes?" And he said, "What's playing at Loew's 86th Street tomorrow?"

Q *Was Sen. John F. Kennedy's book,* Profiles in Courage, *for which he accepted a Pulitzer Prize, ghost-written?—J.N., Hampton, Va.*

A It was not.

WALTER SCOTT'S

PERSONALITY PARADE®

December 27, 1959

Anna Magnani

Hiram Fong

Nelson Rockefeller

Q *Is there a feud between Marlon Brando and Anna Magnani?*—G.P., Newark, N.J.

A After their last film together, it's doubtful whether each will work with the other again.

Q *What is the famous crack made by Hermione Gingold concerning Arthur Murray?*—C.Y., Chicago, Ill.

A Miss Gingold looked at Murray, a tall, lean, cadaverous-type man, and reportedly said, "Are you alive—or just taped?"

Q *Is it true that the name "Uncle Sam," now used in reference to the United States, was based on a real person?*—N.E., Tucson, Ariz.

A Yes, Samuel Wilson of Troy, N.Y., a provisioner for the U.S. Army in the War of 1812, stamped his barrels of beef and pork with the letters, "U.S." An employee, asked what the initials stood for, shrugged and said, "Uncle Sam, I think." The story spread.

Q *Can you reveal how much voting power the Ford family retains in the Ford Motor Co.?*—R.L., Detroit, Mich.

A 40 percent.

Q *Senator Hiram Fong, the millionaire lawyer representing the State of Hawaii in the U.S. Senate—is he the first person of Chinese descent to sit in the upper house of Congress?*—E.P., Portland, Ore.

A Yes. A Congressional colleague of Fong's, also from Hawaii, Daniel Inouye is the first person of Japanese descent to sit in the House of Representatives.

Q *Is it true that if a motion picture critic panned one of his films, the late Cecil B. DeMille used to have the critic investigated for possible communist affiliations?*—G.P., Oakland, Calif.

A Yes. In many ways DeMille was a small man.

Q *Have President Eisenhower and ex-President Truman ever met face to face since Ike took office, or is their feud still in effect?*—H.E., Washington, D.C.

A They met for the first time in more than six years at the funeral of their mutual friend and colleague, General of the Army George Marshall. They murmured cordial greetings, went their separate ways. Between these two proud, sensitive men, the so-called "feud" is still "on."

Q *Can you tell me if Governor Nelson Rockefeller has on his political staff the same men who backed Eisenhower for the presidency?*—H.M., Newark, N.J.

A Rockefeller has on his team Judson Morhouse, N.Y. State Republican Chairman, R. Birdell Bixby, law partner of Thomas E. Dewey, Russel Sprague, Long Island GOP leader, Emmet J. Hughes, former adviser and speech writer for Eisenhower, Hugh Morrow, another speech writer, and other experts from the Eisenhower campaign.

Q *Ever since Jean Peters supposedly married Howard Hughes, nothing has been heard of her. What's happened to the girl?*—L.P., Columbus, Ohio.

A Affairs and persons connected with Howard Hughes are always shrouded in mystery. Miss Peters' whereabouts are currently unknown.

Q *Senator Kennedy of Massachusetts was a World War II hero, also his brothers. Can you tell me what Peter Lawford, the Senator's brother-in-law, did in World War II? Was he in the British or the U.S. Army?*—F.P., Boston, Mass.

A Actor Lawford saw no military service.

Pearl Buck

John Wayne

Princess Margaret

Q *When Pearl Buck heard that she had won the Nobel Prize for literature, the story is that the first words she uttered were: "O pu sing sin." Is the legend true? If so, what do these Chinese words mean?—Morris Wiener, Miami, Fla.*

A The story is true. The sentence means, "I don't believe it."

Q *Can you tell me how old Dorothy Thompson is and whether she is recognized as America's outstanding female journalist?—Venetia Conklin, Chicago, Ill.*

A Dorothy Thompson was born on July 9, 1894. In the 1940s she was regarded as the U.S. woman journalist with the most prestige. She gave up her newspaper column, but still writes a monthly article for the *Ladies' Home Journal.*

Q *Florenz Ziegfeld introduced many beautiful and talented women to the public, among them Nora Bayes, Fanny Brice and his wife, Billie Burke. What were the real names of these women, and when did they first appear in the Ziegfeld Follies?—F.L., Newark, N.J.*

A Nora Bayes—real name: Leonora Goldberg; appeared: 1907. Fanny Brice—real name: Fanny Borach;

appeared: 1910. Billie Burke—real name: Mary Burke; she was married to Ziegfeld in 1914, never appeared in a *Follies* production.

Q *Does John Wayne wear a hairpiece in movies? Is that also true of Jimmy Stewart?—M.N., Marion, S.C.*

A True of both actors when before the cameras.

Q *Does anyone know the exact rate of population growth and how many people there will be on this earth say 100 years from today?—Arthur Enright, New York, N.Y.*

A In 1950 the world population was about 2.5 billion. The present doubling rate (once every 50 years) means that by the year 2000 there will be 5 billion people, by the year 2050 there will be 10 billion.

Q *Would you please detail Frank Sinatra's connection with the notorious Fischetti mob of Chicago?—P.T., Buffalo, N.Y.*

A Sinatra has on occasion been seen with one of the Fischettis, but otherwise has no known connection with them.

Q *Antony Armstrong-Jones of Princess Margaret fame—did he have a trade or any formal education before he became the photographer of royalty?—Lois McKendrick, Oakland, Calif.*

A Mr. Antony Armstrong-Jones was educated at Cambridge, studied architecture, failed several exams in the subject. He dabbled in clothes design and interior decoration before taking up photography.

Q *Darryl Zanuck helped to discover such stars as Marilyn Monroe, Peggy Cummins, Bela Darvi, Juliette Greco and dozens more. Which is his favorite?—G.L., Hollywood, Calif.*

A According to Zanuck, "the best star I ever had was the late Rin Tin Tin."

Darryl Zanuck

Herbert Hoover

Shelley Winters

Marlon Brando

Q *I understand that when Herbert Hoover was president he refused to accept any salary. Is this true?—Clyde French, Miami, Fla.*

A Hoover when in the public service, both as secretary of commerce and president, earmarked all his salary for charities and public service activities. He did the same in 1958 with the $25,000 annual pension voted by Congress to former presidents.

Q *How much does Natalie Wood get for a motion picture? How much does her husband make?—Norma Kositcheck, Chicago, Ill.*

Natalie Wood

A Natalie: $150,000 a film; husband Bob Wagner: $75,000.

Q *Which one of President Roosevelt's children has been divorced the most?—Fred Kline, Denver, Colo.*

A Elliott Roosevelt.

Q *Is it true that in America the rich are getting richer and the poor poorer?—*

Harry Conklin, London, Eng.

A The rich are getting richer, according to a survey by the National Bureau of Economic Research, but so are the poor.

Q *Could you tell me what Shelley Winters' real name is?—T.R., Brooklyn, N.Y.*

A Shirley Schrift.

Q *Is it true that Senator Kennedy disagrees violently with his father, Joe Kennedy, on domestic and foreign politics?—Maude Collins, Boston, Mass.*

A According to the Senator: "My father has a wholly different view of what role the U.S. should play in the world from the one I've had in the 14 years I've been in Congress."

Q *Can you tell me how many R.A.F. pilots took part in the Battle of Britain in World War II and how many of these are still alive?—Kenneth Moore, Toronto, Can.*

A Approximately 2,500 pilots helped save Great Britain. Of this number about 320 are still alive and now in middle age.

Q *What wise man said: "It is not the lack of love but the lack of friendship*

which makes unhappy marriages"?—Natasha Pearlson, Oakland, Calif.

A The German philosopher, Nietszche.

Q *Can you reveal the name of Marlon Brando's secret French sweetheart?—J.N., Fort Worth, Tex.*

A French starlet Renee Dinah, who resembles Brando's former wife, Anna Kashfi.

Q *Is it true that Alec Guinness was offered $500,000 to play Jesus Christ in a movie and turned it down?—Betty Dinston, Washington, D.C.*

A True.

Q *Helen Hayes recently returned to the Catholic Church. When did she ever leave it?—Brian O'Brien, Boston, Mass.*

Helen Hayes

A The 59-year-old First Lady of the American theater was brought up in the Catholic faith but left the Church in 1928 when she married the divorced playwright, Charles MacArthur, who died four years ago.

WALTER SCOTT'S
PERSONALITY PARADE®

August 28, 1960

Audrey Hepburn

Lana Turner

Walter Winchell

Harpo Marx

Q *Can you tell me what Audrey Hepburn named her baby and its weight at birth?—Elaine Davis, Peoria, Ill.*

A Sean Ferrer. The baby weighed nine pounds.

Q *I've been told that business is so good in Konrad Adenauer's West Germany that the government there is recruiting overseas workers. Is this correct?—James Easterling, Erie, Pa.*

A There is practically no unemployment in West Germany today. The result is that the government is seeking skilled workers from nearby countries.

Q *Could you tell me how long TV's Ed Sullivan has been married to the same woman?—K.L., Port Chester, N.Y.*

A Thirty years.

Q *Is it true that Fidel Castro is one of Cuba's greatest Casanovas?—B.F., Daytona Beach, Fla.*

A Where women are concerned Cuban dictator Castro reputedly is not backward.

Q *What's happened to Lana Turner's daughter, Cheryl Crane, the one who ran away from that Los Angeles County School for Girls?—D.T., Boston, Mass.*

A Cheryl Crane, at this writing, is back at the El Retiro School for Girls at Sylmar, California, under court supervision.

Q *Of the so-called "Big Three" of psychoanalysis—Freud, Adler, Jung—which developed the "introvert-extrovert" and "inferiority complex" concepts?—Carol Byron, Miami, Fla.*

A Dr. Carl Jung, 85, last living member of the Big Three.

Q *How many Nazi war criminals are still at large in the Argentine?—Milton Golden, Ellenville, N.Y.*

A The reply of President Frondizi of the Argentine: "I cannot say. I do not know. I am not the chief of police, but merely president."

Q *Who is the most successful female playwright in America?—Frances Reynolds, Columbia, S.C.*

A Many critics favor playwright Lillian Hellman, author of *The Little Foxes*,

The Children's Hour, Watch on the Rhine and the current prize-winner *Toys in the Attic*.

Q *Why does Walter Winchell always wear a hat? Is it because he's bald or because he's a newspaperman?—J.Y., Chicago, Ill.*

A Because he's a bald newspaperman.

Q *Would you please list the real names of the Marx Brothers?—Frank Litchek, Minneapolis, Minn.*

A Chico (Leonard), Groucho (Julius), Harpo (Adolph), Gummo (Milton) and Zeppo (Herbert).

Richard Nixon

Eliot Ness

Louis Armstrong

Q *Vice President Nixon and Sen. John Kennedy—has either of these two ever worked for a living in a non-government job?—A.Y., Dayton, Ohio.*

A Kennedy was a newspaper correspondent, Nixon a practicing attorney for a short time before each went to Congress.

Q *What ever happened to screen star Jean Arthur? I see her old movies on television all the time.—Claire Reed, Beaumont, Tex.*

A Jean Arthur has retired from films, lives in Carmel, California.

Q *Wasn't Eliot Ness, on whose crime-busting career The Untouchables is based, once mayor of Cleveland?—Jack Roster, Youngstown, Ohio.*

A The late Eliot Ness ran unsuccessfully for mayor of Cleveland on the Republican ticket in 1948. Before that, he investigated corruption in the Cleveland police department, forced 200 resignations, sent many top officials to state prison.

Q *Was Anatomy of a Murder with James Stewart and Lee Remick based on a real murder case, or are the book*

and film pure fiction?—F.P., Holland, Michigan.

A Mrs. Hazel Wheeler of Three Rivers, Michigan, recently filed a $9-million libel suit against Dell Publishing Co. and Columbia Pictures alleging that *Anatomy of a Murder* was a true story. The suit claims that John Voelker, who wrote the book under the pseudonym of Robert Traver, had been the real-life defense attorney who won an acquittal for a Lieut. Coleman Peterson, accused of murdering Mrs. Wheeler's tavern-owning husband, Maurice Chenoweth.

Q *Which First Lady was the youngest in the White House?—E.K. Donlon, El Cajon, Calif.*

A Frances Folsom was 22 when she married President Grover Cleveland in the White House in 1886.

Q *How old is Louis Armstrong? How many wives has he had?—Natalie Grudsen, Milwaukee, Wis.*

A Trumpet-player Armstrong, 60, has had four wives.

John Kennedy

Prince Rainier

Jane Fonda

Nikita Khrushchev

Q *Is it true that Prince Rainier plans to drum up business for his Monaco by staging an international television festival at Monte Carlo?—Peter Owens, Chicago, Ill.*

A True; first festival starts in November.

Q *Can anyone tell me what has happened to Barbara Payton, once married to actor Franchot Tone?—Lurlean Kemp, Los Angeles, Calif.*

A Miss Payton was recently divorced from her third husband, George Provan. She has been living in Searchlight, Nev.

Q *What proof is there that the riots in Japan against Eisenhower's visit last spring were Communist-inspired?—H.T., Ft. Worth, Tex.*

A The Japanese government has on hand a long secret report from its security authorities, revealing that 300 Japanese Communists, aged 30 to 45, and trained in revolutionary technique in China, have taken over control of subversive activity in Japan. Their job is to inflame the current mood of neutralism in Japan against the United States. Twenty

of these men—the Japanese code word for them is *Gakushu*—masterminded the Tokyo demonstrations that canceled out President Eisenhower's intended visit.

Q *How many times has Henry Fonda been married? Who is the mother of his actress-daughter Jane, and where is she?—L. Bornke, Chicago, Ill.*

A Four times. Fonda's second wife, Frances, who took her own life, was the mother of Jane Fonda.

Q *What are the correct figures on how many men we have in our Army and how many are stationed overseas?—George Cobbold, Detroit, Mich.*

A As of this writing the Army consists of 870,000 men, 63 percent of whom are stationed overseas.

Q *Can you tell me if Richard Greene, the actor who plays Robin Hood on television, is married or single?—Marion Cooke, Toronto, Ont.*

A Greene married Mrs. Beatriz Robledo Summers, a South American million-heiress on July 28, 1960.

Q *I read that Khrushchev buys all his personal guns in London. Don't they manufacture sidearms in Russia?—John Chapin, Washington, D.C.*

A Khrushchev recently purchased from James Purdey, a London gunsmith, a pair of double-barreled sporting guns for duck hunting. They cost him approximately $3,000 and were quietly ordered through the Soviet Embassy in London. The Russians do manufacture sidearms.

Q *Who in show business is really named Daniel Kuminsky?—Geraldine Fisher, Buffalo, N.Y.*

A Comic Danny Kaye.

Danny Kaye

Allen Dulles

Lawrence Welk

Q *I read that Allen Dulles, chief of the Central Intelligence Agency, picks all his aides from the Ivy League colleges. Is this correct?—F.P., Baton Rouge, La.*

A A recent check showed that most of Mr. Dulles' top 20 aides are graduates of Yale, Harvard or Princeton. Mr. Dulles is a Princeton alumnus.

Q *What's happened to Dr. Klaus Fuchs, the scientist who was imprisoned in British jails for nine years for passing atom secrets to the Russians? I know he was discharged from prison, but is he working for the Russians?—Kenneth Townes, Washington, D.C.*

A Fuchs is working for the Communists in East Germany.

Q *Do you know anything about a film called* Black Tights? *Isn't it being made secretly?—Lyle Hansen, Chicago, Ill.*

A *Black Tights* is no secret. It is a film now being shot in Europe, which consists of four original sexy-type ballets by Roland Petit. It has an international cast starring Petit's wife, Zizi Jeanmaire from Paris, Cyd Charisse from Hollywood and Moira Shearer from London.

Q *Is Cyrus Eaton, the millionaire from Cleveland, a member of the social register?—Ames Salisbury, Chicago, Ill.*

A Eaton has been dropped from the 1961 Social Register, reportedly because of his friendship with Nikita Khrushchev. The mining tycoon gave a large lunch for Mr. K in New York earlier this year.

Q *How old is bandleader Lawrence Welk?—Lona Greenson, Newark, N.J.*

A Welk is 57.

Q *How come married men always fall in love with actress Lauren Bacall? Actor Jason Robards plans to marry her as soon as his divorce is final. To whom was actor Humphrey Bogart married when he started going with Bacall?—N.Y., Pasadena, Calif.*

A Bogart was married to actress Mayo Methot when he first met Miss Bacall.

Q *I understand that because of sodium fluoride in the water there, the children of Jacksonville, Florida, have no tooth decay. Is this true?—Harold Waters, Saginaw, Mich.*

A Dr. Floyd DeCamp, director of the Florida Bureau of Dental Health, claims that a study reveals that 45 percent of the children who have lived in Jacksonville since birth never suffered tooth decay. Jacksonville water has a high level of fluoride.

Q *Which is the biggest baby month?— George Hopkins, Portland, Ore.*

A During the past 10 years, the average points to the month of August.

Q *Can you publish or identify the first female medical student in the U.S.?—Brian Thomas, Fort Worth, Tex.*

A Elizabeth Blackwell, who entered the Medical Institution, Geneva, New York, on October 20, 1847.

Q *Why is it that Copenhagen, Denmark, has never had any polio cases? Isn't this because Danish medicine is better than ours?—G.F., Rye, N.Y.*

A According to Dr. H. E. Knipschildt, Copenhagen has sporadically experienced attacks of infantile paralysis. For the past year and a half, however, the city has had no reported polio cases. Its immunization program was begun several years ago.

Q *How old is J. Edgar Hoover? How tall? How much does he weigh?— G.P., Washington, D.C.*

A Hoover at 65 is just under six feet, weighs 170.

Q *How many of the Congo people are college graduates?—B.O., Miami, Fla.*

A Fewer than 50.

J. Edgar Hoover

Queen Elizabeth

Lloyd Bridges

Vivien Leigh

Q *Is it true that the Queen of England never wears the same dress twice in public?—Betsy Wales, Lincoln, Neb.*

A No. Queen Elizabeth has worn the same dress on occasions.

Q *Is it true that David Lloyd George, England's prime minister in World War I, was a woman chaser?—Helen Crenshaw, Los Angeles, Calif.*

A Says Richard Lloyd George, his son: "My father was probably the greatest natural Don Juan in the history of British politics. His entire life, including the 53 years of marriage with my mother, was involved with a series of affairs with women, some romantic, some deeply obsessive, some cynical and worldly, and most of them fruitful."

Q *Which college has provided America with the most presidents?—Bill Gershorn, Boston, Mass.*

A Harvard. It has given us the two Adamses, the two Roosevelts, and President-elect Kennedy.

Q *How old is Lloyd Bridges, star of* Sea Hunt? *Is he married?—Dora Albin, Newark, N.J.*

A Lloyd Bridges is 47 and married. He and his wife Dorothy have three children, Lloyd, 18; Cindy, 17; Jeff, 10.

Q *How old is Vivien Leigh? Is it true, now that Sir Laurence Olivier is divorcing her, that she has already picked out a third husband?—Clare Williamson, Detroit, Mich.*

A Vivien Leigh, 47, has been seeing a good deal of John Merivale, 42, Canadian-born actor.

Q *Can you tell me why the works of Victor Hugo are included in the Index, the list of books Roman Catholics are forbidden to read?—T.P., Santa Fe, N.M.*

A Victor Hugo held strong anti-clerical opinions. The present pope, however, has ordered a special commission to revise the Index. It is expected that of the 5,000 titles on the list, approximately 2,500, including the works of Victor Hugo, will be removed.

Q *Was the late Errol Flynn a dope addict? Is that why he was turned down for military service?—H.G., Pasadena, Calif.*

A Flynn was a dope addict. But his addiction began after he was rejected for military service because of a heart murmur.

Errol Flynn

WALTER SCOTT'S
PERSONALITY PARADE®

December 25, 1960

Clark Gable

Syngman Rhee

Gamal Abdel Nasser

Jacqueline Kennedy

Q *Were the first two wives of the late Clark Gable younger or older than he?*—Avis Giles, Chicago, Ill.

A Both older.

Q *Is it true that Arlene Dahl's new husband, Christopher Holmes, is the owner of the world's largest ranch?*—Merle Moncrief, Hobbs, N.M.

A Holmes is part owner of a 2,175,000-acre ranch in Paraguay. This ranch is said to be the biggest enclosed ranch in the world.

Q *Is Brigitte Bardot really man-crazy?*—Carol Gertz, Newark, N.J.

A Like many motion-picture actresses, she prefers the companionship of men.

Q *What's happened to Dr. Syngman Rhee of Korea?*—Myrtle Hunt, Tucson, Ariz.

A At this writing the 85-year-old former Korean president is living in luxurious exile on Oahu, Hawaii, as guest of Mr. and Mrs. Wilbert Choi of Honolulu. Dr. Rhee refuses to discuss with newsmen the recent happenings in Korea. It is said that he has a tacit understanding with the U.S. State Department not to grant interviews or discuss Korean internal politics.

Q *Isn't it true that President-elect Kennedy's wife has been married twice? Wasn't her first husband, Michael Canfield, private secretary to former U.S. Ambassador Winthrop Aldrich in London?*—G.P., Washington, D.C.

A No, you are mistaking Mrs. Kennedy for her sister, Princess Lee Radziwill, who has been married twice, first to Michael Canfield and now to Prince Stanislaw Radziwill, who arrived in London after the war, a virtually penniless Polish refugee. Mrs. John F. Kennedy, the former Jacqueline Bouvier, has been married only once.

Q *How close is President Nasser to completing the Aswan Dam?*—Bertram Kerns, Detroit, Mich.

A According to informed sources, Nasser has been having trouble with Russian technicians in Egypt, can't possible hope to complete the dam before 1970 unless he gets help from the Western democracies.

PERSONALITY PARADE®

January 8, 1961

Lady Bird Johnson

Elizabeth Taylor

Mohandas K. Gandhi

Q *Everyone calls Mrs. Lyndon Johnson "Lady Bird." What is her real name and where did she get that nickname?— Edith Bird, Baton Rouge, La.*

A Mrs. Johnson, born in Karnack, Texas, on December 22, 1912, was christened Claudia Alta Taylor. She acquired her nickname from the Taylor family maid when she was a baby. When she entered St. Mary's Episcopal School for Girls in Dallas, she wanted to use the name Claudia. But old friends insisted upon calling her Lady Bird. The Johnsons have two daughters, Lynda Bird and Lucy Baines, and the family home is known as the LBJ Ranch, initials of all the family members.

Q *Before anyone goes to work for the British Royal Family, does he have to sign a contract agreeing not to publish any information about the Royal Family acquired during service?—Fred Hartwig, Portland, Ore.*

A Yes. This agreement between employer and employee was put into effect after World War II when a Royal governess wrote a book about the young princesses, Elizabeth and Margaret. Recently the Queen Mother obtained a High Court injunction against an ex-foot-

man who was proposing to publish his memoirs.

Q *On a movie like* Cleopatra, *with Elizabeth Taylor, how much is the insurance premium?—F. Lertsy, Oakland, Calif.*

A Somewhere between $300,000 and $400,000.

Q *Is it true that years ago Lena Horne and Pearl Bailey both danced in the same chorus line?—Rachel Flowers, New York, N.Y.*

A Yes, in 1933 at the old Cotton Club in Harlem.

Q *Is John Wayne a grandfather?—Dick Ely, Reno, Nev.*

A Yes, he has four grandchildren.

John Wayne

Q *Who is the author of the following quotation: "There is more to life than increasing its speed"?—Arthur Hanley, Fort Worth, Tex.*

A Mohandas K. Gandhi.

Q *I understand that one of the richest men in the world is Charles Stewart Mott of Flint, Michigan. Who is he?— Joseph Piotrowski, Los Angeles, Calif.*

A Mott, 85, is one of the few surviving automotive pioneers. He has been a director of General Motors since 1913, owns 2,458,000 shares of that company. His dividend income from General Motors approximates $5 million a year. At the turn of the century he started to manufacture bicycle wheels. Later he switched to auto wheels. In 1909 he sold a 45-percent interest in his firm for $1,481,000 worth of GM stock.

Q *Is Robin Hood a true or fictional character?—Frank Folsen, Boston, Mass.*

A There is evidence that Robin Hood was an Englishman who lived in the early 14th century. The first ballad about him, called "A Lytell Geste of Robyn Hode," was printed in 1495.

Nikita Khrushchev

Alan Paton

Q *Is it true that Khrushchev possesses details of West Germany's defense plans through 1963?—C.S., Miami, Fla.*

A Yes. The information was contained in a document known as "MC-70," which was passed to the Russians by a German parliamentary deputy, a member of the Russian espionage ring operating in West Germany.

Q *Did Wernher von Braun invent the rocket propulsion system used by the Nazis in their V-2 bombs?—Clayton Wile, Oakland, Calif.*

A No. The system was devised by Dr. Rudolf Nebel of Germany, who began to work on it in 1930. Nebel took out the first patent on fluid propulsion. Later, the Nazis forcibly purchased his rights for $7,500.

Q *I thought that phony, canned laughter was ruled out on TV shows. Recently I've watched several big TV programs in which the audience howled at jokes that weren't funny. Is some mechanical device used?—B.P., Hollywood, Calif.*

A No, but reportedly several entertainers demand large blocks of studio tickets when they are taping a show. They distribute these tickets to friends with orders to "laugh it up." This is what is known in the trade as the "stacked audience."

Q *Why has the South African government seized the passport of its most distinguished citizen, Alan Paton?—Fred Croll, Washington, D.C.*

A Paton, author of *Cry, the Beloved Country,* is a political opponent of the present South African government, which wants to confine him to the country of his birth. Says Paton: "It is indicative of the weakness of the government's position that they cannot allow people to express what they believe to be the truth about the policies of apartheid."

Q *I understand that Queen Elizabeth has ordered that the automobiles of the British Royal Family be equipped with safety belts. Is this true or sales propaganda?—Ben Cronin, Newark, N.J.*

A So far only Princess Margaret has ordered safety belts for her personal cars, two Rolls-Royces, a Rover and a Morris Mini-Minor.

Q *Has anyone won the Nobel prize twice?—Saul Franklin, Oakland, Calif.*

A Yes, Marie Curie of France. She and her husband, Pierre, shared the physics prize with Henri Becquerel in 1903. Later, in 1911, she won the Nobel prize for chemistry on her own.

Q *How old are conductors Bruno Walter, Pierre Monteux, Sir Thomas Beecham and Leopold Stokowski?—Ann Richards, Raleigh, N.C.*

A Bruno Walter is 84; Pierre Monteux is 85; Beecham is 81; Stokowski is 73.

Q *Isn't the Netherlands Royal Family quietly killing the romance between Princess Beatrix and an unknown commoner?—Roberta G., Tucson, Ariz.*

A Princess Beatrix has been seeing a good deal of Robert Steensma, a fellow student at the University of Leiden, and a commoner. Should she marry Steensma, Beatrix would give up her right to the Netherlands' throne, a situation that her mother, Queen Juliana, faces uneasily.

Q *When was Ann Blyth married to Dennis Day, and how many children does she have?—Doris Cook, Chicago, Ill.*

A Ann Blyth married Dr. James McNulty, brother of Dennis Day, in 1953. They have four children.

Q *Will you tell me whether the president's wife, Jacqueline Kennedy, is a graduate of Smith College?—Penelope Ward, Newark, N.J.*

A No. Mrs. Kennedy was graduated from George Washington University, Washington, D.C.

Jacqueline Kennedy

WALTER SCOTT'S

PERSONALITY PARADE®

February 12, 1961

HILAI / Globe

Farouk I

Globe

Robert Frost

Cutler / Globe

Doris Day

Q *Ex-King Farouk of Egypt—where is he now and with whom?—Peter DeBrun, Chicago, Ill.*

A Farouk commutes between Lausanne, Switzerland, and Rome, Italy, is frequently seen with Irma Capece Minuto, his sometimes fiancée.

Q *Can you reveal the woman who was the great love in Maurice Chevalier's life?—Martha Baum, Newark, N.J.*

A Mistinguett, glamorous French dancer who helped him achieve his first popularity.

Q *Is it true that Cadillac is coming out with a compact car?—James Doran, Detroit, Mich.*

A It is planning a Town Sedan (factory list price: $5,040), which is seven inches shorter than any other Cadillac, but not a compact.

Q *Is it on the level that no details of an infant's race or color are recorded on birth certificates of babies born in New York City?—G.Y., Laurel, Miss.*

A As of January 1, 1961, it's true. New York City is the first community in the U.S. to eliminate this

information from birth certificates, although racial and color details are still maintained in Department of Health records.

Q *Who said: "A diplomat is a man who remembers a woman's birthday but not her age"?—George Bristol, Baltimore, Md.*

A Poet Robert Frost.

Q *What is comedian Joey Bishop's real name and real birth date?—Al Schwartz, Philadelphia, Pa.*

A Joseph Abraham Gottlieb, born in New York City on February 3, 1918.

Q *I understand that Henry Luce of Time-Life has ordered his company to enter the book publishing business in a big way. Is this true?—H.P., Newark, N.J.*

A Yes, Time, Inc., has entered the book publishing business, intends to sell books through direct mail. Its book publishing division is headed by Jerome Hardy, former vice-president of Doubleday in charge of advertising for 13 years. Its editor is Norman Ross, for-

merly with *Life*. *Time* hopes to sell 4 million books in 1961, which would make it the fifth largest book publisher in the U.S.

Q *Is producer Darryl Zanuck married to French actress Juliette Greco?—Mildred Cousins, Fort Worth, Tex.*

A No, Zanuck is married to Virginia Fox Zanuck.

Q *How many times has All-American girl Doris Day been married?—Bernard Fox, Los Angeles, Calif.*

A Three times.

Q *Who is Ted Sorensen and exactly how close is he to President Kennedy?—Henry Tritus, Washington, D.C.*

A Sorensen, 32, is Kennedy's special counsel at the White House, and one of his closest friends and most trusted advisers.

WALTER SCOTT'S

PERSONALITY PARADE®

April 9, 1961

Beaton / Globe

Tina Onassis

Harris and Ewing / Globe

Eliot Ness

Dwight Eisenhower

Q *Is it on the level about actor Louis Jourdan and Tina Onassis, whose husband left her for Maria Callas?—Georgia Falmouth, Chicago, Ill.*

A At this point it's a definite possibility.

Q *On TV's* Candid Camera, *is there a feud between Allen Funt and Arthur Godfrey?—B.U., Newark, N.J.*

A They did not get along, and Godfrey has quit the show.

Q *Where is Diane Lennon, eldest of the Lennon sisters of the Lawrence Welk band? Is she legally an adult?—Lydia Gray, E. St. Louis, Ill.*

A In Los Angeles. Diane wed Dick Glass last October 16 and legally became an adult at that time. Since then, she has become 21 years old.

Q *I understand that every Jerry Lewis motion picture except one has made money. Which Lewis film hasn't?—Frank Rowalsky, Miami, Fla.*

A Cinderfella is not doing well at this writing and may become the first Lewis box-office flop.

Q *Please advise the cause of death of Eliot Ness of* Untouchables *fame.—H.H., New York, N.Y.*

A Ness died of a heart attack at age 54, in 1957, at Coudersport, Pa.

Q *A French newspaper carried the story that Brenda Lee, the singer, is not a 16-year-old girl but a 32-year-old midget. Please tell us the truth.—Louise Bechmann, Waianae, Hawaii.*

A Brenda Lee was born outside Atlanta, Georgia, on December 4, 1944.

Q *I am an old classmate of Norma Shearer from Montreal High. What happened to her? Is she married? Is she a grandmother?—Mrs. M.S., N. Miami, Fla.*

A Norma Shearer, 57, is married, lives in Los Angeles, is a grandmother.

Q *To whom are Audrey and Jayne Meadows married?—Mrs. J.B.H., Knoxville, Tenn.*

A Jayne is married to Steve Allen. Audrey may take the marital step with Robert Six of Continental Airlines, former husband of Ethel Merman.

Q *Is it true as I hear so often that ex-President Eisenhower's profits from his book* Crusade in Europe *were tax free?—Mrs. Fred Barber, Oakland, Calif.*

A No, they were not. The former president paid a capital-gains tax on the income from the book.

Q *I read that when his wife lay dying of a lung infection, Mohandas Gandhi refused to let her be injected with penicillin. Is this true? If so, why?—Geraldine Nugent, Los Angeles, Calif.*

A It's true. According to Gandhi, injections were not permitted strict practitioners of the Hindu religion.

Mohandas Gandhi

Yuri Gagarin

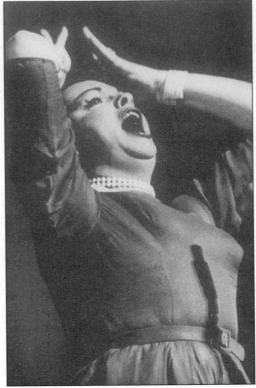

Judy Garland

Queen Elizabeth

Q *Yuri Gagarin, the first man in space, isn't his wife a Russian celebrity in her own right?—Milton Fox, Los Angeles, Calif.*

A Valentina Gagarin is a practicing physician.

Q *Who is the world's richest jockey—Sir Gordon Richards of England or our own Eddie Arcaro?—Dennis S., Fresno, Calif.*

A Neither. Richest jockey is millionaire Johnny Longden, 54, who's been riding winners for 34 years.

Q *Is noted author and cartoonist James Thurber blind?—T.L., Washington, D.C.*

A Yes.

Q *I understand that Bettina, whose heart was crushed when Aly Khan was killed, has been dating another man. Can you identify him?—Dina T., Greensboro, N.C.*

A Italian diplomat Lorenzo Attolico, Count of Adelfia.

Q *Can you tell me what sort of role Judy Garland plays in* Judgment at Nuremberg?—*Evelyn Romack, Madison, Wis.*

A She plays a girl sent to a concentration camp on a false charge that she had an affair with a Jewish man.

Q *How many Republican and Democratic presidents has this country elected since the Civil War?—Alan Hurlbut, New Haven, Conn.*

A Five Democrats, eleven Republicans.

Q *Why does de Gaulle of France refuse to help the UN in the Congo?—Edna Skinner, Portland, Ore.*

Charles de Gaulle

A Says de Gaulle: "The UN has transferred to the Congo its global incoherence. France does not wish to participate either with her men or money in any enterprise now or later of this organization or should I say disorganization."

Q *Who is the highest paid corporation executive in England?—Frank Rainey, St. Louis, Mo.*

A Sir William Lyons, chief of Jaguar cars, at an estimated $150,000 a year.

Q *How does Dr. Hendrik Verwoerd of South Africa regard Japanese in that country—as white or colored?—M.J., Boston, Mass.*

A Henceforth Japanese in South Africa are to be treated as white so they can live in white areas. This is reportedly a concession because South Africa wants to make friends with Japan for commercial reasons.

Q *Is it true that Queen Elizabeth pays the largest water, gas, light and heating bills in the British Empire?—Claude Hoeven, Des Moines, Iowa.*

A One of the largest. Household bills for water, gas, light and heating at Windsor Castle, Buckingham and St. James Palaces total approximately $144,480 a year.

WALTER SCOTT'S
PERSONALITY PARADE®

June 11, 1961

Lister Hill

Walt Disney

Q *Is it true that Mamie Eisenhower suffers from a rheumatic heart and that this was kept from the American public?—J.P., Washington, D.C.*

A It's been no secret that Mrs. Eisenhower has a rheumatic heart.

Q *Sen. Lister Hill of Alabama—did he really study medicine under Sir Joseph Lister of London, father of surgical antisepsis?—Don Spier, Los Angeles, Calif.*

A No. His father, Dr. Luther Hill, studied under Lister, was so impressed by his teacher that when a son was born on December 29, 1894, he named him Lister. Today Sen. Lister Hill is recognized as the man currently most responsible for federal assistance to medical research.

Q *Prince Rainier and Princess Grace of Monaco have been married five years. What change has five years of marriage brought about in the Prince?—Flora Williams, Miami, Fla.*

A He no longer races automobiles.

Q *I understand that Eartha Kitt, the colored singer, is expecting her first child. Is her husband, Bill McDonald, white or Negro?—Helen M., Knoxville, Tenn.*

A McDonald is white.

Q *How much does Walt Disney earn per week?—Bill Delaney, Burbank, Calif.*

A His salary in 1960 was $3,000 a week. This year it may be boosted to $5,166.

Q *Can you tell me which men own the new Los Angeles Angels baseball team?—Frank Corelli, Oakland, Calif.*

A Major stockholders are Bob Reynolds, Gene Autry, Leonard Firestone and Robert Lehman.

Q *What's happened to Yves St. Laurent, Dior's dress-designing prodigy, whose health crumbled after he had been drafted into the French Army?—Marianne Benet, Madison, Wis.*

A He's designing costumes for French ballet star Zizi Jeanmaire, may open an independent fashion house with the support of many rich female clients.

Q *How many Jews in Norway were executed by the Nazis during World War II?—Jonas Rosen, Chicago, Ill.*

A Norway had 1,450 Jews in 1940; 650 were deported by the Nazis, the rest escaped. Of the 650, only 13 ever returned to Norway.

Q *Who is the author of the statement: "Life is either a daring adventure or nothing"?—N. Adams, San Diego, Calif.*

A Helen Keller.

Q *I would like to know if singer Nelson Eddy is still living. If so what does he do?—K.P., Detroit, Mich.*

A Eddy sings on the supper-club circuit.

Q *What connection does Franklin D. Roosevelt, Jr., have with Jaguar cars?—Victor Carlson, Minneapolis, Minn.*

A He distributes Jaguars in several states.

Q *Who is the Rachel Roberts who's been seen so much with actor Rex Harrison?—E.P., Evansville, Ind.*

A She is a British actress who recently won the British Academy Award as the best actress of the year. She has a leading role in *Saturday Night and Sunday Morning*, now playing U.S. theaters.

Rachel Roberts and Rex Harrison

Q *Are there conditions strongly associated with emotional problems for which tranquilizers do little if any good?*

A Yes. I don't think they can be of much help in getting the overweight individual to lose unwanted pounds. Nor can they do much to clear up certain skin conditions which are thought to be caused by mental unrest. I doubt also whether they can do much in ulcer cases, because ulcers, I feel, are caused not by tensions but by chemical factors in the body.

Q *Tranquilizers have been used increasingly in the past five years. Is there anything new about them?*

A Yes. We have learned a great deal about whom they can help, whom they cannot help, their strengths, limitations and what might be developed in the future.

Q *Aren't people overusing—and doctors overprescribing—these drugs?*

A In my opinion, no. Of course, the drug can be abused in individual cases. However, in general, the normal healthy individual avoids dosing himself with pills. As for doctors, they generally prescribe tranquilizers for people they believe can be helped by them.

Q *Can these drugs really cure mental illness?*

A They do not cure anything. They may alleviate symptoms and open the way to more complete treatment and understanding of the problem.

Q *Do tranquilizers create a feeling of happiness?*

A No. However, they can make your problem seem less forbidding by removing or decreasing unreasonable anxiety. This is a basic virtue of the drugs.

Q *What is their actual effect?*

A They relieve anxiety, calm you down, make you better able to endure the situation you find upsetting. The "situation" may involve anything from visiting the dentist to sweating out a new job.

Q *Are there emotional conditions for which tranquilizers simply don't work?*

A Certainly. If a mother is anxious because her child is sick, she's not likely to be helped by tranquilizers. Hers are normal, healthy jitters. Tranquilizers work best when there is no real cause to justify emotional distress.

Q *What kind of anxiety does yield to tranquilizers?*

A Doctors call it "free-floating anxiety." The individual is always on edge, but cannot tell why. He feels vaguely uneasy. Added stress becomes the final straw that makes him extremely nervous and excitable.

Q *What types of troubled patients gain benefits?*

A Those who are extremely jittery or overexcitable and psychotics who have delusions and who fall out of touch with reality.

Q *How many different tranquilizers are available today for prescription use by disturbed patients?*

A More than 40. They fall into three basic chemical categories: meprobamate, chlorpromazine, reserpine.

Q *Do these drugs produce any ill effects?*

A All drugs, tranquilizers included, may have harmful effects when taken by people who cannot tolerate them. However, when carefully prescribed, tranquilizers do not produce serious side effects.

Q *Is it dangerous to take an overdose?*

A An overdose of any drug is dangerous. Skin blotches, weakness, drowsiness and changes in vision have been reported as occasional effects of ordinary tranquilizer doses. In rare cases, blood disorders have developed.

Q *Should you drive a car after taking a tranquilizer?*

A Most people can do so safely. However, a few may find that their efficiency is somewhat impaired. Such persons should be cautious about driving or operating any machinery which can be life-endangering.

Q *Can tranquilizers make you outdo yourself on the job or in an emergency?*

A I doubt it. I doubt that they can make a slugger out of a mediocre ballplayer. These drugs don't increase your natural capacities. They may help you to realize them.

Q *Haven't tranquilizers changed the mental hospital picture?*

A They have helped. Since tranquilizers and psychic energizers have come on the scene, mental hospital patient loads have decreased slightly, reversing a trend of many years.

Q *What is a psychic energizer?*

A A drug which, unlike the tranquilizer, can lift the patient out of the doldrums of depression.

Q *Will research produce more and better drugs to combat emotional disorders in the years ahead?*

A We hope so. We need new and effective drugs to treat criminal behavior, which I'm sure results very often from brain abnormality.

Q *Is there any new evidence to that effect?*

A Yes. Doctors in England have found that in 90 percent of certain groups of convicted criminals, there are abnormal wave patterns as shown by standard measurement techniques. Perhaps drugs of the future might be able to make these brain waves normal and thus prevent the individual from committing crime.

Q *Are there any other frontiers for new drugs in this field of emotional well-being?*

A There are experiments with drugs aimed at improving your performance in tasks which you know produce anxiety and tension.

Q *Can you take tranquilizers safely for life?*

A I believe that the majority of patients can—providing they are closely supervised by their doctors.

Q *You hear that tranquilizers are good for almost everything from overweight to heart trouble to ulcers. Do they have that wide a range of effectiveness?*

A They are not "good for almost everything." They can help in cases where anxiety arises from physical illness. Thus, tranquilizers are prescribed often for symptoms of menopause, certain types of headache, chest pain associated with heart trouble, insomnia, some menstrual disorders and muscular spasm.

Henry Fonda

Q *Henry Fonda is scheduled to do a TV spectacular on the American family. Can you tell me how many times Fonda has been married?—Mrs. Roland McGill, Levittown, N.Y.*

A Four times.

Q *What's happened to the late Aly Khan's girl friend, Bettina?—Anna Levin, Newark, N.J.*

A She's gone into the dress business, opened a shop in Paris on the Place Gastand called "Bettina."

Q *Where is Mrs. Bruno Richard Hauptmann, whose husband was executed for kidnapping the Lindbergh baby?—T.R., Trenton, N.J.*

A Mrs. Hauptmann was living in Kamenz, Germany, in 1954, then moved to Bautzen. Since both cities are in the East Zone, occupied by the Russians, no news has been forthcoming of Mrs. Hauptmann.

Q *Which book is the all-time best-seller in the U.S.?—Dorothy West, Oakland, Calif.*

A *The Holy Bible.* Since 1900, about 500,000,000 copies have been sold.

Q *Would you please tell me the real name of Dean Martin and where he was born?—Virginia Benzek, Chicago, Ill.*

A Dino Crocetti, Steubenville, Ohio.

Q *Does former Vice President Nixon send his two daughters to private or public schools?—Loren Lundigan, Buffalo, N.Y.*

A The Nixon girls go to Marlborough, a private school in Los Angeles.

Q *Who succeeds the president and vice president of the U.S. should they both die in office?—B. Beer, Columbus, Ohio.*

A The Speaker of the House. Prior to the Presidential Succession Act of 1947, the secretary of state was third in line, but no longer.

Q *Recently Art Linkletter was stopped near Bakersfield at the beginning of dove-hunting season with 124 doves. What was the penalty?—Steve Giacomazzi, Hartford, Calif.*

A No truth whatever to that story. Linkletter never goes hunting, probably wouldn't recognize a dove if he saw one.

Q *Does the Duke of Windsor still own a large cattle ranch in Canada?—Charles Coulter, Seattle, Wash.*

Duke of Windsor

A A few weeks ago the Duke of Windsor announced through his ranch manager that he was prepared to sell his real estate near High River, Alberta, which he has owned for 42 years.

Q *For 15 years I've been trying to get the answer to this question: How come in 1941, nine hours after news reached General MacArthur in the Philippines that the Japanese had attacked Pearl Harbor, almost all our aircraft in the Philippines were lined up like sitting ducks on the airfields of Luzon waiting to be destroyed by Japanese bombers—and they were, too. Who was responsible for this shocking negligence and why have the American people never been told the full truth?—P.B., Fort Bragg, N.C.*

A Congress has investigated every aspect of the Japanese attack on Pearl Harbor, has reported on the alleged poor judgment of the Army and Navy officers then and there in command—but it has never investigated what happened in the Philippines on December 8, 1941, or apportioned blame for military ineptness there.

Q *Why does Carol Burnett of the* Garry Moore Show *rub her finger under her nose or twitch her ear at the end of the show? Is she giving some secret message to someone?—Jo Szymanski, Richmond Hill, N.Y.*

A It's a sign to relatives back home that she's OK.

Q *What was Premier Nikita Khrushchev's position in the Communist Party during the regime of Josef Stalin?—Adrian Gitana, U.S. Navy.*

Nikita Khrushchev

A Khrushchev was the party's first secretary in the Ukraine, also a member of the presidium of the U.S.S.R. Supreme Soviet.

Q *Please tell me if Miss Norma Shearer ever remarried after being widowed, and also how old she is.—Mrs. Nicholas Stanislo, Dayton, Ohio.*

A Miss Shearer, 57, is the wife of one-time ski instructor Marti Arrouge, whom she married in 1942 six years after the death of her first husband, producer Irving Thalberg.

Q *I would like to ask if Dorothy Provine is married. Also, what is her age, and is that her real name?—Debbie Griffin, Madison, Wisc.*

A Miss Provine is 24. She is not married and does use her real name.

Dorothy Provine

WALTER SCOTT'S
PERSONALITY PARADE®

January 7, 1962

Q *On* The Jack Paar Show *I heard Zsa Zsa Gabor tell how she had lost "everything" in the Hollywood fire. Now I read that many of her paintings were saved as well as her jewels. Which version is true?—M.Y., Dallas, Tex.*

Zsa Zsa Gabor

A Several of her paintings were saved including two valuable Renoirs. She was also traveling with her most valuable jewels when the fire occurred. In addition, her house, which had been given to her by Conrad Hilton as part of a divorce settlement, was insured for $185,000 although it would cost about three times that amount to rebuild it today.

Q *Will you please tell me the yearly pension General MacArthur receives?—Jack Linhenhoher, Eagle Rock, Va.*

Douglas MacArthur

A According to the Army, General MacArthur is technically still on active duty, draws $1,700 per month base pay, $171 per month quarters, $47.88 per month subsistence allowance—roughly $24,000 a year.

Q *Why has nothing been carried in the press about the Dorothy Provine-Frank Sinatra romance?—Selma Diamond, New York, N.Y.*

A Both parties have tried to keep it quiet.

Q *Can you tell me anything about a great woman scientist named Charity Waymouth?—H.Y., Dublin, N.H.*

A Dr. Charity Waymouth is a prominent biochemist who formulated a nutrient at the Jackson Laboratory, Bar Harbor, Maine, which keeps healthy and cancerous cells growing outside the human body—one of the foremost developments in cancer research.

Q *Now that the Dinah Shore-George Montgomery marriage has broken up, will Montgomery marry Ziva Rodann?—Kenneth George, Los Angeles, Calif.*

A Dinah's divorce will be obtained in California, which means that neither party will be able to marry for at least one year after the interlocutory decree is granted.

Q *Does Tony Martin wear a hairpiece?—Josephine K., Springfield, Mass.*

A When performing.

Q *I read in a Hollywood gossip column: "Amanda Blake and Milburn Stone sold their* Gunsmoke *residual rights to CBS for $1,000,000 each..." Can this be true?—Milton Robinson, Los Angeles, Calif.*

A CBS paid the two of them a combined sum of $200,000 for their residual rights.

Q *Why is it that Winston Churchill will not permit exhibition of the great portrait of him by Graham Sutherland, one of England's most distinguished painters?—Olive Verchianni, Miami, Fla.*

A The Sutherland portrait of Churchill, described by art critics as "a truly great work," was painted in 1954 after Sir Winston had suffered a stroke and had been voted out of office. Both of these developments were reflected in his face and bearing when Sutherland painted him; thus the finished portrait was not to Sir Winston's liking. After it was published in newspapers at the presentation, Churchill banned all future publication.

Q *How old are Governor and Mrs. Rockefeller? Also, has any U.S. president ever been divorced?—Thomas Price, Eureka, Calif.*

Nelson Rockefeller

A The governor is 53; Mrs. Rockefeller is 54. No president of the U.S.A. has ever been divorced although two presidents, Andrew Jackson and Warren G. Harding, were married to divorcées.

Q *How old is John L. Lewis of the United Mine Workers?—Louis Gates, Alexandria, Va.*

A Lewis is 82.

Q *Is it on the level that Mary Martin turned down the lead in the Broadway hit,* Oklahoma?*—George Deidrich, El Paso, Tex.*

A Yes, it's true.

Mary Martin

Q *Is it true that blind pianist-singer Ray Charles is a drug addict?—Lola Dupre, New Orleans, La.*

A Charles admitted to detectives in Indianapolis recently that he'd been "hooked" since he was 16.

Q *Thomas Jefferson had a library of 10,000 volumes, one of the greatest in colonial America. Do you know what happened to it?—Evans R., Durham, N.C.*

A Congress paid $25,000 for the Jefferson Library, which later became the nucleus of the Library of Congress.

Q *What connection does President Charles de Gaulle have with "the four gorillas"?—June Hanover, Chicago, Ill.*

A Les gorilles, as they are known in France, are de Gaulle's four bodyguards, who go with him everywhere.

Q *What was the cause of Rudolph Valentino's death and who claimed his body?—Mrs. George Kemper, Hollywood, Calif.*

A Valentino died in New York City of a perforated ulcer. His body was claimed and brought back to Hollywood by Pola Negri, to whom he was to have been married one week later.

Q *Who invented the hot dog?—Alice Fremd, Rye, N.Y.*

A Many people have claimed credit but it is popularly agreed that British-born Harold Stevens, who died recently at age 83, began the custom of selling frankfurters in rolls to baseball fans in New York.

WALTER SCOTT'S

PERSONALITY PARADE®

February 4, 1962

Q *I understand that showman Billy Rose, once married to Fanny Brice, Eleanor Holm, and twice to Joyce Matthews, is now the single largest stockholder of American Telephone & Telegraph stock in the world. If this is true, how did Rose get all that dough?—Evans Michaels, Chicago, Ill.*

Billy Rose

A Rose owns 80,000 shares of A.T. & T., worth approximately $11,000,000. He is the second largest individual shareholder of record, made his money as a show business producer.

Q *Can you tell me which is the best-selling disk in the history of the record business?—Roger Levy, Burlingame, Calif.*

A Bing Crosby's recording of "White Christmas." To date 20,000,000 copies have been sold.

Q *Would you please give the name of the man who broke the Japanese purple code, which permitted us to defeat the Japanese at the Battle of Midway? I have never seen the name of this great man in print.—Harry Wolff, Miami, Fla.*

A A cryptographer named William Friedman in conjunction with others reportedly broke the code in 1942.

Q *Is one of President Kennedy's sisters mentally retarded?—L.Y., Boston, Mass.*

A One of the Kennedy girls was stricken with cerebral palsy as a child, placed in an institution. The president's father, Joseph Kennedy, thereupon established a foundation to finance research in the treatment and education of retarded persons. Recently the president appointed a panel of lay and medical people to study the problem and prepare a report.

Q *Jane Fonda, daughter of Henry Fonda—who was her mother? I've been told Jane's mother left her $10,000,000. What about it?—Victor Marco, Monroe, La.*

A Miss Fonda's mother was Frances Seymour Brokaw Fonda, who committed suicide when Jane was 12. Jane was left money and jewelry. One pair of emerald and platinum earrings, for example, which she received last December on her 24th birthday, is valued at $30,000. She was not left $10,000,000, however. Closer to one percent of that figure would be more accurate.

Q *We have been long-time appreciative listeners of Howard K. Smith. An inquiry to the CBS station in Los Angeles has elicited no answer as to Smith's present or future activities. Can you help?—Eveline M. Hutchinson, Alhambra, Calif.*

A Howard K. Smith has joined the ABC network to report news and to present analysis and interpretation. His first half-hour report is scheduled for February 14.

Brigitte Bardot

Q *One of Brigitte Bardot's most successful films, And God Created Woman, was written and directed by her then husband Roger Vadim. I've been told that Vadim was paid only $500 for writing and directing. Could you verify?—Dennis Raffa, New York, N.Y.*

A Vadim was paid $5,000 for both jobs by producer Raoul Levy who had previously loaned him various sums of money.

Q *Who said: "The best portion of a good man's life is his little, nameless, unremembered acts of kindness and of love"?—Thomas Kline, Knoxville, Tenn.*

A Poet William Wordsworth (1770-1850).

Q *Radio Free Europe keeps asking the public for funds. Is this a private organization or the one run by Edward R. Murrow?—O.E.M., Scranton, Pa.*

A Edward R. Murrow heads the United States Information Agency, a government organization. Radio Free Europe is technically a private organization.

Q *Is it on the level that Francoise Sagan, 26-year-old French novelist, is broke?—N. Newman, Oakland, Calif.*

Francoise Sagan

A Not broke— just hard-up. Miss Sagan, who in six years has written five best-sellers in France and two plays and earned $750,000 in the process, says, "I frittered away my money...now I have a business manager who I hope won't."

Q *Did Jackie Gleason ever go steady with June Taylor? With whom does he go steady now? Will he ever marry again?—L.U., Allendale, N.J.*

A Gleason was a close friend of Marilyn Taylor, sister of choreographer June Taylor. He is now an equally close friend of Honey Merrill, former showgirl and one of his associates. Since Gleason, a Roman Catholic, is separated but not divorced from his wife, the chance of a second marriage for him in the near future is not likely.

Q *I understand that General Alfred M. Gruenther's salary from the American Red Cross is $50,000 per year. Also that he draws army retirement pay and lives in a $75,000 home provided by the Red Cross. Is this true?—Herford T. Cowling, USAF Ret'd., Arlington, Va.*

Alfred Gruenther

A As president of the American Red Cross (a $100,000,000-a-year voluntary welfare organization), General Gruenther receives $30,000 per year, making him less well-paid than most corporation presidents. His army retirement pay is $1,275 per month. The estate on which he lives was provided by a wealthy Washingtonian in 1922 and is maintained by a trust fund established at that time for this purpose.

Walt Disney

Q *Is it true that Walt Disney has gone into the bowling business?—Dana Atherton, Dallas, Tex.*

A Walt Disney Productions has invested $927,000 in Celebrities Bowling Co. which operates a recreation center in Denver, complete with bowling alleys, swimming pool, restaurants, etc.

Q *Did Gracie Allen get furious at George Burns when George decided recently to team up with Carol Channing?—Henrietta Adelman, New York, N.Y.*

A No. Gracie has retired from show business. George, tired of doing a single, signed with Carol on a 50-50 basis. They will work together for the first time at the Seattle World's Fair in June.

Q *When I was in Budapest recently I was told that Sir Laurence Olivier had been born there, the son of a rabbi, that his real name is Louis Levy. Is this so?—R.L., Watertown, N.Y.*

A Sir Laurence Kerr Olivier is descended from French Huguenots who fled to England in 1572 to escape religious persecution. Olivier was born in Dorking, Surrey, England, on May 22, 1907, the son of the late Reverend Gerald Kerr Olivier, an Anglo-Catholic clergyman, and his wife, Agnes Louise Crookenden. Originally Sir Laurence planned to succeed his father in the ministry. What they told you about him in Budapest is baloney.

Q *Lita Milan, the Hollywood actress who became such a good and close friend of Rafael Trujillo—what's happened to her now that the Trujillos have been thrown out of the Dominican Republic?—Fred Heinrich, Pasadena, Calif.*

A In knowledgeable quarters it is said that she and Rafael have had it.

Q *What are the chances of a reconciliation between Dinah Shore and George Montgomery?—Harold Frisch, St. Louis, Mo.*

A Chances are good if Dinah will swallow just a wee bit of pride.

Dinah Shore

Q *I've been watching Ed Sullivan on TV for years. His talent escapes me. Does he have any? If so, please describe.—L.L., Pt. Chester, N.Y.*

A Over the years Sullivan has developed a stage presence. He has little performing ability of any type. His talent lies in putting together week after week an excellent variety show, and this definitely takes talent.

Q *How many times has Loretta Young been divorced, and is she through with TV?—George L., Monroe, La.*

A Loretta Young, 48, is currently separated from her second husband, Tom Lewis, was divorced from her first, the late Grant Withers. She is currently preparing a new TV series, *Christina's Children,* to be directed by her brother-in-law Norman Foster.

Q *Frederick Loewe who wrote the music for* My Fair Lady, Gigi, Brigadoon— *has he retired from musical composition?—Unity V., Washington, D.C.*

A Loewe recently toured Japan in connection with his next show, for which he will undoubtedly write the music.

Q *Bill Harrah, who does $40,000,000 worth of gambling business each year at his Lake Tahoe and Reno gambling casinos, is the acknowledged gambling king of the world. Why has his background been kept such a secret?—B.O., Sacramento, Calif.*

A Harrah, 50, dislikes publicity. Originally he came from Venice, California, where he ran a bingo parlor which was then legal. He studied engineering at the University of California in Los Angeles, eventually came to Reno where in a few short years he became the town's number-one gambling entrepreneur. Harrah collects old cars, gives no interviews, is said to be not particularly proud of the fact that he has devoted his fine mind and the best years of his life to the establishment of the world's largest gambling casino where thousands of people each week are separated from their hard-earned money.

Q *The daughter of Aristotle Onassis who went to live with her mother, now the Marchioness of Blandford—how old is the girl and is she worth a fortune?—Leona Ashton, Los Angeles, Calif.*

A Christina Onassis, 11, spends six months of each year with her mother and six months with her father who set up a $20,000,000 trust fund for her.

Q *Who will play the Rex Harrison role of Henry Higgins in the movie version of* My Fair Lady?—Enid Conklin, Memphis, Tenn.

A Best bet: Cary Grant.

Q *When Sargent Shriver married Eunice Kennedy, old Joe Kennedy took care of him by putting Shriver in charge of Chicago's Merchandise Mart. Is it true that Kennedy also gave Shriver and the rest of his sons-in-law a million bucks each?—F.L., Peoria, Ill.*

A No. Kennedy established million-dollar trust funds for his own children, no trust funds for his sons-in-law.

Sargent Shriver

PERSONALITY PARADE®

April 8, 1962

Gina Lollobrigida

Q *Can you tell me if Gina Lollobrigida and her husband, who were becoming Canadian citizens a year or so ago, are still living in Toronto?—L.T., Detroit, Mich.*

A No, they've pulled out of Canada, have returned to Rome for good.

Q *Is it true that Bing Crosby is producing a series of 15 record albums to be called "Bing's Hollywood Story"?—David Larrimore, Chicago, Ill.*

A Decca is turning out the series. It will contain 189 songs from 40 Crosby motion pictures.

Q *Will the U.S. Navy permit a Negro to command any of its ships?—V. Bostic, Birmingham, Ala.*

A Negroes have commanded patrol-type boats. The *USS Falgout*, a destroyer escort, is currently commanded by Lt. Commander Samuel L. Gravely, 39, a Negro.

Q *Who is the authority for the statement that it cost the late Clark Gable $500,000 to divorce his second wife, Ria Franklin Prentiss Lucas Langham of Houston?—Manny Franklin, Miami Beach, Fla.*

A According to Charles Samuels, author of *The King,* a biography of Gable, the actor asked Carole Lombard, his third wife, after they were married in Kingman, Ariz., if she had any money in her purse. He had just given the preacher $100, claimed it was all the money he had in the world. "What happened to the rest of your loot?" Lombard asked. "I gave it all to Ria," Gable confessed. "More than a half a million." Carole took her husband in her arms. "You silly son of a —," she cried ecstatically. "To think you paid half a million bucks for me."

Q *I have been told that Tito of Yugoslavia and Nasser of Egypt are close friends. Is this true?—J.G., Washington, D.C.*

A Tito has made a number of trips to Cairo to see Nasser, and the two men appear to get on well with each other.

Q *Can you tell me how much Chubby Checker will earn from the Twist this year?—Donald Richards, Los Angeles, Calif.*

Chubby Checker

A Checker, 20—real name Ernest Evans—will earn approximately $200,000 this year, according to his court-appointed guardian.

Q *Who is considered the leading dress-designer in Paris?—Sandra Bryan, New York, N.Y.*

A Cristobal Balenciaga, an unmarried, publicity-shy Spaniard, is generally considered pre-eminent.

Q *What's happened to Brigitte Bardot's husband, Jacques Charrier?—Lois H., Camden, Ark.*

A Jacques Charrier, 26, was recently recalled to complete his army service but is in a hospital suffering from a nervous breakdown. He was temporarily discharged from the French army in 1959 after three weeks in a psychiatric ward.

Q *Why do we land our astronauts in the ocean, and why do the Russians land theirs on land?—James Nebel, Washington, D.C.*

A We believe it is safer. The Russians apparently eject their astronauts from their space capsules and let them parachute to earth.

Q *I understand that Danny Thomas could have had a long-term contract at MGM years ago if he had agreed to a nose-job. Is this true or publicity?—Mrs. J. Sherman, Springfield, Ohio.*

A True. According to Thomas, he refused to let plastic surgeons alter his nose, thereby lost the contract.

Q *Ingemar Johannson's secretary and traveling companion—a beautiful babe named Birgit Lundgren—haven't she and Ingemar been secretly wed since 1954?—B. Olson, Chicago, Ill.*

A No, they've been friendly since 1954, plan to marry later this year.

Q *Ford is turning out a new small car, the Cardinal, to compete with the Volkswagen. Will it be made in America? When will it come out? How much?—T.R., Lansing, Mich.*

A The Cardinal will be manufactured domestically with a German-imported engine. It will be shown this fall, will probably sell for around $1,750.

Q *How does Robert McNamara, the present secretary of defense, rank in Washington?—J. Bray, Marion, Iowa.*

A Ace-high. In one year on the job, he has made more basic improvements in the nation's military organization than any other defense secretary of recent years. Currently, he is determined to improve the nation's reserve forces, most probably by streamlining them.

Robert McNamara

Jackie Gleason

Q *Could you please tell me if Paul New-man and Jackie Gleason shot their own pool in* The Hustler?—*Kathy Thornton, San Marino, Calif.*

A Gleason (a top-notch billiard player) and Newman did some of the scenes, but the close trick-shots requiring a master's touch were done by the World Champion of Pocket Billiards, Willie Mosconi, who also acted as technical advisor on the film.

Q *One of the richest and most famous families in the world is the Wallenberg family. Who are they, what do they do, where do they come from?—Evelyn Solvesen, Bennington, Vt.*

A Marcus, Jacob, and Marc Wallenberg are leading bankers and industrialists in Sweden. They head many companies such as Swedish Match, SKF ball bearings, L.M. Ericcson Telephone Co. The Wallenberg family is one of the oldest and reputedly the richest in Sweden.

Q *Is Prime Minister Macmillan of Great Britain a martini man or, like Churchill, a scotch and soda man?—B. Price, Enid, Okla.*

A Macmillan is a martini man.

Q *Does Joan Crawford receive payment for the publicity she gets for Pepsi-Cola—or is her work just a "labor of love" in memory of her late husband Al Steele, who was president of the company?—Gloria Samuels, El Paso, Tex.*

Joan Crawford

A Miss Crawford's five-year contract with Pepsi-Cola, signed last fall, sets her annual salary at $35,000 for the first two years with a raise to $50,000 annually for the last three. In addition, she receives $3,600 a year as a director.

Q *How much money has this country given Tito's Yugoslavia in the past dozen years?—Joe Filene, Orlando, Fla.*

A Approximately $2,200,000,000 in military and economic aid.

Q *I can't believe that singer Johnny Mathis is a millionaire. How come?—Faith Gordon, San Francisco, Calif.*

A Record royalties and nightclub fees wisely invested by his manager Helen Noga in real estate properties are responsible for making Mathis one of 35 Negro millionaires in the U.S. today.

Q *Isn't it a fact that Fidel Castro, his brother Raul, and three other Castro children were illegitimate, which you failed to mention in a previous written background of the Castro family?—Betty J. Schellenberg, Ft. Worth, Tex.*

Fidel Castro

A Castro's father, Angel, was married to two women. His first wife was a Cuban schoolteacher by whom he had two children, Lidia and Pedro Emilio. Subsequently, he fell in love with the cook in his household, Lina Ruz Gonzales, by whom he had five additional children—among them Fidel and Raul, who were born illegitimately. When Angel Castro's first wife died, Angel married his cook.

Q *How much does Hugh Hefner, publisher of* Playboy, *pay those models to pose in the nude?—R.R., Moline, Ill.*

A $3,500 a sitting.

Q *Who was the first person in the U.S. saved by penicillin?—Nathan Douglas, Buffalo, N.Y.*

A Twenty years ago Mrs. Ogden Miller, wife of a former Yale University faculty member, was given an injection of penicillin by Dr. Thomas Sappington which saved her life.

Bob Newhart

Q *I would like to know if the Bob Newhart TV show will appear next season.—T. Bristol, Wallingford, Conn.*

A The Newhart show has been dropped by Sealtest but may pick up another sponsor for next season.

Q *Why did President Kennedy order a resumption of nuclear tests?—H.P., Washington, D.C.*

A Because of progress made by the Soviet Union in developing new nuclear weapons and the need to test our own weapons development program so as not to fall behind.

Q *Is it true that hosiery manufacturers have developed runless ladies' hose and will not market them?—Henry Altman, Hempstead, N.Y.*

A Runless hose for ladies will be marketed next month at $1.75 per pair.

Q *What's happened to Alger Hiss since he was released from prison?—Sally Allen, Camarillo, Calif.*

A He works as a printing salesman in New York City.

WALTER SCOTT'S
PERSONALITY PARADE®

July 8, 1962

Rita Hayworth

Q *What happened to Rita Hayworth and Gary Merrill in Hong Kong? Will you tell the truth?—Carolee Lansing, Stockton, Calif.*

A After touring Southeast Asia together for a month, they had a spat and Merrill flew out of Hong Kong, leaving behind a note which said: "Rita, I'm sorry it has to be this way. I'm leaving."

Q *Is it true that the* Christian Science Monitor *would not report anything dealing with "materia medica" even if the medical world announced the authenticated news of a cure for cancer?—Irving M. Sandberg, Miami Beach, Fla.*

A Untrue. While not inclined to carry speculative reports on unproved "wonder" drugs or cures, the *Monitor* prints factual medical news, fully covered the Salk vaccine development.

Q *Who is the author of the expression "He is a foul-weather friend"?—Bernadine Howard, Atlanta, Ga.*

A Winston Churchill said it of his close friend, Lord Beaverbrook.

Q *I'm a Little Leaguer and would like to know what was the longest home run ever hit—how far did it go, and who hit it?—G. Owens, Springfield, Ohio.*

A Babe Ruth's 587-foot home run, made in 1919 in an exhibition game between the New York Giants and the Boston Red Sox in Tampa, Florida.

Q *I would like to know the official home residence of both Richard Burton and Elizabeth Taylor.—A. Hirsch, Newark, N.J.*

A Switzerland.

Q *Has Franco of Spain signed with an American press agent to get him a better public image? Please identify the press agent if true.—N. Rosler, Duluth, Minn.*

Francisco Franco

A Communications Counsellors, Inc.

Q *Several weeks ago a family in Detroit sold $23,000,000 worth of General Motors stock. Which family, and where did they earn their money?—T.T., Ann Arbor, Mich.*

A Members of the Louis Mendelssohn family of Detroit sold 430,000 shares. Louis Mendelssohn was secretary-treasurer and a director of the Fisher Body Corporation before it was taken over by General Motors in 1926.

Q *Why was William Faulkner absent from the White House Nobel Prizewinners' Dinner?—B.C., Washington, D.C.*

A Faulkner, in Charlottesville, Virginia, at the time, declined, saying the trip to Washington was "a long way to go just to eat."

Q *Which major network TV shows have been canceled so far for the coming season?—J. Hoffman, Seaford, N.Y.*

A GE Theater, Pete and Gladys, Window on Main Street, Ichabod and Me, Frontier Circus, Hennesey, Father Knows Best, Father of the Bride, Groucho Marx, The Investigators, Checkmate, Bob Cummings, Gertrude Berg, Follow the Sun, Lawman, Bus Stop, Adventures in Paradise, Expedition, Surfside Six, Calvin and the Colonel, New Breed, The Hathaways, Bachelor Father, The Roaring 20s, Target: the Corrupters, Top Cat, Straightaway, Margie, The Real McCoys, National Velvet, 87th Precinct, Thriller, Cain's Hundred, Outlaws, Robert Taylor's Detectives, Wells Fargo, Tall Man, Bob Newhart.

Q *How old is Tito of Yugoslavia, and is he really a great Don Juan?—Ronald Alvarez, Santa Barbara, Calif.*

A Tito is 70. He had that Don Juan reputation as a young man.

Q *Can you tell me anything about the feud between Samuel Goldwyn and William Wyler?—Ed Leavis, Baltimore, Md.*

A Wyler is suing Goldwyn for approximately $400,000, an amount allegedly due him. Wyler claims that as its director he was promised 20 percent of the net profits of *The Best Years of Our Lives*.

Q *Wilhelmina, former Queen of the Netherlands—how old is she, and what is her current rank?—Jan Havenred, Chicago, Ill.*

A Wilhelmina, who will be 82 next month, is now Princess Wilhelmina, having relinquished the throne to her daughter, Queen Juliana.

Q *The new Lucille Ball TV program—what will it be about? Is Desi in it?—Jerry Weingarten, Oklahoma City, Okla.*

A Desi is not in it. Lucille Ball and Vivian Vance play two young widows with children, on the prowl for husbands.

Lucille Ball

Arnold Palmer

Q *Is it true that Arnold Palmer, the great golfer, flies his own plane to golf tournaments? Also how much will he earn this year and from what?—Laverne Mitchell, Helena, Mont.*

A Palmer flies his own plane, a two-engine, seven-seat job, to most tournaments. His income this year from all sources will approximate $350,000. He receives a $6,500 guarantee from Wilson Sporting Goods plus royalties on clubs bearing his endorsement. His syndicated newspaper column brings in another $20,000. His minimum fee for golf exhibitions is $3,000 plus a percentage of the gate. At this summer's end he had already won approximately $100,000 from golf victories. Further fees come from his endorsement of shoes, shirts, slacks, socks, windbreakers, golf clothes of all types.

Q *I heard that Anita Ekberg has gained 70 pounds, now weighs 200. Is that really true?—T. Dolci, Pittsburgh, Pa.*

A Miss Ekberg has reportedly

Anita Ekberg

gained 50 pounds, went to Lausanne recently for a secret slimming cure at a Swiss clinic.

Q *Dr. Martin Luther King—in what subject did he receive his doctorate and from which university and where was he ordained?—Wm. Kirkland, Macon, Ga.*

A Martin Luther King was ordained a minister in Atlanta at age 19 by his father, pastor of Atlanta's Ebenezer Baptist church. Later, he earned his doctorate in theology at Boston University.

Q *What is the relationship between Madame de Carbuccia of St. Tropez and Darryl Zanuck of 20th Century-Fox?—A.J., Long Beach, Calif.*

A Madame de Carbuccia is the owner of a villa on the French Riviera in which Mr. Zanuck formerly resided with his newest protégée, Irina Demich, and her mother.

Q *Has Dick Clark of American Bandstand been divorced? If so, has he taken a second wife?—R.L., St. Louis, Mo.*

A Clark divorced his first wife of nine years in November 1961. In April of this year he married his former secretary, Loretta Martin.

Dick Clark

Q *General Trujillo of the Dominican Republic was assassinated on May 30, 1961. Who runs the Dominican Republic today?—T. Pomerantz, Wilmington, Del.*

A A seven-man council of state under President Rafael Bonnelly.

Q *Does anyone know how much fashion models are paid in Paris? Take someone working at a place like Dior's.—D.E., Santa Fe, N.M.*

A Maggie Griffiths, 23, a top British model, recently quit Dior's claiming that in season she worked from 10 a.m. to 10 p.m., averaged only $42 per week.

Q *Can you tell me what position Pierre Salinger's brother occupies in the government?—Claude Ransom, Chicago, Ill.*

A Herbert E. Salinger, brother of the White House press secretary,

resigned as a special assistant to former Labor Secretary Arthur Goldberg this past August.

Q *Do women have the vote in Japan and are there any women in government?—Janet Lord, Akron, Ohio.*

A Women vote in Japan, recently sent two of their sex to the Japanese senate—Mrs. Shizue Kato and Mrs. Aki Fujiwara, both 64.

Q *Why has nothing been said in the press of Bob Hope and his "housekeeper"?—R.V., Vancouver, B.C.*

A Bob Hope has never been involved with his housekeeper. You are mistaking him for his older brother, Jim Hope, 70. James Hope, a real estate dealer, was recently divorced by his wife who testified that when she asked her husband to fire their young housekeeper, he allegedly replied: "If anybody's gonna get fired around here, it's gonna be you."

Q *How old is dancer-choreographer Martha Graham?—Geo. Capri, Dallas, Tex.*

A 69.

Q *As a result of our high altitude hydrogen blast over Johnston Island on July 9 a new radiation belt has been established at high altitudes that may last for years. Who was responsible for this mistake?—M. Monahan, Pittsburgh, Pa.*

A The Defense Department and the Atomic Energy Commission have jointly admitted their misjudgments about the effects of the July 9 blast in the Pacific.

Q *I've read that the best actress in Hollywood is a girl named Susan Oliver who has never made a single motion picture, only TV. Is this so?—Dana Penney, Zanesville, Ohio.*

A No, it is not. Miss Oliver worked in *Butterfield 8* and *The Caretakers* and several other films.

Susan Oliver

Edward Villella

Q *I am told that the most exciting new ballet dancer in Russia is an American named Edward Villella. Can you tell us anything about him?—Maria Dunnison, New York, N.Y.*

A Villella on tour in Russia with the New York City ballet was described by Moscow dance critics as "one of the most exciting new male dancers of our time." A native New Yorker, Villella is a former boxer who trained for the merchant marine, gave it up for dancing.

Q *Raymond Massey, the actor, has a daughter, Anna, 25, who is extremely talented. I saw her on the London stage. Is she married and if so, to whom?—Lillian Plant, Denver, Colo.*

A Anna Massey, alleging misconduct by her 29-year-old husband, English actor Peter Huggins in London, recently was awarded a divorce and custody of their three-year-old son.

Q *Where will the 1964 and 1968 Olympic Games be held?—Anthony M. Ford, Chicago, Ill.*

A 1964 in Tokyo—1968 as yet undecided but probably Lyons, France, or Detroit, Michigan.

Q *Is it true that most of the world's great financiers end up unhappy, miserable suicides? How about men like Insull, Hopson, Kreuger, Livermore and others?—J. Christopher Stallings, San Francisco, Calif.*

A It is true that many, but not most, of the world's financial giants have come to an unhappy end. Jesse Livermore and Ivar Kreuger were suicides. Insull died a fugitive. Howard Hopson died insane. Money frequently brings unhappiness.

Q *Republican National Chairman William Miller said recently that the Republican Party in his opinion did not have "anything to worry about." In the last 32 years how many times has the Republican Party controlled Congress?—T.L., Tucson, Ariz.*

A Twice—in 1946 and 1952.

Q *I understand that C. P. Snow, the author-scientist, recently died on the operating table. Details, please.—Anna Gold, New York, N.Y.*

A Sir Charles Snow is very much alive. During an operation on the retina of his eye, his heart suddenly stopped beating. Dr. Lorimer Fison, the ophthalmic surgeon, opened Snow's chest, massaged the heart by hand. After two minutes it began to beat again. Snow recovered, but lost the sight of one eye.

Q *Does anyone know how much money Khrushchev has poured into Cuba?—Stephen M., St. Louis, Mo.*

Nikita Khrushchev

A An estimated $1,000,000,000 in arms; an estimated $912,000,000 in economic aid, for Castro's Cuba.

Q *Is Senator Hubert Humphrey the only pharmacist in Congress? What are his degrees?—Janet Mollifson, Minneapolis, Minn.*

A Humphrey, 51, is the only pharmacist in Congress. He attended the Denver College of Pharmacy, but got his Bachelor of Arts degree from the University of Minnesota and an M.A. from Louisiana. He was elected mayor of Minneapolis at the age of 34 and a United States senator at 37.

Q *Is it true that Yehudi Menuhin, the great violinist, is now in the food business?—G. Kirk, Springfield, Ohio.*

A Yes, the health-food line in London.

Q *I would like to know the minimum wage for members of the Screen Actors Guild who work in Hollywood.—Susan Leonard, Evansville, Ind.*

A $100 a day or $350 a week, but work is so scarce in films that last year 70 percent of Guild members earned less than $2,500 from motion picture work.

Q *What is the relationship between President Kennedy and pollster Lou Harris?—J. Leylan, Dallas, Tex.*

A Lou Harris, 41, of Louis Harris & Associates, is a close friend of President Kennedy's. His samplings of public opinion have helped guide Kennedy since he was a U.S. senator. Harris is known figuratively as the president's private pollster. He employs 25 assistants and 3,000 part-time interviewers. Reportedly the Democratic National Committee paid Harris $76,000 in the first five months of 1962.

Q *Is it true that Premier Stalin planned to exile the entire Mikoyan family to Siberia during World War II?—J. Palmer, Wheeling, W. Va.*

A There was some talk of it. Eventually one or more of Mikoyan's four sons were exiled to Siberia, which is why there was never any love lost between Stalin and Mikoyan.

Joseph Stalin

WALTER SCOTT'S

PERSONALITY PARADE®

March 31, 1963

Q *When Elizabeth Taylor's third husband, Mike Todd, was killed in a plane crash, he was flying a rented plane. Elizabeth and Mike Todd's son have sued the company, Ayer Lease Plan, Inc., for $5,000,000. Have they been paid the $5,000,000 yet?—Eric Duncan, Santa Fe, N.M.*

Elizabeth Taylor

A They sued for $5,000,000 but were awarded only $40,000. Of this sum, $13,000 went in attorneys' fees. The remaining $27,000 went to Elizabeth Frances Fisher, daughter of Elizabeth Taylor and Todd, later adopted by Eddie Fisher following his marriage to the widow Todd.

Q *What is Richard Nixon's present occupation?—Mike Stern, Portland, Ore.*

A As of this writing he is a lawyer and author.

Q *Was it Rita Moreno who sang in* West Side Story, *or was it not?—Claire French, Los Angeles, Calif.*

A She sang one number, but it was Betty Wand who "ghost-sang" two songs for her.

Q *Who said: "Easy-crying widows take new husbands soonest; there's nothing like wet weather for transplanting"?—Charles Longo, Tucson, Ariz.*

A Oliver Wendell Holmes, American author and physician (1809-1894).

Q *Is it true that Governor George Romney of Michigan will talk for five minutes to anyone who comes to see him?—P.T., Iron Mountain, Mich.*

George Romney

A When Governor Romney is in Lansing he sets aside the morning hours to talk to visitors on a first-come, first-heard basis. He limits each caller to five minutes.

Q *Can you tell me if the Duke of Edinburgh is in line to the Greek throne?—Louis Peters, Richmond, Va.*

A The Duke of Edinburgh is third in line of succession to the Greek throne.

Q *I heard Grace Kelly on television a few weeks ago, and her accent was as phony as a four-dollar bill. She comes from Philadelphia, but I'd like to know what sort of accent she's adopted.—H. Garber, Scranton, Pa.*

Grace Kelly

A It is known as the "international diplomatic accent."

Q *I would like very much to find out if Joseph P. Kennedy, the president's father, has regained the power of speech.—Jayne Reese, Pasadena, Calif.*

A Mr. Joseph P. Kennedy unfortunately has not yet regained his power of speech. He was deprived of it by a stroke he suffered on December 19, 1961.

Q *Which one wears a hairpiece, George Chakiris or George Maharis?—Diana Dellos, Chicago, Ill.*

A George Maharis. George Chakiris' hair is all his own.

Q *I understand that before Moise Tshombe left Katanga he had $15,000,000 flown to Swiss banks. Is this true?—George Hutterman, Columbus, Ohio.*

A The story is that 60 boxes of money were flown out of Katanga by Jan van Rissengen, a Belgian flyer working for Tshombe, and that the money was handed over to Portuguese officials in Angola. What happened to it from there is not yet known.

Q *Is Esther Williams married to Fernando Lamas?—Freda Ranansky, Oakland, Calif.*

A They were reported wed in Europe some time ago.

Q *How much does the Kingston Trio earn in recording royalties each year?—R. Ford, Detroit, Mich.*

A Close to $300,000.

Q *Montgomery Clift's niece admitted shooting and killing her Italian lover. How come the judge let her go free? Is this justice?—Enrico Salto, Atlantic City, N.J.*

A Suzanne Clift, pregnant by her dead lover, was placed on probation for 10 years by Massachusetts Superior Court Judge Lewis Goldberg, with the stipulation that she voluntarily commit herself to the Massachusetts Mental Health Center for treatment. Judge Goldberg said the case involving Miss Clift was one of the most "troublesome" he had ever deliberated. No one has been executed in Massachusetts since 1947, and Miss Clift, according to her attorneys, has been a mental case for some time.

Q *I have been told that although she is almost 50, Loretta Young still wears braces on her teeth. Is this so?—Hannah Knowles, Dallas, Tex.*

A Occasionally she does.

Q *Who is LeRoy Johnson, and why is he so prominent in Georgia?—Vita Johnson, Gulfport, Miss.*

A Johnson is the first Negro to have been elected to the Georgia senate in 92 years. He has also been named by the Atlanta Junior Chamber of Commerce as one of the five most outstanding young men of the year.

Q *I would like to know if Bobby Kennedy's seven children attend public or parochial school.—J.F., Bethesda, Md.*

A All of Robert Kennedy's children attend parochial school except Michael, four, and Mary, three, who are too young.

Robert Kennedy

Peter O'Toole

Q *Peter O'Toole, who stars in* Lawrence of Arabia—*doesn't he have a different nose than the one with which he was born?—Helene Carter, Winnetka, Ill.*

A It's the same nose except that it's been straightened by plastic surgeons.

Q *King Saud of Arabia recently took his four wives and 15 concubines to the French Riviera on vacation. What I'd like to know is if he's abolished slavery and polygamy in his country.—Ann Hersholt, Miami, Fla.*

A In 1936 the King's father, Ibn Saud, forbade the importing of slaves into Saudi Arabia. In 1962 the present King Saud formally abolished the buying, selling and owning of slaves in Saudi Arabia. Polygamy, however, has not been abolished. Mohammedan law still allows a man four wives.

Q *Does anyone have any idea how much the U.S. has spent to date enforcing the education of James Meredith of Mississippi?—T.P., Mobile, Ala.*

A Almost $5,000,000.

Q *Why has nothing ever been printed about Elvis Presley's twin? Why has his identity been kept in the dark?—Lois Evans, Monroe, La.*

A Elvis' twin brother died at birth.

Q *Who said "Conceit is God's gift to the little man"?—Victor Agry, Buffalo, N.Y.*

A Advertising executive and writer Bruce Barton.

Q *Screen star Deborah Kerr—is her marriage to writer Peter Viertel on the skids?—Jamie Wilsson, Brownsville, Tex.*

A According to Miss Kerr, she is sublimely happy. "I am truly alive for the first time in my life," she says. "Cary Grant often talks about searching for the truth within himself. I don't think you find it in yourself. You find it in someone else, and that's when you give them everything you've got. That's the secret of happiness. And that's why I'm so happy now."

Q *Is it true that when Eddie Fisher played Las Vegas he dropped $150,000 at the gaming tables which he did not have?—G. Prentiss, Sacramento, Calif.*

A The figure is much too high. Insiders say he dropped one week's salary, $25,000.

Q *I would like to know to whom actress Leslie Caron is married and whether she owns the Caron drugstore in Paris.—Corinna Murville, Fayetteville, N.C.*

Leslie Caron

A Leslie Caron is married to British stage director Peter Hall. Her father owns the pharmacy in Paris.

Q *What about the Princess Soraya-Maximilian Schell romance? True or publicity?—Susan Ferriere, Carson City, Nev.*

A True.

Q *In that mess about the TFX plane contract and Defense Secretary McNamara, I'd like two things explained: (1) what does TFX stand for, and (2) how wealthy is McNamara, and does he have any stock holdings in General Dynamics, which was awarded the TFX contract?—G.H., Akron, Ohio.*

A TFX is the name of a fighter plane ordered by the government. T stands for tactical, F for fighter, X for experimental. As of March 1, 1963, Defense Secretary McNamara was worth approximately $1,278,200. He had $294,100 in federal and municipal bonds, $982,795 in common stocks and $1,035 in cash. None of his holdings was in General Dynamics. When McNamara joined President Kennedy's cabinet in 1961, he relinquished his job as president of the Ford Motor Co., which paid him an annual salary and bonus approximating $500,000. He also sold 24,705 shares of Ford stock for $1,500,000. As secretary of defense, McNamara receives $25,000 a year, and from various congressional committees a thorough going-over.

Robert McNamara

Q *I would like to find out once and for all why* Cleopatra, *the motion picture extravaganza, wasn't filmed in Hollywood where it started out. Why was it moved to England and Italy?—Ben Kahn, Philadelphia, Pa.*

Elizabeth Taylor

A Elizabeth Taylor reportedly wanted to work overseas so as to take advantage of the favorable tax setup. Spyros Skouras, then head of 20th Century-Fox, foolishly assented, a move which subsequently led to his downfall.

Q *Can you tell me if Romano Mussolini, jazz pianist son of Benito Mussolini, has been booked into Las Vegas?—Louise Schneider, Fort Dodge, Iowa.*

A Not yet. He's expected to play Mexico and South America first.

Q *Is it true that Governor Nelson Rockefeller of New York will become Joan Crawford's fifth husband?—Carl King, Washington, D.C.*

A Not likely.

WALTER SCOTT'S
PERSONALITY PARADE®

May 19, 1963

Anita Ekberg

Q *Is it true that Federico Fellini will divorce his wife to marry Anita Ekberg?—Lois Haldemann, Cleveland, Ohio.*

A Anita Ekberg was recently married in Switzerland to an American film bit-player, Rich Van Nutter, from Pomona, Calif.

Q *Why aren't the American people told the truth about President Kennedy's illness? Isn't it a fact that his aching back has practically crippled him?—P.L., Coronado, Calif.*

A He is not crippled. Extraordinary precautions are constantly taken to protect his weak back. Frequently, for example, he wears a small corset or girdle. When he travels, a special horsehair mattress is sent along so that he can have a night of comfortable sleep. He also has a specially built leather seat which lends support to his lower spine. The truth is that the president must baby his back, keep his muscles strong and supple, which is why he tries to get in a few minutes of swimming each day in the White House pool, which is heated to about 90 degrees. Two years ago in Ottawa, when he bent down to shovel some dirt, he hurt his back, had to go around on crutches, submit to the moist pack treatment.

Q *Who is the richest woman in Great Britain after the Queen?—Leona Richardson, Fairfield, Conn.*

A Probably the Countess of Seafield, who owns 800 square miles of Scotland, including 10 towns, three castles.

Q *Recently I saw the movie, Nine Hours to Rama, about the assassination of Mahatma Gandhi. In the movie Gandhi blesses Naturam Godse, the man who shot him. Is this true or fictional?—Al Weisler, Chicago, Ill.*

A It is fictional. When Gandhi was shot, he died almost instantly. He muttered only two words, "He, Ram!" (Oh, God!) The film is a distortion of history.

Q *What's happened to writer Dorothy Parker, and how old is she?—Nord Brecklin, Miami, Fla.*

A Dorothy Parker, 69, teaches literature at Los Angeles State College.

Q *Why has former Vice President Richard Nixon signed to write a series of articles for* The Saturday Evening Post?—G.Y., Whittier, Calif.

A One reason: money.

Q *What is the true scan on the Vince Edwards-Juliet Prowse romance?—Adrian Bronston, Jean, Nev.*

A They started dating when both were working in Las Vegas.

Q *Would you kindly tell me the names of the wives of the late Tyrone Power? Where are they now, and what are they doing?—Alice Richmond, Denver, Colo.*

Tyrone Power

A Annabella resides in Paris, Linda Christian is playing the field in Hollywood, Debbie Minardos is also playing the field.

Q *What I cannot understand is how someone like singer Dorothy Dandridge, who earns more than $100,000 a year, can now be bankrupt. Will you please explain?—Kenneth Yorkes, Toronto.*

A Miss Dandridge has spent more than she earned.

Q *Jane Powell and her husband Pat Nerney have separated, which is par for Hollywood marriages. How many children are involved?—L.T., Phoenix, Ariz.*

Jane Powell

A The Nerneys have a daughter, Lindsey, seven. Miss Powell has two children by a previous marriage to Geary Steffen. Nerney has a daughter by a previous marriage to actress Mona Freeman.

Q *Is it true that a liquor license is impossible to obtain in New York State without a pay-off to the "right" politicians?—M.P., Buffalo, N.Y.*

A There have been irregularities in the issuance of such licenses, and Governor Nelson Rockefeller has undertaken to investigate and correct the scandalous conditions pertaining thereto.

Q *Who is the Israeli secret service chief who engineered the capture of Adolf Eichmann and recently tried to have killed the German scientists working in Egypt?—F.L., Brooklyn, N.Y.*

A Iser Helperin was in charge of the Israeli secret service when Eichmann was captured. He was also in charge when attempts were made via explosives on the lives of German scientists working for the Egyptian government. He recently resigned.

Q *How good are the chances of Vice President Lyndon Johnson running for the presidency in 1968?—George Hunt, Dallas, Tex.*

A Pretty good.

Grace Kelly

Q *Earl Mountbatten is one of those upper-class Britishers. I've been told that Grace Kelly was his secret guest in London not too long ago. Why was this not reported by our press?—L.T., New York, N.Y.*

A Princess Grace and her husband were the recent guests of Earl Mountbatten on a private visit to his home in Romsey, Hampshire. The press carried reports of their visit.

Q *On TV I heard Congressman John Bell Williams—it was on the* Today *program—he said that the attorney general of the U.S. sends his children to white, segregated schools, and lives in the segregated neighborhood of McLean, Virginia. Is this so?—D.H.P., Denver, Colo.*

A The attorney general's three school-age boys attend Our Lady of Victory parochial school in Washington, D.C., which is committed to a policy of nonsegregation. His one school-age daughter, Kathleen, attends the Stone Ridge Convent of the Sacred Heart parochial school in Bethesda, Maryland. This school is attended by a Negro student. The attorney general and his family live in a nonsegregated neighborhood in McLean, Virginia, less than 1,000 yards away from a Negro family.

Q *How many appointments has President Kennedy made to the U.S. Supreme Court?—Fred Watters, Pasadena, Calif.*

A Two, Justice White and Justice Goldberg.

Q *Who chooses the colored people to register at various southern universities? For example, who decided that Vivian Malone would attempt registration at the University of Alabama?—G.T., Birmingham, Ala.*

A Vivian Malone from Mobile was selected by the NAACP from a dozen female Negro volunteers.

Q *Is comedian Lenny Bruce really a dope addict?—Florence Kahn, Chicago, Ill.*

A Such was the ruling of a California Superior Court in a recent psychiatric hearing.

Q *Recently Lord Beaverbrook, 84, the British press king, got secretly married. Who and how old is his wife?—Louis Prilt, Boston, Mass.*

A His wife, Lady Dunn, 52, was the widow of Sir James Dunn, British steel magnate who died in 1956, left an estate valued at $65,000,000. Lady Dunn inherited one half after taxes.

Q *The Lucille Ball show on TV this past season was not very good. Has Lucy lost her appeal?—Vincent Marco, Pittsburgh, Pa.*

Lucille Ball

A Miss Ball, around a long time, is no longer a new attraction, but she remains one of the foremost comediennes of this era.

Q *Is it true that Bing Crosby was originally scheduled to star in* To Kill a Mockingbird *instead of Gregory Peck?—Patricia Wayne, Detroit, Mich.*

A No. Crosby tried to buy the screen rights to the novel but was one day too late.

Q *Is Nöel Coward still writing plays, or has he retired?—Paul Vesian, Poughkeepsie, N.Y.*

A Coward says he will never retire, is working on a new musical, *The Girl Who Came to Supper.*

Q *In Shakespeare's day I understand that* Antony and Cleopatra *was a big flop. Is this true?—Ann Seldman, Cedar Rapids, Ia.*

A It was performed, according to authority Ivor Brown, only once or twice and then forgotten for a long time.

William Shakespeare

Q *Can you tell why the shares of 20th Century-Fox went down after* Cleopatra *opened?—Kenneth Hyman, Montreal, Que.*

A Before *Cleopatra* was released, 20th Century-Fox stock boomed from a low of 20 to a high of 37. Wall Street anticipated a great, memorable and immensely profitable motion picture. After the film was released, the stock went down.

Q *I would like to know how much Christine Keeler obtained from the sale to the British press of her memoirs of life and love with Profumo?—L.T., Tucson, Ariz.*

A $42,000.

Q *How old is Danny Kaye, and in what branch of the service was he in World War II?—Althea Ross, Miami, Fla.*

A Kaye is 50, was not a member of the armed forces in World War II.

Q *Does David Selznick produce motion pictures any more?—Hy Fishman, Passaic, N.J.*

A In the past 15 years Selznick has personally produced only one film, and not a very good one at that, *A Farewell to Arms.* It starred Rock Hudson and Mrs. Selznick, Jennifer Jones.

David Selznick

WALTER SCOTT'S
PERSONALITY PARADE®

August 18, 1963

Judy Garland

Q *I've been told that Judy Garland's Thanksgiving Day TV show was taped this July 4th. True or false?—Tom Kline, Hastings, Neb.*

A Judy's Thanksgiving Day show was taped over the July 4th weekend.

Q *Who was the last non-Italian Pope?—David Gold, Passaic, N.J.*

A Adrian VI of Holland, 1522-23.

Q *William Vassall, the British Admiralty clerk who sold secrets to the Soviet Union after being compromised as a homosexual—wasn't he once convicted of molesting an 11-year-old English boy? How could the British employ such a man?—David Watts, Concord, N.J.*

A You are mistaking William Vassall for his brother Richard, who was so charged and convicted.

Q *Is it true that Shakespeare's wedding was a shotgun wedding? I need the information for a term paper.—J.P., Lancaster, Pa.*

A Yes, according to many authorities.

Q *Who said, "The misfortunes hardest to bear are those which never come"?—F. Wirsig, Richmond, Va.*

A James Russell Lowell (1819-1891), American poet, essayist, editor and diplomat.

Q *Is singer Frankie Avalon paying off on a paternity accusation?—H.P., Newark, N.J.*

A He makes regular support payments.

Q *I would like to know from which U.S. medical school Dr. Stephen Ward, mentor of Christine Keeler, was graduated.—G.T., London, Eng.*

A No medical school, but from the Kirksville College of Osteopathy in Missouri in 1938.

Q *Is it true that the French have a minister of sport? If so, who is he?—Allen Wilshire, Los Angeles, Calif.*

A True. France's High Commissioner of Youth and Sports is Maurice Herzog, first man to conquer Annapurna, the Himalayan peak. His job: to organize government-sponsored youth clubs, athletic facilities, camping trips, etc.

Q *The rumor has been widespread for months that Marilyn Monroe's last phone call before her suicide was to the attorney general, Bobby Kennedy. Is this so?—P. Ward, Washington, D.C.*

A No, it was to her psychiatrist, Dr. Ralph Greenson.

Maya Plisetskaya

Q *I know this is a matter of opinion, but among critics who is considered the world's greatest ballerina? I mean among those ballerinas now living and working.—Louise Weber, Tucson, Ariz.*

A Probably Maya Plisetskaya, 37, prima ballerina of Russia's Bolshoi Ballet. Critics compare her to the great Ulanova.

Pat Patterson and Charles Boyer

Q *Is Charles Boyer still married to Pat Patterson? Isn't this something of a record for Hollywood?—D.S.K., N. Miami Beach, Fla.*

A They were married in 1934, have a son Michael who works at Four Star TV productions. For Hollywood it's something of a record.

Q *I would like to know if the American public has ever been told how the CIA under Allen Dulles set up and paid for the West German Federal Intelligence Agency headed by Reinhard Gehlen. Were we ever told that this organization was infiltrated by Red agents who transmitted to Moscow all our top secret information?—T.L.P., Falls Church, Va.*

A The American public is told practically nothing of CIA activities, because such disclosure would nullify the Agency's effectiveness. As for Russian infiltration of the Gehlen organization, it was amazing. Three of the organization's most trusted men, Heinz Felfe, Hans Clemens and Erwin Tiebel, turned out to be Soviet agents, who in 10 years delivered more than 15,000 photos of the Gehlen files to Soviet contacts in East Germany.

Q *What is the age of actress Patricia Neal? Is she now married?—John Baker, Lowry A.F.B., Colo.*

A Patricia Neal is 37. She is married to writer Roald Dahl.

Q *What has become of British cinema queen Shirley Anne Field? Last reports had her going to Mexico to make Kings of the Sun with Yul Brynner.—Ralph H. Martin, San Jose, Calif.*

A After finishing *Kings of the Sun*, Miss Field returned to London.

PERSONALITY PARADE®

August 25, 1963

Q *When President Kennedy was journeying around Europe a few weeks ago, did he take time out to visit his sister's grave in Derbyshire?—L.T., New Rochelle, N.Y.*

John F. Kennedy

A He did.

Q *In 1948 a Negro girl, Edith Irby, was the first of her race to enroll in a southern medical school. I believe it was at the University of Arkansas. Can you tell me what's become of her?—O. Calderon, San Antonio, Tex.*

A She is now Dr. Edith Jones, chief of cardiology at St. Elizabeth's Hospital, Houston, Texas. She is also a clinical instructor at Baylor University Hospital. She is married to Dr. J. B. Jones, a dean at Texas Southern College. They have two children.

Q *As a stockholder in CBS I would like to know if the network has built two $75,000 dressing rooms for Danny Kaye and Judy Garland. And if so, why?—F.T., White Plains, N.Y.*

A The TV network spent $75,000 on a penthouse for Kaye and $75,000 on a trailer dressing room setup for Judy Garland. Reason: to keep them happy.

Q *When did the great silent star Rudolph Valentino die? And wasn't there a rumor at the time that he was shot by a jealous husband?—R.G., New York, N.Y.*

A Valentino died in 1926 when he was on a visit to New York. There were plenty of rumors about the cause of his death. He died of Peritonitis.

Q *I understand that Roger Kahn, the sportswriter who wrote* Calories Don't Count, *is writing the autobiography of Mickey Rooney. When will it appear?—Ilse Freund, Baltimore, Md.*

A Kahn was hired to ghost the Rooney autobiography, delivered 80 percent of the book, then filed a $75,000 breach of contract suit against Rooney for calling off the deal. The actor counterclaims Kahn breached the contract because the manuscript "contained many grievous and serious misstatements of fact." Result: no book.

Q *A New York furrier named Lou Ritter was once married to actress Carroll Baker. Was he also married to Zsa Zsa Gabor?—F. Bloom, Hempstead, N.Y.*

A Gabor and Ritter, who is now deceased, were never married.

Q *I would like to find out where screen star Stella Stevens was born, what was her name at the time of her birth and who the man was who gave her a start in motion pictures.—E.P., Memphis, Tenn.*

Stella Stevens

A Stella Stevens was born in Hot Coffee, Mississippi. Her real name is Estelle Eggleston. Her original sponsor was a Philadelphia theater-owner named Marty Shapiro.

Juliet Prowse

Q *What's happened to Juliet Prowse? Is she really returning to South Africa?—Helen Adams, Chicago, Ill.*

A She is starring in *Irma La Douce* in summer stock, plans to film in Europe, claims, "After my romance with Sinatra was over, 20th Century-Fox shoved me right into the ground with four triple-C pictures. Now I have to start all over again."

Q *What is the setup between Dame Margot Fonteyn, the ballerina, and Rudolph Nureyev? They've been doing the ballet tour everywhere. Doesn't she ever see her Panamanian husband?—H.T., Dallas, Tex.*

A Dr. Roberto Arias, former Panamanian Ambassador to Great Britain, spends most of his time in Panama supervising his investments. Miss Fonteyn is accompanied by her 74-year-old mother on these ballet tours. She and Nureyev are colleagues.

Q *Recently Charles Wrightsman rented the 680-ton yacht,* Radiant, *from Basil Mavroleon, the Greek shipping king. He paid $10,000 a month rent for the yacht. I would like to know who is Charles Wrightsman that he can afford such rates.—Ellen Charles, Indianapolis, Ind.*

A He is an oil millionaire, Palm Beach neighbor of the Kennedys, father of Charlene Wrightsman Cassini, who earlier this year took her life.

Q *Is Jerry Lewis an egomaniac?—Bernard Roth, Passaic, N.J.*

A He is extremely confident.

Q *Who is Marie Cui, who recently named Marlon Brando as the father of her four-month-old daughter? How much money does she want?—Carla O'Kane, Frankfort, Ky.*

A Marie Cui is a Philippine dancer who gave birth to a daughter, Maya Gabriella, on February 27, 1963. She charges Brando is the father of her child. She wanted $775 a month, but a few weeks ago a court announced that Brando was not the child's father.

Q *I read in PARADE that Gary Player, 28, is well on his way to becoming a millionaire. Is this really true? How come there is so much money in professional golf? The prizes don't seem that large.—Tom Winston, Raleigh, N.C.*

A It is true. The big money in golf for professionals like Player, Palmer and Nicklaus lies in endorsements and television, not prize purses.

Q *Who said: "The husband who's always busy as a bee may some day find his honey missing"?—Vic Healy, New York, N.Y.*

A Bob Hope.

Bob Hope

PERSONALITY PARADE®

November 10, 1963

Q *Gene Autry, the cowboy star, just bought the Mark Hopkins Hotel in San Francisco. Where is he getting all the money?—G.L.P., Baltimore, Md.*

Gene Autry

A Autry heads an investing syndicate which owns the Los Angeles Angels, the Los Angeles Rams football team, the Sahara Inn in Chicago, the Continental Hotel in L.A., and several other properties. He is a millionaire in his own right.

Q *Is it true that if Neville Chamberlain had not capitulated to Hitler in 1938 on the Sudeten crisis the anti-Hitler generals in Germany would have used the crisis as an excuse to get rid of Hitler?—R.C. Walsh, Bethesda, Md.*

A True. The fact is that anti-Hitler generals sent an emissary, General Ewald von Kleist, to London to urge Chamberlain to take a strong stand against Hitler. But General von Kleist was ignored by Chamberlain, and consequently Europe was thrown into war.

Q *What individual owns the most telephone stock in the U.S.?—Penny Ward, Denver, Colo.*

A One of the largest shareholders is showman Billy Rose, who owns 80,000 shares of American Telephone and Telegraph, worth $10,000,000.

Q *The movie* Stolen Hours *with Susan Hayward—isn't that a remake?—Jen Babcock, Portland, Me.*

A Yes, of the Bette Davis starrer, *Dark Victory.* It concerns a woman with an incurable brain disease who marries her doctor.

Q *Does anyone know the average number of advertisements the average American is exposed to every day?—Fred Paul, Louisville, Ky.*

A A good guess: 1,500.

Q *I would like to know if*

Audrey Hepburn

Audrey Hepburn ia a millionaire and where her home is. Can you help?—Ellen Ostrup, Newark, N.J.

A She is easily a millionaire; lives in Burgenstock, Switzerland.

Q *Who is responsible for the Jerry Lewis TV show on Saturday nights? I mean, who authorized it?—T.R., Los Angeles, Calif.*

A Leonard Goldenson, chief of the ABC-TV network.

Q *Has singer Kate Smith retired?—Harvey Ditson, Chicago, Ill.*

A No, she recently made a Carnegie Hall appearance and does occasional guest shots on TV.

Q *I would like to know why ex-President Eisenhower, when recently giving a list of 10 possible Republican presidential candidates, omitted the name of Richard Nixon.—Ernest Gent, Rockingham, N.C.*

A Eisenhower says he was convinced that when Nixon announced he was finished running for political office the former vice president meant it.

Q *Is it on the level that Shakespeare's famous love sonnets were written by him to a boy and not to a girl?—Ted Switzer, Cambridge, Mass.*

A Among authorities that is the generally held belief. The two earliest known editions of the sonnets are the Thomas Thorpe quarto of 1609 and the John Benson octavo of 1640. Benson went through the sonnets changing "he" to "she" and "him" to "her" in all cases; the sonnets were subsequently printed and reprinted in that manner. The sonnets were dedicated to "W.H.," who variously has been identified as William Herbert, Henry Wriothesley, William Hall and William Holgate, this last the 17-year-old son of an innkeeper at Saffron Walden where Shakespeare was supposed to have acted in 1607.

Q *Is Ezra Taft Benson, secretary of agriculture under Eisenhower, chief of the John Birch Society in Utah?—Ole Hansen, Salt Lake City, Utah.*

A No, his son is.

Q *How much did sportsman John Galbreath pay for Swaps? Wasn't it the highest price paid for any horse?—John Lee Pennell, San Diego, Calif.*

A Galbreath paid $2,000,000 for Swaps, the highest price paid to date for any thoroughbred.

John Galbreath

Q *Who said: "Love is the delusion that one woman differs from another"?—Dave Gates, Miami, Fla.*

A H. L. Mencken, American writer, editor and critic (1880-1956).

Q *Where does Howard Hughes hang his hat now?—Bette Stockman, Friendship, N.Y.*

A In Los Angeles County.

Q *Errol Flynn's son, Sean—why no word about the young lover from Hollywood and his riotous doings?—Diana Merlow, New York, N.Y.*

A Sean Flynn is in Venice working in a low-budget Italian film, *See Venice and Die.*

Q *I understand that Bing Crosby has put up for sale his Palm Desert house with a sign, "The President Slept Here." How much does Crosby want for his house, and is that sign really there?—J.T., Riverside, Calif.*

A The Crosby house in Palm Desert carries no such sign. It is for sale, however, at $186,000. Five years ago it cost $40,000 to build, but Crosby has made several improvements. President Kennedy slept there twice.

Bing Crosby

WALTER SCOTT'S
PERSONALITY PARADE®

November 24, 1963

Q *Can you tell me if* The Enemy Within, *supposedly written by Bobby Kennedy, was actually written by John Seigenthaler of Nashville?—L.R., Nashville, Tenn.*

A Seigenthaler, a former reporter, helped Kennedy with the book.

Q *How old is June Allyson, and how old is her new husband? Doesn't she have him by 15 years?—Eli Gottesmann, New York, N.Y.*

A Miss Allyson is 41; her husband, Glenn Maxwell, is 31.

Q *I caught Frank Sinatra, Jr., on an Ed Sullivan TV show, and the kid was awful. What is the critical opinion of the boy's voice?—J.T., Hoboken, N.J.*

A That it's small.

Frank Sinatra, Jr.

Q *Does anyone really know why Sonny Liston ran out of London a few months ago? Producers in England had to return all that money.—Stanley Cullaghan, Baltimore, Md.*

A "I left," explains Liston, "because I was tired about the Birmingham questions. I've never been afraid in the ring, but I get real nervous when people ask me questions about race relations. I got a bad headache from all those questions they asked, and I just decided to come home."

Q *Is it true that Fidel Castro once tried to murder his father because his father wouldn't marry his mother?—Hector Ramirez, Miami, Fla.*

A Castro disliked his father but never attempted to kill him. Fidel was born August 13, 1926. Until he was 12, he was the illegitimate son of Angel Castro and his mulatto housekeeper, Lina Rez. When Castro's first wife died, Angel married the housekeeper, thereby legitimizing his son, Fidel. Between Castro father and son there was reportedly little love. Fidel

Fidel Castro

accused his father of exploiting his laborers, but he never tried patricide

Q *How much does Jimmy Hoffa spend on politics?—Harry Knox, Chicago, Ill.*

A Hoffa says he plans to spend between $5,000,000 and $8,000,000 this year to elect pro-Teamster politicians. Next year he plans to spend more to defeat President Kennedy.

Q *I've just learned from a reliable source that Pat and Shirley Boone have separated. Is this true or false?—Mabel Page, Desert Hot Springs, Calif.*

A False.

Q *Linus Pauling, the only American to win the Nobel Prize twice, was denied a passport by the State Department in 1952. What reason was given?—George Lanfield, Pasadena, Calif.*

A "Not in the best interests of the U.S." Later Pauling's passport was reinstated.

Q *Were Joan Crawford and Douglas Fairbanks, Jr., ever married to each other?—B.K., Ironton, Mo.*

A They were married in 1929, divorced in 1933.

Q *Who said: "The 100 percent American is 99 percent an idiot"?—Carl Keeler, Tucson, Ariz.*

A The late George Bernard Shaw.

Q *Dolores Hart, the Hollywood star who is becoming a nun—where is she in residence?—K.T., Los Angeles, Calif.*

A In the Monastery of Regina Laudis, Bethlehem, Conn.

Q *How much did President Kennedy receive for the motion picture rights to his life story,* PT-109, *and was the film any good?—D. Higgins, Columbia, S.C.*

A The deal for the movie rights to the book *PT-109* by Robert Donovan was in part negotiated by the president's father, Joe Kennedy, a former movie tycoon himself. The president got nothing; each of the crew members of the original *PT-109* or their widows got $2,500 each. Author Donovan, now with the *Los Angeles Times*, got $120,000.

Q *I would like to know if it's true that Elizabeth Taylor has set up a trust fund for David Rennie, son of film star Michael Rennie.—David Rutland, San Antonio, Tex.*

A Yes, she is his godmother and set up a $10,000 trust fund for the boy.

Elizabeth Taylor

Q *Which television station does Jack Paar own?—Hilda Gresham, Brattleboro, Vt.*

A Paar recently agreed to purchase a 60 percent interest in TV station WMTV, Poland Spring, Maine.

Jack and Joan Benny

Q *I would like to know how many times Jack Benny's daughter has been married. Also, is she adopted, and does Benny have any other children?—Hannah Payne, Washington, D.C.*

A Joan Benny, adopted, is the only child of Jack and Mary Benny. Joan has been married three times, has two children.

WALTER SCOTT'S
PERSONALITY PARADE®

February 2, 1964

Lady Bird and Lyndon Johnson

Q *How old is President Johnson's wife, and is it true that she secretly buys her dresses in Paris?—Bertha Franklin, Laurel, Miss.*

A Mrs. Johnson is 51, buys her clothes domestically.

Q *Who was the Secret Service agent in charge of the Kennedy trip through Dallas? Where was he when President Kennedy was shot?—J.K.M., Madison, Wis.*

A Agent Roy Kellerman was riding in the right front seat of the president's car when Kennedy was shot.

Q *How much money has the film* Lawrence of Arabia *made to date?— Vi Fromme, Tenafly, N.J.*

A Approximately $14,000,000, which is what it cost to make.

Q *I've heard that Peter Lawford's wife, Pat, will divorce him to marry Porfirio Rubirosa. Any truth to that story?— B.R., Washington, D.C.*

A None.

Q *Winston Churchill, who wrote a best-seller,* The Crisis, *in 1901—is he the same Winston Churchill of World War II fame?—Florence Soman, Chicago, Ill.*

A No, the Winston Churchill who wrote *The Crisis* was an American, raised in St. Louis, who attended the Naval Academy at Annapolis, subsequently wrote several historical novels.

Q *Why was Jack Webb, in charge of TV at Warner Brothers, fired and replaced by Jack Warner's son-in-law, Bill Orr?—V. Fleming, Burbank, Calif.*

A Warner, an extremely difficult man to work for, was dissatisfied with Webb's record. Warner Brothers is a studio with a long history of nepotism.

Q *How old is Pope Paul?—Ann Glenn, Zanesville, Ohio.*

A He is 66.

Q *Mme. Nhu of South Vietnam was one of the richest ladies in that country. Did she ever get her fortune out?—Ed Swinnerton, Kansas City, Kan.*

A No. Most of her multimillion-dollar fortune was in real estate which was confiscated by the new military regime.

Q *How much is Eddie Fisher's swag from his marriage to Liz Taylor?— Roy Dino, Las Vegas, Nev.*

A At least a million; more if *Cleopatra* is a rousing success.

Q *Was the John Birch Society in favor of impeaching the late President Kennedy?—E.J.F., Salem, Mass.*

A In the December 1963 issue of *American Opinion*, a monthly magazine published by the John Birch Society, an article by Charles Tansil asserted that President Kennedy should have been impeached for proposing a disarmament program to the United Nations.

Q *Who said, "A rich man and his daughter are soon parted"?— Clarence Enfield, Denver, Colo.*

A Frank Hubbard, America newspaper humorist (1868-1930).

Q *Who devised the first crossword puzzle in the U.S.?—Jan Feldman, Philadelphia, Pa.*

A Credit is generally given to Arthur Wynne, an editor of the N.Y. *World* in 1913.

Q *Is Jill St. John publicity-crazy? Is that why she's been dating Baby Pignatari, Frank Sinatra and the rest of that crowd?—Sal Douglas, Baltimore, Md.*

A Miss St. John is not publicity-shy, likes male company.

Jill St. John

Q *I saw George Hamilton in the movie version of* Act One, *and he is awful. Who is responsible for hiring this baby?— Bernard G., Miami, Fla.*

A He was hired for *Act One* by Dore Schary.

Q *In how many states are citizens under the age of 21 allowed to vote?— Claire Allen, Des Moines, Iowa.*

A In four: Georgia and Kentucky, where the voting age is 18; Alaska, 19; and Hawaii, 20.

Q *How long has Fidel Castro been in power in Cuba?—D.N. Jones, Wheeling, W.Va.*

A Five years.

Q *Why does Mamie Eisenhower always go west via private railroad car?— Henry Tinney, Urbana, Ill.*

A The former First Lady does not like to fly.

Mamie Eisenhower

Q *President Johnson has such a busy schedule, when does he sleep? Also how much does he weigh?—V. Roth, Richmond, Va.*

A President Johnson weighs approximately 205 lbs., sleeps at night, generally four to six hours.

Q *How much older than Ernest Borgnine is Ethel Merman? How many husbands has she had? Why do these stars marry younger men?—Lois Petersen, Denver, Colo.*

A Ethel Merman is 55; Borgnine is 47. Miss Merman has previously been married to Bill Smith, a publicist at 20th Century-Fox; the late Bob Levitt, a newspaper executive; and Bob Six, head of Continental Airlines. Some female celebrities marry younger men because these men are frequently weak, tractable and, of course, available. This is not true of Borgnine, who says, "We met and happened to fall in love."

Q *Does anyone know how much money the American public has contributed to Mrs. Lee Harvey Oswald, widow of the suspected assassin of President Kennedy?—B.M. Lewis, Louisville, Ky.*

A To date, approximately $24,000.

Q *How old is Speaker of the House John McCormack?—Charles Haddon, St. Paul, Minn.*

A He is 72.

Harris & Ewing / Globe

John McCormack

Q *I would like to know how many times Alfred Dreyfus in the Dreyfus Affair was tried.—Frieda Deutsch, Asbury Park, N.J.*

A Twice. In 1894 Dreyfus, a French Jew, was court-martialed on charges of selling French army secrets to the Germans. Sentenced to Devil's Island for life, he was retried in 1899 because it was felt the evidence against him was trumped up and partly a product of strong anti-Semitic feeling. He was again found guilty, but by this time, public opinion in favor of Dreyfus was so high and the evidence against him so obviously fraudulent, that the French government decided to pardon him.

Q *Is the Paul Newman-Joanne Woodward marriage headed for the rocks?—N.H., Reno, Nev.*

A There have been rumbles.

Q *Whatever happened to Fabian?—Ginger Welton, Upper Darby, Pa.*

A He's in Hollywood, was recently signed for a film.

Q *Is it true that in France if a writer strongly criticizes General de Gaulle, he can be fined and imprisoned? I have reference to the case of Alfred Fabre-Luce.—W. Rutledge, Charlotte, N.C.*

Globe

Charles de Gaulle

A Alfred Fabre-Luce, a French author, was recently fined $300 for having defamed de Gaulle in his recent book, *High Court*, which puts the French president on imaginary trial for having violated the constitution. Among other things, the author said that General de Gaulle belongs to "the psychiatric category of paranoiacs," a statement the court considered defamatory. The book was ordered destroyed. The publisher was also fined $300.

Q *Is it true that Rex Harrison will play the King Arthur part in the movie version of* Camelot *which Richard Burton portrayed on Broadway?—Anne Ellis, Chicago, Ill.*

A Harrison has been offered the part.

Q *Jackie Kennedy's mother, Mrs. Hugh Auchincloss—does she have any children by Auchincloss?—G. Tierney, Arlington, Va.*

A Yes—Jamie, 16, and Janet, 18.

Q *Can you tell me how many children Cyd Charisse has?—Ben Price, Amarillo, Tex.*

A Two boys, one by dancing master Nico Charisse, her first husband, one by Tony Martin, her second and current husband.

Q *Was Inger Stevens ever engaged to Tony Quinn, the actor?—D.P., Los Angeles, Calif.*

A Never engaged; but they did for a while have a tumultuous friendship.

Q *Who said: "Keep your eyes wide open before marriage, and half-shut afterward."?—Alva Churchill, Ojai, Calif.*

A Benjamin Franklin.

Q *Who are the executors of the John F. Kennedy will?—Dave O'Brien, Danvers, Mass.*

A Mrs. Jacqueline Kennedy, and the late president's two brothers, Robert and Edward.

Q *What is the title of Grace Metalious' new novel, which supposedly outdoes* Peyton Place*?—Cora Angier, Naples, Me.*

A *No Adam in Eden.*

Q *How many children do Charles and Anne Lindbergh have? Why is there a news blackout on these children? Can you tell us anything about them?—F.T., Darien, Conn.*

A The Lindberghs have five children: Jon, 31, married, father of four; Land, 26, married, father of one; Anne, 23, recently married to French student Jacques Feydy; Scott, 21; and Reeve, 18, these last two, unmarried. Ever since the notorious Lindbergh kidnapping, the Lindbergh children have not been exposed to the public press.

Q *Mary Martin recently folded in a Broadway play called* Jennie*. How much was lost on the play?—Irv Pincus, Jersey City, N.J.*

A About $600,000.

Globe

Mary Martin

Q *I question your allegation that the late President Kennedy ever attended Princeton University. Every record shows he is a graduate of Harvard. What is the truth?—Charles Ormes, Miami, Fla.*

John F. Kennedy

A President Kennedy enrolled as a freshman in Princeton in 1935. He roomed until midterm exams in #9 South Reunion with two former classmates from Choate Preparatory School, Rip Horton and LeMoyne Billings. He then became ill with an adrenal insufficiency and left Princeton. Later he entered Harvard, from which college he was graduated.

Q *How many times has Tommy Manville been married, and what's the funny message you get when you call his house?—Amy Lyons, Hyde Park, Ill.*

A Manville, 69, has been married 13 times. When he is not at home, a tape recorder gives out with: "Mr. Manville is out. He will return shortly. At the sound of the 'beep,' please leave your name and the reason for your call. If you are an ex-wife of Mr. Manville's, don't bother to leave any message."

Q *The so-called "hot line" between Washington and Moscow—has Khrushchev or Johnson used it yet for any purpose?—Frank Richardson, Bangor, Me.*

A Not as of this writing.

Q *Captain Eddie Rickenbacker, 73, recently retired as head of Eastern Air Lines. Can you tell me how much money Eastern has made since 1960?—F.J., Mineola, N.Y.*

Eddie Rickenbacker

A From 1960 through 1963 Eastern lost more than $40,000,000.

Q *When June Allyson married that young barber, Glenn Maxwell, was her monthly family allowance from the Dick Powell estate reduced? If so, how much?—Penelope Douglas, Tucson, Ariz.*

A Yes, it was reduced from $5,000 a month to $2,500.

Q *What is Greer Garson's married name, and does she own a ranch near Las Vegas, N. Mexico?—D.J.T., Hale Center, Tex.*

A Her married name is Fogelson; she and her husband own such a cattle ranch.

Q *Can you tell me what John Jacob Astor, heir to the great Astor real estate fortune, does for a living?—D.R., Baltimore, Md.*

A Astor lives on his inheritance.

Q *How much does Barbara Hutton weigh?—Louise Long, Darien, Conn.*

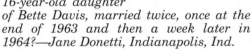

Barbara Hutton

A At this writing, less than 100 pounds.

Q *Why was Barbara Sherry, 16-year-old daughter of Bette Davis, married twice, once at the end of 1963 and then a week later in 1964?—Jane Donetti, Indianapolis, Ind.*

A Tax advantages. By marrying ahead of the scheduled 1964 date, the bride became a 1963 dependent.

Q *Is there a world's woman chess champion?—Katherine Peterson, Madison, Wis.*

A Yes, Nona Gaprindashvili of Russia.

Q *Could you please tell me what the lapel emblem that Lyndon Johnson wears stands for?—Gordon Closway, Winona, Minn.*

A The Silver Star which Johnson won for wartime duty in the Pacific.

Q *I read where Albert Schweitzer recently celebrated his 89th birthday. How many of his years has he spent in Africa?—L. Josephs, Los Angeles, Calif.*

A Dr. Schweitzer set up his hospital outpost 50 years ago at Lambaréné, in what is now the African Republic of Gabon.

Q *Why didn't Princess Grace of Monaco and her prince show up at President Kennedy's funeral when the rest of the world's true royalty showed up?—Lois Revere, Dayton, Ohio.*

A Princess Grace later came to mourn at the president's grave.

Q *There is a woman named Rae Jeffs involved with Irish poet Brendan Behan. Who is she, and what is their relationship?—Claire E.Y., Medford, Mass.*

A Mrs. Jeffs, an Englishwoman, lives with her parents in Sussex. Formerly she worked for a publishing company which printed Behan's manuscripts. A close friend of both the poet and his wife, Rae Jeffs is devoting herself to "keeping Behan working."

Q *Evelyn Lincoln, secretary of our assassinated President Kennedy—was she given any of his personal effects?—Clara Emiss, Baton Rouge, La.*

A Yes, the American and presidential flags which had stood in his office.

Q *Lady Jean Campbell, ex-wife of novelist Norman Mailer—is she a member of British royalty?—Gene Flint, Denver, Colo.*

A No, she is the granddaughter of British publisher Lord Beaverbrook.

Q *Can Jackie Gleason read music, write music or play any musical instrument? If not, how can he compose?—B.T., Ithaca, N.Y.*

A He picks out a tune on the piano with one finger, has an arranger write down the notes.

Jackie Gleason

WALTER SCOTT'S
PERSONALITY PARADE®

February 23, 1964

Q *How many millionaires in the U.S. pay the 91 percent income tax rate on real income?—Stan Seidman, Chicago, Ill.*

A According to the Treasury Department's Office of Tax Analysis, "None."

Q *Is it true that 25 percent of the SS guards in Hitler's Nazi Germany were holders of the doctor's degree?—Lise Peters, Oakland, Calif.*

A Yes, according to paragraph three, page 4, of *Science, Scientists and Politics*, issued by the Center for the Study of Democratic Institutions of the Fund for the Republic, Inc., Santa Barbara, California.

Q *What connection does Bobby Baker, formerly of the U.S. Senate, have with the Las Vegas gambling syndicate?—D. Frank, Denver, Colo.*

A He and several Las Vegas figures were involved in financial deals.

Q *Are there any wholly dry states in the Union?—George Henschel, Butte, Mont.*

A Only one, Mississippi.

Q *Is it true that Hollywood is going to make a film about a bordello madam called* A House Is Not A Home *and that Shelley Winters will play the madam?—Ken Wolper, Atlantic City, N.J.*

A True.

Q *Can you identify Sewsunker Sewgolum?—Dan Golden, Buffalo, N.Y.*

A He is an Indian, 35, from Durban, South Africa, classified there as a nonwhite, who plans to come to America in the near future. Sewgolum is a golfer. He is self-taught, uses a cross-handed grip, is considered the best nonwhite golfer in South Africa.

Q *Has any British prime minister ever been assassinated?—Dora Offer, Oil City, La.*

A Yes—Spencer Perceval, in 1812.

Q *Would it be possible to learn the name of*

Judy Garland

Judy Garland's clothes designer?—Joanna Pappas, Brockton, Mass.

A Ray Aghayan.

Q *To settle an argument, who won the Hollywood Oscar last year for the best performance by an actress?—S. Adams, La Jolla, Calif.*

Anne Bancroft

A Anne Bancroft, for her work in *The Miracle Worker.*

Q *Madame Joliot-Curie, who did such outstanding radium work—when did she die and of what?—V. Leone, Princeton, N.J.*

A In 1956, of leukemia, which she had contracted as a result of her work with radioactive matter.

Q *Could you tell to whom Kay Kendall was married at the time of her death?—C.F., Granite City, Ill.*

A Actor Rex Harrison.

Q *June Allyson's 31-year-old husband, a barber named Glenn Maxwell, went into bankruptcy with liabilities of $19,000 against assets of $8,000. Can a man go into bankruptcy when his wife is worth a small fortune, which is true of June?—T.P., Glencoe, Ill.*

A Yes. In this case Maxwell's debts were incurred before his marriage to Miss Allyson.

Q *Can you tell me if Dean Martin and Milton Berle have had their faces redone?—Pen Adams, Los Angeles, Calif.*

A Their noses have been remodeled.

Q *Does anyone know how much it has cost Richard J. Reynolds, heir to the tobacco fortune, to divorce his wives?—D.L. Evans, Winston Salem, N.C.*

A He paid Elizabeth Dillard, mother of his first four children, approximately $9,000,000. Marianne O'Brien, his second wife and mother of two children, got $3,000,000. Wife number three, Muriel Marston, got $2,000,000.

Q *William McKnight and Archibald Bush, the multi-millionaires from Minnesota Mining and Manufacturing—don't they live in St. Paul?—K.L., Duluth, Minn.*

A They do.

Q *I would like to know what's happened to Dizzy and Daffy Dean, the former star baseball players.—Joe Frick, St. Louis, Mo.*

A The Dean Brothers are currently working at the Dean Poladian Carpet Company in Phoenix, owned by Dizzy.

Q *On TV I heard a candidate for the Republican presidential nomination say he would, if elected, withdraw U.S. recognition of the Soviet Union but that before he made such a move, he would have to have the Senate agree. Does a president need Senate consent to withdraw recognition?—Dan Mackenzie, Chicago, Ill.*

A The candidate was in error. A president has the right to withdraw recognition without Senate consent.

Q *How old is Alfred P. Sloan, Jr.?—James O'Connor, Boston, Mass.*

A He is 88.

Q *Does Jack Benny wear lifts in his shoes, and how old is he really?—Sara Lee Harris, Greenville, N.C.*

A At 70, Jack Benny does not wear lifts in his shoes.

Q *Is it true that Col. John Glenn's entry into Ohio politics was met with no regret by his fellow astronauts? Is it true that there was some discord between him and the rest of the astronauts?—H.T. Smith, Houston, Tex.*

John Glenn

A Before Glenn resigned to enter the senatorial race in Ohio, there was a feeling among several of the astronauts that he wasn't pulling his weight as a member of the team, that he had become a goodwill ambassador, infected by the virus of fame.

Q *I understand that the only thing Senators Hubert Humphrey and Barry Goldwater agree on is the Peace Corps. They're both in favor of it. True or False?—Elaine Klein, New York, N.Y.*

A True. They both favor the Peace Corps.

Q *Has Debbie Reynolds gone into the hospital business?—G.F. Henry, Glendale, Calif.*

A Yes, her company has bought the Oceanside Hospital in Oceanside, California, for $1,000,000, plans to turn it into a profitable business venture.

Q *Can you please tell me how gamblers rig dice games so that the innocent player doesn't have a chance?—Fred Keeloy, Des Moines, Iowa.*

A Federal agents who raided a gambling casino in White Sulphur Springs, West Virginia, owned by William Gearhart, found wires running from a dice table to a foot treadle in the cashier's cage. The dice used contained bits of metal. By operating the foot treadle, the cashier could magnetize the table after the player's first throw so that he would then roll a seven and lose his bet.

Q *Lady Bird Johnson—did she suffer four miscarriages? Is it true she was married 10 years before she had her first daughter?—E.T., Corpus Christi, Tex.*

A True on both counts.

Adolphe Menjou

Q *How much money did Adolphe Menjou, who recently died, leave in his estate? Did he have any children?—Peter Greengold, Passaic, N.J.*

A Menjou left an estate valued at $700,000. He had two sons: Harold 51, adopted; Peter, 27.

Q *Actress Paula Prentiss—her real name please?—Ian Balzer, Iron Mountain, Mich.*

A Paula Ragusa, now married to actor Richard Benjamin.

Q *Who has conducted more nuclear explosions—the U.S. or the U.S.S.R.?—John Kase, Miami, Fla.*

A As of this writing the score is U.S.—302, U.S.S.R.—145.

Q *William IV, King of Great Britain before Queen Victoria, had 10 illegitimate children by an actress, Dorothea Jordan. Are the descendants of those children still living?—T. Rentschel, New Haven, Conn.*

A Yes. William IV raised his eldest son to the peer age and named him Earl of Munster. The fifth Earl of Munster, Geoffrey FitzClarence, lives now in London, has long been a distinguished member of the British Foreign Service. Other descendants also use the name Fitz-Clarence.

Q *Was Henry Cabot Lodge ever a newspaper writer?—D.F. Kennedy, Boston, Mass.*

Henry Cabot Lodge

A Yes. First for the old *Boston Evening Transcript*, before he received his Harvard degree, then from 1925 to 1931 for the *New York Herald Tribune*, for which he worked in Washington, D.C.

Q *Before he died, wasn't William Faulkner planning to leave Mississippi for good?—G.T.G., Biloxi, Miss.*

A Before his death Faulkner bought a home on Rugby Road in Charlottesville, Virginia, where he was a writer-in-residence at the University of Virginia. He was preparing to sell his house in Oxford, Mississippi, when he died.

Q *Who is Lamar Hunt in the world of sports?—Victor Kalish, Salem, Ore.*

A Lamar Hunt, 32, is the son of Texas oil millionaire H. L. Hunt. Young Hunt is owner of the Kansas City franchise of the American Football League, which he founded.

Q *If Prince Charles, heir to the British throne, converted to Catholicism or married a Catholic girl, would he be banned from ever wearing the Crown?—Van McIntyre, Daytona Beach, Fla.*

Prince Charles

A Yes. A British law passed in 1700 states: "Any person who shall be reconciled to, or hold communion with, the See or Church of Rome, or profess the Popish religion, or marry a Papist, is excluded from inheriting...the Crown."

Q *The late Alan Ladd—did he have a weakness for the bottle? Tell the truth, now.—B. Morris, Palm Springs, Calif.*

A Yes, but he was a fine man.

Q *Is Samuel Goldwyn planning to film the James Joyce classic,* Ulysses?—*Joe Brody, New York, N.Y.*

A Goldwyn has no such plans.

Q *Isn't it a fact that Allen Dulles was removed from the CIA by the late President Kennedy as a result of his incompetence in the Cuban fiasco? If this is so, then why would President Johnson select him as a member of the Warren Commission, investigating the assassination of Kennedy?—Eileen Salmon, Ft. Wayne, Ind.*

Allen Dulles

A Dulles was a top intelligence agent in World War II, did a brilliant job as chief of the Central Intelligence Agency, resigned from that Agency and was not removed, is recognized as a man of character, probity, sagacity and unblemished reputation.

Q *Is the Robert Goulet-Carol Lawrence marriage in trouble?—P.T., Hollywood, Calif.*

A No.

WALTER SCOTT'S
PERSONALITY PARADE®

April 5, 1964

Q *Is it true that the late President Kennedy could have easily survived the wound from his assassin's first bullet, but that the third bullet, allegedly fired by Lee Harvey Oswald, really did him in? I've read so many conflicting reports about the shooting. Is there an authoritative autopsy report or something?—A.T., Arlington, Tex.*

John F. Kennedy

A The autopsy report given to the Secret Service and the Warren Commission reveals that Kennedy was struck first in the upper part of the right back shoulder. The bullet caused a hematoma, a swelling containing blood, inside the neck and shoulder muscles. Physicians believe the president might easily have recovered from that wound. The second bullet to hit the late president, thought to have been the third shot fired by the assassin, hit Kennedy in the lower right back side of the head. It caused such immediate and violent destruction to his head as to be "completely incompatible with life." That bullet destroyed considerable brain tissue, severely damaged the forehead, and a fragment from that bullet exited through the throat. The throat wound, first observed by Dallas physicians who tried to save the president, gave rise to the speculation that two assassins might have been involved in the murder, one shooting from the front and one from the rear. The autopsy report proves conclusively, however, that the shots which killed the president were fired from behind. The Dallas doctors who treated him at Parkland Memorial Hospital were unaware that the president had been first shot in the shoulder since he was on his back at all times while at the hospital. An autopsy was performed on the late president's body on November 22, 1963, at the Bethesda, Maryland Naval Hospital.

Q *Will Dolores del Rio ever see 60 again?—Diane Home, El Paso, Tex.*

A Never.

Q *Will Mrs. J. D. Tippit of Dallas pay income tax on the more than $600,000 in gifts she's received?—Mrs. D. Gregory, Portland, Ore.*

A No.

Q *On what grounds did Princess Lee Radziwill, sister of Jackie Kennedy, receive an annulment of her 1953 marriage to Michael Canfield?—Leon Guterman, Miami, Fla.*

A The annulment was granted on a charge that Canfield, a non-Catholic, had entered the marriage with no intention of having children.

Q *Does the Austrian police force consist of Nazis? Is that why they roughed up our Olympic stars at Innsbruck?—Heidi Gunther, Oakland, Calif.*

A Says sportscaster Tom Harmon, who covered the Winter Olympics: "It was a brutal mish-mash. Some of the Austrian police reminded me of the Storm Troopers in Hitler Germany. They are completely totalitarian. Their dislikes were not confined to Americans, but included everyone visiting there. They set the tourist trade in Austria back 10 years."

Q *How old is Lana Turner? Does she drink?—Ina Kurtz, Columbia, S.C.*

A Miss Turner, 44, has been known to indulge.

Q *Ernest Hemingway left an estate valued at more than a million bucks. My question is, how much of the estate was in stocks and bonds?—K. Peters, Sun Valley, Ida.*

Ernest Hemingway

NBC/Globe

A The estate included $418,933 in stocks and bonds; $801,766 in real estate; $189,611 in notes, cash and mortgages. Stocks held by Hemingway included 304 shares of Eastman Kodak, 504 shares of General Motors, 280 shares of American Tobacco, 240 shares of Bethlehem Steel and 336 shares of AT&T.

Q *Why has the press consistently refused to tell the story of Father Donald Runkle?—T.R.S., Washington, D.C.*

A The press has carried the story of how Father Runkle, 50, was ordered by a Chicago judge to pay damages to 38-year-old Robert McArdle for alienating the affections of Mrs. McArdle, 36. She was the organist at Father Runkle's church and was divorced last summer because of an affair with the priest from 1958 to 1962. After doing penance, Father Runkle was transferred from Chicago to Odessa, Texas.

Q *How long has Gunsmoke been on the air? Is it true that Jim Arness and Amanda Blake have been made millionaires by the show?—Chuck Adams, Las Vegas, Nev.*

A Gunsmoke has been on the air 11 years. Both Arness and Blake as a result are in the millionaire class or soon will be.

Q *Does Zsa Zsa Gabor have any ability as an actress—I mean as a serious actress?—Elaine Hammer, Jersey City, N.J.*

A Practically none.

Q *Is Frank Costello still the leader of the Mafia in this country?—Dino Landi, Philadelphia, Pa.*

A Police authorities believe the leader still to be Vito Genovese.

Q *Which one of these is the most disliked actor in Hollywood: Glenn Ford, Burt Lancaster, Kirk Douglas?—Lou Oliver, Los Angeles, Calif.*

A Douglas insists he's the most disliked.

Q *One of the British Beatles, Paul McCartney, dated actress Jill Haworth in New York and Miami. Is this serious or just publicity? Isn't Jill the girl friend of Sal Mineo?—Dolores Finch, Hempstead, N.Y.*

A Jill and Paul are friends. The Beatles don't need any more publicity. Jill and Sal are not as close as they once were.

Q *Is the David Susskind marriage breaking up?—G.T., Swampscott, Mass.*

A Yes.

Q *Can you tell me if the State of New York pays Governor Rockefeller his full salary while he's running around the country?—R.W. Wales, Syracuse, N.Y.*

A Yes. Potential presidential candidates are not taken off salary because they aspire to higher office.

WALTER SCOTT'S

PERSONALITY PARADE®

April 12, 1964

Q *Judy Garland's husband claims Judy has tried to commit suicide at least 20 times during her life. Obviously such a girl does not really want to take her life. What is it that the poor soul really wants?—H.V., Racine, Wis.*

A Judy wants a man to love her truly for herself, not for her earning capacity or former fame. "All I'd like," she has said, "is a happy, married life."

Q *The famous line by the late President Kennedy: "Ask not what your country can do for you but what you can do for your country"—wasn't that line written by speechwriter Ted Sorensen?—David Small, Baltimore, Md.*

A No, it was written by Kennedy and first used by him in a campaign speech in Juneau, Alaska. Sorensen liked the line so much that he suggested the president include it in his inaugural address, and Kennedy did.

Q *Who said: "The two most beautiful words in the English language are, 'check enclosed' "?—Roy Brandy, Miami, Fla.*

A Writer Dorothy Parker.

Q *Is it true that Bob Hope, Bing Crosby and Cary Grant are all 60 or over?—Felicia Esar, San Antonio, Tex.*

A Each is 60.

Q *Joe Valachi, who told the Justice Department about the Cosa Nostra, the national crime syndicate—where is he? Is it true he has sold his life story to* Life *magazine?—Charles Steadman, Chicago, Ill.*

A Valachi is in the District of Columbia jail. He is writing his memoirs to pass the time. These memoirs are being carefully read by the Justice Department's criminal division. Valachi's story has not been sold at this time to any magazine or publisher.

Q *Among musicians, which girl singers are regarded as tops?—Tiny Taylor, Memphis, Tenn.*

A Ella Fitzgerald and Lena Horne are always listed among the best.

Q *Carol Burnett's child—boy or girl?—Dolores Visocky, Johnson City, N.Y.*

A Girl.

Q *I understand that when German magazines now run cover pictures of Adolf Hitler they purposely blur the portraits. Is this so, and if so, why?—Willa Wagner, Hanover, N.H.*

Adolph Hitler

A It is so. The objective is to make the cover shots unprintable for framing, so that portraits of Adolf Hitler are no longer hung throughout Germany.

Q *Does Prince Charles, heir to the British throne, play any musical instrument?—N. Knox, Chicago, Ill.*

A Charles plays the trumpet.

Q *Do the Beatles wear wigs?—Enid Brinkman, El Paso, Tex.*

A They do not.

Q *Is it true that Martin Luther King has refused L. B. Johnson's offer of a Johnson-King ticket in the coming presidential election?—G.L. Brown, Ft. Worth, Tex.*

A No such offer was ever made Martin Luther King.

Q *Judge Joe B. Brown, who presided over the murder trial of Jack Ruby—I've been told that as a lawyer Brown never acquired or tried a single case. Exactly what is his legal background?—F. Paul, Atlantic City, N.J.*

A Judge Brown was born in Dallas on June 9, 1908. As a young man he worked as a railroad rate clerk. At age 25 he enrolled in night law courses at Jefferson University, three years later was graduated and ran for Justice of the Peace in the Oak Cliff section of Dallas. He was elected, thus never had the opportunity to acquire or argue a single case as a lawyer.

Q *Is the U.S. Chamber of Commerce still against trade with Communist nations?—Louis Marabini, New York, N.Y.*

A The Chamber under Edwin P. Neilan is abandoning that stand.

Q *I cannot believe that Hollywood intends to make a film of Edward Albee's play,* Who's Afraid of Virginia Woolf? *Say it isn't so.—Lidia Rossi, San Francisco, Calif.*

A It is so.

Q *Does Lance Reventlow, Barbara Hutton's only child, work for a living?—Ken Darby, Los Angeles, Calif.*

A He does not.

Q *Before he married Deborah Kerr, did Peter Viertel live with Bettina the model and Ava Gardner the actress?—F.T., Paris, France.*

A For a time he was most friendly with both.

Q *Was the Liston-Clay fight a fix? How come Liston's company made a re-match deal with Cassius one day before Cassius took the title?—Elley Rich, Las Vegas, Nev.*

Cassius Clay

A Liston owns 22 percent of a company called Intercontinental Promotions, Inc. One day before the Liston-Clay fight, Intercontinental signed a deal with Clay giving Intercontinental the right to promote Clay's first defense of the title for $50,000. Jack Nilon, Liston's manager, is also a large shareholder of Intercontinental. Bill Cherry, the company's lawyer, says: "We took a gamble. There was nothing illegal about it. We were just being smart businessmen. We made the agreement, which gives us a 365-day option, until February 25, 1965, just in case Clay should become champion—which he did." Liston has two of five votes on the board of directors at Intercontinental. The three other are controlled by Bob Nilon, Jack Nilon and Cherry himself.

WALTER SCOTT'S

PERSONALITY PARADE®

June 21, 1964

Mary Pickford

Q *How old is Mary Pickford? What is she doing these days?—Beatrice Joyner, Columbia, S.C.*

A Miss Pickford, 71, has been touring Europe, searching for her old silent films, which she plans to present to the Hollywood Film Museum.

Q *Who is "Scooter" Miller, and what connection does she have with the First Lady?—Robert Gibbons, Atlanta, Ga.*

A "Scooter" Miller is Mrs. Dale Miller, whose husband represents the Dallas Chamber of Commerce in Washington, D.C. She is a close friend and confidante of Mrs. Johnson's.

Q *Who is the general counsel for James Hoffa's Teamsters' Union?—L.C. Johnson, Garden City, Kan.*

A Edward Bennett Williams.

Q *Who said: "A statesman is a dead politician"?—Jon Barrington, Des Moines, Iowa.*

A Former President Harry Truman.

Q *How come the American press has avoided printing any news about the libel suit filed by Dr. W. A. Dering against Leon Uris, author of* Exodus?*—P.G. Purvis, Lafayette, Ind.*

A The suit was filed in England. Dr. Dering was accused in the book of sterilizing and experimenting medically on the bodies of Jewish women. After listening to his wartime activities, the British court awarded him damages of one half-penny, ordered him to pay costs of $56,000.

Q *What's happened to King Umberto, whom the Italians threw out after World War II?—Nicholas Bocalli, Utica, N.Y.*

A Umberto, 59, separated from his wife, ex-Queen Marie-José, lives in Portugal, frequently travels in Europe under the pseudonym "Mr. Sarr."

Q *What did Henry Cabot Lodge do when he worked for Time magazine a few years ago?—Ilo Katawaya, San Francisco, Calif.*

A He was listed as a foreign affairs consultant.

Henry Cabot Lodge

Q *How old was Grace Kelly when she got married?—Laura Dennison, Ardmore, Pa.*

A 26.

Q *Are the Beatles swingers?—Jo Babcock, Sacramento, Calif.*

A They swing.

Q *How old is cosmetics queen Helena Rubinstein?—Mann Epstein, Ithaca, N.Y.*

A Good bet: 92.

Q *What sort of man was Rupert Brooke, the British poet who wrote: "If I should die, think only this of me, that there's some corner of a foreign field that is forever England"?—Lloyd Canford, Cambridge, Mass.*

A Brooke, who died in 1915 of a mosquito bite on his upper lip, was vain, immature, self-centered, a hypochondriac, a Narcissus, a poet of potential. For authentic biographical details read *Rupert Brooke*, by Christopher Hassall, published in London by Faber.

Q *How many copies of her mystery thrillers has Agatha Christie sold?—Len Albert, Miami, Fla.*

A Approximately 300,000,000.

Q *Ernest Hemingway, in his book* A Moveable Feast, *writes about Gertrude Stein and her companion in Freudian overtones. Was Gertrude Stein's "companion" male or female?—Peter de Rivers, Carbondale, Ill.*

Ernest Hemingway

A Female Alice B. Toklas.

Q *Is Adlai Stevenson fond of actresses? How about him and Mercedes McCambridge and Ava Gardner and others?—T.S., Chicago, Ill.*

A Stevenson admires feminine beauty.

Q *Will the Roman Catholic Church ever okay contraceptive pills?—Lon Smith, Berlin, N.H.*

A Dr. John Rock, Roman Catholic professor emeritus of gynecology at Harvard, author of *The Time Has Come* and pioneer of the oral contraceptive, said recently: "I have great confidence in the sagacity of my Church. It will not fail to see the necessity of this measure for human welfare. In the past the Church has sometimes moved slowly, but this question is so urgent for the benefit of the human race that I am hopeful that even as soon as September, when the Vatican Council reconvenes, there may be a favorable pronouncement."

Q *Joe Louis, the heavy-weight boxing champion—was he defeated or did he retire unbeaten?—Chris Desmond, St. Paul, Minn.*

Joe Louis

A Louis retired unbeaten in 1949, but later in an attempted comeback was defeated by Ezzard Charles.

Q *What relationship does Elizabeth Taylor's husband, Richard Burton, have with Walter Jenkins, the former Presidential assistant?*—George Taylor, Philadelphia, Pa.

Elizabeth Taylor

A No relationship except that Richard Burton's real name is Richard Walter Jenkins.

Q *I would like to find out what happened to Fabrizio Ciano, son of Mussolini's daughter and Mussolini's one-time foreign minister.*—B. Thoren, Oak Park, Ill.

A Fabrizio Ciano operates a slide-fastener factory in Caracas, Venezuela.

Q *Is it true that the late Willa Cather's will specifically prohibits the sale of any of her novels to Hollywood?*—F.T. Lewis, Poughkeepsie, N.Y.

A A motion picture was made from her novel, *A Lost Lady*. It was so bad Miss Cather forbade all future film versions of her works. The prohibition is specifically mentioned in her will.

Q *I am wondering how much it cost old man Kennedy to win the election for Bobby Kennedy in New York.*—D. Roberts, New York, N.Y.

A Approximately $2 million was spent by the Kennedy forces in the recent senatorial campaign. Of this sum $1,206,207 was paid to the advertising agency, Papert, Koenig and Lois, the bulk of which was spent on the purchase of television time.

Q *Is Julie Andrews getting $1 million to star in the film, Hawaii, or is that just publicity?*—Nat Friedman, Jersey City, N.J.

A $700,000 is closer to the truth.

Julie Andrews

Q *Would you please list the television stations owned entirely or in part by President Johnson or his family.*—F.S., Yakima, Wash.

A KTBC, Austin; KBTX Bryan; KWTX, Waco, all in Texas. In addition, KXII, Ardmore, Oklahoma, KLFY, Lafayette, Louisiana.

Q *Is it true that Stanley Marcus of the department store here will be our next ambassador to Great Britain?*—G.T., Dallas, Tex.

A Good possibility at this point to replace retiring David Bruce.

Q *Jack London, the writer, was an intellectual drunk who spent his life in search of adventure. He wrote a book called* Assassination Bureau, ltd. *What's it about? Was London illegitimate? Did he commit suicide?*—Andrew Gaines, Berkeley, Calif.

A London, born illegitimate, committed suicide at age 40. His novel tells the story of an organization of murderers who for $50,000 would kill a personal or political enemy, providing they considered the killing socially justifiable.

Q *I've been told that a three-year-old Volkswagen now sells in Havana for $10,000. Is that so?*—Victor Huerta, Miami, Fla.

A Current price: $9,000.

Q *The late President Kennedy was an ardent movie fan. I had the pleasure of serving as projectionist for him. On his last visit to Palm Beach, on Sunday, November 17th, 1963, I ran the film* Tom Jones *for him. I'm wondering if that's the last film he ever saw.*—Charles C. Dodds, W. Palm Beach, Fla.

John F. Kennedy

A It was.

Q *Who are the most widely read authors in the world?*—Connie Haber, Chicago, Ill.

A According to the UN survey on translations: (1) Shakespeare, (2) Tolstoy, (3) Dickens.

Q *I know we don't recognize Red China, but haven't we had foreign policy discussions with Red China for the past 10 years very secretly in Poland?*—C.T.L., Washington, D.C.

A For the past nine years our ambassador to Poland and the Chinese ambassador to Poland have held periodic talks on a variety of subjects.

Q *I've read that Natalie Wood is restricted to a spending allowance of $25 per week. Who makes such restrictions on her budget?*—Lois Epstein, Port Chester, N.Y.

A Her business manager, Irving Leonard, allows her $25 per week for pocket money. She charges everything else.

Liberace

Q *What is Liberace's first name?*—Nola Jinsen, Milwaukee, Wis.

A Walter.

Q *I've been informed on good authority that John Lennon, the Beatle, is so nearsighted he can't even see his fans. Why doesn't he wear glasses?*—Susan Fields, Beverly Hills, Calif.

A Lennon was recently fitted with contact lenses.

Q *When I was in Germany I was told by ordnance experts that German's explosives in World War II were 80 percent more powerful than those of the Allies. If true, how come?*—Manfred Henschel, Hempstead, N.Y.

A True. The Germans added small quantities of aluminum powder to their explosives, thus increasing their efficiency.

Q *Is it true that there is a United Network Command of Law Enforcement (UNCLE) which the TV series, The Man from UNCLE, is based on?*—John Moore, Silver Spring, Md.

A Pure fiction.

WALTER SCOTT'S
PERSONALITY PARADE®

May 16, 1965

Q *Why are we spending $30 billion to put a man on the moon? Isn't that a stupid waste of the taxpayers' money?—K.T., Princeton, N.J.*

A It is part of our space program which in turn is a continuation of man's quest for new knowledge. Man has always been interested in the nature of his world. Modern science figuratively began in space—from the observations of Galileo with his telescope, the mathematical calculations of Kepler on planetary motions, the laws of gravitation and motion devised by Newton.

Q *Where was ex-King Farouk finally buried?—J. Burch, New Cumberland, W. Va.*

A He was quietly buried near the grave of his father, King Fuad, at a mosque near the citadel of Saladin in Egypt.

Q *How far is the moon from the earth? How far is Mars from the earth?—Ralph Irwin, Ft. Worth, Tex.*

A The moon is 240,000 miles from the earth. Mars is 34 million miles from earth.

Q *In their second movie do the Beatles actually ski? Or are doubles used?—Edith Coleman, Washington, D.C.*

The Beatles

A The Beatles tried to ski at Obertauern, Austria, for their second film, but local skiers were eventually used instead. Fritz Lang, their ski instructor, said without mentioning names: "Some were eager to learn, and some were plain lazy."

Q *George V and Queen Mary had a son named Prince John. How come no one ever hears of him or reads about him?—G. Elson, New York, N.Y.*

A He died in 1919, age 13.

Q *How many people in the U.S. are on some form of public relief?—L. Donovan, Croton, N.Y.*

A At this writing one in every 25, or approximately 7,900,000.

Q *Does Sean Connery get any profit percentage from the James Bond films he stars in?—S.H., Bangs, Tex.*

A He owns 5 percent of *Goldfinger* which reportedly will gross $40 million world-wide.

Sean Connery

Q *I read that Eartha Kitt married her white husband, Bill McDonald, now her manager, on the rebound. Is this on the level?—A.L.T., Birmingham, Ala.*

A Miss Kitt recently told a London reporter: "I'll be quite honest with you. I was never really in love with Bill. I've only loved one man in my life, Arthur Loew, and when he married someone else, I married Bill on the rebound, you might say. But he knew what the score was from the beginning."

Q *Anything to the Patty Duke-Frank Sinatra, Jr., romance?—Helen James, Knoxville, Tenn.*

A It has possibilities.

Q *Has anything authoritative ever been written on who are the worst tippers?—F.L., Washington, D.C.*

A Nothing authoritative. A recent survey of bartenders, however, has them choosing baseball players, doctors, dentists, lawyers and women.

Q *Bing Crosby's four sons by his wife Dixie—all divorced? How many times?—Gigi French, Palo Alto, Calif.*

A Phil Crosby has been divorced twice. Linnie and Dennis once. Son Gary still happily married to his first bride.

Q *I would like to know what roles the following people played in the popularization of the Ku Klux Klan: D. C. Stephenson, Elizabeth Tyler and Edward Clarke.—R.T., Indianapolis, Ind.*

A D. C. Stephenson was the Klan organizer in Indiana in the early 1920's. In 1925 he was convicted and sentenced to life imprisonment for the rape of a young secretary who later died. According to the testimony of C. Anderson Wright, former Klan kleagle in New York state before a 1921 congressional committee: Elizabeth Tyler and Edward Clarke owned the Southern Publicity Association in Atlanta, which was hired to boost Klan membership.

Q *Elizabeth Montgomery, daughter of film star Robert Montgomery, is herself the TV star of* Bewitched. *How many times has she been married? Who were her husbands?—L.T., Troy, N.Y.*

A Elizabeth has been married three times. First husband, Frederick Camman; second husband, Gig Young; third husband, Bill Asher.

Q *Does the Welch Grape Juice Company of Westfield, New York, have any connection with the Robert Welch of the John Birch Society?—Jene Nathans, Miami Beach, Fla.*

A No connection.

Q *Is Yul Brynner naturally bald, or does he have to have his head shaven?—Robert L. Macchia, Ozone Park, N.Y.*

A Brynner is not completely bald, has to have his head shaven regularly.

Yul Brynner

Q *Who is the Chief Butler of England? Is it true that the Chief Butler is in charge of conducting all state functions, such as coronations and burials?—George Kent Baker, Cambridge, Mass.*

A The Chief Butler of England is Bernard Marmaduke FitzAlan-Howard, 16th Duke of Norfolk. In addition to arranging two royal funerals and coronations, he has organized the proclamation of three monarchs—Edward VIII, George VI and Elizabeth II—plus the funeral of Winston Churchill. The Duke was born in 1908 and is the leading Catholic layman in England. In 1937 he broke with family custom and married a Protestant, the Hon. Lavinia Strutt without persuading her to become a Catholic. They have four daughters. The Duke is one of the wealthiest men in England, an aristocrat who detests publicity. He performs his functions as Earl Marshal of England and not as Chief Butler. The sole function of the Chief Butler of England is to pass a cup of wine to the sovereign at coronation banquets. Last such banquet was held in 1821.

Q *Is it true that President Johnson buys Lady Bird's dresses?*—R.V.L., Medford, Ore.

A He used to, and Lady Bird in gallant sacrifice would wear them despite LBJ's penchant for loud colors. Nowadays, however, the New York buyers for Neiman-Marcus of Dallas consult with the First Lady on her choice of clothes.

Q *In a recent Supreme Court case, Pointer v. Texas, the "confrontation clause" was made basic to all state criminal trials. What does that mean? I have to know for my government class.*—Elaine Ritchie, Miami, Fla.

A The Sixth Amendment of the U.S. Constitution guarantees that anyone accused of a crime shall "be confronted with the witnesses against him." Many states in the past have refused to uphold that right, have convicted defendants in part on absentee testimony. They no longer can do that. A defendant now has the right to cross-examine the witnesses in court so that a jury can determine from the manner in which the testimony is given who is telling the truth and how much of it. Along with *Gideon v. Wainwright* and *Malloy v. Hogan,* the decision in *Pointer v. Texas* is part of a trend on the part of the U.S. Supreme Court to hold that the protections guaranteed the individual under the Federal Constitution are binding on the state courts as well as the Federal ones.

Q *Jacqui Chan, the Chinese actress who used to date Tony Armstrong-Jones before he married Princess Margaret, she has a baby daughter named Abigail. I would like to know who the father is.*—K.L., Cumberland, Md.

A The father is actor David Saire, who secretly married Jacqui three years ago.

Q *Did Gary Cooper ever play Gen. George Patton in movies? When was the film released?*—Everett Cromer, Tazewell, Va.

A Cooper never played the role. Twentieth Century-Fox is now preparing a film on the life of Patton.

Q *Would you tell me the ratio of whites to Negroes in the U.S.?*—Debby Wolfe, Gallagher, W.Va.

A According to 1960 census, 158,832,000 white, 18,872,000 Negro.

Q *Is it true that most of the persons murdered in the United States are killed by mail-order guns?*—Morton Stevens, Chicago, Ill.

A About 50 percent.

Q *Former Presidents Herbert Hoover and John F. Kennedy gave their government salaries to charity. Has President Johnson? How about other presidents?*—H. Powers, Buffalo, N.Y.

Herbert Hoover

A Only Hoover and Kennedy to date.

Q *I've been told that producer Joe Levine has become disenchanted with actress Carroll Baker, will make no more films with her. What is the status of that rumor?*—D.L., Hollywood, Calif.

A The disenchantment is mutual; if continued there will be a definite break.

Q *Are self-employed physicians under social security?*—John Given, Denver, Colo.

A Under the Medicare bill, self-employed doctors will start paying social security taxes next year, making them eligible for pension and survivors' benefits.

Q *Which state of the Union has the largest number of drunks? Where in this country is more alcohol consumed?*—V.L.T., St. Louis, Mo.

A California with approximately 900,000 alcoholics ranks number one. Nevada and Washington, D.C., have residents who consume the most alcohol per person.

Q *Who said, "Three things cannot be taught—generosity, poetry and a singing voice"?*—A.L. Wagner, Chicago, Ill.

A Author unknown—it's an old Irish proverb.

Q *When and where were Dorothy Kilgallen and Richard Kollmar divorced? Why do you refuse to answer this question?*—Ferdinand W. Smith, Irvington, N.J.

A They have not been divorced, recently celebrated their 25th marriage anniversary, live together in a townhouse on East 68th Street in New York City.

Q *Is it true that the Roman Catholic Church is the richest church in the world? Can you give a comparison of other resources and wealth?*—C.E.S., Huntington, N.Y.

A A recent tax dispute between the Vatican and the Italian state has revealed some of the Roman Catholic Church's great wealth. Its portfolio of securities is estimated at $5.6 billion, compared to the portfolio of the Church of England which is worth approximately $580 million. The Vatican is an international financial power using such bankers as the Rothschilds, Hambros, Samuel Montagu, and the Morgan Guaranty group in this country. In Italy it has interests in Il Banco di Santo Spirito, Il Banco di Roma, La Societa Generale Immobiliare, Sogene, and through them extensive holdings in hotels, transportation companies, mills, etc. Its complete wealth in terms of real estate, art treasures, etc., is unrivaled by any other church.

Q *Nicholas Katzenbach, the U.S. Attorney General—is he really the best educated attorney general we've ever had in this country?*—F.L., Rice, Knoxville, Tenn.

Nicholas Katzenbach

A One of the best. Katzenbach was educated at Princeton, Yale Law School, Oxford where he was a Rhodes Scholar. He worked for a while in his father's law firm, quit to join the law faculty at the University of Chicago, then received a Ford Foundation grant for a project in international law at the University of Geneva, Switzerland, came to the Department of Justice in the Kennedy administration as an assistant to his former Yale roommate, "Whizzer" White, now a Supreme Court justice. His qualifications and background are outstanding; one of his most notable qualities: ability to get along with people.

WALTER SCOTT'S

PERSONALITY PARADE®

June 13, 1965

Q *Is it true that there's a big fight going on in Hollywood to see who will play the leading role in the film version of* Hello, Dolly!?—*H.G., Newark, N.J.*

A Leading contenders to date are: Doris Day, Shirley MacLaine, Julie Andrews, Carol Channing, Lucille Ball, all possibilities.

Q *What is Soupy Sales' real name?—K. Jeran, Huntington, N.Y.*

A Milton Hines.

Q *Are the contestants in* General Electric's College Bowl *TV program given any clues or hints about upcoming questions?—W.H. Van Tifflin, Hendersonville, N.C.*

A No clues or tips on questions, just tips on the procedure to be followed.

Q *Could you tell me how much of an estate the late President Kennedy left to his wife and children?—L.T.D., Albany, N.Y.*

A Somewhere around $10 million—all of it from trust funds established by his father, Joe Kennedy.

Q *Isn't it true that Chief Justice Earl Warren spent one or more of his vacations with ex-Premier Khrushchev at K's home in Russia?—Mrs. E.J. Andors, Arlington, Va.*

A Not true. Warren and columnist Drew Pearson several years ago visited Khrushchev as have many other Americans in the line of diplomatic and journalistic duty. But Warren has never spent a vacation with Khrushchev.

Q *I understand that the late President Kennedy would permit only Cuban refugees who were Catholic to enter the U.S. Is this correct? Please use only my initials.—C.W.B., Loveland, Colo.*

A Complete falsehood.

Q *Has Connie Francis (r.) ever won a beauty contest?—D.G., Augusta, Me.*

A Never.

Q *Is Tony Curtis twice the age of*

Connie Francis

his wife, Christine Kaufmann?—Joyce Johnston, St. Paul, Minn.

A Yes; Curtis is 40, Christine 20.

Q *What is wrong with the state of California when it runs for office or considers running for office such men as Pierre Salinger, George Murphy, and now Ronald Reagan, none of whom was ever previously elected to any government office? Does Ronald Reagan who used to be a liberal Democrat—does he actually have a chance to become the Republican governor of the state?—S.T.L., Sacramento, Calif.*

A Many Californians do not vote on the issues or the candidate's qualifications. They vote on the basis of his personality. Since Reagan, despite his former political affiliations, has a pleasing personality, he stands a good chance of receiving the Republican gubernatorial nomination.

Q *What does Maureen O'Sullivan have to say about Frank Sinatra, a man going on 50, dating her daughter, Mia Farrow, a girl going on 20?—R. Nagel, Little Ferry, N.J.*

A She has stayed out of it, once jokingly remarked, "If there's any female in this family Frank Sinatra marries, it should be me."

Q *Dinah Shore's parents—was one a Negro or had Negro blood?—Virginia Beres, Detroit, Mich.*

A No Negro blood in the family.

Q *Can Jimmy Durante have any babies? The baby daughter he has—is it his natural daughter or adopted?—S.S., Ely, Minn.*

A Adopted.

Jimmy Durante

Q *Of which country is Danny Kaye a native?—Mrs. Lee Pettrine, Denver, Colo.*

A Danny Kaye was born in Brooklyn, New York in January, 1913.

Q *I would like to find out what Raymond Burr—he plays Perry Mason on TV—what he does when he goes to Vietnam to entertain the boys?—T. Sturm, Dallas, Tex.*

A He sits around with the servicemen, swaps stories, raises their morale.

Charlton Heston

Q *What is the advance word in the film,* The Agony and the Ecstasy *with Charlton Heston?—Russell Hayward, Vallejo, Calif.*

A On the basis of its sneak preview in Minneapolis—excellent.

Q *Is it true that there is no love lost between Chet Huntley and David Brinkley? Do they have a friendly relationship?—Johnny Bell, Jr., Baton Rouge, La.*

A Most friendly relationship.

Q *This boy Mark Herron whom Judy Garland goes around with—does he have an occupation? Or does Judy keep him on an allowance? Doesn't she earn a thousand times what he does?—B.T., Miami, Fla.*

A Herron is an actor who has played bit parts from time to time. Judy, of course, earns much more.

WALTER SCOTT'S
PERSONALITY PARADE®

July 4, 1965

Q *Two questions about Queen Elizabeth's tour of Germany. Why wasn't she greeted by Konrad Adenauer? Did she really bring along her own dressmaker to dress her?—Carlotta Gonzales, Los Angeles, Calif.*

Queen Elizabeth

A Adenauer, 89, was injured in a train accident before the Queen arrived and was ordered to bed. Mr. Hardy Amies, the Queen's dressmaker, accompanied her on the tour.

Q *Why did President Johnson send Marines into the Dominican Republic? Wasn't this a violation of Article 15 of the OAS charter?—Louis Slott, Jersey City, N.J.*

A Article 15 of the charter of the Organization of American States says: "No state or group of states has the right to intervene directly or indirectly for any reason whatever in the internal or external affairs of any other state." In sending U.S. Marines to the Dominican Republic, the President violated the charter. But he was also confronted by two major responsibilities: (1) to protect the lives of American citizens in Santo Domingo (2) to prevent a Communist infiltration and possible takeover of the Dominican government. Intervention in foreign lands is one of the agonizing problems of the presidency and is generally motivated by what the president considers the best interests of the American people.

Q *Cassius Clay, the heavyweight champion—it's hard to believe that such a bruiser could be declared unfit for the draft. How come?—David Henry, Chicago, Ill.*

A Clay was declared unfit for military service not on physical grounds but on mental ones. His behavior at times is not the most stable.

Q *Richard Burton's ex-wife, Sybil—was she ever a brunette?—F. T., Chicago, Ill.*

A Early in their marriage.

Q *Is it true that President John*

Burton and Family

F. Kennedy and author Aldous Huxley both died on the same day?—Elaine Gavin, Washington, D.C.*

A Yes, November 22, 1963.

Q *Who is the Roosevelt who ran for mayor of Miami Beach? Mayor of Los Angeles? How many times has each been married? What are their business backgrounds?—Chas. Wolfe, Port Chicago, Calif.*

Elliott Roosevelt

A James Roosevelt, insurance man and congressman, ran for mayor of Los Angeles. He has been married three times. Elliott Roosevelt, 54, business consultant, was elected mayor of Miami Beach. Elliott has been married five times.

Q *If you call Franco of Spain an insulting name in Spain, can they throw you in jail even though you're a tourist?—V.T., Detroit, Mich.*

A Yes. Alan Chatsworth, 22, a British sailor, was recently sentenced to a month in jail for referring to Franco as "an old bastard."

Q *Who is President Johnson's personal lawyer? Who drew up the trust agreement whereby Johnson's TV empire is run by his friends?—D.T., Baltimore, Md.*

A The president's personal lawyer is Abe Fortas of the Washington, D.C. law firm of Arnold, Fortas and Porter, which firm drew up the trust agreement.

Q *I would like to know where Ronald Reagan was stationed in World War II and when Jane Wyman divorced him.—C.R., Bakersfield, Calif.*

A Reagan was stationed with the Army Air Force motion picture unit in Culver City, California, during World War II. He was divorced by Jane Wyman in 1948.

Q *I have been told that Australia will not permit a nonwhite to become an Australian citizen, that the country bans nonwhite immigrants. Is this true?—Alan McDonald, Phoenix, Ariz.*

A Australia permits nonwhites to visit, not to stay.

Q *The real name, please, of actress Anne Bancroft.—R. Richardson, Raleigh, N.C.*

A Anne Italiano.

Q *Who said: "Democracies are most commonly corrupted by the insolence of demagogues"?—Henry Altman, Brooklyn, N.Y.*

A Plato.

Q *In World War II, did the British arrest Italian residents of London and put them in internee camps?—Frank Orsatti, New York, N.Y.*

A When the German army routed the French and its troops were a few miles outside of Paris, Mussolini on June 10th, 1940, declared war on Great Britain and France. This cowardly "stab in the back" by Italy aroused the fury of the British public to the point where Italian-owned shops were attacked, their owners threatened. In London more than 600 Italians were arrested as enemy aliens, and many long-term Italian store-owners hung up such signs as: "The proprietors of this restaurant are British subjects and have sons serving with the British Army."

Q *Why is a man named Red Adair famous?—S.L. Marshall, Houston, Tex.*

A Red Adair, 50, is recognized as an oil fire-fighting expert. When an oil well catches fire, generally it can be extinguished by setting off a large enough explosion to deprive it of its oxygen. After that is done, the well has to be capped. These two procedures are extremely dangerous, and Adair specializes in both. He has flown all over the world to extinguish oil fires.

Q *After her fight with producer Ross Hunter, is Lana Turner washed up in films?—F.R., Hollywood, Calif.*

Lana Turner

A No longer the box-office draw she once was, Lana of late has been investing her surplus funds in real estate, has confided to friends that insofar as films are concerned she's just about had it.

WALTER SCOTT'S

PERSONALITY PARADE®

July 25, 1965

Q *For months now Frank Capra, the great motion picture director, has been involved in a top secret project at Columbia Pictures. Very hush-hush. No publicity. Do you know what it is?—Allen Bowles, Los Angeles, Calif.*

Frank Capra

A Capra has been working on an unpublicized production, tentatively entitled *Marooned*, the story of an astronaut lost in space.

Q *Jersey Joe Walcott, the referee of the Clay-Liston fiasco fight—is it true that he cannot count to 10 and cannot read?—G.R. Guyer, Miami, Fla.*

A Walcott can count and read.

Q *Two questions concerning medicine: (1) Gertrude Stein—the writer and art collector, did she not receive her medical degree from Johns Hopkins, class of '01? (2) What publishing company prints reasonable original, not reprint paperback medical books?—G. Weaver, Baton Rouge, La.*

A Gertrude Stein was graduated from the Johns Hopkins Medical School in 1901 but was not awarded a degree in medicine. Lange Medical Publications, Los Altos, California, probably sells more original paperback medical books in this country and abroad than any other publishing house. Other prominent publishers of medical paperbacks are Little, Brown & Co. of Boston and Blakiston Division of McGraw-Hill, New York.

Q *Can you tell me what to do with unordered merchandise sent to me through the mails? I don't order this merchandise. Next thing I get is a bill which says, "Please remit at once."—Mrs. Charles Bristol, Cornwall, N.Y.*

A According to postal authorities the recipient of unordered merchandise is under no obligation to pay for it. The only requirement is to hold the merchandise for a reasonable length of time, say 30 days, then throw it away. It must be returned only if the mailer sends you return postage in advance. If you use any of the merchandise, it must be paid for.

Q *Do not use my name, but isn't it a fact that after a reasonable length of time*

Jackie Kennedy will marry Adlai Stevenson?—T.W., Ohiowa, Neb.

A No such fact; moreover, highly improbable.

Q *I would like to know if President Johnson and Defense Secretary Robert McNamara have been honest with the American public in disclosing the full truth about our involvement in Vietnam. Isn't it true that we have been carefully spoonfed just enough information from time to time? Who is responsible for the spoon-feeding information program?—D.T., New York, N.Y.*

A The spoon-feeding information program from the Defense Department may be attributed to the Defense Secretary, Robert McNamara; the reluctance to inform the public about the eventual escalation, the number of U.S. troops necessary for a holding or offensive action, the prospect of mounting U.S. casualties in Vietnam to President Johnson.

Q *Would you please run a picture of the Russian ballet dancer Rudolf Nureyev?—Linda Gallo, Bellevue, Wash.*

A Yes.

Rudolf Nureyev

Q *What public relations firm has been hired by the Kennedy family to keep news about its members continually in the press? Initials only please.—E.B., Washington, D.C.*

A The Kennedy family does not employ a public relations firm to publicize the Kennedy family members, but each Kennedy involved in politics or with a semi-public agency has a press officer.

Q *How old is Chet Huntley, and is he really a great lover and ladies' man?—F.T., Washington, D.C.*

A Huntley, 53, happily married for the second time, was recognized as a ladies' man in his more youthful days, is now a serious news commentator.

Q *In the film, The Dolls, is Gina Lollobrigida nude, or does she wear flesh-colored tights?—Fred Maione, Hempstead, N.Y.*

A Flesh-colored tights.

Q *Now that she's no longer on TV regularly, what is Dinah Shore doing?—Ellie Fein, Chicago, Ill.*

Dinah Shore

A She is entertaining regularly in Nevada gambling hotels.

Q *Whatever happened to singer Johnny Ray?—Alan Horowitz, No. Miami Beach, Fla.*

A Johnny Ray has been working in England for the past few years. Recently Lou Walters of the Latin Quarter night club in New York announced he was giving Ray a comeback opportunity in this country.

Q *Where in the Bible does it say: "Love your enemies, for they tell you your faults"?—Mrs. Ben Schafer, Newark, N.J.*

A The quotation comes from Benjamin Franklin, American statesman, author, and scientist (1706-1790).

Q *Does actor Richard Burton wear lifts in his shoes?—Vivian Eaton, Hagerstown, Md.*

A When acting.

Q *Why in his autobiography does Charles Chaplin refuse to say anything about his first two wives?—Helen Guilfoyle, Urbana, Ill.*

A He had to marry them, and the memories of those unhappy days have caused him to "block" them out.

Charlie Chaplin

Q Yul Brynner, the actor, recently renounced American citizenship. Wouldn't it be a good idea for American citizens to now renounce Yul Brynner films? Also what makes the Swiss tax setup so advantageous that so many film stars like Brynner, Elizabeth Taylor, Bill Holden, Richard Burton, etc., establish residence in Switzerland?—Gertrude Klein, Chicago, Ill.

Yul Brynner

A Brynner is worth comparatively little at the U.S. box office. Film stars establish residence in Switzerland where they form personal corporations and have their incomes paid into them. Such corporations pay only two-tenths of one percent corporate tax. No tax is collected on undistributed profits, and the profits never have to be distributed. As for Swiss income taxes, they are negligible. One tax authority estimates that by renouncing her U.S. citizenship and maintaining residence in Switzerland, Elizabeth Taylor will pay less than one-tenth of what she had to pay in U.S. taxes.

Q Is it true that photographers covering Lyndon Johnson have been ordered to photograph only his left profile, that in fact the president is a most vain man?—D.L., Washington, D.C.

A In San Francisco when Johnson spoke at the 20th anniversary of the United Nations, Secret Service agents grouped all the photographers so that only the president's favorite side, his left profile, could be photographed.

Q Can you tell the inside story of how Frank Sinatra's son got slapped by that actress in South America when he got too fresh?—A. Cousins, Miami, Fla.

Frank Sinatra, Jr.

A Young Sinatra did not get fresh with anyone. In Buenos Aires, a blonde young starlet Mabel Luna, probably searching for publicity, squeezed through a mob of autograph hunters who were milling around Sinatra. Suddenly she slapped the young singer twice, screamed, "Send that to your father—for all he has done to women."

Q Hasn't Jackie Kennedy secretly been dating orchestra leader Leonard Bernstein?—F.L., New York, N.Y.

A Bernstein is a happily married man, an old friend of Mrs. Kennedy's. There has been no secret dating. They have attended several public functions.

Q What is the ration of doctors to people in this country and in the Soviet Union?—Don Clark, Baltimore, Md.

A There is one doctor for every 714 people in the U.S., one doctor for every 350 persons in the Soviet Union.

Q Was Doris Day ever married to a Negro? Has any member of her family ever been married to a Negro?—Harry T., Columbus, Ohio.

A Miss Day has been married three times but none of her husbands is a Negro. Her father some years ago married a Negro barmaid.

Q How is Groucho Marx doing in England with his TV quiz show?—Leon Gordon, Hollywood, Calif.

A He's laid a bomb. Typical criticism: "Groucho's quiz show is just one big yawn."—Clive Barnes in the *London Daily Express*.

Q Barbara Walters of the Today TV program—is she married? Is she any relation to Lou Walters who owns the Latin Quarter night club in N.Y.?—Lou Garber, Staten Island, N.Y.

A She is married to producer Lee Guber, is the daughter of Lou Walters.

Q I would like to know if Robert Welch of the John Birch Society who has accused former President Eisenhower, his brother Milton, Supreme Court Justice Earl Warren and other patriots of being Communist sympathizers, I would like to know how much Welch gets for lecturing and if he himself ever ran for political office and on what ticket.—V.T., Boston, Mass.

A Welch reportedly receives $1,000 per lecture fee, ran unsuccessfully in 1950 for the Republican nomination for lieutenant governor of Massachusetts.

Q There is a very famous anecdote about actress Katharine Hepburn and her reluctance to have anything to do with press agents, especially Hollywood press agents. Would you find out what it is and print it? Thank you.—Lois James, Denver, Colo.

A Several years ago when she reported to work at Paramount Studios for her role in *The Rainmaker*, Katharine Hepburn was greeted politely by a young man who said: "I am Bob Fender, press agent on this picture." The actress quickly replied: "I am Katharine Hepburn, actress on this picture. And you realize, of course, that this is the last conversation we will have." It was.

Q The late Marilyn Monroe left an estate of $500,000 when she died. In the creditors' claims on the estate, I understand there is one by her former drama coach, Paula Strasberg. I would like to find out how much Mrs. Strasberg is asking for her lessons.—Diana Clark, Oakland, Calif.

Marilyn Monroe

A Her claim on the estate for drama coaching is $22,209. The estate, however, is virtually bankrupt owing to large federal and state income tax and estate tax payments. Mrs. Strasberg and other creditors will probably get little or nothing.

Q Who said: "Avoid popularity. It has many snares and no real benefits"?—Frieda Henschel, Wellesley, Mass.

A William Penn.

Albert Einstein

Q Is it true that Albert Einstein, the great scientist, never wore socks?—Sal Fiore, Atlantic City, N.J.

A It was true while he lived and worked at Princeton.

Fang and Phyllis Diller

Q *Would you please publish a picture of "Fang," Phyllis Diller's husband?—R.S., Mt. Vernon, Iowa.*

A Yes.

Q *The rumor is that Elizabeth Taylor will do almost anything legitimate for money which is why she is writing her autobiography. Is Richard Burton writing the book for her? If not, who is?—D.R.R., Greenwich, Conn.*

A The book is being ghosted by Richard Meryman who is expanding a *Life* article he wrote on the actress some time ago.

Q *You made a serious error in your June 20th column when you reported that Madame Chiang Kai-shek attended and was graduated from Wellesley College. She attended and was graduated from Wesleyan College in Macon, Georgia. Isn't that so?—Judith Caulfield, Orlando, Fla.*

A Not true. Mayling Soong, later Madame Chiang Kai-shek, was graduated from Wellesley—not Wesleyan—with an A.B. degree, class of 1917. When she was 12 years old she arrived in Macon, Georgia, and according to W. Earl Strickland, president of Wesleyan, "was tutored through her high school work by Wesleyan faculty and completing her freshman year of college at Wesleyan." She then transferred to Wellesley of which college she regards herself an alumna. She regards Wesleyan with great warmth and respect. Her two sisters were graduated from

John F. Kennedy

there, but she considers Wellesley her collegiate alma mater.

Q *The late President Kennedy could speak no foreign languages. Yet one of his most memorable speeches was the one he gave in Germany in which he cried out, "Ich bin ein Berliner." My question is who wrote the speech for him and was it written phonetically?—Ed Henry, Cambridge, Mass.*

A Kennedy asked his speech-writers to draft a short message, to be spoken in German, after he finished his scheduled speech in Berlin. The writers suggested two sentences: *"Ich freue mich in Berlin zu sein."* (I am happy to be in Berlin) and *"Ich bin dankbar fuer den herzlichen Empfang."* (I am grateful for the cordial reception). Kennedy asked that these sentences be translated phonetically so that he, not knowing any German, could speak them. He then asked what they meant. When he was told, he quickly said, "I can't say that. It's trite and empty." Whereupon he sat down with McGeorge Bundy, one of his advisers. They began a new draft. Hastily in his almost illegible handwriting, the President scrawled, "I am a Berliner." The interpreters then wrote out the phonetic translation to fit Kennedy's Massachusetts accent: *"Ish bin ine bear-Lean-ar."* When Kennedy spoke that line in front of West Berlin's city hall, the crowd answered with a roaring ovation whereupon the president turned to his interpreter, smiled as if to say, "It went across O.K."

Q *I would like to obtain some truth about the war in Vietnam. Is it a revolution, a civil war, a war of aggression? Is it true that all the Vietnamese both North and South hate the Americans? Do we have any definite policy for winning the war?—J.D. Schwartz, Brooklyn, N.Y.*

A The war in Vietnam is basically a revolution grounded in the discontent of peasants who have been cheated, exploited, and deprived of the primary necessities of life. The revolution is being abetted from the outside by the Communists of North Vietnam. It is a civil war, too, in that Vietnamese is pitted against Vietnamese. Americans are disliked by both North and South Vietnamese, because they are white and wealthy. At the present time we have no policy for winning the war, hope by the use of additional troops to develop a military stalemate which will lead to acceptable negotiated settlement. This, of course, is an oversimplification.

Q *How much did Henry Ford and his new wife, Cristina, pay for their new yacht, Shemara?—A. Jennings, Grosse Pointe, Mich.*

A Ford chartered the yacht, *Shemara*, for the summer from Sir Bernard and Lady Docker.

Fess Parker

Q *Recently saw Sound of Music with Julie Andrews. Noticed that Marni Nixon who sang for Audrey Hepburn in My Fair Lady was also in the cast. What part did she perform?—Mrs. Max M., Salem, Ore.*

A One of the singing nuns.

Q *Has Fess Parker ever played the movie role of Tarzan?—Judy Kleefisch, Alexandria, Va.*

A He has not.

Q *What is the basis of the feud between Lyndon Johnson and Bobby Kennedy?—S.T. Hunt, Ft. Worth, Tex.*

A Their personalities clash.

Q *Would you please describe the special Rolls-Royce that Beatle John Lennon has bought for himself? Thank you.—Amy Ford, Greenville, Ohio.*

A It boasts smoked windows which permit Lennon to look through them from the inside but prevents pedestrians on the outside from looking inside.

Q *Is it true a legitimate son was born to Brigitte Bardot a few years ago? If so, why has it been hushed up?—W.B.J., Patrick A.F.B., Fla.*

A It has not been hushed up. She poses with the boy occasionally, but tries to keep him out of the limelight.

Brigitte Bardot

WALTER SCOTT'S
PERSONALITY PARADE®
January 2, 1966

Q *You cannot tell me that someone hasn't put the fix in with the Selective Service for heavyweight champion Cassius Clay. How can this man be classified 4F, unfit for military service, and knock out such fighters as Sonny Liston and Floyd Patterson?—Charley Hennessy, Boston, Mass.*

Cassius Clay

A Cassius Clay has been examined twice, once at the Armed Forces Examination Station in Coral Gables, Florida, a second time at the Station Louisville, Kentucky. His physical condition is excellent, but on both occasions he was unable to pass the mental and aptitude tests given by the Army. His level of intelligence does not meet the minimum military standards.

Q *Who is the most influential Washington correspondent? I mean the man whose writings command the most respect.—Athena Brooks, Evanston, Ill.*

A Best bet: Walter Lippmann who lucidly explains some of the most complicated issues of our time.

Q *Is it true that the White House is trying to prevent Bobby Baker from writing his memoirs because of possible embarrassment to Lyndon Johnson?—L.T., Chillicothe, Ohio.*

A No. Baker has begun his book, has hired the Ashley Famous Agency to represent him.

Q *Has Marlene Dietrich ever been divorced from Rudolf Sieber, her husband? Is she really hated in her native Germany? Does she have any talent?—M. Hartog, Baltimore, Md.*

Marlene Dietrich

A Dietrich has n o t b e e n divorced. She was against Hitler and the Nazis in World War II and is therefore not widely loved by the Germans, some of whom regard her as unloyal. She has scant singing or dancing talent but great stage presence.

Q *The story wasn't carried in the American press, but didn't Princess Margaret and Tony have a quarrel with plane passengers on their trip home from Bermuda after their tour of the U.S.A.? I believe the fight was with a Colonel Scott. Would you print the truth?—Asa Jackson, New York, N.Y.*

A On the BOAC flight that carried Princess Margaret and her husband home, first-class passengers were told they would have to accept tourist-class seats for that particular flight. Col. Murray Scott and his ill wife refused to give up their first-class seats in the compartment reserved for Princess Margaret and her party. There was no quarrel. Margaret and Tony were most gracious to the Scotts en route to London.

Q *Barry Goldwater's wife—wasn't she operated on for cancer in St. Joseph's, Phoenix?—Helen Alarcon, Carlsbad, N. Mex.*

A No, it was a hysterectomy, also a non-malignant tumor was removed.

Q *Bobby Kennedy and his wife do so much traveling. Who minds the store when they're away?—Louis Morantz, Portland, Ore.*

A The Kennedys have 17 in help.

Q *What does "laser" stand for? Who invented it?—V.C. Allen, Lubbock, Tex.*

A "Laser" stands for "light amplification by stimulated emission of radiation." The ownership of the basic laser patents is currently in legal dispute involving three physicists, Richard Gould, Charles H. Townes, Arthur L. Schawlow.

Q *It seems incredible to me that Elizabeth Taylor and her husband are each paid $100,000 a week overtime. Say it isn't so.—Elaine Margolis, Madison, Wis.*

A It isn't so. Miss Taylor gets $100,000 per week overtime, but Richard Burton gets only $75,000 per week overtime.

Q *How many war veterans in the U.S.?—G.T. Knox, St. Louis, Mo.*

A Approximately 21,625,000.

Q *Who was America named after—an Italian or an Englishman?—Brad Foster, New Haven, Conn.*

A It is popularly assumed that it was named after Amerigo Vespucci, the Medici shipping tycoon, but some historians now claim it was named in honor of an Englishman, Richard Amerycke, a high sheriff of Bristol who was the principal backer of John Cabot's voyage of discovery to the North American mainland.

Q *What is the truth about Kim Novak's back? I heard she hurt it on her honeymoon which is why she had to quit the movie she was making in England.—Bonnie Gray, Baltimore, Md.*

Kim Novak (left)

A The actress hurt her back when she fell off a horse in France where she was filming *The Eye of the Devil* with David Niven.

Q *There's a simply marvelous story about Swifty Morgan, the guy who hangs around comedians, and J. Edgar Hoover of the FBI. If the story can be printed, will you print it?—A.P.S., Del Mar, Calif.*

A One version: Swifty Morgan is a lovable old character who peddles watches from time to time. He is well-known, well-liked in show business circles. One afternoon at the Del Mar race track Swifty spotted J. Edgar Hoover who regularly attends the races. He approached Hoover and offered to sell him a diamond wrist watch for $1,500. Supposedly Hoover examined the watch, listened patiently to Swifty's sales pitch, then offered Morgan $500 for the timepiece. "You must be kidding!" exclaimed Swifty. "The reward on it alone is $750."

Q *Recently I saw a photo of the late President Kennedy with the following poem beneath it:*
"When he shall die
Take him and cut him out in little stars.
And he will make the face of heaven so fine
That all the world will be in love with night,
And pay no worship to the garish sun."
Who is the author, his wife, Jackie?—R.E. Young, Buffalo, N.Y.

A The lines are from Act III, scene II of *Romeo and Juliet* by William Shakespeare.

WALTER SCOTT'S
PERSONALITY PARADE®

May 22, 1966

Q *Since you are such a know-it-all, would you classify as "hawk" or "dove" the following men: Robert McNamara, Walt Rostow, Henry Cabot Lodge, George Ball, all working for the Johnson administration.—Stanley De Marco, Los Angeles, Calif.*

A Robert McNamara—dove; Walt Rostow—hawk; Henry Cabot Lodge—hawk; George Ball—dove.

Q *I would like to know which is the bestselling record album of all time.—Elizabeth Snodgrass, Bend, Ore.*

A Probably the Columbia album of *My Fair Lady.* More than six million copies have been sold to date.

Q *The real names, please, also ages, of Sonny and Cher.—Henrietta Weinberg, Hoboken, N.J.*

A Sonny, 26, is Salvatore Bono, born in Detroit, raised in Los Angeles. She is Cheryl LaPiere, 19, of Fresno, California.

Q *Several weeks ago you cast aspersions on the manhood of the late Somerset Maugham. On what evidence did you base your conclusions?—A.T.T., Buffalo, N.Y.*

A Maugham's homosexuality was for years well recognized in British and American literary circles. In his recently released book, *Somerset and All the Maughams,* author Robin Maugham, the novelist's nephew, quotes his uncle as saying: "I've been such a fool. My greatest mistake was this: I tried to persuade myself that I was three-quarters normal and that only a quarter of me was queer—whereas really it was the other way round."

Q *I understand that Walter Reuther, the labor leader, went to school in Russia. If so, how long? What was he taught in the U.S.S.R.? What school did he attend?—E.T.S., Oakland, Calif.*

A Reuther and his younger brother, Victor, toured Russia during the Depression, worked for 16 months in the Gorki automobile factory built by the Ford Motor Company for the Soviet government. They did not attend school.

Q *Is it true that Ernest Hemingway's tombstone in Ketchum, Idaho, bears the titles of all his books? I've been told it's the largest tombstone in Idaho.—Doris Johnson, Oakland, Calif.*

A Not true. The tombstone is a seven-foot-long slab of marble on which is simply lettered "Ernest Miller Hemingway, July 21, 1899-July 2, 1961."

Q *Who was Dean Martin's first wife? Why do Martin and his present wife, Jeanne, have custody of his four children from his first marriage?—Florence Simon, Dayton, Ohio.*

A Martin was divorced from his first wife, Elizabeth Ann McDonald, in 1949. He sued for custody of their four children, Craig, Claudia, Gail, Deana, in 1957 on charges of neglect and was awarded them in an uncontested case.

Q *I've heard tell that Gov. George Wallace of Alabama has ordered his wife not to watch color television for fear she'll lose the white vote. True or a joke?—D.L., Mobile, Ala.*

A Joke.

Q *I read that Elizabeth Taylor looks positively shrewish in her next film,* Virginia Woolf. *Would you run a picture?—Vera Lee Hopkins, Marion, S.C.*

Elizabeth Taylor

Q *Two questions, please, about* Marvin Watson, one of the president's White House Texans:(1) Does he have all the White House telephone calls tape-recorded? (2) Is he anti-union and anti-labor?—Charles F.F., Wichita Falls, Tex.

A Watson says he has never had any White House telephone calls tape-recorded, is neither anti-union nor anti-labor.

Q *Is there really such an organization as Interpol? When and where was it formed? Where are the headquarters?—P.W., Richford, N.Y.*

A Interpol stands for International Criminal Police Commission. Headquarters are in Paris. It was founded in 1923 in Vienna by Dr. Johann Schober, chief of the Vienna police, reestablished after World War II by F. E. Louwage, Inspector General of Belgium's Ministry of Justice. Its function is to gather and circulate records of international criminals in order to help police forces of member nations. It tries to keep tabs on the world travels of dope smugglers, counterfeiters, white slavers, etc. Interpol is neither a super police nor an international detective agency, but rather a public service central records bureau.

Q *Prince Charles, heir to the British throne—how much loot will he come into?—Dan Rivers, Parkersburg, W. Va.*

A Prince Charles as Duke of Cornwall inherited 80 acres of London property as well as 120,000 acres in west England. At 18 he will draw an estimated annual income of $120,000. When he reaches 21 this will jump to $400,000 annually plus $1 million accumulated from 10 percent of the land revenues collected since his birth. When he ascends the throne he will inherit the entire Windsor fortune which by then should be worth $1 billion or more.

Q *Newsweek magazine quotes President Johnson as saying the following to Sen. Vance Hartke of Indiana: "Now you look here. I remember you when you were just a two-bit mayor of a two-bit town in Indiana and I made you a United States senator." Is this the way the President of the United States talks to senators? It sounds like a line of dialogue from a third-rate Hollywood movie. What is the truth?—D.E.L., Terre Haute, Ind.*

Lyndon Johnson

A The quotation is a reasonable facsimile of the truth. When aroused the president has been known to fight back with brass knuckles on his tongue.

Q *Can you tell me if Jimmy Hoffa, the Teamsters Union president, has hired his son to defend him?—F.T., Detroit, Mich.*

A Hoffa's son, James Jr., a brilliant student at the University of Michigan law school, has not yet passed his bar exam. Recently, however, he won a state senate research position in Lansing, Michigan, on the basis of his outstanding academic record.

Q *For years I've read that the producers who run the Hollywood studios were not too bright. Can you tell me why they would hire for $125,000 per year a man like Jack Valenti who admittedly has had no motion picture experience at all? Also why would presidential assistant Valenti, so deeply and emphatically attached to Lyndon Johnson, want to leave him?—W.E.R., McLean, Va.*

Jack Valenti

A Jack Valenti was recommended to the producers by his good friend, President Johnson. One suggested reason: Valenti and Bill Moyers, another White House assistant, were overlapping in duty areas and a conflict was inevitable. Johnson therefore asked Lewis Wasserman of Universal Pictures and Arthur Krim of United Artists to get for Valenti the job as president of the Motion Picture Producers Association. Last September Johnson appointed Wasserman a member of the Peace Corps' National Advisory Council, while Krim, of course, is chairman of the National Democratic Party Finance Committee. To protect Valenti, who first has to learn the film business, the producers hired at $200,000 per year for the next five years as their general counsel attorney Louis Nizer, who knows the financial end of the film industry, having taken part in several major proxy fights. As to why Valenti is willing to leave the White House, he says: "I have certain economic obligations which I undertook before I came to Washington. When I joined the president in 1963 I cut myself loose from all my income-producing properties, and I went to work at $21,000 a year. It's only been in the last year that presidential assistants have earned $30,000 per year. I love the president very much. Our country will have been much better for his being president. To leave him is a wrenching emotional experience, because my life has been entwined so closely with his. I have mixed feelings compounded of hope and anguish. But I also have a wife [the former Mary Margaret Wiley, LBJ's long-time private secretary] and a daughter, Courtenay Lynda, and we're expecting another child in August. I'm 44, and I must think of my future. I'd love staying with the president whom as you know, I love very much, but I would then be 50. And what industry wants to hire a man of 50? I must say I've been offered jobs which pay better than this one, especially through stock options, but this one will constitute a challenge. I've always loved motion pictures."

Q *Is it true that Omar Sharif, supposedly from Egypt, is really Moses Schwartz from Palestine, and that the Egyptians hate him as a film star?—Helen Epstein, New York, N.Y.*

A Sharif's real name is Maechel Shalhoub. He was raised as a French-speaking Catholic by Syrian-Lebanese parents. When he married Faten Hamama, the Egyptian screen idol, he converted to the Moslem religion. Now that they are divorced, he is widely disliked in Egypt where in many sources he is known as "Cairo Fred."

Q *There is a new French actress, successor to Brigitte Bardot and Jeanne Moreau, who stars in a film named* Galla. *Supposedly she is the hottest. Can you reveal her name and photo?—John Gold, Chicago, Ill.*

Brigitte Bardot

A Name: Mireille Darc.

Q *I understand that Sen. Robert Kennedy is building up a nationwide machine so that he can run for the presidency in 1972. Is this so?—Dan Ehrenberg, Los Angeles, Calif.*

A Substantially true. Bobby Kennedy has friends like Lieutenant Governor Patrick J. Lucey in Wisconsin, John Hooker in Tennessee, Jess Unruh and Tom Braden in California to whom he looks forward for political support in the years ahead.

Q *A college economist says that Parkinson's Law will in time nullify the good done in the war on poverty and that anyway the poverty war is practically party politics. What is Parkinson's Law?—C.W. Wirsted, Sioux Falls, S. Dak.*

A The first Parkinson's Law, originated by British writer C. Northcote Parkinson, concerns the belief that bureaucracy creates work for itself in order to insure its own survival. Once established, a bureaucracy will increase at a rate unrelated to the amount of work to be done. The forces at work will tend to prevent any decrease in the number of bureaucrats. "Under a monarchy the process may be undone when the King wants the money for something else. But no one can reduce the civil service in a democracy."

Q *Is it true or false that Red Skelton had a son who died in Europe?—Mrs. Bud Mitchell, Rochelle, Ga.*

A Red Skelton's son died of leukemia, May 10, 1958, in the UCLA medical center. The previous summer his parents had taken him on a world tour.

Q *Can you tell me how much the Beatles are worth?—Charlene Kemp, Elgin, Ill.*

A Each is a millionaire, listed among the 99 Britishers who earn $300,000 or more per year. Every day of the year they earn roughly $5,000 from all sources.

Q *The crewcut hairpieces worn by Hugh Downs and Frank Sinatra—who manufactures them? What are they called?—Louis Dembitz, Boston, Mass.*

A The hairpieces worn by Downs and Sinatra are manufactured by Max Factor; they are called "the Celebrity," contain no lace, are held to the scalp by a double-faced adhesive tape.

Q *Ever since Vivien Leigh divorced Sir Laurence Olivier five years ago, her constant escort has been actor John Merivale. Can you tell us anything about him?—Diane Knox, Allentown, Pa.*

Vivien Leigh

A Merivale is four years younger than Miss Leigh, 52. At one time he was married to American actress Jan Sterling. He and Miss Leigh are currently playing in the Broadway play, *Ivanov*. They have never made any secret of their affiliation. Friends say Miss Leigh is unwilling to chance marriage for the third time, prefers being known in England as Vivien Lady Olivier, likes to drive around in the Rolls-Royce she and Olivier once jointly owned which still bears the license tags—VLO-123, for Vivien and Laurence Olivier.

WALTER SCOTT'S
PERSONALITY PARADE®

July 10, 1966

Q *Is it true that the U.S. Army is now operating Dachau, Hitler's oldest concentration camp in Germany, as a stockade for American GI's?—E.L.T., New York, N.Y.*

A Eastman Barracks, a prison for American GI's, is located on the same land that encompassed the Dachau concentration camp. From time to time GI inmates report a strong nauseating stench wafting up from the nearby crematorium where the Nazis murdered approximately 28,000 Jews and anti-Nazis. Dachau today is divided into two areas: one consists of the memorial to victims of the German atrocities, headed by Ruth Jakusch of the Dachau International Committee; the other consists of the Eastman Barracks, which once was used to incarcerate important enemies of the Third Reich. GI's in Germany refer to the Eastman barracks as "the Dachau stockade." It is a neat, whitewashed jail that houses GI's who have been sentenced to six months of imprisonment or less.

Q *Were Henry Wadsworth Longfellow and Nathaniel Hawthorne college classmates?—Watson Henry, Evanston, Ill.*

A Yes, both were graduated from Bowdoin College, Maine, class of 1825.

Q *I've read that most of the fatal accidents in private flying are caused by drunk pilots. Is this so?—Vernon Richards, Paducah, Ky.*

A One of the first formal studies of general aviation accidents, made by Drs. Charles Harper and William Albers of the Federal Aviation Agency, shows that in 158 of 477 fatal general aviation accidents in 1963—this has nothing to do with commercial airline flying—56 or 35.4% of the 158 pilots registered positive at autopsy as regards alcohol in the blood.

Q *Does Barry Goldwater plan to run for the U.S. Senate again?—Dan Lloyd, Tombstone, Ariz.*

A Probably in 1968 or when Senator Hayden of Arizona retires.

Q *Not long ago while I was in Europe, I was told that most major European countries deliver the mail faster and more frequently than the U.S. Post Office does. Is this true? If so, please use only my initials as I would still like to get my mail.—M.P.G., Bal Harbour, Fla.*

A True.

Q *How many years have Chet Huntley and Dave Brinkley been with NBC, and who was responsible for putting them together?—R. Espinard, Chicago, Ill.*

A Brinkley has been with NBC since 1943, Huntley since 1955. The original pairing suggestion came from the late Fred Wile of NBC-TV, Los Angeles, was implemented by Pat Weaver, formerly in charge of NBC-TV.

Q *I've heard that Robert Goulet was married before his marriage to Carol Lawrence and that he has a child from that first marriage. Is that so?—A.T.E., Jamaica, N.Y.*

Goulet and Lawrence

A Yes, he was married to Louise Longmore in 1956, has a daughter, Nicolette, by her.

Q *How many times has columnist Drew Pearson been sued for libel? Has he ever lost? Is it true Gen. Douglas MacArthur planned to sue him for libel because he reported that MacArthur every now and again touched up his hair?—Arthur Holt, Los Angeles, Calif.*

A Pearson has been sued approximately 25 times, has lost only one suit. MacArthur resented Pearson's intimations that he was a vain man.

Q *Who said: "In America there are two classes of travel—first class, and with children"?—J. Robert Jenkins, Cambridge, Mass.*

A The late Robert Benchley, U.S. humorist—1889-1945.

Q *In 1961 President Kennedy sent his vice president, Lyndon Johnson, and his sister and brother-in-law, Jean and Stephen Smith, to Vietnam. What was Johnson's report on Vietnam? What did he recommend back then?—S.L., Washington, D.C.*

A He then reported that the number-one danger in Southeast Asia was not Communism but "hunger, ignorance, poverty and disease," went on to say that we must "make imaginative use of our scientific and technologic capacity." He favored military training missions but no commitment of American troops on the grounds that such commitments would revive anticolonial demonstrations in Vietnam. The major supporter for troop and combat escalation in Vietnam was Walt Rostow, who with Gen. Maxwell Taylor followed Johnson to Vietnam in October 1961. Both gentlemen suggested U.S. troop commitments. Despite demurrers by Averell Harriman and J. Kenneth Galbraith, President Kennedy reluctantly agreed to send combat troops to Vietnam. In May 1962, when Defense Secretary Robert McNamara flew into Saigon for his first assessment of the situation, he said after a two-day stay: "Every quantitative measurement we have shows we're winning this war."

Q *Is Petula Clark married? Does she have any children? Is she English or French?—Claire Diamond, Jersey City, N.J.*

A Petula Clark, British, is married to a Frenchman, has two daughters.

Q *In Vietnam many American soldiers are referred to by their buddies as "Straight Arrows" and "Broken Arrows." What do these expressions mean?—Viola Rushmer, Baltimore, Md.*

A "Straight Arrow" signifies a married man who remains faithful for his entire stretch of duty in Vietnam. "Broken Arrow" refers to a married soldier who succumbs to temptation.

Q *When Senator Fulbright was president of the University of Arkansas, is it true he was given the choice of resigning or being fired, and that he chose resignation?—C.H.B., Deming, N.Mex.*

William Fulbright

A No. Fulbright was fired by Gov. Homer Adkins on the grounds that he was not an educator but a political hack. This occurred immediately following Adkins' election against which Fulbright's mother had strongly fought in her reform newspaper, *The Northwest Arkansas Times*, describing Adkins as a "blowhard" and a "handshaker."

WALTER SCOTT'S
PERSONALITY PARADE®

July 31, 1966

Q *Is there a feud between J. Edgar Hoover and Sen. Bobby Kennedy? I have read that there is no love lost between them.*—H.T. Lewis, Seattle, Wash.

A No feud. When Senator Kennedy was attorney general in charge of the Justice Department, he did not see eye-to-eye with Hoover on several problems and procedures. Mr. Hoover, because of his long government service, established national reputation and wide political influence, has long been regarded as a law unto himself.

Q *Everybody knows that Ursula Andress has been fooling around with Jean-Paul Belmondo. My question is: Does Belmondo's wife know about this? Also how many children do the Belmondos have?*—Lois Jenkinson, Upper Darby, Pa.

A Belmondo's wife, former club dancer Renee Constant, has long been aware of her husband's extracurricular activities. The Belmondos have three children.

Q *Is it true that Beatle John Lennon, a millionaire, won't give a dollar to his father who earns $20 a week?*—Nola Green, Vancouver, B.C.

John Lennon

A Fred Lennon, who earns $22 a week as a bartender at the Tony Jug Hotel in Surrey, says: "John has forgotten me all right. We've only met once since he became famous." John Lennon's parents were divorced, and the Beatle has been most generous to his mother.

Q *How many U.S. presidents were Army generals before they reached the White House?*—Bernard Riche, Newark, N.J.

A Of the 35 U.S. presidents, 11 were generals: Washington, Jackson, W. H. Harrison, Taylor, Pierce, Grant, Hayes, Garfield, Arthur, Benjamin Harrison, Eisenhower.

Q *A friend of mine says that neither he nor any other ordinary person is allowed to be tattooed in New York state. Isn't it a constitutional right for a man to get tattooed if he wants to?*—Pierre Joffre, New York, N.Y.

A New York City's new health code outlaws tattooing. New York state's Court of Appeals has upheld the constitutionality of the code on the grounds that

"The record shows...that the prohibition of lay tattooing was an advisable procedure for the security of life and health."

Q *I would like to know if a pocketbook version of Ralph Nader's book, Unsafe at Any Speed, is available.*—F. Tremaine, Ann Arbor, Mich.

A It will be in November.

Q *Is Helen Keller still alive? If so, how old, and where does she live?*—Bennett C. Alvarez, San Diego, Calif.

A Miss Keller, 86, resides in Easton, Conn.

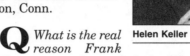
Helen Keller

Q *What is the real reason Frank Sinatra was banned from Mexico? Is it because he tried to introduce gambling on behalf of the Las Vegas syndicate?*—E.L.E., Chicago, Ill.

A Sinatra was banned from Mexico because he produced *Marriage on the Rocks*, a film which held Mexicans up to ridicule.

Q *What's happened to young John Barrymore?*—Vicki Henstchel, Wichita, Kans.

A Young Barrymore is working in television.

Q *In 25 years of movie-going I have never heard more obscene dialogue than in the film* Virginia Woolf. *Will you please explain to me how Warner Brothers obtained official producers' approval of the film?*—D.L., Denver, Colo.

A Originally, approval was denied. Pressure was then brought to bear upon the Motion Picture Producers' Association. The denial was reversed by a group of outside producers.

Q *Is it true that in the present Bing Crosby marriage, Bing goes his way and his wife, Kathryn, goes hers? What is she doing now, still working as a nurse?*—Julian Knox, Palo Alto, Calif.

A Kathryn Crosby has been playing summer stock throughout the country. She is a professional actress although she has qualified as a nurse.

Q *Is it true that Isabella Rossellini, one of the twins Ingrid Bergman had with Roberto Rossellini, is quietly dying of a mysterious bone disease in Rome? Why has nothing appeared in the American press?*—Diane Hyams, Jersey City, N.J.

A Reportedly Isabella, 13, is suffering from scoliosis, an abnormal curvature of the spine, making her appear smaller than she really is. She is being treated by Professor Scaglietti in Florence, may require a fusion operation. Her mother, Ingrid Bergman, who gave custody of her three children by Rossellini to their father, has canceled her acting commitments, will stay in Italy at Isabella's side for the length of her recovery.

Q *Who said: "When you become used to never being alone, you may consider yourself Americanized"?*—Roberta Vaughn, Princeton, N.J.

A Andre Maurois, born 1885, French writer.

Q *Max Schmeling, former heavyweight boxing champion—where is he living? Is he married?*—Victor Weiss, Baton Rouge, La.

A Schmeling is in Hollenstedt, south of Hamburg, with new wife Anny Ondra.

Q *A few questions, please, about Lorne Greene of* Bonanza. *Is he an American or Canadian citizen? How many times married? How many children? How old is he? His present wife?*—Dan Froley, Superior, Wis.

A Greene retains his Canadian citizenship. He has been married twice, has 21-year-old twins by his first marriage, which ended in divorce in 1960. His son Charles is a student at MIT. His daughter Linda is now Mrs. Robert Bennett, lives in Santa Monica, California. Greene is married to Nancy Deale, who once acted under the name Liza Cummings.

Lorne Greene

Walter Scott's
PERSONALITY PARADE®

August 7, 1966

Q *The Vietnam war policy now being followed by President Johnson—is it any different from the policy advocated by Barry Goldwater when he ran against Johnson in 1964?—E.L., Washington, D.C.*

A Essentially it's the same policy.

Q *The late Ed Wynn—is his grandson Ned in films? Was Wynn ever estranged from his son Keenan? Was Keenan ever married to Van Johnson's wife?—Louis Devers, Bridgeport, Conn.*

A Ed Wynn's son and grandson are both in films. Keenan Wynn was married at one time to Evie Wynn. Evie Wynn divorced him to marry Van Johnson, later divorced Van Johnson, is currently unmarried. Ed Wynn and son Keenan were not estranged.

Q *Does Joe DiMaggio, former star outfielder of the New York Yankees, own DiMaggio's restaurant on Fisherman's Wharf in San Francisco, or does he just permit the use of his name for royalties?—Henrietta Johnson, Lincoln, Neb.*

A DiMaggio's restaurant is owned by Joe's brothers, Dominic and Tom. Joe is part owner of Continental Television, a northern California retail chain of eight stores.

Q *Jane Wyman, once married to Ronald Reagan—has she abandoned her acting career?—Dorothy Richardson, Raleigh, N.C.*

Jane Wyman

A Jane Wyman has not retired, works in TV, plans to appear shortly in a Broadway play.

Q *The first two films starring the Beatles—how much money have they earned?—Dorothy Channing, Albany, N.Y.*

A Each has grossed approximately $20 million.

Q *I understand that Grace Kelly recently introduced a new dance step called the Stop-Op. Can you describe it?—Emma Fontaine, Rutland, Vt.*

A When the music stops, both partners freeze, then try to sense when the music will start again by jumping high in the air. A group of Cuban dancers demonstrated the step in Monte Carlo where Princess Grace tried it with her partner, actor David Niven.

Q *Is President Johnson grooming George Christian, former press secretary for Texas Gov. John Connally, to replace Bill Moyers?—T.T., Dallas, Tex.*

A Christian is being groomed to assist Moyers.

Q *Nancy Sinatra's hair—I have a bet it's bleached. Am I right or wrong?—Lois De Leo, New Orleans, La.*

A Right.

Nancy Sinatra

Q *Is it true that pop singer Roy Orbison and his wife were both killed in a July 4th auto accident?—George Harrison, Short Hills, N.J.*

A Roy Orbison was not killed. His wife, Claudette, was killed in Gailatin, Tennessee, on June 6th in a collision involving her motorcycle and an automobile. Orbison was riding a few feet in front of her on his own motorcycle. Three children survive.

Q *One of the funniest movies, The Russians Are Coming—is there a book by that name? Who wrote it?—Elaine Dougherty, Boston, Mass.*

A The film was adapted from a novel, *The Off-Islanders,* by Nathaniel Benchley.

Q *A Song at Twilight by Nöel Coward— is this new play about Nöel Coward and homosexuality?—B.J.J., Rochester, N.Y.*

A The play, written by Nöel Coward, concerns a homosexual writer, thought by many to be the late Somerset Maugham. It probably will come to New York later in the year.

Q *I've read that of the 40,000 South Vietnamese workers employed by American contractors in Vietnam, a good 10 percent are members of the Viet Cong. Is this so?—Leon A. Goldman, Chicago, Ill.*

A The four leading U.S. contractors in Vietnam are Brown & Root of Houston, Texas; Morrison-Knudsen, Boise, Idaho.; J.A. Jones, Charlotte, North Carolina; Raymond International, New York, New York. At this writing the combine employs 38,745 South Vietnamese. An estimated 10 percent are considered members of the Viet Cong.

Q *When Lynda Bird Johnson took her graduation gift trip to Europe, she was accompanied by eight Secret Service men. Who paid for these men?—T.R., Baltimore, Md.*

A The U.S. Government.

Q *After World War II, Sen. Thomas Dodd helped with the prosecution of Nazi war criminals at Nuremberg. Since Dodd flunked the Connecticut bar exam, how could he be allowed to practice law?— A.L.T., Hartford, Conn.*

A Dodd, of course, was not a U.S. senator at the time; neither was he practicing law in Connecticut. He was a Department of Justice employee who from all accounts did an excellent job at Nuremberg.

Q *Who said: "In prosperity our friends know us but in adversity we know our friends"?—Lester Sims, Cambridge, Mass.*

A Writer Churton Collins.

Q *Is it true that after The Countess from Hong Kong, Charles Chaplin will never again make a film with Marlon Brando?—T.R.F., Miami Beach, Fla.*

A It is not likely that Chaplin will ever again direct Brando.

Charlie Chaplin

PERSONALITY PARADE®

September 11, 1966

Q *Why is President Johnson so disliked and mistrusted when, after all, he is trying so hard?—William Marsh, Washington, D.C.*

A Unfortunately Mr. Johnson's personality and background do not inspire love, warmth and trust.

Q *Whatever happened to Mandy Rice-Davies, the blonde British model who figured so prominently in the Profumo scandal that rocked England three years ago?—Ronald Thorp, New York, N.Y.*

A Her romance with a French nobleman, Baron Pierre Cervello, is finished. Mandy says now that she is waiting to marry an Israeli airline steward, Raphael Shaul, whose parents own a chain of discotheques in Israel. She met him on a recent cabaret tour. Mandy Rice-Davies has been barred from working in the U.S.

Q *Richard Burton and Liz Taylor received no salary for filming* The Taming of the Shrew. *How come?—S.L., Newark, N.J.*

Taylor and Burton

A The Burtons will share in the profits, if any. Six previous versions of the Shakespeare play have been filmed, many unprofitably.

Q *Marshal Ky of Vietnam has said over and over again: "We will never accept negotiations with the Communists." If this is so, how then is peace possible, unless we kill all the Viet Cong?—T.T., Boston, Mass.*

A Marshal Ky says many things, but when the chips are down he will do what the U.S. tells him to do. We are running the war in Vietnam, not Marshal Ky, although he is a very fast draw from the lip.

Q *Is Cassius Clay the owner of a jet transport named "Irene"?—Louise Pretchett, Louisville, Ky.*

A No, but he plans to buy one, "because, after all, kings and presidents have their own personal planes and they are just kings and presidents of one country. I am champion of the whole wide world."

Q *Who is George Livanos? I understand he's the world's most eligible bachelor.—Kay Menzies, Baltimore, Md.*

A George Livanos, 31, is one of the world's wealthiest men. When his father died three years ago, Livanos inherited a $300 million Greek shipping empire. His sister, Tina, was once married to Aristotle Onassis. His other sister, Eugenie, was once married to Stavros Niarchos, now the husband of Charlotte Ford. George Livanos was recently engaged to a 16-year-old Greek girl, Lita Voivoda, whose father is the wealthiest tobacco magnate in Greece. Livanos is no longer considered the world's most eligible bachelor.

Q *How old is actress Cyd Charisse who has the best legs in the world?—Joseph Sharif, Rutland, Vt.*

A 43.

Cyd Charisse

Q *Since the U.S. is not officially at war with North Vietnam, why can't our fliers be treated and tried as criminals, spies, space pirates or whatever Hanoi wants to call them?—T.R., Fort Benning, Ga.*

A Article Two of the 1949 Geneva Convention, which the U.S. and North Vietnam both have signed, says, "The Convention shall apply to all cases of declared war or of any other armed conflict..."

Q *Whose idea was it to stage Luci Johnson's wedding in the National Shrine of the Immaculate Conception, the largest Roman Catholic Church in the U.S.?—Gloria Truscott, San Antonio, Tex.*

A The idea of a wedding spectacular was Luci's.

Q *Afdera Franchetti, one of Henry Fonda's wives—the one who was arrested allegedly for smuggling marijuana from London into Rome—which number wife was she? Is it also true she was the late Ernest Hemingway's sweetie?—Leona Georgi, East Orange, N.J.*

Franchetti and Fonda

A Baroness Afdera Franchetti, 33, was the fourth of Fonda's five wives. Daughter of Baron Raimondo Franchetti, an Italian scientist-explorer, she is said to have been Hemingway's close friend.

Q *Does one have to pay to sit in French parks?—Ilona von Hallen, Brooklyn, N.Y.*

A In many French parks it costs from two to five cents to rent a chair from a concessionaire.

Q *Approximately 10 years ago President Nasser of Egypt nationalized the Suez Canal. How has it done?—Dennis Harrison, Winnetka, Ill.*

A Under the Egyptians the Suez Canal has been run efficiently and profitably.

Q *Is it true that the average female brain weighs less than the average male brain?—Doris Devereaux, Naples, Me.*

A Yes, the average male brain weighs a little more than three pounds, the average female brain a little less than three pounds.

Q *I've been told that Vice President Hubert Humphrey is finished as a Democratic Party presidential possibility in 1972. Is this so?—L. Williams, St. Paul, Minn.*

Hubert Humphrey

A Humphrey in many quarters is considered a Johnson mouthpiece, is no longer regarded as the liberals' favorite. Political veterans claim Bobby Kennedy will be the Democrats' 1972 standard bearer.

Q *Actor Stephen Boyd had the cutest little Jamaican housekeeper named Esther in London. Is it true that Marlon Brando stole her away, now keeps her in his Hollywood hillside home?—L.F.S., Los Angeles, Calif.*

A The girl voluntarily left Mr. Boyd's employ in London to work for Brando while he was filming in London. Later she came to Hollywood, stayed at Brando's home when he went off to Tahiti to visit Simon, the son he had by a Tahitian girl.

Q *When Baron James Rothschild, 70, the Paris banker, married that 27-year-old usherette, did any of the other Rothschilds show at the wedding? Also, who is the richest Rothschild?—Nicole Lapin, Miami, Fla.*

The Rothschilds

A None of the Rothschilds attended the wedding. They claimed they were otherwise occupied. The wealthiest Rothschild is Edmond, of the family's French branch, DeRothschild Fréres. From a rather nondescript building at 45 Rue de Fauborg St. Honoré, he runs an empire called Compagnie Financiere. It controls investments in real estate, oil, pipe lines, factories, hotels, etc.

Q *Why is it that Americans are doing most of the fighting in Vietnam, and the South Vietnamese are sitting on their butts?—F.R., Albany, N.Y.*

A The Army of the Republic of Vietnam, A.R.V.N., the South Vietnamese, are not capable of beating the Viet Cong and the North Vietnamese. They lack the dedication, the ability, the willingness, the leadership. They have, therefore, been assigned to pacification duties while the Americans do the bulk of the fighting.

Q *I would like to know if Bobby Kennedy was ever a heartless bill and rent collector.—Mrs. J.R. Quinn, Boston, Mass.*

A For a short while he collected rents from his father's apartments in Boston. But heartless? No.

Q *How many remaining monarchs in Europe? Please list and tell which ones are the richest.—Lois Van Every, New York, N.Y.*

A There are seven reigning monarchs in Europe: Queen Elizabeth of Great Britain, Queen Juliana of the Netherlands, King Baudouin of Belgium, King Constantine of Greece, King Frederik of Denmark, King Olav of Norway, King Gustaf of Sweden. Queen Juliana is by far the wealthiest with an estimated $600 million fortune. Queen Elizabeth comes next with an estimated $300 million.

Q *Is Mrs. Lurleen Wallace of Alabama the nation's first woman governor?— Frank Fletcher, Mobile, Ala.*

A No. Texas and Wyoming both have previously known women governors.

Q *Two questions, please, about the Selective Service: (1) What does the 1Y classification mean? (2) What is the legal minimum mental standard necessary to get into the Army?—Ben Jenkins, Rock Hill, S.C.*

A 1Y is the classification given mental rejectees. Minimum legal mental standard for military induction is a fifth grade education or its equivalent.

Q *Julie Christie makes no secret of the fact that she is living with a man, that she prefers their arrangement to marriage. My question is why, if she flaunts her immorality, do theaters release her films?— Vivian W., Long Beach, Calif.*

A Her films are profitable. If the public is outraged by her private life, it has the choice of patronizing or not patronizing her films.

Q *I have an argument with my wife. She claims Ronald Reagan is the first show business character to sit in a governor's chair. I say she's all wet. Who's right? Supply evidence to your answer.— James L. Talcott, Fresno, Calif.*

A You are right. John Lodge, like Reagan an actor, served as governor of Connecticut. Jimmie Davis, a minstrel, served as governor of Louisiana.

Q *When Jack and Jacqueline Kennedy were first married, they bought a lovely mansion in McLean, Virginia, which was once the headquarters of Union Army Gen. George McClellan during the Civil War. Has the house been torn down?—Mrs. Faith H. George, Danville, Va.*

A No. It's called "Hickory Hill," was sold in 1957 to Ethel and Robert Kennedy. It consists of a 15-room house and ten acres of land. The house was sold at the request of Mrs. Jacqueline Kennedy, who, depressed at having miscarried in a pregnancy, decided to move into Washington, D.C.

Q *Is it true that in Spain no adultery may be shown or suggested on the screen?—Dee Sanford, New Orleans, La.*

A Not true. Adultery may be shown, but under no circumstances may the adultress be Spanish. She can be American, British, French, etc., but never Spanish.

Q *How much money did the late Billy Rose leave in his estate? How much*

went to his ex-wife, Eleanor Holm?— D.E.L., Orlando, Fla.

A Rose's estate is estimated at $40 million. When Eleanor Holm divorced him, she accepted $200,000 as a full property settlement. Even so, Rose left her $10,000 in his will. Miss Holm, however, has filed a $15 million claim in the U.S. District Court of New York. She charges that in 1953 as part of a separation agreement prior to her divorce, she accepted two Renoirs from Rose supposedly worth $1 million. She says the Renoirs were not Renoirs, that Rose duped her; now she wants $15 million from his estate.

Q *Is it true that Arnold Palmer and Jack Nicklaus are quietly buying up the best golf clubs in England?—E.P., Cleveland, Oh.*

A Palmer is interested in buying the Prince's Golf Club at Sandwich and the Royal Cinque Ports course at Deal as golfing clubs for traveling Americans.

Q *In the 1968 presidential election, is it true that Romney and Nixon will kill each other off, and Reagan will win the Republican candidacy?—Ted Hershberg, Atlantic City, N.J.*

A Conjecture.

Q *Defense Secretary Robert McNamara has said over and over again that the U.S. is not employing mercenaries in Vietnam to fight for us. And yet I read all the time in the newspapers that we are paying mercenaries to fight for us. What is the truth?— E.L., Washington, D.C.*

Robert McNamara

A The truth is that mercenaries are fighting on our side in Vietnam. The mercenaries are composed of ethnic Chinese Nungs, evacuated from North Vietnam in 1954 and resettled in the south. These Chinese mercenaries are known as "Mike Force" companies. Technically they have been hired by the government of South Vietnam, but they are paid with American funds.

WALTER SCOTT'S
PERSONALITY PARADE®
February 19, 1967

Q *Recently a boy from our town was killed in Vietnam. Now his brother has been drafted. I say he cannot be sent to Vietnam because he is the last boy in the family, but my friends say he can. Who is right?—L.M., Dillsburg, Pa.*

A The boy is not obliged to go to Vietnam—but he must take the initiative to prevent it. Under Pentagon policy, the sole surviving son of a family is not required to serve in a combat zone (which includes all of Vietnam) if at any time since September 16, 1940, another member of the family (father, son or daughter) has been killed, is missing or was totally disabled while in service. Under another rule, not more than one member of a family is required to serve in Vietnam at the same time, regardless of casualties in the family. Neither of these rules applies automatically, however. A person covered should make his status known to every available authority: draft board, induction center, company clerk, top sergeant, company commander.

Q *Please settle an argument. I think the first Mrs. Sinatra—Nancy— married after her divorce from Frank. I know it didn't last long. My friend claims it isn't so. Who's right?—A.M., Hollis, N.Y.*

Nancy Sinatra

A Your friend.

Q *On December 8, 1941, Congress declared war on Japan without debate and with only a single dissenting vote. Who cast this vote?—William L. Wilson, Lemon Grove, Calif.*

A Jeannette Rankin, then a Republican representative from Montana.

Q *Rep. L. Mendel Rivers, the House Armed Services Chairman—is he a member of the John Birch Society?—G.H., Newark, N.J.*

A Rivers (D., S.C.) has defended the John Birch Society on the House floor, but he professes not to be a member.

Q *Does Jacqueline Kennedy receive payment for use of her photo on various magazine covers?—L.M. Norling, Vista, Calif.*

A No.

Q *F. Lee Bailey, the attorney who got Sam Shepard and Dr. Carl Coppolino acquitted—isn't he under investigation for unethical conduct by the Boston Bar Association?—J.P., Norwalk, Conn.*

F. Lee Bailey

A He is being investigated, but no formal action has been taken. Bailey notes that many successful criminal lawyers have been investigated.

Q *Please tell me why the Harlem Globetrotters aren't in the National Basketball Association. Is it because they aren't good enough to survive in the league?—J.V., Syracuse, N.Y.*

A The Globetrotters find vaudeville more profitable than basketball.

Q *Who said, "Tis better to have loved and lost, than never to have loved at all"?—B. Key, Fort Collins, Colo.*

A Alfred Lord Tennyson (1809-92), appointed England's poet laureate in 1850.

Q *What is the most valuable coin in the world, and how much is it worth?— Douglas Senseman, Warren, Ohio.*

A Probably the 1804 silver dollar, which was purchased by a rare-coin agent for $36,000 in 1963.

Q *Please print what the letter U stands for in the name U Thant.—M.I.H., El Cajon, Calif.*

A In Burmese, U before a name means "Mr." or "Uncle." When it follows a name, it signifies first-born. The U.N. Secretary General, like most Burmese, has only one name.

Q *Bess Myerson, TV personality—how old is she? How many times has she been married? Any children? What year was she Miss America?—D.S., Charleston, W. Va.*

A Miss Myerson (left) is 42, has a 19-year-old daughter, Barbara, recently

Bess Myerson

divorced her second husband, wealthy international lawyer Arnold Grant. She won her title in 1945.

Q *Where does the Queen of England keep her crown jewels?—Karen Swanston, Novato, Calif.*

A In the Tower of London.

Q *I read recently that Cardinal Spellman is "Military Vicar of the Armed Forces." How can the Pentagon give such a title to the representative of one denomination?—R.T.T., New York, N.Y.*

A The title is a religious one, given him by the Holy See, not by the U.S. government.

Kurt Russell

Q *Could you please give me some information on Kurt Russell?—Carole Newsom, El Paso, Tex.*

A Fast-rising movie-TV actor Kurt Russell is a 15-year-old sophomore at Thousand Oaks (Calif.) High School who would rather make the varsity baseball team (he's a second baseman) than get a big acting assignment. His contracts have always included a clause that his acting commitments would not interfere with baseball. His father, Bing, a deputy sheriff on *Bonanza*, was a promising minor league outfielder until a beaning ended his career at 22. Kurt is under contract to Walt Disney Studios for two pictures a year, gets $1,500 to $2,000 for a TV guest appearance.

Raquel Welch

Q *Does actress Raquel Welch owe her publicity buildup to Darryl Zanuck? Did she have a thing with Tony Franciosa in Spain? Is that why Tony's marriage broke up?*—R.T.T., San Diego, Calif.

A Darryl Zanuck saw possibilities in Raquel Welch and utilized her talents. Tony Franciosa acted in Spain with Miss Welch on a production, *Fathom*. Miss Welch owes her publicity buildup to her manager-husband, Pat Curtis, had nothing to do with the Franciosa marital breakup.

Q *Rumor here has it that* Life *magazine is preparing a major exposé of a Hollywood star to be entitled "King of the Paternity Suits." Can you check that one out?*—D. Baer, Los Angeles, Calif.

A No truth to the rumor. *Life,* however, is preparing a major story on Marlon Brando with which he is cooperating and probably will approve.

Q *Is General de Gaulle slowly losing his eyesight? Isn't he just about blind?*—Louise Lundy, Richmond, N.Y.

A De Gaulle sees poorly, frequently stumbles, sometimes falls, but is not going blind.

Q *Did Jack LaLanne, star of his own exercise show on TV, die a couple of years ago from too much exercise? How old was he?*—Jean Lemay, DeKalb, Ill.

A LaLanne, 54, is still on TV.

Q *Several weeks ago Lynda Bird Johnson was on the Stanford University campus interviewing students. About what?*—R.E.E., Palo Alto, Calif.

A She was preparing a magazine article on the generation gap, wanted to find out how students feel about their parents, etc.

Q *The Korean soldiers in Vietnam—are they all volunteers? How much do they get? Doesn't the U.S. pay them?*—. Charles Hall, Dallas, Tex.

A They are volunteers, receive $45 a month combat pay, which comes from U.S. funds.

Q *Does Hugh Downs of the* Today Show *wear a hairpiece?*—Penny Cohn, New York, N.Y.

A Yes, a small one in front.

Q *Now that Sandy Koufax has retired as a baseball pitcher, what does he plan to do—sell insurance?*—Dan Harkness, Urbana, Ill.

A Koufax has been signed by NBC as a sportscaster.

Q *What goes with the Warren Beatty-Vanessa Redgrave friendship?*—Lonnie Rice, Pacific Palisades, Calif.

A It's warming up.

Q *In the 20th century, who were the richest U.S. presidents?*—Sam Carlson, St. Paul, Minn.

A Herbert Hoover, John F. Kennedy, and Lyndon Johnson—thus far.

Q *How long has Ray Charles been blind?*—David Swasey, Hialeah, Fla.

A Charles started going blind at five, was totally blind by seven.

Q *I understand the Sheraton Corporation is quietly taking over two of the biggest hotels in Paris—the George V and the Plaza Athenée. Is that so?*—Georgette Yule, New Haven, Conn.

A Madame Francois Dupré, widow of the racehorse owner, was left the hotels by her husband, is quietly negotiating to sell them.

Q *Who has the most gold records?*—Raymond Ohea, Astoria, N.Y.

A Elvis Presley—31.

Q *I would like the military-service record of J. Edgar Hoover.*—C.D.D., Garland, Tex.

A No military service.

Q *Can you tell me if Ronald Reagan has demoralized the forces of free higher education in California since becoming governor?*—Mrs. R.T. Stevens, Chicago, Ill.

A Having spent 30 years learning his craft, Reagan is basically an actor. Actors are exhibitionists who like to dramatize problems and events. Instead of taking a long, hard, quiet study of education in California, that state's most valuable resource, Reagan opened up in panicsville with a melodramatic announcement of abolishing California's tuition-free educational system. The result is that his panic has communicated itself to some educators, and some demoralization has set in.

Q *Is Jack Paar returning to TV?*—A.L. Thomas, Bangor, Me.

A Paar will do a funny documentary on Hollywood early in May. NBC-TV will carry it.

SMP / Globe

Jack Paar

Q *Now that Danny Kaye is finished on TV, is he really returning to the New York stage?*—Fran Winters, Chicago, Ill.

A Not the New York stage. Kaye has agreed to appear at the Chichester Festival Theatre in England for six weeks at $75 per week. It will mark his first stage play in 20 years.

Q *Is there anyone who started out as an associate of Frank Sinatra 25 years ago who is still with him? I mean guys like Hank Sanicola, Bobby Burns and others who helped him up the ladder.*—D.E., Hoboken, N.J.

A They have all left.

Q *Is it true that Candy Bergen refused to have anything to do with the screen version of* Valley of the Dolls *because she hated the book?*—S.T., Salt Lake City, Utah.

A True.

WALTER SCOTT'S
PERSONALITY PARADE®

July 9, 1967

Q *Is it true that Sen. Thomas Dodd of Connecticut failed the Connecticut bar exam and is now permitted to practice law in that state only through special legislative dispensation?—L.V., Norwich, Conn.*

A Senator Dodd failed the Connecticut bar examination in 1933. He then went to South Dakota and passed the bar exam there. In 1945 he applied on motion as an out-of-state attorney in New London County, Connecticut, to practice law. The bar admitted him, but the admission was appealed to the Connecticut Supreme Court of Errors, and Dodd's admission by the local bar was overruled. Subsequently the judicial rules were changed, and Dodd was allowed to practice in Connecticut, where he is now a recognized member of the bar, serving as counsel on leave for the Hartford law firm of Pelgrift, Dodd, and Stoughton. Details of his case are available in 43 Atlantic 2nd, p. 224 (June 1945).

Q *I have asked several times if it is not true that the name of the young Aga Khan appears as the father on the secret birth certificate of a boy born this past February in Paris to the Aga's former girl friend, Anouchka von Meks. Why do you refuse to answer when the whole thing is being hushed all over Europe, and you promise to tell the facts?—Louise E.T., Hartford, Conn.*

A The child's birth certificate does not list the Aga Khan or any other man as father. Anouchka von Meks, 24, still a good friend of the Aga Khan, named her son Karel Ismail Ali von Meks. For further information see the not so secret birth extract.

Q *How come a state like Arkansas has produced three such respected and powerful men in Washington as Sen. William Fulbright, chairman of the Foreign Relations Committee; Sen. John McClellan, chairman of the Committee on Government Operations; and Rep. Wilbur Mills, chairman of the Ways and Means Committee?—Sally Rowe, Little Rock, Ark.*

A Arkansas voters consistently return these men to office. By virtue of their seniority they then take over the high-ranking committee chairmanships. Senator Fulbright was elected to the Senate in 1944, Senator McClellan in 1942, Representative Mills to the House of Representatives in 1938.

Q *When writer Mary McCarthy was married to Edmund Wilson, the New Yorker magazine critic, did he beat her regularly?—R.S.E., Stamford, Conn.*

A Not regularly. In her petition for separation Miss McCarthy claimed that on one occasion she slapped her husband when he refused to help her with the garbage, and mocked her. When she finished her chores, Wilson thereupon hauled off and let her have it.

Q *Some time ago I read that if Jackie Kennedy marries again, she will marry the architect from Oakland, California, John Warnecke. Are these two romantically involved or friends?—E.L., Bethesda, Md.*

Warnecke and Jackie

A They claim to be friends with a mutual interest in architecture.

Q *Why is Beatle John Lennon's Rolls-Royce called a "freak out"? How much does it cost? Is it equipped with a bed?—Nancy Lee Conway, Henderson, N.C.*

A John Lennon's $17,000 Rolls-Royce is called a "freak out" because Lennon had it painted yellow with a zodiac sign on the roof, wheels of orange, blue, red, and white, colorful flowers and scrolls on the sides. It is not equipped with a bed.

Q *I would like to ask a very simple question about the war in Vietnam. Are we winning it either militarily or politically?—Mrs. Carl Allen, Philadelphia, Pa.*

A At this point we have prevented the South Vietnamese from losing the war, but as yet we are not winning it for them either militarily or politically.

Q *Does Mia Farrow smoke cigars?—Hilda Knowles, Miami, Fla.*

A Just little ones.

Q *I would like to know the highest sum the Book-of-the-Month Club has ever paid for the rights to any book.—Janice Talcott, New York, N.Y.*

Mia Farrow

A The club paid $250,000 for William Manchester's *The Death of a President*, will pay a record $325,000 for the rights to Svetlana Stalina Alliluyeva's memoirs.

Q *Who gave this piece of advice to young people: "If you are not very clever, you should be conciliatory"?—Hardy Andrews, New York, N.Y.*

A British prime minister and novelist Benjamin Disraeli (1804-81).

Q *How old is Tito of Yugoslavia, and who will be his successor?—Bernadine Gershenson, Newark, N.J.*

A Marshal Tito is 75; his successor has not yet been chosen.

Q *I understand that there is a marriage bureau in London which provides white wives for colored African and Asian leaders. Isn't this how Kwame Nkrumah, former dictator of Ghana, got his white wife?—Therese Fontaine, Montreal, Quebec.*

A In 1958 Nkrumah of Ghana married Helen Ricz Fathia, an Egyptian Coptic girl he had seen only in photographs. But she was not registered with any London marriage bureau, nor is there any such bureau specializing in wives for the leaders of African governments.

Q *Is it true that Lorne Greene, Dan Blocker, and Mike Landon all plan to quit the* Bonanza *TV program? Is it true they want higher salaries?—Helen Davidson, Jersey City, N.J.*

A Each now receives $11,000 per week; each plans to leave after the 1969-70 season at which time they will have been on the show 12 years.

Q *Did President Franklin Roosevelt know on the basis of intercepted messages that Japan planned to bomb Pearl Harbor or merely that Japan planned to wage war against the U.S.?—V.L. Pritchard, New Haven, Conn.*

A According to William H. Franklin, director of the State Department's historical office, there is no evidence that President Roosevelt knew in advance of Japan's plan to bomb Pearl Harbor. What he did realize on December 6, 1941, however, after reading a long decoded, intercepted secret Japanese message, was that war with Japan was inevitable.

Q *Who finances Richard Nixon's trips all over the world?*—Henry Moore, Newark, N.J.

Richard Nixon

A Some are paid for by his law clients, some by himself, his latest by *Reader's Digest* for which he plans to write some articles.

Q *How old is singer Betty Hutton? Was she abandoned by her father? When she recently declared bankruptcy, how much did she list in assets and liabilities?*—P. Lund, Detroit, Mich.

A Betty Hutton, 46, recently filed for bankruptcy in the federal court in Los Angeles, listing $150,000 in liabilities, practically no assets. She filed for bankruptcy, she declared, because her creditors bugged her, sitting around nightclub tables every time she performed, waiting backstage to collect from her. Miss Hutton's father abandoned his family when she was a child growing up in Detroit.

Q *The new Negro justice of the U.S. Supreme Court, Thurgood Marshall—isn't he married to a white woman?*—Ann Goodson, Richmond, Va.

A Thurgood Marshall is married to the former Cecilia Suyat, a Hawaiian of Filipino descent. His first wife, Vivian Burey Marshall, died in 1955.

Q *Why did Nasser lie so brazenly to the world about U.S. and British intervention in the Arab-Israel war when British aircraft carriers were 1500 miles away from Egypt and the U.S. Sixth Fleet was 400 miles away?*—Dana Muench, Miami, Fla.

A Losers need alibis. Nasser hoped to entrap Soviet Russia into rushing troops and aircraft to his aid; he could not bear the humiliation of telling his people the truth.

Q *Richard L. Strout of the* Christian Science Monitor *writes a column in* The New Republic *entitled T.R.B. What do those initial stand for?*—H. Fuller, Salem, Mass.

A T.R.B. are the initials in reverse of the words Brooklyn Rapid Transit, the subway line on which Bruce Bliven of The New Republic used to ride into Manhattan many years ago when the column of comment was originated.

Q *Who is Lyndon Johnson's personal and private secretary?*—T. L. Taylor, Amarillo, Tex.

A Mrs. Juanita Duggan Roberts, who started out as one of his volunteer campaign workers in 1938.

Q *I am told that the U.S. Government Printing Office sells more printed matter than any other publisher in America. How many publications does it print per year? How much money does it gross? What are the bestsellers?*—Louise Shepard, Louisville, Ky.

A In the last fiscal year the Government Printing Office sold approximately 67 million copies of government publications, grossing $14,800,000. Traditional bestsellers are publications on infant care and the federal income tax.

Priscilla and Elvis Presley

Q *Did Elvis Presley pay his wife $1 million to marry him? Where did he first meet his wife? Now that he's married, will he lose his box-office appeal?*—Jeannie Anderson, Provo, Utah.

A Eight years ago when Presley was a draftee in Germany, he was invited to the Wiesbaden apartment of Capt. and Mrs. Joseph Beaulieu, like him from Memphis. There he met Priscilla Beaulieu, their 14-year-old daughter. Over the years, these two fell in love, were married in Las Vegas this past May. Presley did not give his wife $1 million. His marriage is expected to have no adverse effect on his popularity.

Q *Dean Rusk and President Johnson maintained from the beginning that what is involved in Vietnam is our national honor. Each has said that if we fail to honor that commitment, all our alliances will crumble, no nation will believe us. Why then did we evade our commitment to Israel in the Gulf of Aqaba crisis? Surely Israel, the only country which stands in the way of Soviet Russia's communizing the entire Middle East, is more important to us than Vietnam.*—J. E. Nettleton, Bangor, Me.

A The U.S. has 42 military commitments throughout the world. Having committed so much money and so many men to Vietnam, we are not in a strong position, without mobilization or calling up the reserves, to meet more than one substantial military commitment at a time. The truth is that the extent of our commitment in Vietnam was miscalculated by the late President Kennedy and the same advisers who later counseled President Johnson. The security and protection of the U.S. is the President's first obligation, and he honors the nation's commitments according to his best judgment.

Q *Please identify the following quotation: "In the field of observation, chance favors only the prepared minds."*—Una Ellis, Montgomery, Ala.

A French scientist Louis Pasteur (1822-95).

Q *In watching the UN debates on TV during the Middle East crisis, I was very much taken by the deportment of the Israel foreign minister Abba Eban. Can you tell us something about this man?*—Mrs. Roger Hewlett, Evanston, Ill.

Abba Eban

A Abba Eban, 52, was born in South Africa, raised in London, was a brilliant debater at Cambridge, later became a Cambridge don. Abba's father was Abraham Solomon, who died in South Africa when his children were very young. Mrs. Solomon took the family to London where she subsequently married Dr. Isaac Eban, a radiologist. At this time, Abba Eban called himself Aubrey Solomon Eban. When Israel became an independent state, he observed the Israeli custom of taking the Hebrew form of his given name, has since been known as Abba Eban. Eban enlisted in the British army in 1939, rose from private to major. He speaks English, Arabic, Hebrew, French, German and Persian, is married to the former Suzan Ambache, a student he met at the American University in Cairo. They have two children.

Q *I have been told that the Republicans will field Rockefeller and Reagan against Johnson and Humphrey in 1968. Does this make sense? What happens to Richard Nixon in this shuffle?*—H.R.T., San Diego, Calif.

Ronald Reagan

A Generally it is conceded that Richard Nixon will control at the outset the largest block of delegates to the Republican convention. He may, in return for a promise to be appointed Secretary of State in a Republican administration, release his support if after the first few ballots he feels he cannot win the presidential nomination. A Rockefeller-Reagan team would give Johnson and Humphrey a stiff fight, especially if there is no appreciable change in the Vietnam war situation.

Q *Is it true that the Beatles are on LSD and other drugs?*—Wanda Kulik, Brockton, Mass.

Paul McCartney

A Paul McCartney, 25, only bachelor Beatle, revealed in a recent interview that he had used the drug LSD four times. "I took it," he said, "just to see what it was like. I had read a lot of sensational stories about it, like calling it the 'heaven or hell' drug. But that's nonsense. I am not, never have been, and never will be a drug addict. Neither am I advocating that anyone else should try the drug."

Q *Please identify the author of the lines: "Laugh and the world laughs with you. Snore, and you sleep alone."*—Juanita Forman, Jackson, Miss.

A Mrs. Patrick Campbell, the actress who played Eliza in George Bernard Shaw's *Pygmalion*, wrote those lines in a letter to the playwright, complaining of the difficulties she encountered in finding a perfect lover.

Q *Several weeks ago the foreign press carried reports about Tony Curtis and Virna Lisi. Anything to them?*—Dana Landers, Newark, N.J.

A Filming together in Italy, Curtis and Miss Lisi got to know each other well.

Q *Does the average Egyptian or Arab know the truth about the recent Arab-Israeli war? If not, what does Nasser tell his people?*—Raoul Adams, Washington, D.C.

A Nasser refers to the Arab defeat as a "reverse," exhorts his people to prepare themselves for the "next round" and the annihilation of the Israelis. There is no admission of defeat, no willingness to sign a peace treaty, only a policy aimed at regaining through Russian diplomatic intervention and threats as much of the lost Arab territories as possible.

Q *Actor Warren Beatty has sailed through dozens of girls, including Natalie Wood, Leslie Caron, and others who hoped to marry him. I now understand his latest victim is Julie Christie. Is it true that Julie carries her own mattress around with her? Also what is the Beatty technique?*—E.T., Baltimore, Md.

A When she was a near penniless actress in England a few years ago, Miss Christie used to carry her own air mattress around with her. She would inflate it and sleep on the floors of various friends' apartments. Beatty's Don Juan technique is a study of concentration. Like all great lovers he has the ability of convincing the girl of the moment that for him she is the only woman in the world. It is a most effective technique on undereducated, nonintellectual film actresses.

Q *When the Jane Russell-Bob Waterfield divorce reaches the courts, won't Howard Hughes take the witness stand to testify that he has been paying Jane $1,000 a week for the past 20 years?*—E.L.S., Las Vegas, Nev.

Waterfield and Russell

A Hughes will never testify; process servers will never be able to serve him in person.

Q *What's happened to Hjalmar Schacht, Hitler's finance minister? Is he dead or alive?*—T.L. Crane, Rutland, Vt.

A Schacht, 90, is still alive, recently finished another book on finance, *The Magic of Money.*

Q *Rita Hayworth has a daughter by the late Aly Khan. What relation is Rita's daughter to the present Aga Khan?*—Jennifer Helmick, St. Paul, Minn.

A Rita Hayworth's daughter, Yasmin Khan, is a half sister to the present Aga Khan, who was Aly Khan's son.

Q *Jack Paar recently sold the TV station he owned in Maine for $5 million. Is it because he's soon going back into network TV?*—Charles Garner, Utica, N.Y.

Jack Paar

A Paar says his future plans include much traveling abroad, making it difficult for him to own a TV station. He claims he has no intention of returning to network TV in the near future, although all three networks would like to sign him.

Q *Many times I've heard the story that President Johnson does not approve of Lynda Bird's romance with actor George Hamilton and would much prefer that she marry someone else. Is this so?*—T.L. Lewis, Erie, Pa.

A The president is too wise to get involved in Lynda Bird's romances, and she is too prudent to do anything which would adversely affect her father's popular support.

Q *I understand that NBC plans to break up the Huntley-Brinkley team. Is this so?*—S.T., East Orange, N.J.

A There have been many rumors and some discussion, but such a breakup is not likely until after the 1968 presidential election.

Q *I would like to know what's happened to a sexy actress of yesteryear named Virginia Mayo.*—D. Hutton, Burbank, Calif.

A Virginia Mayo, film actress of the 1950's, still works in motion pictures, is currently appearing in a play in Las Vegas.

Q *Is the Ursula Andress-Jean Paul Belmondo affair still going strong?*—Elaine Trundel, Philadelphia, Pa.

A Still going.

WALTER SCOTT'S

PERSONALITY PARADE®

August 13, 1967

Q *There is an anecdote about the late Marilyn Monroe and the spelling of Mississippi that was told to me on a recent trip to Hollywood. I have forgotten it. Can you give it?—Mrs. H.T. Keller, Baltimore, Md.*

Marilyn Monroe

A Applying for a job, Marilyn was asked by an interviewer to spell Mississippi. "Do you want the river or the state?" she reportedly asked.

Q *Is Hayley Mills living with a 60-year-old British director? What's the story?—E.T.T., Los Angeles, Calif.*

A Hayley Mills, 21, fell in love with director-producer Roy Boulting, 54, while they were filming *The Family Way*, in which she plays a newlywed who tries desperately to have her impotent husband consummate their marriage. One of Hayley's costars in the film is her father, actor John Mills. During the course of the production it was obvious to John Mills that his daughter was falling in love with the director, who not only is old enough to be her father, but who has children Hayley's age. Boulting plans to marry Hayley Mills as soon as he can obtain a divorce from his third wife. As an actress under contract to the late Walt Disney for five films, Hayley Mills found these films gushy and restricting, resented Disney's ruling that she could not be seen drinking or smoking in public lest she spoil the image of her Disney had established. Had the true, sophisticated Hayley Mills been exposed to the public, her romance with Boulting might not come now as such a surprise.

Q *I am very much puzzled about the statistics given out by the U.S. in the Vietnam war. We say that the South Vietnamese have 600,000 troops. We have about 500,000 troops. Thus on our side we have a total of 1,100,000 troops. We say that the enemy, the Viet Cong and the North Vietnamese, has a total of 295,000 troops opposing us in Vietnam. We also say that in the last seven years we have killed 200,000 of the enemy, wounded or caused to defect another 200,000. Is any of this true? If so, how come 1,100,000 of our troops can't defeat 295,000 of their troops?—E.L. White, Detroit, Mich.*

A The 600,000 A.R.V.N. (Army of the Republic of Vietnam) troops are virtually worthless as combat or pacification troops. We pay their salaries, but they have no esprit de corps, in many cases no will to fight. The approximately 500,000 U.S. troops are spread thin on foreign terrain, are fighting against guerrillas who are supplied with the best intelligence by friendly natives and the most sophisticated weaponry by Soviet Russia. U.S. figures as to the number of enemy killed, wounded, or deserted are highly inaccurate.

Q *When Queen Elizabeth and Prince Philip visited Ottawa to celebrate Canada's centenary this summer, Philip got in a fight because someone spoke to his wife. Is it true that no one is allowed to speak to the queen unless she speaks first? What happened up there?—Louise Cheshire, Conway, N.J.*

A A press photographer wanted to photograph the queen from a favorable angle. He asked an official to convey the message to the queen. When the official did, Philip angrily ordered him to stop, pointed to the photographers, and said, "Peel off and get those bloody people away." The queen thereupon ordered him not to lose his cool. Generally the queen must not be spoken to unless she speaks first. This, of course, does not apply in cases of fire or other emergencies.

Q *Is Chuck Connors really getting $25,000 a week to appear on his new series, Cowboy in Africa?—Bee Lowry, Denver, Colo.*

A Connors will receive $20,000 a week, his production company an additional $5,000.

Chuck Connors

Q *What is the truth about Marlon Brando? Is he married to Tarita, that girl in Tahiti who is the mother of his son, or is he married to Movita, the Mexican actress?—V.T., San Diego, Calif.*

A Brando and Movita were married on June 4, 1960, in Xochimilco, Mexico. They have two children, Segio Brando, six, and Rebecca Brando, ten months. Movita is seeking a separate maintenance agreement from Brando, asking $8,000 a month for support of herself and her children. Brando's son, Simon, by Tarita, is the result of an extra-marital affair. He has another son by his first wife, an Irish girl who took an Indian name, Anna Kashfi.

Q *Can you tell me on what grounds Vanessa Redgrave obtained a divorce from her husband, Tony Richardson, and who got custody of the children?—Willa Thomas, Atlanta, Ga.*

A Actress Vanessa Redgrave charged that her husband committed adultery with actress Jeanne Moreau in 1965 when they were working in Ethiopia on a film, *The Sailor from Gibraltar*. Miss Redgrave asked the court's discretion over her own later adultery. She was granted custody of her two daughters, a two-year-old and a three-year-old, with reasonable visitation rights for the father.

Q *Chubby Checker, Harry Belafonte, Sammy Davis—why do these Negro entertainers marry white girls? Why do they not marry within their own race?—P.T., Philadelphia, Pa.*

A A matter of individual preference.

Q *Who was the youngest First Lady in the U.S. history?—Roberta Neufelt, Jersey City, N.J.*

A Frances Folsom, 22, ward of President Grover Cleveland, who married him in the White House in 1886.

Q *Who said the following: "Whenever I hear anyone arguing for slavery, I feel a strong impulse to see it tried on him personally"?—Frances Miller, Montgomery, Ala.*

A Abraham Lincoln.

Q *I've read that Mamie Eisenhower and Lady Bird Johnson are deathly afraid of airplanes. Is that true? Is it also true that on commercial airlines Lady Bird will never travel first class?—Eleanor Patterson, San Antonio, Tex.*

A Mrs. Johnson and Mrs. Eisenhower are not enthusiastic airline passengers. Mrs. Johnson considers first-class airline passage an extravagance, generally travels coach when she is not flying with her husband on the presidential jet.

WALTER SCOTT'S
PERSONALITY PARADE®

October 22, 1967

Q *Why did Elizabeth Taylor renounce her U.S. citizenship last year?—Penny Parker, Los Angeles, Calif.*

Elizabeth Taylor

A As a British citizen residing in Switzerland, she will save millions in taxes, may even help husband Richard Burton secure a knighthood.

Q *I understand that while Russia is supplying North Vietnam with missiles, it is also supplying the U.S. with titanium, which we must have for aircraft engines subjected to high temperatures. Is this so?—Leon Jackson, San Diego, Calif.*

A It is true. The Harvey Aluminum Corporation of Torrance, California, buys raw titanium sponge from Russia. It makes titanium bars and billets from this sponge. The bars are transported to the Thompson Ramo Woolridge factory in Cleveland. TRW fabricates the titanium into parts for Pratt & Whitney engines which go into the McDonnell F4 UH (Phantom) aircraft, on duty over Vietnam.

Harvey Aluminum buys the Russian raw titanium sponge for 95 cents a pound. This is considerably cheaper than American-manufactured titanium which costs about $1.40 per pound. At the same time the Russians are supplying titanium for American aircraft, they are supplying Ho Chi Minh with missiles to shoot down these same aircraft.

Q *Sen. Everett Dirksen—is it true that he is the only U.S. Senator who has a son-in-law serving with him in the Senate?—F. Lewis, Pekin, Ill.*

Howard H. Baker Jr.

A Yes. Sen. Howard H. Baker, Jr. (R., Tenn.) is married to Dirksen's only daughter.

Q *I know that Howard Hughes now spends all his time in Las Vegas. Is his wife with him?—Charles W. Davis, Reno, Nev.*

A Jean Peters Hughes spends most of the week in Los Angeles, where she owns a home in the Bel Air district, occasionally flies up to see her recluse husband.

Q *I would like to know who the better athlete is, Bobby Kennedy or his wife, Ethel?—Francis Kelly, Brockton, Mass.*

A Ethel.

Q *On the Joey Bishop TV show I heard Sen. George Murphy of California claim that the elections in South Vietnam were fair. Murphy showed as evidence a ballot which had photos of Thieu and Ky on page 9, instead of page 1. Doesn't Murphy know that nine is the favorite number of the Buddhists? Doesn't Murphy know it represents to most Vietnamese the nine heavens of Buddha and is their most favored number, which is why Thieu and Ky gave it to themselves?—David Morgan, San Francisco, Calif.*

A As an expert on Southeast Asia, Senator Murphy is an excellent song-and-dance man.

Q *Now that Lynda Bird Johnson is going to marry a Marine, isn't it true that President Johnson is sighing with relief? Isn't it true that he never really liked actor George Hamilton? Now that Hamilton is no longer going with Lynda Bird, will the Hollywood studios drop him?—D.L. Lee, W. Palm Beach, Fla.*

A President Johnson was gracious to Hamilton so long as he thought there was a chance Hamilton might pop the question to Lynda Bird. He did not want to interfere with her romance. He feels better about her future wedding to Capt. Chuck Robb of the Marines. Robb is more Johnson's type. Hamilton was dropped by MGM just before he started dating Lynda Bird. Their romance certainly enhanced his box-office value, and he was cast in several films which otherwise might not have gone to him. Chances are that Hamilton's show business career will now decline, that he will probably marry some heiress. He is partial to girls with money.

Q *Please identify the following quotation: "Children begin by loving their parents; as they grow older they judge them; sometimes they forgive them." I believe it is a quotation from either George Bernard Shaw or Charles Lamb.—Viola Smart, Chicago, Ill.*

A The quotation is from Oscar Wilde, British wit and dramatist.

Q *Who is Edsel Ford?—Bryan McCarthy, Bridgeport, Conn.*

A He is the 18-year-old son of Henry Ford of the Ford Motor Company, attends the Gunnery School, Washington, Conn.

Q *I had planned to take my children to the famous Moscow Circus when it visited this country. Now I hear the appearance has been canceled because of the Vietnam War. Is this true?—P.K., Westport, Conn.*

A No. During the Middle East crisis, the Soviet Union cut off almost all scheduled cultural exchanges with the U.S., including the exchange of the Moscow Circus and the Great American Circus. Now some of the exchanges have been restored, and the Moscow Circus is scheduled to visit 13 American cities beginning this month.

Q *My wife caught the sneak preview of the movie Dr. Dolittle, in Minneapolis, and she says it is slow. Did this movie really cost 20th Century-Fox $27 million?—D.T.L., St. Paul, Minn.*

A The film cost approximately $17 million, but with sales and promotion costs added, the company needs $27 million to break even. The *Dr. Dolittle* sneaked in Minneapolis, admittedly too long, has now been edited into a shorter, faster-moving version.

Q *Did the Beatles really go to India to mourn the death of their manager, Brian Epstein? Are they now retiring? If not what are they doing?—Charlee Deane, Henderson, N.C.*

A The Beatles canceled their mourning trip to India, instead finished a TV spectacular which they have now offered for sale in the U.S.

The Beatles

WALTER SCOTT'S
PERSONALITY PARADE®

November 12, 1967

Q *Why is it that Sidney Poitier, the Negro actor, insists upon playing the hero in all his films? I, for one, am finding him tiresome.—Lily Ann Clark, Raleigh, N.C.*

Sidney Poitier

A Says Poitier: "I'm the only Negro actor who works with any degree of regularity. I represent 20 million people in this country, and millions more in Africa. I'm the only one for these people to identify with on the screen, and I'm not going to do anything they can't be proud of. Wait till there are six of us; then one of us can play villains all the time."

Q *Was John Maynard Keynes, the economist who thought up deficit financing—was he a homosexual?—George T. Franciscus, Cambridge, Mass.*

A Keynes was a homosexual, one of the many who attended Cambridge University in the early 1900's. Others in his group were writer Lytton Strachey, artist Duncan Grant. A good account of these men and their homosexuality is available in *Lytton Strachey, The Unknown Years*, by Michael Holroyd (Holt, Rinehart, Winston).

Q *How come there are no billboards in Honolulu? Why can't other cities do the same thing and banish them?—Lane Eckelman, New Orleans, La.*

A Several years ago a group of civic-minded Honolulu residents bought up the last major outdoor advertising company on Oahu, convinced the local government to ban billboards in order to preserve the remnants of island beauty. Other city governments are not willing to do this, largely because in many cases the outdoor advertising companies provide free billboards to campaigning politicians.

Q *Are the Mamas and the Papas breaking up?—Sally Michaels, Sioux Falls, Iowa.*

A No, the rock 'n' roll group has been playing Europe recently.

Q *Who is the single largest shareholder of 20th Century-Fox stock, Darryl Zanuck or Spyros Skouras?—Peter Hodgedon, Boston, Mass.*

A Skouras recently sold out all his holdings, 104,000 shares at $54 per share, leaving Zanuck the largest shareholder with 100,000 shares.

Q *Will you please list those Hollywood stars who have renounced their American citizenship in favor of lighter taxes in Europe?—Ramona Garcia, San Diego, Calif.*

A Elizabeth Taylor, Yul Brynner, director John Huston.

Q *After Frank Sinatra was knocked out by Carl Cohen of the Sands in Las Vegas, there was a gag about the fight which made the rounds in Hollywood. Can you repeat it?—Faye Crowley, New York, N.Y.*

A One of the best was cracked by comedian Pat Buttram who said: "Sinatra should have had better sense than to pick a fight with a Jew in the desert."

Q *What is the relationship between the Broadway producer David Merrick and David Margolis of St. Louis?—T.L., St. Louis, Mo.*

A Merrick was Margolis before he became Merrick.

Q *Judy Garland's personal appearance tour—did it bomb? Is she washed up?—Lois Tucker, St. Louis, Mo.*

A The tour bombed in several cities. Critics agree that Judy has just about had it.

Q *Is Ronald Reagan a Catholic?—James M. Elder, Macon, Ga.*

A His father was Irish Catholic, his mother Scottish Presbyterian. He, like Lyndon Johnson, is a member of the Christian Church.

Q *Is it true that Eastern Airlines is buying up the Laurance Rockefeller hotels?—Les Kannon, Far Hills, N.J.*

A Eastern has purchased a 60 percent interest in the Mauna Kea Beach Hotel in Hawaii, and an 80 percent interest in the Dorado Beach, the Rockefeller hotel in Puerto Rico.

Q *What's happened to Loretta Young? Is her acting career over?—Ellen Welch, San Francisco, Calif.*

A Miss Young has become a fashion consultant for a chain of bridal salons but has not forsaken acting. If a good film part of TV series comes along, she is available.

Q *Is it true that the Catholic Church in Spain no longer prohibits birth control pills?—Luis Gomez, Miami, Fla.*

A True; the pill is now available in Spanish drugstores without prescription, and the Catholic Church in Spain believes it is now a matter of individual conscience whether any married woman chooses to use it.

Q *The Nielsen rating service which reports on the popularity of the different TV programs—how large a sampling do they use?—Ron Unger, Newark, N.J.*

A About 1,200 families.

Q *Who designs Elizabeth Taylor's clothes? I understand she is now size 16. Is this so?—Leah Altman, Larchmont, N.Y.*

A Elizabeth Taylor's clothes come from Tiziani of Rome, owned by Evan Richards, a Texan. Miss Taylor, who now refers to herself as a "nice, fat, middle-aged woman," ranges in size from 12 to 16. Of late, she's been 16, weighs in at 134.

Q *Some of my friends say Vincent Price is a fine actor, but is not an art critic. Am I correct or incorrect in defending Mr. Price's knowledge of art? Please comment.—Geo. W. O'Brien, St. Louis, Mo.*

A Price is a fair actor but one of the most knowledgeable art collectors and critics in the country. He was educated in the fine arts at Yale, studied abroad, is a member of many art councils.

Q *Is Walter Winchell writing his autobiography?—Irving Turkel, Jersey City, N.J.*

A Yes, *The Private Papers of Walter Winchell*, for which he's received a $75,000 advance from Doubleday & Co., will be published next year or in 1969.

Walter Winchell

WALTER SCOTT'S

PERSONALITY PARADE®

January 21, 1968

The Supremes

Q *The Supremes—have they broken up? I noticed a new girl singing with the group on TV. What's the story?—Karen Holbert, Clinton, Md.*

A The Supremes are now called "Diana Ross and the Supremes." Of the original trio, Diana Ross and Mary Wilson remain. The third member, Florence Ballard, has been replaced by Cindy Birdsong. Motown Records claims Miss Ballard left because she was tired of traveling. Others claim she did not like the new billing.

Q *Lynda Bird Johnson's wedding was done in excellent taste. It was joyful yet dignified. Who was responsible for running the show that well?—Nanette Hopkins, Raleigh, N.C.*

A Mrs. Lyndon B. Johnson; the bride; Mrs. Elizabeth Carpenter, the First Lady's press secretary; Mrs. Bess Abell, the White House social secretary; and, of course, all their many assistants.

Q *Can you tell me if Jean Francois Steiner, the Jewish author of the bestselling book,* Treblinka, *about concentration camps, recently married a Nazi?—Henry Kitzakowski, Milwaukee, Wis.*

A Steiner, whose father died at Auschwitz, was secretly married several months ago to Grit von Brauchitsch, granddaughter of Field Marshal von Brauchitsch who commanded the Wehrmacht in Poland, France, and Russia from 1939 to 1941, but was later fired by Hitler. Steiner and his bride first met at the Sorbonne several years ago and fell in love. Miss von Brauchitsch was never a Nazi.

Q *I understand that Egypt is bankrupt and is being supported by King Faisal of Saudi Arabia. Is this so?—R.T. Malouf, New York City, N.Y.*

A Faisal in partnership with the government of Libya contributes about $70 million to Egypt every 90 days. In that way King Faisal keeps Nasser in line.

Q *When Bobby Kennedy was a schoolboy, didn't he flunk out of St. Paul's, a fashionable prep school in Concord, New Jersey?—Dean Hartrack, Rutland, Vt.*

A He did not. St. Paul's is an Episcopal school. Its daily chapel services are Protestant. As a youngster Kennedy thought seriously of becoming a priest. He wrote his mother about the Protestant services at St. Paul's and requested that he be sent to some other school. Mrs. Kennedy thereupon enrolled him in a Roman Catholic preparatory school, Portsmouth Priory in Rhode Island.

Q *Isn't Julie Andrews secretly wed to director Blake Edwards? Aren't they on their honeymoon?—Evie Underwood, Phoenix, Ariz.*

A Miss Andrews' California decree will not be final until November this year. She and Mr. Edwards have been traveling in Europe, will start a film next month.

Harris and Ewing / Globe

Robert Kennedy

Q *Gen. David Shoup, retired commandant of the U.S. Marine Corps, says that President Johnson's contention that the Vietnam war is vital to U.S. interests is "pure, unadulterated poppycock." Shoup says it is really a civil war among the Vietnamese. Would you give us some background on Shoup? Is he a crackpot or a respected member of the corps?—A.T. Davis, Indianapolis, Ind.*

Globe

David Shoup

A Gen. David Monroe Shoup, 63, was the 22d commandant of the U.S. Marine Corps, 1960-1963, and a respected member of the Joint Chiefs of Staff. He was born in Battle Ground, Indiana, educated at De Pauw University, commissioned a second lieutenant in the Marines in 1926.

In World War II he was awarded the Congressional Medal of Honor for leading the Marines in the attack on Tarawa. In 1959 he stood tenth on the list of Marine officers, but President Eisenhower thought so highly of Shoup that he advanced him over nine senior Marine officers, including three lieutenant generals, to the position of Marine commandant.

Q *Who said: "Our foreign dealings are an open book—generally a checkbook"?— Olive Williamson, Seattle, Wash.*

A Will Rogers (1879-1935), American humorist.

Q *I have a bet about Nancy Sinatra, Frank's daughter. I say she has had a nose job and a hair job. My husband says I am a jealous cat, and it's not so. Who is right?—Louise Altman, Miami Beach, Fla.*

Globe

Nancy Sinatra

A You are right about the nose and hair jobs.

Q *What percentage of student scientists in Russia are girls?—Rowland Crawford, Cambridge, Mass.*

A Approximately 40 percent.

Q *I would like to find out what Col. John Eisenhower, son of the ex-president, does for a living now that he's no longer in the Army. Also, will he inherit Gen. Eisenhower's millions?—Patricia Altonberry, Merion, Pa.*

A Col. John Eisenhower works as an editor for a publishing company. As the ex-president's only child, he will inherit eventually his parents' considerable wealth.

Q *George Meany of the AFL-CIO—doesn't Lyndon Johnson have labor leader Meany in his hip pocket?—Bernard Wolfson, Newark, N.J.*

A Meany believes firmly in going all the way with L.B.J.

Q *Ringo Starr, the Beatle drummer—I understand his wife is furious because Ringo is making out with Miss Sweden in Italy. What's the scoop?—Ellen James, Des Moines, Iowa.*

A Ringo is acting in the film, *Candy*. In several scenes he plays opposite Ewa Aulin, 18-year-old Swedish actress. He plays the part of a sex-driven Mexican gardener who has an affair with Candy. Ringo's wife understands it is all make-believe.

WALTER SCOTT'S
PERSONALITY PARADE ®

February 11, 1968

Q What is the basic difference between President Johnson and his predecessor, President Kennedy? Certainly Johnson has been a more effective president, certainly a greater achiever.— Frank Donovan, Durham, N.C.

John F. Kennedy

A Johnson's achievements in the field of domestic legislation—civil rights, Social Security, poverty programs, etc.— surpass Kennedy's by far. Possibly the major difference between the two men is that Kennedy inspired a large share of the nation's youth while Johnson has alienated it.

Q Didn't Tony Curtis give wife Christine Kaufmann her freedom so that she might marry Dino Martin, 17-year-old son of Dean Martin? Isn't that the real reason the Curtises agreed to disagree?—L. Davis, Los Angeles, Calif.

A Freedom or not, it is highly improbable that Mrs. Curtis will marry a 17-year-old boy, however musical, long-haired, and attractive he may be. Surely, his mother would object.

Q Did rocket specialist Wernher von Braun marry his cousin?—K.T., Huntsville, Ala.

A Yes. In 1947, von Braun was married to Maria Louise von Quistorp, his 18-year-old second cousin.

Q Can you tell me if Robert McNamara plans to rejoin the board of directors of the Scott Paper Company?—Louis Brophy, Wilmington, Del.

A If there is no conflict with his position as president of the World Bank.

Q I have a letter from a nephew fighting in Vietnam. He writes that one function of the South Vietnamese army, the ARVN, is to supply the American troops with commercial girls. Can this be so?— Mrs. T.M., San Marino, Calif.

A There is one ARVN regiment in South Vietnam known as "The Brothel Regiment." In the past it has set up a profitable field brothel for the use of neighboring American soldiers, who are charged outrageous prices. But this is a unique case involving only a handful of ARVN noncoms and one regimental staff officer.

Q Who is Queenie Epstein? She is the girl to whom Brian Epstein, the Beatles' manager, left his entire estate. I mean is she his wife, sister, or what?— Henrietta Marks, Jersey City, N.J.

A His mother, to whom he left an estate valued at $1,167,000—$638,400 after taxes.

Q What is the "big sleep" treatment for drug addicts?—Mavis R., Bloomington, Ind.

A It is a treatment used at All Saints' Hospital in Birmingham, England, and other places. The patient is put into a near-coma for days while the body accustoms itself to getting along without drugs.

Q Can Ann-Margret act? I went to Northwestern with her, and she could sing up a storm, but has she learned to act?— F.R.R., Lake Forest, Ill.

Ann-Margret

A Ann-Margret has always been kind to her mother.

Q Does Gov. Nelson Rockefeller have an even-money chance of becoming the Republican candidate for the presidency, or is it just a bunch of talk?— William O'Brian, Albany, N.Y.

A Richard Nixon is the Republican frontrunner at this writing. According to several polls, however, he is the one Republican President Johnson can be fairly sure of beating. These same polls on the other hand indicate that Rockefeller can give Johnson a tough fight. Therefore, if President Johnson's popularity rating continues to rise, the Republican delegates may decide that only Rockefeller can beat him. In short, the stronger President Johnson becomes, the stronger Governor Rockefeller's chances.

Q David Hemmings, the young British actor who starred in Blow-Up—I'd like to know if he and an actress from here, Gayle Hunnicut, were married.—L.T., Fort Worth, Tex.

A Several months ago they announced they had been married in Sorrento, Italy. Says Hemmings, who has two children from his first marriage to English actress Genista Lewis: "Gayle and I were in Sorrento together. The atmosphere was so romantic that we went into a little church and between ourselves exchanged marriage vows. There was no priest or anything like that. Later we decided to have a legal ceremony in London and another in Texas, but we just couldn't go through with it." Says Gayle: "We simply realized that a real marriage between us wouldn't work out. The ceremony we had was emotional and impetuous, and we realized later it wasn't valid."

Q Does anyone know how many members of the Ku Klux Klan there are in the U.S.? Isn't it a fact that the Klan has a larger membership than the U.S. Communist Party?—H.L., Mobile, Ala.

A According to the House Un-American Activities Committee, there are approximately 17,000 KKK members, 10,000 Communist party members.

Q The gossip columns have been having a field day with items about Barbra Streisand and Omar Sharif. Did these two fall in love while filming?—E.R., Rochester, N.Y.

A Streisand and Sharif became fast friends during the filming of Funny Girl, worked closely together, but Miss Streisand is happily married to actor Elliot Gould.

Q Dr. Christiaan Barnard and Dr. Norman Shumway, the heart transplanters—aren't they both products of the great University of Minnesota Medical School?—Ky Westin, Duluth, Minn.

A They both did graduate work in surgery there under the tutelage of the great Dr. Owen Wangensteen, but Barnard obtained his M.D. degree in South Africa at the University of Capetown and Shumway his M.D. at Vanderbilt.

Christiaan Barnard

WALTER SCOTT'S
PERSONALITY PARADE®

March 10, 1968

Q *Who is the richest woman in television and how much is she worth?—Efisio Gentile, Oak Park, Ill.*

Lucille Ball

A Probably Lucille Ball who has earned an estimated $30 million from TV and thanks to capital gains has kept a large part of it.

Q *What choice does an average voter like myself have between Lyndon Johnson and Richard Nixon regarding the war in Vietnam? Aren't they both Hawks?—M. Fox, Los Angeles, Calif.*

A President Johnson has expanded our commitment in Vietnam and nearby countries from approximately 20,000 to 600,000 U.S. servicemen, including 40,000 U.S. troops in Thailand. Richard Nixon is a traditional Hawk. As far back as 1954 he said at a meeting of the American Society of Newspaper Editors: "If in order to avoid further Communist expansion in Asia and particularly in Indochina, if in order to avoid it we must take the risk now by putting American boys in . . . I personally would support such a decision." It is possible, of course, that Nixon will alter his position on Vietnam in the future, but as of this writing his candidacy would offer the average voter no primary alternative in the Vietnamese war.

Q *If the U.S. ever went to war against North Korea, would the Russians come in on the side of North Korea?—William Gage, New Canaan, Conn.*

A Soviet Russia is pledged to defend North Koreans should the North Koreans ask for aid.

Q *Has Hollywood signed Corin Redgrave, brother of the Redgrave sisters?— Marianne Hodges, Orlando, Fla.*

A Corin Redgrave, 27, brother of actresses Vanessa and Lynn, recently signed a five-year contract to make five films for film director Fred Zinnemann, director of *High Noon, From Here to Eternity, A Man for All Seasons.*

Q *A divorce judge once told me, "The faults of husbands are often caused by the excess virtues of their wives." Was this original or is it a famous quote?—Angelo di Salle, Clifton, N.J.*

A The quote is from Sidonie Gabrielle Colette, the prolific French novelist who died in 1954.

Q *Gov. George Romney of Michigan—is he a child of a polygamous marriage? Didn't his parents believe in polygamy?—E.T., Lansing, Mich.*

A Miles Park Romney, the governor's grandfather, came to the Territory of Utah as a child of 7 in 1850. He came from England and, like a good Mormon at the time, adopted the practice of polygamy and took four wives. In 1883 when the U.S. Supreme Court banned polygamy, Miles Romney and his wives fled to a Mormon colony in Mexico.

In 1887 his 18-year-old son, Gaskell, came from Utah to join the family in Mexico. In 1895 Gaskell Romney married a Mormon girl in Chihuahua. Their fourth child, George Romney, was born in Mexico in 1907. Five years later when civil war broke out in Mexico, the family fled to El Paso, Texas, thence to Utah. Governor Romney is not the child of a polygamous marriage.

Q *There is a funny anecdote about Robert McNamara trying to speak Vietnamese. Can you tell it?—Halford Blakesley, New York, N.Y.*

Robert McNamara

A Vietnamese is a language with six tonal levels. The same word spoken in different tones results in different meanings. McNamara is not a particularly good linguist. He speaks a smattering of French with a California accent, but he has tried to learn a few words of Vietnamese in deference to his Vietnamese audiences. One of his favorite gambits is to say to the Vietnamese, "Vietnam for 1,000 years." The audience always smiles and frequently laughs in response to this, because what McNamara actually is saying in the tone he uses is, "The duck wants to lie down."

Q *Why did President Johnson make the Joint Chiefs of Staff sign a memorandum saying that they okayed the defense of Khe Sanh in Vietnam? Doesn't he trust them?—Morley Pritchard, Asheville, N.C.*

A Not completely. He knows full well what the Joint Chiefs did to the late President Kennedy in recommending the Bay of Pigs fiasco in Cuba. He knows full well what the Joint Chiefs did to him in recommending the expansion of the war in Vietnam. He does not want history to hold him exclusively responsible for any sizable defeat in Vietnam.

Q *Is it true that J. Edgar Hoover runs the Justice Department, and that the Justice Department does not run him?—M.L., Sacramento, Calif.*

J. Edgar Hoover

A For years Hoover has been a power unto himself in the Department of Justice. When Bobby Kennedy was Attorney General, attempts were made to keep Mr. Hoover in line. The result was a Hoover-Kennedy feud, particularly on the subject of wiretapping.

Q *A few weeks ago I saw Lee Radziwill, Jackie Kennedy's kid sister, in Palm Springs with Truman Capote. Before that she was in Cannes and Stockholm with Rudolf Nureyev. Doesn't she ever stay home with her husband, the prince?— R.T., Palm Desert, Calif.*

A The Radziwills have an understanding. He does not object to her man friends and she does not object to his.

Q *When I first saw Elke Sommer in European films, she was as flat-chested as a pancake. Now, she seems so well-rounded. Has she been taking silicone injections or has plastic surgery been performed on her chest apparatus?—Tina Stackpole, Columbia, Mo.*

A Silicone injections.

Q *My son in Vietnam was recently hospitalized with a case of wet-foot. He says most soldiers get this from slogging in the mud and water, but that the enemy doesn't. How come?—Mrs. Randall Phillips, Chicago, Ill.*

A The Viet Cong do not suffer from wet-foot because they wear sandals or go barefoot. U.S. servicemen are now equipped with a water-proofing agent which has markedly reduced the incidence of wet-foot injury, which consists of a whitening and wrinkling of skin across the metatarsal area.

Ethel Kennedy

Q *How old is Ethel Kennedy? Is she as young-looking as people say? Is it true that she wears size-6 clothes? Does her family have more money than Bobby's?— Ethel Maureen Davis, Chicago, Ill.*

A Ethel Kennedy is a youthful 40. She wears size-nine clothes. She is the sixth of the seven children of multimillionaire George Skakel who owned the Great Lakes Carbon Corporation. The Skakels and the Kennedys are two of the wealthiest families in the nation with fortunes estimated to exceed $200 million.

Q *Is Stokely Carmichael a Communist or a Communist agent?—Sam Tarloff, Los Angeles, Calif.*

A Carmichael toured Communist Cuba, Czechoslovakia, North Vietnam and other Communist capitals last summer. He may not be a registered member of the Communist Party, but he has consistently preached the bitter anti-Americanisms of the Communist line.

Q *Can you tell me how much money Mike Nichols earns when he directs a film?— Anne Lucas, Asheville, N.C.*

Mike Nichols

A Nichols was paid $150,000 plus almost 17 percent of the profits for directing *The Graduate*. He was paid $400,000 for directing *Who's Afraid of Virginia Woolf*? He will be paid $1 million and 10 percent of the prof-

its for his third film.

Q *Since* Time *magazine owns an $18-million piece of MGM, can we believe any future reviews in* Time *and* Life *of MGM motion pictures?—Helen Gomberg, Philadelphia, Pa.*

A So long as the reader knows that Time, Inc. has a large interest in MGM productions, he can judge the reviews accordingly.

Q *Actress Joanna Pettet says she is expecting a baby in September and that actor Alex Cord is the father. My question is, are they married?—Barbara Hammer, Carlsbad, N.M.*

A Not at this writing, but of her friendship with Cord, actress Pettet says, "I don't want to hurt what we have now by getting married in a way we don't want to." Miss Pettet, currently filming *The Best House in London* opposite David Hemmings in London, plans to marry Cord prior to September.

Q *Why didn't President and Mrs. Johnson attend the funeral of the Reverend Martin Luther King, Jr.?— Margaret Orloff, Jersey City, N.J.*

Martin Luther King, Jr.

A The Secret Service advised the president that his attendance at the funeral would make for a security nightmare. He agreed.

Q *Who is a man named Henry Loeb? Why is he so passionately disliked by the Negro people?—E.T.L., Mobile, Ala.*

A Henry Loeb, 47, is the present mayor of Memphis, Tennessee. He declined to grant sanitation workers in his city union recognition and a dues checkoff until after the assassination of Martin Luther King, Jr. Loeb is a member of a wealthy Memphis family who sent him to preparatory school at Phillips Exeter and to college at Brown University where he captained the tennis team. He is known as a stubborn, hard-line resister to liberal civil rights legislation.

Q *My son was flown to Vietnam in a crowded troop transport. President Johnson's son-in-law was flown to Vietnam in Ambassador Bunker's private jet*

equipped with berths. Why did President Johnson permit such obvious favoritism?—R.G., Dallas, Tex.

A He exercised a prerogative of office and in the process possibly diminished his standing with the public.

Q *Is it true that the CIA was responsible for the death of the Cuban Che Guevara? Also I understand that the U.S. secreted his body into this country. Is that true?—Thomas Antos, Lackawanna, N.Y.*

A CIA agents were definitely in the area of Bolivia where Guevara was captured, probably questioned him before his death. But they opposed his execution, which was carried out by a Bolivian army sergeant under orders from the Bolivian High Command. Guevara was buried in a shallow grave not far from the place where he died.

Q *Bobby Darin the singer who was married to Sandra Dee—will he marry Barbara Howar, the Raleigh, North Carolina, chick who used to do Lynda Bird's hair?—T.R. Evans, Durham, N.C.*

A Darin and Howar have been dating.

Q *How much did ABC-TV pay for the television rights to the Oscar show?— Margaret Jean Ullman, Buffalo, N.Y.*

A Approximately $750,000.

Q *Faye Dunaway—how much did she get for* Bonnie and Clyde? *Is it true that she was once married to the late comedian, Lenny Bruce?— Edwina Lester, New York, N.Y.*

Faye Dunaway

A Miss Dunaway received $30,000 for her Bonnie role. Of her relationship with Bruce, she recently told a British reporter, "I think one of the most wonderful periods in my life was when I lived with Lenny Bruce. Why did he have to die to be appreciated? I call this the great American tragedy." Miss Dunaway is currently engaged to photographer Jerry Schatzberg.

Robert Kennedy

Q *I would like to know who paid for the Robert Kennedy funeral train from New York City to Washington, D.C. Is it not true that on specific orders from President Johnson, the entire bill was taken care of by the federal government to the tune of $30,000?—Alice Lake Carruthers, Sea Island, Ga.*

A Not true. The special funeral train cost approximately $15,000, was paid for by the Kennedy family.

Q *When actress Faye Dunaway was living with the late comic Lenny Bruce, was he not on the heavy stuff?—C.T., New York, N.Y.*

A For years prior to his death comedian Bruce was a narcotics addict, tried pretty nearly everything.

Q *The chaplain of Yale University, William Sloane Coffin—how do the Yale students and faculty feel about him? Are they for or against him in the federal indictment charging him and Dr. Spock with conspiracy to help young men avoid the draft?— William Gilhooley, Stamford, Conn.*

William Sloane Coffin

A At the Yale commencement exercises last month, a religious ceremony was interrupted when Coffin approached the podium to lead the congregation in prayer.

The graduating class of '68, their parents, and the Yale deans gave Coffin a thunderous, spontaneous, standing ovation. Said Coffin, "I thank you and I appreciate this, but you are letting your generosity exceed your judgment."

Q *Does the U.S. spend more on chemical and germ warfare than it does on cancer research?—Helen Roberts, Charlotte, N.C.*

A Yes. The government spends approximately $300 million on chemical and biological warfare, much less on cancer research.

Q *I am interested to know if Lyndon Johnson has interceded in the case of Bobby Baker to keep him out of jail. Baker is now serving time at The Carousel Motel, Ocean City, Maryland.—John C. Crumbaugh, Washington, D.C.*

Bobby Baker

A President Johnson has scrupulously avoided interfering in the Bobby Baker case. Baker owns The Carousel Motel which is why he spends time there.

Q *I read the other day that Julie Christie and Warren Beatty have been living in a Los Angeles penthouse. Isn't there something the studios can do about this?—Georgianna Scott, Gainesville, Fla.*

A Neither Miss Christie nor Mr. Beatty is under exclusive contract to any one studio. Hollywood studios no longer control the private lives of their players. Miss Christie has explained many times that she prefers living with a man to marrying him.

Q *Now that Lurleen Wallace has passed on, isn't George Wallace finding it tough to raise funds for his presidential campaign?—Red Peters, Laurel, Miss.*

A Many industrialists report privately that a contribution to Wallace's campaign never hurt when it came to selling their wares to the state of Alabama during the gubernatorial incumbency of the Wallaces. Since Mrs. Wallace's death, however, and the ascendancy of Albert Brewer to the governor's job, several of these industrialists are not quite so ready to support Wallace financially.

Q *Jim Brown, the former Cleveland Browns football star turned actor, was recently involved with a model in Los Angeles. The newspapers said he threw her off his balcony. Hasn't Brown been involved with lots of women on assault charges which have been hushed up because he's in films?—Ed Casey, Toledo, Ohio.*

A Brown, father of three, has been cleared of previous assault and paternity charges several of which have been well publicized.

Q *The late Sen. Robert Kennedy—did he volunteer to become U.S. Ambassador to Vietnam?—Frederick T. James, Elkton, Md.*

A Yes, in 1964, but President Johnson declined the offer.

Q *My son who has just returned from Vietnam tells me that most of the corruption there springs from the fact that the PX employs 5,000 Vietnamese women who steal us blind and sell everything to the black market. Is this the source of corruption in South Vietnam?—Mrs. Harold Chase, Madison, Wis.*

A The U.S. does employ 5,000 Vietnamese clerks in its PX system but these clerks are small fry. The major corruptions emanate from the South Vietnamese elite and military castes.

Ava Gardner and Frank Sinatra

Q *Is Ava Gardner still in love with Sinatra? Was he not the great love of her life?—Eloise Jenkins, Smithfield, N.C.*

A Gardner and Sinatra are still good friends. They were married at a time when Sinatra's career was at low tide. Otherwise it might have worked out.

Q *I know that the rightists and the John Birch Society wanted Chief Justice Earl Warren impeached, but from the viewpoint of the educated American moderate, what sort of chief justice was Warren?—Walter Rilla, San Antonio, Tex.*

Earl Warren

A Prof. Alpheus T. Mason, 43 years on the faculty of Princeton University, one of the nation's outstanding authorities on constitutional interpretation, believes history will probably record Earl Warren as one of the greatest chief justices of the Supreme Court, second only to Chief Justice Marshall.

In the three areas of race relations, reapportionment, and rules concerning criminal procedure, the Warren Court helped improve the lot of the ordinary man.

Professor Mason, who has penned biographies of Justices Brandeis, Stone, and Taft and is now working on Warren's, says: "I think Warren meets Woodrow Wilson's test of statesmanship—visions of things to come—insight into the central purposes of our society, capacity, and determination to make judicial power a chief instrument for their realization."

Q *I understand that Ava Gardner is washed up in Hollywood films because she has lost her sex appeal and is just too old. How old is she?—Mrs. William Scofield, Raleigh, N.C.*

A Ava Gardner was born in Smithfield, North Carolina, on December 24, 1921.

Q *Who said, "I don't know who my grandfather was. I am much more concerned to know what his grandson will be"?—Oliver Urquardt, Lexington, N.C.*

A Abraham Lincoln.

Q *What is the "terrible tragedy" in the life of Texas Governor John Connally who has been mentioned as a possible running mate for Hubert Humphrey? Supposedly no one is allowed to mention this in Texas.—J.E.E., Tulsa, Okla.*

A In 1959 at age 16, John Connally's daughter, Kathleen, eloped. Several months later when her husband returned home one night, he says she had a shotgun in her hands and was threatening to take her life. He fought with her for the gun, but it went off, killing her.

Elizabeth Taylor

Q The New York Times, The Washington Post, The Los Angeles Times *all carried advertisements endorsed by show business personalities, advocating more strict gun laws. My question is—who paid for these expensive ads?—Frances MacDonald, Hartford, Conn.*

A They were paid for by Elizabeth Taylor, a film star and former U.S. citizen but now a citizen of Great Britain.

Q *I am a student of political science, and I have read that in the Kennedy-Nixon presidential race of 1960 Nixon would have won had there been an honest count in two states—Illinois and Texas. Is this so?—George Davidson, Newark, N.J.*

Kennedy and Nixon

A In Illinois Kennedy won by less than 9,000 votes. In Texas out of 2,311,845 votes, he won by 46,233 votes. In both states Republicans claimed a dishonest count had cost their candidate the election.

In Texas a federal court in Houston rejected the formal Republican complaint.

Q *Is it true that when Douglas Dillon was Secretary of the Treasury our $10 bills did not print "In God We Trust" and that it was restored by Henry Fowler in series 1963?—H.A. Kastner, Southport, Me.*

A The expression, "In God We Trust," first appeared on U.S. coins in 1864, arising out of Civil War religious sentiment. In the succeeding century the phrase was reprinted on various coins as they were minted. It was not until 1955 that the 84th Congress passed Public Law 140, adapting the slogan to currency. Under this law the inscription did not appear on $10 bills until 1963 when the new series was issued.

Walt Disney, with friend Mickey Mouse

Q *Is it true that Mickey Mouse's real name was originally Mortimer Mouse? If so, who changed it?—Lena Ralston, Orlando, Fla.*

A The late Walt Disney called his character Mortimer Mouse, but Mrs. Disney and film distributors did not think Mortimer was commercial or catchy enough. The character was thereupon renamed Mickey Mouse.

PERSONALITY PARADE®

October 6, 1968

Brigitte Bardot

Q *Do real estate agents give free houses to celebrities in order to popularize their holdings? I believe that Brigitte Bardot has been given free houses all over the world in order to promote sales. What's the story?—Charles Le Boutillier, Westport, Conn.*

A In Bardot's case she has been given homes at St. Tropez, Deauville, Almería, and Cabo Frio, near Rio de Janeiro, at favorable rates. But, if she does not pay her taxes on the house at Cabo Frio, the city fathers there plan to take back the house and private beach they gave her three years ago.

Q *Is it true that President Johnson has done more for the blacks of this nation than any other U.S. president?—Elaine Merrill, Raleigh, N.C.*

A He has opened many doors for blacks. He placed the first black man in the history of this nation on the U.S. Supreme Court, the first black man in a presidential Cabinet, the first black man on the Federal Reserve Board, the first black lady to be a high official in the U.S. State Department. His record on civil rights during his administration has been superb.

Q *Lloyd's of London, the great insurance syndicate—does it have any Americans, or are Americans banned?—Nedrick Loomis, Cambridge, Mass.*

A For the first time in its history, Lloyd's of London this year admitted two American underwriters, Bernard Daenzer of New York and Philip Berman of Allentown, Pennsylvania.

Q *I have been told that it is a standard procedure in the U.S. military if a lower-ranking officer questions the orders of a superior officer to have the lower-ranking officer committed to an asylum for psychiatric examination. Can you verify or deny?—E.H. Ettinger, Chicago, Ill.*

A In some cases the lower-ranking officer is examined by a psychiatrist, but he is not committed to an asylum. For example, when a Naval officer doubted the official version of reported attacks on two U.S. destroyers in the Gulf of Tonkin—a version which is open to much doubt—the Navy ordered him to take a psychiatric examination, but he was not sent to an asylum.

Q *I see by the papers where Vanessa Redgrave is starring in the life story of Isadora Duncan, the dancer. Didn't Isadora have two famous illegitimate children? Who were their fathers?—O.L., Oakland, Calif.*

A The first child, Deirdre, born in 1905, was fathered by Gordon Craig, son of actress Ellen Terry. The second, Patrick, born in 1910, was fathered by Paris Singer of the sewing machine family. Both children were drowned in 1913 with their British governess when the family car rolled into the Seine while Isadora was at rehearsal.

Q *What is French ski champion Jean-Claude Killy doing now? Is it true he gave up skiing to become an actor or race-car driver?—Louis Baker, Long Island, N.Y.*

Jean-Claude Killy

A No. At present Killy is under contract ($300,000) to General Motors to publicize cars, not to race them (expressly forbidden). His acting is limited to television commercials for his sponsor. By all accounts he is bored.

Q *I thought that Sargent Shriver was Hubert Humphrey's first choice as a running mate. How come he chose Senator Muskie? Also what is Muskie's real name?—Bennett Groves, St. Louis, Mo.*

A Humphrey's first choice as a running mate was Sen. Ted Kennedy, who turned down the offer. Humphrey then sounded Ted out on what he thought of his brother-in-law Sargent Shriver as a possible vice presidential candidate. After listening to Ted, Humphrey decided to offer the job to Senator Muskie of Maine. Muskie is the son

of Stephen Marcizewski, a Catholic tailor who emigrated from Poland, later Americanized his name.

Q *Braniff Airlines began paying passengers a dollar every time one of their flights was late. The scheme started in April and lasted three months. How much did it cost Braniff?—Fred Hirsch, Ft. Worth, Tex.*

A Approximately $123,000.

Q *Can you tell me why Jackie Kennedy took her son John-John out of a Catholic school in New York City and enrolled him in an interdenominational one?—V.T., Springfield, Mass.*

A It is traditional for the Kennedy male children to be enrolled in racially and religiously integrated schools. The Kennedy female children are generally sent to parochial schools.

Q *Something happened on a TV show in which Zsa Zsa Gabor was finally silenced. I believe it happened on the Johnny Carson or Joey Bishop show and involved a comedian named Irwin Corey. Can you tell what happened?—Patricia Benn, Jersey, City, N.J.*

Zsa Zsa Gabor

A Zsa Zsa, who loves to talk endlessly about herself, appeared on a recent Joey Bishop program. She began to talk about a new diamond some man had given her. Her soliloquy seemed endless. Suddenly, comedian Irwin Corey interrupted. "How did you get that diamond," he demanded, "on the lay-away plan?" For a fast 30 seconds, Zsa Zsa was stunned into silence.

Q *What politician first made the statement, "A chicken in every pot and two cars in every garage"?—C.B., Jamestown, N.D.*

A Henry IV of France (1533-1610) said, "I want there to be no peasant in my realm so poor that he will not have a chicken in his pot every Sunday." More recently, Adolf Hitler promised a car in every garage, collected installment payments for his Volkswagen or "People's Car" in advance, and turned the factory over to armaments production.

Q *There is a rumor in Hollywood that Raquel Welch plans to leave her husband and discoverer, Pat Curtis, for black actor and former football pro Jim Brown. I understand that Curtis and Brown got in a big fight in Granada, Spain, and that Curtis was arrested. Is any of this true?— R.T., San Diego, Calif.*

Welch and Brown

A Conceivably Miss Welch may drop her husband, Pat Curtis, one day and take a third, but it will not be actor Jim Brown. There was no fight between Brown and Curtis in Granada. There was a fight between Curtis and a Spanish actor who was ardently courting Miss Welch. Curtis was reportedly arrested while his wife and Brown were filming *100 Rifles*, but 20th Century-Fox has tried to quash the entire affair.

Q *Has Lady Bird Johnson been offered a job as a television commentator to appear on TV soon?—Theresa Klinc, Newark, N.J.*

A Mrs. Johnson has not signed with any network as a telecaster. She will appear on ABC-TV in December to describe her life in the White House and her duties as the president's wife. The show has already been taped.

Q *Has Dr. Benjamin Spock retired as an author after selling more than 20 million copies of his Child Care?—Mrs. Laura Keys Carruthers, Shaker Heights, Ohio.*

A Dr. Spock, 65, is working on two books at this time: *The Meaning of Life* and *Love for Teenagers*, and an untitled work on faith, mankind, and major American problems.

Q *When Fulgencia Batista left Cuba, how much did he take with him in loot? What does he do nowadays? Also, what is the Kennedy-Khrushchev treaty?—Murray Wheeler, Indianapolis, Ind.*

A Batista, 67, who stole millions from Cuba, lives in exiled luxury in Estoril, Portugal. He also has a house he rents in Madrid from where he runs his investments.

The Kennedy-Khrushchev agreement— it is no treaty—rarely publicized in the U.S., called for the Soviets to remove their ballistic missiles from Cuba in 1962 in return for a U.S. promise not to invade Cuba.

Q *Is it on the level that President Johnson has received more threats against his life than any other U.S. president? Also isn't Johnson the first U.S. president not to run for re-election?—Marie De Lucca, Atlantic City, N.J.*

A President Johnson has been averaging about 7,000 actual and potential threats against his life each month, an all-time high. Johnson is one of two incumbent U.S. presidents since 1884 who did not submit himself for re-election. The other was Truman.

Q *What really happened in that French Riviera slugfest between Lana Turner and her producer?—E.T., Des Moines, Iowa.*

Lana Turner

A Miss Turner, starring in the TV series, *The Survivors*, became upset after many disputes and slapped producer William Frye. Promptly, Frye slapped her back. Miss Turner thereupon refused to work so long as Frye was her producer. Frye is no longer producer, and Miss Turner is no longer the most popular member of the crew.

Q *Which self-employed group in the U.S. commands the highest annual income?— Dan Holstead, Warm Springs, Ga.*

A The medical doctor, with an estimated annual income ranging from $25,000 to $40,000.

Q *Who is the author of the timely comment, "The world is weary of statesmen whom democracy has degraded into politicians"?—Sarah E. Kalnin, New York, N.Y.*

A Benjamin Disraeli (1804-1881), British statesman and author who became Queen Victoria's prime minister in 1867.

Q *Which is the largest city in Latin America?—Ella Martinez, Chula Vista, Calif.*

A Mexico City with over 7 million people and a population increasing by 300,000 per year.

Q *Is it true that Florence Nightingale, the pure, moralistic British nurse, died of syphilis?—Leona Mirsch, Miami Beach, Fla.*

A Florence Nightingale reportedly acquired syphilis while treating the wounds of infected patients.

Q *I understand that Sen. Everett Dirksen, the Illinois spellbinder, has taken millions out of the Peoria law firm of Davis, Morgan & Witherell for bringing in major corporation accounts. What's the story?—Ed Bennett, Chicago, Ill.*

A Dirksen has been "of counsel" to David, Morgan & Witherell for the past 24 years. According to senior partner Arleigh Davis, "Our agreement with the senator prohibits him from taking part in any federal case. We pay him fairly nominal sums only in those cases to which he makes a contribution via consultation. We do not use the senator to appear in court or prepare briefs. He is more of a consultant than anything."

Q *Have the Black Panthers ever attacked Catherine Basie, wife of bandleader Count Basie?—Stephen Evans, Mobile, Ala.*

A Mrs. Basie recently testified that she had been threatened by extremist groups in Queens, New York, has resigned from the South Jamaica Community Council which she headed for 16 years.

Q *Does Barbra Streisand have any children, and who is the father?— Eleanor Fingerspan, Brooklyn N.Y.*

A Miss Streisand is married to actor Elliott Gould. They have a son, Jason Emanuel, born December 29, 1966.

Barbra Streisand

Q *Is it true that Burt Lancaster's wife has finally thrown him out because she learned about his girl in France?— L.E., Los Angeles, Calif.*

A The Lancasters have separated at this writing. Theirs has been a most stormy marriage for a variety of reasons.

Maria Callas

Q *Maria Callas and Aristotle Onassis—were they lovers or just good friends? Also what happens when Jackie Onassis meets Maria?—E.P., Scranton, Pa.*

A They were lovers. When Mrs. Onassis meets Miss Callas, each will probably say, "How do you do?"

Q *How many Mormons in the Nixon Cabinet, and isn't this a record?—O.V. Neilsen, Provo, Utah.*

A Secretary of the Treasury David Kennedy and Secretary of Housing George Romney are both practicing Mormons. This is the first time two members of the Church of Jesus Christ of Latter-day Saints have been appointed to any presidential cabinet.

Q *When will Detroit start selling the new small cars to compete with the foreign ones?—Victor Wolff, Wallingford, Conn.*

A Ford plans to sell its two-door "Maverick" starting some time in April for close to but under $2,000. American Motors will follow with a similar model later in the year, and General Motors will sell one in 1970.

Q *I would like to know how large the U.S. Navy's 7th Fleet is. It is now in the Pacific.—Peter Yount, Asheville, N.C.*

A The 7th Fleet consists of approximately 80,000 men, 190 ships, 750 aircraft.

Q *Is it true that in the presidential election of 1968 Richard Nixon lost all the major cities in the U.S.?—Deena Woolrad, Miami Beach, Fla.*

A Yes, Nixon lost the cities but won the election with 43 percent of the popular vote. Had George Wallace not been a third candidate, it is possible that Nixon would have won 53 percent or thereabouts.

Q *I've been told that when Jerry Lewis' son, Gary, got out of the Army, Jerry gave him a yacht, a house, and a private plane. Is this so?—Carla de la Pena, Los Angeles, Calif.*

A No, he gave Gary a $150,000 home for him and his family.

Q *Who said, "True friendship is a plant of slow growth"?—Mrs. Wilson W. Blanding, Quincy, Ill.*

A George Washington.

Q *How long has Lawrence Welk been on TV? How come he still talks with a German accent?—D.L.T., Mobile, Ala.*

A Welk is starting his 15th year on TV, was reared in a German-speaking community, Strasburg, North Dakota, by his German immigrant family, learned German long before he learned English.

Q *Is there a rule that no motion picture actress may be photographed nude in bed with an actor unless they are married?—Vera Dunphy, Eugene, Ore.*

A Years ago the motion picture producers' code forbade scenes of a couple in bed whether married or not, nude or not. Nowadays, however, nudity is par for the course.

Q *What is the truth? Do the Russians have as many intercontinental ballistic missiles as we have?—Bernard Fine, Newark, N.J.*

A Best estimate: we are ahead 1,054 to 900. The Soviets, however, will achieve parity with us later this year. They will then seek to halt the armament escalation, which is both senseless and expensive.

Q *Did Henry Ford ever run for the U.S. Senate? Is it true that he could not read?—Fern Hamline, Des Moines, Iowa.*

A Ford was a man of little formal education, only a few years in grade school. In 1918, however, at Woodrow Wilson's suggestion, he ran in Michigan against Republican Truman H. Newberry and lost by a few thousand votes.

The Nixon family

Q *Can you tell me if Richard Nixon wore pancake makeup at his daughter's wedding?—Eleanor Parkinson, San Diego, Calif.*

A The president always wears makeup when he knows he will be televised. While the wedding in this case was not telecast, Nixon was, entering and leaving the church.

Q *I have heard it said often that the two greatest lovers in the history of the U.S. Senate were George A. Smathers of Florida and John F. Kennedy of Massachusetts. Is this true?—P.W., Washington, D.C.*

A As young, single men, both cut a wide swath through the forests of femininity.

Q *Is Sidney Poitier, the Negro actor, the most popular movie star in the world?—Herbert Barris, New York, N.Y.*

A According to motion picture exhibitors, Poitier was the number-one box-office attraction of 1968.

Dotti and Hepburn

Q *Why would Audrey Hepburn, who is 39, marry an Italian psychiatrist ten years her junior?—Elaine Timmons, Lubbock, Tex.*

A Miss Hepburn's screen career is declining. Afraid of growing old, she needs constant reassurance, both physical and mental, that she is still desirable. At 29, psychiatrist Andrea Dotti is capable of providing such assurance.

Q *Is Jackie Kennedy Onassis with child?—Bertha Franklin, New Orleans, La.*

A Natives of Skorpios in Greece as well as much of the European press believe she is. As of this writing, neither Mr. nor Mrs. Onassis has confirmed or denied the happening.

Q *U.S. Supreme Court Justice Warren—was his father murdered?—Melanie Harris, El Camino, Calif.*

A Yes. In 1938, Mathias H. Warren, wealthy real estate dealer of Bakersfield, California, was bludgeoned to death in a home he occupied alone. The murder has never been solved.

Q *Can you tell me, please, how much Lyndon Johnson receives from the government now that he has retired?—Nicholas Ballantine, Denver, Colo.*

A Johnson was paid $375,000 to tide him over during the transition period, January to June, 1969. In addition, he receives $80,000 in retirement pay and expenses for life.

Q *There is a movie with Peter Sellers called, I Love You, Alice B. Toklas. Who the heck is Alice B. Toklas?—Frances Bienstock, Oakland, Calif.*

A Alice B. Toklas and Gertrude Stein, American expatriates in Paris, were reputedly lovers. Miss Stein, a writer and art connoisseur, befriended many young painters and writers, including Pablo Picasso, in the early years of this century. She died in 1946. Her good friend, Alice B. Toklas, died a pauper in 1967, was buried next to Miss Stein.

Q *Are the Beatles and the Monkees breaking up?—Johnnie Wheeler, Springfield, Ill.*

A The Monkees are breaking up. Peter Tork has quit the outfit. Mickey Dolenz and Davy Jones are being drafted. The Beatles are fighting among themselves, will probably stay together so long as the arrangement is financially rewarding. Their "Apple" holding corporation is in financial trouble.

Q *I have heard so much about a miraculous youth pill called KH3. It is on sale in England and in France but not in this country. Do you know anything about it?—Mrs. Ellis Marcus, Pittsburgh, Pa.*

A It consists largely of a procaine compound introduced in Rumania ten years ago. The Food and Drug Administration has not accredited the drug for sale in the U.S.

Q *All the Nixon women—Pat, Julie and Tricia—do they all wear size-eight clothes?—Leona Greenspan, Las Vegas, Nev.*

A Mrs. Nixon and daughter Julie wear size eight, Tricia Nixon, size four.

Ernest Hemingway

Q *Why did novelist Ernest Hemingway kill himself? Was it not because he fell in love with a nurse at the Mayo Clinic?—Jessica Wagner, Staten Island, N.Y.*

A Hemingway killed himself because he was out of his mind. No nurse was involved.

Q *Whatever happened to that little Filipino girl who was the sole survivor of the massacre in Chicago when Speck murdered eight nurses in a dormitory?—Ollie Atkinson, Springfield, Ill.*

A Corazon Amurao, 25, recently was married to her childhood sweetheart in San Luis, the Philippines.

Q *Have Maria Callas and her ex-lover Aristotle Onassis called it quits?—N.M., Silver Spring, Md.*

A Callas told Onassis in the apartment of Baroness Maggie van Zuyland, their mutual friend, that henceforth she was devoting her life to her career, no longer could afford to be seen in public with Onassis.

Duke Ellington

Q *Was Duke Ellington born in the U.S.A.? If so, how come his portrait is on stamps issued by the Republic of Togo?—Nellie Hutchins, Ft. Mill, S.C.*

A Ellington, 69, American-born Negro, appears with his musical instruments on a stamp of the Republic of Togo as a measure of honor and acclaim.

Q *I have been told that no one in South Vietnam wants the war to end, because they will then be out of a job. Is this so?—Ed Simmons, Seattle, Wash.*

A When the war ends, the South Vietnamese economy will have to be completely reconstructed. Those South Vietnamese, including army officers, who have prospered from the war, would like it to continue. But the men who are doing the fighting and the dying, most of them Americans, want it to stop.

WALTER SCOTT'S

PERSONALITY PARADE®

March 9, 1969

Q *How old are Bing Crosby and Bob Hope? Which one is richer? Are they really close friends or merely appear so for commercial purposes?—Donna Lane, Santa Monica, Calif.*

Bing Crosby and Bob Hope

A Each is 65. Crosby's wealth is estimated at $75 million. Hope is worth at least twice as much. They are old buddies who genuinely enjoy each other.

Q *I cannot believe that more than 25 Secret Service Agents are still paid to look after Lyndon Johnson. Why is this necessary?—Mrs. Patricia Lockhart, Fort Wayne, Ind.*

A The law passed by Congress requires the Secret Service to provide protection to former presidents and members of their families living with them. A minimum of three agents, each working an eight-hour shift, is generally necessary at each location. Since Lyndon Johnson, his wife, their daughters and grandchildren get around a good deal, at least 25 Secret Service agents are required to cover them.

Q *Is Tiny Tim a daffodil? How much did he earn last year?—Claire Todd, Cedar Rapids, Iowa.*

Tiny Tim

A Tiny claims to be a "normal, healthy, virginal young man." Last year he earned approximately $375,000.

Q *When an oil company pollutes a seaside with its oil, which is what happened off Santa Barbara, California, creating damage and havoc, who pays for the damage done?—William Fryer, Los Angeles, Calif.*

A Federal law does not require the responsible oil company to pay for cleanup or the damages.

Q *Can you tell me why Onassis didn't give Jackie Kennedy a wedding gift of diamonds instead of rubies? Surely he is rich enough to afford diamonds.— Paula Glenn, Portland, Ore.*

A The ruby is the birthstone of July, and Mrs. Jacqueline Bouvier Onassis—she no longer uses Kennedy in her name—was born on July 28.

Nancy and Ronald Reagan

Q *I've been told that Ronald Reagan's wife, Nancy, wore a $1,500 James Galanos see-through dress at the presidential inauguration. Weren't people shocked?— T.E., Bakersfield, Calif.*

A Nancy Reagan wore a $1,200 Galanos see-through dress at the inauguration but the see-through portion was covered with two squares of black lace. Mrs. Reagan is always sedate and well dressed at public functions.

Q *Can you tell me why Senator Gore of Tennessee was the only U.S. senator to oppose the confirmation of David Packard, the millionaire defense industrialist, as Deputy Secretary of Defense?— Tom French, Palo Alto, Calif.*

A Packard is a brilliant man of probity, sagaciousness and unblemished reputation, but he is also a former member of the board of General Dynamics, manufacturer of the TFX fighter-bomber plane. He is a leading member of the military-industrial complex with a particular philosophy of defense spending. Senator Gore felt that Packard might suffer from a conflict of attitude, that the conflict of interests law should apply equally to cabinet members of great as well as moderate wealth. It was not until Gore began objecting to Packard's appointment that Packard agreed to appoint an independent trustee to oversee his $300 million of Hewlett-Packard stock.

Q *Can you tell us something about Alfred Nobel, founder of the Nobel Awards? We understand he was one of the world's most fascinating men.—Mr. and Mrs. Lars Swensen, Provo, Utah.*

A Alfred Nobel, son of a Swedish architect-engineer, was born in Stockholm in 1833. He was reared and educated by private tutors in St. Petersburg, Russia, where his father was working on the explosive fluid, nitroglycerine.

Nitro had 100 times the power of traditional gunpowder but no one knew how to handle it. Working beside his father, young Alfred Nobel invented a detonator, patented the device, started the first factory for the mass production of dynamite.

He quickly became a multimillionaire but throughout his life remained a moody bachelor and recluse. He supported socialism, hated war, sneered at the human race. "I regard large inherited wealth," he wrote, "as a misfortune which merely serves to dull men's faculties."

In 1895 Nobel wrote his will which consisted of 302 words, ordering all his property to be invested in safe securities. Dividends from these stocks were to go in cash awards to men who achieved the most in the fields of peace, chemistry, physics, medicine, and literature. Nobel died in San Remo, Italy, on December 7, 1896. *The London Times* considered that he was worth a four-line obituary.

Duchess and Duke of Windsor

Q *Has the Duke of Windsor done any meaningful work in the last 20 years?— Bernard Hays, Mesa, Ariz.*

A The Duke of Windsor at 74 is an old man. He performed creditably as a prince and monarch, fulfilled his diplomatic duties in World War II, but for the past two decades seems to have led a dreary life, consisting in part of attending meaningless parties thrown by wealthy people.

WALTER SCOTT'S
PERSONALITY PARADE®

March 23, 1969

Lady Bird Johnson

Q *I understand that Lady Bird Johnson has sold her memoirs to McCall's magazine for $1 million because McCall's was the magazine which hired her daughter Lynda Bird. Is this so?—B.E., McLean, Va.*

A If Lady Bird Johnson sells her memoirs to anyone, she will sell to the highest bidder.

Q *Is Ingrid Bergman making a Hollywood come-back?—Valerie Crutchfield, Tucson, Ariz.*

A She is making a film in Hollywood for the first time since 1949. The film is *Cactus Flower*, in which she co-stars with Walter Matthau.

Q *How come the White House in Washington, D.C., is now referred to by politicians as J. Walter Thompson East?—E. Feeney, San Francisco, Calif.*

A Three of President Nixon's top White House aides formerly worked in the Los Angeles branch of the J. Walter Thompson advertising agency. They are H. R. Haldeman, the president's staff and scheduling chief; Dwight Chapin, the president's appointments secretary and Ronald Ziegler, the president's press secretary.

Q *Who said, "A woman's mind is cleaner than a man's because she changes it more often"?—Lena Glover, Shreveport, La.*

A Oliver Herford (1863-1935), American humorist.

Q *Is it true that there are more lesbians in Great Britain proportionately than in any other country?—E.S., Orlando, Fla.*

A There are no conclusive figures on the subject. A recent article in the *British Medical Journal* estimates that one of every 40 British women has lesbian tendencies, blaming that development on Britain's system of boarding schools and girls' colleges in which females are deprived of masculine company for long periods of time.

Q *I would like to find out if Fred Hartley, that tactful, diplomatic head of Union Oil whose offshore drilling polluted our beautiful beaches, is a U.S. citizen.—T.L., Santa Barbara, Calif.*

A Hartley, 51, born in Vancouver, British Columbia, reared and educated there, became a U.S. citizen in 1950.

Q *What does Richard Chamberlain, the ex-Dr. Kildare of TV fame, do nowadays?— E.C., El Paso, Tex.*

A Some time this month Chamberlain will play *Hamlet* with the Birmingham Repertory Company in England. Few Americans have dared to play the role in front of exacting British audiences. If Chamberlain succeeds in not killing Hamlet,

Richard Chamberlain

perhaps he will succeed in killing his image as Dr. Kildare—which he would like very much.

Q *The true story of the S.S. Pueblo—wasn't it a case of divided command, a case in which the high command is to blame?—E. Henline, Norfolk, Va.*

A That is true in part. Thirty men aboard in the intelligence section were not accountable to the Pueblo's skipper, Comdr. Lloyd "Pete" Bucher, but to their 30-year-old intelligence officer, Lt. Stephen R. Harris. He in turn was accountable to the National Security Agency and not to Bucher. The Navy no doubt will revise this system of divided command on future intelligence ships.

Q *Now that Barbra Streisand has put the skids on her husband, Elliott Gould, will she go back to actor Omar Sharif?—Nancy Glenn, Grand Rapids, Mich.*

A She will probably play the field.

Omar Sharif

Q *Is it true that Jack Palance and Omar Sharif had fist fights on the film,* Che? *Is it true that they are feuding?—Helen Levitt, Columbus, Ga.*

A No fist fights but feuding.

Q *James Farmer, the new Assistant Secretary of Health, Education, and Welfare, was the first Negro to accept a high position in the Nixon Administration. Wasn't the job offered Farmer because his wife is white?—Robert Maxwell, Chicago, Ill.*

A Farmer's wife, the former Lula Peterson of Chicago, is white. But the job would have been offered him no matter the color of his wife's skin. Farmer is a civil rights activist who founded the Committee of Racial Equality, later CORE. Son of a Texas college professor who was the state's first Negro Ph.D., and a mother who was a schoolteacher, Farmer was graduated from Wiley College in Texas at age 18 with a B.C. in chemistry, later won a Divinity Degree at Howard University. He knows as much about Negro problems as probably any man in the nation, is eminently qualified to hold his present position.

Q *I read in the* Wall Street Journal *that Henry Kissinger, the president's chief foreign policy adviser, can work day and night because he has no wife to come home to. When I knew Kissinger he not only had a wife but two lovely children. What's he done with them?—K.G., Cambridge, Mass.*

A Kissinger and his wife, the former Ann Fleischer, were divorced in 1964. Mrs. Kissinger has custody of their two children, Elizabeth, nine, and Dan, seven, in Belmont, Massachusetts.

Bob Evans and Ali McGraw

Watson / Globe

Q *Is Bob Evans, the Romeo who runs Paramount studios, making out with Ali MacGraw who was such a hit in Good-bye, Columbus?—May Walsh, Pekin, Ill.*

A Miss MacGraw and Mr. Evans have gotten together.

Q *I have read that our Secret Service no longer protects Jackie Kennedy and her kids, that old money-bags Onassis shells out a small fortune to Pinkerton's for private detectives. Is that on the level? How much does it cost Onassis?—Mildred Kulick, Williamson, Pa.*

A It is not true. The U.S. Secret Service is charged with protecting the Kennedy children until they are 16 or until Mrs. Onassis requests the agency to desist. To date, she has not. The result is that Secret Service agents still travel with the offspring of the late president to Greece and wherever else they may go.

From time to time Onassis hires a Pinkerton guard to look after Jackie in New York, but the charge for this service is $7.50 per hour. Abroad and on the Island of Skorpios, Onassis employs his own security force to protect Jackie while U.S. Secret Service agents protect her children.

Q *How come Doris Day, Ava Gardner, Kim Novak, and other Hollywood stars have never acted on the stage?—Myra Turlington, Dunn, N.C.*

A Stage acting calls for considerable dramatic talent. Screen acting does not.

Q *Is it a fact that Groucho Marx makes all his wives sign pre-marital financial agreements limiting their alimony in the event of divorce?—Louis Schecter, Los Angeles, Calif.*

A He did with his last wife, the former Eden Hartford. Eleven days before their marriage in 1954, she signed an agreement which, in the event of divorce, limited her alimony payments to $15,000 a year plus her half of community property.

This past January, however, when Mrs. Marx filed for divorce, she asked for approximately $5,000 per month. Groucho subsequently countered with his own divorce suit, pointed out that when they first married both parties agreed that their 38-year age difference might eventually lead to a divorce, in which case Mrs. Marx would be satisfied with yearly alimony of $15,000.

Q *Five years ago some Englishman bet $25 at 1,000 to 1 that a man would land on the moon before 1971. Who was he, and did he ever get paid off?—Laura Engelbaum, Tenafly, N.J.*

A He is David Threlfall of Preston, Lancashire. After the astronauts landed on the moon, the London bookmaker, William Hall Ltd., promptly paid young Threlfall, 26, his due, a check for $25,000.

Q *Elizabeth Taylor's oldest son Michael—is he a hippie as I have read? Where does he go to school?—Mindy Haines Lockwood, Amarillo, Tex.*

A Michael Wilding, 16, dresses colorfully but is no hippie. He attends school in Hawaii.

Q *Sen. Russell Long of Louisiana—I understand the press is investigating his drinking habits, his love-life, and his connections with the oil industry. Isn't this rip-roaring son of Huey Long vulnerable on all three counts?—R.T., Baton Rouge, La.*

Russell Long

Harris and Ewing / Globe

A Senator Long's love-life is negligible at this point. His drinking habits are no secret. He may be vulnerable, however, as a conduit for campaign contributions from the oil industry. For example, Harold M. McClure, Jr., president of the McClure Oil Co. of Alma, Michigan, and president of the Independent Petroleum Association of America, has given money to Senator Long's office to be distributed to senators friendly to the oil interests. McClure is also the Republican national committeeman from Michigan.

Q *The rumor that Marlon Brando will not date a white girl, prefers instead to date blacks like Mary Wilson and Diana Ross—is there any truth to that?—Neva Sloane, Augusta, Ga.*

A Brando is color-blind where it comes to race. He thought his first wife, Anna Kashfi, was Indian. After his marriage he learned she was Welsh. His second wife was Movita Castenada, a Mexican. The mother of his son, Simon, is a Polynesian girl who acted with him in *Mutiny on the Bounty*. From the record, Brando seemingly prefers to date young women of minority races and nationalities, but generally he is willing to give them all a try regardless of color or creed. In this regard he is most democratic.

Q *Bill Cosby, the Negro comic—doesn't he own four apartment houses in Brooklyn which do not allow black tenants?—Liza Levitt, Brooklyn, N.Y.*

Bill Cosby

Korbin / Globe

A An article to that effect appeared in the September issue of *Sepia* magazine, a publication edited by Negroes. The author of the article was Frank Peterson. The editorial staff of *Sepia* as well as Mr. Peterson insist the condition was true at the time the article was written. Undoubtedly it has changed by now, and Negroes have been allowed to rent apartments in the buildings.

Q *My wife has been reading an advance copy of a book called The Lost Prince. Its author is Hank Searls. The book is a biography of Lt. Joseph P. Kennedy, Jr., the oldest Kennedy brother who was killed in a dangerous air mission in World War II. The book claims that young Kennedy was madly in love with a beautiful married British girl at the time of his death. Is the girl still living? Is her identity well known?—F.E., Nantucket, Mass.*

A She is still living. Her name is Pat Wilson. Her husband, an Army officer, was killed in Italy in World War II in an automobile accident. She subsequently remarried. In London circles she is fairly well known, will become even better known after *The Lost Prince* goes on sale.

October 26, 1969

Q *Can you tell me if it is true that soul singer Johnny Cash earned $2 million last year? Is he an ex-prisoner himself? Is that why he likes to entertain for other prisoners?—Norman Freed, Newark, N.J.*

Johnny Cash

A Cash earned approximately $2 million last year. Over the years he has been imprisoned on a variety of charges. He feels a great kinship with men behind bars, likes to perform in prisons.

Q *I understand that the offspring of many top government officials have been "busted" for smoking pot. Would you please print their names?—E.D.L., Washington, D.C.*

A It is true that the children of top government officials in Washington, D.C., have been cited either smoking marijuana or having been present where it was smoked, but it would serve no good to publish their names. In government circles it is widely acknowledged that marijuana-smoking has become endemic among the young and that the so-called narcotics laws must be revised on a more realistic basis.

Q *Neiman-Marcus, the Dallas department store which services the Texas oil millionaires—who owns that store? Is it becoming a national chain?—Maurice Wetzler, El Paso, Tex.*

A Since last May, Neiman-Marcus has been owned by Broadway-Hale Stores, Inc. Stanley Marcus, 64, of Dallas, still runs Neiman-Marcus. He plans to open another branch in Bal Harbour, Florida, in November, 1970. If that one is successful, other out-of-state stores will follow.

Q *Has the house in which Sharon Tate was murdered really doubled in price since her death? Did Sharon and her husband Roman Polanski own the house?—Lee Rivers, Honolulu, Hawaii.*

A The house is owned by Terry Melcher, son of actress Doris Day. It was Melcher who rented the house to the Polanskis. The house was on the market at one time for approximately $200,000. The asking price has since jumped to $300,000.

Q *I have been told that each year 10 percent of the freshman class of the U.S. Naval Academy in Annapolis resigns because of unbearable adolescent physical hazing: True or false?—Martha Klein, Birmingham, Ala.*

A Last year 10.2 percent of the plebes at Annapolis resigned from the Academy, the highest percentage of resignations that Academy has known since it was founded 123 years ago. Major reason for the resignations: physical hazing of plebes by upper classmen. In 1969 only 3.6 percent resigned. In 1966 only 5.3 percent resigned.

Under Rear Adm. James F. Calvert, new superintendent of the Academy, the hazing has been minimized and so has the resignation rate.

Q *In a book,* The Trial of Dr. Spock, *author Jessica Mitford says that Spock and others were tried by the government merely to salvage the pride of General Hershey. Why should General Hershey's pride be salvaged? The truth, if possible, please.—Lacey W. Edwards, Bethesda, Md.*

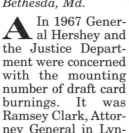

Benjamin Spock

A In 1967 General Hershey and the Justice Department were concerned with the mounting number of draft card burnings. It was Ramsey Clark, Attorney General in Lyndon Johnson's Ad-

Hershey

ministration, who decided to prosecute Dr. Spock and four others on the charge of conspiring to counsel, aid, and abet violations of the Selective Service Act. General Hershey's pride, his punitive and illegal instructions to draft boards to induct Vietnamese war protesters—these had nothing to do with Clark's decision. Miss Mitford is in error in her interpretation of the Justice Department's motivation.

Q *Who is the one-armed member of the U.S. Senate who goes around without a prosthetic? Why doesn't he wear an artificial arm, and where did he lose the original?—Mary Line Anderson, Greensboro, N.C.*

A He is Sen. Daniel K. Inouye (D., Hawaii). He lost his right arm in World War II on Mt. Marchiaso in Italy two days before the war's end. He was hit by an enemy rifle grenade. Senator Inouye wore a prosthetic until 1952 "when I decided I didn't need it and it didn't fit in with the warm Hawaiian climate."

Darryl Zanuck & Genevieve Gilles

Q *I am a stockholder in 20th Century-Fox. It has been my experience that every time our leader, Darryl Zanuck, comes up with a new protegee, he casts her in picture. Generally these pictures with Bella Darvi, Juliette Greco, Irena Demick are flops. Now that Darryl has Genevieve Gilles, what are we to expect?—M.T., Chicago, Ill.*

A We are to expect a film, *Hello-Goodbye*, starring Genevieve Gilles and Curt Jurgens.

Q *How come the Nixon Administration has kept Sargent Shriver on as the U.S. Ambassador to France when Shriver is a Democrat and so many rich Republicans are clamoring for his job?—Eloise Phillips, Los Angeles, Calif.*

A It suits the Nixon Administration to have a member of the Kennedy family as U.S. Ambassador at this time. If Shriver has political ambitions, and he most certainly has, next year is the time for him to go into action. Until then he has found a safe harbor, far from the trials of brother-in-law Ted Kennedy.

Q *Who said: "Little children, little joys; big children, big cares"?—James Wincott, Dallas, Tex.*

A It is an old anonymous proverb.

WALTER SCOTT'S

PERSONALITY PARADE®

November 2, 1969

Q *Is it true that Abraham Lincoln was illegitimate, that Lawrence of Arabia was illegitimate, and that the late Winston Churchill was conceived out of wedlock?—M.L. Warner, Greenwich, Conn.*

Abraham Lincoln

A Lincoln probably was illegitimate. Lawrence of Arabia certainly was. Winston Churchill was said to have been a premature, seven-months baby, but researchers suspect that his mother, Jennie Jerome, was pregnant at the time of her marriage to Randolph Churchill, both of whose parents adamantly refused to attend their son's wedding.

Q *What make and year of car does the crusader, Ralph Nader, drive?—T.Y., Imperial Beach, Calif.*

A Crusader Nader owns no car, takes taxis.

Q *President Nixon keeps talking about his desire to end the war in Vietnam. Is it not a fact that he planned to draft more men in 1969 than Lyndon Johnson did in 1968?—Terry Koontz, Portland, Ore.*

A Last year the Johnson Administration inducted 296,000 draftees into the armed forces. This year the Nixon Administration planned to induct approximately 340,000 draftees. Had Nixon not canceled planned draft calls for November and December of 1969, the Defense Department would have called up 44,000 more men in 1969 than it did in 1968. As the figures now stand they will show 296,000 men drafted in 1968, 289,000 men drafted in 1969.

Q *What is the lowdown about the Belgian Princess Paola and the prostitutes of Brussels? I know the story has been suppressed in Europe. Can you tell it?—Louise McGuire, Springfield, Mass.*

A Princess Paola, beautiful wife of Prince Albert, younger brother of Belgium's King Baudouin, agreed to attend a film premiere in Brussels. It was a charity performance designed to raise funds for a home for repentant ladies of the night. These women were put out of business 20 years ago when prostitution was outlawed in Belgium.

The Belgian court objected to the princess attending such a function for such a purpose, so she did not attend. The story was not suppressed anywhere.

Q *I understand there is a sexy connotation in the title of a movie,* Easy Rider, *which all the kids are flocking to. What is the underground meaning of the term easy rider?—Walt David, Berkeley, Calif.*

A To hip musicians easy rider signifies a man who lives on the immoral earnings of his wife.

Q *How old is Joseph P. Kennedy, Sr.? Has he ever regained the power of speech?—Al Dubin, Miami Beach, Fla.*

Joseph Kennedy

A Mr. Kennedy is 81, has never regained the power of speech.

Q *Authoress Jacqueline Susann—I hear her real name is Mandelbaum, that she is 62 years old, and that her books are ghost-written. Can you confirm?—Dora Klein, New York, N.Y.*

A Jacqueline Susann's husband, Irving Mansfield, was born Irving Mandelbaum in Brooklyn. Miss Susann writes every word of her novels herself. Most probably she is in her early 50's, having played ingenue roles on Broadway in the 1930's.

Q *When U.S. forces kill native Vietnamese by accident and error as they have during the course of the war, do we pay compensation to the families of the victims?—Merle Sherman, Gary, Ind.*

A We pay about $35 a body.

Q *Can you tell us anything about Michael Parks, the young actor in the* Then Came Bronson *TV series?—The Broughton Girls, Raleigh, N.C.*

A Michael Parks was born in Corona, California, education in Sacramento, is married to the former Kay Carson, a choreographer. The couple have a one-year-old son. Parks lives in Ojai, about 60 miles from Los Angeles, avoids the Hollywood scene. A one-time drifter, he displays little articulation or emotion, is supposed to personify today's young generation.

Q *Since I live here, I would like to find out once and for all if the Defense Department uses Hawaii as a testing site for nerve gases?—Maury Gaines, Kona, Hawaii.*

A The Pentagon, after first denying it, has admitted that the Army tested nerve gases in Hawaii on four occasions between 1966 and 1967. The Pentagon claims it has no future plans for testing any chemical or biological weapons in the islands.

Q *What have the Russians done to the children Svetlana Alliluyeva, Stalin's daughter, left behind in Moscow?—P.E., Princeton, N.J.*

A The Soviets have done nothing to them. Daughter Katya attends Moscow University. Son Joseph is a doctor.

Q *I note that Lauren Bacall and Katharine Hepburn will soon be starring in Broadway musicals. Can either sing? Also what shows are they going into?—Tina Fitzpatrick, Phoenix, Ariz.*

A Miss Bacall will star in a musical comedy version of the film, *All About Eve.* Miss Hepburn will star in *Coco,* a musical based on the life of French dress designer Coco Chanel, now in her 80's. At the moment both Miss Bacall and Miss Hepburn are hard at work trying to find singing voices.

John Mitchell

Q *Attorney General John Mitchell of the Nixon Cabinet is described as Nixon's strong man. Is this because Mitchell never smiles?—A.L. Thomas, Camden, N.J.*

A Mitchell has been known to smile on occasion. He is considered the strong man in Nixon's Cabinet, because the president seems to place great stock in his judgment and advice on a growing variety of subjects.

PERSONALITY PARADE®

December 14, 1969

Q *I would like to know how David Brinkley, the NBC-TV commentator, feels about the war in Vietnam. Is he a hawk or a dove?—Kay Hillinger, Pine Bluff, Ark.*

A At a recent University of Arizona lecture in Tucson, Brinkley told his young audience: "It's hard to disagree that the Vietnam war is wrong. Two-thirds of the U.S. tax income is for the military when American cities rot. There is nothing to be won in Vietnam worth the danger of World War III or worth the damage done to the internal structure of our country."

Q *Some time ago Paul Newman, Sidney Poitier, and Barbra Streisand announced that they were forming their own motion picture company and would produce their own films. What, if anything, has happened to their company?—Frank Perry, Reading, Pa.*

A The company, First Artists Production Company, recently signed a distribution deal with National General Pictures to produce at least nine films in six years. Newman, Poitier, and Streisand each plan to star in a minimum of three.

Q *The story of Funny Girl is based on the life of Fanny Brice. Whatever happened to her gambler husband Nicky Arnstein, played by Omar Sharif in the movie. And what about her daughter?—Barbara Sobko, N. Attleboro, Mass.*

Omar Sharif

A Nicky Arnstein died on October 2, 1965. Fanny Brice's daughter is married to Ray Stark, a former agent and now the film producer who turned out *Funny Girl*.

Q *My son sent me a few weeks ago the following quotation: "If an award were given to the government department or agency displaying the most ignorance, stupidity, laziness, cowardice, incompetence and venality, third prize might go to the Subversive Activities Control Board, second prize to the Post Office Department, but surely first prize would go, with no dissenting votes, to the Federal Trade Commission." Can you please identify the quotation? A man named Thayer had something to do with it.—Mrs. J.L. James, Danville, Va.*

A The quotation is from a review by George Thayer of a book, *The Nader Report on the Federal Trade Commission*, written by Edward Cox, Robert Fellmeth, and John E. Schulz. The book review was syndicated by the Los Angeles Times-Washington Post Service.

Q *Why are Natalie Nevins, Steve Smith and Frank Scott no longer on the Lawrence Welk Show? Natalie once said the show was her life.—Mrs. D.D.M., Longmeadow, Mass.*

Lawrence Welk

A Welk insists that all show performers go on yearly summer tours. Natalie Nevins felt strongly that her primary obligations were at home with her husband and family; so she retired as a regular, Steven Smith has returned to college, and Frank Scott, because of an illness in his family, has moved back to North Dakota.

Q *Is there any chance of Gov. Ronald Reagan being defeated for reelection in California in 1970 either by Assemblyman Jesse Unruh or San Francisco Mayor Alioto?—Ben Mars, El Centro, Calif.*

Ronald Reagan

A Gov. Reagan is over-whelmingly popular in the state of California except in student and academic environments. There is practically no chance of his being defeated by any Democratic candidate unless he should goof badly, which is most unlikely. Reagan is shrewd, intelligent, personable, and learns quickly.

Q *How many North Vietnamese or Viet Cong have we killed and wounded in Vietnam in an effort to bring peace to that country? How many South Vietnamese soldiers have been killed by the enemy?—R.T., Biloxi, Miss.*

A As of November 1, 1969, we and our allies in South Vietnam killed 566,501 Vietnamese. In addition, we have wounded another 3,500,000. As of November 1, 1969, 96,456 South Vietnamese soldiers were battle casualties. As of that date, approximately 700,000 soldiers on both sides had lost their lives.

Q *Is it true that the Army uses human guinea pigs to test drugs and gases for chemical and biological warfare?—S.R., Berkeley, Calif.*

A Yes, the Edgewood Arsenal in Maryland tests various sprays, gases, irritants, and hallucinogens on 70 full-time Army volunteers. The men take two months out of their normal Army assignments for these tests. Over the last 14 years approximately 5,200 men have participated in the testing programs.

Q *How old is Kyle Johnson, the black youth in the movie, The Learning Tree? Can you tell something about him?—Bertha Kamm, Chicago, Ill.*

A Kyle, 17, attends Pierce Junior College in Los Angeles. In spite of his success in *The Learning Tree*, he considers acting secondary to education. His mother, Nichelle Nichols, played in the TV series, *Star Trek*.

Q *Isn't Joan Kennedy secretly planning to divorce Sen. Ted Kennedy? Isn't that the reason she went to Europe?—Dana X, Swampscott, Mass.*

Joan Kennedy

A Joan Kennedy is planning no divorce. She went to Europe to recuperate from her miscarriage and to avoid persistent newsmen.

Q *I have been told that the federal government plans to legalize homosexuality in this country. What is the story?—E.F. Flute, San Francisco, Calif.*

A A government task force has recommended that homosexual behavior between adults should no longer be considered a crime. The government is studying the recommendation, has made no decision whether or not to endorse it. There are an estimated four. million homosexuals in the U.S., and the task force, appointed by The National Institutes of Health, suggests that the repeal of laws against homosexuals would no doubt reduce their emotional stress and trauma.

1970
1971
1972
1973
1974
1975
1976
1977
1978
1979

WALTER SCOTT'S

PERSONALITY PARADE®

March 1, 1970

Q Has President Nixon obtained a job for his kid brother, Donald Nixon, in the Federal government yet?—E.L., Whittier, Calif.

Richard Nixon

A J. Willard Marriott, a close friend of the president and one of the major contributors to the Republican party, recently hired F. Donald Nixon, the president's brother, as a vice president of his restaurant, hotel, and airline catering company. Donald Nixon, 55, will not be involved in any dealings on behalf of the Marriott Corporation with the federal government.

Q Can you tell me why Rex Harrison is called "Sexy Rexy"? He is 61 years old and seems to have as much sex appeal as a grape.—Bernadine Goldschmidt, Long Beach, Calif.

A Harrison, 61, has lost much of his hair and sex appeal; but in his 20's and 30's he cut a wide swath among the women of the world. Married four times, he has proven his virility on countless occasions, some embarrassing and others not. The appelation, "Sexy Rexy" was a journalistic concoction, founded on the testimony of Hollywood actresses who loved and told.

Q What's happened to actor Don Ameche? He was very popular 30 years ago when I was in love with him.—Charlene Williams, New York, N.Y.

Diahann Carroll

A Ameche acts occasionally. He recently became a TV director and directed Diahann Carroll in an episode of the TV series, Julia.

Q Who was responsible for the FBI opening an office in Jackson, Mississippi, during the civil rights disputes? Was it J. Edgar Hoover or the late Bobby Kennedy?—L.T., De Soto, Miss.

A It was Lyndon Johnson who insisted upon it.

Q Is it a fact that the Jesuits, long recognized as the most intellectual and educated elite of the Roman Catholic priesthood, are banned from working in Switzerland?—Morley Knox, Gainesville, Fla.

A Article 51 of the Swiss constitution so bans the Jesuits. The issue, more than 100 years old, has been revived by many Swiss educators who want Article 51 repealed.

Q Who said: "The real great man is the man who makes every man feel great"?— David Fleischmann, Cambridge, Mass.

A G. K. Chesterton (1874-1936), British essayist.

John F. Kennedy and Richard Nixon

Q I have heard that the late President John F. Kennedy owned the Merchandise Mart in Chicago. Is this so?—Morris Brody, Detroit, Mich.

A The late President owned a $577,341 interest in the Merchandise Mart, the building in Chicago originally purchased by his father.

Q If a citizen of the U.S. resides overseas, does he have to pay federal income tax?—Allen Lescoulie, Oakland, Calif.

A For Americans who reside overseas for 17 or 18 consecutive months, the first $20,000 of earned income is tax exempt. This exemption rises to $25,000 for those Americans living abroad more than three years.

Q It is said that Carlos Marcello of the Mafia owns and runs the Mardi Gras in New Orleans. True?—B.C., Monroe, La.

A Carlos Marcello owns several enterprises which profit from the Mardi Gras but he neither owns nor runs the festival.

Tony Curtis and Christine Kaufmann

Q Christine Kaufmann, Tony Curtis' second wife—did she give Tony the air for Dean Martin's young son, Dino? What's happened to Christine?—Harriet Kale, Miami Beach, Fla.

A Christine Kaufmann, 25, German-born actress who became the wife of actor Tony Curtis when she was only 18, now lives in Munich. At one time she was most friendly with Dino Martin.

Q Is it true that RCA and other American companies have their color TV sets manufactured in Japan?—O.T., Camden, N.J.

A Many of the components are of Japanese manufacture as are many of the cheaper color TV sets.

Q Does President Nixon carry with him at all times a special device which alarms the Secret Service in case of personal attack?—Maurice Tuchmann, Muncie, Ind.

A No, but in the kneewell of his White House desk there is an aluminum-pronged alarm. All the president need do is lean his knee against that device, and the Secret Service agents will burst into the room at once.

Alan Cranston

Q *Who are the outstanding rookies in the U.S. Senate?—Myra Goodell, Altadena, Calif.*

A According to veteran senatorial observers, four new members of the U.S. Senate who to date have displayed outstanding diligence, industry, imagination, and intelligence are Sens. Alan Cranston (D., Calif.), Harold Hughes (D., Iowa), William Saxbe (R., Ohio), and Charles Mathias (R., Md.).

Q *I read in the newspapers that an abortion in Singapore costs $1.50. How much does the average abortion cost in the U.S.?—Nancy Fredrickson, Atlanta, Ga.*

A It has been estimated by many investigators that the average legal abortion in this country costs somewhere between $750 and $1,500. The average illegal abortion costs somewhere between $500 and $1,000.

Q *Who said: "In America the president reigns for four years, and journalism governs forever and ever"?—Lonnie Ashenaze, Winter Park, Fla.*

A Oscar Wilde, (1854-1900), Irish playwright and poet.

Q *Does Jane Hart, wife of Sen. Philip Hart of Michigan, own the Detroit Tigers baseball team?—E.L., Grosse Pointe, Mich.*

A No, her father, the late Walter Briggs, owned the Detroit Tigers and Briggs Stadium.

Q *Is it true that prices on all British motor cars will rise 20 percent next week?—Dan Henderson, Sutersville, Pa.*

A Starting soon, most British cars will cost more in Great Britain to cover the rise in wages, steel prices, other raw materials.

Q *Attorney General John Mitchell said recently that the air freight trucking industry at a large U.S. airport was under the domination of the crime syndicate. Which airport did he have reference to?—A. Thomas, Baldwin, N.Y.*

A It is popularly supposed that he meant the John F. Kennedy International Airport which serves New York City and environs.

Paul and Linda McCartney

Q *I would like to know if Beatle Paul McCartney's American wife is again pregnant.—Jane Frankel, Teaneck, N.J.*

A She is.

Q *Ron Ziegler, President Nixon's press secretary—did he have any experience in journalism when Nixon gave him the job?—Allen Asher, Baltimore, Md.*

A Ziegler, 30, used to work at Disneyland in Anaheim, California, as a jungle guide aboard the Disneyland jungle cruise boats. At the University of Southern California when he was a student in 1960, he campaigned for Nixon. After graduation he campaigned again for Nixon in 1962 when Nixon ran unsuccessfully for governor of California. During this campaign he met Harry Haldeman, also a Nixon campaign worker and manager of the Los Angeles office of the J. Walter Thompson advertising agency. Haldeman hired Ziegler as a junior account executive. When Nixon won the presidency in 1968, Haldeman recommended Ziegler as press secretary with Communications Director Herb Klein watching over him.

Q *Is Charles Atlas, the body developer, still alive? If so, what about him?—Al Hicks, Newark, N.J.*

A Charles Atlas, 77, is alive and well. He lives in New York and Florida. Atlas was born Angelo Siciliano in Italy and brought to America at age 10. He was reared in Brooklyn and changed his name to Atlas after the Atlas Hotel in Rockaway, Long Island.

In 1921 he won the title the World's Most Perfectly Developed Man in a contest sponsored by *Physical Culture* magazine. Subsequently he entered the physical culture mail order business himself with Charles Roman as his managing director. Roman still runs the business which advertises, "You, too can have a body like mine."

Martin Luther King, Jr.

Q *Wasn't Martin Luther King, Jr. almost assassinated by a black woman ten or twelve years ago? I believe it was in 1960.—Mrs. Kenneth Reisch, New York, N.Y.*

A In September, 1958, King was stabbed in a Harlem department store while autographing his book, *Stride Toward Freedom*. A 42-year-old black woman plunged a letter-opener into his chest. King did not panic. He sensibly insisted that the knife be left in his chest until he was taken to the hospital where a physician removed it.

Had he removed it himself or moved suddenly, he might have died instantly. The woman who tried to kill King was later committed to an insane asylum.

Rock Hudson

Q *Has Rock Hudson left Hollywood to become a recording star?—Ellen Arnold, Colorado Springs, Colo.*

A Hudson has not left Hollywood. For the past three years he has been taking vocal lessons, recently formed a corporation, R & R Productions, to produce films and recordings of which Hudson recently completed two, *Rock Gentle* and *Rock for the Fun.*

Q *Was David Eisenhower ever engaged to an attractive, young divorcee named Judy Tegethoff before he was married to Julie Nixon?—E.T., Philadelphia, Pa.*

A He was not. Judy Tegethoff was his father's private secretary. When Col. John Eisenhower, David's father, was appointed U.S. Ambassador to Belgium, Mrs. Tegethoff subsequently joined the U.S. Embassy in Brussels where she is now a member of the Ambassador's secretarial staff.

Q *Is it true that Shirley Temple Black has been given an armed bodyguard by the Secret Service because she represents us at the United Nations?—Louise Herman, Tucson, Ariz.*

A Shirley Temple Black, a member of the U.S. delegation to the 24th General Assembly of the United Nations, was given an armed bodyguard by the City of New York. She has received crank mail from time to time.

Q *Who said, "It's bad to suppress laughter. It goes back down and spreads your hips"?—Abe Dieterle, Cincinnati, Ohio.*

A The quip was made by the late Fred Allen, American comic.

Q *Who is older, President Nixon or his wife?—Bernardine Kelly, Boston, Mass.*

A Richard Nixon was born on January 9, 1913. His wife was born on March 16, 1912.

Q *Is it true that Brandon Cruz who plays "Eddie" on* The Courtship of Eddie's Father *was killed in an automobile accident?—Jean Bucher, Philadelphia, Pa.*

A No. The eight-year-old actor is alive and well, working at the ABC-TV studios in Hollywood.

Q *My American history professor says that in 1942 the Rose Bowl football game was held in the South because of fear the Japanese would invade southern California. Is this the truth?—M.P.H., University, Miss.*

A In 1942 fear of Japanese attack caused the Rose Bowl game to be transferred from Pasadena to Durham, North Carolina. There, without the benefit of the customary Rose Parade, Oregon State upset Duke University, 20-16.

Q *Will film star Albert Finney marry Anouk Aimée?—Jill Fothergill, Detroit, Mich.*

A Albert Finney, 33, currently filming *Scrooge* in London, and Anouk Aimée, 37, who watches him on the set each day, are indeed friends and lovers. But Miss Aimée has already been married three times and Mr. Finney once, to actress Jane Wenham. Both are understandably chary of marriage. But spring is in the air, and who knows?

Q *Is there any chance that Charles Manson, allegedly the mastermind behind the Sharon Tate murders, will beat the rap?—Eve Conde, Youngstown, Ohio.*

A There is a slight chance. But now in this year of 1970, juries are not particularly sympathetic or understanding where the non-conformist young of the nation are involved.

Q *A prominent Wall Street broker tells me that Richard Nixon is eternally indebted to a man named Peter Flanigan. Who is Mr. Flanigan and how did Mr. Nixon get in his debt?—R. Young, Scarsdale, N.Y.*

Richard Nixon

A Peter Flanigan, 46, is one of President Nixon's top White House aides. The son of "Hap" Flanigan, former head of the Manufacturers Hanover Trust Company, Peter Flanigan was born with the proverbial silver spoon in his mouth. He was educated at the Greenwich (Conn.) Country Day School, Portsmouth Priory (which prep school Bobby Kennedy attended) and Princeton University.

A vice president at 30 of the prestigious Wall Street firm of Dillon, Read & Co., Flanigan, unlike other wealthy Irish Catholic members of the Eastern Establishment, declined to support John F. Kennedy in the 1960 presidential race. Instead, he contributed his money and support to Richard Nixon, organized the nationwide Volunteers for Nixon & Lodge organization.

As a result of his loyalty and personal friendship, Nixon appointed him a trusted adviser. An authoritative man of Gaelic charm and some abrasiveness, Flanigan helped set up in Bermuda the successful Barracuda Tanker Corporation of which he was president. Barracuda financed and owned the oil tanker, Torrey Canyon, which broke in half on the reefs of southern England, contaminating British and French shore waters. Barracuda also financed the tanker Sansinena which, like the Torrey Canyon, flies the Liberian flag, thus avoiding payment of U.S. taxes.

Mr. Flanigan was recently a mild source of embarrassment to the administration in connection with a waiver of the Jones Act first granted the Sansinena but later revoked.

Mr. Flanigan has aroused the curiosity of several members of the Washington press corps who are investigating his various pursuits, past and present.

WALTER SCOTT'S
PERSONALITY PARADE®

June 7, 1970

Q *Does · Sen. Edward Kennedy have a weak character? His cheating episode at Harvard. His tragedy with Mary Jo Kopechne. What is his fatal flaw?—R.E.S., Cambridge, Mass.*

Edward Kennedy

A The Senator's character is wanting in some respects. But whose is not? He is much too young for any of his flaws to be fatal—yet.

Q *Richard Nixon campaigned for the presidency on a promise to "bring us together." Has he abandoned that policy? In all my 71 years I have never known this nation in war or peace to be more divided.—Edmund Cates, Santa Barbara, Calif.*

A President Nixon and his chief advisor, Attorney General John Mitchell, have seemingly chosen to follow the policy of government by support of the white middle-class householders at this time. After more than one year in office, it is safe to say that both men have failed to unify the Republic. Neither, however, has abandoned the hope.

Q *Was Queen Elizabeth of England ever in love with anyone before she married Prince Philip? Is it true that Philip suffers from the roving eye?—Albert Quincy, Miami, Fla.*

A Elizabeth met Philip when she was 13 and he was a young student at Dartmouth Naval College. She had never loved any other man except her father and the love she felt for him she transferred to Philip. In his time Philip has appreciated the delights of feminine companionship.

Q *How much older than his wife is Aristotle Onassis? Isn't he twice the age of Jackie Kennedy?—Penelope War, Wilmington, N.C.*

A Onassis gave his age as 40 in 1946 when he married 17-year-old Tina Livanos. Jackie is 40.

Q *Inger Stevens, my favorite actress, recently took her life. Does anyone know why? Was she ever the lover of Bing Crosby and Anthony Quinn? Why did she take her life?—A.T. Anderson, Mason City, Iowa.*

A At various times actress Stevens expected that first Bing Crosby and then Anthony Quinn would marry her. Nei-

ther did. She thereupon took up with other men who declined to marry her. No doubt a contributory cause to her suicide. Ike Jones, a 40-year-old Negro, claims he was secretly married to Miss Stevens in Tijuana in 1961. Jones, former football star at UCLA, wants to administer her $162,000 estate.

Q *I note that Dr. Christiaan Barnard, the heart transplant man, is against legalized abortion unless the mother's life is endangered or the baby might be seriously malformed. Is Barnard a Roman Catholic?—Mrs. Evelyn Richmond, Fort Smith, Ark.*

A No, he is the son of a Protestant South African minister, but his present wife is a Roman Catholic.

Dennis Hopper

Q *What's happened to Michelle Phillips, formerly with The Mamas and the Papas?—Heidi Hindusmith, Chicago, Ill.*

A She has become the girlfriend of film-maker Dennis Hopper of *Easy Rider* fame. Hopper recently cast her in another of his films, *The Last Movie*.

Q *When Stavros Niarchos, the Greek shipping magnate, married Charlotte Ford of the automobile family in 1865, was that marriage recognized by the Greek Orthodox Church?—Raines Halliday, Los Angeles, Calif.*

A No, it was not. The Greek Orthodox Church generally allows a man only three marriages. Niarchos' third wife was

the late Eugenie Livanos, sister of Tina, ex-wife of Onassis, and the church continued to regard her as Niarchos' wife even after Niarchos had married Charlotte Ford, from whom he was divorced after the birth of a child, Elena.

Q *Was John Maynard Keynes, the economist, a homosexual as well as a conscientious objector?—L.G., Princeton, N.J.*

A Keynes was a homosexual and a conscientious objector against conscription in World War I. But he was also a very great economist, one of Britain's finest.

Q *Is it true that because of student objections Dow Chemical Company has given up its napalm contract with the government?—U. Titterton, Detroit, Mich.*

A Dow stopped manufacturing napalm in May, 1969, when its contract with the Defense Department ran out, bid on a new contract, which was awarded to another company.

Vladimir Lenin

Q *Can you tell me if Lenin and Kerensky, the Russian revolutionaries, were both born on April 22 in the same Russian city?—Peter Young, Durham, N.C.*

A Yes. Lenin was born on April 22, 1870. Kerensky was born on April 22, 1881, both in the same Russian village, Simbersk, now known as Ulyanovsk, after Lenin's family name. Kerensky is alive and living in New York City.

Jack Dempsey

Q *How old is Jack Dempsey? Is he still a restaurant king?—Louis Weiss, Jersey City, N.J.*

A Jack Dempsey, former heavyweight champion, is 75, still attends to his restaurant business.

Q *Richard Nixon's first love in Whittier, California, was a delightful girl named Ola Florence Welch. My mother says they went together for six years and were supposed to get married. Why didn't they? And have they seen each other since their breakup?—V.T., Whittier, Calif.*

A Ola Florence Welch and Richard Nixon first met in 1930 at Whittier High School in a Latin play. They both went on to Whittier College. All their friends expected they would marry. After graduation, Miss Welch got a teaching job, "and we began to drift apart. He stepped out on me," she recalls, "and I stepped out on him."

In 1936 Ola Florence Welch married one of Nixon's classmates, Gail Jobe. The Jobes now have three children: Brenda, 31; Brent, 29, and Dennis, 25, live the retired life in Sedona, Arizona.

"We had a class reunion in 1959," Mrs. Jobe recalls, "our 25th, and it was then I saw Richard Nixon for the first time in more than 20 years. He looked very well. He was most cordial, friendly, and polite. But I must say I'm glad I married whom I married.

"If Dick had married me, I'm sure he would not have become president of the United States. My fun-loving ways did not mix with his high and serious ambition."

Q *Marjorie Merriweather Post who inherited the General Foods fortune is 83. Does she plan to marry someone half her age?—Anne Reles, W. Palm Beach, Fla.*

A Mrs. Post, the breakfast cereal heiress, is reportedly contemplating marriage to Robert Wilson, 58, of Palm Beach. A durable lady, Mrs. Post has survived four husbands.

Q *Is it a fact that of 13,000 General Motors dealers, all but seven are white?—E.F., Detroit, Mich.*

A That is approximately correct, but the corporation is doing everything possible to franchise minority entrepreneurs.

Q *Can you tell me if actress Joan Collins has renounced marriage for all time?—Evelyn Brandt, New Rochelle, N.Y.*

A Joan Collins, 37, recently divorced from Anthony Newley, announced recently, "From now on I'm going to have my cake and eat it, too. No more marriage for me. I'm all for free love. I honestly can't see how a woman with a life expectancy of 70 to 75 years could want to spend it all with one man."

During her Hollywood days it was said of Miss Collins that she threw herself away but she always seemed to take careful aim while doing so. She zeroed in on such men as actor Robert Wagner, Sammy Davis, Jr., Rafael Trujillo and, of course, Warren Beatty of whom she says frankly, "We were living together and we were very happy. Then as soon as we thought about making it legal, we started having terrible fights."

Q *Has any Englishman in modern history ever been appointed prime minister of Great Britain for three consecutive terms?—Ron Walker, St. Paul, Minn.*

A No, but Harold Wilson may be the first after Thursday's election, accomplishing a feat which escaped Disraeli, Gladstone, Baldwin and others.

Q *I hear that venereal disease is turning California into a disaster area. Is Governor Reagan doing anything about this?—A.L., Roanoke, Va.*

A According to Ronald Cremo, an adviser to the California Department of Public Health, venereal disease cases in the state numbered more than 100,000 last year. More than 90 percent of these were cases of gonorrhea, with more than half the victims under 25 years of age. In an effort to stem the tide of such infections, a new California law empowers physicians to treat minors for venereal disease without notifying their parents.

Q *Do you know anything about the so-called "Royal Hunt Scandal" involving Prince Bernhard of the Netherlands and Lee Radziwill, sister of Jackie Onassis? It took place in Italy last year.—Robert Q., Silver Spring, Md.*

A Last December in Novi Ligure, Italy, some 2,000 head of game were alleged to have been killed illegally by a party of jetsetters including Prince Bernhard, Stavros Niarchos, Walter Chiari, Dominguin, the bullfighter, and Lee Radziwill. The hunt took place on the estate of the Marquis Edilio Raggio. He and his guests have been charged with pursuing and shooting game on snow-covered terrain which makes the game highly vulnerable. Worse yet, Prince Bernhard of the Netherlands is president of the International Wildlife Fund.

Bobbie Gentry

Q *Is Glen Campbell the real reason Bobbie Gentry left her millionaire husband Bill Harrah?—Hank Rice, Reno, Nev.*

A No. Bobbie and Harrah were simply incompatible, largely because of their age difference. Bobbie is 27, Harrah is 58.

Q *Does Henry Kissinger know about Jill St. John's friendship with Attorney Sydney Korshak? Will Kissinger marry the actress? What is Jill St. John's real name?—Evelyn Berlin, Van Nuys, Calif.*

A President Nixon's adviser, Henry Kissinger, knows Miss St. John casually, not intimately. Chances are he knows little about her purchase of Parvin-Dohrmann stock or her affiliation with attorney Korshak. Miss St. John's real name is Jill Oppenheim.

Q *I am a homosexual. I have been told that homosexual relations between two consenting adults are legal in Europe. Is this true?—E.E., Chicago, Ill.*

A Austria and Finland are the two West European countries where homosexuality is still illegal. The Austrian cabinet, however, recently approved a bill legalizing homosexual relations between consenting adults. The Austrian Parliament will vote on the bill any day now.

The Nixon family

Q *How does Mrs. Richard Nixon compare to Mrs. Lyndon Johnson?—R. Voight, Fitchburg, Mass.*

A Mrs. Nixon is a much warmer and giving personality. She lacks Mrs. Johnson's great drive, ambition, and sense of thrift.

Q *Which industry in the U.S. pays its executives the highest salaries? Who last year got the most loot?—M. Mead, Cortez, Colo.*

A Generally the automobile industry awards its executives with top compensation in the form of salaries and bonuses. Last year James Roche, chairman of General Motors, was paid $790,000 in salary, bonus, and stock purchase credits. Henry Ford II, chairman of Ford Motor Company, was paid $515,000. Other well-paid executives: Howard J. Morgens, president of Procter & Gamble, received $425,000. Harold Geneen, president of International Telephone & Telegraph received $639,724. Philip B. Hofmann of Johnson & Johnson received $576,383. William S. Vaughn, chairman of Eastman Kodak, received $348,000.

Q *I would like to know who said, "War is hell."—Margaret Medford, Lake City, Fla.*

A The statement is attributed to Civil War Gen. William Tecumseh Sherman (1820-1891), the Union general who led the march from Atlanta to the sea in 1864. But what he actually said in 1880 was: "There is many a boy here today who looks on war as all glory but, boys, it is all hell."

Q *When Lyndon Johnson, our ex-president, appears on television, how much does he get paid for the interview?—Nellie Richards, Dallas, Tex.*

Lyndon Johnson

A CBS-TV pays him $100,000 per interview in a package deal which includes the publication of his memoirs by a CBS subsidiary, Holt, Rinehart & Winston.

Q *What happened to Abigail McCarthy, the Senator's wife? Is she divorced or what?—Cathy McGuire, Portsmouth, Va.*

A Mrs. Eugene McCarthy is separated from her husband, is writing a book about his 1968 campaign.

Q *Was the great country-western-soul singer Ray Charles born blind? If not, when did he become blind?—Gina Pock, Yakima, Wash.*

A Charles, 39, lost his sight at age 7, after a two-year bout with glaucoma.

Q *I would like to find out if Spiro Agnew was ever a manager of a supermarket and from which law school if any he was graduated. And at what age? And wasn't he originally a Democrat?—Arthur Ackley, Washington, D.C.*

A Spiro Agnew (original family name—Anagnostopoulos) worked as manager of a supermarket, claims adjuster for the Lumberman's Mutual Casualty Company, and as a clerk for the Maryland Casualty Company. World War II interrupted his law studies and he finally earned his law degree in 1947 from the Baltimore Law School at age 28. Originally a Democrat, he switched to the Republican Party on the advice of a law partner, E. Lester Barrett.

Josef Stalin

Q *Is it true that Josef Stalin imprisoned the world-renowned aircraft designer, Andrei Tupolev, in the purge of the 1930's?—Walter Edelstein, Cleveland, Ohio.*

A Yes, Stalin suffered from maniacal suspicions, sent thousands of Russia's most talented men to Siberian concentration camps. Tupolev was rescued from prison by Chief Marshal of Soviet Aviation Alexander Golovanov. He went to Stalin one day and asked why Tupolev had been imprisoned. Stalin said there was some suspicion concerning Tupolev's friendship with foreign governments. Said Golovanov in amazement, "Surely you don't believe that nonsense?" Stalin agreed that it sounded ridiculous. A month later Tupolev was released from jail, is today the Soviet Union's most honored and revered aircraft designer.

Golovanov's memoirs are appearing in the Soviet literary magazine, *Oktyabr.*

Q *Is Shirley MacLaine, the movie star, dumping her husband to marry the NBC-TV commentator Sandy Vanocur?—F.G., New York City.*

A Miss MacLaine and Mr. Vanocur are the closest of friends, but Miss MacLaine has a tacit understanding with her husband, Steve Parker, which permits free-wheeling on the part of each.

Q *I have read that there was a feud between Gen. Douglas MacArthur and Gen. Ike Eisenhower, that they really detested each other. Was this so?—Claude Easterley, Providence, R.I.*

Dwight Eisenhower

A MacArthur was jealous of Eisenhower, was once reported to have described Eisenhower as "the best clerk who ever served under me." Eisenhower considered MacArthur a melodramatic ham whose word was not his bond, said many times sarcastically that he had "studied dramatics" under MacArthur.

Q *Is Richard Nixon a member of the Lakeside Golf Club in North Hollywood? I was in the locker room the other day, and I noticed that locker #381 had his name on it. How long has Nixon been a member of this club?—John Palmieri, Los Angeles, Calif.*

A Nixon does not belong to the Lakeside Golf Club. Once in a great while he plays there with member Bob Hope who has locker #386. Actually, the name Richard M. Nixon on locker #381 is a gag, used to impress visitors. When a guest checks in at Lakeside and asks to play a round of golf, he is frequently told, "Sure thing, just throw your clothes in Dick Nixon's locker. It's #381, and it's open. The president won't be going around today."

Q *Is it true that actress Lee Remick has become the femme fatale of Europe, that she is bowling over every man in her path, that she was recently named "the other woman" in a famous divorce case, that she has never recovered from her friendship with John F. Kennedy?—T.P., Philadelphia, Pa.*

A Actress Lee Remick, 34, divorced from her husband, TV producer Bill Colleran, in Mexico last year, was recently named as "the other woman" in London by British actress Valerie Gearon. Miss Gearon was granted a divorce on the grounds of her husband's alleged adultery with Miss Remick. Valerie Gearon's ex-husband is William "Kip" Gowans, an assistant film director, who charms women with his tenderness, understanding, and attention. He is 30. Valerie Gearon appeared in the film, *Nine Hours to Rama*, and more recently as Anne Boleyn's sister in *Anne of the Thou-*

sand Days. Miss Remick has known or met many men in her time, among them the late John F. Kennedy, Gov. Nelson Rockefeller and others.

Q *Shocking, isn't it, that Olof Palme, prime minister of Sweden, was not invited to the White House when he was in Washington some weeks ago. How come?—Peter Olafson, St. Paul, Minn.*

A Palme, 43, a graduate in 1948 of Kenyon College, Gambier, Ohio, is against the U.S. involvement in Vietnam. Sweden has given sanctuary to U.S. Army deserters. President Nixon was showing his disagreement with the Swedish attitude by not inviting Palme to the White House. The Swedish prime minister, however, did spend a few hours with Secretary of State William Rogers.

Q *Is the Catholic Church gaining or losing membership in the U.S.?—Xavier Collins, Chicago, Ill.*

A For the first time in this century the Roman Catholic Church in the U.S. has suffered a decline in membership. There are now 47,872,089 Catholics in the U.S.A., a decrease of 1,149 from a year ago.

Q *Sophia Loren and Marcello Mastroianni are making a film called* The Priest's Wife. *A drama or a comedy?—Neil d'Angelo, Atlantic City, N.J.*

Sophia Loren

Marcello Mastroianni

A A comedy about a priest who has an affair with a woman he passes off as his sister.

Q *I am a resident of Alabama. During the recent political campaign between George Wallace and Governor Brewer we were told that Brewer's wife is an alcoholic, that the Brewers' two daughters were pregnant by Negroes, and that the State of Alabama was in danger of Negro domination unless we voted for George Wallace. Was any of this true?—D.L., Huntsville, Ala.*

A None of it.

Q *Why would a man like Howard Hughes become the largest gambling operator in the world? I mean gambling just involves money. It doesn't produce real goods. Surely Hughes is not interested in making more money.—Owen Roberts, Lake Tahoe, Nev.*

A Hughes owns six casinos in Las Vegas, one in Reno, with 221 tables for roulette, craps, and blackjack, plus 2,275 slot machines. His casinos account for about 15 percent of the $550 million wagered annually in Nevada. Hughes moves in mysterious ways. Why at this point he should devote the remaining years of his life to the organization of a gambling empire, only he knows. He is already a billionaire.

Q *Is Audrey Hepburn washed up as a screen star? Did she have a menopausal baby? How old is she?—Edna Hutchins, Monroe, N.C.*

Audrey Hepburn

A Audrey Hepburn, 41, mother of a new son, may be finished as a film star but there is still a place for her in television.

Q *How much is Lawrence Welk worth? Is he a skin-flint and penny-pincher as I have heard? Does he pay his musicians more than union scale?—Louise Allenberg, Pittsburgh, Pa.*

A Welk, 67, is worth at least $20 million, much of it in real estate. He is a penny-pincher, largely because he has never forgotten the traumatic poverty of his early youth in Strasburg, North Dakota. Welk has been known to pay some musicians more than union scale, but not many, and not frequently.

Q *Who was Charles Carroll in American history? I know he signed the Declaration of Independence.—Lena Tryon, Baltimore, Md.*

A Charles Carroll of Carrollton, Maryland (born in Annapolis, 1737, died in Baltimore, 1832), was the last signer of the Declaration of Independence to die. He was also at age 95 reputed to be the wealthiest man in the U.S. A lawyer who served as a senator from Maryland, he was one of the great patriots and landowners of the Revolutionary War period.

WALTER SCOTT'S
PERSONALITY PARADE®

October 4, 1970

Caroline and John-John Kennedy

Q *I would like to know what Jackie Kennedy's kids, Caroline and John, call Onassis. Do they call him "Daddy"?— Mrs. Myron Knight, Seattle, Wash.*

A No, they call him "Ari," short for Aristotle.

Q *I understand that a close friend of Madame Thieu has made more money from the war in Vietnam than any other single individual in Southeast Asia. Can you identify him?—Roland Clark, Cambridge, Mass.*

A Most probably you have in mind Nguyen Thi Hai, an importer of pharmaceuticals in Saigon. Hai is President Thieu's leading financial backer and a close friend indeed of President Thieu's wife.

Q *What's happened to Ron Ridenhour, the soldier who broke the story and disclosed the truth about the Mylai massacre?—Alex Pipley, Phoenix, Ariz.*

A Ridenhour is in Vietnam writing a series of articles on the American GI for Dispatch News Service.

Q *Is legalized gambling coming to New Jersey?—Roger Fianetti, Asbury Park, N.J.*

A A bill has been introduced in the New Jersey Legislature which would legalize gambling in Atlantic City only.

Q *Is Herb Klein, President Nixon's communications director, an Oriental?— L.T., La Jolla, Calif.*

A No, he merely looks and on occasion behaves like one, inscrutable, secretive and impenetrable.

Q *Why does Ronald Reagan, the governor of California, refuse to release a financial statement of his worth?—Norton Higgs, Sacramento, Calif.*

A Reagan is a millionaire, largely through real estate deals involving ranch land near Los Angeles. He has been accused of having millionaires as political associates, prefers as of this writing not to reveal his financial worth.

Q The Wall Street Journal *claims that U.S. soldiers looted a village in Cambodia. Is that story true? If so, have the troops responsible been punished?— Philip Colman, Los Angeles, Calif.*

A The story is true. It was filed by Peter Arnett, the Pulitzer Prize-winning correspondent of the Associated Press who was an eyewitness. Arnett's report, however, was deleted from the AP wire in the U.S. The AP sent the story out on its foreign wires, later admitted that it was denied to U.S. readers because of an "error in judgment." To date, none of the U.S. soldiers who looted the Cambodian village has been punished.

Eddie Fisher

Q *Eddie Fisher used to earn $700,000 a year. How could such a man go bankrupt?—Ellen Singleton, Ft. Lauderdale, Fla.*

A Fisher is a compulsive gambler, used to drop tremendous sums at Las Vegas gambling casinos. He also spent money as if it were going out of fashion. Among the debts listed in his bankruptcy petition: $40,980 to a jeweler.

Q *Where does most of the heroin in the United States come from, Mexico, France, or Turkey?—Ann Lillis White, Asheville, N.C.*

A Turkey is the primary source of illicit opium. Most of the laboratories where crude morphine is refined into heroin are located in and around Marseilles, France. "If we can eliminate Turkey as a source of opium," says John Ingersoll, director of the U.S. Federal Bureau of Narcotics and Dangerous Drugs, "we estimate that we could reduce by 50 percent the amount of heroin coming into the United States."

Pat Nixon

Q *I have heard it said many times that Pat Nixon is unhappy in the White House and regrets the day her husband entered politics. Is this true?—Mrs. Emma Little, New York, N.Y.*

A Pat Nixon hoped in 1962 after Nixon was defeated in the California gubernatorial election that her husband would retire from running for elective office. But she is reconciled to the fact that essentially Nixon is an incurably political personality. She anxiously looks forward, however, to the day when they will be living in San Clemente, California.

Q *Now that Otto Preminger has confessed to his affair with the late Gypsy Rose Lee, explaining that she gave birth to his son out of wedlock—what effect will this have upon Preminger's film career?—Diane Hutter, Terre Haute, Ind.*

Otto Preminger

A It will probably cost him an invitation to the White House.

Q *Why do historians blame the Cuban Bay of Pigs fiasco on President Jack Kennedy? Wasn't it really President Eisenhower's fault?—David Leeds, Cambridge, Mass.*

A It was President Eisenhower who gave Allen Dulles, then in charge of the Central Intelligence Agency, the go-ahead on the agency's plan to train and equip Cuban exiles in the United States to invade Cuba and overthrow Castro.

When President Kennedy took office, he foolishly followed the advice of his military and permitted what was obviously an ill-prepared invasion of Cuba. This resulted in the Bay of Pigs fiasco for which he generously assumed the blame. Similarly, when Lyndon Johnson succeeded to the presidency, he, too, followed the advice of the military and continued the fiasco Kennedy had begun in Vietnam. The reluctance of incumbent presidents to alter the foreign policy of their predecessors is one of the great weaknesses of the American presidency.

Q *I hear that Priscilla Presley has given Elvis the final warning—one more extracurricular dame and she's had it. Your comment, please.—T.R., Memphis, Tenn.*

A It is not the happiest of marriages, but the Presleys have a darling daughter, Lisa, three; and both are trying to work out a modus vivendi under particularly trying circumstances—especially since Elvis is primarily a sexual creature.

Q *Does anyone know how much the General Motors strike which began September 14, 1970, and lasted ten weeks, cost the nation?—Mrs. Richard Delaney, Boston, Mass.*

A According to James Roche, chief executive officer of General Motors: "Exact measurements are impossible, but it is estimated that every working day of the strike there were production losses of about 26,000 cars and trucks in the U.S. and Canada.

"The employees lost $12 to $14 million a day in wages. The corporation lost $90 million a day in sales. Suppliers lost $40 million a day. And governments lost $20 million a day in taxes just from the manufacture and sale of vehicles alone."

Q *Who said, "The silliest woman can manage a clever man," and who said, "Marriage must be a relation either of sympathy or of conquest"?—Mrs. Peter Elson, Palo Alto, Calif.*

A First quotation: poet Rudyard Kipling. Second quotation: writer George Eliot.

Richard Nixon

Q *Is it true that President Nixon has asked Golda Meir for the loan of Israeli General Moshe Dayan?—Freda Welborne, San Leandro, Calif.*

A No, it's part of a popular joke. Supposedly the president said to Mrs. Meir on a recent visit, "How come a small country like Israel can win a war in six days and a large country like ours can't win in Vietnam after ten years?" And supposedly Mrs. Meir said it was because her country was blessed with many great generals.

President Nixon is then supposed to have said, "Suppose we borrow from you General Moshe Dayan and General Itzhak Rabin. Whom would you want in return?"

Golda Meir thought for a moment, then said, "General Motors, General Foods, General Electric, and General Telephone."

David Frost and Diahann Carroll

Q *If David Frost marries Diahann Carroll, will Westinghouse cancel his TV contract because of the interracial marriage?—E.T. Ulster, Pittsburgh, Pa.*

A TV cancellations depend almost entirely on ratings. Should Frost marry Miss Carroll and his ratings thereupon decline, that would constitute grounds for cancellation, but not the marriage per se.

Q *I would like to know something about Edward Gierek, the new leader of Poland who succeeded Gomulka.—Robert Olszowski, Cleveland, Ohio.*

A Gierek was born in Poland on January 6, 1913. After his father died in a mine accident he and his mother emigrated to France where he worked as a miner at age 13. In 1931 he joined the French Communist Party, was deported to Poland in 1934. In 1939 he went to Belgium where he joined the Belgian Communist Party and again fomented labor and political troubles. After World War II, he returned to Poland where he began working in the Central Committee of the Polish United Workers Party.

WALTER SCOTT'S
PERSONALITY PARADE®

April 11, 1971

Henry Kissinger

Q *Recently Sen. Stuart Symington of Missouri said that according to the Washington cocktail party circuit, Henry Kissinger had more power than Secretary of State William Rogers. In reply, President Nixon described Symington's allegation as a "cheap shot." Two questions: (1) Does Symington know what he is talking about? (2) Was the president correct in his "cheap shot" assessment?—Marshall F., McLean, Va.*

A It is probable that more people in the United States have heard of Henry Kissinger, the president's national security adviser, than have heard of William Rogers, his secretary of state. Certainly, Kissinger of Harvard (Class of '50) has been more widely and intensively publicized than Rogers of Colgate (Class of '34).

Moreover, Kissinger is the White House intellectual-in-residence and President Nixon's personal "intellectual ghost." His background, education, and expertise on foreign affairs surpass Rogers'.

As to their relative importance in the presidential hierarchy, it is significant that a federal grand jury in Harrisburg, Pennsylvania, recently indicted a group of anti-war priests and nuns for allegedly planning to kidnap Dr. Kissinger as the *eminence grise* of the Administration. No group of priests, nuns, rabbis, ministers, or even students has ever been indicted for plotting to kidnap Bill Rogers.

The Kissinger vs. Rogers controversy is of President Nixon's making. Until recently he has afforded Kissinger far more visibility than Rogers. Symington's statement—"Wherever one goes in the afternoon or evening around this town, one hears our very able secretary of state

laughed at. People say he is secretary of state in title only"—was an exaggeration. So, too, it appears, was President Nixon's denigration of it as a "cheap shot."

Symington, however, was not far off the mark. He was reflecting the fear, held in many academic and political circles, that the power to make and affect U.S. foreign policy was being concentrated in the Kissinger White House enclave without any accountability to Congress on Kissinger's part. Whenever senators want to question Kissinger about his role, advice, position papers and predilections, especially on Indochina, Nixon invokes his "executive privilege," and advises Henry to say nothing.

What must be remembered, of course, is that all men of power, including Kissinger, Symington, Rogers and Nixon, are subject to vanities, frustration, hurts and irritations. In the heat of the moment they occasionally make a remark which in the later cool of reflection they would have preferred to have left unsaid.

Q *Has Ryan O'Neal, the star of* Love Story, *traded in his wife for Barbra Streisand?—Leona Paige, Dallas, Tex.*

O'Neal and Young

A Sadly, Ryan O'Neal and LeighTaylor-Young who met and married while working on the TV version of *Peyton Place*, have agreed to a trial separation. The O'Neal-Streisand friendship should be considered at this point as merely "interlude."

Barbra Streisand

Q *Hans Schmidt-Horix, the West German Ambassador to Portugal, was found dead with his wife last November, apparently the result of a suicide pact. The East Germans allege that the couple was actually murdered by an organization called "Odessa." What is Odessa?—B.D., Glendale, Calif.*

A Odessa stands for "Organisation Der Ehemaligen SS Angehoerigen," or organization of former members of the SS, founded after the war to smuggle war criminals out of Germany and provide them with new identities and new lives.

According to the "Democratic German Report," published in East Berlin, Schmidt-Horix was a former SS intelligence officer who served the Hitler regime in Paris, Washington and Lisbon.

The East Germans charged that since 1945 Odessa has arranged a number of "suicides" of former Nazis, including Schmidt-Horix, who were believed ready to name accomplices. There is no proof to back up these allegations, however.

John Wayne

Q *We have heard that John Wayne is only five feet three inches tall and that he wears elevated boots. Also that extra-small saloon doors make him appear taller. Can you tell us how tall he really is?—Jeanne Sagan and Denise Kessler, Clarion, Pa.*

A John Wayne is six feet four, weighs 240 pounds.

Q *I would like to know how many of the United States presidents were Freemasons. Please name them.—Claudia Simonoma, Sacramento, Calif.*

A Thirteen American presidents were acknowledged Freemasons: George Washington (Master of the Alexandria, Virginia, lodge), James Monroe, Andrew Jackson (Grand Master of Tennessee), James Polk, James Buchanan, Andrew Johnson, James Garfield, William McKinley, Theodore Roosevelt, William Howard Taft, Warren G. Harding, Franklin D. Roosevelt and Harry S. Truman. Other famous American Masons: Benjamin Franklin, Paul Revere, John Hancock, Davy Crockett.

Eddie Fisher

Q *How much did Eddie Fisher owe when he declared bankruptcy? Did he blow his roll on dames or gambling?—Peter Sherman, Atlantic City, N.J.*

A On August 14, 1970, Fisher filed for bankruptcy in San Juan, Puerto Rico. He listed $916,300 in debts and $40,000 in assets in municipal bonds held by the Bank of America as security on a loan. He spent a million in high and fancy living.

Q *I've heard that Roger Vadim got tired of kooky Jane Fonda and has gone back to his first wife, Brigitte Bardot. What's the story?—Helen Wicker, Norfolk, Va.*

A Vadim and Bardot, who were married from 1952-1957, have decided to make another film together. Most probably it will be based on *Creezy*, a novel dealing with the unhappy love affair of a politician and a model. Bardot and Vadim have been seen together in France, but Brigitte says no love affair is taking place. She is in fact in love with another man, hopes to make him her fourth husband. Vadim, who just directed a resounding flop at MGM, *Pretty Maids All in a Row*, is estranged from Jane Fonda, espouser of various causes.

Q *Is former heavyweight champion Joe Louis on relief?—Mary Ann Motley, Chicago, Ill.*

A No, he is working as a greeter at Caesars Palace in Las Vegas.

Joe Louis

Q *Why is it that some politicians say 45,000 U.S. troops have been killed in Indochina since 1961 and others say 55,000? Is there not an exact or more accurate accounting? Which figure is true?—Mrs. L.E. Nelson, Jamestown, Va.*

A Approximately 54,500 American servicemen have lost their lives in Indochina since 1961. The Defense Department explains that approximately 45,000 have been killed in combat. Approximately another 9,500 have died in non-hostile incidents such as drownings, slayings, and traffic accidents. In addition, approximately 300,000 U.S. servicemen have been wounded in ten years.

Q *Has any American ever been nominated for the presidency three times by a major party and lost each time?—Claire Ricci, Utica, N.Y.*

A Yes, Henry Clay and William Jennings Bryan, the only three-time losers in American history.

Q *On the back of every U.S. one-dollar bill there are three sayings: (1) In God we trust; (2) Annuit coeptis; (3) Novus ordo seclorum. What do the last two mean?—Oron Jackson, Ft. Worth, Tex.*

A Annuit coeptis means in rough translation, "He has smiled on our undertakings (or plans or beginnings)." Novus ordo seclorum translates into "A new order of the ages."

Frank Sinatra

Q *They say that more than anything else in his life Frank Sinatra is most proud of his friendship with the late President John F. Kennedy, that all over his house Sinatra has signs which read, "President John F. Kennedy Slept Here." Is any of this on the level?—Eva Vance, Cathedral City, Calif.*

A Sinatra, 56, has one plaque on a bedroom door in his Palm Springs home. It reads, "John F. Kennedy Slept Here: November 6 and 7, 1960." At one time John F. Kennedy and Sinatra were friendly. After Kennedy was elected president, however, the FBI sent down to Robert Kennedy, the president's brother and attorney general, a dossier on Sinatra and his underworld associations. John F. Kennedy thereupon kept his distance from Sinatra. When he visited Palm Springs he preferred to occupy the Bing Crosby residence in nearby Palm Desert.

Fidel Castro

Q *Fidel Castro's sister, Juanita, claims that the new Russian envoy to Cuba is an expert in nuclear rocketry. Is this capable of verification?—Adolfo Gomez, N. Miami, Fla.*

A Juanita Castro, an outspoken opponent of her brother's Communist policies in Cuba, is correct. The Soviet Ambassador to Cuba is Nikita Pavlovich Tolubeyev, an expert in the installation of nuclear rockets. Before his assignment to Havana, Tolubeyev was stationed in Cyprus where he helped run the Soviet's Near East espionage network.

Q *Is Pan American Airways still accepting reservations for trips to the moon?—Celia Gordeen, Los Angeles, Calif*

A No, Pan Am closed its books for that trip after accepting 90,000 reservations, commencing in 1964 up through March 3, 1971.

WALTER SCOTT'S

PERSONALITY PARADE®

May 23, 1971

Q *I understand that Hollywood does not like Ali MacGraw, her husband Bob Evans, or actor Ryan O'Neal. Is this why* Love Story *failed to win an Academy Award?—Lois Sonnenfeld, Larchmont, N.Y.*

A Ali MacGraw and Ryan O'Neal are personally well-liked in the motion picture industry. *Love Story* won an Oscar for its musical score, but members of the Academy regard the film as successful commercial claptrap and little else. There is no correlation between films of distinction and their box-office draw.

William Calley

Q *How do the South Vietnamese feel about Lieutenant Calley and his sentence?— Henry Bowman, Riverside, Calif.*

A President Thieu, who originally described the My Lai massacre as phony Viet Cong propaganda, declared Calley's life imprisonment sentence to be "well-deserved." When President Nixon ordered Calley removed from the Fort Benning stockade and placed him under house arrest, however, Catholic and Buddhist newspapers in South Vietnam objected to such leniency. An editorial in *Duoc Nha Nam*, a neutral and widely respected religious newspaper, denounced American justice as "justice for white Americans, despising and trampling upon all mankind."

According to a poll conducted for the American Broadcasting Company by the Lou Harris organization, however, 77 percent of the people in the U.S. believe that Lieutenant Calley was singled out for court-martial and punishment even though the My Lai massacre involved others, including his superior officers. Only 24 percent agreed with the guilty verdict. Some 81 percent believed that other incidents such as My Lai have occurred in the war.

Billy Graham

Q *Does Evangelist Billy Graham suffer from cancer of the throat? Isn't that why he was hospitalized?—P.T., Asheville, N.C.*

A According to Graham, 52, he underwent surgery on February 10, 1971, for the removal of some salivary glands, "the doctors then ordered me to take an extended period of rest because they found I was going too fast."

Q *I note that President Nixon has spoken out against abortion, reversing the liberal Defense Department posture on termination of unwanted pregnancies. In doing this, is the president supporting the position of the Roman Catholic Church or his own Quaker faith?—Mrs. T.Y.O., Whittier, Calif.*

A The Quaker faith has no ruling on abortion. Each Quaker is free to make up his or her own mind on the subject. President Nixon's position, however, was made evident in the following statement released at the Western White House, San Clemente, California, April 3, 1971:

"Historically, laws regulating abortion in the United States have been the province of the states, not the federal government. That remains the situation today, as one state after another takes up this question, debates it and decides it. That is where the decisions should be made.

"Partly for that reason, I have directed that the policy on abortions at American military bases in the United States be made to correspond with the laws of the states where those bases are located. If the laws in a particular state restrict abortions, the rules at the military base hospitals are to correspond to that law.

"The effect of this directive is to reverse service regulations issued last summer, which had liberalized the rules on abortions at military hospitals. The new ruling supersedes this—and has been put into effect by the Secretary of Defense.

"But while this matter is being debated in state capitals, and weighed by various courts, the country has a right to know my personal views.

"From personal and religious beliefs I consider abortion an unacceptable form of population control. Further, unrestricted abortion policies, or abortion on demand, I cannot square with my personal belief in the sanctity of human life—including the life of the yet unborn. For, surely, the unborn have rights also, recognized in law, recognized even in principles expounded by the United Nations.

"Ours is a nation with a Judaeo-Christian heritage. It is also a nation with serious social problems—problems of malnutrition, of broken homes, of poverty, and of delinquency. But none of these problems justifies such a solution.

"A good and generous people will not opt, in my view, for this kind of alternative to its social dilemmas. Rather, it will open its hearts and homes to the unwanted children of its own, as it has done for the unwanted millions of other lands."

Tommy Corcoran

Q *Is there any chance that Tommy Corcoran, the old New Dealer, will marry Mrs. Anna Chennault?—Ed Wade, Washington, D.C.*

A There is always a chance, but at this time, not much. Says Mrs. Chennault: "I am very happy being single."

Marie Dressler

Q *Please identify if possible the following quotation: "It's not how old you are but how you are old."—Patricia St. Cloud, Kenosha, Wis.*

A It was a favorite saying of the late film star, Marie Dressler.

Q *Is it true that President Nixon's first girlfriend, Ola Welch Jobe, has all his love letters in the Bank of America vault in Whittier, California?—Mrs. E.L. Kline, Tucson, Ariz.*

A Mrs. Jobe, who saves everything from old twine to old newspapers, has naturally saved the Richard Nixon letters from 1930-1936. They make fascinating reading, indicating as they do the full range of Nixon's character as a young man. The letters, however, are not stored in the Whittier branch of the Bank of America. Mrs. Jobe keeps them elsewhere.

Q *Actress Patty Duke recently gave birth to a son whom she named Sean Duke. Who is the father, her husband, Mike Tell, or Desi Arnaz, Jr.?—T.G., Denver, Colo.*

A At this point no one is sure. Her legal husband, Mike Tell, believes the child was fathered either by him or by Desi Arnaz, Jr.

Q *Ronald Reagan, the millionaire governor of California, paid no state income tax last year. He claims a lawyer made out his income tax. Who was the lawyer? I would like to hire him myself.—Mrs. Louise Smith, San Francisco, Calif.*

A Roy Miller of the Los Angeles law firm of Gibson, Dunn & Crutcher.

Q *Henry Kissinger, the president's foreign affairs adviser—is he a Republican or a Democrat?—Newton Binder, Cambridge, Mass.*

A Neither. He is an independent, voting the man and not the party.

Q *Has Richard Nixon ever been in North Vietnam?—Olga Hennessey, Hempstead, N.Y.*

A Says the president: "I am one of the few people, at least in public life, who has been to Hanoi. I was there in 1953 and then came back in 1956."

Q *Is Elliott Gould quitting movies? What caused his crackup? Is he really going with an 18-year-old girl?—Vee Darby, Philadelphia, Pa.*

A Gould blew his stack on the set of *A Glimpse of Tiger*, a picture which has been canceled. He was a victim of physical and emotional exhaustion. He has since gone off with his new girlfriend, Jennifer Bogart, age 18.

Gould and Bogart

Q *Children of college professors—are they given free tuition when they attend college?—V. Thomas, Seattle, Wash.*

A "Professional courtesy" in private universities is extended to the offspring of university faculty. In some cases tuition is entirely forgiven, in other cases 50 percent discounts are offered, or sums up to $1,500.

Q *I would like to know the role occupied by Johann Winckelmann in history.— Mrs. Dora Lewis, New Orleans, La.*

A Johann Winckelmann (1717-68), the homosexual son of a Prussian cobbler, grew up to become the "Father of Archaeology," a great classical scholar, and one of the world's foremost art historians.

Lana Turner

Q *Can you tell me why Lana Turner gave her seventh husband, Ron Dante, $200,000 and now wants it back?— Judy Strange, El Paso, Tex.*

A Miss Turner insists that the document she signed turning $200,000 over to Dante for helping her through a trying emotional time is not valid because of the condition she was in when she made the grant.

Woody Allen and Louise Lasser

Q *Louise Lasser—who's in Woody Allen's film, Bananas—is she the same girl who does those "good daughter" and "good wife" television commercials for a cough medicine?—S.G.R., Staten Island, N.Y.*

A Yes. Also, she's Woody Allen's ex-wife.

Q *Will General Abrams or President Nixon or Ambassador Bunker ever tell the American public the truth about Lam Son 719, the Laos invasion—how many troops the South Vietnamese lost, how many of our helicopters were lost, how many of the enemy were killed, whether or not the invasion was a victory or a defeat?—Charles W. Peters, Arlington, Va.*

A The fact that to date none of these gentlemen has made such an announcement indicates that possibly the Laos invasion was anything from a disappointment to a disaster. Foreign sources classify it as a defeat for the ARVN (Army of the Republic of Vietnam) but it is fatuous to expect President Nixon to use that word to describe the incursion since it was he who gave the go-ahead. The White House position is that it is still too early to tell. President Thieu of South Vietnam called it "a great victory," but his vice-president, Marshal Ky, says it was not. Some American officers in Vietnam diplomatically describe Lam Son 719 as "counterproductive." Others maintain it helped stem the flow of supplies down the Ho Chi Minh Trail.

Q *What are Charles Lindbergh's five children doing today?—Mrs. P. Edwards, Oakland, Calif.*

A Lindbergh's son Jon, 38, is a marine biologist near Seattle directing a "fish-farming" project; his son Land, 34, is a Montana rancher. Both are married.

Daughters Anne, 30, and Reeve 25, both married, live respectively in France and Vermont. Son Scott, 28, is a student in Europe.

Q *What has happened to the singing group called the Monkees? I hear they joined other groups—is this true?—Claire McKenzie, Schenectady, N.Y.*

A The Monkees have gone separate ways since they busted up in 1969. Mike Nesmith has formed his own group, The First National Band, which records for RCA. Davy Jones has made recordings solo and with Mickey Dolenz.

Daniel Patrick Moynihan

Q *I've heard a lot about the "Moynihan Report." Can you tell me something about the person who wrote it and its purpose?—E.C.H., Springfield, Gardens, N.Y.*

A Daniel Patrick Moynihan was LBJ's assistant secretary of labor when he wrote the controversial report in 1965, then served Nixon as a presidential counselor, resigned last November to return to his teaching post at Harvard. Purpose of the report was to analyze the high rate of failures by Negroes in Selective Service exams. Many black spokesmen objected to its major conclusion: that the instability of the Negro family and the absence of fathers in many of them was a main cause of ghetto poverty, illiteracy and despair.

Christiaan Barnard

Q *Dr. Christiaan Barnard, the heart transplant man, says fellow doctors have been boycotting him, sending patients "home to die" rather than letting them undergo heart transplants. Is Barnard right?—Evelyn Layne Underwood, Chicago, Ill.*

A There is some doubt at this point as to whether heart transplants are worth what they cost in time, money, travail, and treatment, since most die within 18 months. Among some physicians Dr. Barnard has earned the reputation of being a publicity hound.

Q *Regarding the appointment of three girls, ages 14, 15 and 17, as pages in the U.S. Senate—what education and training do they have that would entitle them to the salary of $7,380 a year?—Ruth G. Guisti, Sacramento, Calif.*

A The only qualifications for senate pages are that they be 14 to 17 years old and have completed the eighth grade. In the case of a female page, the appointment senator is responsible for her safety in travel between the Capitol and her place of residence.

Q *I understand that Dr. Samuel Johnson, the great 18th-century English writer, once made a crack that applies to the Women's Lib campaign today. Do you know what it could be?—D. Lapey, Newark, N.J.*

A The bearish Johnson growled: "Nature has given women so much power that the law has very wisely given them little."

Q *Retired Maj. Gen. Carl C. Turner—charged with income tax evasion and selling government firearms—will he still receive his U.S. Army retirement pay?—Helene A. Ellison, Orlando, Fla.*

A Yes, at the rate of $1,770.75 per month.

PERSONALITY PARADE®

July 25, 1971

Q *There has been talk of starring those two delightful actors, Rock Hudson and Jim Nabors, in The Odd Couple. Would those two stars consider playing with each other? Can you reveal anything about their married lives? I thought Jim Nabors was married to his two dogs, Goober and Baby.—Mrs. R.S., Mobile, Ala.*

Jim Nabors

A TV star Jim Nabors of *Gomer Pyle* fame, born in Sylacauga, Alabama, 40 years ago, has never been married. Rock Hudson, born Roy Scherer, Jr., 45 years ago in Winnetka, Illinois, was married for a short time to Phyllis Gates, his agent's secretary. They were divorced on August 13, 1958. Hudson and Nabors are

Rock Hudson

mutual admirers and would probably consider playing together in *The Odd Couple* except that Tony Randall and Jack Klugman already star in the TV series of the same name.

Q *Is it true that Lyndon Johnson deliberately deceived the American public on the Vietnam war? Is that not the true substance of the Pentagon Papers?—George Haggerty, Palo Alto, Calif.*

A One of the great and grand old men of the U.S. Senate is Clinton P. Anderson, 75 (D., N. Mex.). A former Congressman and Secretary of Agriculture, Anderson has served in the Senate since 1948. He knows Lyndon Johnson well, supported Johnson in his drive for the Democratic presidential nomination against John F. Kennedy in 1960.

An outstanding legislator of unshakable integrity and unblemished reputation, Anderson in his book of memoirs, *Outsider in the Senate* (World Publishing Co., 1970), writes the following on PP. 315-316:

"President Johnson, I think, might even have survived the disaster of the Vietnam war but he failed utterly to understand the feelings of the American people about it. It seemed to me that he insisted on treating the people as children, who could not be told the truth and who had no right to make their own views known on policy. In a way, this was how he ran the Senate during his years as Majority Leader. It never occurred to him to accommodate himself to the will of the Senate. . . Lyndon was always concealing instead of revealing openly what he was doing and what was at stake. I believe he was not forced out of office because he lost the Vietnam war, but because he lost the confidence of the American people in how he was conducting it. The tragedy was that his defeat was so unnecessary, for Lyndon Johnson behaved with the public good as his goal, but he hid so much from view that the public was never sure that was so."

Q *If the North Vietnamese will return all of our men who are prisoners of war, why won't President Nixon withdraw all U.S. forces from Vietnam by December, 31, 1971?—Ann Kennedy, Lexington, Mass.*

A According to President Nixon's press secretary, Ron Ziegler, the withdrawal of U.S. forces by the end of the year would be "so precipitous it would not give the South Vietnamese an opportunity to determine their own destiny."

The Nixon policy in Vietnam is not dedicated solely to the recovery of our men who have been taken prisoners of war. It is aimed at providing the Saigon government with a "reasonable chance" to survive after the U.S. withdraws. Mr. Nixon refuses, however, to define "reasonable chance" in terms of time. His option to retain the U.S. presence in Vietnam remains open-ended.

Q *Was actor Audie Murphy under contract to the Teamsters Union when he was killed in a plane crash?—Thomas Lloyd, Glendale, Calif.*

A He was not; he was working, however, for the release of Teamsters Union boss James Hoffa from jail. Murphy, who filed for bankruptcy in 1968, was hoping to get a Teamsters Union pension fund loan to reconstruct his financial base. He felt that if he could effect the release of Hoffa, the Teamsters boss would help him.

Q *I understand that Erich Segal, the author of* Love Story, *has been*

Erich Segal

laughed off the Yale campus. Is it because his students are jealous of him?—Mrs. Ronald Armstrong, East Haven, Conn.

A No. It's simply because they consider Segal's talent as a novelist microscopic and his post-*Love Story* behavior inexcusably immodest.

Q *I read that the U.S. will not allow British actress Vanessa Redgrave to enter this country. Isn't the true reason her unusual sex life?—Betty Scaife, Jersey City, N.J.*

A Vanessa Redgrave has given birth to a child out of wedlock which may raise the question of moral turpitude. But she is also a well-known supporter of the black power and anti-Vietnamese-war movements. Moreover, it has been reported recently that she was organizing a group to pressure the British government into granting asylum to American deserters. She is also said to be the financial backer of an underground military newspaper at an American airbase in England.

The visa section of the U.S. Embassy in London probably regards her as a probable troublemaker, and on such grounds is reluctant to grant her a visa. The intervention of Sen. Jacob Javits (R., N.Y.), however, may make a difference if it hasn't already.

WALTER SCOTT'S
PERSONALITY PARADE®
October 31, 1971

Spiro Agnew

Q *Would President Nixon dare appoint Spiro Agnew to the U.S. Supreme Court?—D.L., Baltimore, Md.*

A Nixon will appoint to the Supreme Court those individuals whose conservative judicial philosophy is most akin to his. Politics, of course, will play a major role in the appointment.

Q *If and when Eugene McCarthy divorces Abigail, won't he marry Marya McLaughlin, CBS commentator?— Peter Hayes, Montecito, Calif.*

A It's a possibility. Former Senator McCarthy and Miss McLaughlin have been and still are closest of friends.

Q *Is it true that to make up for the poverty of his youth, Nixon has always been attracted to men of wealth?— Ed Wales, Syracuse, New York.*

A True of Nixon, true of Johnson, true of Eisenhower.

Q *About the U.S. Supreme Court justices. How much do they earn? Also, how many judges on the federal bench, and how many of these are women?—Louis Miller, Freeport, N.Y.*

A The chief justice, Warren Burger, earns $62,500 per year, the other Supreme Court justices $60,000 annually. There are approximately 500 federal judges, four of whom are women: Shirley Hufstedler, 46, of Los Angeles and the 9th Circuit Court of Appeals; and U.S. District Judges Cornelia Kennedy, 48, of Detroit; Constance Motley, 50, of New York City; and Sara Hughes, 75, of Dallas.

Q *Is it not a fact that most of the riots in our federal prisons are started by blacks? What percentage of prisoners in federal prisons are Negro?—Harry Rademacher, Salt Lake City, Utah.*

A Most riots in federal prisons are not begun by blacks. Although blacks account for approximately 12 percent of the total U.S. population, they comprise 27.6 percent of all federal prisoners.

Q *The other day I heard one black man call another black man "a no-good Oreo." Can you tell me what that expression signifies?—Mrs. Helen Lawrence Kent, Greenwich, Conn.*

A It is a synonym for an Uncle Tom, named after the cookie, Oreo, which is black on the outside, white on the inside.

Q *I understand that Senator Ted Kennedy is very much interested in certain angles pertaining to Alaska Airlines. Is this so?—K.L., McLean, Va.*

A Senator Kennedy flies a good deal, meets the pilots and stewardesses of many different airlines, appreciates beauty and competency wherever he finds them.

Angela Davis

Q *Does Angela Davis wear an Afro wig?—Dianne McAvity, Philadelphia, Pa.*

A She does.

Q *Now that Look magazine has expired, is it true that Time, Inc. in bringing out two magazines called Well and Money?—Laura Williston, Buffalo, N.Y.*

A Time, Inc. is polling 500,000 of its book and record customers, asking if they would pay nine dollars per year to become charter members of these two projected monthlies. If Time, Inc. receives enough "yes" replies, it will publish *Well* which deals with preventive health care, and *Money* which deals with management of household finances and personal investments.

Mamie Eisenhower

Q *How old is Mamie Eisenhower?— Edith Gilhorn, Erie, Pa.*

A Seventy-five on November 14.

Frank Sinatra

Q *Does Frank Sinatra plan to enter politics now that he has given up show business?—E.L., Palm Springs, Calif.*

A Sinatra, 55, had little formal schooling, about six months of a high school education in Hoboken, New Jersey. Now that he has retired from show business, he seeks to compensate for his lack of formal schooling. Most recently he has embarked on a crash program dealing with political science. Since Ronald Reagan and George Murphy made it to the top in California politics, there is no reason why Sinatra might not also enter the field. Because of television, politics has become more receptive to actors.

WALTER SCOTT'S
PERSONALITY PARADE®

January 16, 1972

Deneuve and Mastroianni

Q *Is actress Catherine Deneuve carrying actor Marcello Mastroianni's child?— Kay Evans, Asbury Park, N.J.*

A She claims she is.

Q *When I first knew John Tunney, now U.S. Senator from California, his name was Varick Tunney. When did he change it?—Louis Allen, Charlottesville, Va.*

A Tunney was christened John Varick Tunney. He was always called Varick, because he had a brother named Jonathan. When Tunney entered politics he had a polling outfit, Opinion Research of California, poll residents of the Indio-Imperial Valley area on what they thought of the name Varick. Many of them thought it sounded "foreign, Russian, or un-American." He therefore decided to use John, where-upon his brother Jonathan decided to use the name Jay.

Q *I understand that one of the world's richest cities—Beverly Hills, California, has neither a hospital nor a cemetery. Is this true?—Richard Classon, Tucson, Ariz.*

A True.

Q *It is quite obvious that President Nixon is a football "nut." Did he play any other sports in school, such as golf or tennis?—Leif Christianson, Ogden, Utah.*

A At Whittier College, Nixon made the football squad but not the team. He was not what one would call a natural athlete. He plays no tennis. His golf is mediocre because he doesn't play enough. At this point in life, bowling is probably his best sport.

Q *Was Henry Ford II, chairman of the Ford Motor Company, ever thrown out of Yale for cheating?—Stan Earle, New Haven, Conn.*

A Ford, a member of the Class of 1940, turned in a sociology paper written for him by someone else. He did not graduate with his class. Had he repeated the sociology course and written his own paper he would have been permitted to do so. He decided not to accept that option.

Q *Who are the two most prominent and popular conservative columnists in the country?—Hank Loeb, Belmont, Mass.*

A Probably William Buckley and Joseph Alsop.

Angela Lansbury

Q *Has Angela Lansbury, the star of* Mame, *had heroin trouble in her family?— Maxine Ford, Ft. Lauderdale, Fla.*

A Yes, her teenage son, Anthony, now 19, became addicted to heroin whereupon Miss Lansbury relinquished her role in *Mame*, courageously moved her family to a small village in Ireland, Ballycotton, near Cork, where no heroin was available, and her son bravely "kicked the habit."

Q *The late Spyros Skouras, head of 20th Century-Fox, and other Greeks frequently play with beads. There are 33 beads on their strings. Why 33?—Elon Haggard, Haverford, Pa.*

A The number 33 signified the number of years Christ supposedly lived on earth.

Q *Why did James McNeill Whistler call the famous painting of his mother, "Arrangement in Grey and Black" instead of "Whistler's Mother"?—Louis Albertini, Hayward, Calif.*

A Whistler always insisted that a painting be judged by the harmony of its form, color, and line—not by its subject matter.

Q *When I was drafted in the U.S. Army in 1941, I was paid a salary of $21 a month. What's the starting salary for recruits today?—Ted Bernstein, Bergen, N.J.*

A Rookies get $268.50 per month.

Q *Is it true that Julie Andrews has called it quits in Hollywood and is returning to England?—Sylvia Bright, San Jose, Calif.*

A No—the rumor began when she offered her Beverly Hills mansion for sale—asking price: $525,000.

Julie Andrews

WALTER SCOTT'S
PERSONALITY PARADE®

April 30, 1972

Q *What are the statistical chances for Spiro Agnew's eventual elevation to the presidency, assuming (a) that he's retained by President Nixon on the 1972 ticket and (b) that the Republicans win in November?—Arnold Burke, Chicago, Ill.*

A Of the 35 presidents before Nixon, 12 were succeeded by their vice presidents—eight as a result of the president's death, and four by election in their own right. That adds up to historical odds of 1 in 3.

With two-term presidents, the odds are even better. Of the 12 who served two or more terms, six were succeeded by their vice presidents, three by death and three by subsequent election. So if a Nixon-Agnew ticket is reelected, according to history there's a 50-50 chance that Agnew will become president.

Princess Grace and Princess Caroline

Q *Does Princess Grace allow her daughter to be photographed in a bikini, but forbid swimsuit photos of herself because she has a potbelly?—T.G., Binghamton, N.Y.*

A Judge for yourself.

Q *That Japanese sergeant who hid in a cave on Guam for nearly 30 years—did he get a huge lump sum in back pay from the Japanese Army?—L.B.B., San Diego, Calif.*

A Shoichi Yokoi's back pay was $128.10. He also received $324 from the Ministry of Health and Welfare, will get an annual pension of $418. In addition, his countrymen have contributed $15,000 to date.

Q *What are the physical, moral and mental qualifications required to be a Washington lobbyist?—Violet M. Gonzalez, Bogota, N.J.*

A He must be able to hold his liquor, keep his mouth shut, and sell his viewpoint while making the men in Congress think he is helping them serve the public. The best lobbyists are shrewd, discreet, charming salesmen.

Billy Graham

Q *I have faith in Billy Graham—even when I hear people say he's a millionaire. Is it true that he takes only $18,000 in annual salary?—J.E. Abraham, Allentown, Pa.*

A Though annual operating expenses for Graham's organization run over $15 million, the evangelist draws an annual salary of $26,500. He also has personal income from family property in Charlotte, North Carolina, and book royalties, which go into a trust for his wife and children. An inheritance from the sale of his father's farm gave him money to build a 10-room house atop a mountain outside the resort town of Montreat, North carolina. When he leads a crusade, a corporation is set up in each city to receive and dispense all monies. It publishes an audited accounting as soon as the crusade is over.

Q *Is Joseph P. Kennedy III a student? Do all his travels mean he is getting into politics?—Linda Taylor, Bridgeport, Conn.*

A Joe is 19 and not now attending school. He has been to several—Our Lady of Victory School and Georgetown Prep in Washington, Milton Academy in Milton, Massachusetts, and Manor Hall Tutoring School in Cambridge, Massachusetts, where he earned his high school diploma. He is deeply interested in politics, has worked for his uncle, Sen. Ted Kennedy.

Q *Could you please tell me how many motor vehicles are registered in the U.S.? Also how many are cars, trucks or buses?—James A. Poole, Erie, Pa.*

A Automobiles: 88,840,541; buses: 189,085; trucks: 17,789,280; publicly owned vehicles: 1,616,997; total: 108,435,903.

Q *Has Richard Nixon traveled more miles than any other president in history?—Elmo Menetre, Truth or Consequences, N. Mex.*

A No, but he's working at it. As of last March, Nixon had logged 312,173 miles, including his China trip. Lyndon Johnson racked up 523,060 miles while in office.

William Westmoreland

Q *Why do they call the Army Chief of Staff William C. Westmoreland "Wind Dummy Westy"?—D.B., Washington, D.C.*

A The general got his nickname when commanding the 101st Airborne Division at Fort Campbell, Kentucky. After several of his men were injured during training, Westmoreland himself led more than 100 jumps. Dummies were tossed out to check wind conditions, and thus the title—one of respect. The general is slated to retire July 1.

Liza Minnelli and Desi Arnaz, Jr.

Q *What's with Liza Minnelli? Is she as kooky as her mother Judy Garland? Is she married, divorced, or separated? Is she living with Desi Arnaz, Jr.? Is she a husband-stealer? What is the truth?—Ben Young, Charlotte, N.C.*

A Liza Minnelli, 25, is an enormously talented entertainer. Considering her Hollywood background, rearing, and heritage, she is lucky to be functional. Anything she says is open to question. She is no stickler for truth. She is estranged at this writing from her husband, the Australian rock musician and singer, Peter Allen. Liza has also been accused by Mrs. Margaret Louise Kulbeth, wife of an obscure musician from Houston, Texas, of alienating her husband Rex Kulbeth who goes by the name Rex Kramer.

Mrs. Margaret Kulbeth alleges that Liza met her husband in Houston on November 1, 1969, subsequently entered into a contract with his musical group, The Bojangles, later made love with her husband in Toronto, Houston, and Puerto Rico. She is asking $556,000 in damages from Liza.

As for Liza's friendship with Desi Arnaz, Jr., he is six years her junior but sexually advanced for his age. Liza is an escapist who has long been in love with love.

Q *When Richard Nixon first became president of the U.S. he said to the American people: "I pledged to end this war in a way that would increase our chances to win true and lasting peace in* Vietnam, in the Pacific, and the world. I am determined to keep that pledge. If I fail to do so, I expect the American people to hold me accountable for that failure." If President Nixon expects to be held accountable, why do Vice President Agnew and others in the administration denounce those Americans who seek to hold Nixon accountable for escalating the war?—Paul Fox, Los Angeles, Calif.*

A This is a political year, and Nixon supporters naturally prefer all-out support for their man instead of doubt and disagreement. Such partisanship is understandable where it involves the longest, most controversial and confused war in U.S. history.

Q *Can you tell me if Billie Jean King, the greatest female tennis pro in the world, and Barbara Tuchman, one of the world's greatest historians, are among the list of American women who have had abortions? I refer to the list which appeared in Gloria Steinem's magazine, Ms.—J.K.L., Columbus, Ohio.*

A Billie Jean King and Barbara Tuchman are both on the list along with Kay Boyle, Judy Collins, Lee Grant, Mary Rodgers, Viveca Lindfors, Lillian Hellman, Elizabeth Janeway, many other outstanding women of accomplishment. In publishing such a list Gloria Steinem seeks to ridicule the social stigma, paranoia, and the guilt complexes traditionally associated with women who have had abortions.

Q *Does Elvis Presley wear a girdle, and why has he never played New York?— Otto Klein, Cleveland, Ohio.*

A Presley does not wear a girdle. He will make three appearances at Madison Square Garden in New York City, opening June 9 and doing matinee and night shows June 10. Tickets are priced at $10, $7.50, and $5.

Q *Was Adolf Hitler a degenerate who engaged in relations with his own niece who was named Geli Raubal? Is it not a fact that he murdered her when he found her in bed with a Jewish artist?— Theresa Montoya, Phoenix, Ariz.*

A Angela "Geli" Raubal, Hitler's niece and for a time his mistress, was found dead in her Prinzregentenplatz apartment in Munich on September 19, 1931. Hitler had been with her the evening before and his revolver was found at her side.

An examination of the body showed a freshly broken nose and other contusions. Someone had beaten her severely. The corpse was quickly sealed in a lead coffin, however, and shipped to Vienna for burial.

Geli Raubal was notoriously promiscuous. Hitler hired her as his Berchtesgaden housekeeper when he was 36 and she was 17. During this period of his life, Hitler, according to such early associates as Dr. Otto Strasser and Ernst "Putzi" Hanfstaengl, was a sexual deviate. Hanfstaengl reports that Hitler used Nazi party funds to buy up from blackmailers a collection of obscene drawings he had done of his niece. Of her relationship with her uncle, Geli Raubal once told friends: "My uncle is a monster. No one can imagine the sort of things he expects me to do."

As to Geli's Jewish lover, the *London Sunday Times* reports: "Brigid Hitler, widow of Adolf's half brother Alois, disclosed. . . that Geli, who admittedly had a number of lovers in addition to Hitler, had told Hitler on the evening she died that she was pregnant by a Jewish artist whom she wanted to marry. One can image the effect on Hitler's Aryan blood pressure."

Adolf Hitler

WALTER SCOTT'S
PERSONALITY PARADE®

July 16, 1972

Q *Why is President Nixon giving John Connally of Texas such a big buildup? Does he plan to drop Agnew for Connally?—Richard Costello, Galveston, Tex.*

John Connally

A President Nixon will pragmatically decide on his 1972 running mate. If the polls show Nixon substantially in the lead against his Democratic opponent, he will stay with Spiro Agnew as his Veep. If the polls reflect a tight presidential race, he may exercise the option of replacing Agnew with Connally, hoping that Connally will generate enough clout to swing Texas and several Southern and border states into the Republican fold. Connally at this point is Nixon's vice presidential insurance, if and when he needs him; hence the Connally buildup.

Q *Can you tell me if Diana Ross and her white husband are expecting a second child?—Lee Owen, Detroit, Mich.*

A Yes. Their first child, Rhonda Suzanne, was born in August, 1971. Their second should arrive in December, 1972.

Q *Why has Martha Mitchell left show business?— R.L., Washington, D.C.*

A Mrs. Mitchell's retirement is only temporary. As soon as she regains her voice the public will again become the beneficiary of her pronouncements, and in fact has.

Martha Mitchell

Q *Is it not a fact that the Duke of Windsor died of cancer and that his widow will shortly marry John Utter? Can you tell us something about Mr. Utter?—David Hilton, Boston, Mass.*

A The Duke of Windsor died of cancer. His widow has no intention of marrying John Utter who was private secretary to the Duke for the past 13 years. Utter, 67, ten years younger than the Duchess, is an American diplomat who quit the State Department because of McCarthyism in the early 1950's. Prior to that he worked for diplomat Robert Murphy, served as political adviser to General Eisenhower in World War II, was stationed in our embassies in Cairo and Paris, served for a while as head of the U.S. State Department's North African desk. A former director of the Simmons Company and independently wealthy, Utter went to work for the Windsors in 1959 upon the recommendation of Mrs. Sommerville Tuck, wife of the former U.S. Ambassador to Cairo. Utter is charming, distinguished, diplomatic, will no doubt continue to manage the Duchess of Windsor's affairs.

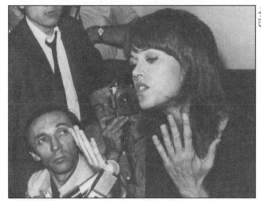

Jane Fonda

Q *Nancy Sinatra, Marlo Thomas, and Jane Fonda—which of these three daughters of stars has the most talent, and which one could have made it on her own?— Marianne Schloss, Westbury, N.Y.*

A Of the three Jane Fonda is the most talented and could probably have won stardom on her own. The other two are doubtful.

Q *Who are Sen. George McGovern's biggest financial backers?—Peter Pratt, San Francisco, Calif.*

A A few are Stewart Mott, who inherited a General Motors fortune; Max Palevsky, a Xerox executive from Los Angeles; Joe Sinay of RB Furniture Stores in Los Angeles, and Miles Rubin, a Los Angeles textile company executive.

Q *Why does the Congressional House Committee on Crime hound a good Republican like Frank Sinatra? Why do they treat him as if he is some sort of hood trying to avoid subpoenas? Why do they want him anyway?—M.R., Hoboken, N.J.*

A Sinatra is not a Republican. He is a veteran Democrat turned independent. It has been said that he has a long history of alleged friendships with alleged Mafia figures. It is about these relationships and collateral ownership of racetracks, hotels, and gaming establishments that Rep. Claude Pepper (D., Fla.) wishes to question him. Pepper's committee was prepared to subpoena Sinatra in Baltimore several weeks ago at a tribute dinner to Spiro Agnew who is a Sinatra crony. Mickey Rudin, Sinatra's attorney, as well as Sen. John Tunney (D., Calif.) assured the committee that Sinatra would appear voluntarily. Subsequently Sinatra escaped subpoena by flying to London in a private aircraft. The House committee therefore no longer regards him as a potentially cooperative witness and seeks to question him on July 18th.

Q *I understand that when President Nixon was in Moscow he invited Brezhnev and the other Soviet leaders to come to Washington. When may we expect Brezhnev, Podgorny, and Kosygin?—Neal Clayton Woods, Cambridge, Mass.*

A Next May, exactly one year after Nixon's 1972 summit meeting in Moscow, Brezhnev and Company will arrive in Washington, D.C., providing, of course, Nixon is reelected, which the Soviets feel is inevitable.

Jaqueline Kennedy Onassis

Q *Why does Jackie Kennedy Onassis favor pants over skirts?—Ann Bernard, Bangor, Maine.*

A Because she is slightly bowlegged.

Susan and Peter Fonda

Q *I understand that Andy Griffith, Peter Fonda and Johnny Carson were all recently divorced in the same week. On what grounds?—Paula Travers, Carbondale, Ill.*

A All three were divorced in the third week of June, 1972. Griffith, after 23 years of marriage, lost wife Barbara because of "irreconcilable differences." Peter Fonda lost his wife of 10 years on the same grounds. Joanne Carson charged "cruel and inhuman" treatment after eight years of marriage.

Q *How much did it cost Father Daniel Berrigan and the other defendants at Harrisburg to defend themselves against the U.S.? How much will it cost Daniel Ellsberg and Tony Russo to defend themselves? How much does it cost the government to prosecute these cases?—Ron Miller, Berkeley, Calif.*

A The Father Berrigan defense came to $600,000. The Ellsberg-Russo defense will cost approximately the same. No one knows exactly how much it costs the government to prosecute these cases. A safe estimate is three times the cost of the defense.

Q *What happened to that $500,000 action against Liza Minnelli? She was accused of enticing a band drummer and breaking up his marriage.—Anne Craig, Dallas, Tex.*

A Mrs. Margaret Kulbeth of Houston, Texas, wife of Rex Kulbeth who played with the Bojangles musical group under the name of Rex Kramer, accused Liza Minnelli of enticing Rex to leave her. Miss Minnelli originally denied the allegations of the alienation of affection action. Several weeks ago, however, her attorneys quietly settled the suit out of court.

Q *Three years ago in Washington, D.C., Henry Kissinger told Quaker representatives: "Give us six months. If we haven't ended the war then, you can come back and tear down the fence." How come Kissinger has been so wrong about the war?—Robert Dolan, Bryn Mawr, Pa.*

A Kissinger has tried but has consistently failed to understand the North Vietnamese mind.

Q *Why did the FBI "bug" football star Joe Namath's sex life?—M.N., New Rochelle, N.Y.*

A The FBI never bugged Joe Namath's sex life. At one point Namath's business associates were under FBI surveillance. In the course of that surveillance Namath and his friendship with an airline hostess came under review. The FBI, as an investigational agency, believes in gathering more material than less.

Q *Did Marcello Mastroianni ever leave his wife for an airline hostess? Is it on the level that this Italian Romeo has all the constancy of a rabbit?— Theresa Novelli, Chicago, Ill.*

Marcello Mastroianni

A Actor Mastroianni generally falls in love with his leading lady. Several years ago, however, after he finished *La Dolce Vita*, he engaged in a protracted love affair with a stewardess, flying with her from one European city to another.

Q *Has Oleg Prokofiev, son of the Russian composer, defected to the U.S.?— R.L.L., Washington, D.C.*

A Oleg Prokofiev, 44, artist son of the late Russian composer, Sergei Prokofiev, has been permitted to stay in England for another year even though he has exceeded his Soviet permission to stay abroad. Prokofiev, who has been lecturing at Sheffield University, is defying a Soviet order to return to Moscow, but he has not defected or requested political asylum. His English wife, Camilla Gray, daughter of Basil Gray, former keeper of Far Eastern art in the British Museum, died in Moscow last December after suffering a miscarriage. Prokofiev currently resides with his in-laws in their country home, Long Wittenham, Berkshire.

Q *President Nixon said in a recent press conference, June 29, 1972, that the North Vietnamese never accounted for the 15,000 French prisoners of war they took in 1954. Is that statement accurate? I understand it is not.—W.E., Cambridge, Mass.*

A According to the French government, President Nixon was in error. The Viet Minh returned approximately 9,200 prisoners of war after their victory at Dien Bien Phu in 1954. Another 6,000 members of the French army who were ethnically Vietnamese were unaccounted for. But the North Vietnamese say these were allowed to return to their homes, a statement which may or may not be true.

The Arthur Murrays

Q *What's happened to Arthur Murray, the dancing teacher, and his wife?— Mavis Kennedy, Waltham, Mass.*

A Arthur Murray, 77, and his wife, Kathryn, 65, have been married 47 years, live in a Honolulu penthouse apartment. Murray—real name, Teichman—has retired but spends some of his time as an investment counselor.

WALTER SCOTT'S
PERSONALITY PARADE®

September 24, 1972

Steve McQueen and Ali McGraw

Q *I see that Steve McQueen and Ali MacGraw have been dating, since they've dumped their respective spouses. Any chance of these two getting together?—Mavis McGrath, Roxbury, Mass.*

A They've already been together. Whether their togetherness will lead to marriage is difficult to determine, especially in Hollywood where constancy is not one of the constants.

Q *Would it be safe to assume that the two presidential candidates in 1976 will be Spiro Agnew for the Republicans and Ted Kennedy for the Democrats? It is difficult for me to believe that in this great country of more than 200 million, these are the two best men the nation has to offer.—Mrs. Leroy Grange, San Jose, Calif.*

A At this point it would be reasonable to assume Agnew vs. Kennedy in 1976 as presidential rivals. Agnew and Kennedy are, of course, not the best qualified men in the nation for the presidency. But one must remember that in the U.S.A., politics has not necessarily been equated with statesmanship. In the era of television, men have often been chosen for office mainly on the basis of charisma.

Q *What is the life expectancy rate for males and females in the United States?—Daniel Rich, Charlotte, N.C.*

A According to the National Center for Health Statistics on the basis of final 1970 mortality statistics, the average life expectancy for the total U.S. population was 70.8 years. Life expectancy at birth was 68.1 years for males and 75.4 for females.

Q *Ted Kennedy's speech at the Democratic National Convention—wasn't it written by Richard Goodwin and not Milton Gwirtzman, the Kennedy family lawyer?—Charles Young, Cambridge, Mass.*

A You are right. Veteran speechwriter Goodwin was the author.

Henry Kissinger

Q *Isn't it a fact that Henry Kissinger now has the FBI check out a girl before he dates her? Isn't it a fact that the girl must then sign a document saying she will write nothing about Henry or tell about their affair?—H.D., Birmingham, Ala.*

A Nonsense. Henry has a hangup for show business personalities and will date almost any starlet with two eyes. One of his latest is Samantha Eggar, a British actress of provocative past.

Q *Defense Secretary Melvin Laird says that our fliers over Vietnam bomb only military targets. If this is true, why do our planes drop thousands of anti-personnel weapons whose major objective is to kill people?—D.N., Somerville, Mass.*

A Mr. Laird is not the most truthful Defense Secretary we have had in this country. In all fairness, however, and as regards the war in Indochina, he has been lied to by the military, and in turn has transmitted those lies to the public. A classic example, of course, concerns our so-called "protective reaction strikes" over North Vietnam, falsified by Gen. John Lavelle and others. Moreover, in modern war, civilians are considered legitimate military targets no matter what the Geneva Convention says. In World War II, U.S. Air Forces consistently bombed civilian populations as did other nations. More civilians than military personnel were killed in our atomic bombings of Hiroshima and Nagasaki and the same holds true for the German bombings of Rotterdam, London and Warsaw.

Q *How old is Queen Mother Elizabeth of Great Britain? How tall? Was she a commoner by birth? Is she healthy?—Ann Higgins, Portland, Oreg.*

A The Queen Mother Elizabeth is 72. She is 5 feet 1/2 inch tall. She is in excellent health. She was a commoner by birth when she married the Duke of York, a shy, stuttering, rather dull man who became George VI when his brother King Edward VIII abdicated the British throne in 1936.

Q *Dionne Warwick, the black singer—how old? How wealthy? How educated? How married?—Benton Lacey, Detroit, Mich.*

A Dionne Warwick, 31, born in Orange, New Jersey, attended Hartt College of Music, Hartford, Connecticut, is married to actor William Elliott. She is worth at least a million. Dionne has one son, David, three. She is pregnant, plans to return to Hartt College for her master's degree in music.

Mr. and Mrs. Sammy Davis, Jr.

Q *Was Sammy Davis, Jr., the black entertainer who is now campaigning for President Nixon, ever engaged to actress Kim Novak?—E.L,, Chicago, Ill.*

A He was in love with her, but they were not engaged. Miss Novak at the time was a star of Columbia Film Studios, whose then despotic president, Harry Cohn, raged apoplectically when he learned of the love affair. Quickly, he pressured Sammy to stay away from his star. Reacting to that pressure, Davis married a woman of his own race, jumped next into a marriage with Swedish actress Mai Britt, is again married to a member of his own race.

Coco Chanel

Q *Can it be a fact that in World War II, the great French designer, Coco Chanel, was really a Gestapo agent, holed up in the swank Ritz Hotel along with the Nazi occupiers?—D.L., Denver, Colo.*

A In World War II, Coco Chanel lived in Paris, in the Ritz Hotel, with a high-ranking German officer. How much information she gave him no one will ever know. She certainly, however, was no Gestapo agent. Her lover, Baron "Spatz," is still alive. A biography on Chanel, written by Edmonde Charles-Roux, will be published in this country next year by Knopf and will undoubtedly shed some light on Chanel's behavior during World War II. Understandably this portion of Chanel's life was omitted from the stage play, Coco, starring Katharine Hepburn.

Q *Is the Central Intelligence Agency worth to this country what it costs?— B.S., Los Angeles, Calif.*

A That is difficult to tell, since practically no man knows what the CIA costs the U.S. taxpayer annually. Its budget is so inextricably mingled with defense appropriations that the truth of the agency's expenditures is virtually beyond the determination of Congress. Sen. John Stennis (D., Miss.), head of the Armed Services Committee, and a few other senators are supposed to keep a watchful eye on the CIA, but Stennis has long been regarded as a cooperative captive of the intelligence and defense communities.

Q *Where in New York does Martha Mitchell live? Is it true that if her husband, John, doesn't behave himself, she will blow the whistle on him in her book in which she promises to tell all?—George H., Staten Island, N.Y.*

A Martha and John Mitchell live in the Essex House in New York City. Martha is unpredictable. If and when she writes her book, chances are she will incriminate no one, least of all husband John.

Q *Would you please explain to me how Richard Kleindienst became attorney general of the United States? Was it politics or talent?—S.L., Tucson, Ariz.*

A Mr. Kleindienst is a talented conservative lawyer. He was ROTC freshman honor cadet at the University of Arizona, president of the Harvard Conservative League, a member of Phi Beta Kappa. He is considered by many to be a more knowledgeable attorney than his predecessor John Mitchell, a graduate of the Fordham Law School who specialized in municipal bonds. Kleindienst, however, is basically a politician. He entered Arizona politics in 1953 as the youngest member of the state legislature. He became chairman of the Republican State Committee in 1956. In 1964 he became field director on the Barry Goldwater for President Committee. In 1964 he ran for Governor of Arizona and was defeated. Three years later he became Nixon's Arizona campaign manager and then his national director of field operations. After the election Nixon showed his gratitude by appointing Kleindienst deputy attorney general under John Mitchell. When Mitchell resigned last February, Kleindienst succeeded him. The top positions in the U.S. Justice Department are regrettably part of the American spoils system. It will be recalled that in 1960 President Kennedy rewarded his brother, Robert, with the position of U.S. attorney general after Robert successfully served as his campaign manager.

Q *What's happened to Gloria Swanson, and what's happened to Perry Como?—Diane Hackman, Detroit, Mich.*

A Gloria Swanson is in London acting in a play entitled *The Gathering of the Clan.* Perry Como opens in Las Vegas on November 7 at the Hilton.

Perry Como

Q *When Jean-Paul Belmondo got tired of actress Ursula Andress and bounced her, didn't she fly to Hollywood and latch onto Ryan O'Neal? Isn't the O'Neal-Andress love affair the talk of the film colony?—Frances Bishop, San Diego, Calif.*

Belmondo and Andress

A Ryan O'Neal is a handsome young actor who has plucked many grapes from many vines. Several weeks ago he and Ursula cooed on the sands of Malibu Beach. Hollywood no longer takes these cooings seriously. For the most part, they are transient, especially where O'Neal and Andress are concerned.

Ryan O'Neal

Q *How many fraggings have American soldiers committed in the awful, endless Vietnam war which drags on and on, poisoning the life blood of this nation?— Mrs. Henry Altschuler, New York, N.Y.*

A When a soldier throws a fragmentation grenade at a superior officer on his own side in an attempt to kill or wound that officer, such an incident is called "a fragging." In the past four years U.S. soldiers in Vietnam have committed approximately 550 fraggings, resulting in 86 deaths.

Q *What has Charlton Heston ever done to Australia that his films should be banned in that country? I refer to his latest, Skyjacked.—Mary Lois Woodward, Chapel Hill, N.C.*

A Australia has not banned Charlton Heston movies. The reason *Skyjacked* has been banned from Australia, according to Donald Chipp, a customs and excise minister, is that "the film deals with the hijacking of a crowded civil airliner by a mentally disturbed United States Army sergeant. The methods of hijacking and of holding a crew and passengers hostage are explicitly and vividly depicted. . . .The experience of airlines and civil aviation authorities have shown that the hijacking techniques employed in films are reproduced in real life a short time later."

WALTER SCOTT'S
PERSONALITY PARADE®

November 19, 1972

Liz Taylor and Richard Burton

Q *Is it a fact that Elizabeth Taylor now pays bodyguards $1,000 per week to watch her round the clock? What is she afraid of?—Jane Cohen, New Rochelle, N.Y.*

A When Elizabeth Taylor married Mike Todd, she became a convert to the Jewish faith. Palestinian terrorists regard her as one of the enemy. Recently when Elizabeth and her husband, Richard Burton, were in Rome, working on a two-part TV movie, *Divorce His—Divorce Hers*, they insisted upon the tightest security precautions. Rumors were flying in Rome that the Black September gang of Arab terrorists was determined to kidnap her, hold the actress as hostage in an attempt to barter her release for the exchange of Arab prisoners in Israeli hands.

Q *Isn't Richard Nixon's personal lawyer, Herbert Kalmbach, the most potent behind-the-scenes figure in the Republican Party in charge of fund-raising and all undercover operations? Can you tell us anything about Mr. Kalmbach?—J.L., San Diego, Calif.*

A Herbert Kalmbach, 50, is a senior partner in the Newport Beach, California, and Los Angeles law firm of Kalmbach, De Marco, Knapp & Chillingworth. He is one of Nixon's top political strategists and fund-raisers. He is also secretary of the Nixon Foundation. Kalmbach runs the little-known but powerful Lincoln Club of Orange County which consists of many millionaires—C. Arnholt Smith, Arnold Beckman, Clement Hirsch—who contribute large sums to the Republican party. Because of his well-known White House influence, Kalmbach is responsible for the growth of his law firm. It numbers among its clients United Air Lines, Dart Industries, Travelers Insurance, the Marriott Corporation, Music Corp. of America, and many others. The FBI has questioned Kalmbach intensively on his knowledge of the political skulduggery performed by Republican operatives during the recent presidential campaign.

Q *I understand the richest man in Nevada is Bill Harrah, the Hotel Casino mogul who was married to singer Bobbie Gentry. How many times has he been married, and is it true that he settles $5 million on each bride?—T.L. Layne, Lake Tahoe, Nev.*

A Bill Harrah, 61, recently took Roxanne Carlson, 32, for his fifth bride; his fourth was Mary Burger. As a rule Harrah makes no extravagant settlements on his brides, although he was exceedingly generous with Scherry Teague, who was both his first and second wife and who saw him through his alcoholism.

Q *Two years ago Chet Huntley left national TV for his home state of Montana to build a tourist attraction, Big Sky. Since then I've heard him on radio, also doing TV commercials for American Airlines. Whatever happened to the Big Sky project?—Anne Preston, Louisville, Ky.*

A The first buildings of the 10,648-acre resort, located 15 miles from Yellowstone National Park, are nearing completion. The resort is owned by a consortium of corporations, including Chrysler, General Electric, Burlington Northern, Continental Oil, and several others. Huntley says that if he exercises all his options he will own less than 2 percent of Big Sky. He serves as board chairman and chief promoter.

Q *Is it true that when Henry Kissinger goes to Moscow, the Soviet secret police, the KGB, always offers to fix him up with Russian girls of the night?—R.L., Washington, D.C.*

A In the past the Soviets have offered such hospitality, but Henry has always wisely declined. On one occasion he told a Soviet officer jokingly, "For three or four days I can get along without women."

Henry Kissinger

Doris Day

Q *Who said, "I knew Doris Day before she was a virgin"?—Ken Larsen, San Diego, Calif.*

A The late pianist-author Oscar Levant.

Q *There is an heir of the Woolworth family who gets his kicks by beating up on girls. He was recently thrown in jail in England. Why has the case been hushed up in the U.S.?—Leola French, Miami Beach, Fla.*

A The character in question is Anthony Hubbard, a wealthy Woolworth heir who was sentenced to 15 months for assault and battery. According to charges on which he was convicted, he took a girl to dinner, brought her home to his apartment, beat her up when she said no. Says Hubbard: "I will give $25,000 to anyone who can cure my bad temper."

Q *Remember that little nine-year-old girl in South Vietnam who was napalmed? Her photo ran in all the papers showing her nude and screaming in pain. What's happened to her?—T.T., Charlotte, N.C.*

A Phan Thi Kim Phuc, nine, burned in an accidental strike several months ago by South Vietnam bombers, is recovering at the Barsky Center, a hospital for plastic and reconstructive surgery in Saigon. Three skin grafts have already been performed.

PERSONALITY PARADE®

January 14, 1973

The Marx Brothers

Q *Erin Fleming, the chick who is looking after Groucho Marx, 82—will she inherit his fortune?—Anne Fielding, Torrance, Calif.*

A For managing Groucho, ex-actress Erin Fleming, approximately 35, receives 15 percent of Groucho's yearly income. Groucho has a son and other progeny, and most probably they will inherit the bulk of his estate. He also has a brother Zeppo, recently divorced by Barbara Marx good friend of Frank Sinatra and vice president Spiro Agnew.

Q *I understand that several French publishers have offered Le Duc Tho, Hanoi's peace negotiator, a large fortune for his memoirs. What will this do to Kissinger's?—Anne Kruger, Jacksonville, Fla.*

A If Le Duc Tho's memoirs are published first and encompass the story of the secret negotiations with Kissinger, they will undoubtedly detract from the book Kissinger will probably write one day.

Q *Anything serious between Ava Garner and Sal Mineo? I know she's 50 and Sal's only 33. But these days the older women are picking on the younger stallions.—L.E., Smithfield, N.C.*

A Ava Gardner and Sal Mineo are neighbors in London, live in Ennismore Gardens, Kensington, occasionally dine with each other. Nothing serious.

Q *Can you tell me why Dr. Christiaan Barnard, the South African heart transplant surgeon, and his brother Dr. Marius Barnard are leaving the medical profession to enter politics?—Victor Rosen, New York, N.Y.*

Dr. Christiaan Barnard

A They are not leaving the medical profession. The Barnard brothers plan to run for Parliament as members of the United Party which opposes the ruling Afrikaner Nationalist party.

Explains Dr. Christiaan Barnard: "South Africa has to discard this government in the same way as this country has discarded the ox wagon and moved into the jet age. The Nationalist government has a stigma just as the Nazis had a stigma. The world now associates it with racialism. The only way we can change our image and gain friends is to rid ourselves of it."

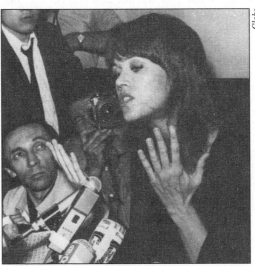

Jane Fonda

Q *What does Henry Fonda, who is a millionaire, have to say about his daughter Jane marrying a radical like Tom Hayden?—Milton Gordon, New Orleans, La.*

A Fonda, who has been married five times, has nothing to say about Jane's plans to marry Hayden, 32. Jane is 35 and capable of making her own marital decisions. She must first divorce Roger Vadim, her present husband from whom she is separated.

Q *Is it a fact that Louisiana is the single most influential state in the United States Congress?—Laura McKinney, Shreveport, La.*

A Because of congressional committee seniority Louisiana used to be. Last year before Sen. Allen J. Ellender (D., La.) died, he was chairman of the Senate Appropriations Committee. Before Rep. Hale Boggs (D., La.) disappeared in an Alaskan plane accident, he was the House Majority Leader. As things now stand, Sen. Russell Long (D., La.) is chairman of the Senate Finance Committee, and Rep. Edward Hebert (D., La.) is chairman of the House Armed Services Committee. Louisiana, Mississippi and Arkansas maintain great clout in the Congress by constantly re-electing their senators and congressmen.

Q *Which corporations in the United States employ the most people?—Charles Schreiber, Chicago, Ill.*

A (1) American Telephone & Telegraph; (2) General Motors; (3) Ford; (4) ITT.

Q *Why do such foreign actresses as Leslie Caron, Julie Christie and Liv Ullman fall for Warren Beatty? Are they gullible, of low intelligence or is Beatty simply irresistible?—Diane Jenkins, Salt Lake City, Utah.*

Warren Beatty

A Leslie Caron truly expected actor Beatty to marry her at one point. Julie Christie is not the most perceptive, discriminating or intelligent girl in the world. Liv Ullman, formerly the mistress of Swedish director Ingmar Bergman, is a free soul who finds Beatty's approach to life and love entrancing. Beatty has a way with women. His technique consists largely of concentrating on their cares and desires so that they come to believe he really means to establish an enduring relationship.

WALTER SCOTT'S
PERSONALITY PARADE®

January 21, 1973

Shakira Baksh and Michael Caine

Q *Michael Caine, the English actor, is supposed to be the greatest stallion in the British Empire. Who is his latest girlfriend?—Ben Wasserman, Rochester, N.Y.*

A Caine currently goes with Shakira Baksh, the former Miss Guyana.

Q *I would like to know if the Secret Service or the FBI is charged by law with the protection of the U.S. attorney general and his wife, Mr. and Mrs. Richard Kleindienst. Didn't the Secret Service accompany Martha Mitchell and her husband, John, when he was attorney general?—Robert Wise, Los Angeles, Calif.*

A Neither the Secret Service nor the FBI is charged by law with the protection of the attorney general. When John Mitchell held that office from 1969 to 1972, he was under periodic threat. It was feared that the antagonism he engendered might spread to his stimulating wife, Martha, and their lovely daughter, "Marty." FBI protection was therefore accorded the Mitchells on their many trips. From March 14, 1969, to March 17, 1972, seven FBI agents were assigned at different times to protect the Mitchells. The seven agents were: Dennis F. Creedon, J. Gerard Hogan, Henry A. Schutz, Dan A. Frant, Frank J. Illig, Frederick Woodworth and Francis M. Mullen, Jr.

Q *Why is Executive Order 9066 referred to as "the shame of the nation" and who was responsible for it?—T.E., Evanston, Ill.*

A Executive Order 9066, issued by President Franklin D. Roosevelt, on Feb. 19, 1942, permitted in the United States the organization of concentration camps, politely referred to as "relocation camps." In the spring of 1942, the U.S. Government began the removal and internment of 110,000 residents, two-thirds native-born Americans, into relocation camps. The order applied to all citizens and resident aliens of Japanese ancestry who resided in the Pacific Coast states of California, Oregon and Washington. After the Japanese attack on Pearl Harbor, the government as well as many Americans were filled with hysteria, outrage and fear of sabotage. Although not one incident of sabotage was traced or attributed to these persecuted Japanese-Americans, they were forced to sell their farmland, their property and possessions at prices far below market value, and then incarcerated behind barbed wire in such God-forsaken sites as Tule Lake, California; Topaz, Utah; Gila River, Arizona; Minidoka, Idaho; Jerome, Arkansas; Heart Mountain, Wyoming; and Granada, Colorado. No Italian-Americans or German-Americans were similarly incarcerated during World War II, only Japanese-Americans.

Q *How many law firms has Richard Nixon worked for and what was his legal specialty?—Anita Atkins, Buffalo, N.Y.*

A Most of Nixon's adult life has been spent in politics as congressman, senator, vice president and president. When out of office he worked for Wingert & Bewley, a small law firm in his home town of Whittier, California (1938-1940); for Adams, Duque & Hazeltine, a Los Angeles law firm in 1961, and for Mudge, Rose, Guthrie & Alexander, a New York City law firm, from 1964-1967. He has no legal specialty.

Q *I have heard that the second highest group incidence of venereal disease is the senior citizen group. Is this true?—John H. Waddell, Hemet, Calif.*

A Not true. Venereal disease is an affliction of the young and the sexually active. Its incidence is understandably lowest among senior citizens.

Q *I have read recently in* Reader's Digest *that members of the U.S. Senate and House of Representatives are pro-* hibited from smoking during congressional sessions. Is this rule actually enforced?—Michael E. Davis, Huntsville, Ala.*

A Members are not allowed to smoke on the House or Senate floors. In the House, however, where there are no assigned seats, Representatives are permitted to smoke "behind the railing" but not on the floor. In the Senate, smoking is permitted in the adjacent hallways, cloakrooms and conference rooms.

Q *Can you tell me why Jackie Kennedy or her husband "Sam" Onassis doesn't sue those Italian photographers who took pictures of Jackie in the nude?—Mel Bentley, Mineola, N.Y.*

A Legally there is scant opportunity for redress. The photos were taken by Italian photographers known as "paparazzi," who have no great love for Mrs. Onassis. They were published in the Italian pinup magazine *Playmen*. In Italy, there is at best only a hazy legal conception of invasion of privacy. Brigitte Bardot once sued the "paparazzi" and was awarded $75 in damages. Soraya, formerly married to the Shah of Iran, also sued, only to have her case thrown out of court. Apparently, the "paparazzi" consider Jackie and her husband "Sam" fair game.

Jackie Kennedy Onassis

Richard Nixon

Q *When President Nixon vacations at Key Biscayne, Florida, does the U.S. Air Force fly cover over Cuba just in case?—Harry Parks, Boca Raton, Fla.*

A It does, to prevent a surprise attack on the presidential quarters.

Q *I read recently that Mark Spitz, the Olympic swimming champion, is having his nose and chin re-formed through plastic surgery. Is this because he plans to become a film star, or his fiancée Susan Weiner made him do it?—Madeleine Schwartz, Los Angeles, Calif.*

A Spitz and his fiancée are both satisfied with his face as it is. No plastic surgery is about to be performed on Spitz.

Q *Where did Lyndon Johnson die—at the LBJ ranch or en route to San Antonio in a helicopter ambulance?—T.S., Austin, Texas.*

A Most probably at the LBJ ranch in his bedroom. He suffered a heart seizure, called for Mike Howard, his Secret Service agent. Howard and two other Secret Service agents applied a resuscitator, heart massage, every emergency procedure they knew—all to no avail. There was no sign of life while LBJ was being flown from his ranch to Brooke Army Medical Center in San Antonio where he was pronounced dead on arrival.

Q *When Henry Kissinger departs the Nixon administration, will he head for All Souls College in Oxford?—Ben Walters, Cambridge, Mass.*

A Kissinger once investigated the possibility of a visiting fellowship at All Souls—but that was when he was still at Harvard. At this writing, Kissinger doesn't know specifically where he will go when he leaves the Administration. Most probably he will accept a publisher's hefty advance for his memoirs and write them in an environment of maximum conduciveness—where the girls are.

Henry Kissinger

Q *The Watergate scandal in which two officials, Gordon Liddy and James McCord, of President Nixon's campaign organization, were found guilty of criminal conspiracy, burglary and wiretapping—has the public been told the whole truth about this case or has much of it been swept under the rug?—R.R., Bethesda, Md.*

A Since John N. Mitchell, the former attorney general, and Maurice Stans, the former secretary of commerce, are on record as having personally approved the disbursement of $199,000 to one of the convicted defendants, it is probably true that the whole truth concerning Watergate will not be told until Mitchell, Stans, Herbert Kalmbach, the president's lawyer, Charles Colson, Donald Segretti, Dwight Chapin, and others are called to testify by Sen. Sam Ervin's Special Senate Committee which is investigating the case.

Q *Now that he has lost his only son, to whom will Aristotle Onassis leave his billion-dollar fortune? Will it go to his wife Jackie, to his daughter Christina, or to his son's 39-year-old girl friend Fiona Baroness Thyssen?— Theo Karakis, Sea Girt, N.J.*

A When Alexander Onassis, 24, died as a result of an air crash, he had already broken off with Fiona Baroness Thyssen, 40, once Great Britain's loveliest model under her maiden name, Fiona Campbell-Walter. Aristotle Onassis was opposed to his son's love affair with the older woman and therefore it is unlikely that he will leave her anything in his will. Most of his vast fortune—estimated at between $500 million to $1 billion—will probably go to Jackie Kennedy Onassis, his daughter Christina and charity.

Q *Friends in England tell me that the name of Joseph P. Kennedy, father of the late assassinated John F. Kennedy, is one of the most despised in their country. Is this true? If so, why?—R.T.S., Berkeley, Calif.*

A "Despised" is too strong a word. Papers recently released from official British wartime files show that in 1939 when Joseph P. Kennedy was U.S. ambassador to Britain his support for appeasement and U.S. nonintervention in World War II made him a significant danger to Britain's war effort. As ambassador, Kennedy was so pessimistic about Britain's chances of survival against Hitler's Germany that President Franklin D. Roosevelt had to send "Wild Bill" Donovan, a trusted friend, to England for a more objective assessment of the war.

Robert Vansittart, chief diplomatic adviser to Lord Halifax, the British foreign minister, wrote in 1939: "Mr. Kennedy is a very foul specimen of double-crosser and defeatist. He thinks of nothing but his own pocket. I hope that this war will at least see the elimination of this type."

After World War II British opinion of Joseph P. Kennedy mellowed, especially since he lost his oldest son, Joe, in a highly dangerous secret mission over the French coast, and another son, John, fought courageously in the Pacific. Today in Britain it makes a great deal of difference which Kennedy one discusses. The sons are admired, the father is not.

Joe Kennedy

Elvis Presley

Q *How old is Elvis Presley? Is it true that he is a functional illiterate and that his wife left him because of that reason?—T.E.L., Memphis, Tenn.*

A Presley is 38. He was graduated from high school in Memphis, Tennessee, and can therefore read and write. He rarely reads an entire book, however, but that is not why his wife Priscilla, 28, left him. She fell in love with a karate instructor from Hawaii.

Q *How much money did Edward G. Robinson leave, and who will get it?—Hazel Barker, Raleigh, N.C.*

A Robinson who died on January 26, 1973, at age 79 left an estate valued at approximately $2.5 million. It consists largely of 88 works of art including masterpieces by the French impressionists Renoir, Manet, Monet, Pissarro and others. The paintings will be auctioned, and the proceeds will go into trusts for Robinson's widow, Jane; his son, Edward G. Robinson, Jr., and his granddaughter, Francesca.

Q *A few weeks ago a federal grand jury indicted two sons of the Texas millionaire H. L. Hunt on charges of tapping telephones. Why should two guys, both multimillionaires, go around tapping telephones? Are Bunky Hunt and Herb Hunt a little nuts in the belfry?—F. L., Dallas, Tex.*

A The six-count indictment charged W. Herbert Hunt and Nelson Bunker Hunt, both sons of H. L. Hunt and executives in Hunt Oil Co., as well as two other defendants, with tapping telephones in the homes of six individuals. When the case comes to trial the public will learn if the government's charges are true, and if they are, presumably, why the Hunt brothers arranged to bug the telephone of Juanita Edwards, their father's private secretary, and five others.

Q *Is John Connally, former Governor of Texas, building a $70-million commercial and cultural center in Dallas? Where is Connally getting all that loot?—E.L., Houston, Tex.*

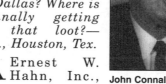

John Connally

A Ernest W. Hahn, Inc., contractors in Hawthorne, California announced recently that in partnership with John B. Connally, former Secretary of the U.S. Treasury, and Pollard Simons, a Texas developer, that they planned to build a $68-million commercial and cultural center in Dallas. The three men, Hahn, Connally, and Simons, have formed a partnership, Prestonwood Associates. Their center will consist of a regional shopping complex with six department stores, an entertainment court with restaurants, cinemas, a theater for plays, and community living facilities. Financing will come from banks and insurance companies

Q *I read recently that Ronald Reagan plans to run for president of the U.S. if the Republicans will nominate him in 1976. How old will he be by then? Won't he have to alter his political philosophy? And will it be possible for a divorced man to get elected president of this country?—E.L.L., Sacramento, Calif.*

A Reagan will be 65 if and when he runs for the presidency. He is currently in the process of moving politically from the right wing of his party to a more centrist position. If Reagan is elected president, he will become the first divorced man to win the honor. His first wife was actress Jane Wyman. His second is former actress Nancy Davis whom he wed in 1952. Politicians, however, no longer consider divorce an obstacle to elective office.

Q *Is Audrey Hepburn finished with motion pictures? If so, why?—Candy Courtland, Mason City, Iowa.*

Audrey Hepburn

A Audrey has agreed to come out of her five-year retirement to star in *The Survivors,* largely because the film will be made in Rome where she lives with her psychiatrist-husband and two sons, and will not be separated from them.

Q The Chicago Tribune *claims that four U.S. Senators—John Tower (R., Tex.), Dewey Bartlett (R., Okla.), Pete Domenici (R., N. Mex.) and Ted Stevens (R., Alaska)—are owned by the oil industry and vote accordingly. Is this a matter of fact or allegation?—B.W., Chicago, Ill.*

A *The Chicago Tribune* never said that the four senators you name were "owned" by the oil industry. What it did say on February 18, 1973, in an article by Jim Squires, is: "At least four members of the Senate—John Tower of Texas, Dewey Bartlett of Oklahoma, Peter Domenici of New Mexico and Ted Stevens of Alaska—who received oil industry support last fall, are now sponsoring legislation to deregulate the price of natural gas." That particular statement is true.

Q *Why is it that the Japanese won't give a visa to Mick Jagger of the Rolling Stones?—Evelyn Graves, Kinston, N.C.*

A The Japanese Foreign Office says Jagger was convicted of possessing marijuana in 1970. Foreigners who have been convicted on drug charges are banned from entering Japan.

Mick Jagger

Walter Cronkite

Q *Is it true that CBS plans to replace Walter Cronkite with Roger Mudd?—Emily Frankel, Hempstead, N.Y.*

A Cronkite recently signed a five-year deal with CBS which permits him a three-month vacation during which time Mudd would step in as his substitute. At the end of five years if Cronkite has had it, Mudd would be on hand to take over. But Walter will remain around for years.

Q *How should one rate Scott Fitzgerald as a writer? Will he last?—Irving Upchurch, Chicago, Ill.*

A He was a man of shallow Princeton education. There is no appreciable depth in any of his novels. He was inspired by the jazz age era. He believed in craftsmanship as a writer, and could write like an angel. He filled notebooks with phrases, descriptions, memories and trivia. In one of his letters he writes: "One time I had a talk with Ernest Hemingway, and I told him against all the logic that was then current that I was the tortoise and he was the hare, and that's the truth of the matter, that everything I have ever attained has been through long and persistent struggle while it is Ernest who has a touch of genius which enables him to bring off extraordinary things with facility. I have no facility...."

Q *Can you tell me if Ola Welch Jobe, Richard Nixon's first girlfriend, is putting up for auction at Parke-Bernet Galleries the love letters she received from Nixon during the 1930-37 period of their courtship?—R.L., Prescott, Ariz.*

A She is not.

Q *With the great increase in counterfeiting why hasn't the United States government turned to multicolored money to make it more difficult for the counterfeiter?—Augustus C. Baker, Hemet, Calif.*

A Precisely because the color of the currency doesn't make the counterfeiting any more difficult.

Q *Several months ago you were asked your opinion of the three best and the three worst appointments in the first Nixon Administration. As I recall, you picked the three best as Henry Kissinger, who obviously has you in his pocket; Daniel Moynihan, now the U.S. Ambassador to India, and Pat Gray who resigned as acting head of the FBI. The three worst appointments, you said, were John N. Mitchell as attorney general, Maurice Stans as secretary of commerce, and William Rehnquist as associate justice of the Supreme Court. How do those choices hold up in retrospect? Or have you changed your mind?—Leslie Bellamy, Los Angeles, Calif.*

A In retrospect they seem fair. Rehnquist is a brilliant justice, but he is an extreme right-wing idealogue. Intellectually however, he is far superior to Mitchell and Stans and perhaps should not have been linked with them. Otherwise the same selections hold.

John Mitchell

Daniel Moynihan

Q *I have read many times that during World War II only Japanese-Americans were incarcerated in concentration camps. Isn't it true that Italian-Americans and German-Americans were also placed in such concentration camps?—Vega Wimmer, Detroit, Mich.*

A Unfortunately it is true. Italians and Germans were interned in Minnesota and Texas and other states.

Q *Frank Sinatra's first wife, Nancy—is she in love with producer Ross Hunter, producer Jacques Mapes, or both?—Helen Burns, Monaca, Pa.*

A She is in love with neither but accords both her friendship.

Nancy Sinatra (Frank's first wife)

Q *Who murdered the gangster Johnny Stompanato—was it Lana Turner or her daughter Cheryl? Wasn't it Lana who plunged the knife and Cheryl who took the blame?—Louis Katz, Hollywood, Calif.*

A It was Miss Turner's daughter, Cheryl, who, seeking to protect her mother, stabbed Stompanato.

Q *I read in the newspapers where the White House hatchetmen, Hans and Fritz, have chopped down Herb Klein, one of our local boys, who was President Nixon's communications director. Is that true? Also, how long will it take them to get Kissinger?—J.T., San Diego, Calif.*

A Hans and Fritz have gotten Klein. They will probably not get Kissinger.

Raquel Welch

Q *Has Raquel Welch had her fanny re shaped?*—*Virginia Johnson, Chicago, Ill.*

A Her nose and her bust but not her fanny.

Q *Is it true that to enter the U.S. Armed Forces a female has to be a high school graduate while a male need not?*—*Anne Whitaker, Raleigh, N.C.*

A Women have to be high school graduates or the equivalent. Men do not. But it is not a question of law, merely preference by the services.

Q *Ex-Cabinet members and his closest associates have been involved in such crimes as burglary, illegal wire-tapping, perjury, and the obstruction of justice. Yet President Nixon has the temerity to go on TV and describe the Watergate scandal as a "deplorable incident." Is he kidding or what?*—*M. Klein, New York, N.Y.*

A From time to time Nixon practices self-deception, understandably seeks to underplay what is most damaging to him and his Administration.

Q *I would like to know who financed the trip of Shirley MacLaine and 11 other Women's Libbers to the People's Republic of China. Wasn't it the Communist Party?*—*Mrs. G.R., Boston, Mass.*

A Shirley MacLaine financed most of it.

Q *Is it not a fact that the major sin of H. R. Haldeman and John Ehrlichman, former members of the White House palace guard, was that they isolated President Nixon from Congress, the American public, and the Republican Party?*—*W.M., Tucson, Ariz.*

A Haldeman and Ehrlichman are combative men. They were corrupted by power into arrogance and reportedly isolated Nixon from others who disagreed with them.

Q *I heard Gov. Ronald Reagan say on TV that the people involved in the Watergate jazz were "stupid and foolish but not criminal." Is Reagan naive or deceptive?*—*E.T. Thomas, Berkeley, Calif.*

A Governor Reagan of California is an actor not a lawyer. He is also a Nixonian apologist who plans to succeed Nixon as president of the U.S.A. Under the circumstances he is not about to denounce as criminals several fellow members of the Republican party.

Q *Is there any difference in character traits between John Connally of Texas and the late Lyndon Johnson? Don't the oil interests in this country own Connally as they once owned Johnson?*—*F.R., Houston, Texas.*

A Connally, a protégé of the late president, has many of Johnson's strengths and weaknesses. Connally is closely allied to and supported by the major oil corporations, which was also true of Johnson.

Q *How old is Fred Astaire? Does he wear a hairpiece? What is his real name? Will he make a comeback?*—*Henrietta Kerby, St. Louis, Mo.*

Fred Astaire

A Fred Astaire, at least 73, was born Fred Austerlitz, wears a hairpiece, has no intention of making a film comeback.

Q *How good or bad are the chances that President Richard Nixon will be impeached? Do the Democrats really want his scalp?*—*N.M.L., Philadelphia, Pa.*

A At this writing the Congress seems to prefer that Nixon run out his remaining 1,300-odd days in office in a weakened and ineffective manner rather than involve Congress in lengthy impeachment proceedings, which, if successful, would result in the ascendancy to the presidency of Spiro Agnew.

Richard Nixon

Q *Is Martha Mitchell writing a book in which she will tell all?*—*E.L. Ramsey, Rutland, Vt.*

A Mrs. Mitchell is collaborating on a book with writer Winzola McLendon, but she is not about to tell all, surely not about the former U.S. Attorney General John Mitchell, her second husband.

Q *Bernie Cornfeld, the Brooklyn social worker who made millions selling mutual funds overseas—how did he come out on that rape charge filed against him in London?*—*Ed James, Los Angeles, Calif.*

A Cornfeld pleaded guilty to indecently assaulting Valli Davis, 19, in his London town house. He claimed that a friend had introduced Miss Valli to him, and he understood that she was to become his mistress. He therefore walked naked into her bedroom one night in an effort to make love to her whereupon the girl fled half-clothed and barefooted into the street and hailed a cab driver who drove her to the police. Cornfeld was fined approximately $1,125 on two counts of unlawfully assaulting and beating the girl. To add to his troubles, the Swiss charged him on May 14th with fraud and mismanagement.

WALTER SCOTT'S
PERSONALITY PARADE®

June 24, 1973

William Westmoreland

Q *What's happened to Gen. William Westmoreland of the Vietnam controversy?— Clark Edwards, San Francisco, Calif.*

A General Westmoreland is employed by the state of South Carolina. He is a special assistant to Gov. John West, advising on foreign trade. Mr. and Mrs. Westmoreland plan to build a home in Charleston.

Q *Has Mussolini's widow, Rachele, ever written her memoirs about that phony male nymphomaniac she was married to? I mean Il Duce. Where and when was her book published? And how could the talented Italian and German people permit themselves to be led by such obvious psychopaths as Mussolini and Hitler?—Arlene Kelly, East St. Louis, Ill.*

A Mrs. Mussolini's memoirs are scheduled for publication in Italy by Charles Orengo, which means that some U.S. publishing house will follow with an English translation. Politically the Italian and German people were unsophisticated, lost control of their governments to mentally unbalanced orators who quickly took over governmental machinery and viciously eradicated almost all dissent. Industrialists of influence went along

with the dictators in an effort to preserve their individual wealth. In the end they, too, were destroyed.

Q *Did Peter Sellers break up the Liza Minnelli-Desi Arnaz, Jr. romance? Aren't all these acting types more than a little kookie? Your opinion, please?—Louise Altschuler, San Jose, Calif.*

A They are three immensely talented performers, but they are not the most emotionally mature people in the world. Sellers has small idea of his true identity. Liza is unstable and in love with love. Young Arnaz, six years her junior, is handsome, well-mannered, undereducated and spoiled by having achieved success without struggle. As for Sellers, he is chronically bedeviled by the specter of advancing years and reportedly cannot differentiate between infatuation and love. All three characters would make superb case studies for a psychiatrist. Peter Sellers did not break up the romance. It was Liza who decided that Desi was not for her. She is after all the daughter of Judy Garland who went through at least five marriages in a fruitless search for true and lasting love. And the apple does not fall too far from the tree. Next week, however, Liza may change her mind about everything; she is nothing if not quixotic.

Q *Sen. Howard Baker, Republican of Tennessee, is the cutest, smartest little guy I've seen on TV in a long time. He is the star of Watergate. Can you tell me anything about him? Most important, is he married?—Elaine Harvey, Los Angeles, Calif.*

A Howard H. Baker, Republican, was born in Huntsville, Tennessee, November 15, 1925. Both his father and stepmother served in the U.S. Congress. Baker is a lawyer, served in the U.S. Navy from 1943-46. He is married to the former Joy Dirksen, daughter of the late senator from Illinois. They have two children, Darek and Cynthia.

Q *Can you find out why the late J. Edgar Hoover hated the late Martin Luther King so much? Was it because King enjoyed a free-wheeling sex life, and Hoover had none? Was it because Hoover was white, and King was black? Why did Hoover wiretap King so consistently and leak evidence of King's sex life to the press?—N.L., Macon, Ga.*

A In 1962 and 1963 Dr. King criticized the FBI for dragging its feet in civil rights cases. Enraged by the criticism of his bureaucratic child, the FBI, and suspicious of King's associates, Hoover had the civil rights leader tailed and wiretapped throughout the country. A man of strong sexual appetites, King was an easy mark for electronic surveillance. When Dr. King won the Nobel Peace Prize, Hoover was further enraged, sought to undermine the achievement by highlighting King's marital infidelity. Arthur Murtagh, 51, of Constable, New York, a lawyer who retired from the FBI after 21 years of service, 11 of which he spent in Atlanta, King's hometown, is writing a book which deals in part with the battle of Hoover versus King.

Martin Luther King, Jr.   **J. Edgar Hoover**

Q *Would you buy a used car from Attorney General Elliot Richardson?—D. Evans, Cambridge, Mass.*

A Yes, anytime—especially if his wife, one of the loveliest women in the nation, held joint title to it.

Q *I understand that for years Henry Kissinger and Bob Haldeman despised and sought to annihilate each other in the White House struggle for power. Now that Kissinger has won, is he licking his chops?—M.R., Washington, D.C.*

A It is no secret that Haldeman detested Kissinger for his life style, his publicity, his fame, his influence with the president. Kissinger, in turn, regarded Haldeman as his number-one enemy in the White House. Kissinger, however, did not destroy Haldeman. A man of arrogance, strangely capable of a deep, visceral hate, Haldeman may have severely harmed himself. But surely Kissinger has not played "Mr. Clean" in the Nixon melodrama, currently entitled, "Malice in Blunderland." Henry, too, has been stained by the widening disclosures of staff and newsmen wiretaps in which he played a part.

Joseph Kennedy

Q *I have read in a book called* The Kennedy Case *that Mrs. Rose Kennedy, matriarch of the Kennedy family, is notoriously tight with a nickel, runs around her house turning out the lights, wears adhesive plasters on her face to remove the wrinkles—also that her son, the late John F. Kennedy, had to use a cane in order to walk, but that fact was hidden from the U.S. public just like Franklin Roosevelt's paralyzed legs. Is any or all of this true?—L.C., Washington, D.C.*

A It is all true, and it is all part of the eyewitness observations of author Rita Dallas. Mrs. Dallas was head nurse to family patriarch Joseph P. Kennedy during the last eight years of his life, and she saw plenty. She has written, along with Jeanire Ratcliffe, a compassionate book which reveals some of the most intimate details of the Kennedy tribe.

Q *Why has Richard Nixon been so reluctant to tell the truth from the very beginning of how he acquired and improved his estate at San Clemente?—R.L., San Diego, calif.*

A Mr. Nixon by nature is a very private, secretive, involuted man, the product of his insecure boyhood with its years of semi-genteel poverty. Obviously the acquisition of his San Clemente prop-

erty was for him so good a deal that he declined to disclose its very special ramifications to the public for fear the public would consider the transaction suspect— which, of course, it now does. Suspicion is always the handmaiden of secrecy.

Q *Is Burt Lancaster going to star in a remake of* Moses? *If there is any actor whose private life bears no resemblance to Moses, it is Lancaster's. How idiotic can those Hollywood producers be, casting Lancaster as Moses?—Willa Castillo, Phoenix, Ariz.*

A Sir Lew Grade, British TV executive, is joining with Radio Televisione Italiana to co-produce a six-part TV series entitled *The Law Giver—Moses*, which will star Lancaster. Do not blame Hollywood for this one.

Q *Was Marilyn Monroe murdered because she was having an affair with President John F. Kennedy?—Terry Bee, Boston, Mass.*

A Nonsense, Marilyn Monroe died of a pill overdose. Rumors that she was murdered are being circulated in an attempt to sell books based on her tragic life.

Marilyn Monroe

John F. Kennedy

Q *Would you please tell me something about Bobby Riggs, the tennis player who beat Margaret Court for $10,000? I understand that Riggs was paid $1 million by his first wife, Kay, for a divorce. What's the truth about him?—Lane Edwards, Rye, N.Y.*

A Bobby Riggs, 55, one of the great tennis champions of the century, was born in Los Angeles, the sixth son and seventh child of Gideon and Agnes Riggs. His father was a minister of the Church of Christ. As a youngster Bobby became the protégé of Dr. Esther Bartosh, a university anatomy professor, who bought him his first tennis racket. Riggs never had much money as a teen-ager and had to hustle to survive. As he grew older, winning one tennis championship after another, he became an expert in hustling and winning bets both on the tennis court and golf course.

Before he was 22, he was married to Kay Fischer, a student at Manhattanville College who played in minor tennis tournaments. She was the daughter of a Chicago builder. Bobby and Kay had two sons in their marriage, which lasted 12 years. The first Mrs. Riggs is now Mrs. Max Tauber of Los Angeles, and she claims she never settled anything on Bobby.

The second Mrs. Riggs is the former Priscilla Whelan whose family owned the American Photographic Studios, a chain-store operation. She and Riggs were married for 23 years, had four children, were divorced last year. Riggs reportedly received some financial settlement as a result of that divorce, but not a million dollars. The second Mrs. Riggs lives in Port Washington, Long Island, claims, "We are still the best of friends."

Q *Several years ago British actress Vanessa Redgrave had a child out of wedlock with Italian actor Franco Nero. Is their love affair still in effect?—Mary R. Holmes, Philadelphia, Pa.*

A No. Nero, 40, has separated from Redgrave, 36, who has custody of their four-year-old son. She has taken up with another man whose marital state is tottering, while Nero's new love is actress Marisa Mell, 30.

Franco Nero

Barbara Hutton

Q *Is it true that Barbara Hutton loans her fabulous jewelry to her domestic help for parties?—Gale Lane, New York City.*

A Barbara Hutton frequently loans jewelry to her secretaries and other domestic personnel, requires them to sign a receipt for the borrowed jewelry. Several months ago she says she loaned $25,000 worth of jewelry to her young French nurse, Chantal Chaignon, for a dinner party. Miss Chaignon contends the jewelry was a gift, not a loan, and has refused to return it. Recently a French court upheld Mademoiselle Chaignon's contentions. As a result Barbara Hutton may no longer loan out her jewelry.

Q *Is it true that Ronald Ziegler, President Nixon's press secretary, was a "Mouseketeer" back in the 1950s?—J.J. Richmond, Washington, D.C.*

A Ziegler, 34, was never a "Mouseketeer." He did work at Disneyland, however, as a guide on the Jungle Ride.

Q *Sam Goldwyn, the Hollywood producer who passed away on January 31 at 91, was famous for many Goldwynisms originated by his press agents. Which ones did he originate himself?—Anne Ferris, Pittsburgh, Pa.*

A Goldwyn, like the other pioneers of the motion picture industry—the Schencks, Mayers, and Warners—was a Jewish immigrant from Eastern Europe with little command of the English language. When his story editor, after reading Lillian Hellman's play, *The Children's Hour*, said to him: "We can't film this, Sam. It's all about lesbians," Goldwyn replied: "Forget it, we'll make 'em all Mexicans." He was also famous for the remark, "Include me out." And in the later years of his life when he reminisced about his early days in Hollywood, he mused: "We have all passed a lot of water since then."

Q *Why did California Democratic Sen. John Tunney's wife divorce him after 15 years of marriage and three children?—Karl F. Cockrane, Santa Clara, Calif.*

A According to Mieke, his Dutch-born ex-wife, the fault was the political system of the U.S. which compels a politician's wife to repress her own identity and independence.

"The wife either becomes a cliche . . . or she stays in the background trying not to be provocative," Mrs. Tunney wrote in last month's *Ladies' Home Journal*. ". . . It's a stifling life, it's very repressive, and a fair number of these people become slightly out of kilter and have to seek psychiatric help."

Q *Does anyone know why President Nixon had his brother, Donald, tailed by the Secret Service, the Treasury Department, and the Central Intelligence Agency?—D.R., Seattle, Wash.*

Richard Nixon

A For years the president has been afraid that his brother's business contacts and acquaintances—especially with the Howard Hughes organization—might embarrass the White House. He therefore had the Secret Service place F. Donald Nixon under surveillance. Some sources say that a variety of agents shadowed the president's brother on orders from Bob Haldeman, John Ehrlichman and John N. Mitchell, all no longer with the government.

Q *Is Lawrence Welk retiring from show business?—Clair Bosworth, Tulsa, Okla.*

Lawrence Welk

A After 50 years in the band business, Lawrence Welk, in his 70's, has decided to "slow down" but not to retire. A multimillionaire real estate operator, Welk has no financial incentive to continue as a bandleader but will play occasional dates.

Q *I am fascinated by the relationship of E. Howard Hunt, who bungled the Watergate robbery, and William Buckley, the conservative commentator who is godfather to three of Hunt's four children. What is the basis of their friendship? Also how could our Central Intelligence Agency hire a man of Hunt's character? Are there many others like him in the CIA?—T.W., Mclean, Va.*

A In 1951 and 1952, when William Buckley, Jr. was doing some work for the CIA in Mexico, his superior was E. Howard Hunt, then assigned by the CIA to its station in the American Embassy in Mexico City. Hunt and Buckley soon became fast friends. Buckley is not only godfather of three Hunt children but the executor of Dorothy Wetzel Hunt's estate. Mrs. Hunt, who was involved in the Watergate payoffs, was killed in a United Air Lines plane crash in 1972.

Hunt was hired by the CIA in 1947 because he had been a member of the OSS (the Office of Strategic Services) in World War II. For the best insight into his career and character, read *Compulsive Spy—The Strange Career of E. Howard Hunt*, by Tad Szulc.

William Buckley

Q *Isn't Richard Nixon the strongest president the U.S. has ever had? Do you know of any other who has withstood such fierce, concentrated and continuous fire?—H.L.S., Houston, Tex.*

A Nixon has the guts, fight, fortitude, and loneliness of the long-distance runner.

Q *TV personality David Frost has been jilted at least three times: first by actress Janette Scott who married singer Mel Torme, then by actress-singer Diahann Carroll who married a Las Vegas clothier, and now by model Karen Graham who married Las Vegas operator Del Coleman. What's wrong with Frost?— Stefanie Troy, Providence, R.I.*

David Frost

NBC/Globe

A Nothing's wrong with him. He's just unlucky in love.

Q *Two questions about the British Royal Family: (1) Are they allowed to vote? (2) Have Princess Margaret and her husband Lord Snowdon each taken a lover?— E.E.E., Westport, Conn.*

A No member of the British Royal Family nor any peer in the House of Lords is permitted to vote in a general election. Princess Margaret's marriage to photographer Snowdon is reportedly foundering, but no extracurricular lovers are yet involved.

Q *Sen. James Buckley of New York and his brother William Buckley, the TV commentator—what is the origin of their wealth? Isn't it Texan?—Eva Hogan, New York City.*

A The Buckley father, William Senior, was the founder with his two brothers of the Texas law firm of Buckley, Buckley & Buckley. He bought up many Mexican oil leases only to have more than a million dollars of his oil properties expropriated by the Mexican government in 1921. A year later Buckley came to New York, invested heavily in the stock of oil companies, amassed a fortune estimated at $100 million. He bought a home, "Great Elm," in Sharon, Connecticut, and another in Camden, South Carolina. He and his wife had 10 children. Before his death in 1958 at the age of 77, William Buckley, Sr.,

managed to distribute practically all of his wealth to his wife Aloise, whom he had married when he was 36, and their offspring, eight of whom are alive.

Q *Charles Rhyne who is representing Rose Mary Woods, the president's secretary, in various court proceedings—who pays his fee, Miss Woods or the U.S. government?—K.G., Washington, D.C.*

A Miss Woods.

Q *How many illegitimate children did the late artist Pablo Picasso sire? Do all or none get part of his $100 million estate?—Richard Holmes, Eureka, Calif.*

A According to a law passed in France in 1972, illegitimate offspring are entitled to a share of their parents' estate. Picasso had at least three illegitimate children, Claude and Paloma Picasso by writer-artist Francoise Gilot, and Maya Widmaier, 38, illegiti-

Pablo Picasso

mate daughter by his third mistress, Marie-Therese Walter. The court recently ordered Picasso's widow Jacqueline to give one-eighth of the estate to Claude and Paloma. Maya's case is pending.

Q *Does homicide run in families? I note that Sirhan Sirhan assassinated Robert Kennedy, and his brother Sharif Sirhan threatened to assassinate Golda Meir. What's happened to them?—B.P., Newark, N.J.*

A Mental instability frequently runs in families. Sirhan Sirhan is in San Quentin. Sharif Sirhan, 40, is at this writing in a Los Angeles jail serving his six-months sentence for threatening to kill Mrs. Meir.

Q *Is the California Bar Association doing anything about the California attorneys involved in the Watergate mess, or is it simply looking the other way?— M.T., Riverside, Calif.*

A According to Seth M. Hufstedler, president of the association, "hundreds of man hours" have been spent in a preliminary investigation of possible misconduct by the following attorneys: Richard Nixon, John Ehrlichman, Herbert Kalmbach, Robert Mardian, Donald Seg-

retti and Gordon Strachan. Twenty-five lawyers have been disbarred in California in the last three years. It is possible some of the above may be added to the list, providing the State Supreme Court rules that moral turpitude was involved in any of the offenses they may have committed.

Q *While walking on a crowded street in Paris recently I ran into Jackie Onassis apparently unescorted. Doesn't she have a bodyguard provided by her husband or the U.S. government?—Robert Lunsford, Reedville, Va.*

Jackie Onassis

Globe

A Mrs. Kennedy relinquished U.S. Secret Service protection when she married Aristotle Onassis. She then became her husband's responsibility. From time to time he has provided her with a guard, but she goes frequently unescorted.

Q *Is it true that even though she was supposed to receive more than a million-dollar divorce settlement from Elvis, his ex-wife Priscilla hasn't yet received a penny and supports herself by working in a Hollywood dress shop?— T.E., Memphis, Tenn.*

A Not true. Priscilla Presley, 27, and dress designer Olivia Bis have opened a boutique in Beverly Hills, which is probably how the rumor started. Priscilla works because she wants to, not because she has to.

Priscilla and Elvis Presley

Globe

Q *Since Richard Nixon has been hit with a whopping $450,000 tax bill, will he have to play the piano for a living in his old age?—Lucille Hatch, Miami Beach.*

A Not likely. Nixon will receive for life a pension based on his federal service as naval officer, congressman, senator, vice president and president. It should approach or exceed $75,000 per year. In addition, he will get $96,000 a year for life to run and staff an office.

Q *Adolf Hitler's sweetheart and wife, Eva Braun—did she save thousands of Jews from the gas chambers by intervening with Hitler on their behalf?—Lean Gross, Philadelphia.*

Adolf Hitler

A Eva Braun did not intervene with Hitler on behalf of the Jews. She was, however, deeply involved in saving the lives of hundreds of Allied prisoners of war. When the war began going badly for Hitler in 1944, he ordered the execution of all prisoners of war, especially American fliers who had so devastatingly bombed Germany. Hitler's officers tried to reason with der Fuehrer, but he was maniacally obstinate.

Eva Braun, however, employed a different tack. She arranged for the execution assignment to go to Gottlob Berger, general of the *Waffen SS,* who secretly promised her that the executions would not be carried out. Berger kept his word. An American author, Glenn Infield, of Beaver Falls, Pennsylvania, discovered these facts in a heretofore undisclosed interview of Berger by the late Judge Michael A. Musmanno, who was a jurist at Nuremberg. Infield has just finished a book on Hitler's Germany and the Musmanno Archives which will be published by Grosset & Dunlap later this year.

Q *Is it true that Clare Boothe Luce is losing her eyesight? I have heard many rumors to that effect.—Christine Chun, Honolulu, Oahu.*

A No. Mrs. Luce recently had cataract surgery, now sees better than she formerly did.

Q *Is there still a feud between Aristotle Onassis and Prince Rainier of Monaco? Is Jackie Onassis jealous of Princess Grace?—L.S.G., Atlantic City, N.J.*

A In March, 1967, Prince Rainier pressured Onassis into selling his shares in the Société des Bains de Mer, a gambling casino in Monte Carlo, for some $9 million. He claimed Onassis was too conservative. Onassis then, hurt, promised he would never again return to Monte Carlo. Several months ago, however, Onassis returned to collect the effects of his 24-year-old son Alexandre, who was killed in a plane crash. Alexandre had an apartment in Monte Carlo.

Rainier and Onassis met again, renewed acquaintances, decided to heal their rift. Rainier invited Onassis and his wife to spend more time in Monaco, but reportedly Jackie is not too fond of the place. She is not jealous of Princess Grace. But she is mindful of the fact that many years ago when Onassis was married to his first wife, Tina, the first Mrs. Onassis was recognized as the leading hostess of the French Riviera, throwing one fabulous party after another at their Château de la Croe. Ironically enough, Tina and Stavros Niarchos, her new husband, have taken over the same château outside Cannes.

Prince Rainier

Q *Why does Sen. James Buckley, the conservative Republican of New York, want Nixon to resign as president? Does he believe he is guilty? Doesn't he believe he is entitled to a fair trial?—John Donovan, Staten Island, N.Y.*

A Senator Buckley does not know whether President Nixon is guilty or not. He wants him to resign to spare the United States the national trauma of impeachment proceedings, a televised trial in the Senate, a possible conviction, and, even should the president be acquitted, a continued loss of prestige and effectiveness overseas. Senator Buckley is asking the president to place country above self. This is precisely what Edward VIII, King of Great Britain, did in 1936 when he performed an act of noblesse oblige by stepping down as monarch and permitting his brother to succeed to the throne. The U.S. is currently cleaved. Senator Buckley believes it will remain so for the length of the scandal-ridden Nixon administration, win, lose, or draw. Under the circumstances he suggests that Vice President Ford take over for Nixon. His mail at this writing is running 2 1/2 to 1 against his stand.

Q *Does Katharine Hepburn drink? On the Academy Awards telecast this year I noticed her shaking something terrible. Was it drink or nervousness?—Louise Baker, Los Angeles.*

Katharine Hepburn

A According to several physicians who watched the program, there is a possibility that Miss Hepburn, 64, may be suffering from Parkinson's disease, or shaking palsy. Miss Hepburn fiercely protects her privacy, and although she is a physician's daughter, she is the last to communicate any word about her health.

Q *What is the CIA Domestic Contact Service? Is it a service through which William E. Colby, head of the Central Intelligence Agency, supplies domestics for his men, or is it a domestic espionage service not allowed by law?—L.T., Washington, D.C.*

A The CIA Domestic Contact Service is an information-gathering operation. American businessmen, returning to the U.S. from foreign trips, are asked to pass on useful information gleaned in their overseas visits or tours of duty. "There is no payment of money," Richard Helms, former CIA director, testified before the Senate Foreign Relations Committee on February 7, 1973. "There is no effort to twist anyone's arm. We simply are giving them an opportunity as patriotic Americans to say what they know . . ." The CIA-businessmen relationships are kept top secret so as not to endanger the business executives or their companies.

Walter Scott's
PERSONALITY PARADE®

June 2, 1974

Q *Isn't it correct that Henry Kissinger proposed to Diane Sawyer of the White House press staff before he proposed to Nancy Maginnes, the present Mrs. Kissinger?—O.T., McLean, Va.*

Diane Sawyer

A Says Miss Sawyer: "That's absurd, he never proposed—not marriage, anyway."

Q *President Nixon has accused John Dean of playing a "criminal" role in Watergate, of offering clemency and bribery and coverup to the Watergate defendants. Who brought John Dean into the Justice Department and who made him President Nixon's lawyer?—R.O., Dover, Del.*

A John Dean was a protégé of John Mitchell, President Nixon's friend, law partner, campaign manager and attorney general. It was Mitchell who sponsored Dean.

Q *Why does the Wall Street crowd call William Simon, the new secretary of the treasury, "Popeye"?—Norma Parker, New York City.*

A Simon, multimillionaire former bond salesman for Salomon Brothers, has protruding eyeballs, and like the comics character he is named after, eats creamed spinach by the bucket.

Q *What's happened to Greer Garson? How many times married?—Frances Crouch, Redlands, Calif.*

A Greer Garson, 65, starred recently on television in the play *Crown Matrimonial*. She is still married to her third husband, New Mexico rancher Buddy Fogelson. Her other husbands were Edwin Snelson and Richard Ney, who 32 years ago played her son in her most popular film, *Mrs. Miniver.*

Q *So far in this administration we have had four U.S. attorneys general: John Mitchell, Richard Kleindienst, Elliot Richardson, and William Saxbe, and one acting attorney general, Robert Bork. Which one in your opinion was the best?—E.W.L., Cambridge, Mass.*

A A likely candidate for excellence is Elliot Richardson of whom President Nixon said on April 30, 1973: "As the new attorney general I have today named Elliot Richardson, a man of unimpeachable integrity. . . . I have given him absolute authority to make all decisions bearing upon the Watergate case and related matters. . . he has the authority to name a special supervising prosecutor. . . he will be fearless in pursuing this case wherever it leads."

Q *Is O. J. Simpson, football star on the Buffalo Bills, leaving football for a movie career?—Peter Underwood, Long Beach, Calif.*

A Simpson, who last season broke the National Football League's rushing record (the first man to gain 2,000 yards in a season) has no intention of quitting football. In the off-season, O. J. simply picked up a little spare cash by working in *The Klansman* with Richard Burton and Lee Marvin.

Q *Did Howard Hughes ever keep Gina Lollobrigida a Hollywood love captive? Was Gina ever in love with Dr. Christiaan Barnard, the heart transplanter? How old is Gina anyway, and is she finished in films as a leading lady?—Josephine Flores, Clifton, N.J.*

A Gina, 45, says that in 1950 Howard Hughes sent her a cable in Rome which said, "LET ME MAKE YOU A STAR." Gina explains: "Back then I had just married Dr. Milko Skofic, but I came to Hollywood where Howard insisted that I divorce Milko and marry him. I was locked up in his tremendous mansion for days, but I finally signed a contract, then flew back to Rome and Milko." Of Dr. Barnard, whose first wife published Gina's love letters to her husband, Gina says: "He is an idiot, a cheap publicity-seeker. I am a top film star. I know what publicity is and how it works." Replies Barnard: "She can say anything she likes. I don't care." Gina's film career is on the wane, but recently she has achieved some notoriety as a still photographer.

Howard Hughes

Gina Lollobrigida

Spiro Agnew

Q *Did Richard Nixon know that Spiro Agnew was "on the take" when he chose him as his running mate in '68? Did he know that Spiro Agnew was taking bribes while he was vice president of the United States? Why did Agnew keep telling lies up to the last minute, saying "I will not resign. I will not resign"? Also, is it true that the public has paid Agnew's lawyers?—David Evans, Baltimore, Md.*

A Nixon had no idea Agnew was crooked when he accepted him as his running mate. When he learned that Agnew was taking payoff money while still vice president of the U.S. he had his chief of staff, Gen. Alexander Haig, work on Agnew to resign. Agnew's lies to the American people about not resigning were part of his plea-bargaining technique. Approximately $178,000 of Agnew's legal fees have been paid through public contributions to his defense fund. A superb book, accurate and detailed, on the entire Agnew affair is *A Heartbeat Away: The Investigation and Resignation of Vice President Spiro T. Agnew*, by Jules Witcover and Richard M. Cohen (published by Viking).

PERSONALITY PARADE®

June 16, 1974

Clark Gable

Q *How old is Clark Gable's only child? Was he ever kidnapped? Is that why he is never seen in public?—Pamela Thomas, Encino, Calif.*

A John Gable, born four months after his father's death, is 13. He lives a highly protected life. His mother, Kay, four times married, says, "For years I've made it a practice to keep John out of the public eye. We had a kidnap threat a few months after he was born, and I've been afraid of another one ever since." Young John inherited approximately $400,000 from his father.

Q *Julia Child—who runs the cooking program on public television—was that nice matronly woman ever a spy for our Central Intelligence Agency?—Earl Adams, Reading, Pa.*

A Mrs. Julia McWilliams Child, now known as TV's "French Chef," worked for the Office of Strategic Services in Chungking, China, during World War II, maintained the OSS intelligence files there. She was never a spy for the Central Intelligence Agency, the organization which succeeded OSS.

Q *When Spiro Agnew goes to Greece as he recently did, does he have to clear*

such overseas trips with his probation officer? Also, why was Dale Anderson, who was Baltimore County Executive just as Agnew was, sent to jail for five years, and Agnew didn't pull a single night in the pokey?—Mrs. Allen L., Baltimore, Md.

A Spiro Agnew is on unsupervised probation for three years, which means he can go anywhere anytime he wants to without the permission of any probation officer. As regards Dale Anderson's sentence of five years in jail for the same kind of crimes Agnew was connected with, one must remember that justice in this country is frequently unequal, depending upon one's position and finances.

Q *Why is it that Mia Farrow and Robert Redford both refused to do promotional work on* The Great Gatsby? *Is David Margulies of St. Louis the same David Merrick who produced* The Great Gatsby?*—L.F., Joplin, Mo.*

Mia Farrow

A Reportedly Farrow and Redford dislike the film. David Margulies and David Merrick are one and the same.

Q *Can you tell me if it is true that Jews were barred from the jury which tried John Mitchell and Maurice Stans in New York City several weeks ago?— Harry Schwartz, Philadelphia.*

A They were not barred. They simply were not chosen by the Mitchell-Stans attorneys, who hired Marty Herbst of Conceptual Dynamics, Inc., to help them in jury selection. Having been guided by Herbst's research into the jurors' background, attorney Peter Fleming, Jr., chose those jurors who were non-Jewish, who were politically to the right, who read the *New York Daily News* instead of *The New York Times*, who had high school educations instead of college degrees. His selection of the jury was brilliant, the government's selection not.

Q *The U.S. Constitution says the president can be removed only for "treason, bribery, high crimes, and other misdemeanors." Does this mean that he can be removed only if he is a proved criminal? Suppose he is shown to be a profane, vindictive, incompetent, tax-cheating man who allowed his office to be used to destroy his*

political adversaries through wiretapping, surveillance, illegal entry, fraud, bribery, and other illegal means? Does he, despite all this, remain immune from removal?— D.T., Washington, D.C.

A There are two schools of thought on removing the president from office. James St. Clair, the Boston attorney obtained by Gen. Alexander M. Haig to save the president, believes in the strictest interpretation of the Constitution that evidence must be offered which conclusively proves the president guilty of a crime. Others maintain that the president can be removed if he does not meet his constitutional duties so that his conduct in office is detrimental to the welfare of the nation. There are historical precedents for both interpretations of the law.

Q *Alain Delon, 38, the French film star, and Mireille Darc, 32, the French film actress—married or living together?— Connie Halpern, Jamaica, N.Y.*

A After seven years of togetherness, no marriage yet.

Q *Does conservative columnist William F. Buckley agree with his brother, New York's Sen. James Buckley, that President Nixon should resign?— Anne C. Fisher, Fort Wayne, Ind.*

William Buckley

A Bill Buckley's "dream scenario" of how Nixon should leave the government calls for the House of Representatives to impeach Nixon, for Nixon then to remove himself voluntarily from office under provisions of the 25th Amendment, for the U.S. Senate to exonerate him, and finally for Nixon to resign. "There would be a certain amount of coitus interruptus in the whole thing," Buckley conceded, "but on the whole everybody's feelings would be taken care of . . . I don't think anybody would dispute the fact that if he ceased to be president today the country would be a whole lot better off."

The 25th Amendment permits a U.S. president to acknowledge that he is temporarily incapable of discharging the duties of his office and to be replaced by the vice-president. Subsequently he can declare that he has overcome his disability unless by a two-thirds vote, Congress decides otherwise.

WALTER SCOTT'S
PERSONALITY PARADE®

June 23, 1974

Q *A recent Gallup poll shows that 73 percent or almost three-fourths of the American people believe Richard Nixon was involved in Watergate or the coverup. Does this mean that the U.S. Congress feels the same way and wants Nixon removed from office?—Stephen Adams, Oakland, Calif.*

A In a general way Congress belatedly reflects U.S. public opinion. That does not mean, however, that 75 percent of the Congress wants Nixon removed from office at this time. It may mean that 75 percent of the Congress believes Nixon was involved in the Watergate coverup—two separate matters. At this writing, national polls reveal that 25 to 27 percent of the American people remain hard-core Nixon supports. A Gallup poll taken in May showed that of the Americans surveyed, 48 percent believe President Nixon should be removed from office; 37 percent believe he should not, and 15 percent have no opinion on the subject.

John Connally

Q *If former Gov. John Connally of Texas has become a dedicated Republican, why does he hire a Democratic law firm like Williams, Connolly & Califano to defend him in the dairy operators' scandal in which allegedly he is involved with Jake Jacobsen?—P.E., Alexandria, Va.*

A If Gov. Connally were sick, presumably he would hire the best physician he could get without inquiring into the doctor's politics. He feels the same way about lawyers. He obviously believes that the Washington, D.C., law firm, in which the senior partners are Edward Bennett Williams, Paul R. Connolly and Joseph Califano, is the best qualified to defend him in his alleged involvement with Jacobsen in the milk operators' scandal.

Q *Who are the 10 most eligible bachelors in the United States?—S.M., Ann Arbor, Mich.*

Ryan O'Neal

A Arbitrarily: U.S. Sen. John Tunney (D., Calif.); U.S. Sen. Joseph Biden (D., Del.); basketball stars Wilt Chamberlain and Walt Frazier; consumer advocate Ralph Nader; football star Joe Namath; film star Ryan O'Neal; TV performer David Frost; *Playboy* magazine founder Hugh Hefner; heir to General Motors fortune Stewart Mott.

Q *How old is Grace Kelly? How long has she been married to Prince Rainier of Monaco? How old is he? Is he still a playboy? Is their marriage secure?—Alma Zack, Silver Hill, Md.*

A Grace Kelly is 44. Rainier is 51. They have been married 18 years, have three children: Princess Caroline, 17; Crown Prince Albert, 16; Princess Stephanie, 9. Prince Rainier stopped playing around when he got married. His marriage to Princess Grace is from all accounts successful and happy.

Q *A stripper from Mingo County, West Virginia, named Blaze Starr claims to have been the mistress of the late Earl Long, governor of Louisiana, and the girlfriend of Frank Rizzo, now mayor of Philadelphia. Is there any truth to her claims?— D.L., Philadelphia, Pa.*

A Blaze Starr (real name—Sissie Fleming) has written her autobiography, *Blaze Starr—My Life Story as told to Huey Perry*, published by Praeger. In her book Blaze details her spicy relationships with Long and Rizzo. If she is not telling the truth, Mayor Rizzo may sue her and her publishers for libel.

Q *The real reason, please, why Willy Brandt resigned as chancellor of West Germany? Wasn't it because he was afraid his private life would be revealed rather than because his aide, Gunter Guillaume, turned out to be a Communist spy?—F.R. Becker, Cincinnati, Ohio.*

A Brandt gave three reasons for his resignation: (1) He let top secret papers fall into the hands of Guillaume even though he knew Guillaume was suspected of being an East German spy; (2) He felt he would hinder Bonn's relationships with East Germany and the Warsaw Pact nations; (3) He was afraid various aspects of his private life, particularly his campaign travels during which he was interviewed by female journalists who found him fascinating, would be drawn into speculation.

Q *When are Moshe Dayan's memoirs coming out?—Herbert Robinson, New York City.*

A Moshe Dayan, who was paid $107 a week as Israel's defense minister, has signed a contract with a British publisher, Weidenfeld and Nicholson, for his memoirs. Dayan will receive, if he hasn't already, an advance of $450,000 for the book which will be published in 1976.

Q *I understand that actor Henry Fonda had a pacemaker implanted to help his ailing heart. What other celebrities use pacemakers and how do they work?— Louise Brown, Ft. Lauderdale, Fla.*

A Among the more than 150,000 Americans using the battery-powered device are Supreme Court Justice William O. Douglas and President Nixon's close friend Elmer Bobst, the honorary chairman of Warner-Lambert Company. The pacemaker works by sending out steady electric impulses that stimulate the heart to beat at the proper rhythm.

Q *Was Doris Day's son, Terry Melcher, ever married to Sen. Barry Goldwater's daughter?—L. Harman, Douglas, Ariz.*

A No, for a short time he went with Senator Goldwater's niece, Wendy Johnson, 24.

Doris Day

Jackie and Aristotle Onassis

Q *I have heard it said that ever since he married Jackie Kennedy, Aristotle Onassis has been saddled with bad luck. Is there any truth to this story?— Edward Hawk, Philadelphia, Pa.*

A Since his marriage to Jackie, Onassis has lost his son Alexander in a plane crash; his airline, Olympic Airways, has gone into the red; he has failed to win permission to build a refinery in New Hampshire; his longtime friendship with opera star Maria Callas has gone sour; his privacy has been violated by the omnipresent paparazzi hounding him and Jackie for photographs. On the other hand, being married to the former Jackie Kennedy has undoubtedly brought Onassis moments of pride and pleasure.

Q *Is it not a fact that Richard Nixon never wanted Gerald Ford as his vice president, that his first choice after the Spiro Agnew scandal was Governor John Connally of Texas?—K.F., San Antonio, Tex.*

A Nixon preferred Connally to Ford. It was Melvin Laird, however, who convinced Nixon that Connally was a too new convert to the Republican Party to win congressional approval as vice president. Under the circumstances it was lucky that Nixon listened to Laird since Connally was subsequently indicted on five counts in the milk support scandal. One of Mr. Nixon's major weaknesses was his incredibly bad personnel judgment.

Q *What's happened to William Rogers who was secretary of state under Nixon?— Maybelle Johnson, El Paso, Tex.*

A Mr. Rogers is a partner in the New York and Washington law firm of Rogers & Wells, handles legal affairs for the government and Shah of Iran, and many others. He is also a director in the brokerage firm of Merrill Lynch Pierce Fenner & Smith. He is one Nixonian who got out before the Nixon administration collapsed.

Q *Is it true that in the United States, your ambassadorships are for sale to the largest political campaign contributors? Is it true that Ruth Farkas was named ambassador to Luxembourg after she and her husband donated $400,000 to the president's campaign in 1972?—L.F., Montreal, Canada.*

A It is a stupid, evil and traditional practice, hopefully on the way out. In 1963, for example, 34 percent of our ambassadors were political appointees. By 1972 the figure was down to 22 percent. It is true about Mrs. Farkas and her husband George. But the practice is also true of Harry Truman and Perle Mesta and Dwight Eisenhower and Clare Boothe Luce. Mrs. Luce, at least, had some international background which qualified her as an ambassador to Italy. But Mrs. Mesta's main qualification was money.

Cass Elliot

Q *Cass Elliot, the singer of "Mamas and the Papas" fame—did she really choke to death on a sandwich in England?—Elise Conrat, Portland, Me.*

A Cass Elliot died of a heart attack. Prof. Keith Simpson, pathologist for the British Home Office who performed the autopsy, revealed that Mama Cass weighed 225 pounds, twice the normal weight for a woman of her size, and was suffering from advanced fatty degeneration of the heart muscle.

Q *Isn't it true that His Holiness, the Pope, has never seen Jesus Christ Superstar and that PARADE's "Keeping Up . . . With Youth" editor fell for phony publicity that he had and liked it?—R.R.S., Tucson, Ariz.*

A The Pope has not seen the film and any publicity to the effect that he has is untrue.

Q *Before the Nixon administration came into power, how many federal officials were impeached by the House of Representatives?—Claude Ettinger, Baltimore, Md.*

A Thirteen, including President Andrew Johnson. Only four resulted in conviction by the Senate. All four were judges.

Q *I would like to know if the Secret Service still guards Mamie Eisenhower, if she has ever been threatened, and how much, if there is any Secret Service surveillance, it costs?—K.L., Gettysburg, Pa.*

A Mamie Eisenhower is protected by 14 Secret Service agents. She has never been substantially threatened. The annual cost of her protection to the federal government is an estimated $300,000.

Q *It seems to me in retrospect that Richard Nixon's two major mistakes were (1) hiring Bob Haldeman as his chief of staff and (2) tape recording so many of his presidential conversations. My question is why did he take these two actions?—Lois Jenkins, Salt Lake City, Utah.*

A Haldeman was a veteran Nixon supporter, fanatic in his loyalty, a characteristic Nixon apparently values above candor. Nixon planned to use the tape recordings in the writing of his memoirs.

Q *Some questions, please, about Patty Hearst. Her grandfather was the late William Randolph Hearst. Who is her paternal grandmother? And is she still living? Also did Patty get along with her parents? Also did William Randolph Hearst ever win an elective office?—L.T., Hillsborough, Calif.*

Patty Hearst

A Patty Hearst's paternal grandmother is ex-showgirl Millicent Willson Hearst, now in her 90's and living in New York. Patty Hearst got along with her parents, more so with her father, Randolph, than her mother, Catherine. William Randolph Hearst was a member of the U.S. House of Representatives from 1903-07. Was subsequently defeated when he ran for mayor of New York City and governor of New York State.

WALTER SCOTT'S
PERSONALITY PARADE®

September 22, 1974

Q *Is Sally Quinn of* The Washington Post *writing a book attacking CBS for firing her from the Morning News?—Alice Walsh, Staten Island, N.Y.*

A Sally Quinn is writing a book, *We're Going To Make You a Star*, which Simon & Schuster will publish early next year. Originally planned as an article for *The Atlantic Monthly*, the manuscript was expanded into an 80,000-word book. Miss Quinn

DM / Globe

Sally Quinn

has received a $70,000 advance on the book and will receive 60 percent of the paperback sales. "I've named all the people I dealt with," she explains. "But I haven't tried to do anyone in. I think the corporate system comes out the villain."

Q *Isn't Mrs. Gerald Ford the first divorcée in U.S. history to become the nation's First Lady? And if she isn't, who is? And what can you tell us about her?—Denise Richardson, Raleigh, N.C.*

A The first divorcée to become the nation's First Lady was Florence Kling Harding, the nagging, domineering wife of Warren G. Harding, 29th president of the U.S. Florence Mabel Kling was born in Marion, Ohio, in 1860, the daughter of Amos Kling, one of the wealthiest men in town. In 1880, "Flossie" Kling eloped with Henry de Wolfe, a local playboy. Six months later on Sept. 22, 1880, their son, Eugene Marshall, was born in Prospect, Ohio.

In 1886 Florence de Wolfe was granted a divorce, was permitted to use her maiden name. She turned over her son to her parents. Her ex-husband, Henry de Wolfe, became a thief and an alcoholic and died in 1894 at age 35. He was buried in an unmarked grave in Marion, Ohio.

In 1891, Florence Kling married Warren G. Harding. She was 30. He was 25. In 1921, when Harding was sworn in as president of the U.S., Florence "The Duchess" Harding became First Lady in an administration which was to become stigmatized as one of the most corrupt in U.S. history. Harding died in San Francisco in August, 1923, whereupon his widow stupidly burned most of his files and papers. She died in November, 1924, the American public having learned little of her true background. History has recorded her a shrew, her husband as a good-natured, immoral, incompetent president, one of the nation's two worst.

Q *Can you tell us anything about Joe Albritton who has bought into* The Washington Star-News?—*Peter Lord, Arlington, Va.*

A Joe Lewis Albritton, 49, is a Texas lawyer and banker who runs the Houston Citizens Trust Company. He also owns a majority interest in Pierce Bros. Mortuaries of Los Angeles, is chairman of the board of Pierce National Life Insurance Co. of Los Angeles and is chairman of the executive committee of First International Bancshares of Dallas. He is a religious Baptist, a conservative Democrat. He was born in D'Lo, Mississippi, the sixth of seven Albritton children. He is married, has an eight-year-old son.

Q *Can you tell what's happened to actress Angie Dickinson who, I understand, knew the late President John F. Kennedy in his Hollywood salad days?—T.T., Washington, D.C.*

A Angie Dickinson, married to composer Burt

Ormitz / Globe

Angie Dickinson

Bacharach, recently finished starring in *Big Bad Mama*, the first film to exploit the public interest in the Patty Hearst affair.

Q *It is my understanding that when a president retires from his office, only he and his wife are entitled to Secret Service protection. How come then that President Nixon's two daughters were accorded Secret Service protection long after Nixon left the White House?—Martin Bernstein, Miami, Fla.*

A They weren't accorded Secret Service protection "long after" Nixon left the White House. President Ford as a courtesy to the Nixon girls and their parents asked the Secret Service to look after Tricia and Julie for a few days.

Q *Wasn't Adolf Hitler able to take over the German army for his Nazis because most of the army generals were homosexuals, especially their leaders, Generals Von Blomberg and Von Fritsch?—Hans Dietric, Milwaukee, Wis.*

A Most of Germany's generals were not homosexual. The two most important in 1937, Von Blomberg and Von Fritsch, were opposed to Hitler's plans for a European war. Hitler thereupon decided to remove them. In Von Blomberg's case this was fairly easy because Von Blomberg

had married "a girl of the night" and could easily be blackmailed on the basis of her morals. To engineer Von Fritsch's resignation was more difficult, because Von Fritsch was widely respected. Hitler, however, had him arraigned on a trumped-up homosexual charge in a stacked court presided over by Goering. The charges were completely false and never proven, but Von Fritsch resigned anyway, whereupon Hitler proceeded to take over the army and lead it into a disastrous war.

Q *Is there no end to the Watergate scandal even with Nixon's resignation? How much of the taxpayers' money has been spent on the Watergate mess, anyway?—Robert Blake, Cambridge, Mass.*

A It should be over by the end of the year. To date approximately $10 million of the taxpayers' money has been spent on the scandal.

Q *What was the secret of Winston Churchill's greatness? Wasn't it a "gift for gab" rather than a brilliant intelligence?—Morton Edward, Raleigh, N.C.*

A Churchill was primarily a great orator. As his physician Lord Moran wrote: "Without that feeling for words he would have made little enough in life, for in judgment, in skill, in administration, and the knowledge of human nature he does not at all excel." Churchill was frequently rude, ill-mannered and self-obsessed. He was always conservative and strongly anti-labor. In 1910 he called out the troops to break the strikes. Following World War II he was voted out of office by people who unlike himself had no desire to preserve and pay for the old British Empire. He was, however, a truly great wartime leader who all his life aspired to glory and leadership.

Winston Churchill

Q *When I was in Hollywood some weeks ago I heard someone say, "Peter Bogdanovich is pulling another Anna Sten with Cybill Shepherd." Can you interpret that statement?—K.L., San Diego, Calif.*

Cybill Shepherd

A Many years ago the late film producer Sam Goldwyn tried to make a star of an actress named Anna Sten. He failed. The public simply refused to accept her. Director Peter Bogdanovich may be trying the same trick with his girlfriend, Cybill Shepherd. He starred her in *Daisy Miller*, a bomb, and has starred her again in a $7 million production, *At Long Last Love*. Cybill Shepherd is a top model. She is kind to her mother. But to date, the acting talent she has shown is minuscule.

Q *Has Rose Mary Woods, the famous secretary of Richard Nixon, retired, or is she employed elsewhere?—A.M.B., Madison, Wis.*

A Rose Mary Woods is still Mr. Nixon's secretary, working at this writing out of the White House in connection with transition affairs.

Q *Lenny Bruce, the comedian whose life served as the basis for the Dustin Hoffman film* Lenny—*is it true that Bruce was so foul-mouthed that he was banned from performing in overseas countries?—Jean Catt, Newark, N.J.*

A Lenny Bruce was an addict who died in Hollywood in 1966 from a drug overdose. He was a "sick" comic whose raw routines made him unacceptable in Great Britain.

Q *What is the Azores Fixed Acoustic Range? I believe it has something to do with the Navy.—M. Ellis, Salem, Mass.*

A The Azores Fixed Acoustic Range located in the Azores, a group of islands in the Atlantic owned by Portugal, consists of a group of sonars mounted on submerged towers. These sonars monitor submarine traffic through the Strait of Gibraltar and other waters and are linked by computers to Washington. They are designed to prevent an enemy nuclear attack upon the U.S.

Q *I would like to know how much money Chris Evert, the 20-year-old tennis player from Fort Lauderdale, earned last year.—Cissie Clark, Miami, Fla.*

A Approximately $300,000 in prize money and endorsements.

Q *What's happened to the marriage between Peter Lawford and Mary Rowan, daughter of comedian Dan Rowan?—Elsie Kitchener, Ventura, Calif.*

A Miss Rowan, 23, was granted an interlocutory decree from actor Peter Lawford, 51, on grounds of "irreconcilable differences" after 18 months of marriage. Miss Rowan asked for and was awarded the couple's double bed, automobile, and dishes, all gifts to her from her father. She was awarded no alimony.

Pablo and Marta Casals

Q *Pablo Casals, the great cellist, was 97 when he died in 1973. He left a beautiful wife, 60 years younger. Where is she? What's happened to her? She was a knockout.—Chuck Sullivan, West Palm Beach, Fla.*

A Marta Casals, 38, was Casals' star cello pupil when they fell in love in October, 1954, in the south of France. Mrs. Casals lives in San Juan, Puerto Rico, where she presides over the Casals Festival, a public corporation financed by the Puerto Rico government. Mrs. Casals oversees the summer Casals concerts, supervises the Puerto Rico Symphony Orchestra, and the Puerto Rico Conservatory of Music. Until a few weeks ago when she announced plans to wed pianist Eugene Istomin, she was working 12-14 hours a day, seven days a week, too busy to write her memoirs for which so many publishers are importuning.

Q *Abortion is illegal in Italy. Yet I understand 1.5 million Italian women had abortions last year. Who is responsible for this travesty?—D.L. Leone, Trenton, N.J.*

A The Italian Ministry of Health says there were 800,000 abortions in Italy last year. The World Health Organization says there were 1.5 million. Other informed sources place the number at 3 million. In Italy anyone involved in an abortion, whether therapeutic or not, faces a prison sentence of two to five years. Despite this provision of the Italian penal code, many Italian women insist upon the right to abortion. Their leader is Gianfranco Spadaccia, 39, leader of the Radical Party, supporter of the Florence abortion clinic, which provides operations by competent surgeons for $150. Spadaccia has been arrested, and the Florence clinic has been shut down. As a result backroom abortions, dangerous and unhygienic, thrive.

Q *William Powell who used to play the sophisticated Thin Man in those movies with Myrna Loy—is he still alive? Where? How old?—Lynn Baer, Raleigh, N.C.*

A William Powell, 82, retired, resides at this writing in Palm Springs, Calif.

Q *Isn't there a chance that Miss Vicki, the estranged wife of Tiny Tim, will be jailed for falsely accepting relief money in New Jersey?—D.F., Camden, N.J.*

Tiny Tim

A There's a small chance since county officials are investigating possible welfare fraud. Vicki Budinger, formerly of Haddonfield, New Jersey, allegedly worked as a go-go dancer in a New Jersey nightclub while she was on the welfare roles at $235 a month. Moreover, her husband Tiny Tim claims that he was sending her $100 a month for the support of Tulip, their three-year-old daughter. Miss Vicki is currently in London where she expects to marry Amos Levy if she hasn't already.

Sophia Loren

Q *I understand that many film stars with children who live in Italy are moving out of that country because of all the kidnapping going on. Is this so?—Milo Craig, Pittsburgh, Pa.*

A To date it's true of Sophia Loren, who has taken her two sons, Eduardo, two, and Cipi, six, and moved to Paris. Both boys have been registered for enrollment in Eton, so that eventually Sophia, 40, and her husband, Carlo Ponti, may well move to London.

Q *Since President Ford was so quick to give Richard Nixon a full and complete pardon for all the crimes he may have committed, including income tax evasion, obstruction of justice, telling lies to the American people, masterminding the Watergate coverup, and who knows what else—why won't Ford give the same sort of pardon to Nixon's fellow conspirators: John N. Mitchell, Bob Haldeman, John Ehrlichman, and Robert Mardian?—F.G., Phoenix, Ariz.*

A President Ford's reasoning is as follows: Mr. Nixon is the only president in U.S. history who was forced to resign from office. The pardon for him was intended to end the national focus on Watergate and to put the bitterness and divisiveness surrounding Watergate behind us so that the nation could focus on its difficult problems. Ford contends that these circumstances do not apply to Mitchell, Haldeman, Ehrlichman and Mardian and that these convicted men must pursue the normal judicial processes. This is specious reasoning, of course, having little to do with equal justice under law and pointing up the proclivity of relating prior pardon to high office. But according to White House spokesmen this is what President Ford contends.

Q *What's happened to Dixy Lee Ray, former chairwoman of the Atomic Energy Commission?—Beulah Eagleton, Orlando, Fla.*

A Dixy Lee Ray has moved over to the State Department where she is assistant secretary for oceans and international environmental and scientific affairs. The Energy Reorganization Act of 1974 created two new agencies to replace the Atomic Energy Commission: The Energy Research and Development Administration (ERDA) and the Nuclear Regulatory Commission.

Q *Is it true that when Pat Gray was acting director of the FBI, several FBI agents tried to blackmail him?—R.R., Hartford, Conn.*

A One special agent transferred by Gray said to him: "We're going to keep a black book on you, you son-of-a-bitch, until we get you good." Gray's reply: "You just try and see what happens to you."

Q *Having seen Barbra Streisand and James Caan in* Funny Lady, *the story of the late comedienne, Fanny Brice, I wonder how much truth there is in the picture. For example, didn't Fanny Brice have two children? And when she married Billy Rose, wasn't he the most ill-bred, crude, money-grubbing promoter on Broadway and only 4 feet 10?—P.T., Hempstead, N.Y.*

Billy Rose

Steinberg / Globe

A There is an outline of truth to the film. Fannie Borach was born on New York City's Lower East Side in 1891. Her father was a saloon owner. She won amateur singing contests at age 14, took her first show business job as a chorus girl at 15. In 1910 she sang in burlesque, was subsequently hired by Ziegfeld who starred her in his *Follies* over the years. By the 1920's she was an international stage star. Her first marriage was annulled. Her second was to the gambler and conman Nicky Arnstein with whom she had two children, Frances, now married to Ray Stark, producer of the Barbra Streisand film, and William, a top Los Angeles artist. Fanny Brice married Billy Rose, a brash Broadway promoter in 1929. He was 5 feet 3; she was 5 feet 8. They were divorced in 1938. Fanny Brice developed into a superb interior decorator, an outstanding artist, and a woman of impeccable taste and character. Rose became a multimillionaire in AT & T stock after producing many Broadway hits.

Bob Hope

Q *How old is Bob Hope? How long has he been known as "Mr. Republican," and when did he stop being politically neutral?—Martin Hyatt, Cathedral City, Calif.*

A Bob Hope, born Leslie Townes Hope in Eltham, England, on May 29, 1903, was advised by his late agent, Jimmy Saphier, to keep his political life private. Until the Nixon administration, which Hope supported morally and monetarily, the comedian did not live his political life in public. Once Nixon came to power in 1969, however, Hope, by then the richest man in show business, decided that he no longer would keep his Republican Party affiliation a secret.

WALTER SCOTT'S
PERSONALITY PARADE®

May 11, 1975

Nelson Rockefeller

Haarris and Ewing / Globe

Q *Is it true that Vice President Nelson Rockefeller cannot read because he suffers from some kind of disease?—E.H.C., Wallingford, Conn.*

A Rockefeller used to suffer from dyslexia, a reading difficulty in which he read words in transposed position. He long ago overcame the difficulty.

Q *I would like to know if Bing Crosby has retired; also his age.—Jan Walker, Sioux Falls, S.D.*

A Crosby, 71, has not retired, recently showed up in London where he cut two record albums consisting of his old favorites such as "Some Sunny Day," "The Best Things in Life Are Free," "Breezing Along With the Breeze." The old groaner also makes an occasional TV appearance or commercial but spends most of his time fishing, playing golf, and leading a relaxing life.

Q *When are the Emperor and Empress of Japan coming to the U.S. to reciprocate President Ford's visit to Japan?—Eloise Schaeffer, Akron, Ohio.*

A The Emperor and Empress will fly to Anchorage, Alaska, on October 1, 1975, will visit Washington, D.C., Woods Hole, Massachusetts; New York City, Chicago, Los Angeles, and on October 9th, the Scripps Institute of Oceanography at La Jolla, California, near San Diego.

Q *During President Ford's Easter vacation in Palm Springs, he occupied at $100 a day the residence of his good friend Fred Wilson. Who is Fred Wilson?—D.L., San Bernardino, Calif.*

A Fred Wilson, 55, is a successful insurance broker with branches in Beverly Hills and the Bahamas who likes to golf with Ford.

Q *How is Shirley Temple Black doing as U.S. ambassador to Ghana?—T.E., Salinas, Calif.*

Shirley Temple Black

Globe

A The word in diplomatic circles is that after only a few months on the job, Shirley Temple Black has become "the most popular U.S. ambassador to Ghana the Americans have ever sent us." The one-time child movie star not only tries to speak Ashanti but she dresses from time to time in Ghanaian clothes and has become one of the most charming and industrious diplomates in West Africa.

Q *Now that events have humbled Henry Kissinger somewhat, any chance he might show enough courtesy to the rest of us by taking English lessons from the Actors Studio or Berlitz? When it's so easy for actors to shed their accents, why has Dr. Kissinger been so adamant about retaining the Dr. Strangelove sound?—E. Wagner, Denver, Col.*

Henry Kissinger

Globe

A Dr. Kissinger does not make his living as a professional actor. He is a foreign policy expert. His accent, such as it is, does not handicap his performance. "The Dr. Strangelove sound" you refer to lies in the ear of the listener. Dr. Kissinger has been adamant on many points, but the retention of his slight accent is not one of them.

Q *The illegal political activities of several major airlines have in my opinion been criminal. Is someone like Harding Lawrence of Braniff Airways going to jail, or will these secret slush funds be covered up?—G.L., Dallas, Tex.*

A The Civil Aeronautics Board, the federal agency charged with regulating the nation's airlines, recently charged that American Airlines and Braniff Airways maintained and manipulated secret political slush funds and violated various reporting procedures. Harding Lawrence of Braniff will have to account to the CAB, his stockholders, the Internal Revenue Service, and possibly the Securities and Exchange Commission as well as the Justice Department for his responsibility in the mess.

Q *I understand that Rabbi Baruch Korff, Richard Nixon's fund-raiser, has been offering Nixon for lectures and TV interviews at $250,000 per. Have there been any takers? Why does Nixon need so much money?—T.R.R., Arcadia, Calif.*

A According to Rabbi Korff, Nixon has run up some $300,000 in legal bills in order to keep control of his presidential tapes and papers. Public contributions as of last month paid about $145,000 of those bills. No networks have offered Nixon $250,000 for an interview.

Q *Evonne Goolagong, the Australian tennis champ who is part aborigine —what does her name mean in her native tongue, if anything?—Carl Mayer, Madison, Wis.*

A According to Miss Goolagong, who is one-fourth aborigine, "My name translates into 'tall trees by still waters.' "

Q *Does Warren Beatty hate Frank Sinatra? Did they have a fight on the night of the Academy Awards? Didn't his sister Shirley MacLaine have a fight with Sammy Davis, Jr., that same night?—C. Bradfield, Santa Cruz, Calif.*

A On April 8, 1975, at the Academy Awards telecast, Warren and Shirley made comments concerning Sinatra's and Davis'

Frank Sinatra

support of the Republican Party—both Sinatra and Davis were staunch Richard Nixon supporters—but there was no fight, just good-natured kidding.

WALTER SCOTT'S
PERSONALITY PARADE®

June 15, 1975

Q *I understand that Columbia Pictures is secretly negotiating with Victor Marchetti, author of* The CIA *and* Cult of Intelligence, *to write a film called* The Director. *It would be based on the clandestine activities in Italy of William Colby, director of the CIA. In this film Colby would be depicted as having fallen in love with Clare Boothe Luce, who was U.S. ambassador to Rome when Colby was CIA chief there. Is any of this so?—L.G., McLean, Va.*

A Marchetti and a Hollywood studio have been discussing a screenplay to be entitled *The Director*.

John Wayne

Q *I would like to know if John Wayne is really a duke?—Charles A. Thurman, Vancouver, Wash.*

A Wayne was born Marion Michael Morrison in 1907 at 404 E. Court St. in Winterset, Iowa (pop. 2,956), and was named "Duke" after an Airedale he owned.

Q *There have been two blots on Gerald Ford's congressional career. Do you know what they were, and will they be used against him in the 1976 presidential campaign?—Allen Wood, Grand Rapids, Mich.*

A One was his ill-advised and widely publicized attempt to impeach Supreme Court Justice William O. Douglas, and his second was recommending Gordon Liddy, the zany Watergate burglar, for a job in the Treasury Department. Of these two, only the first was serious, because it reflected a vindictiveness which is uncharacteristic of Ford's basic good nature. The second was purely accidental.

Q *Who is the beautiful blonde Sen. Ted Kennedy has been squiring about? She's a dead ringer for his wife, Joan, except that she's a whole lot younger.—F.J.D., Bethesda, Md.*

Page Lee Hufty

A You probably have in mind Page Lee Hufty, tall, beautiful, shapely, blonde artist-daughter of a Palm Beach, Florida investment banker. Page lives in Washington, D.C., is an old tennis-playing crony of the senator, and is 27.

Q *How long have Fred MacMurray and June Haver been married, and what are they doing?—Letty Franciscus, Staten Island, N.Y.*

A Fred MacMurray and June Haver, shown here at the opening of the Sheraton Paris Hotel, have been married 20 years. He's working in films and commercials. She's retired.

Q *Is it true that it takes an average of 15 months to get a telephone in Paris? What sort of civilized country is France?—J. Jewis, Miami, Fla.*

A When it comes to telephone installations the French are hopeless. It takes 15 months to get a phone in Paris. By 1980 the French hope the waiting time will be reduced to a month.

Q *Now that Clyde Tolson is dead, will the nation ever know the truth about his relationship with the late J. Edgar Hoover? Why really did Hoover bequeath Tolson his $500,000 estate?—Ellen Patten, New York City.*

J. Edgar Hoover

A Clyde Tolson, a bachelor like Hoover, was Hoover's most intimate friend. Through most of his 44-year career in the FBI, Tolson was Hoover's second in command. He and Hoover socialized, traveled, and worked together. They were virtually inseparable. After Hoover died on May 2, 1974, Tolson was importuned to write about and disclose the history of their relationship. Tolson refused. He did not, however, refuse to accept as principal beneficiary the $550,000 estate Hoover left him. Many FBI veterans regarded Tolson as the single most knowledgeable man concerning the secret life of J. Edgar Hoover.

Q *Did Harry Belafonte ever drop $700,000 at the Las Vegas crap tables? Is his wife white? Is Maya Angelou, the black writer, married to a white? Is Diana Ross married to a white?—L.L., Roxbury, Mass.*

A Belafonte reportedly once dropped $70,000 at the Vegas gaming tables. Belafonte, Ross, and Angelou all have white mates.

Burt Reynolds

Q *Is it true that actor Burt Reynolds has ditched Dinah Shore for Liza Minnelli because Liza is younger?—Bobbie Jenkins, Philadelphia.*

A After four years the Reynolds-Shore romance has petered out. Dinah is 58. Reynolds is 39. While it lasted their affair was mutually rewarding. As regards Reynolds and Liza Minnelli with whom he's just finished filming, she is married to Jack Haley, Jr.

Q *President Ford's trip to Helsinki—did it accomplish anything for this country? Didn't the number of newsmen who attended the Helsinki conference outnumber the delegates?—M. Lewis, New York City.*

A The European summit at Helsinki provided more show than substance for the United States. Newsmen who covered the summit outnumbered the delegates, 1,550 to 1,111. What President Ford and Secretary of State Kissinger have to negotiate with the Soviets is an agreement on strategic nuclear armaments. Without that, détente begins to wane. No such deal was made at Helsinki.

Q *When James Hoffa was sent to prison for jury tampering, the Teamsters Union settled his pension claims. For how much?—T.E., Detroit.*

A For $1.7 million.

Q *Howard Hughes' Glomar Explorer—why was it not sent back into the Pacific to raise the rest of that sunken Russian submarine? Isn't that $400 million of the taxpayers' money going right down the drain?—L.R., Redwood City, Cal.*

Howard Hughes

A Obviously a high-level intelligence decision was made not to nettle the Soviets. Obviously it was made by President Ford, Secretary of State Kissinger, and Secretary of Defense Schlesinger with input from CIA director William Colby.

Q *Tip O'Neill, the congressman from Cambridge, Mass.—isn't he about to succeed Carl Albert, the Democratic Speaker of the House who plans to resign?—F.T., Cambridge, Mass.*

A If Albert decided to resign—and he very well may—Tip O'Neill has the job.

Q *When the Organization of American States voted to normalize trade relations with Cuba, which American countries voted against the resolution?—Louis Sala, Miami, Fla.*

A Chile, Paraguay and Uruguay voted against removing the trade embargo. Brazil and Nicaragua abstained.

Q *I see that Elizabeth Taylor has agreed to tell all in her autobiography. Who is publishing it? And can the actress write? What is the extent of her formal education?—N. Kawashima, Los Angeles.*

Elizabeth Taylor

A Elizabeth Taylor has signed with the British publishing house of W. H. Allen to handle her autobiography. A ghost writer will be assigned to help her. Miss Taylor was graduated from the MGM Studio High School. She would very much like to show the facility in writing and wit that her fifth husband, actor Richard Burton, once demonstrated.

Q *Can you tell me anything about Jack Nicholson, the screen star? How old, where from, background?—Nell Lavery, Rochester, N.Y.*

A Nicholson, 38, was born in Neptune Park, New Jersey, a few months after his alcoholic father deserted the family. He was reared by his mother, a successful beauty shop owner. He came to Hollywood after high school, spent the 1950's and 60's playing bit parts in horror movies and on TV shows. Subsequently he hit it big in *Easy Rider, Five Easy Pieces, Carnal Knowledge, The Last Detail* and *Chinatown*. He was married in 1962 to actress Sandra Knight from whom he is now divorced. Nicholson has won four Academy Award nominations, earns $1 million a picture, is currently working with Marlon Brando in a western, *Missouri Breaks*.

Q *Since David Frost, the British TV interviewer, has agreed to pay Richard Nixon $600,000 to $1 million for a series of four interviews, and Nixon is getting a $2 million advance from book publishers, and his estates in San Clemente and Key Biscayne are worth at least $1.5 million and he gets a government pension for life—doesn't this mean he has no financial worries?—F.L., Knoxville, Tenn.*

A With Rabbi Korff raising money to pay his legal battles plus what he has and will get, Richard Nixon, it would appear, has no financial worries at this time.

Q *Indira Gandhi, prime minister of India—how long will the army support her? Will the Indian army permit her to turn India into a Fascist dictatorship?—Harold Schmidt, Milwaukee, Wis.*

A The Indian army will probably support Mrs. Gandhi so long as she does not try to turn the army on the Indian people.

Q *Who is Kim Roosevelt? What is his connection with the CIA?—Rose Hendry, Charlottesville, Va.*

A Kermit "Kim" Roosevelt, 60, is a former chief of the CIA's Middle East Department. In 1953 he was responsible for ousting Mossadegh, then Premier of Iran, and restoring power to the present Shah. Roosevelt retired from the CIA around 1959, has since worked as a consultant and adviser to such corporate giants as Northrop, Gulf, Tenneco, and Raytheon. Out of Groton and Harvard, class of '37, a former history professor at Cal Tech, Roosevelt joined the OSS (Office of Strategic Services) in World War II, wrote its history, became pro-arab, and rejoined the intelligence community in 1950. In 1964 he started Kermit Roosevelt and Associates, a power in Middle East contacts. A grandson of President Theodore Roosevelt, "Kim" is well-known in corporate circles as "a man who can get things done in the Middle East."

Joe DiMaggio and Marilyn Monroe

Q *Who is the man who sends flowers to Marilyn Monroe's burial-site three times a week, year in and year out?—Jeanne May, Rockford, Ill.*

A Her second husband, ex-baseball star Joe DiMaggio.

WALTER SCOTT'S

PERSONALITY PARADE®

September 28, 1975

Henry Kissinger

Q *What does Nancy Kissinger do when she accompanies her husband on those overseas trips? He is so busy negotiating.—M.R., McLean, Va.*

A Mrs. Kissinger provides serenity, comfort, and an altogether civilizing influence to a husband frequently wracked by mounting frustration.

Q *Would I be accurate in saying that our men who lost their lives in Vietnam died for absolutely nothing?—J.L.W., Waupun, Wis.*

A Opinion is largely a matter of judgment—not a statement of fact.

Q *What sort of man is Gov. Edmund G. Brown, Jr., of California? I hear conflicting reports ranging from "great" to "flop."—Helen Wood, Tucson, Ariz.*

A Like all politicians, Brown, 37, has supporters and detractors. His supporters say he is shrewd, intelligent, perceptive, pragmatic, finely tuned in to the anti-political music of the people who have little faith at this time in politicians and their promises. Brown's detractors claim he is super-ambitious, wants to be president, is basically a loner without warmth, heart, love, compassion, tenderness, or rudimentary manners. They say that had the California gubernatorial campaign of 1974 continued for two more weeks, Brown would have surely lost to Republican candidate

Houston Flournoy. It is too early to pass any valid judgment on Brown. But certainly he is a young governor to watch.

Q *Are women allowed to join the U.S. Coast Guard?—Gwen F., Palo Alto, Ca.*

A The U.S. Coast Guard Academy at New London, Connecticut, will start admitting young women in July, 1976. Women must apply by December 15, 1975.

Q *I am 18 years old and would like to know what the following two quotations mean: (1) "Gerald Ford is a man for the twenties." (2) "President Ford apparently prefers guns to butter."—P. Ricker, Augusta, Maine.*

A The first statement probably refers to the opinion held by some people that Gerald Ford would have made a good president in the unchallenging and prosperous era of Calvin Coolidge. Their judgment is that Ford is not by philosophy, background, and nature a creative, innovative or imaginative leader but rather a standpatter who lacks vision and the great dream. The second statement refers to the fact that Ford is more quick to favor increased Defense Department appropriations than he is to favor social welfare programs.

Q *Is there any truth to the rumor that Bianca Jagger is leaving husband Mick for President Ford's son, Jack?—C.D., Mission Viejo, Cal.*

Mick Jagger

A Nonsense, Bianca Jagger is primarily interested in publicity.

Q *What's happened to millionaire playboy-financier Bernie Cornfeld? Is he back in a Swiss jail?—Jerry Dean, Miami, Fla.*

A Cornfeld some months ago fled his Beverly Hills mansion for London. He is under indictment for fraud in this country, having been accused of using an electronic device, a so-called "black box" to place free some 350 overseas telephone calls from his Beverly Hills residence. U.S. Attorney Robert Bonner in Los Angeles has prepared the necessary papers for Cornfeld's extradition. Whether the U.S. State Department will follow up on the case remains to be seen.

Q *Who is the best young portrait painter in America?—Claire Ogilvie, Eugene, Oreg.*

A One of the best is Jamie Wyeth, 29, son of painter Andrew Wyeth and grandson of illustrator Newell Convers Wyeth. Young Wyeth of Chadds Ford, Pennsylvania, and Monhegan Island, Maine, paints in oil and watercolor, now gets $25,000 and up for an oil. His portrait of the late President John F. Kennedy is said to be moving, profound, and unique, depicting a pensive personality far different from Kennedy's popular image.

Q *Has Bess Truman lived longer than any other First Lady?—Joseph T. Kasprzak, Baltimore, Md.*

A Yes—she observed her 90th birthday on February 13.

Nancy and Ron Reagan

Q *Is Maureen Reagan no longer speaking to her father, Ronald Reagan, because they differ over the Equal Rights Amendment?—T.C., Washington, D.C.*

A Reagan is opposed to the Equal Rights Amendment; daughter Maureen favors it. They are still good friends.

PERSONALITY PARADE®

October 19, 1975

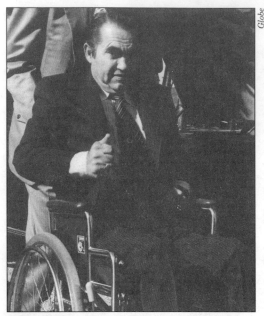

George Wallace

Q *Due to Governor Wallace's terrible tragedy, is his sex life over?—V.A., Buna, Tex.*

A According to the governor, it is not.

Q *Does the U.S. still have the largest army in the world?—Mavis Cornsweet, Providence, R.I.*

A The U.S. Army with 785,000 troops stands fourth in size behind the Soviet Union, the People's Republic of China, and India.

Q *One of the hottest scandals in London involves playwright Harold Pinter. He has left his wife actress Vivien Merchant for an affair with Lady Antonia Fraser who is married to Member of Parliament Hugh Fraser. Are all these characters using their real names?—T.T., Washington, D.C.*

A Before he took the name Harold Pinter, playwright Pinter was David Baron. Before she took the name Vivien Merchant, actress Merchant was Ada Thompson. They were married 19 years before Pinter decided to change affiliations.

Q *Who designed or invented the Volkswagen Beetle?—Thomas Levy, Denver, Col.*

A The VW Beetle was the brainchild of designer Ferdinand Porsche, son of an Austrian tinsmith. Professor Porsche exhibited his first car in 1900 in Paris. He began testing the VW, the "People's Car," in Germany in 1935. Porsche died in 1951 at age 75.

Q *When does Henry Kissinger plan to leave the government, or does he intend to stay on indefinitely?—Victor Rosen, New York City.*

A No one knows at this point, most probably including Kissinger. In many ways Dr. K has become a captive of his own power, publicity, prestige and creature comforts. Should Ford and Rockefeller be elected in 1976 there is a good chance that Kissinger will stay on. He has so structured things that no Kissinger replacement is waiting in or out of the State Department wings.

Q *Is fluoride in water good for people or does it cause harm?—Angie Hathaway, Asheville, N.C.*

A Many medical authorities declare that fluoride strengthens the structure of dental enamel, helping to prevent decay. It is particularly effective during childhood when teeth are being formed. Opponents of fluoridation say it is everything from a Communist plot to a cause of premature baldness.

Q *How much farther to the right than Gerald Ford is Ronald Reagan?—Daniel Lang, Concord, N.H.*

A As much as he has to be to win whatever office he wants.

Q *The late Chief Justice Earl Warren hated Richard Nixon with a terrible hatred and denounced him many times in private. What was the origin of the hatred?—L.A.L., Fresno, Calif.*

Earl Warren

A Warren regarded Nixon as a politician who did not play the game fairly.

Q *I have been told by someone who should know that the FBI is in serious trouble because of the Jack Kennedy assassination coverup. I am also informed that Clarence Kelley, director of the FBI, is largely a figurehead, and that the bureau is actually run by three officials named Callahan, Jenkins and Adams. Is any of this true? Are there any such men in the FBI? If there are, who are they?—S.S., Kansas City, Mo.*

A Nicholas P. Callahan is associate director of the FBI. Thomas J. Jenkins and James B. Adams are deputy associate directors of the FBI. All three are subordinate to Clarence Kelley in position but not in knowledge, influence or experience. The FBI, of course, is in trouble for destroying a threatening note delivered to its Dallas office by Lee Harvey Oswald a few days before he assassinated President Kennedy. Worse yet, the FBI subsequently withheld this information from the Warren Commission investigating the assassination.

Miss Vicki and Tiny Tim

Q *What's happened to Miss Vicki, the wife of the weirdo singer, Tiny Tim?— Helen Justice, Newark, N.J.*

A Miss Vicki recently returned to Camden, New Jersey, after a stay in London. She plans to resume her career as a go-go dancer in order to support her daughter, Tulip, four. Miss Vicki, 23, says she has no plans to divorce Tiny Tim, Tulip's father. "He doesn't want a divorce, and neither do I."

Q *I would be interested in knowing how many children Supreme Court Justice William Douglas and his current wife have. Thank you.—Linda Myrick, Oakland, Cal.*

A None.

Q *In your opinion what was Gerald Ford's major accomplishment during his first year as president?—Francine Cates, Tallahassee, Fla.*

A The restoration of civility and decency to the office of the presidency.

PERSONALITY PARADE®

December 7, 1975

Q *How old is actor Paul Newman? How long can he go on playing the virile stud?—Bennett Livermore, Scottsdale, Ariz.*

Paul Newman

A Newman at 50 is in good shape, can last for another 10 years at least as a film hero unless he falls into a vat of beer, his favorite drink.

Q *So many people in the American intelligence community keep talking about "The Family Jewels." What are they, and who owns them?—F.L., Lexington, Ky.*

A On May 9, 1973, James Schlesinger, then director of the CIA, distributed a memo asking past and present members of the agency to "report to me immediately on any activities now going on, or that may have gone on in the past, which might be construed to be outside the legislative charter of the agency."

Within two weeks Schlesinger received almost 700 pages of information which were turned over to the CIA's inspector general's office. There a secret report on the CIA's alleged illegalities was compiled. That ultrasecret report in time was referred to as "The Family Jewels." On July 12, 1973, James Schlesinger was sworn in as secretary of defense, leaving his successor, poor Bill Colby, holding the bag of "Family Jewels." Before Gerald Ford fired him, Colby spent days trying to explain the CIA sins Schlesinger had uncovered.

Q *I notice that Nobel Prize winner Linus Pauling accepted from President Ford this country's highest science award, the National Medal of Science. Why was chemist Pauling twice turned down for the award when Richard Nixon was president?—D. Givens, Pasadena, Cal.*

A Pauling, no Nixon admirer, was strongly opposed to the U.S. involvement in the Vietnamese War.

Q *Is the William Holden-Stefanie Powers love affair still blazing?—Minna Lewis, Sacramento, Cal.*

A Not blazing—just continuing on course.

Q *Have Bob Woodward and Carl Bernstein, authors of* All the President's Men, *come to the parting of the ways? When is their book,* The Final Days, *coming out?—O.T., Richmond, Va.*

A Woodward and Bernstein of *The Washington Post* are no longer collaborators. Their book on the last days of the Nixon administration is scheduled for publication in the spring of 1976.

Confucius

Q *Why has there been such a vicious anti-Confucius campaign in the People's Republic of China?—Helen Chin, Honolulu, Oahu.*

A Largely because Mao Tse-tung considers the basic Confucius philosophy non-revolutionary and many of Confucius' statements ridiculously outdated. For example, Confucius said of women: "Women are worthless people who are difficult to keep . . . It is most difficult to get along with mean persons and women . . . It is a virtue if a woman has no ability . . . "

Q *Is it true that the invention of gin gave rise to the development of the police system?—Maude Praeger, Minot, N. Dak.*

A Gin, which used to be called "Geneva," was concocted by a Dutch chemist in the 17th century. It became the first hard liquor for the masses, who used to drink only beer, ale, and wine. According to Jonathan Rubinstein in his book, *City Police*, "gin democratized drunkenness and brought new terrors to London and then subsequently to all cities." The crime which resulted from this drunkenness stimulated the founding of the police forces.

Q *Is there any truth to the rumor that Sarah Churchill, daughter of the late Winston Churchill, has been banned by the airlines? Where is she, how old, and her occupation, please?—Janine Card, Salt Lake City, Utah.*

A Sarah Churchill, 61, second daughter of Winston and the Baroness Spencer-Churchill, lives in New York where she is reportedly working on a book, *A Word in Your Eye*. After visiting her mother in London a few weeks ago, Sarah allegedly was involved in several altercations at Heathrow Airport. Reportedly she hit one airline employee with a flight bag, tugged at a passenger's beard, was finally denied passage on two flights. Next day, however, Air India flew Sarah, the widow of Lord Audley, to New York. She is a highly spirited woman.

Q *They say that one of the world's greatest spies is an Arab named Isar Harel. For which Arab country does he work?—Nathan Lefko, Brooklyn, N.Y.*

A Isar Harel, 63, is a Russian-born Jew who for 10 years was head of Mossad, Israel's intelligence service. It was Harel who 15 years ago masterminded from Buenos Aires the abduction of the Nazi mass murderer Adolf Eichmann, who was flown to Tel Aviv, tried, convicted and executed.

Q *Julie Andrews hasn't had a hit movie since The Sound of Music. She bombed in her TV series. Why then is Caesars Palace in Las Vegas signing her at $250,000 a week?—Ed Henderson, Searchlight, Nev.*

Julie Andrews

A Caesars Palace has not signed Miss Andrews at $250,000 a week. The Las Vegas hotel at this writing is negotiating with the singer-actress to appear on stage next August at a figure not yet agreed upon, but certainly less than $250,000 a week.

Frank Sinatra

Q *Was it ever Frank Sinatra's function to introduce girls to the late President John F. Kennedy? Also, what was Sinatra's relationship to the late Sam Giancana, alleged head of the Chicago Mafia?—P.A., Chicago.*

A It was never Sinatra's function to introduce girls to Kennedy. In the early days of the Kennedy administration, however, Sinatra was an enthusiastic Kennedy supporter. According to testimony in the possession of the U.S. Senate's Select Committee on Intelligence, Sinatra introduced an attractive 26-year-old, Judy Campbell, to the then Senator Kennedy in Las Vegas on February 7, 1960. Subsequently, Judy Campbell, now Mrs. Judith Exner, 41, came to enjoy a close personal relationship with Kennedy. That relationship was aborted when Kennedy learned through J. Edgar Hoover that Judy Campbell was also a close personal friend of Sam Giancana, to whom Sinatra had introduced her in March, 1960, in Miami.

As to Sinatra's relationship with Giancana, Sinatra in 1963 surrendered his license to run a Lake Tahoe gambling casino and hotel to the Nevada Gaming Commission "because of his relationship with Giancana and the Mafia chief's vis-

its to the gambling casino." Sinatra broke with the Kennedy clan when it became apparent that they no longer considered him persona grata and declined to stay in his desert home at Rancho Mirage, California.

Q *I would like to know how old Rock Hudson is and was he ever married and what is his real name?—F. Gardener, Oak Park, Ill.*

A Hudson is 50. In November, 1955, when he was 30, he married Phyllis Gates, a secretary at Universal Studios. The marriage didn't work, and Phyllis obtained a divorce in August, 1958. Hudson's real name is Roy Scherer.

Q *Ralph Nader—is he a public citizen or a megalomaniac workaholic? What tangible good has he done?— P. Samuel, Rockville, Md.*

A Nader is a public citizen and a "workaholic." He is the single most important citizen in the consumer movement and a young man who has spent his adulthood and his earned fortune in the cause of participatory democracy.

Q *How many First Ladies are under the protection of the Secret Service?— Benjamin Young, Philadelphia.*

A Mrs. Betty Ford, Mrs. Bess Truman, Mrs. Dwight Eisenhower, Mrs. Lady Bird Johnson, Mrs. Richard Nixon. Mrs. John F. Kennedy was under Secret Service protection until she married Aristotle Onassis. As his widow she is not

Lady Bird Johnson

entitled to Secret Service protection. Her son John, however, is accorded such protection until he reaches the age of 18.

Q *How much was writer Peter Benchley paid for the film rights to his sensational best-seller, Jaws?—Nita Cavanaugh, Hartford, Conn.*

A Benchley was paid $175,000 for the book and screenplay with escalator clauses that brought the total for the film rights to $250,000. In addition, he gets 10 percent of the production's net profits, or approximately $10 million. He will reap another $1 million in foreign sales of the book. In *Jaws* Benchley has it made—for life.

Q *Is it true that Grace Kelly is worried sick about her daughter Caroline and that Jackie Onassis is worried sick about her daughter Caroline?—Eleanor Woods, Roxbury, Mass.*

A The two Carolines, each 18, constitute a justifiable source of worry to their mothers. Caroline of Monaco uses too much makeup, sees too many boys. Caroline Kennedy lives in dangerous London.

Grace Kelly

Q *Did President Ford make a deal with Alexander M. Haig, Jr., former Nixon chief of staff, that he, Ford, would pardon Nixon?—E.G., Washington, D.C.*

A Ford had several talks with Haig, who suggested and pleaded for a Nixon pardon—talks which Ford failed to tell his own staff about, one talk particularly on August 28, 1974, 10 days before Ford announced the Nixon pardon—and Haig felt sufficiently assured that Ford would grant the pardon. It has been suggested in many quarters that the president has not been completely open and candid with the public or fully disclosed to a congressional subcommittee the complete background of the pardon. There was talk, for example, that if Ford did not grant the pardon and Nixon was dragged through criminal proceedings, a Nixon suicide was a possibility. There was much else that Ford and Haig have not disclosed about the pardon.

Q *Was the late Errol Flynn ever a heroin addict?—H.G., Vancouver, B.C.*

A Flynn tried everything. He was on heroin for a while when his friend, director Raoul Walsh, heard of the addiction. Walsh remained with Flynn until he got him to break the habit. When Flynn finally made it, he

Errol Flynn

turned to Walsh and said, "I'm glad you got me off that kick. It cost so damn much."

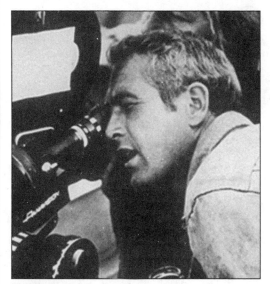

Paul Newman

Q *Is it true that Paul Newman is playing the lead as the track coach in a movie based on the best-selling novel* The Front Runner *in which a gay track coach falls in love with his charge? Didn't Robert Redford turn down the role of the runner because he refused to kiss a man, even Paul Newman?—Lila Gornick, Oakland, Cal.*

A It is not certain at this point whether Paul Newman will go through with *The Front Runner* even though Academy Award winner Jeremy Larner has written a creditable script. Robert Redford was never asked to perform in the movie. The role in question calls for a younger actor.

Q *They say the bloodiest feud in Washington, D.C., is between Don Rumsfeld, the secretary of defense, and Robert Hartmann, who is President Ford's chief speechwriter. Why do these two men hate each other?—G.P., Arlington, Va.*

A Hartmann and Rumsfeld were and probably still are rivals for President Ford's ear. Now that Rumsfeld is headquartered in the Pentagon, the feud has waned. Hartmann was Gerald Ford's legislative assistant when Ford was House minority leader. Rumsfeld was a congressman from Illinois who helped make Ford House minority leader. Thus both men enjoyed a friendly history with Ford. When Ford was appointed president, he in turn appointed Hartmann one of his counselors and appointed Rumsfeld as assistant to the president with Cabinet rank. Under the circumstances both Hartmann and Rumsfeld jockeyed for the position of Ford's number one adviser. In addition, the chem-istry of attraction does not exist between their individual personalities.

Q *Judith Exner, who is writing a book about her dalliances with the late John F. Kennedy—wasn't she once married to Lucille Ball's husband, Gary Morton?—Frank Hutchinson, Los Angeles.*

A She was not, but her sister, actress Susan Morrow, once was. Susan married Morton in December 1953, separated in August 1954; their marriage was annulled in 1957. In November 1961, Gary Morton married Lucille Ball following her divorce from Desi Arnaz.

Q *I am a fan of Marvin Kalb, the CBS diplomatic correspondent who used to travel with Henry Kissinger. A few months ago Marvin Kalb suddenly disappeared from radio and TV and was replaced by his brother, Bernard. Why?—Lettie Greenberg, New Rochelle, N.Y.*

A Last September Marvin Kalb came down with what doctors diagnosed as a herniated spinal disk. He was confined to bed, should be back to work in the near future.

Michael Douglas and Brenda Vaccaro

Q *Michael Douglas—he's the son of actor Kirk Douglas and he also produced* One Flew Over the Cuckoo's Nest*—is he living with actress Brenda Vaccaro?—F.R., North Hollywood, Cal.*

A They had a spiff and separated for a few hours, but a small reconciliation gift, a $3,000 diamond ring, has helped bring them back together.

Q *Is it a fact that the CIA paid prostitutes to service Jordan's King Hussein, the Shah of Iran, and President Mobutu of Zaire on their various visits to the U.S.?—G.T., Washington, D.C.*

A According to *The New York Times*, which leaked a Congressional report, the CIA commissioned a former aide of billionaire recluse Howard Hughes to find girls for the above-mentioned dignitaries. Whether the girls were prostitutes or mere conversationalists, the report does not say. It was the CIA, however, which provided federal funds for the female companionship.

Q *I notice that Gloria Swanson, like Zsa Zsa Gabor, has been married six times. Who were Gloria's six husbands, and was one of them the late Joseph P. Kennedy?—Louise Newman, Troy, N.Y.*

A Actress Gloria Swanson, at least 76, was married to movie star Wallace Beery, restaurateur Herbert Somborn, the Marquis Henri de la Falaise de la Coudray, Michael Farmer, William Davey and William Dufty, 60, her current husband. Gloria was never married to Joseph P. Kennedy although they were friendly partners for years.

Q *If Hubert Humphrey is elected U.S. president, will he free the American draft resisters in Canada? — K. Bauer, White Plains, N.Y.*

A Senator Humphrey is opposed to unconditional amnesty for draft evaders and resisters.
"I have been consistent in my support of a repatriation program which would heal the wounds created during the Vietnam era while at the same time avoiding the inadequacies and operational difficul-

Hubert Humphrey

ties of the president's clemency program," says Senator Humphrey. "Persons repatriated under such a program would not be placed under any legal disability, nor would they lose any rights of citizenship, including equal protection of the laws. But they would be required to perform some form of alternative service to the nation in such fields as health, education and social welfare.
"A program of unconditional amnesty, without some accommodation on the part of the beneficiaries, would be a disservice to the memory of those who fought and died in Vietnam."

WALTER SCOTT'S
PERSONALITY PARADE®

May 30, 1976

Q *How does Clarence Kelley, current head of the FBI, compare to J. Edgar Hoover? I realize comparisons are frequently invidious and based on opinion. Even so, I would like to know.—D.L., Media, Pa.*

J. Edgar Hoover

Harris and Ewing/Globe

A Sanford J. Ungar, author of *FBI*, one of the most thoroughly researched books on the bureau and also one of the most objective, says that Hoover was "prejudiced and narrow-minded, overtly biased against black people." Hoover once promised that so long as he was head of the FBI, it would never have a black agent. He was also, according to Ungar, "intolerant of women in any but subservient positions." Hoover also conspired to break the law by countenancing burglaries, break-ins, and mail intercepts of organizations and people with whose politics he disagreed. Although Clarence Kelley worked under Hoover, he is of a different breed. Kelley is more honest, open, tolerant, understanding and democratic. To him has fallen the Herculean job of restructuring the morale, image and organization of the FBI. Under Hoover, the FBI was an authoritarian agency beyond the control of the Congress and in whose ranks men rose by virtue of sycophancy rather than merit. *FBI*, by Sanford J. Ungar, is published by Atlantic Press-Little Brown.

Q *Was the late Field Marshal Viscount Montgomery of World War II fame a practicing homosexual?—T.E.E., Berkeley, Cal.*

Viscount Montgomery

A There is no evidence that Montgomery was a practicing homosexual. He had an unhappy childhood, feuded with his mother, and when his wife passed away after 10 years of marriage, displayed relatively little need for other women. He was rude, brusque, cocky, domineering, emotionally immature, incapable of giving love. Montgomery felt that his mother had denied him love, and as he grew into manhood he never learned how to bestow it upon others. He was, however, friendly and sympathetic to junior officers, and this behavior stimulated rumors concerning his sex life. One of the most revealing and controversial books on Montgomery is *The Field Marshal*, by Alun Chalfont.

Q *People say that the richest man in the South is a man named Claude Canada. Can you tell anything about him, or if there even is such a man?—Mary Lerner, New Orleans, La.*

A Claude Canada, 57, of Kimper, Kentucky, is owner of the Canada Coal Co. in Pike County. He is worth about $250 million, owns eight Rolls-Royces, a $2-million home, pays his employees a minimum of $50 a day, provides each of his foremen with a company Cadillac for personal use. He is one of the new so-called "Coal Multimillionaires."

Bette Davis

Q *How old are Gregory Peck and Bette Davis? I know they share birthdays.—Lena Harris Gould, Hickory, N.C.*

A Gregory Peck and Bette Davis are respectively 60 and 68. Peck was born April 5, 1916; Davis, April 5, 1908.

Q *Is Chris Evert, the tennis star, suffering from a broken heart because Jimmy Connors dumped her for Marjorie Wallace?—P.T. Owens, North Las Vegas, Nev.*

A Last year Chris Evert won $323,977 in tennis tournament prize money. At 21 she held 16 major championships, had won 56 consecutive matches, was well-liked and widely respected. She is still 21, and while she may have lost Jimmy Connors as a sweetheart, such a loss may eventually prove a blessing. Connors is playing the field. No one woman deserves what he has to offer in charm, manners and intellect.

Q *I recall a Jimmy Carter who was a country and western singer. Is this the same Jimmy Carter who wants to be president of the U.S.?—Carol Trombly, Wyoming, Minn.*

A It is not. The Jimmy Carter who wants to become president is non-guitar-playing. He is in the peanut-farming business. He is also a good old country boy.

Q *I wonder if you can tell me what happened to Sam Bowers, who used to be the Imperial Wizard of the Ku Klux Klan in Mississippi?—T.P., Laurel, Miss.*

A Samuel Bowers and six others were convicted by an all-white jury in 1967 of depriving citizens of their constitutional rights in the shooting to death in 1964 of three civil rights workers, Michael Schwerner, 23; James Chaney, 21, and Andrew Goodman, 20. Bowers was sentenced to a 10-year term in the federal penitentiary. This past March, after serving six years, Bowers was released from McNeil Island federal penitentiary in Washington. He was granted time off for good behavior and placed on probation.

Q *Is it true that the late Humphrey Bogart used to slap his wives around just so that he could get in a tough-guy mood?—Louise Richardson, Raleigh, N.C.*

Humphrey Bogart

A Bogart and his third wife, Mayo Methot, when alcoholically stimulated, would haul off at each other. After Bogie married Lauren Bacall in 1945, however, and she gave birth to two children, Stephen and Leslie, Bogart nipped less and softened his lifestyle.

Q *Bill Wyman, guitarist for the Rolling Stones, has been living with a Swedish chick for years. What's her name, where do they live, and is Wyman really 45?—Ann W., Darby, Pa.*

A Bill Wyman, 38, is a British tax exile, recently built a $750,000 home near Vence, in the South of France, where he lives with Swedish girlfriend Astrid Lundstrom.

WALTER SCOTT'S

PERSONALITY PARADE®

August 8, 1976

Q *Marlene Dietrich's husband died a few weeks ago at age 79. Is it true that Dietrich kept her marriage to this man a secret for 52 years?—Patty Bergson, Phoenix, Ariz.*

Marlene Dietrich

A Rudolf Sieber, an assistant motion picture director, married Marlene Dietrich in Berlin on May 13, 1924. She was then an extra in German films. It was Sieber who nurtured, promoted and recommended his wife to director Josef von Sternberg for the leading role in *The Blue Angel*, the film which made her an international star. When Paramount Pictures signed Miss Dietrich and brought her to Hollywood, it was thought best not to mention her husband. Rudolf Sieber subsequently became a chicken farmer in the San Fernando Valley while his wife was promoted to screen stardom. Although Sieber and Dietrich lived apart for decades they remained good friends. They had a daughter in 1925 who became an actress under the name Maria Riva. When Sieber died in Sylmar, California, June, 24, 1976, his wife was in Paris. She flew to California to make the funeral arrangements. Sieber died in a rocking chair at his ranch, was found by his maid. He was a good and kind man.

Q *Is it a fact that the most poverty-ridden city in Europe is Glasgow, Scotland?—Curt Gunther, Chicago.*

A Glasgow is not the most poverty-ridden city in Europe, but it is probably the most poverty-ridden major city in Great Britain. It suffers the highest death rate, the highest unemployment rate, the highest infant mortality rate, the highest tuberculosis rate of any large city in the British Isles.

Q *Why is Gen. William Westmoreland against permitting women to enroll at West Point?—Josey Henderson, Charlotte, N.C.*

William Westmoreland

A Westmoreland, former commander of U.S. troops in Vietnam, believes it's "silly" to enroll women in the U.S. Military Academy. His explanation: "The purpose of West Point is to train combat officers, and women are not physically able to lead in combat. Maybe you could find one woman in 10,000 to lead in combat, but she would be a freak, and we're not running the Military Academy for freaks . . . I don't believe women can carry a pack, live in a foxhole, or go a week without taking a bath."

Q *Why did singer Diana Ross drop her white husband Robert Silberstein after he fathered three lovely daughters for her? Wasn't he a good husband and a good press agent?—G.T.T., Detroit.*

A Singer Ross has not been particularly forthcoming on the causes of her divorce. Friends suggest she outgrew Silberstein, no longer found in him the qualities she once needed. She is a determined, driving young woman, knows what and whom she wants in life.

Bob Waterfield and Jane Russell

Q *Was Jane Russell, the actress discovered by the late Howard Hughes, recently involved in a murder?—F.L., Miami Beach, Fla.*

A Jane was not, but Robert Waterfield, the adopted 20-year-old son of the actress and Bob Waterfield, her ex-husband and former professional football star, was. Young Waterfield has been charged with murder in Santa Maria, California, in the shooting of Oscar Hernandez, 26.

Raquel Welch

Q *Raquel Welch claims she is really in love for the first time—and this time it's a Brazilian press agent. Who is the lucky fellow?—N. French, La Jolla, Cal.*

A Raquel Welch, 35, met press agent Paulo Pilla, 33, while touring Brazil in her nightclub act. He followed her to Hollywood, has succeeded her last boyfriend, dress designer Ron Talsky. Raquel is generally kind to her lovers, finds them jobs.

Q *I was recently told by a former FBI agent that under Clarence Kelley the morale of the FBI has now plummeted to zero. Is this correct?—L.K., Alexandria, Va.*

A Morale in the FBI is admittedly low. But director Clarence Kelley is not to blame. The true culprit was the late J. Edgar Hoover, who in some cases hired pliant, uncreative men and in many instances had them break the law they swore to uphold. Also responsible for the deterioration of morale within the bureau were the Congresses who over 48 years permitted J. Edgar Hoover to run the FBI without any valid congressional oversight. Like the CIA, with whom it frequently feuded, the FBI not only consistently broke the law but lied about its transgressions. Like his predecessor, L. Patrick Gray, FBI director Clarence Kelley may still not know what is really going on in his organization. The FBI remains heavily staffed in the upper echelons by J. Edgar Hoover appointees, and unless Attorney General Edward Levi—who runs the Justice Department—sweeps the FBI with a new broom, the bureau's morale will continue to languish as will the public's faith in its integrity.

PERSONALITY PARADE®

August 15, 1976

Q *Singer Connie Francis was awarded $2.5 million for having been raped in a Howard Johnson Motor Lodge in Westbury, New York, in 1974. Her husband was awarded $150,000. Can you please explain?—N.L., Far Rockaway, N.Y.*

A Miss Francis claimed that the Howard Johnson Motor Lodge was negligent in failing to provide adequate security and adequate locks on the door. She claimed the rape had all but ruined her marriage. Her husband was awarded $150,000 in damages because his marriage, too, has apparently suffered from his wife's trauma, a trauma which she insisted had wrecked her planned comeback. The rapist has yet to be caught. Miss Francis claims she will never be the same.

Q *The New York State Supreme Court has barred Richard Nixon from the practice of law. I would like to know on which charges they found him guilty.—G.W., San Diego, Cal.*

Richard Nixon

A The charges alleged are related to the Watergate scandal. Specifically Nixon was charged with: (1) Improperly obstructing an FBI investigation of the illegal entry into the Democratic national headquarters in Washington, D.C., on June 17, 1972; (2) Improperly approving the blackmail payments of money to E. Howard Hunt, indicted in the break-in; (3) Improperly concealing evidence relating to members of his staff and the Committee to Re-Elect the president; (4) Improperly interfering with the legal defense of Daniel Ellsberg of Pentagon Papers notoriety; (5) Improperly attempting to obstruct a Justice Department investigation of the illegal break-in of the offices of Dr. Lewis Fielding, the Beverly Hills psychiatrist who treated Ellsberg.

Q *My understanding is that actor Peter Lawford, once married to Pat Kennedy of the Kennedy tribe, is now secretly married to a 16-year-old Florida beauty. What's the truth?—Helen Dupont, Santa Monica, Cal.*

A Peter Lawford, 52, was quietly married to Deborah Gould, 25, of Miami, Florida, in a brief civil ceremony in Arlington, Virginia, a few weeks ago. It was Deborah's first marriage and Lawford's third.

His first wife was Patricia Kennedy, sister of the late President John F. Kennedy, and his second wife was Mary Rowan, daughter of Dan Rowan, the comedian.

Q *Is it a fact that Frank Blair, who was co-host with Barbara Walters on the Today show for 12 years, hated her?—L.T., Riverside, Cal.*

A Blair says that during the 12 years he worked with Barbara Walters, she was "rude and inhospitable . . . I never felt close to her. She was aloof, very cold, very aggressive."

Elizabeth Taylor

Q *Is Elizabeth Taylor an American citizen? I mean does she vote and pay taxes here?—Owen Henry, Baltimore, Md.*

A Elizabeth Taylor is a British subject, cannot vote in this country. She is a British tax exile with a Swiss residence in Gstaad.

Q *Many professors have told me that the best novelist in the world today is Vladimir Nabokov. Can you tell me something about him?—Anne Reynolds, Charleston, S.C.*

A VlaDEEmir NaBOAKoff, which is how he pronounces his name, is a 77-year-old Russian-born novelist, best known for his novel *Lolita,* who lives in the Montreux-Palace Hotel in Montreux, Switzerland. Nabokov, author of 18 novels, describes himself as "an American writer born in Russia and educated in England, where I studied French literature before spending 15 years in Berlin." Nabokov was born in St. Petersburg in 1899, raised in Czarist Russia, the son of wealthy aristocrats. As a young man he inherited $2 million from a rich uncle, lost it to the Communist revolution. In the 1920's and 30's he lived in Berlin and Paris, two cities of exile for Russian emigrés. He married Evssevna Slonim, the daughter of a Russian Jewish industrialist. They have a son, Dimitri, who is an opera singer.

In 1940 Nabokov came to the U.S., taught Slavic languages at Stanford University, taught other subjects at Wellesley, Harvard and Cornell. In 1955 he wrote *Lolita,* the story of a middle-aged professor's obsession for a 12-year-old nymphet. It was turned down by American publishers, was eventually brought out by Olympia Press in Paris. The novel rocketed Nabokov to worldwide acclaim. Literary critics consider Nabokov the most original and talented stylist since the late James Joyce. He is not an easy novelist to read but surely a worthy one.

Q *Actress Luise Rainer, who won Oscars for* The Good Earth *and* The Great Ziegfeld—*does she still live in Vienna? How old is she? Is she finished with pictures?—Carl Sternweiss, Clifton, N.J.*

A Luise Rainer, 63, quit films, lives in London's Belgravia district with second husband Robert Knittel, a book publisher.

Q *I am shocked to read that Queen Elizabeth of England, who is given $2.52 million a year by her subjects, pays no income tax. Is this so?—Clarence Devine, St. Louis, Mo.*

A The British Royal Family pays no income tax, which allows the Queen to amass a fairly hefty sum. A

Queen Elizabeth

few weeks ago the Queen bought her daughter, Princess Anne, an estate for $1,350,000.

WALTER SCOTT'S
PERSONALITY PARADE®

September 26, 1976

Q *I've read Bob Dole, the Republican vice presidential candidate, described as "a slasher, an attack dog, a Doberman pinscher, a gut fighter." The New York Times says of him: "During the Senate Watergate hearings in the summer of 1973 it was disclosed that while Mr. Dole was at the Republican committee he received $3,000 from the same secret cache of money that later financed the Watergate burglary." In view of Senator Dole's past—marital and political—why did a gentle, decent human being like President Ford choose him in preference to Senators Brooke, Weicker, Percy, Baker, Hatfield as well as Bill Ruckelshaus, William Scranton, and John Connally? Also, was Dole checked out by the FBI?—P.Y., New York City.*

A Dole was chosen not because he was necessarily the most qualified man for the job. Sens. John Tower of Texas and Bob Griffin of Michigan, advisers to Ford, felt that Dole was most politically expedient for the Republican ticket, and apparently their opinion swayed Ford. Dole was not checked out by the FBI. In view of his former campaigning tactics, Senator Dole will probably refrain from acting "the hatchet man" in this one.

Zsa Zsa Gabor

Q *Zsa Zsa Gabor was recently married for the seventh time. She gave her age in Las Vegas as 56. Her seventh husband, attorney Mike O'Hara, gave his age as 47. For her last three marriages, Zsa Zsa has been 56. How come?—Dolly Owens, Las Vegas, Nev.*

A For Zsa Zsa Gabor time stands still.

Q *Can you tell me if Julie Nixon Eisenhower has secretly signed a deal for $1 million to write a biography of her mother, Pat Nixon? My understanding from a good source is that it's true.—I.O.P., Garden City, N.Y.*

Julie Nixon Eisenhower

A Not true to date. Julie Nixon Eisenhower has signed with Simon & Schuster to write a book consisting of eight personality pieces about interesting people she's met. But she has not signed the deal you suggest. No doubt her publisher hopes for such a book from her.

Q *Is it a fact that the FBI and the CIA have committed more burglaries than any other two law enforcement agencies in the federal government?—F.L., Frankfort, Ky.*

A The Central Intelligence Agency is not a law enforcement agency. The FBI, however, is. Both agencies have consistently violated the law in an effort to uphold it. The CIA has for years burgled the premises occupied by Americans abroad. It has also wiretapped U.S. citizens abroad. The FBI has illegally wiretapped and burgled domestically. Whether both agencies have committed more violations of the law than any other government agencies is unascertainable.

Q *Billy Dee Williams, the black Clark Gable, is he married to a white or black woman?—Amos Tucker, Charleston, S.C.*

A Actor Billy Dee Williams, one of Hollywood's first black matinee idols, is married to Teruko Williams, a Japanese-American. They have three children. Williams starred in *Lady Sings the Blues* and *The Bingo Long Traveling All-Stars and Motor Kings.*

Q *Would like to know how the government of Romania rewarded Nadia Comaneci, the little gymnast who won three gold medals, one silver, and one bronze at the Montreal Olympic Games.—D. Lupescu, Los Angeles.*

A The government offered her father, who is a mechanic, a one-month family vacation and a new Mercedes.

Q *The Lockheed bribery, which has scandalized Japan—wasn't there a similar bribery scandal in Japan during World War I? I believe it was known as "The Siemens Case." Can you amplify?—Ben Lerner, Cambridge, Mass.*

A In 1914 Siemens-Schueckertwerke AG of Germany and later Vickers Armstrong Ltd. of England bribed high-ranking Japanese Navy personnel into placing large orders for communications equipment with Siemens and warships with Vickers. There was a trial, and several Japanese scapegoats were sent to jail, but two top Japanese politicians, Prime Minister Yamamoto and Navy Minister Saito, were merely retired to the Navy reserve although they were held "morally responsible." Despite the Siemens-Vickers scandal, Yamamoto became prime minister of Japan again in 1923, and Saito made it to that office in 1932.

Henry Kissinger

Q *Isn't Henry Kissinger scheduled to work for CBS-TV as a commentator after he leaves the government? My understanding is that when he was at Deauville, France, last month as a house guest of Loel Guinness of the banking family, William Paley, head of CBS, was a guest at the same time. And that's where the deal was made. Is this true?—L.T., New York City.*

A It's true that Kissinger and Paley were guests of Mr. and Mrs. Loel Guinness at their home outside Deauville. But no deal between Kissinger and Paley was consummated.

WALTER SCOTT'S
PERSONALITY PARADE®

November 7, 1976

Q *I am amazed reading about the extramarital affair the late President John F. Kennedy had with Judith Campbell. Where were the assignations held—in the White House? And did not Kennedy realize that Judy Campbell was reporting each time to the late Sam Giancana, head of the Chicago Mafia? Really! This whole thing is so shockingly sordid it is beyond my comprehension. Why didn't the Secret Service do something about it? Surely they must have known that Kennedy was playing around.—Mrs. J.B.W., Philadelphia.*

John F. Kennedy

A Before he was elected president, John F. Kennedy was introduced to Judith Campbell by Frank Sinatra in Las Vegas. Later, in Miami, Sinatra introduced Judith Campbell to Sam Giancana of the Mafia. He introduced Giancana as Sam Flood. For many months the showgirl did not know Giancana's real name or his position as leader of the Chicago crime syndicate. Judith Campbell's first assignation with Kennedy, then a U.S. senator, took place in the Plaza Hotel, New York City, about March 7, 1960. After Kennedy was elected president in November 1960, further assignations took place in the White House and elsewhere. The Secret Service, charged with guarding Kennedy, surely knew of the liaison but was powerless to prevent it, since extracurricular sex activity did not endanger Kennedy's life.

Reportedly, Judith Campbell told Giancana of her affair with Kennedy. Giancana did not mind sharing her favors with the president. He may well have thought of using his knowledge to blackmail Kennedy at some later date. The CIA also made the monumental error during that same period of enlisting Giancana and his late henchman John Rosselli in efforts to assassinate Fidel Castro of Cuba.

FBI agents subsequently wiretapped Giancana, learned about his and Kennedy's sexual relationships with Judith Campbell. They reported it to J. Edgar Hoover. Director Hoover in turn reported it to Robert Kennedy, then attorney general of the U.S. Hoover also notified President Kennedy of the Giancana-Campbell relationship. Kennedy thereupon severed his friendship, not only with Judith Campbell, but with Frank Sinatra as well.

Q *I've been told that people in the hometown of the late Field Marshal Bernard Montgomery speak disparagingly of his memory. True?—Victor Newmarket, New York City.*

A They consider Montgomery "cheap and niggardly" in Bentley, England. Montgomery, who died there in March, 1976, at age 88, left $270,000 in his will. Of that sum, he bequeathed only $165 each to five members of the Cox family, who spent their entire working lives in his service. Apart from this bequest, the Montgomery estate went to Monty's son, the new Viscount of Alamein. Michael Cox, Monty's chauffeur, said of him: "Monty never gave more than he had to. What he left our family is a paltry sum. It will pay for a few rounds of beer."

Muhammad Ali

Q *What is the marital status of heavyweight boxer Muhammad Ali? Didn't one of his girlfriends just give birth to a baby by him?—Morton Ingliss, Chicago.*

A Khalilah Ali, married to Ali for nine years, filed suit in Chicago recently for divorce on grounds of mental cruelty and desertion. They have four children. Ali acknowledges that he is the father of an illegitimate daughter born August 6, 1976, to his long-time traveling lover, Veronica Porche. The baby girl, Hana Yasmeen Ali, was born in Berrien (Michigan) General Hospital, according to a parenthood certificate filed with the Berrien County registrar of deeds.

Q *Is it true that the two highest-paid baseball players are both black?—Ron Gamble, Birmingham, Ala.*

A Hank Aaron, now retired, was paid $240,000 in 1976 by the Milwaukee Brewers, Dick Allen $225,000 by the Philadelphia Phillies. Both are black and reportedly the highest-salaried players in big league baseball last season.

Q *Has anyone in this country made more money from broadcasting than Lowell Thomas, who is 84? I am told he is worth $100 million. True?—K.G., Pawling, N.Y.*

A Lowell Thomas has earned millions as a broadcaster, but it was not until the mid-50's—when he helped found Capital Cities Communications—that he could amass his present fortune, estimated at $10-15 million. Capital Cities owns some 14 radio and TV stations, also newspapers in Fort Worth, Texas, Pontiac, Michigan, and Belleville, Illinois. Capital Cities also owns Fairchild Trade Papers, which publishes *Women's Wear Daily, Home Furnishings Daily*, and other trade papers of that ilk. At last count, Lowell Thomas owned approximately 175,000 shares of Capital Cities stock, worth more than $8.5 million.

Q *Why has Susan Ford moved out of the White House—because she is tired of Secret Service surveillance?—Monty Campbell, Charlotte, N.C.*

Susan Ford

A Susan Ford and three other sophomores from Mt. Vernon Junior College for Women have moved into an Alexandria, Virginia, townhouse, the basement of which houses the Secret Service persons assigned to guard Susan. So long as she is the president's daughter, Susan cannot escape the Secret Service. None of the Ford children particularly likes living in the White House.

WALTER SCOTT'S

PERSONALITY PARADE®

December 12, 1976

Q *After J. Edgar Hoover died on May 2, 1972, 35 file drawers of material were removed from his office to his home. Much of this material was then shredded by Hoover's secretary, Helen Gandy. My question is: Who authorized Helen Gandy to shred those files?—David D., Arlington, Va.*

J. Edgar Hoover

A Miss Gandy has testified under oath before a House subcommittee that she shredded the contents of the files in accordance with Mr. Hoover's expressed wishes.

Q *How much did NBC charge for commercials when the network showed* Gone With the Wind?—Carol Woolf, Des Moines, Iowa.

A $234,000 per minute.

Q *When is the trial of Claudine Longet, ex-wife of Andy Williams? She was the one who shot her lover, "Spider" Sabich, the ski champion, in Aspen, Colorado—Mrs. J.T.W., Williamstown, Mass.*

A The trial of Claudine Longet Williams is set for January 3, 1977. Until then the Paris-born, Las Vegas show-girl will stay with her three children by Andy Williams, Noelle, 12, Christian, 11, and Robert, seven, in the Palm Springs residence of Mr. Williams.

Q *Two questions about Ronald Reagan: At 65, has he abandoned his ambition to be president; and who syndicates his newspaper column?—Florence Rigby, Pacific Palisades, Cal.*

A Reagan has not yet taken himself out of any future presidential role, despite his age. His weekly newspaper column is handled by King Features Syndicate.

Q *Where is Nguyen Van Thieu, former president of South Vietnam, living these days, and what is he living on?—H.L., Davenport, Iowa.*

A Thieu lives in the town of New Malden, south of London, in a recently purchased four-bedroom house. Thieu and his wife went into exile in April, 1975, a few days before South Vietnam surrendered to the Communists. They have been

living for the last year in England, where their 13-year-old son goes to school at Eton. The Thieus are living on the money they managed to acquire in South Vietnam.

Evita Peron

Q *Can you tell where Evita Peron, the second wife of the late Argentine dictator Juan Peron, is buried?—Vito Lalle, New York City.*

A Evita Peron died of cancer in Buenos Aires in 1952 at the age of 33. She was proclaimed "the spiritual chief of the nation," and a special mausoleum was built for her. In 1955, after a military uprising, her embalmed body was stolen from Buenos Aires and its location remained a mystery for 15 years. Then it was found in a cemetery in Milan, Italy. In 1971 it was sent to Juan Peron, who was then living in exile in Madrid. The body was finally brought back to Argentina in 1974 and placed in a chapel in Olivos, a suburb of Buenos Aires. A few weeks ago it was again buried in an exclusive cemetery in Buenos Aires—hopefully, the end of its macabre odyssey.

Q *How come Arthur Ashe is the only black player in big-time tennis?—Carlton March Fredericks, New Rochelle, N.Y.*

A Ashe, 33, says: "The key to black progress in tennis lies in the public schools. If we don't beef up the tennis programs there, only the parents of the middle-class black child will be able to afford to kick out the extra dough needed for him or her to compete." Ashe also feels that blacks have limited access to private clubs and are thus handicapped in developing their tennis skills. Ashe, originally from Richmond, Virginia, is the only black man to have been ranked No. 1 in the tennis world. In the 1950's a black woman, Althea Gibson, triumphed at Wimbledon and Forest Hills.

Q *Why did the Shah of Iran return to the Soviet Union a Russian pilot who flew a small plane across the border and asked for asylum in the U.S.? Isn't the Shah a friend of the U.S.?—G.K., Denver, Colo.*

A Mrs. Svetlana Peters, daughter of late Soviet dictator Joseph Stalin, who herself defected to the West in 1966, cabled the Shah and asked him not to send the pilot back to Russia. Nobel Peace Prize-winner Andrei Sakharov and four other leading Soviet dissidents also issued an appeal to the Shah. But the Shah was unmoved. Under terms of an anti-hijacking agreement between Iran and the Soviet Union, Lieut. Valentin Zasimov of the Soviet Air Force was handed over to Soviet authorities this past Oct. 25. The Shah considers himself a friend of the U.S., but he does what he considers best for the country he rules with an "Iran hand."

Q *There is a nightclub in Rome frequented by the beautiful people. It's called "Jackie O." Is it owned in whole or in part by Jacqueline Kennedy Onassis?— Charles Solow, New York City.*

A It is not.

Jacqueline Onassis

Q *How much money did the late J. Paul Getty leave the Getty Museum, which is located on the Pacific Coast Highway between Santa Monica and Malibu?—Claire Weintraub, Los Angeles.*

A A codicil in the Getty will bequeaths to the museum 21 percent of the Getty Oil stock, worth approximately $700 million.

Q *Now that Henry Kissinger is no longer secretary of state, can we find out the true story of the wiretaps he was instrumental in having placed on his colleagues and friends?—E.D., Bethesda, Md.*

Henry Kissinger

A Kissinger, of course, is ashamed of the wiretapping episodes, which took place from 1969 to 1971. He has said repeatedly that he regretted ever having been part of them. In 1969, however, he was "a new boy" in the Nixon administration and was currying favor with Nixon. He was fearful of John Ehrlichman and Bob Haldeman, and so he adopted the Nixonian phobias and suspicions of the time.

Among the names he provided to the FBI for wiretapping and surveillance purposes were those of several men he had hired for the staff of the National Security Council, including Morton Halperin, Helmut Sonnenfeldt, Daniel Davidson, Winston Lord, Richard Moose, Richard Sneider and Anthony Lake. Others included Lt. Gen. Robert Pursley, a military assistant to Melvin Laird, Nixon's defense secretary; William Safire, a Nixon speechwriter; William H. Sullivan, former U.S. ambassador to Laos; Henry Brandon, Washington correspondent for the *Sunday Times of London*, and Hedrick Smith of *The New York Times*. Wiretaps on Marvin Kalb of CBS, William Beecher, then of *The New York Times*, and John Sears, a Nixon campaign aide, were ordered by John Mitchell.

The wiretaps were fruitless. None of the men wiretapped revealed national security secrets. Recently a federal judge ordered Richard Nixon, John Mitchell and Bob Haldeman to pay damages (the amount not yet ascertained at this writing) to Morton Halperin and his family for having maintained wiretaps on their conversations.

A book which describes the wiretapping episodes in detail is *The American Police State* by David Wise (published by Random House).

Q *The present version of* King Kong *cost approximately $23 million to make. My understanding is that producer Dino De Laurentiis and Paramount Pictures have to give Universal Studios 11 percent of their profits. Why is that?— Maurice Blitzstein, Chicago.*

A Because Universal agreed to cancel its own King Kong production plans.

Q *In 1875 Eli Black, who was head of United Brands Co., leaped to his death from the 44th floor of the Pan American Building in New York City. Has the true story of Black's management and corporate raiding ever been told?—M.P., New Rochelle, N.Y.*

A For the inside story of Eli Black and United Brands, read *An American Company* by Thomas McCann. It gives a sad, sorry and full account of what Black and United Fruit, the world's largest producer and seller of bananas, did to Central America. United Fruit is a division of United Brands, was involved with the CIA in mounting a secret invasion of Guatemala and a lot of other shocking and unsavory deeds.

Dr. Benjamin Spock

Q *How many medical doctors ran for national office in last year's election? How did they make out? What office did Dr. Benjamin Spock run for?—Jack McMillan, Orlando, Fla.*

A Dr. Benjamin Spock ran for vice president of the U.S. on the People's Party ticket. He lost. Twenty-five other M.D.'s ran for national office, and 23 lost. The two victorious physicians are members of the House of Representatives: Dr. Tim Lee Carter (R., Ky.), who won his seventh term; and Dr. Lawrence P. McDonald (D., Ga.), a Marietta urologist and member of the John Birch Society, who was returned for a second term.

Q *I have been told that Jack Nicholson is rapidly becoming the richest actor in the motion picture business, that he is now worth $50 million. How much did he earn from* One Flew Over the Cuckoo's Nest?—*Arlene Mae Watkins, Philadelphia.*

A Nicholson earns a minimum of $1 million per film plus a hefty percentage of the film's gross. He gets 15 percent of *Cuckoo's* gross, which should bring him about $15 million. The richest actor in the motion picture business is Bob Hope, whose fortune is estimated at above $100 million. But such actors as Steve McQueen, Paul Newman, Robert Redford, Marlon Brando and Jack Nicholson are rapidly approaching Hope's record.

Q *I would like to know if* Robinson Crusoe, *the classic by Daniel Defoe, was based on a true-life story. Thank you.— Owen Johnson, Watertown, N.Y.*

A *Robinson Crusoe* is based on the real-life adventures of Alexander Selkirk, a Scottish navigator who cast himself away on the Chilean island of Juan Fernandez for 52 months. He was rescued by Capt. Woodes Rogers in 1709 and written up by the captain in *Cruising Voyage Round the World* in 1712.

Q *Amy Carter, nine, is the first child of a U.S. president to attend a public school in 70 years. What is the racial breakdown of the Stevens School little Amy attends in Washington, D.C.?—Joan Manley, New York City.*

A About 60 percent of the students are black, about 30 percent were born abroad and are the offspring of diplomats and other foreigners.

Q *Indira Gandhi, prime minister of India, claims she is bringing "guided democracy" to her country. Is "guided democracy" a new synonym for dictatorship?—Jean Taylor, Winston-Salem, N.C.*

Indira Gandhi

A India is drowning in a sea of overpopulation. Indira Gandhi has become a despot—some people say "a benevolent despot"—in an effort to keep her country afloat. Democracy in India may well be a thing of the past. "Guided democracy," of course, is no synonym for dictatorship.

Laura Baugh

Q *Is it true that Laura Baugh earned $300,000 winning golf tournaments last year? If so, why haven't we heard more of this golf champion?—Fred Ricket, W. Palm Beach, Fla.*

A Laura Baugh, 21, of Del Ray Beach, Florida, earned approximately $29,000 in tournament prize money last year. A beautiful, photogenic young blonde, she earned about $250,000 appearing on TV commercials and other advertising vehicles. To date she has not won a professional tournament but, through the efforts of agent Mark McCormack, has made a fortune promoting various products. As an amateur, Laura won the U.S. amateur title in 1971.

Q *About Sen. Barry Goldwater—why didn't he do something to stamp out the corruption and crookedness in his own state, or did he insidiously find himself wrapped up in it?—H.T., Tucson, Ariz.*

A Goldwater and his brother Bob are members of the Arizona Establishment. Perhaps they were political innocents unmindful of the corruption which was developing in their state. Surely a man of Goldwater's character would not knowingly traffic with owners of massage parlors, crooked land speculators, and members of the underworld. Senator Goldwater may not be the most admired member of the U.S. Senate, but he is an honest man.

Q *How does Zbigniew Brzezinski, head of the National Security Council, compare to Henry Kissinger? Is Zbig chang-* ing his name to Big Bear?—G.T., Cambridge, Mass.

A Brzezinski is not changing his name. In contrast to Kissinger, he has much less power. From all appearances, Carter is very much his own foreign policymaker. Under Gerald Ford it was Kissinger who pretty much made foreign policy.

Q *Is it true that President Jimmy Carter is considering a face-lift because of sagging jowls and a double chin and has sought the advice of Ronald Reagan on this question?—M.P., San Diego, Cal.*

A Carter is considering many problems, but a face-lift is not one of them.

Q *What is the true story about actress Sophia Loren and the Italian police authorities? Why don't they want her to leave Italy? Is she a smuggler?— G. Beckett, Deal, N.J.*

A Sophia Loren, 42, and her husband Carlo Ponti, 62, became citizens of France in 1963 to avoid bigamy suits in Italy. Divorce was then illegal in Italy, and the Italians declined to regard as legal the divorce Ponti had obtained in Mexico in 1957. Thus, for a long while Ponti and Loren were regarded in Italy as living in sin.

Sophia Loren

When Loren and Ponti moved to Paris, Italian police suspected that they might be transferring their assets to France, particularly large amounts of Italian currency, which is illegal.

This past March when Sophia Loren was about to board a Paris-bound plane at Rome's Da Vinci Airport under an assumed name, the Finance Police, who enforce the Italian foreign exchange regulations, detained her. They recalled her luggage, searched it thoroughly, confiscated three large sealed envelopes which contained records of her various banking transactions and those involving her husband's "alleged currency violations."

After several hours of interrogation they permitted Miss Loren to catch a plane to Paris, where she was met by her husband.

In February of this year a dozen members of Rome's Finance Police raided the Ponti villa outside Rome, conducted a search for financial documents, and found some they considered relevant to their investigation.

Loren and Ponti were for years considered one of the wealthiest couples in Italy, and Italy seems determined to prevent them from removing all their assets. Sophia, her husband and their two sons may eventually move to Montreal or California.

Q *Is it a fact that the two leading Don Juans of the Carter administration are Hamilton Jordan, Carter's former campaign manager, and Jody Powell, Carter's press secretary?—F.K., Bethesda, Md.*

A Jordan and Powell appreciate female beauty in all its forms, which is why each has an attractive wife.

Q *Anna Manahan of Charlottesville, Virginia—has she ever been recognized as Anastasia, youngest daughter of Czar Nicholas II, who was murdered with his family at Ekaterinburg in 1918?—Lois Brown, Richmond, Va.*

A Moritz Furtmayr, one of Germany's top forensic experts, claims that he has positively identified the former Anna Anderson, 75, as the Russian Grand Duchess Anastasia. Furtmayr contends that Anderson's right ear is identical to that in a photo of Anastasia's right ear. Anna Anderson is currently married to former University of Virginia history professor John Manahan. She has petitioned for the last 50 years, in various German court fights, that she be legally recognized as the late czar's youngest daughter. Furtmayr's views may give rise to still another court case.

Q *I understand there is no truth in the report Olympic swimmer Mark Spitz and his wife are separated. Am I right?—S.R., Los Angeles.*

A You are right.

The Spitzes

Q *I keep reading that there is a chance Gerald Ford will run for U.S. president in 1980. How much of a chance?—Sam Reilly, Oak Park, Ill.*

A Practically none. Gerald and Betty Ford now enjoy the best of all possible worlds, and they are not about to forsake it.

PERSONALITY PARADE®

May 29, 1977

Q *Now that Vivien Leigh and Peter Finch have both passed on, is there anyone who will tell the truth about their tempestuous love affair? Is there anyone who will tell the truth about Vivien Leigh? Is it not true that she was mad and died insane?—D.D.L., Denver, Col.*

Vivien Leigh

A So long as films endure, Vivien Leigh (1913-1967) will be remembered for her magnificent performance as Scarlett O'Hara in *Gone With the Wind.*

Unfortunately, Vivien Leigh in her adulthood developed into a tubercular manic depressive whose mental illness was hidden from her adoring public by friends and colleagues. One of these was actor Peter Finch, who was discovered and first employed by Miss Leigh's husband, Laurence Olivier.

In 1953 Leigh and Finch starred in a movie, *Elephant Walk,* shot in Ceylon. During the course of the production, Vivien Leigh broke down. Lovingly, Finch took care of her. They flew back to Hollywood where Vivien was replaced by Elizabeth Taylor.

Vivien Leigh, when seized by mental malady, was subject to fits in which she fantasied sexual relations with tradesmen and others not of her station. On occasion she would attempt to disrobe, throw herself out of planes and trains, suffer horrible hallucinations. For years she was given therapy.

When not ill she was a lady of kindness, gentility, courage and tremendous generosity; as an actress she was enormously talented but not the equal of her longtime husband, Lord Olivier. She won two Academy Awards as best actress—for Scarlett O'Hara in *Gone With the Wind* (1939) and for Blanche du Bois in *A Streetcar Named Desire* (1951).

She was a good and gallant lady, tormented by an unstable mind which periodically could not find itself. She died July 8, 1967, of tuberculosis.

Q *Who were the top individual contributors in the 1976 presidential campaign?—Frances Matthews, Beverly Hills, Cal.*

A According to the Federal Election Commission, a Mr. Henry Grover of Houston, Texas, spent $63,000 of his own money supporting the candidacy of former California Governor Ronald Reagan. Ranked second among the spenders was Colorado beer magnate Joseph Coors, who contributed $33,782 to Reagan. Gov. Milton Schapp of Pennsylvania contributed $28,001 to Jimmy Carter and others.

Q *It is my understanding that one of our congressmen from Alabama used to take a daily "sex break" when he was in the House of Representatives. Can you identify him?—F.H., Montgomery, Ala.*

A In his forthcoming autobiography, *Fishbait,* William "Fishbait" Miller, who guarded the door of the House of Representatives, points to the late Rep. Frank Boykin (D., Ala.) as the 275-pound congressman who was well recognized for taking "sex breaks." Boykin campaigned on the slogan "Everything is Made for Love." He died in 1969.

Q *Is it true that, after Fidel Castro, the most popular heroes in Cuba are athletes?—Bill Ross, Monroe, La.*

Fidel Castro

A Generally, that seems to be true. For example, Teofilo Stevenson, two-time gold medal winner in the Olympics and the world's amateur heavyweight champion, is enormously popular in Cuba. So, too, is Alberto Juantorena, who won the 400- and 800-meter runs at Montreal in 1976. The most popular sport in Cuba is baseball, followed by boxing, track and field, and basketball. The Cubans insist that their Teofilo Stevenson can beat Muhammad Ali.

Q *Why has the American press killed or played down the story of Victor Dubrowsky, the Soviet orchestra leader jailed in Indianapolis a few weeks ago? What really happened?—K.L., Akron, Ohio.*

A Dubrowsky, conductor of the 75-member Oslupov Balalaika Orchestra and one of the leading musical directors in the Soviet Union, was apprehended by detectives in the J.C. Penney department store in Indianapolis. He was accused of shoplifting and turned over to the local police, who jailed him for about five hours. The Soviet embassy in Washington, D.C., phoned the Indianapolis police and explained to Deputy Police Chief Jack Cottey that Dubrowsky was a great musician who'd been invited by the U.S. State Department to give a concert tour. They demanded his immediate release. Cottey checked with Penney's and arranged Dubrowsky's freedom contingent upon his signing a release that he would not sue J.C. Penney. Dubrowsky signed the release, was escorted from the jail, later directed a concert in Cincinnati. The entire incident is not one the Russians, the executives at J.C. Penney, the Indianapolis police or the U.S. State Department care to publicize.

Charlie Chaplin

Q *Charlie Chaplin celebrated his 88th birthday on April 16, 1977. Is it a fact that he can no longer walk? How many times has he been married? Where does he live?—Sara Long, Ithaca, N.Y.*

A Sir Charles Chaplin is confined to the wheelchair in which Queen Elizabeth II of Great Britain knighted him in 1975. He lives in Vevey, Switzerland. He has been married four times. His current wife, to whom he has been married 34 years, is Oona O'Neill, daughter of playwright Eugene O'Neill, who bitterly opposed the marriage. To celebrate his 88th birthday, Chaplin bought a new Silver Shadow Rolls-Royce.

WALTER SCOTT'S
PERSONALITY PARADE®

June 19, 1977

The Rolling Stones

Q *The inside word is that there is a porn film on the Rolling Stones which is a knockout. Have the Rolling Stones ever starred in England in a series of pornographic flicks?—Maude L., Pittsburgh, Pa.*

A No, they have not. But in 1972 the Stones commissioned Robert Frank, 52, a Canadian film producer, to make a documentary feature of their North American tour. Mick Jagger planned to release it in Great Britain and the U.S. After Jagger saw the finished product, he banned the film from ever being shown in public. The Stones went to court to prevent British newspapers from describing the film, which Sir Hilary Gwynne Talbot of the High Court described as "wholly unfit for public exhibition." And with good reason—it allegedly contains scenes of group sex, nudity, and sexual activity photographed backstage, on the airplane, in hotel bedrooms, and elsewhere. Reportedly there have been private showings of the film.

Q *Isn't there bad blood between Hamilton Jordan, President Carter's patronage chief, and Joe Califano, Carter's HEW Secretary? How long will it be before Jordan ousts Califano?—D.L., Alexandria, Va.*

A Jordan was surprised when Califano chose John Ellis, an Ohio Republican, as his executive deputy commissioner of education. But Jordan is much too shrewd to make overt and traceable moves against Califano at this stage of the game. Perhaps down the road a piece.

Q *What is the story about comedian George Kirby? Is it true that he was discovered in Las Vegas with five pounds of heroin worth $3 million?—G.F., Reno, Nev.*

A Kirby and four others were arrested in Las Vegas a few weeks ago by federal agents who allegedly found some cocaine and 1.1 pounds of heroin worth $400,000 on the premises. Kirby has been charged in federal court with possession of heroin and intent to distribute. He pleaded not guilty, will be tried July 6.

Q *I have been told that since Betty and Gerald Ford left the White House, each has become a millionaire. Is that true?—D.L., Bethesda, Md.*

A This is not true. What is true is that the William Morris Agency has negotiated TV and book deals for the Fords which eventually will place them in the millionaire category.

Q *Even though Italy is a Roman Catholic country, doesn't the Italian government distribute free oral contraceptive pills to women?—F.R., Syracuse, N.Y.*

A According to the Italian Health Ministry, such pills are distributed free provided the women obtain a prescription for the pill from a family planning center.

Q *It is my understanding that Leonid Brezhnev, leader of the Soviet Union and secretary-general of the Communist party, has Communist party card #1. Who has Communist party card #2?—F.D.L., Hartford, Conn.*

Leonid Brezhnev

A No one knows. You are probably mixing up membership in the Soviet Journalists Union with membership in the Communist party. According to Tass, the Soviet news agency, Brezhnev was issued card #2 in the Soviet Journalists Union. Card #1 was issued in the name of Vladimir Ilyich Lenin, founder of the Communist party and the Soviet state.

Q *I cannot for the life of me understand why Jimmy Carter sends top secret government and CIA reports to Richard Nixon. What is the reason?—Dean Winter, Los Angeles.*

A Carter also sends such reports to former President Gerald Ford. It is a courtesy extended to former U.S. presidents and reflects a presidential continuity of sorts. Both Nixon and Ford possess background knowledge which President Carter may one day find useful.

Globe

Lady Bird Johnson

Q *Was Lady Bird Johnson offered the U.S. ambassadorship to Mexico? I have heard that story many times. Supposedly, President Carter offered her the job, and she turned it down.—M. Molina, San Antonio, Tex.*

A President Carter never offered Lady Bird Johnson the U.S. ambassadorship to Mexico. He offered her a place on the commission to choose White House fellows, and Lady Bird has accepted that position.

Q *Is professional tennis, with players like Connors, Nastase and others, going the way of boxing? Is the "fix" becoming an integral part of what was once regarded as a gentleman's game? Do players like Connors and Nastase bet on themselves? Are these players controlled by gamblers?—L. Lewis, New Rochelle, N.Y.*

A Connors and Nastase were involved in a tennis match in Puerto Rico in which the prize money distribution was untruthfully announced. It was not a "$250,000 winner-take-all" match. Connors was guaranteed $500,000 and Nastase $150,000. The promotion of professional tennis matches may be suspect, but the tennis players themselves must be regarded as honest until proved otherwise. However, some fans will regard professional tennis that involves big money with a jaundiced eye.

Michael Sarrazin and Jacqueline Bisset

Q *How old is actress Jacqueline Bisset? Before she lived with lovers Michael Sarrazin and then Victor Drai, was she not a protégée of Darryl Zanuck, one of the founders of 20th Century-Fox?—E.L.P., N. Hollywood, Cal.*

A Jacqueline Bisset, 32, was never a protégée of Darryl Zanuck, although she did work at 20th Century-Fox in his final days there.

Q *Is it a fact that Woodward and Bernstein, authors of the two best Watergate sellers,* All the President's Men *and* The Final Days, *have fallen out because of money and have abolished their collaboration?—Sara Patrick, New York City.*

A There was no falling out, just an agreement that each would go his separate way. Bernstein is working on a book about the Joe McCarthy era, and Woodward is collaborating with Scott Armstrong on a book dealing with governmental institutions. Woodward and Bernstein remain friends.

Q *Why would the Shah of Iran give Pepperdine University in Malibu a gift of $1 million?—Louis Haynes, Malibu, Cal.*

A In April 1977 a delegation of educators from Pepperdine flew to Tehran and awarded the Shah an honorary Doctor of Laws degree. A month later he endowed for $1 million an Empress Farah of Iran chair in education at Pepperdine, which will provide scholarships for Iranian students and others.

Q *David Eisenhower, Ike's grandson—doesn't he plan to run for congressman from Pennsylvania?—V. Lewis, Downingtown, Pa.*

A Young Eisenhower is toying with the idea. Meanwhile, he is hard at work gathering material for a biography of his famous grandfather.

Q *The millionaire German playboy Gunther Sachs, who gave Brigitte Bardot a tumble—is he married and of what nation is he currently a citizen?—Heinz Schwartz, Elizabeth, N.J.*

A Gunther Sachs and his new wife, Mirja, have become naturalized Swiss citizens, reside in Gstaad. Taxes, you know.

Q *I would like to know what two of the wealthiest men in the U.S. Senate—John Heinz of Pennsylvania, heir to the Heinz Foods fortune, and Edward Kennedy of Massachusetts, heir to the Kennedy real estate fortune—did with their recent $12,900-a-year pay raise?—Peter Gallagher, Pittsburgh, Pa.*

A Heinz plans to set up a scholarship program for students, and Kennedy plans to contribute his raise to various charities.

Q *When Secretary of Defense Harold Brown was recently awarded an honorary degree at Brown University, many of the students who were being graduated turned their backs on him. Why?—B.T., Cambridge, Mass.*

Harold Brown

A Brown was Secretary of the Air Force during part of the Vietnam war, and some students undoubtedly disagreed with his policy on bombing, his handling of the Ernest Fitzgerald C-5A overcost case and other war-related matters.

Q *Can you tell me anything about Isaac Singer, inventor of the sewing machine? My understanding is that he led an evil and wicked life.—Evangeline Flynn, Staten Island, N.Y.*

A Isaac Merritt Singer had five wives and mistresses who gave him a total of 24 children. Singer (1811-75), son of a poor immigrant, was a frustrated actor who became an inventor. He patented a practical sewing machine in 1851, became a leading manufacturer of sewing machines and an extravagant womanizer. His partner, Edward Clark, devised the idea of selling machines on the installment plan. Toward the end of his life, Singer moved to England, lived stylishly. When he died he was honored with a mile-long funeral procession, his bier drawn by 12 horses. He insisted upon being buried in three coffins, one inside the other. Strange, talented, hedonistic man.

Jimmy and Rosalynn Carter

Q *They say that after Jimmy Carter and his wife rode on the nuclear sub U.S.S. Los Angeles—I believe Mrs. Carter was the first woman allowed to take over the controls—Jimmy wrote something funny in the ship's log. Can you find out what he wrote?—L.F., Americus, Ga.*

A After emergency maneuvers were carried out aboard the submarine, the president reportedly wrote in the log: "Emergency maneuvers for the president and First Lady—excellent job." Then he signed it "Jimmy Carter."

Q *Who is Alan Jay Lerner, who has been married seven times? Does he own Lerner Stores, the well-known dress chain?—Mary Karp, Chicago.*

A Alan Jay Lerner, a member of the Lerner merchandising family, is a well-known lyricist ("My Fair Lady," "Camelot," "Gigi"). He recently took his seventh bride, Nina Bushkin, 28, daughter of famous jazz pianist-composer Joe Bushkin. Lerner is 58.

Alexandros Andreadis and Christina Onassis

Q *What's happened to the marriage of Christina Onassis, daughter of the late shipping magnate Aristotle Onassis, and Alexandros Andreadis, heir to the Greek banking fortune?—M. Janis, Salem, Mass.*

A After less than two years, the marriage was dissolved in Athens, Greece, in July 1977.

Q *Has any U.S. official ever stated how we keep track of Soviet missiles? Do we actually know how many missiles the Soviets have; and if so, how do we know that?—D.G., Silver Spring, Md.*

A Several techniques are used to track the number, launching, and location of Soviet missiles. President Carter has acknowledged the use of "aerial surveillance from space." And as *Aviation Week & Space Technology* magazine revealed, President Lyndon Johnson on March 15, 1967, told an audience in Nashville, Tennessee, "I wouldn't want to be quoted on this, but we've spent $35-40 billion on the space program. And if nothing else had come out of it except that knowledge we've gained from space photography, it would be worth 10 times what the whole program cost. Because tonight we know how many missiles the enemy has."

Q *Gen. Eisenhower's first son—what was his name? How old when he died? Where is he buried?—Clair Hopkins, Denver, Col.*

A Mamie and Ike's first son, Doud Dwight "Icky" Eisenhower, was born in San Antonio while Ike was on assignment at Ft. Oglethorpe, Georgia. He died of scarlet fever at age four, was buried in the Doud family plot in Denver. "Icky" was reinterred in Abilene, Kansas, alongside

his father who died on March 28, 1969. Of his first son's death, Ike wrote in his book *At Ease* that it was "the greatest disappointment and disaster in my life, the one I have never been able to forget completely."

Q *Who said, "There is a foolish corner in the brain of the wisest man"?—Helen Fletcher, Raleigh, N.C.*

A Aristotle.

Q *Last year Cyrus Vance was chairman of the Sargent Shriver for president campaign. Why? And how come Jimmy Carter made Vance secretary of state?—F.L., Bethesda, Md.*

A Vance found many presidential attributes in Shriver. Subsequently, when Carter was elected, Carter realized that Cyrus Vance, who'd been on the Trilateral Commission with him, was a man of tact, probity, and diplomatic experience. He did not hold Vance's early support of Sarge Shriver against him.

Q *I have always been fascinated by the strange life of T. E. Lawrence, the Lawrence of Arabia immortalized by writer Lowell Thomas and actor Peter O'Toole. I have long languished under the opinion that Lawrence was killed in a motorcycle accident in England in 1935. Now I have been told that he was actually murdered by the British Intelligence Service. Is there any credence to that?—Bruce Andrews, Berkeley, Cal.*

T.E. Lawrence

A Speculations about the life and death of World War I hero Lawrence of Arabia continue to grow. In a new Lawrence biography, scholar and author Desmond Stewart offers the thesis that Lawrence was politically murdered. According to Stewart, the British establishment considered Lawrence, with his masochistic sexual habits and his fascist tendencies, a dangerous character, and therefore engineered the "accident" in which Lawrence was killed. Stewart maintains that Lawrence concocted the story of his homosexual rape and torture by the Turks in his book, *The Seven Pillars of Wisdom*. He maintains Lawrence made the whole inci-

dent up, that it was nothing more than a "sado-masochistic phantasy."

Morgan Mason and Louise Fletcher

Q *I've been reading that actress Louise Fletcher, who was so great in* One Flew Over the Cuckoo's Nest, *has been dating Morgan Mason, son of Pamela and actor James Mason. My understanding is that Louise Fletcher is in her 40's while Morgan Mason is in his 20's. Am I right?—F.D.E., Philadelphia.*

A Just about.

Q *I am truly confused about the one-inch Carter peanut farms being sold in Plains, Georgia, for $11. Are these sales the Carter family's idea? Is it Carter land that is actually for sale?—F.L., Macon, Ga.*

A Last year one Carter relative entertained the idea of selling one-inch squares of Carter land, but Jimmy Carter aborted that scheme. However, in 1948 Jimmy's father, James Earl Carter, sold some land 720 feet by 300 feet to black tenant farmer Willis Wright, who in turn sold it to the Plains Realty Co. and David W. Thurmond of Atlanta. Thurmond, through Plains Realty, has been offering for sale at $11 a square inch some of this former Carter land.

These are known as one-inch peanut farms and come with an elaborate brochure about Georgia and the Carter family.

Q *Did Bob Haldeman, Richard Nixon's chief of staff, ever write a Nixon resignation speech in which he pardoned himself, John Mitchell, John Ehrlichman and others?—Mary Pissano, Palo Alto, Cal.*

A At one point in the Watergate crisis, Haldeman drafted a resignation speech for Nixon in which Nixon would pardon himself and all his chief aides. Haldeman also wrote a memo proposing that course of action.

Virginia Woolf

Q *Virginia Woolf was surely one of England's greatest novelists. Was she also gay—in the lesbian sense—and with whom? Are there any books on the subject?—D.D., Bangor, Maine.*

A Virginia Woolf (1882-1941), polished novelist and distinguished essayist, was "gay." Her 1928 novel, *Orlando*, describes her affair with Vita Sackville-West, wife of British diarist and diplomat Sir Harold Nicolson. Three volumes of Virginia Woolf's letters have been published to date. All are revealing of her strange lifestyle and the unique ways of the famous "Bloomsbury Group."

Q *I understand that Marina Oswald, whose husband assassinated John F. Kennedy, has written her autobiography in Russian. When will it be translated for readers in this country?—F.L., Dallas, Tex.*

A Marina Oswald has written no autobiography. Priscilla Johnson McMillan, who interviewed Lee Harvey Oswald in Moscow in 1959, was granted exclusive rights to Marina Oswald's story as far back as 1964. Since then Mrs. McMillan and Marina Oswald have collaborated on a book, *Marina and Lee*, scheduled for publication in the U.S. in October. Mrs. McMillan previously translated into English *Only One Year*, a book written by Joseph Stalin's daughter, Svetlana Alliluyeva.

Q *Does President Carter have the youngest cabinet in history? What is its average age?—Paul Moore, New York City.*

A The average age of Carter cabinet members is a little over 50. It is not the youngest cabinet in history.

Q *How old is Adm. Hyman Rickover, how long has he been in the Navy and what is the source of his power?—Allen Bell, Piedmont, Cal.*

A Adm. Hyman Rickover, 77, is currently enjoying his 59th year in the naval service. He was recently appointed to another two-year term as head of the Navy's nuclear propulsion program. Congress regards him as father of our nuclear Navy and continues to reappoint and keep him on active service as one of the most knowledgeable officers in the service. The source of his power is his nuclear expertise and his congressional admirers.

Q *In 1971 when Henry Kissinger flew to China secretly to invoke Richard Nixon's new China policy, were any U.S. ambassadors apprised of that development?—P.O., Chevy Chase, Md.*

A No, and one who suffered deeply because of that secrecy was Armin H. Meyer, our ambassador to Japan (1969-1972). When Peking disclosed in 1971 that Kissinger had secretly visited China, the Japanese government was furious. For years it had worked with the U.S. to keep Red China out of the United Nations. Japan demanded an explanation from Ambassador Meyer, and he could give none. For the seven months he remained in Tokyo, Meyer's prestige quotient was zero or close to it.

Q *On May 10, 1977, Joan Crawford died. The newspapers said she died of heart failure. About two weeks later People magazine said or implied that Joan Crawford committed suicide. Which is true?—W. Reid, Akron, Ohio.*

Joan Crawford

A There is no evidence that Joan Crawford took her own life.

Q *There is a rumor rife in this community that Boeing Aircraft will soon start manufacturing 600-seat, double-decker air transports. How accurate is that rumor, and if it is, who is in the market for such planes?—J.F., Renton, Wash.*

A Among many other possibilities, Boeing is exploring the manufacture of such super-jumbos for the 1980's. Japan Air Lines might prove a likely customer.

Boeing, however, is constantly in the process of exploring aircraft possibilities, but no announcement has been made of any such double-decker, 600-passenger air transport.

Q *Judge John Sirica, the hero of Watergate—does he plan to retire from the bench and write his autobiography?—V. Everett, Pasadena, Cal.*

A Sirica, 73, recently announced that he was thinking of retirement and "doing a book." Sirica believes that the stress and strain of his judicial role in Watergate brought on his heart attack. He is most grateful to his law clerk who during the lengthy Watergate trials "was the only one I really could talk to. Without his help and advice and patience . . . it would have been pretty difficult for me. I'd go home some nights really down in the dumps and very sad."

Q *When Marlon Brando acts in a film, does he memorize his lines or read them off-camera from idiot cards?—V.H., Los Angeles.*

Marlon Brando

A Brando used to memorize his lines when he first broke into motion pictures. For years now he has read his lines from idiot cards, wall signs, and other devices. Recently he read from idiot cards in making two *Superman* films for which he was paid a minimum of $2.5 million and a profit percentage for 13 days' work.

Q *Do German dentists earn more than German medical doctors? My wife, who is German, says they do. I say she is wrong. Please settle the argument.—O.T.T.O., St. Paul, Minn.*

A Your wife is correct. In 1975 the average West German general practitioner earned $33,055 after expenses. The average dentist cleared $35,275.

Q *David Frost, who interviewed Richard Nixon on TV—his talent escapes me. Exactly what is his talent and vocation?—Bennett Wheeler, Carmel, Cal.*

A David Frost has some talent as an interviewer, is basically a show business promoter.

WALTER SCOTT'S
PERSONALITY PARADE®

October 9, 1977

Juliet Prowse

Q *Juliet Prowse, the beautiful dancer who used to go with Frank Sinatra and Fred Astaire—what's happened to her? I don't see her in films anymore.— Louise Franks, Bayonne, N.J.*

A Juliet Prowse is married to John McCook. They have a five-year-old son, Seth. Juliet earns about $1 million annually, dancing in the Las Vegas hotels formerly owned by Howard Hughes. She works about five months a year.

Q *I have heard a strong rumor that sometime next year Jimmy Carter will pardon John Mitchell and Bob Haldeman. Is it true that Carter will not permit these two men to rot in jail while Nixon enjoys the daily golf and swimming and the other delights of the sporting life in San Clemente?—E.L.P., Long Beach, Cal.*

A Carter has the right to pardon Mitchell and Haldeman at any time and may do so in the future. But only Carter knows whether he entertains any such intention. Mitchell and Haldeman are not rotting in jail. They are working on their respective books. As for Nixon, life for him is no tea party. He may have earned $1 million as his share of the David Frost interviews. He may earn another $2-3 million in royalties from his forthcoming memoirs. But his heart is heavy and, as a primarily mental man, his conscience must surely twinge.

Q *What mystical hold does Howard "The Mouth" Cosell have that he continues to work for ABC Sports especially when he irritates so many fans?— Glenn A. Peil, St. Petersburg, Fla.*

A Cosell is knowledgeable, builds up the people who work with him, has become a TV celebrity by attracting and repelling many television viewers. He is not bland. His voice and style stimulate emotions, some positive, some negative. Roone Arledge, his boss at ABC, considers him valuable to the network. That is the extent of his "mystical hold."

Q *Doesn't Bert Lance have enough information on his fellow Georgians in the White House to pull the plug and sink the Carter Administration?—S.L., alexandra, Va.*

A T. Bertram Lance is the last man in the world to pull the plug of vengeance. Despite all that has happened, he remains one of Carter's closest friends.

Q *Is Bette Midler going to play the life of that weirdo, freaked-out Janis Joplin in the movies?—T.L., Marble Falls, Tex.*

A Twentieth Century-Fox plans to star Bette Midler in a film based somewhat on the life of the late Janis Joplin.

Q *About the late Groucho Marx—did he really drive his three wives to drink? Was he an impossible man to live with?—A.H., Dayton, Ohio.*

Groucho Marx

A The truth about Groucho is that he was not a particularly good husband. His three marriages ended in recrimination and acrimony. In a manner of speaking, he wore brass knuckles on his tongue. From time to time he could not resist the temptation of using his knife-sharp wit to humiliate even those he supposedly loved.

Q *Is there any chance that at 60 Dean Martin will marry a young chick, Phyllis Davis?—Day Silver, Clifton, N.J.*

A Over the years Dean Martin has been partial to marriage. He's had three to date, will undoubtedly, as a creature of habit, progress to a fourth. Whether Phyllis Davis will prove the lucky winner is uncertain at this time. Mr. Martin has been known to change his loves.

Q *How many senators and representatives were offered gifts, girls, campaign contributions, and free trips to South Korea by South Korean lobbyists? And haven't the lobbyists from Taiwan and Israel been offering the same inducements for years?—D.E., Washington, D.C.*

A It's been estimated that more than 100 representatives and senators were approached by South Korean government lobbyists. How many accepted various contributions Leon Jaworski and his staff will determine in the weeks to come. Taiwanese and Israeli lobbyists have also waged lobbying campaigns, but not as blatantly.

Q *Whatever happened to that beautiful Chinese CBS news reporter, Connie Chung?—Helen Ho Walker, Agawarm, Mass.*

A Miss Chung lives in Hollywood, co-anchors the news programs with Joe Benti and Maury Povich on KNXT-TV, the CBS station in Los Angeles.

Q *I cannot believe that Tatum O'Neal is now paid $40,000 a week as an actress. Is this so?—Nina Moore, Los Angeles.*

A Tatum O'Neal is paid by the picture. The Superior Court in Los Angeles recently okayed her $400,000 contract for a 10-week stint in *International Velvet*, a sequel to *National Velvet* in which Elizabeth Taylor starred as a child.

Q *Why won't the Russians sell arms to Egypt? Is it because Brezhnev dislikes Egypt's President Sadat?— C.V., Ocala, Fla.*

A Brezhnev believes that Sadat will be unable to survive Egypt's mounting economic difficulties, sees no

Leonid Brezhnev

reason to sell arms to Egypt, which under Sadat has a pro-American, anti-Soviet foreign policy. The belief is widespread in Europe that Sadat will be overturned unless Saudi Arabia or the United States provides Egypt with large transfusions of cash and credit.

WALTER SCOTT'S
PERSONALITY PARADE®

January 8, 1978

George Bernard Shaw

Q *Many actors hate critics, but haven't many critics developed into great writers whose works the actors performed?—M. Werner, New York City.*

A George Bernard Shaw, Robert Benchley, George S. Kaufman, Graham Greene, Robert Sherwood, James Agee, William Inge, many others were critics before they became writers.

Q *Why is Bert Lance, former Office of Management and Budget director, still allowed to retain his diplomatic passport?—R.O., Washington, D.C.*

A Basically because Lance is one of Jimmy Carter's closest friends and advisers; conceivably because Carter could one day send Lance on some diplomatic mission.

Q *What did Sheila Ryan Caan get from her husband, actor James Caan, in the divorce settlement after two years of marriage?—E.R., Dallas, Tex.*

A The former Mrs. Caan was awarded custody of the couple's young son Scott, $3,000 a month for her and Scott for five years, and then $1,000 a month in child support until Scott reaches 18.

Q *Is it true Alaska residents are free to grow and smoke their own marijuana?—A.L., Seattle, Wash.*

A Alaska is the only state in the union which at this writing affords its resident that freedom without penalty.

Q *How long has Anatoly Dobrynin been the Soviet ambassador to the United States, why is he known in diplomatic circles as "The Red Fox," and is it true that the Soviets plan to recall him in a few weeks?—Victor R., Bethesda, Md.*

A Dobrynin has served as Soviet ambassador to this country for 16 years. He is called "The Red Fox" because he is a sly, tactful Communist. Rumors concerning the date of his return to Moscow are numerous, but the date of his retirement or reassignment is unknown at this time.

Q *Who is responsible for the retirement of Eric Sevareid, 65, from CBS?—R.B.B., Altadena, Cal.*

A It's a company rule okayed by William S. Paley, major CBS stockholder and former chief executive, who stayed in the CBS saddle until he was 75 and still oversees the organization.

Q *How much does Chief Justice Warren Burger of the U.S. Supreme Court earn annually? Do his associates on the bench earn the same salary? What is the reputation of the Burger Court in legal circles—high, low or medium?—Charles Batson, Berkeley, Cal.*

A The Chief Justice is paid $75,000 a year, the associate justices $72,000 a year. Generally the Burger Court is considered "medium" in legal circles. Justice Stevens was nominated by Gerald Ford. Justices Burger, Rehnquist, Powell and Blackmun were Nixon nominees. Justice Marshall, the only black on the court, is a Lyndon Johnson nominee. Justice White was nominated by President Kennedy, Justices Stewart and Brennan by President Eisenhower. The Burger Court is regarded as philosophically unpredictable, intellectually not of the highest stripe.

Queen Elizabeth

Globe

Q *Do you know who the richest woman in Great Britain is?—Jennie Olsen, Richfield, Utah.*

A Most probably the Queen. She has been granted an 18 percent increase in her annual expense allowance—raising it to $3.4 million—to cover the rising wages of her staff and other members of the royal household. The Queen pays no income taxes, no death duties. As a result, the private fortune of the Royal Family grows ever larger.

Q *Cheryl Ladd, who took over from Farrah Fawcett-Majors in* Charlies' Angels, *the TV series—whom is she married to?—Karen Elias, Detroit, Mich.*

A Her actor-husband David is the younger son of the late film star Alan Ladd. His brother, Alan, Jr., is president of 20th Century-Fox Feature Film Division.

Q *Pablo Picasso had a mistress-model, Marie-Therese Walter, who gave birth to an illegitimate child of his. What's happened to Marie-Therese Walter?— Dorothy Zachary, Chicago, Ill.*

Pablo Picasso

A Marie-Therese Walter hung herself October 20, 1977, in her garage at Juan Les Pins, France. She was 68, the mother of Maya Picasso.

Q *I have seen* Mutiny on the Bounty *several times on television. I would like to know if in historical truth there was a homosexual relationship between Captain Bligh, played by Charles Laughton, and Fletcher Christian, played by Clark Gable. Wasn't Charles Laughton a homosexual, and wasn't that why he was cast in the role of Captain Bligh?—V.A.S., Evanston, Ill.*

A Sodomy was a common practice in the British Navy in the late 18th century when Fletcher Christian led the mutiny aboard *H.M.S. Bounty*, commanded by William Bligh. There is no historical record in which either man is even accused of the practice. In his book *Captain Bligh and Mr. Christian*, however, Richard Hough suggests the possibility of a "gay" relationship between Bligh and Christian which originated when they served together on *H.M.S. Britannia*. The late Charles Laughton was a homosexual, but he was not chosen to play Captain Bligh for that reason. His excellence as an actor won him that particular role. The late Clark Gable, of course, was heterosexual.

WALTER SCOTT'S
PERSONALITY PARADE®

March 26, 1978

Stacey Weitzman and Henry Winkler

Q *Henry "Fonz" Winkler—can you tell me anything about the girl he is currently living with?—Ann Gold, New York, N.Y.*

A Winkler, 32, is living with press agent Stacey Weitzman, 30, and her six-year-old son Jed in Los Angeles. Weitzman is an intelligent, career-conscious divorcée who met Winkler in a Beverly Hills clothing store. She is a graduate of the University of Southern California. Winkler is a Yalie. Friends say that if anyone can get Henry down the wedding aisle, it is Stacey.

Q *What Hollywood personality has the most influence with the Carter administration?—Lillian Gross, Encino, Cal.*

A Probably Lew Wasserman, chairman of the Music Corporation of America, one of the leading fund-raisers for the Democratic Party.

Q *It's extremely difficult for me to believe that Donald Duck, the Walt Disney cartoon character, has been banned from the libraries in Helsinki, Finland. Can you find out for what reason? Surely, Donald Duck is not subversive.—Mrs. Peter Harvey, Los Angeles, Cal.*

A Helsinki authorities claim that Donald Duck's lifestyle set a bad example for young people. Matti Holopainen, chairman of Helsinki's Youth Committee, recently told the city council: "Donald Duck has been going steady with the same woman for 50 years without result, and this is hardly a model for the young." Holopainen is not expelling Donald Duck, he is just not renewing library subscriptions to Donald Duck Comics.

Q *Now that Ali MacGraw has gotten rid of husband Steve McQueen, who's her next husband-to-be?—Eve Victor, Indianapolis, Ind.*

A Actress Ali MacGraw, 38, has been dating Rick Danko, 30, a rock musician who played with The Band—once Bob Dylan's outfit—and now has a band of his own. MacGraw and Danko have been seen together on the Malibu sands, which shift almost as quickly as Hollywood love affairs. Ali has also dated Warren Beatty, Hollywood's most insatiable lover.

Q *Is it a fact that Johnny Carson is the highest-paid performer on TV and also TV's most cold, ruthless and conceited star?—F.T., Des Moines, Iowa.*

A That is opinion, not fact. Carson reportedly earns upwards of $3 million annually. At 52, he is a performer of towering ego, but people who think they know him well suggest that Carson suffers more from intellectual insecurity than coldness and conceit. Professionally, Carson is a calculating, talented, demanding performer—or he would never have lasted as long as he has on a medium as ruthlessly competitive as talk-show TV.

Q *Who is the most powerful man in Italy, the Pope?—N. Livetti, Chicago, Ill.*

A At this time it's probably a toss-up between Enrico Berlinguer, Communist Party leader, and Gianni Agnelli, head of the Fiat auto empire. The Pope is the most respected religious figure in Italy.

Q *Is Henry Kissinger money-mad, or is his wife extravagant? I note he has now joined the investment and banking firm of Goldman Sachs & Co. My question is: as what?—V.R., Miami Beach, Fla.*

Henry Kissinger

A As a part-time consultant advising Goldman Sachs & Co. on international affairs. Kissinger is not money-mad, and his wife Nancy is not extravagant. It's just that Dr. Kissinger believes in taking advantage of his fame, which finds him working for Georgetown's Center for Strategic and International Studies, NBC, Chase Manhattan Bank, Goldman Sachs & Co., and Little, Brown & Co.

Jackie Onassis and John Sargent

Q *Why does Jacqueline Kennedy Onassis work for a publishing company like Doubleday when she is worth more than $20 million?—T.T., Philadelphia, Pa.*

A At age 48, Jackie needs to perform meaningful work. As an editor at Doubleday she also has something in common with John Turner Sargent, her sometimes escort who once was married to Nellie Doubleday, heiress to the publishing fortune.

Q *John J. Flynt, Jr., has announced that he's retiring from Congress. He is chairman of the House Ethics Committee that is handling the investigation of influence-buying by the South Koreans. Is there very much ethical about Flynt?—Ed L., Griffin, Ga.*

A Representative Flynt of the Sixth Congressional District of Georgia has been in Congress since 1954, the senior member of the Georgia delegation. At 63, he is known as a "good ole Southern boy."

Regarding ethics, the Ford Motor Company once paid him $12,500 to park 3,000 cars on his farm. Flynt says he would've taken $1 for the rental, but the Ford people insisted. In Griffin, Georgia, Flynt is known for his attempt to avoid a $4,000 tax assessment on a paved road running to his property.

Q *Is it true that in Gallup polls of the women most admired by the American public, the nation's First Lady always wins?—Kate Daniels, Raleigh, N.C.*

A Generally, but not always. In 1951 Sister Kenny was named the most admired. In 1968 Ethel Kennedy was voted No. 1. And in 1971, '73 and '74 Golda Meir placed first. The former Israeli prime minister has made the top 10 every year since 1969.

Olivia Newton-John and John Travolta

Q *Is there anything between Olivia Newton-John and John Travolta, who starred together in* Grease? *Who are the men in her life?—Wendy Wood, Roanoke, Va.*

A Olivia Newton-John, 29, claims none of the gossip concerning her and Travolta is true. She insists there have been only two serious men in her love life: Bruce Welch of the rock group The Shadows, her lover for five years; and Lee Kramer, her manager, with whom she goes on and off.

Q *Does French President Giscard d'Estaing permit the French Foreign Legion to travel with its own brothel? Does he allow French troops fighting in Chad and Mauretania to bring their own prostitutes along?—F.S., Charlottesville, Va.*

A Giscard d'Estaing permits no such thing. In the 19th century the French Foreign Legion was traditionally accompanied by a "bordel militaire de campagne" (military field brothel), but these are no longer allowed. As a matter of fact, 17 men and women recently went on trial in Marseilles for allegedly running a brothel under the guise of a cultural center for the 700 legionnaires in Corsica. Not on trial were the brothel's five prostitutes, each of whom reportedly averaged 60 clients a day and had been shipped to Corsica by their pimps as punishment for not having earned enough on the streets of Paris. Prostitution is tolerated in France, but brothels are not. Giscard d'Estaing is not about to legalize either of the two.

Q *Does Sen. Ted Kennedy (D., Mass.) plan to dump his wife, Joan, and marry Suzy Chaffee, the former Olympic ski champion?—G.B., Pittsfield, Mass.*

A Several months ago Miss Chaffee and Kennedy were skiing together in Aspen, Colorado. But that doesn't necessarily mean the senator is going to "dump" his wife. Over a period of years Kennedy has been seen with many women, Chaffee with many men.

Q *Steve McQueen, the Hollywood superstar, was seen in Japan in person this year. He was supposed to be on some supersecret mission for the Central Intelligence Agency. Can you reveal it?—Amy Henderson, Charlotte, N.C.*

A McQueen was in Tokyo as the plaintiff in a $1 million damage suit. He sued four Japanese companies for using photographs in 1973 from one of his movies, *Le Mans*, without his permission. The four companies were Dentsu, Japan's largest advertising agency; Matsushita Electric Industrial, a major appliance maker; Yakult, a beverage company; and Towa, a film distributor. McQueen claimed that Matsushita and Yakult used photos of him in a car racer's uniform to advertise their products on TV and in print, that Towa and Dentsu planned the ad campaigns. McQueen's presence in Tokyo was neither secret nor connected with the CIA.

Q *Please tell me how President Carter promotes world peace by advocating the sale of U.S. warplanes to Saudi Arabia, Egypt and Israel. Doesn't this violate his solemn campaign pledge?—Catherine Smith, Raleigh, N.C.*

Jimmy Carter

A It does, but campaign pledges are easier to make than to execute. Carter had to express U.S. friendship and gratitude to Saudi Arabia for holding the price on OPEC oil. He had to prove to Egypt that our foreign policy in the Mideast is evenhanded. And he had to assure the Israelis that the U.S. was not abandoning them. Keeping three foreign policy balls in the air simultaneously is a difficult juggle.

Q *On March 6, Larry Flynt, the owner of* Hustler *magazine, was gunned down in Lawrenceville, Georgia. Have the police authorities come up with any suspects?— Linda Brown, Florence, S.C.*

A As of this writing, none. Chief John Crunkleton of the Gwinnett County Police says his men have questioned more than 400 people, "but at this point we don't even have a motive." Flynt is offering a $100,000 reward for any valid information leading to the arrest of the gun person.

Q *How much older is singer Diahann Carroll than her last husband, and whatever happened to him?— Jonnie Burke, Chicago, Ill.*

Diahann Carroll

A Diahann Carroll gave her age as 40 and Robert DeLeon gave his as 24 when they were married in 1975. The marriage ended in tragedy when journalist DeLeon died in an auto accident in 1977.

Q *One of Richard Nixon's most avid defenders and money-raisers was a Massachusetts Rabbi, Baruch Korff. Whatever became of him?—P.R., Springfield, Mass.*

A Rabbi Korff's headquarters are in Washington, D.C., where he founded the U.S. Citizen's Congress Education Foundation. Some weeks ago in Cairo, Egypt, Rabbi Korff revealed that his organization was prepared to finance "Sadat peace fellowships" for young people from the Mideast.

Q *Henry Ford II recently told some of us Ford stockholders that he has a "small town house" in London and that when he comes to London on business he resides in his town house and charges the Ford company a standard daily hotel rate. Who owns the town house? Where is it located? And am I entitled to the same privilege when Henry is not occupying the town house?—C.H., Philadelphia, Pa.*

A The town house is located in the vicinity of Grosvenor Square. It is Mr. Ford's personal property. Stockholders have no rental or visiting privileges.

Q *Has Sam Houston Johnson, brother of late President Lyndon Johnson, fallen in love with Liz Carpenter, former press secretary to Lady Bird Johnson? And doesn't he plan to marry her? That is the rumor we hear in these parts. Any truth to it?—Muriel Evans, Aspen, Col.*

A Sam Johnson, for years in love with "the bottle," claims he is "a born-again Christian in love with religion who has forsaken drink." Johnson is a friend of Liz Carpenter, widow of journalist Les Carpenter. He admires her forcefulness and "light spirit" but has no intention at this time of marrying her or anyone else.

Herbert Hoover

Franklin D. Roosevelt

Q *Herbert Hoover and his wife, Lou Henry, were happily married. Has there been any other happily married couple occupying the White House since the Hoovers? Doesn't the presidency louse up marriages? Your comment, please.—Alice Louise M., Muskogee, Okla.*

A Franklin D. Roosevelt, who followed Hoover into the White House, had an unhappy marriage, largely because of his prior love affair with Lucy Mercer, his wife Eleanor's secretary. Harry Truman, who succeeded Roosevelt, enjoyed his marriage to Bess. They were a "square" couple who loved each other until his death. The Eisenhowers' marriage was scarred by talk of Ike's friendship with his wartime secretary-driver, the late Kay Summersby. Presidents John F. Kennedy and Lyndon Johnson each had an appetite for extramarital activities. Richard Nixon, because of his personality and lust for power, seemed to be a difficult man to live with. Perhaps his daughter Julie will tell some of the truth about the Nixons' marriage in her forthcoming biography of her mother Pat. Obviously the Gerald Ford marriage had its trying times, or why would Betty Ford have turned to alcohol? The Carters appear to have a loving, successful marriage.

Elvis Presley

Q *I would like to know if the late Elvis Presley was ever an informant for the FBI. My friends say that, according to the newspapers, he was. If he was, why was he?—Anne Howard, Florence, S.C.*

A Rock idol Elvis Presley, according to an internal FBI memo, once offered to spy for the FBI and even provided his own undercover name, Col. Joe Burrows of Memphis, Tennessee, but the bureau politely turned him down. Elvis was an insecure young man, badge-and-gun-happy, who longed to be regarded as a pillar of the Establishment, though the image he generated to his fans was quite the opposite.

Q *Has Peter O'Toole's wife, Sian, taken up with a man of 27, almost 20 years younger than she is? And has Peter O'Toole taken up with a 16-year-old girl in retaliation?—T.R., Worcester, Mass.*

A O'Toole's 20-year marriage to actress Sian Phillips, 45, is being dissolved. Sian has taken as a new companion actor Robin Sachs, 27. Peter O'Toole has taken as a new companion former Mexican waitress Malinche Verdugo, 23, whom he brought to Bristol, England, where he's enrolled her in a drama school.

Q *How many times did Gov. Jerry Brown of California fail the California bar exam?—E.S., Fresno, Cal.*

A He passed it the second time.

Q *What happened to the romance between James Coburn and Jean Simmons? I thought they were getting married.—Eleanor Avery, Hendersonville, N.C.*

A Each is already married, but actor Coburn, 50, hopes to marry English singer Lynsey De Paul, 28, when his divorce comes through. Lynsey, 4-feet-11, is a former girlfriend of Beatle Ringo Starr. The romance between James Coburn and actress Jean Simmons, 49, was short-lived.

Q *How old is Rudolf Nureyev, the great Russian dancer who defected? And how old is his mother, whom the Soviets won't release? And what reason do they give?—Barbara Little, Sandusky, Ohio.*

A Nureyev is 40. His mother, Farida, is 75. The Soviets give no reason for their refusal to grant Mrs. Nureyev an exit visa. They are probably punishing Nureyev for his defection in 1961 and holding him up as an example to other potential defectors.

Q *Ursula Andress was one of the sexiest actresses in screen history. Who were the men in her life, and why would none of them marry her? What has happened to Ursula, and how old is she?—T.L., Kinston, N.C.*

A Ursula Andress, 42, was a great and good friend of James Dean, John Derek (to whom she was married for 11 years), Jean-Paul Belmondo, Fabio Testi, Ryan O'Neal and others. She is a resident of Switzerland, generally stars in low-budget European films.

Ursula Andress

Q *I have heard it said frequently that "Big John Connally has gotten himself in bed with the Arabs." What exactly does that mean?—F.D., Houston, Tex.*

A Big John Connally, 61—Democrat-turned-Republican, former governor of Texas, former treasury secretary in the Nixon cabinet—is a partner with Saudi multimillionaires Ghaith Pharaon and Khaled Bin Mahfouz in ownership of the Main Bank of Houston. Connally, a lawyer, was instrumental along with banker Fred Erck in putting that deal together, Connally owning 15 percent of the stock.

WALTER SCOTT'S
PERSONALITY PARADE®
September 10, 1978

Priscilla Presley

Q *Any truth to the story that John Travolta and Elvis' widow, Priscilla Presley, are secretly living it up in Malibu and that if he marries anyone it will be Priscilla?—Diane Kane, Bakersfield, Cal.*

A John Travolta, 24, and Priscilla Presley, 33, reportedly met on the set of *Welcome Back, Kotter*, the TV show in which Travolta stars. She was visiting with her 10-year-old daughter, Lisa Marie, at the time. Priscilla has subsequently seen Travolta, but each is playing the field, and to date no serious romance has developed. Priscilla has been dating Beverly Hills hairdresser Elie Ezerzer and Hollywood model Mike Edwards.

Q *I have come across the name Mary Bancroft in connection with Henry R. Luce, founder of the* Time *magazine publishing empire; Allen Dulles, director of the CIA; and Carl Jung, the great Swiss psychiatrist. Who is or was Mary Bancroft? Certainly she must have been one of the world's most fascinating women to have attracted three such famous men.—G.D., Saratoga Springs, N.Y.*

A Mary Bancroft *is* one of the world's most fascinating women. She was born in Cambridge, Massachusetts, in 1903, daughter of Hugh Bancroft, later publisher of *The Wall Street Journal*. She was educated at Smith College but left to marry journalist Sherwin Badger, whom she divorced. She subsequently married a Swiss banker, moved to Switzerland in the 1930's and became a friend of Carl Jung,

the analytical psychologist who was once a close disciple of Sigmund Freud. When World War II broke out, Allen Dulles became our OSS (Office of Strategic Services) spy chief in Bern, Switzerland, and Mary Bancroft became his secretary and confidante. She was also a confidante of Henry R. Luce and Britt Haden, the Yale graduates who founded *Time* magazine.

A beautiful, sexy, forthright, intelligent and outspoken woman, Mary Bancroft was attracted to strong and talented men, and vice versa. Today, at 75, she is the author of two novels, *Upside Down in the Magnolia Tree* and *The Insufferables*. She lives in New York City, had two children and six grandsons, among them John Taft, reporter for the Lowell (Mass.) *Sun*. Her daughter Mary Jane is married to Horace Taft, dean of Yale and son of the late Sen. Robert Taft. Her autobiography, if Mary Bancroft would write it, would reveal much about many of the most noted men of her time.

J. Edgar Hoover

Q *Can you tell me how many women special agents there are in the FBI and whether the late J. Edgar Hoover was a homosexual who disliked women?—E.L, Washington, D.C.*

A At this writing, there are 96 female special agents in the FBI. J. Edgar Hoover never married, rarely escorted women to social functions. There is no evidence, however, that he was a homosexual. He seemed to prefer the company of his assistant, Clyde Tolson, and it is probable he was a sexual neuter.

Q *Several months ago Arkady N. Shevchenko, the highest-ranking Soviet employee of the United Nations, defected to the United States. Where is he? And what has he told the CIA about Soviet spy activities in this country?—F.E., Lexington, Ky.*

A Yours are exactly the questions the KGB, the Soviet security apparatus, would like answered. Shevchenko is undoubtedly one of the most well-informed defectors to have fallen into the welcome arms of the U.S. intelligence agencies in years. He knows how the Soviets use the United Nations Secretariat as an espionage outpost, and he can identify those Soviet diplomats who are primarily spies. His defection has worried the KGB, which is probably why the Soviets will apprehend "fake" American spies in Russia in order to exchange them for Soviet spies fingered by Shevchenko and apprehended in the U.S.

Q *Which superstars in Hollywood are paid $3 million a picture?—E. Kraus, Charlotte, N.C.*

A Robert Redford, Marlon Brando, Paul Newman and Steve McQueen are said to be worth that much under certain circumstances.

Q *Who is Terry O'Neill? I understand that Raquel Welch, Faye Dunaway. . . every actress who works with Terry wants to marry him. Is he an actor, a writer, a Hollywood director, or what?—Lucy Fox, Bessemer, Ala.*

A Terry O'Neill, 38, is a British still photographer who has worked in films starring Raquel Welch, Faye Dunaway and others. He is a charming man, an excellent photographer particularly adept in photographing female stars with whom he has been romantically linked. O'Neill, however, is married to English actress Vera Day, by whom he has a 10-year-old daughter.

Q *How come the late dictator Juan Peron and his late wife Evita are non-persons in Argentina today?—R.T., Miami, Fla.*

A Because both were venal, conniving, greedy and vengeful. When she died of cancer in 1952, Evita Peron—an ex-prostitute who was born illegitimate—was Argentina's First Lady and had amassed a fortune in jewels and cash worth $10 million, all cached in Switzerland. After her death, Juan Peron consoled himself by taking 13-year-old Nelly Rivas as his mistress. Deposed in 1955, he fled to Spain five years later, subsequently returned to Buenos Aires and the presidency. He died in 1974 and was succeeded in office by his new wife, Isabel, who was arrested in 1976 for financial shenanigans.

WALTER SCOTT'S

PERSONALITY PARADE®

October 22, 1978

Q *Can you tell the truth about Robert Shaw, star of* Jaws *and* The Deep? *Was he an alcoholic who drank himself to death, or did he die a natural death? How many wives and children did he leave?—Martha Nelson, Stroudsburg, Pa.*

A Robert Shaw died at 51 of a massive heart attack on August 28, 1978, two miles from his home in Tourmakeady, County Mayo, Ireland. Shaw was an alcoholic who said he was driven to drink by the pressure of supporting his children and achieving success. He was afraid that he might follow in the footsteps of Errol Flynn ("who died of too much booze at 51, so I don't drink while I'm working"). Shaw was married three times. His first marriage, to Jennifer Bourke, ended in divorce. His second wife, actress Mary Ure, died of a drug overdose in April 1975. His third wife and widow is the former Virginia Jansen, who was his secretary. They married in Bermuda two years ago. In December 1976 she gave birth to a son, Thomas, Shaw's 10th child.

Q *There is a rumor that before she became a sex symbol, Mae West was a man who had a sex-change operation. I also understand she is really 90. What is true?—Leona Rosenzweig, Syracuse, N.Y.*

Mae West

A Mae West was born female on August 17, 1892, in Brooklyn, New York. She is eldest of three children of "Battling Jack" West, a prizefighter, and his wife Matilda, a German-born corset model.

Q *Louise Fletcher, who won an Academy Award for* One Flew Over the Cuckoo's Nest—*I understand she is 44 and terribly in love with actor James Mason's son, who is only 24. What sort of chance do they have for a lasting relationship?—H.F., Bakersfield, Cal.*

A Louise Fletcher and Morgan Mason share a home in Malibu with her two sons from a previous marriage, John, 17, and Andrew, 15. Despite his youth, Morgan Mason is a mature young man, and no one can foretell how long his liaison with Louise Fletcher will last. At this point, the two have been going together for almost two years, are very much in love and virtually inseparable.

Morgan Mason and Louise Fletcher

Q *When will Attorney General Griffin Bell resign, and who will take his place in the Justice Department?—R. Cohen, Washington, D.C.*

A Bell could leave the Justice Department as early as January 1979. Joe Califano, secretary of HEW, is a likely successor to Bell.

Q *Did Gen. Douglas MacArthur steal Louise Cromwell Brooks away from Gen. John J. Pershing and make her his first wife? I would also like to know if MacArthur's mistress, "Isabel," is still living.—Victor Lopez, Los Angeles, Cal.*

A Louise Cromwell Brooks—stepdaughter of Philadelphia banker Edward T. Stotesbury and sister of James Cromwell, husband of Doris Duke—was General Pershing's girlfriend and official hostess following World War I. She made a play for MacArthur, and he succumbed, marrying her on February 14, 1922. Seven years later, the first Mrs. Douglas MacArthur was granted a divorce in Reno. She was worth many millions at the time, but the phony grounds for divorce were the general's "failure to provide support."

While MacArthur was in the Philippines—where Pershing exiled him for having married Louise Brooks—he took a beautiful mistress, Isabel Rosario Cooper, daughter of a Philippine mother and Scottish father. When MacArthur was transferred back to Washington, D.C., he established Isabel in the Hotel Chastelon. An ex-dancer in Shanghai nightclubs, Isabel found MacArthur dull and cheated on him. In 1934 he ended their liaison by paying her passage back to Manila. But she refused to go. Instead she revealed her relationships with MacArthur to columnist Drew Pearson, who was then involved in a libel suit with the general. Eventually Isabel moved to Hollywood and obtained bit parts as an actress, was later reduced to peddling men's ties around the studios.

On June 29, 1960, she took her life via an overdose of sleeping pills. Four years later, on April 5, 1964, MacArthur died at 84 of kidney and liver failure.

Q *What is the true reason Jackie Kennedy Onassis bought up Chappaquiddick Island? Is it because she favors nude bathing or because she wants no one to photograph the spot where Mary Jo Kopechne drowned in 1969 after Sen. Ted Kennedy's car plunged into the water?—P.T., Washington, D.C.*

Jackie Kennedy Onassis

A Jacqueline Onassis has not bought up Chappaquiddick. She paid approximately $1.1 million for 375 acres on Martha's Vineyard, the popular vacation island southeast of the Kennedy family compound at Hyannis Port, Massachusetts. Her land, stretching for almost a mile along the ocean, was purchased to prevent the encroachment of real estate operators and to preserve its wild, natural beauty.

Q *Is sportscaster Howard Cosell the intellectual equal of Muhammad Ali?—D.Y., Newark, N.J.*

A In conversations Cosell has been able to hold his own with Ali—no small feat.

Q *Margaux Hemingway, granddaughter of novelist Ernest Hemingway, is divorcing her first husband, Errol Wetson. For whom, that's the question? And will she marry the guy?—S.E., Boise, Idaho.*

A The new man in Margaux Hemingway's life is Bernard Foucher, a Venezuelan of French origin. At 23, Margaux is ready for marriage number two.

Q *Can one be fined in West Germany for giving a Hitler salute?—Arturo Gonzalez, San Antonio, Tex.*

A Yes. Several months ago Edgar Geiss, 48, of Beckdorf, West Germany, attending the funeral of Herbert Kappler, former SS police chief in Rome, gave the Hitler salute as a final tribute. He was fined $4000 for "using the salute of an organization hostile to the constitution of the Federal Republic of Germany."

Raquel Welch

Q *What is meant by the expression: "Raquel Welch is out of the Dean Martin school of acting"?—Frederika Lawrence, Charlottesville, Va.*

A It means that as an actress she is an excellent golf player.

Q *Who are the four most influential men on Jimmy Carter's White House staff, and are they all playboys?—J.F.R., Albany, Ga.*

A The four most influential members of the "Georgia Mafia" are Hamilton Jordan, Carter's chief of staff; Jody Powell, his press secretary; Frank Moore, his congressional liaison; and Gerald Rafshoon, his image-improver. Powell, Moore and Rafshoon are married; Hamilton Jordan, separated from his wife Nancy, is playing the field circumspectly, since too many media binoculars are focused on him. No genuine playboys among that quartet.

Q *Which one of Bing Crosby's granddaughters works in Hollywood as a topless model?—B.L., Madison, Wis.*

A Denise Crosby, 20, daughter of Bing's son Dennis, has posed semi-topless, hopes to model for *Playboy* magazine. Denise also sings.

Q *I have just finished reading* The Secret Life of Henry Ford, *in which author John Dahlinger claims to be the illegitimate son of the founder of the Ford Motor Company. Is this true?—F.H., Ann Arbor, Mich.*

A Only one person, Mrs. Evangeline Côté Dahlinger—mother of John Dahlinger, who was born April 9, 1923—knows for sure if Henry Ford fathered her son. Mrs. Dahlinger is senile, confined to a nursing home. But even when she was younger and coherent, she refused to discuss the subject with her son. "I simply don't want to talk about it," she would say.

David L. Lewis, a professor of business history at the University of Michigan who spent 19 years researching Henry Ford, writes in his book *The Public Image of Henry Ford:* "He [Ford] shunned the conventional vices, although circumstantial evidence suggests that he had a brief, intense extramarital relationship during the early 1920's."

Lewis lists Evangeline Côté Dahlinger—a pert, attractive, favored friend and employee—as one of the 10 most important persons in Henry Ford's life. Ford gifted a fortune in real estate to Mrs. Dahlinger and took a deep interest in the welfare of her son. The rumor pairing Ford and Dahlinger as father and son has been widespread in Dearborn, Michigan, for years, especially among knowledgeable old-timers.

Q *When Pope John Paul I died after less than 40 days in the Vatican, he was reading a book in bed. I would like to know which book.— N.F., Santa Fe, N. Mex.*

A The book lying by Pope John Paul's bed when he died was *The Imitation of Christ*, by Thomas á Kempis. Two famous quotations from the book are: "Man proposes, but God disposes," and "O, how quickly doth the glory of the world pass away!"

Q *Have Dustin Hoffman and his wife gotten a divorce?—Nan Reese, St. Paul, Minn.*

A Not at this writing.

Q *Is it a fact that Arthur MacArthur, only son of the late Gen. Douglas MacArthur, refused to go to West Point and lives under an assumed name in New York?—F.T.R., Jersey City, N.J.*

A It is true. Arthur MacArthur does not want to be compared to his illustrious and controversial father, does not want to answer questions about him, does not care to submit to interviews. He preferred going to Columbia University rather than seeking an appointment to West Point.

Q *Two years ago Steve McQueen starred in a motion picture based on the Henrik Ibsen play* An Enemy of the People. *Whatever happened to it?—Chris Hooper, Bartlesville, Okla.*

A It was quietly released in this country a few months ago and bombed. It was then released in Europe, where it bombed as well.

John Travolta with Olivia Newton-John in *Grease*

Q *Does John Travolta use bodyguards?—Victoria Ellen, Honolulu, Hawaii.*

A Of late he has been escorted by two bodyguards at public functions.

Q *Is it true that Fiat automobiles are used all over Europe and sold under different names?—Myron Gold, Staten Island, N.Y.*

A Fiat models built under license in the Soviet Union are called Ladas. In Poland they are called Polskis, in Yugoslavia they are Zastavias, and in Spain they are Seats.

WALTER SCOTT'S
PERSONALITY PARADE®

November 26, 1978

Sophia Loren

Brigitte Bardot

Q *Brigitte Bardot and Sophia Loren are both 44. Both are sex symbols, but which is the better actress?—Barbara Butterfield, Honolulu, Hawaii.*

A Critics agree that Loren is by far the better actress.

Q *The gossip on the Harvard campus is that Caroline Kennedy—a Radcliffe junior, daughter of Jackie Kennedy Onassis and the late President John F. Kennedy—is secretly engaged to a writer and will marry him when she is graduated next year. Can you identify the gentleman?—F.T., Cambridge, Mass.*

A Caroline Kennedy, 21 tomorrow, has been seeing a good deal of writer Tom Carney, Yale '71, son of novelist and screenwriter Otis Carney. Young Carney, 29, met Caroline this past summer at the Carney ranch in Cora, Wyoming, and their friendship has apparently ripened into a serious romance. Tom Carney's novel *Daylight Moon* is scheduled for publication early next year.

Q *I have heard that Jerry Lewis is paid $500,000 a year as national chairman of the Muscular Dystrophy Association (MDA). What is the truth?—D.R., Niles, Mich.*

A Lewis receives no salary; many of his expenses are paid by MDA's corporate sponsors. The MDA annual report is open to the public. It shows that 83 percent of its contributions go for medical research, 17 percent for fund-raising.

Q *Whatever happened to Christopher Crawford, Joan Crawford's adopted son? Does he agree with his sister Christina that Joan Crawford was "hateful, cruel, demented and pathological"?—D.B., Detroit, Mich.*

A Christopher Crawford, 35, is an electrical and construction worker who lives on Long Island, New York. "I know it's a terrible thing to say," he concedes, "but I hated J. C. (which is how he refers to Joan Crawford). She was evil and mad, and I don't think she ever cared about me. All she ever cared about was her career. She adopted me and the three other kids because it was good publicity, good for her image." When Christopher was five, Christina dressed him in her clothes, made him up with lipstick and rouge—a harmless, childish prank. "When J. C. saw me," he recalls, "she went wild and whipped me with a three-inch army belt." Christopher and Christina were disinherited by their mother. Christopher is a divorced Vietnam war veteran.

Q *How many of Jimmy and Rosalynn Carter's four children live in the White House?—June James, Tulsa, Okla.*

A At this writing, three: Amy, Jeff and Chip, the latter pair with their wives. The third married Carter son, Jack, resides in Calhoun, Georgia.

Joan Collins

Q *I would like to know what has happened to actress Joan Collins. She wrote a notorious autobiography, Past Imperfect, detailing her love affairs with Harry Belafonte, Warren Beatty, Ryan O'Neal and others. But it was never published in the U.S. Why?—Lane Baker, Salt Lake City, Utah.*

A Joan Collins, 45, continues to work as an actress in England. After starring in the film *The Stud*, she worked with Sir John Gielgud in a new television film, *Neck*, one of the drama series called *Tales of the Unexpected*. Miss Collins decided not to publish her autobiography in the U.S. because she felt it might adversely affect some former lovers who are still active in their pursuits.

Q *Please list the largest private companies in the U.S., their headquarters and what businesses they are in.—Laura Michioku, San Mateo, Cal.*

A Some of the largest are Cargill of Minneapolis, Minnesota, Continental Grain of New York City and Farmers Union Grain of St. Paul, Minnesota, all grain companies. Other leading private companies are Bechtel of San Francisco, California, which specializes in construction; United Parcel Service of Greenwich, Connecticut, which delivers packages; Koch Industries, an oil and gas company headquartered in Wichita, Kansas; Publix Supermarkets of Ft. Lauderdale, Florida; Mars Inc., a candy manufacturer in McLean, Virginia; and *Reader's Digest*, a publishing conglomerate in Pleasantville, N.Y.

Q *Was Barbra Streisand ever named or known as Barbra Goldstein?—Diane Robin, Nashua, N.H.*

Barbra Streisand

A From 1963 to 1971 Barbra was married to actor Elliott Gould, who was born in Brooklyn, New York, on August 29, 1938, and named Elliott Goldstein. Barbra may have been known to intimate friends as "Mrs. Goldstein," but she never used the name publicly.

Q *What is the true story of Richard Wagner, the great German composer, and his wife Cosima? Why have her diaries been suppressed? Is it true that Wagner was the leader of anti-Jewish and anti-Catholic movements in Germany during the last century?—W.T., Butler, Pa.*

A Cosima, daughter of composer-pianist Franz Liszt, was married to Hans von Bulow, a famous conductor and musician, when she fell in love with Richard Wagner. She gave birth to two of Wagner's children in four years, then went to live with him when she was pregnant with a third. Cosima deserted von Bulow in 1868 and married Wagner in 1870. Wagner, a composer of strong emotions, said frequently that "the three J's"—Jews, Jesuits and journalists—constituted the curse of Germany. Wagner died in 1883 at age 70, his wife 47 years later at 92. Her diaries were translated by Geoffrey Skelton and published last month in England by Collins (London) under the title *Cosima Wagner's Diaries*.

Ruth Carter Stapleton

Q *When I was in Tokyo, I caught the president's sister Ruth Carter Stapleton on Japanese TV wearing a kimono. What was she doing in Japan, and who paid for her trip, the U.S. government?—R.F., Fayetteville, N.C.*

A Ruth Carter Stapleton was in Tokyo in October 1978, her trip paid for by several Japanese religious organizations. She was invited to preach on "inner healing." During her stay in Japan, Mrs. Stapleton not only appeared on TV in a kimono, she wore the same kimono when she paid a courtesy call on then Prime Minister Takeo Fukuda. "He was really pleased," she recalls, "when he saw me hobbling toward him inch by inch in my Japanese outfit." Mrs. Stapleton is an irrepressible evangelist.

Q *How large is the principality of Monaco, and who will inherit it when Prince Rainier dies?—R.T.S., Philadelphia, Pa.*

A Monaco consists of about 470 acres. The principality will go to Rainier's son, Albert Grimaldi, when the prince passes on. Grimaldi, 20, is a sophomore at Amherst College in Massachusetts.

Q *I am sure you have heard in medicine of "the placebo effect." Can you tell us anything about Dr. Placebo, who first observed the effect?—Arlene Riggs, Boulder, Col.*

A There was and is no "Dr. Placebo." The word "placebo" is Latin for "I shall please." In medicine placebo is the term for an inactive substance that can have a beneficial effect upon the patient taking it, who believes it is a real drug. "The placebo effect" is an example of mind over matter. Physicians have recognized it since the early 1800's.

Q *Those poor 900 disciples of Rev. Jimmy Jones who followed him in mass suicide—how many were black, how many were white, and how many knew that Jones was a sex pervert, a thief, a charlatan and a fraud?—G.F., Charlotte, N.C.*

A Membership in Jones's Peoples Temple was approximately 70 percent black, 30 percent white. For the most part these trusting disciples were gullible, undereducated, alienated, unsophisticated people who were not prudent enough to have checked on Jones's checkered background. In truth he was little more than a charismatic, psychotic confidence man. Obviously his disciples did not know that, or they would not have sold their worldly goods and followed him to Guyana and death.

Q *Yul Brynner, who keeps strutting the stages of the world in* The King and I, *claims to be 58. Does anyone know his real age?—David Elkins, Pittsburgh, Pa.*

Yul Brynner

A Brynner knows his real age, which he claims is 58. Other sources say that Soviet birth registry records in Vladivostok have him born in 1910, which would make him 68. But these have been unverified. Most probably Brynner, sensitive about his age, is in his middle or late 60's.

Q *Are there any old Bolsheviks alive in the Soviet Union who served in Joseph Stalin's politburo?—Monroe Leventhal, Princeton, N.J.*

A At this writing, three: Vyacheslav Molotov, 88; Lazar Kaganovich, 85; Georgi Malenkov, 72.

Q *I would like to know Ethel Merman's real name, how many husbands she has had, and whether she flattened her last husband, actor Ernest Borgnine, with a right hook.—D.P., Jamaica, N.Y.*

A Ethel Merman's real name is Ethel Zimmerman. To date, she has been married four times. Her first husband was Bill Smith, a Hollywood press agent; her second was Bill Levitt, a Hearst newspaperman; her third was Bob Six, chief of Continental Airlines; her fourth was Ernest Borgnine, an actor with whom she spent a tumultuous few weeks in 1964, the stormy details of which she declines to detail. Those weeks were traumatic, to say the least, and she escaped from the marriage as fast as possible.

Jane Fonda

Q *Who is the guy singer Cher goes out with who wears a mask?—Teeney Andrews, Chicago, Ill.*

A He is Gene Simmons, who appears with the rock group "Kiss."

Q *Jane Fonda's name has been coupled with Ho Chi Minh, Roger Vadim, Timmy Everett, Andreas Voutsinas, Fred Gardner and Tom Hayden. Was she married to any of them?—V.E., Gastonia, N.C.*

A Jane Fonda has been married twice. Her first husband was French film director Roger Vadim. Her second and current husband is writer-politician Tom Hayden.

PERSONALITY PARADE®

February 4, 1979

Prince Charles

Q *Would you please cite the law in the Constitution of Great Britain that prohibits Prince Charles or any other British monarch or future monarch from marrying a Roman Catholic?—F.T., Oshkosh, Wis.*

A There is no written Constitution of Great Britain as there is a written Constitution of the U.S. However, the English Bill of Rights of 1689 and the Act of Settlement of 1701 deny the English Crown to "all and every person and persons that is, are or shall be reconciled to or shall hold communion with the see or church of Rome or shall profess the popish religion or shall marry a papist."

Prince Charles has been linked to Princess Marie-Astrid of Luxembourg, a Roman Catholic, and if he really wants to marry her, the British Parliament can change the 1701 act. It is, after all, not eternal.

Q *I see Orson Welles on TV talk shows all the time, but I never see or hear anything of the Italian countess he married centuries ago or of their daughter Beatrice. Is Welles divorced? Does his family live in Rome?—Mary Baker Welles, Alexandra, La.*

A Orson Welles and the Countess Paola di Girfalco have been married 24 years, are not divorced, live with daughter Beatrice, 23, in Las Vegas. For a time the countess, her daughter and mother resided in Arizona while Welles worked in Hollywood.

Q *What is the connection between a woman named Olga Carlisle and writer Alexander Solzhenitsyn? Is it sexual or literary? I understand they now hate each other, which leads me to believe they once loved each other.—J.K., Cambridge, Mass.*

A The relationship is literary. Olga Carlisle, born in Paris, is the grand-daughter of famed Russian writer Leonid Andreyev. She is also a writer-editor-translator and the wife of writer Henry Carlisle. She met Solzhenitsyn in Moscow in 1967, and it was to her that he entrusted the enormously difficult task of getting his book *The First Circle* published in the West. Solzhenitsyn has allegedly accused her of causing his expulsion from the Soviet Union. Olga Carlisle has written a fascinating book of their relationship, *Solzhenitsyn and the Secret Circle*, published by Holt, Rinehart and Winston. Solzhenitsyn does not come off too well in the book.

John F. Kennedy

Joe Kennedy

Q *Is it true that the only woman John F. Kennedy really wanted to marry was screen star Gene Tierney and that his father, Joe Kennedy, who controlled the family purse strings, ordered him not to because Tierney was politically, socially and religiously unacceptable?—E. Williamson, Houston, Tex.*

A That is not true. Following World War II, in which he gallantly commanded a PT boat in the Pacific, John F. Kennedy was a dashing, wealthy young hero who could have married almost any woman of his choice. The truth is that he engaged in a tempestuous love affair with actress Gene Tierney for a year or so but chose not to marry her.

Tierney may think it was because she'd been married to designer Oleg Cassini, father of her retarded daughter, and that Kennedy as a Roman Catholic could never marry a divorcée. She may think that Old Man Kennedy admonished his son to end the affair. She may have even been told these things. But as a bachelor congressman from Massachusetts 1946-53, John F. Kennedy enjoyed playing the field, and Gene Tierney was only one—albeit a memorable one—of the many flowers he plucked during these years.

No woman—particularly a sensitive, talented beauty like Gene Tierney—wants to believe she was sacrificed to whim. Better for her ego that she lost John F. Kennedy to his lofty political ambition. But if Kennedy had deeply wanted to marry Gene Tierney, he would have done so.

Q *Does Amy Carter go to private or public school in Washington, D.C.?—B.B., Plains, Ga.*

A Amy Carter, 11, is a sixth-grader at Hardy Middle School in Washington, D.C., a public school.

Q *Golda Meir, last of the Israeli pioneers, recently died at 80. Why was the cause of her death kept secret? What was it?—Bertha Cohen, Baltimore, Md.*

A Golda Meir (1898-1978) suffered from leukemia, a form of blood cancer, for her last 15 years. She preferred to keep limited the identity of her illness.

Q *What are the real names of opera singer Beverly Sills, actor Tony Randall and comic Danny Thomas? Are they not all members of the Leon Schwartz family of Dorchester, Massachusetts?—T.S., Lowell, Mass.*

A Beverly Sills (Belle Silverman), Tony Randall (Leonard Rosenberg) and Danny Thomas (Amos Jacobs) are not members of the same family.

Q *An astrologer told me that no U.S. president was ever born in June or was an only child. Is this correct?—Millie McKee, Hickory, N.C.*

A To date, it is true.

Jimmy and Rosalynn Carter

Q *I've been told that the Carters of Plains are a feud-ridden family—that President Carter, for example, has not set foot inside the house of his oldest sister, Gloria Carter Spann, for years; that Carter's brother-in-law Walter Spann has never set foot inside the White House; that Billy Carter hates his brother Jimmy; that the best of the lot is Gloria, who, instead of acting as self-appointed ambassador to the world like Ruth Carter Stapleton, is content to stay at home in Plains as the wife of a dirt farmer, taking care of his house and doing his books. Your comment, please.—J.F., Americus, Ga.*

A The Carter family consists of colorful, extroverted characters. There is not a shy, retiring violet in the lot. It is true that feuds punctuate their interpersonal relationships. Miz Lillian, the president's mother, is an outspoken woman who frequently wears brass knuckles on her tongue. It is true that, to date, Walter Spann has not set foot in the White House. Equally true is the love-hate relationship that exists between brother Billy and the president. Undoubtedly, too, a rivalry of sorts must exist between Ruth Carter Stapleton, the globe-trotting evangelist, and Gloria Carter Spann, wife of a Plains farmer who raises soybeans and wheat. Some day when President Carter writes his memoirs, he may delineate his family relationships, feuds and all.

Q *How many times has Rex Harrison been married? How old is he? Has he ever married an American woman? Did Hollywood star Carole Landis take her life in 1948 because Harrison refused to marry her?—A.K., Chicago Heights, Ill.*

A Rex Harrison, at least 70, has been married six times. Mercia Tinker,

his wife since last December 17, comes from Singapore. Her five predecessors—none American—were Marjorie Colette Thomas, Lilli Palmer, Kay Kendall, Rachel Roberts and Elizabeth Harris. Actress Carole Landis was in love with Rex Harrison, left a suicide note, but its contents were never fully revealed.

Q *Is cartoonist Garry Trudeau abandoning his career to become a designer of postage stamps? Is it also true that he is secretly married to NBC telecaster Jane Pauley?—M.L., New Haven, Conn.*

A Garry Trudeau, Pulitzer Prize-winning creator of the "Doonesbury" cartoon strip, is not married as of this writing to Jane Pauley, nor is he abandoning his career as a cartoonist. He has, however, designed a new set of stamps for the United Nations following in the footsteps of such noted artists as Norman Rockwell, Marc Chagall and Alexander Calder.

Q *Why does William Safire, columnist for The New York Times and other papers, hate Henry Kissinger with such endless passion?—G.R.R., Sea Girt, N.J.*

Henry Kissinger

A Safire disagrees with Kissinger on U.S. foreign policy in the Middle East and detente. When Safire worked with Kissinger in the Nixon administration, Kissinger doubted his loyalty and had Safire wiretapped, then lied about it. Those are three reasons why Safire is no Kissinger admirer. He has others.

Q *Does Farrah Fawcett-Majors have bodyguards to protect her from rape and robbery? What is she doing now?—Laura Lee Edwards, Durham, N.C.*

A Farrah Fawcett-Majors has security protection during production and promotion chores. At this writing she is in England co-starring with Kirk Douglas on a new space movie, *Saturn Three*.

Q *Does Prince Charles have any sort of sex life at age 30, or do the British people expect him to maintain his virginity until he marries?—M.B., Portsmouth, Va.*

A Much is made of the hectic social life of Prince Charles in the British press. He is constantly being photographed with any number of girls, but virtually nothing is written of his sex life. Robert Lacey, author of *Majesty*, once wrote a few lines about the Prince's "normal, healthy sex life." When he submitted the book to Buckingham Palace, however, exclamation marks were placed after the passage. Lacey thought discretion the better part of valor and deleted the few sentences. What they said is that Charles enjoys a normal sex life with young ladies, which is what one would expect in a healthy young man of his years. Most Britons do not entertain false, idealistic or unrealistic hopes concerning his virginity.

Q *I saw John Travolta in a movie in Mexico City called* Vaselina. *When is it coming to this country? Is he also starring in* Saturday Night Fever II?— *Alma Corovado, San Antonio, Tex.*

A *Vaselina* is the Mexican title for Travolta's movie *Grease*. Travolta will undoubtedly star in *Saturday Night Fever II*.

Richard Nixon

Q *Which one of the Watergate conspirators has made the most money to date out of the Watergate scandal?—Harold Marks, Marlboro, Mass.*

A Richard Nixon, who has already received more than $3 million from book royalties, the David Frost interviews, etc.

WALTER SCOTT'S
PERSONALITY PARADE®

May 6, 1979

Q *The rumor is afloat in New York City circles that William Paley, head of CBS, has targeted Jackie Kennedy Onassis for his third wife. Is that true? Is it also true that Paley earns $6 million a year?—B.M., Newark, N.J.*

A William Paley, at 77, is not about to take Jackie Onassis, 50 in July, as his third wife. Paley's earned income is not $6 million a year, though his gross annual income does approximate that figure. In 1978, for example, he received from CBS (Columbia Broadcasting System) a total compensation of $1,009,064 in the form of salary, bonus, stock options and incentive rewards. Since Paley owns 7.2 percent of CBS stock (2,000,084 shares), he also received $4,900,206 in dividends, for a total of $5,909,270. This surely is enough to take care of Jackie Onassis in the style of living to which she or any other woman on earth has become accustomed.

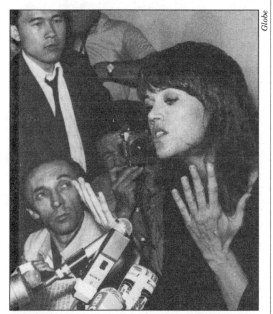
Jane Fonda

Q *I understand that ex-FBI agent Wesley Swearingen claims the FBI bugged Jane Fonda's bed while she was visiting the North Vietnamese in Hanoi during the Vietnam war. Did the FBI bug her bed?—M.L., Washington, D.C.*

A The FBI's Office of Professional Responsibility, charged with investigating the bureau's transgressions, has no record of Swearingen making that complaint. Swearingen says, "I never bugged Jane Fonda, and I don't know anyone who has. But that's not to say she

wasn't bugged during the years she spoke out on the Vietnam war. The FBI kept close tabs on her."

Q *Has Julie Andrews retired from show business? We have not seen her in anything for some time except TV reruns of* Sound of Music.—*Helen Blodgett, Beaufort, S.C.*

Julie Andrews

A After several years of self-imposed retirement, Julie has finished the film 10 for her husband, writer-director Blake Edwards. She will star shortly in a remake of Damon Runyon's *Little Miss Marker*, which brought fame to Shirley Temple decades ago.

Q *Rosalind Russell, the screen and stage star, died in November 1976. She and Freddie Brisson were married 35 years. What did she die of, and has Brisson remarried?—Elsa Craig, Las Vegas, Nev.*

A Rosalind Russell died at 64 on November 28, 1976, a victim of the severest form of rheumatoid arthritis and complications from cancer. Her husband has remarried.

Q *Can you tell us why President Carter sent his college-dropout son Chip to the Mideast with Zbigniew Brzezinski to talk to the Saudis and Jordanians? Is Chip Carter a diplomat? Why should he be sent overseas at taxpayers' expense?—F.T., Frankfort, Ky.*

A Jimmy Carter sent his son to the Mideast along with Brzezinski and Deputy Secretary of State Warren Christopher as a symbolic gesture of his great concern in the cause of peace. Chip did well with the sheiks in Saudi Arabia and the children of Jordan's King Hussein.

Q *Who owns the world's most expensive private airplane?—C. Charles, Austin, Tex.*

A The private plane of the deposed Shah of Iran, a Boeing 707 named Shahin (Falcon), is said to be the most expensive. Its overall cost was $115 million, including $2 million worth of gold toilet fittings and $43 million in other creature comforts. The plane was flown back to Tehran from Morocco and now belongs to the government of Iran.

Q *Gary Player, the golf champion, has been tainted by a "slush money" scandal in his home country of South Africa. How was he involved?—Eric Cox, Pinehurst, N.C.*

A Gary Player admitted accepting government money to play host to American businessmen visiting South Africa. For years the South African government appropriated secret funds to improve the country's image throughout the world. The South African public knew nothing about it and quite naturally resents the use of their money—reportedly $72 million—for such purposes.

George Washington

Q *Who is responsible for the fairy tale about George Washington chopping down a cherry tree?—Lisel Horn, Detroit, Mich.*

A Historians attribute it to Rev. Mason Locke Weems, one of Washington's biographers, who allegedly dreamed it up in 1806, seven years after the first president's death.

Errol Flynn

Q *A book on Errol Flynn says he had a love affair in Hollywood with Tyrone Power in the late 1940's. Was that common knowledge in Hollywood?—H.R., Ontario, Cal.*

A It was not. Unlike Tyrone Power, Flynn never had a reputation in the screen colony as a bisexual. He was indiscriminately heterosexual. Flynn was divorced from Lili Damita in 1942 and Nora Eddington in 1949, married Patrice Wymore in 1950. He fathered four children: son Sean by Damita; daughters Deidre and Rory by Eddington, and daughter Arnella by Wymore. His major extracurricular activity—when not drinking or drugging himself—was participating in sex relations with females of all sizes, shapes and colors.

Q *Which U.S. senators, in your arbitrary opinion, have the best minds? Just name three or four. And which are the most widely respected by their colleagues?—D.H., Baltimore, Md.*

A Jacob Javits (R., N.Y.), Charles Mathias, Jr. (R., Md.), Gary Hart (D., Col.), Ted Kennedy (D., Mass.), John Culver (D., Iowa), and Sam Nunn (D., Ga.), as well as several others, have first-rate minds. Widely respected: Barry Goldwater (R., Ariz.), Edmund Muskie (D., Me.) and Mathias.

Q *Supposedly Margaret Trudeau was the mistress of a prominent Canadian politician before she married Prime Minister Pierre Trudeau in a secret ceremony. Who was her lover?—B.E., Bangor, Me.*

A Pierre Trudeau.

Q *Before Barbra Streisand allowed hairdresser Jon Peters to move in with her, didn't she make him sign a contract in which he agreed never to divulge in print or on air any of the details of their relationship?—D.D., Pasadena, Cal.*

A Domestics employed by Barbra Streisand must first sign a contract not to divulge in print or on air any of her activities or behavior, but Streisand does not make mandatory the signing of such a contract by her lovers.

Q *Around here it is said that Luci Johnson Nugent, the late President Lyndon Johnson's younger daughter, will have to pay her husband Patrick $5 million for a divorce and custody of their four children. Any truth to it?—V.G.C., Austin, Tex.*

A Patrick J. Nugent—who until recently was general manager of radio station KLBJ in Austin, owned by his mother-in-law, Lady Bird Johnson—will undoubtedly agree to a community property settlement worth much less than $5 million. His attorney, James R. Meyers, says: "We hope to settle the whole thing amicably, and I am sure we will."

Mick Jagger

Q *Didn't Bianca Jagger sign a prenuptial agreement with Mick Jagger of the Rolling Stones? Why now*

does she want a financial settlement of $10 million plus $10,000 a month alimony plus $4,000 a month child-support for their daughter Jade?—L.F., Albany, N.Y.

A If and when the Mick-Bianca divorce case goes to court, Bianca Jagger is expected to claim that she signed their prenuptial agreement under duress, that at the time she was four months pregnant with Jade, now seven, and desperately anxious to have her infant born in wedlock.

Q *It is safely assumed that the two greatest British statesmen of the 20th century were David Lloyd George and Winston Churchill. Were both of these men oversexed? Is that a requisite for great statesmanship?—D.E.E., Cambridge, Mass.*

Winston Churchill

A Lloyd George was surely an oversexed womanizer. Most of his biographers refer to his strong sexual appetites. This was not true of Churchill, however, who sexually was pretty much of a straight arrow. There seems to be no positive correlation between sexuality and statesmanship.

Q *It's very fashionable these days to blame Jimmy Carter for everything. But who is most responsible for the failure of U.S. policy in Iran under the departed Shah?—R. De Jesus, Los Angeles, Cal.*

A Henry Kissinger and Richard Nixon instituted the open-ended commitment to the Shah in 1972 so he could purchase an almost endless supply of sophisticated weaponry from the U.S. and be assured of our backing. The pair regarded the Shah as a so-called "regional influential," and their support of him was continued by Brzezinski and Carter. The CIA and State Department under Kissinger reported "no danger ahead signals" for the Shah. And even when former CIA Director Richard Helms was ambassador to Iran 1973-77, there were no warnings that the Shah was being opposed by commercial and religious elements in his country.

WALTER SCOTT'S
PERSONALITY PARADE®

June 24, 1979

Howard Hughes

Q *When Howard Hughes died at 70 in April 1976, we heard that he was a drug addict, that he weighed only 93 pounds at the time of death, that he died of cancer, that he was insane, that at the height of his fame he had a harem of 125 of the most beautiful actresses in Hollywood. Is any of this true?—Sara Davis, Houston, Tex.*

A An autopsy of Hughes's body indicated that he died of "chronic renal failure," kidney disease. He did weigh only 93 pounds when he died and for years had been a cocaine addict. As to his mental health, he suffered from several nervous breakdowns. His behavior, to say the least, was abnormal and obsessive. His fear of germs was psychotic. He was convinced he could buy anyone, had no friends and trusted virtually no one. Before he became a recluse, he would sign aspiring young actresses to contracts at $250 a week. He never had more than 20 girls under contract at any one time and saw them infrequently. He was eccentric to the point of being irrational.

Q *How much does Great Britain pay its prime minister? How many former prime ministers are still living?—G. Allen, Columbia, Mo.*

A Britain pays its prime minister 22,000 pounds (about $44,000) per year. Five former prime ministers—Macmillan, Home, Wilson, Heath and Callaghan—are still living, the largest number in almost two centuries.

Q *Is Karen Ann Quinlan, who fell into a coma four years ago, still living? She's the girl whose parents fought to have her life-support system turned off.—Angela Howard, Buffalo, N.Y.*

A As of this writing, Karen Ann Quinlan, 25, lies alive but motionless on a waterbed in the Morris View Nursing Home in Morris Plains, New Jersey She weighs 65 pounds, receives daily injections of antibiotics and is fed through a nasal tube. Nurses move her periodically to prevent the development of bedsores. Karen lapsed into a coma on April 14, 1975, after leaving a party. Doctors suspect the coma was caused by a combination of tranquilizers and alcohol. In 1976 the New Jersey Supreme Court granted her father permission to remove her life-supporting respirator. When this was done, her parents expected Karen to die. Instead her condition has stabilized and she clings to life in a coma.

Q *Anything going on between Raquel Welch and Burt Bacharach? They recently played here together, and the rumors were flying.—R.T., Las Vegas, Nev.*

A Composer-singer Burt Bacharach is not yet divorced from actress Angie Dickinson and still dates her from time to time. He has no love interest in Raquel Welch.

Jimmy and Rosalynn Carter

Q *Every American president has a close buddy who advises him. Who is Jimmy Carter's number one?—B.T., Syracuse, N.Y.*

A Jimmy Carter is unique in that his number one adviser—even on affairs of state—is his wife Rosalynn. Charles Kirbo, his lawyer, probably ranks number two.

Q *I heard that Elvis Presley once paid Jayne Mansfield $50,000 for one night of love. Or did she pay him? Any truth to the legend?—L.Y., Jackson, Miss.*

Elvis Presley

A No truth. In 1957 Jayne Mansfield wanted Elvis to sing one number in a film in which she was to play the lead. She called Col. Tom Parker, Elvis's agent. Parker said Elvis would sing a number for $50,000. Jayne's producer balked at the figure. Jayne thereupon flew to Memphis, tried to sweet-talk Elvis into her production for a lower amount. Jayne and Elvis spent the night, then she returned to Hollywood. Sure the fix was in, she again phoned Parker. "The price," he said, "is still $50,000." Jayne said later: "I felt somehow that I'd been had."

Q *Is it true that over the years the Gulf Oil Corporation has bought up the U.S. Congress?—T.M., Pittsburgh, Pa.*

A A sworn statement of Claude Wild, Jr., former lobbyist for Gulf, filed in Federal District Court, Washington, D.C., reveals that from 1962 through 1973, Gulf Oil contributed almost $4 million to more than 100 U.S. senators, numerous members of the House of Representatives, 18 governors, state judges and scores of local politicians. Recipients included Jimmy Carter when he was governor of Georgia, and Walter Mondale when he was U.S. senator from Minnesota. It is illegal for corporations to contribute to federal campaigns but not to some state campaigns. In many instances, the contributions were made not to legislators but to their assistants, so that the legislators in many cases never knew the original source of some contributions.

Q *Can you tell me for which motion picture the late actor Edward G. Robinson won an Academy Award? Wasn't it Little Caesar?—Richie Bergen, Luray, Va.*

A Edward G. Robinson never won an Academy Award.

Q *"Jug-Ear" Charlie, Prince of Wales and heir to the British throne—is it a fact that he cannot get married without his mother's consent?—V. Carr, Hartford, Conn.*

Prince Charles

A Prince Charles can marry anyone he chooses, providing he renounces his right to the throne. If he doesn't, he's bound by the Bill of Rights of 1689, the 1700 Act of Settlement, and the Royal Marriages Act of 1772. These acts forbid him to marry a Catholic or a divorcée, or to marry without the consent of his mother or both houses of Parliament.

Q *Who was the man really responsible for firing Andrew Young as U.S. ambassador to the UN?—L. Christian, Austin, Tex.*

A Secretary of State Cyrus Vance, to whom Young had apparently lied or "fudged the truth."

Q *How tall and how old is Vanessa Redgrave? Why did she divorce her first husband, director Tony Richardson, and who is her current love?—A.L., Charlestown, W. Va.*

A Controversial actress Vanessa Redgrave is 42, six feet tall. She divorced Richardson in 1967, charged him with adultery, named actress Jeanne Moreau as his partner. Her current fancy: actor Timothy Dalton, who played opposite her in *Agatha*.

Q *Who are the most probable female candidates for the first woman justice of the U.S. Supreme Court?—Claire Evans, Camden, Maine.*

A Judge Patricia M. Wald of Washington, D.C., Judge Amalya L. Kearse of New York City, Judge Shirley M. Hufstedler of Los Angeles, and Patricia Harris, currently secretary of health, education and welfare, are all possibilities.

Q *Who is or was Ernst Chain, supposedly a great scientist?—Max Fulton, Joliet, Ill.*

A Sir Ernst Chain (1905-79) shared the 1945 Nobel Prize for physiology and medicine with Sir Alexander Fleming and Sir Howard Florey for their work in discovering, applying and developing penicillin.

Chain, a German who settled in England, came across Fleming's original report on penicillin in 1938. By isolating penicillin, he helped develop it in synthetic form so it could be produced en masse.

Q *Isn't Jimmy Carter sure to be nominated for a Nobel Peace Prize for bringing Israel and Egypt together?—Eleanor Heath, Calais, Maine.*

A The nomination is sure, the award less sure but highly probable.

Q *When Lord Louis Mountbatten was buried on September 5, 1979, not a single Japanese dignitary was invited to his funeral in London. Why?—Catherine Mack, Boston, Mass.*

A Mountbatten felt so strongly about the maltreatment of British servicemen by Japanese officers in World War II that he developed a visceral antagonism to the Japanese and specified in his will that none be invited to his funeral. None were.

Harry Hamlin and Ursula Andress

Q *Ursula Andress—the sex bomb who loved John Derek, Jean-Paul Belmondo, Marcello Mastroianni, Fabio Testi, Ryan O'Neal and others—is said to be in love with an 18-year-old boy. Can this be true?—R. Austin, Seattle, Wash.*

A It can, but it is not. Andress, 43, has been dating a young actor from California, Harry Hamlin, 28, who met her this past summer on the set of *Clash of the Titans*.

Richard Nixon

Q *How many people went on the last Richard Nixon trip to China? Can you identify them?—O.P., Philadelphia, Pa.*

A In addition to Nixon, there were Eddie Cox, his son-in-law; Raymond Price, his literary assistant; Jack Brennan, his chief aide; Secret Service men; and friends listed on the aircraft manifest as Britt, Moore, Gleason, Korff, Torey, Hotz, Brackett, Christenson, McDowell, Howell, Endicott and Tulley.

Q *When, where and by whom in this country was the first kidney transplant performed?—Francis Murphy, Norfolk, Va.*

A A team of surgeons—Drs. Joseph Murray, John Merrill and J. Hartwell Harrison—performed the first successful human kidney transplant on December 23, 1954, at the Peter Bent Brigham Hospital in Boston. Dr. Harrison, a Harvard urologist, removed a kidney from donor Ronald Herrick, then in his twenties. Dr. Murray, a Harvard plastic surgeon, then transplanted it into Richard Herrick, the donor's identical twin, who was suffering from end-stage renal disease. Richard Herrick lived for seven years following the operation. Dr. Merrill, a Harvard internist, served as surgical team "anchorman." Also participating were radiologist Dr. James Dealy and pathologist Dr. Gustave Dammin. The operation took five and one-half hours and is regarded today, 25 years later, as a medical and surgical milestone.

WALTER SCOTT'S

PERSONALITY PARADE®

November 25, 1979

Tom Jones

Q *Tom Jones and Engelbert Humperdinck, two of England's top pop stars, live 10 minutes away from each other in Beverly Hills, California, yet they haven't spoken to each other in five years. Please name the woman in the feud.—Janey Browne, Las Vegas, Nev.*

A It's true that Jones and Humperdinck have not spoken to each other in five years, but no woman is involved. Both men refuse to discuss their estrangement. Friends say it has something to do with the fact that both at one time were managed by Gordon Mills, from whom Humperdinck broke away after a bitter court battle involving contracts.

Q *What is the true reason John Travolta backed out of making* American Gigolo *with model Lauren Hutton?—Sari Silverstein, Las Vegas, Nev.*

A Travolta claimed to be depressed by the death of his mother and the cardiac problems of his father and said he needed time to find himself. Another reason might possibly be the adverse reaction to his last film, *Moment by Moment*, in which he played a gigolo to Lily Tomlin. There seems to be little point in his playing a gigolo in two consecutive films—not good for his public image.

Q *Stavros Niarchos, the Greek shipping billionaire—what is his relationship with Lisa Halaby, the American girl who became the latest wife of King Hussein of Jordan?—Victor L., Palm Beach, Fla.*

A Niarchos, 70, has no relationship with King Hussein's wife. He does, however, have a relationship with Princess Firyal of Jordan, who has been married for the past 16 years to Mohammed Hussein, the King's brother. Niarchos and Princess Firyal have been close friends for at least two years. There is talk in Paris that the Princess will divorce Mohammed Hussein and become the sixth Mrs. Niarchos.

Q *Is Princess Ashraf, the Shah of Iran's twin sister, on the Ayatollah Khomeini's "hit list"? Is she known as "The Black Panther"? Where does she live?—F. Rowan, Spokane, Wash.*

A Princess Ashraf, 59, is detested by the Ayatollah Khomeini, who would like her brought back to Iran to stand trial. Because she is dark, domineering and dynamic, Ashraf many years ago was nicknamed "The Black Panther." She owns homes in New York City, the French Riviera and elsewhere. She is married to Mehdi Boushehri, an Iranian lawyer, and is the mother of three children. A notorious high-stakes gambler, Ashraf was almost gunned down by assassins in 1977 en route from a gambling casino to her villa at Juan-les-Pins on the Riviera. In contrast to her brother, she is said to be fearless.

Debby Boone

Q *Did Debby Boone, daughter of singer Pat Boone, marry Gabriel Ferrer, son of singer Rosemary Clooney and actor Jose Ferrer, in order to get away from her strait-laced old man?—F.T., Frankfort, Ky.*

A Presumably she married for love.

Q *Who is responsible for the policy of inviting prominent journalists and their wives to the White House for intimate dinners with President and Mrs. Carter? And what is the purpose of this cozy arrangement?—M.R., Annapolis, Md.*

A The idea is apparently the brainchild of Mrs. Carter, who hopes that such private dinners will result in an improved image for her husband. To date they have not.

Q *I have listened to President Carter on the TV and to a lot of other politicians, but I still do not know the purpose of the Soviet Union in stationing a Russian combat brigade in Cuba. What is the truth?—Charles Bush, Lockport, N.Y.*

Jimmy Carter

A The combat-capable brigade serves several purposes: (1) It provides Castro with a palace guard and a small army of occupation to prevent a takeover by counter-revolutionary Cubans; (2) a Soviet brigade in Cuba assures an immediate Soviet response in the event that the U.S. invades the island; and (3) the brigade trains Cubans in the use of sophisticated Soviet weaponry, while the Cubans train the Soviets in the techniques of jungle warfare. No doubt the presence of Soviet troops in Cuba for the past 17 years has been and is multi-purposed.

Q *Who is Sylvan Goldman? They say he has done more to help the American woman than any man alive.—Lorry Milburn, Canton, Ohio.*

A Possibly your reference is to Sylvan Goldman, 80, inventor of the supermarket shopping cart. Goldman is from Oklahoma City, owned two grocery store chains, the Humpty Dumpty Stores and Standard Food Markets. To help the housewife with her shopping and to increase his business, he put together the first shopping cart and introduced it in his grocery stores in 1937. Later he sold shopping carts to other store-owners at $7 each. Social historians credit Goldman with changing the lifestyle of the American shopper.

1980

1981

1982

1983

1984

1985

1986

1987

1988

1989

Ronald Reagan

Q *Have orders gone out to Ronald Reagan campaign workers to downplay his 69th birthday on February 6?—S.R., Long Beach, Cal.*

A No such orders were ever issued.

Q *Does NBC really pay Johnny Carson $5 million a year? Doesn't that make him the highest-paid entertainer on television? Is he worth it?—B. Fielding, Gloucester, Mass.*

A Carson, reputedly the highest-paid TV entertainer, is worth every dollar he can get. He is a unique talent who helps NBC-TV sell its major product—time.

Q *Mick Jagger seems to lead a life of constant sex, drugs and wild parties. Does he have a special diet that has enabled him to survive these past 15 years?— Fred Davis, New Haven, Conn.*

Mick Jagger

A No special diet, just a strong constitution. Jagger's life for the past 15 years has not been one long, wild party—although publicity might give that impression. If he is throwing his life away, as some people may think, he is taking careful aim. The truth is that Jagger is a prudent multimillionaire.

Q *The newspaper reporters who travel with Rosalynn Carter—do they really refer to her as "the deputy president"?— H.T., Hagerstown, Md.*

A Some of them do.

Q *What is the story behind Jane Fonda and her mother? Who was she in the first place?—Willa D., Wenatchee, Wash.*

A Jane's mother was Frances Seymour Brokaw, young widow of George Brokaw, who previously had been married to author Clare Boothe. Frances Seymour, of prestigious lineage, was the oldest of seven children. She was born in

Jane Fonda

Fairhaven, Massachusetts, in 1905 and took a business course at Katherine Gibbs in Boston. She then met Brokaw, an alcoholic multimillionaire of inherited wealth, and they were married in January 1931. On May 28, 1935, George Brokaw died in a Hartford, Connecticut, sanatorium, leaving his wife $750,000 in life insurance and a trust fund of $4 million.

In 1936 actor Henry Fonda, divorced from actress Margaret Sullavan, met and subsequently married Frances Seymour Brokaw. Their child, named Jane Seymour Fonda, was born in New York City on December 21 1937, and taken to Hollywood when she was a month old. Twenty-six months later, Frances Fonda gave birth to a son, Peter. The Fondas lived on a lovely estate in the Brentwood section of Los Angeles, and in the ensuing years Henry Fonda established his screen stardom. After World War II, Fonda agreed to act on Broadway in *Mr. Roberts,* and the family moved to Greenwich, Connecticut. There the marriage foundered, and Fonda fell in love with Susan Blanchard, 21, stepdaughter of lyricist Oscar Hammerstein II.

Fonda's wife, tortured and haunted by jealousy and loss of ego, suffered periodic nervous breakdowns for which she was confined to various sanatoriums. On April 14, 1950, she slashed her throat and died in her bathroom at Craig House Sanatorium in Beacon, New York. Many months later Jane Fonda, then 12, learned how her mother died when a classmate handed her a movie magazine bearing the stark account. It was not until Peter Fonda was 15 that he too learned the truth of his mother's suicide. He read about it in a magazine that he picked up in a Rome barbershop. Before that, he thought she had died of cancer.

Q *President Carter said he would hold the government of Iran responsible for the safety and return of the hostages at the American Embassy in Tehran. What government of Iran?— C.P.S., Washington, D.C.*

A By "the government of Iran," Carter meant mostly the Ayatollah Khomeini, who at age 80 is prepared to lead his militant followers into death and martyrdom.

Q *Is it true that Ralph Nader does not smoke, drink, curse, own or drive a car, or go out with girls?—Glifford Scull, Graniteville, S.C.*

A Nader does not smoke or own a car, but he does go out with women.

John Travolta

Q *Was Saturday Night Fever based on a true-life story, or was it fiction?— L. Dean, Newark, N.J.*

A Tony Robinson, 21-year-old disco dancer from Brooklyn, New York, claims the role of Tony Manero, played by John Travolta in the film, was based on his life. Robinson has filed a $5 million lawsuit against Paramount Pictures.

Q *Friends in Washington, D.C., tell me that if Jimmy Carter is reelected president, he will purge the government of so many Kennedy supporters and Carter political enemies that he will make Richard Nixon's 1972 purge look like a tea party. Your opinion, please?— K.D., Richmond, Va.*

A Jimmy Carter is an intensively competitive politician who, under stress, has betrayed indications of pettiness. But he is not a venomously vengeful man who would establish an enemies list.

Q *Would you say that since her endorsement of the Palestine Liberation Organization and her leadership of the Workers Revolutionary Party, British actress Vanessa Redgrave is finished in Hollywood?—Louise Montgomery, Lansing, Mich.*

Globe
Vanessa Redgrave

A "Finished" is perhaps too terminal a word. But Vanessa Redgrave— Oscar-winner in 1977 for the film *Julia*— has become so politically controversial that many producers undoubtedly shy away from casting her in their films.

Q *Why has Sen. Herman Talmadge (D., Ga.) taken such great pains to hide the existence of his first wife, Katherine?—T.T., Albany, Ga.*

A Probably because he knows she detests him. Katherine Williamson and Herman Talmadge were married in the Little Church Around the Corner in New York City in 1939, divorced in 1941. There is no mention of her in any of Talmadge's official biographies—only mention of his second wife, Elizabeth Shingler of Ashburn, Georgia, whom he married in December 1941 and from whom he was recently divorced. Talmadge's first wife, now Katherine Talmadge Jenkins, lives in the West Indies and remembers him as "a habitual drunk . . . a terrible womanizer." She claims that Talmadge and his father made life rough for her in Georgia and she does not look back upon that period with happy nostalgia.

Q *They say that Sen. Edward Kennedy's 89-year-old mother Rose is his best fund-raiser, that after she makes her pitch for money there's not a dry eye in*

the house. What does Rose say that's so effective to campaign contributors?— H.L., Springfield, Mo.

A Her most memorable line: "I've lost two sons—it's up to Ted now."

Q *Henry Kissinger and Le Duc Tho of North Vietnam were awarded the Nobel Prize in 1973. Kissinger accepted his. Le Duc Tho did not. Why?—H. Bronson, Arlington, Va.*

A Le Duc Tho refused on the grounds that peace in Vietnam had not been achieved. "Once the arms are silenced and real peace has arrived," he said, "I will be able to consider accepting this prize." American troops departed from Vietnam in 1975, but Le Duc Tho still declines to accept the award—most probably because Vietnamese soldiers are still fighting, this time in Cambodia.

Joe Louis

Q *When Joe Louis was heavyweight champion of the world, did he ever have an affair with Sonja Henie, the late Norwegian skating champion and Hollywood film star?—R. Oates, Las Vegas, Nev.*

A According to Louis, he did.

Q *In her book* Ordeal, *Linda Lovelace of* Deep Throat *notoriety claims her first husband, Chuck Traynor, passed her around to Hollywood celebrities like Sammy Davis, Jr., and Hugh Hefner for sexual purposes. Is this true? If it is not true, have the men she names sued her?— O.L., Washington, D.C.*

A Linda Lovelace Marchiano claims she was used by her ex-husband as a sex slave. He denies it. Sammy Davis, Jr.,

Greta Garbo

admits that he and Linda were "casual acquaintances" but says: "I won't dignify her fantasies with a comment. I don't give a damn what she says, and I don't intend to say anything else about it." To date, Hugh Hefner, founder of the *Playboy* empire, has said nothing about the alleged relationship. Neither man has sued Lovelace—who at this writing lives on Long Island, New York, with her second husband, unemployed construction worker Larry Marchiano. They were on welfare.

Q *I read recently that film star Greta Garbo stopped Nazi Germany from developing the atom bomb in World War II. I also read that she was a secret intelligence agent during the war. Can any of this be verified?—Maury Schaap, New York, N.Y.*

A Greta Garbo was a sometime aide to Sir William Stephenson, chief of British Security Coordination, an arm of the British Secret Intelligence Service. She carried messages to Sweden during World War II and contributed in a small way to the escape of renowned nuclear scientist Niels Bohr from German-occupied Denmark to England, thus preventing Hitler from possibly impressing Bohr into working for the Nazis. Garbo is mentioned in *A Man Called Intrepid*, an account of intelligence operations in World War II, by William Stevenson.

Priscilla Presley

Q *How old is Priscilla Presley, and who is her latest boyfriend?—F.T., Memphis, Tenn.*

A Priscilla Presley, 33, shares her time and habitat with male model Michael Edwards in Beverly Hills.

Q *Who pays for the upkeep of presidential libraries like the Eisenhower Library in Kansas, the Lyndon Johnson Library in Texas, the Franklin D. Roosevelt Library in New York, and all the rest?—Naomi Gringold, Lafayette, Pa.*

A Presidential libraries are built with private funds, but after erected they are operated and maintained by the federal government with taxpayers' money. The cost of maintaining six presidential libraries is now almost $7 million a year. When the Gerald R. Ford Library is completed in Ann Arbor, Michigan, this fall, the total operating cost of all seven facilities will approach $8 million annually, possibly more.

Q *Why is Beatrix of the Netherlands disliked by many of the Dutch?—Louise Morgan, Grand Rapids, Mich.*

A Some consider their new queen abrupt, ambitious, arrogant and authoritarian. Others resent her siding with her father, Prince Bernhard, against her widely loved mother, former Queen Juliana, whose warmth she lacks. There is also a growing anti-monarchical trend in the Netherlands, and if Beatrix rubs the Dutch people the wrong way, they could very well legislate their country into a republic. Beatrix's husband, Claus von Amsburg, was a member of the Hitler Youth and a Wehrmacht panzer division. Fortunately Beatrix has three sons, the oldest of whom, Willem Alexander, 12, was the first male born legitimately into the ruling family in four generations.

Q *I am interested in what happened to Megan Marshack, Nelson Rockefeller's art researcher with whom he was working when stricken with a fatal heart attack. Is Marshack under life contract to the Rockefeller interests, or has she been spirited out of the country?—G.G., Binghamton, N.Y.*

A Megan Marshack—who worked, following Rockefeller's death, for Broadway producer Alexander Cohen and his wife Hildy Parks—has joined the James Wagenvoord Studio as an editor. She is not under any retainer by the Rockefeller interests.

Q *Isn't it true that the Soviet Union has exiled Dr. Andrei Sakharov to the inland city of Gorky to prevent his possible disruption of the Moscow Olympic Games and will send him back to Moscow after the Games are over?—L.B., McLean, Va.*

A Sakharov is the most famous of the 216 dissidents that the KGB has rounded up in advance of the Olympic Games. Whether they will permit him to return to Moscow in the future is not yet known. It is safe to assume, however, that they will not permit him to leave the Soviet Union, since he played a leading part in the construction of the Soviet hydrogen bomb and at 32 was voted the youngest member of the prestigious Academy of Sciences. Gorky is 250 miles from Moscow, and Sakharov may be allowed visits to Moscow after the Olympic Games.

Q *I would like to know the age of famed cardiovascular surgeon Michael DeBakey of Houston and whether he*

Michael DeBakey

secretly underwent surgery at Methodist Hospital in Houston for cancer.—D.G., Del Rio, Tex.

A DeBakey, 71, was operated on in March 1980 at Methodist Hospital. Minor surgery was performed in the rectal area, where sensitive non-cancerous tissues were drained.

Q *I know that Richard Nixon lives at 142 E. 65th St. in New York City. Who lives next door to him? And don't the neighbors mind the Secret Service men?—F.G., Washington, D.C.*

A Nixon's neighbor is David Rockefeller, who himself is accustomed to the trials of security protection.

President Anwar el-Sadat

Q *About President Anwar el-Sadat of Egypt—is it a fact that he will expel any foreign newsperson who writes about his first wife and three daughters? Is it a fact that he is the richest man in Egypt and owns 10 palaces? Is it a fact that he married his present wife, Jihan, when she was only 13 and that she is English?—S.T., El Paso, Tex.*

A It is common knowledge in Egypt that Sadat has been married twice. No foreign newsperson has been expelled for writing about Sadat's first wife and their offspring. Sadat has 10 Egyptian residences available for his use, but they are owned by the state, not by him. In 1949 he married Jihan Raouf, daughter of an Egyptian judge and a British schoolteacher. She was 15 and he 31. They have four children and three grandchildren.

PERSONALITY PARADE®

May 25, 1980

Judy Garland

Elvis Presley

Q *Is it true that the late Elvis Presley will be heard singing duets with Dolly Parton, Judy Garland and others with whom he never sang? I read that a recording company in Nashville is deleting backup tracks from Elvis's old records and dubbing in new voices.—L.D., Memphis, Tenn.*

A Those reports have emanated from Nashville. But Dolly Parton, Elvis's manager Col. Tom Parker and RCA all say they know nothing about any such recordings.

Q *I have been reading about H. L. Hunt, the fabulous Texas oil billionaire whose sons Bunker and Herbert helped run the price of silver up from $6 to $50 an ounce only to have it collapse on them. My understanding is that H. L. Hunt fathered 14 children in all, legal and illegal, via three wives. My question is: How come the old guy was never arrested on a bigamy charge? Did he own the law-enforcement establishment of Texas? Do you have any explanation or know some source that does?—N.T., La Jolla, Cal.*

A Haroldson Lafayette Hunt (1889-1974) had six children by Lyda Bunker, his first wife. He also had four children by Ruth Ray, his secretary. After his first wife died, he married his former secretary and thereby legitimized his second group of offspring. He also had a third family with Frania Tye of Shreveport, Louisiana, who blessed their illegal union with four more children. By virtue of his oil holdings in East Texas, billionaire Hunt had more than enough money to take care of his 14 children and their mothers. As a

result, no charges were ever filed against him.

The Dallas law firm that handles the interests of Hunt's family by Lyda Bunker—led by sons Nelson Bunker Hunt and W. Herbert Hunt—is Shank, Irwin, Conant, Williamson & Grevelle. Ivan Irwin, Jr., of that law firm is a knowledgeable source.

Q *Are Chris Wilding, Elizabeth Taylor's son, and Aileen Getty, granddaughter of J. Paul Getty, still together, or have they split?—B.B.B., Houston, Tex.*

A Still together in Hollywood at this writing.

Q *Has Warren Beatty dropped Diane Keaton for an Italian actress named Ornella Muti? I believe Ornella has a role in the movie* Flash Gordon.—*Antonia Timberlake, Provo, Utah.*

A Ornella Muti, who has starred in seven Italian films and has become Italy's No. 1 sex symbol, is not the latest pigeon in Beatty's flock. She reports that she received a phone call in London from a man who professed to be Warren Beatty and wanted to discuss a film project with her. But as of this writing they have not met, nor has Beatty dropped Diane Keaton.

Q *Is the story true that O. J. Simpson had to settle $5 million on his wife before she would give him a divorce? How much did it cost him?—Cindy Kay, Charlotte, N.C.*

A Under terms of their financial settlement, Mrs. Marguerite Simpson will receive a $500,000 trust fund for herself and the two Simpson children: Arnelle, 11, and Jason, 10. Mrs. Simpson will also receive $600,000 to purchase a new home and 50 percent of O. J.'s deferred income from his pro football employment contracts. The couple divided approximately $3 million in community property.

Q *Actor Dustin Hoffman—does he live in New York or Hollywood? And who is his new love, another dancer like his ex-wife?—Jan Barrett, Jersey City, N.J.*

A Oscar-winner Hoffman, born August 8, 1937, plans to move from New York back to his hometown of Los Angeles and to buy a house there with a tennis court (if he hasn't already). If and when his divorce from dancer Anne Byrne becomes final, Hoffman may marry Lisa Gottsegen, 24, a UCLA Law School student.

Q *Any truth to the vicious rumor that Soviet leader Leonid Brezhnev ordered his hockey team to lose to the U.S. team in this year's Winter Olympics at Lake Placid because he wanted to start a Russian peace offensive?—K.L., Albany, N.Y.*

Leonid Brezhnev

A No truth. The U.S. hockey team was simply better on the ice.

Richard Nixon

Q *Several months ago, former President Richard Nixon flew all the way to the Republic of the Ivory Coast in Africa to open a golf course. The rumor is that he was paid $100,000 to preside over the affair. Is that true?—Chuck Duke, Marion, Ill.*

A It is not true. Nixon is an old friend of President Houphouet-Boigny of the Ivory Coast, having visited that country in 1963 and 1967. A spokesperson for Houphouet-Boigny says that Nixon had only his expenses paid, that he would accept no fee or honorarium for appearing at the golf course opening festivities in Yamoussoukro.

PERSONALITY PARADE®

July 27, 1980

Brooke Shields

Q *Is* Blue Lagoon, *the movie with Brooke Shields and Christopher Atkins, an original or a remake? Did Brooke play the nude scenes in the movie, or was a double used? What did Atkins do before he became an actor?*—Carol Stokes, Washington, D.C.

A Blue Lagoon *is a remake of a 1948 English film starring Jean Simmons and Donald Houston.*

A double for Brooke Shields, Australian diving champion Kathy Trout, was employed in the nude scenes. Atkins worked as a model and a sailing instructor in Rye, New York, before director Randal Kleiser (who also directed *Grease*) chose him for Lagoon.

Q *The rumor is that two old-line American corporations—A&P grocery stores and Colgate-Palmolive—have been sold to General Jahanbani, who used to command the Shah's army in Iran. Can this be verified? Are these two now owned by Arab money or controlled by foreigners?*—T.T., Springfield, Ill.

A A West German company, Tengelmann's, one of the largest grocery chains in the world, owns a controlling stock interest in A&P. Colgate-Palmolive is presided over by Keith Crane, 58, originally from Wellington, New Zealand, but the company is primarily American-owned. The late General Jahanbani, believed killed in the purge following the Shah's overthrow, had no interest in either company.

Q *Friends from Germany tell me that boxer Max Schmeling is the most widely liked sports celebrity in their country because he knocked out Joe Louis in 1936. Can this be right? How old is Schmeling? What did he do in World War II? What does he do now?*—Ron Lieber, St. Paul, Minn.

A Max Schmeling, former heavyweight champion, will be 75 on September 28. He was the first fighter to defeat Joe Louis, knocking him out in the 12th round on June 19, 1936. Louis knocked Schmeling out in a return match in 1938. A paratrooper in World War II, Schmeling injured himself in a drop over Crete in 1941 and was given a medical discharge. After the war, he hit the comeback trail as a boxer but gave it up in 1948. He bought a farm west of Hamburg, which he still occupies with his wife, former screen star Anny Ondra. They have been married 47 years. Schmeling, according to public opinion polls, is the most popular German sports celebrity of the century, which is why he is hired from time to time for promotional work.

Ronald Reagan

Q *Not long after Ronald Reagan was elected governor of California, he underwent a serious and secret operation. Wasn't it for cancer?*—F.T., Glendale, Cal.

A It was not for cancer. In 1967 Reagan suffered from an enlarged, infected and stone-ridden prostate gland. Dr. Burton Smith, his urologist and surgeon, thought it best under the circumstances to perform a transurethral prostatic resection, removing some of the gland. The prostate, however, was not in the slightest cancerous—and there was nothing secret about the surgery, which was performed at St. John's Hospital in Santa Monica, California.

Q *Is former Beatle John Lennon finished with show business?*—Claire Burns, Chicopee, Mass.

A His wife, Yoko Ono, says he is. Lennon recently purchased a 65-foot yacht, plans to sail to various ports with Yoko and their son Sean, four.

John Lennon

Q *Remember Leslie Browne, the ballerina who played Shirley MacLaine's daughter opposite Mikhail Baryshnikov in* The Turning Point? *Whatever happened to her?*—Jamie Fox, St. Paul, Minn.

A After *The Turning Point*, Leslie tried a non-dancing role in the film *Nijinsky*, in which she portrayed the legendary dancer's protective wife Romola. Leslie danced this past season with the American Ballet Theatre. She was an unknown when director Herbert Ross plucked her from the ranks of George Balanchine's New York City Ballet for *The Turning Point.*

Q *Marilu Henner, who used to keep company with John Travolta, is said to be in love with a famous man named Hammett. Is this true? Who is Hammett?*—Wanda Harvey, Seattle, Wash.

A Actress Marilu Henner met actor Frederick Forrest in March on the set of the film *Hammett*, which deals with the life of Dashiell Hammett (1894-1961), writer of "tough" detective stories who used to live with playwright Lillian Hellman. You are obviously confusing Hammett with Forrest, who was nominated for an Oscar for his acting performance opposite Bette Midler in *The Rose*.

Q *Is there really an organization called the Watergate Alumni Association? And is it true that Gordon Liddy is its president, Charles Colson its vice president, and John Ehrlichman its secretary?*—J.G., Red Bank, N.J.

A The Watergate Alumni Association is an organization that exists only in the fertile, funny mind of humorist Art Buchwald.

Shelley Winters

Q *In her recent autobiography,* Shelley: Also Known As Shirley, *Shelley Winters, 58, writes about her affairs with Burt Lancaster, William Holden, and Marlon Brando. Since Shelley must weigh about 250 pounds, are we to assume that these men have a penchant for fat ladies?—Jim Chambers, Wichita, Kan.*

A It means that in her heyday, 30 years ago, Shelley Winters was a trim, well-turned, attractive bleached blonde. Today she is built along the lines of a blocking back, and the lovers she writes about are remembrances of old romances.

Q *Ronald Reagan has a 22-year-old son named Ron or Skippy. He was at Yale for a while but seems to have disappeared from public view. Are the Reagans keeping their son under wraps? And if so, for what reason?—W.P., New Haven, Conn.*

A Ronald Prescott Reagan dropped out of Yale to study classical dancing in California and is now with the Joffrey II Dancers in New York. He has been promoted from a back-up dancer to performing artist. The Reagans are not keeping him under wraps, but they see no point in invading his privacy or interfering with his career.

Q *International gossip has it that Soviet leader Leonid Brezhnev is "the protector" of a beautiful Aeroflot airline hostess. Supposedly Brezhnev and girlfriend were caught in Tricia Nixon's bedroom by Mrs. Richard Nixon in 1973 when* Brezhnev *was staying at the Nixon home in San Clemente. How much of this is true?—Sam Kay, San Diego, Cal.*

A When Brezhnev visited the U.S. in June 1973, he was assigned a guest cabin at Camp David, Maryland. An attractive blonde Soviet stewardess who had flown to the U.S. with Brezhnev was also assigned a guest cabin. A little after midnight, the Soviet hostess left her cabin to join the Soviet premier in his. A week later when Brezhnev and his party flew to San Clemente, Brezhnev was assigned the bedroom formerly occupied by Nixon's daughter Tricia. Again Brezhnev was visited by the same Soviet hostess who reportedly was spotted by Mrs. Nixon. The rumor is that Brezhnev and the hostess conducted or discussed affairs of state.

Leonid Brezhnev

Q *Have Burt Reynolds and Sally Field reconciled? How about his other women? How does he keep all of them straight?—O.L., Daytona Beach, Fla.*

A The computer to keep track of Burt Reynolds and his women has yet to be invented. Sally Field at this writing is reportedly back in the Reynolds fold.

Q *Is Doris Day finished with men? I understand that Doris will never marry again because her husbands beat her up and take her money. Has she become a recluse, as people say?—Helen Mitchell, Houston, Tex.*

A Doris Day, 56, is understandably disillusioned with marriage. Her first husband, Al Jorden, beat her mercilessly; her third, Marty Melcher, cheated, lied and finagled her out of a fortune. After four unsuccessful marriages, Doris prefers the company of dogs in her Carmel and Beverly Hills, California, residences. What she needs in her life is one good man who will love her for being Doris Kappelhoff of Cincinnati, not Doris Day of Hollywood.

Q *It has been said that Jimmy Carter and five other Georgians run America. Personally I don't believe it. But who are the five other Georgians?—Neil Hall, Baltimore, Md.*

A Carter's wife Rosalynn; his lawyer, Charles Kirbo; his chief-of-staff, Hamilton Jordan; his press secretary, Jody Powell, and his domestic affairs adviser Stuart Eizenstat.

Q *Please name the players on the women's professional tennis circuit who are lesbians. Isn't it a fact that the circuit is lesbian-ridden? Isn't that why the parents of 17-year-old Tracy Austin and 15-year-old Andrea Jaeger travel with them—in order to protect them on tour?—S.L., Philadelphia, Pa.*

A Love affairs between some topflight women tennis players are reportedly not uncommon on the circuit. Occasionally an attractive young pro will repel a lesbian overture, but female homosexuality on the tennis circuit is no more widespread than it is in show business or the military or girls' institutions. Moreover, many female tennis champions—Evonne Goolagong and Chris Evert, for example—found husbands while playing the circuit.

Q *Would you be kind enough to run a photo of O. J. Simpson, the former football star, and Nicole Brown? I understand she is one of the most beautiful models in the country. How long have they been going together, and do they plan to marry?—M.H., Lincoln, Neb.*

A Nicole Brown, 23, and O. J. Simpson, 32, have been constant companions for almost a year. There has been no mention at this time of wedding plans.

Nicole Brown and O. J. Simpson

WALTER SCOTT'S
PERSONALITY PARADE®
October 5, 1980

Edward Kennedy

Q *Since Sen. Edward Kennedy failed to get the 1980 Democratic presidential nomination, what does he plan to do with his future?—Ella Cobb, Roxbury, Mass.*

A Senator Kennedy, born February 22, 1932, can (1) retire from political life, which is not likely; (2) run for a fifth term in the U.S. Senate in 1982; or (3) try for the presidency again in 1984, 1988, 1992, and even in 1996, when he will be 64, which is five years younger than Ronald Reagan's current age.

Q *Who said, "I have always been discriminating in my choice of lovers, but once in bed I am like a slave"? Was it Madame Du Barry, the last mistress of Louis XV, or Madame de Pompadour, her predecessor?—G.B., Hartford, Conn.*

A The quotation belongs to neither of those famous French mistresses. The words are those of Swedish actress Britt Ekland, second wife of the late British comedian Peter Sellers.

Q *Hollywood star Natalie Wood has a younger sister Lana Wood, also an actress, who supposedly has been married 10 times and is not yet 30. Can you verify the rumor and list her husbands?—V.T., Los Angeles, Cal.*

Lana Wood

A Lana Wood, 34, has been married only six times: to (1) Jack Wrather III, (2) Carl Brent, (3) Steven Oliver, (4) Stanley Vogel, (5) Richard Smedley and (6) Alan Balter. Her sister Natalie (real name—Natasha Zacharenko) has been married three times: to actor Robert Wagner in 1957, Richard Gregson in 1969, and to Wagner again in 1972.

Q *How old is Russian ballet dancer Mikhail Baryshnikov? How tall? How long has he been in this country? Is he already a millionaire? Who is the Hollywood beauty he has taken as his latest lover?—Needra Orlov, Great Neck, N.Y.*

A Baryshnikov, 32, is five-foot-five when not twinkling on his toes. He has been in the U.S. for six years, is said to be a millionaire or rapidly approaching that status. His love interest at the moment is actress Jessica Lange.

Q *It cost actress Goldie Hawn $25,000 to get a divorce from her first husband, Gus Trikonis, in order to marry singer Bill Hudson. How much will it cost her to divorce Hudson in order to marry that French actor, Yves Renier? Is she willing to give up her two children for Renier?—Chris Ellis, Washington, D.C.*

A Goldie Hawn, 34, has been linked in print with actor Chevy Chase, and Bill Hudson has filed for divorce. A settlement of community property acquired in four years of marriage may well cost Goldie $500,000, but she will probably retain custody of their children Oliver, four, and Kate, one and a half.

Q *What is the secret society—I believe it is known as RIOP, which stands for Right Is Our Principle—headed by the wife of Robert McNamara, former defense secretary and now head of the World Bank?—J.L., Alameda, Cal.*

A Margaret McNamara, 64, is the founder of a charitable organization known as RIF, which stands for Reading Is Fundamental. She founded this nationwide organization in 1966. Since then it has given away millions of books to disadvantaged children. Mrs. McNamara, whose husband is resigning from the World Bank next year to spend more time with his family, is a singularly democratic woman who would never head any secret society. The success of RIF is attributed largely to her industry, organizational skill, and friendly manner with all people, particularly the young.

Elizabeth Taylor

Q *Richard Burton's young wife Susan—is she insanely jealous of Elizabeth Taylor and won't allow any photos or mentions of Liz in her house?—Alice T., Bangor, Maine.*

A "Insanely jealous" is too strong a description. Suzy Hunt Burton feels that she salvaged her actor-husband from an alcoholic grave and wants no reminder of her more-famous predecessor, to whom Burton was twice married. In fact, several weeks ago she ordered a photo of Elizabeth Taylor ripped out of 90,000 programs at the O'Keefe Center theater in Toronto, where Burton was starring in the roadshow revival of the musical *Camelot*.

Q *In World War II, did the Japanese notify Adolf Hitler that they planned to bomb Pearl Harbor, or was Hitler as surprised as everyone else?—Paul Dutton, Ann Arbor, Mich.*

Adolf Hitler

A Hitler was surprised. He expected the Japanese to attack the Soviets from the rear, but the Japanese found the pickings—especially for oil—easier in Southeast Asia, for which resource they first had to neutralize the U.S. fleet in Pearl Harbor. An authoritative book on the subject is *Hitler vs. Roosevelt* by Thomas Bailey and Paul Ryan (Macmillan).

Q *Shirley MacLaine is supposed to be such a brain. How could she have chosen to star in two films like Loving Couples and Change of Seasons?—H.T., Richmond, Va.*

A At 46, MacLaine is not the film attraction she once was. She has to take pretty much what comes along. And what comes along these days in the way of scripts is none too hot.

Tennessee Williams

Q *What's happened to Tennessee Williams, the dramatists who wrote* The Glass Menagerie, A Streetcar Named Desire, The Rose Tattoo, Cat on a Hot Tin Roof *and many other fine plays? Has he lost his touch? He hasn't had a hit play in years and years.—G.T., New Haven, Conn.*

A Tennessee Williams (real name: Thomas Lanier Williams) had his last hit play, *The Night of the Iguana*, 19

years ago. In his most recent comeback attempt, Williams chose as his subject the last visit of novelist Scott Fitzgerald to the sanitarium where his wife Zelda was being treated for mental instability. The play, *Clothes for a Summer Hotel*, starred Geraldine Page and was directed by Jose Quintero. It closed on Broadway this year after 14 performances, losing an estimated $450,000, $20,000 of which was Williams' own money. At this writing, Williams has retreated to his home in Key West, Florida, talks of putting together a repertory company that he'll take to Australia. He is still a talented playwright, will probably come up with another play which will prove both a commercial and critical success.

Q *Is it a fact that all the sheiks of Saudi Arabia are descended from Ibn Saud, who died in 1953, exhausted from taking care of 800 wives?—Helen Asher, Olympia, Wash.*

A Ibn Saud (1880-1953) triumphed over his arch rival, Husein Ibn Ali, in 1924 and declared himself King of the Hejaz and Nejd—which took his name when Saudi Arabia was formally established on September 23, 1932. A warrior of remarkable potency, Ibn Saud admitted in his lifetime to marrying 135 virgins and fathering 43 sons and an undetermined number of daughters. His sons and grandsons are the major sheiks of Saudi Arabia, but there are others who are descended from different lines. Ibn Saud's eldest surviving son is Prince Mohammed, 70, grandfather of Princess Misha'al, whose public execution for adultery in 1977 was the basis of the controversial dramatized documentary *Death of a Princess*, televised earlier this year.

Q *Which is the island in the Bahamas where Henry Ford, William Paley of CBS, Greek shipping tycoon Stavros Niarchos and other millionaires own lavish estates? Is it a private island guarded by special troops?—D.W., Sarasota, Fla.*

A The tycoons you name own property on Lyford Cay in the Bahamas. The island is not guarded by special troops.

Q *How old is Claudette Colbert, if she is still alive? She won an Oscar in 1934 for* It Happened One Night.*—H. Gibson, Seattle, Wash.*

A Claudette Colbert, 75, recently appeared on Broadway in *The Kingfisher* with Rex Harrison, at this writing is very much alive. She was born in Paris,

France, on September 13, 1905, and christened Claudette Chauchoin.

Q *How many people have won the Nobel Prize more than once, and who were the youngest laureates?—Alice Glenn, Lexington, Ky.*

A Only one person, Dr. Linus Pauling, has won two Nobel Prizes alone. Pauling was awarded a Nobel in 1954 for chemistry and another for peace in 1962. Three other scientists have also received two Nobel Prizes, but shared them with co-winners: Marie Curie in 1903 for physics and 1911 for chemistry; John Bardeen in 1956 and 1972 for physics; and Frederick Sanger in 1958 and 1980, also for chemistry. The youngest laureate was Sir William Lawrence Bragg, who in 1915 at age 25 shared a Nobel Prize for physics with his father, Sir William Henry Bragg, for work on X-rays. Theodore Richards of the U.S. won a Nobel for Chemistry in 1914 for work performed when he was 23. Martin Luther King, Jr., was awarded the Nobel Peace Prize in 1964 at age 35, assassinated four years later.

Judy Garland

Shirley Temple

Q *I would like to know if Shirley Temple, Judy Garland and Candy Bergen were all classmates at Westlake School for Girls, a day school in Los Angeles.—Lillian Shields, Costa Mesa, Cal.*

Candy Bergen

A The late Judy Garland never attended Westlake, but Shirley Temple, 52, and Candy Bergen, 34, did. Garland and Temple both attended Ethel Meglin's dance studio in Hollywood in 1931. Temple was then three, and Frances Gumm (later renamed Judy Garland) was nine.

WALTER SCOTT'S
PERSONALITY PARADE®
January 4, 1981

Robert De Niro

Q *Please settle an argument. Actor Robert De Niro, who was so great in* Raging Bull, The Godfather II, Taxi Driver, New York, New York—*is he black or white?—Ella Cutler, Washington, D.C.*

A De Niro, 37, son of painters Virginia Admiral and Robert De Niro, is white. His wife, Diahnne Abbott, however, is a beautiful statuesque black actress and mother of their son Raphael, three.

Q *Is it true that before Ronald Reagan was elected president, his daughter Patti couldn't get arrested in Hollywood, and now every studio in town is offering her $500,000 a film?— F.T., Los Angeles, Cal.*

A Last month, Patti Reagan, 28, who uses the stage name Patti Davis, was signed by NBC to an exclusive acting contract guaranteeing a minimum of $100,000 a year. Before the election, she was largely considered a curiosity attraction of mild interest and cast intermittently in such TV shows as *Here's Boomer*. In the final analysis, she'll be judged by her acting ability and not her father's position.

Q *For some time now, the rumor has been rife that the Unification Church run by Sun Myung Moon has bought out the Proctor & Gamble Company. Is this true?— Marcy L. Ray, Wichita, Kan.*

A Not true.

Q *Who owns the MGM Grand Hotel in Las Vegas? Can you tell me anything about the owner in whose hotel more than 80 people lost their lives in a terrible fire? What does he have to say about that terrible tragedy?—Frank Chase, Seattle, Wash.*

A The MGM Grand Hotel is owned by a public corporation, MGM Grand Hotels Inc. Approximately 50 percent of the corporation's stock is owned by Kirk Kerkorian, 63, a financier who also owns 47 percent of the Metro-Goldwyn-Mayer Film Corporation and 2.4 million shares of Columbia Pictures. The son of an immigrant Armenian farmer, Kerkorian was reared in California's San Joaquin Valley. As a young man, he became a pilot, ferried planes overseas, then organized a charter airline that he parlayed into control of two airlines, Trans International and Western. Kerkorian later bought the Flamingo Hotel in Las Vegas, formed International Leisure Corporation, which he sold to acquire a controlling interest in MGM. He used some of MGM's assets to build the MGM Grand Hotels in Las Vegas and Reno. They were named after Grand Hotel, a 1932 MGM hit starring Greta Garbo and John Barrymore. In 1980 Kerkorian split MGM into two corporations, MGM Grand Hotels Inc., and Metro-Goldwyn-Mayer Film Corporation.

A razor-sharp multimillionaire and stock operator, Kerkorian keeps a low profile, at this writing has said nothing of the MGM Grand Hotel fire of November 21, 1980, instead has let the hotel's executives speak their piece.

Q *Was actor Ryan O'Neal ever busted for drugs? Did he ever have affairs with Margaret Trudeau, Anjelica Huston, Anouk Aimee, Diana Ross, Bianca Jagger, Joan Collins, Ursula Andress and Oona Chaplin? Did O'Neal's own wife ever have an affair with the late David Selznick that drove the producer's wife, actress Jennifer Jones, up the wall?—G.T., North Hollywood, Cal.*

A O'Neal was busted on a drug charge in 1976. He reportedly engaged in affairs with all the aforementioned except Oona Chaplin, widow of the comedian. His first wife, Joanna Moore, admits to an affair with David O. Selznick—which understandably did not overjoy Jennifer Jones, who was married to the producer from 1949 until his death in 1965.

Q *Which newspaper has the largest circulation in the world, and who owns it?— T. McKenzie, New Haven, Conn.*

A Probably *Pravda* (Russian for "truth"), a daily newspaper with an approximate circulation of 10.7 million. Pravda is owned by the Soviet Union, runs from four to eight pages, occasionally more.

Q *The first Beatle drummer was a handsome young devil named Pete Best. Why was he replaced by Ringo Starr, and what's happened to him?—Teena Owens, Dania, Fla.*

A Pete Best, who played drums with the Beatles 1960-62, was replaced at the request of George Martin, a producer for Parlophone Records in London. Reportedly Martin said in 1962 that he preferred another drummer, Ringo Starr, to join Lennon, McCartney and Harrison in their first Parlophone recordings. Brian Epstein, the Beatles' manager, told Best that the other Beatles wanted Ringo in and him out. Thus the dastardly deed was done. Best, 39, currently lives in West Darby, four miles outside Liverpool, plans to work in the U.S. Married in 1963, he has two daughters, Beba, 16, and Bonita, 12. Best is handsomer and more photogenic than any of the other Beatles.

Q *Was there ever a big love affair between the late film stars Judy Garland and Tyrone Power, and is it true that Power was gay?—S.L., San Jose, Cal.*

Judy Garland

A In 1942 Garland and Power were passionately in love. But Power was married to Suzanne Charpentier Murat (Annabella), and she would not give him a divorce—or so, at least, he said. Power was bisexual and reportedly had Garland abort his child.

Dolly Parton

Q *Please answer the question all of America is asking: How large is singer-actress Dolly Parton around the chest?—Bill Crouch, Nashville, Tenn.*

A She measures 42 inches at full expansion.

Q *Now that Chevy Chase has reportedly settled $400,000 on his wife or ex-wife Jacqueline, how much will Goldie Hawn settle on her husband or ex-husband Bill Hudson? Also, will Goldie Hawn marry Chevy Chase or Kris Kristofferson, and will Bill Hudson marry Ali MacGraw?—Frannie McGraw, Mineola, N.Y.*

A As producer and star of the film *Private Benjamin*, a box-office success, Goldie Hawn may have to settle $1 million or more on Hudson if and when they divorce. Goldie at this time is said to favor Kristofferson in the marriage sweepstakes. Ali MacGraw denies any serious involvement with Bill Hudson but continues to go with him.

Q *Twenty-five of the best and brightest men in the Nixon administration served time in jail because of the Watergate conspiracy—men like John Mitchell, Bob Haldeman, Egil Krogh, John Dean,* Charles Colson, John Ehrlichman, Jeb Magruder. Which of these men lost their wives because of Watergate and affiliated reasons? And have they remarried?—F.H., Akron, Ohio.

A Watergate played a role in the dissolution of the marriages of John Mitchell and John Ehrlichman. To date, Mitchell is unmarried. But two years ago, Ehrlichman, 55, domestic affairs adviser for Nixon, married Christine McLaurine, 32, an interior designer. Recently the second Mrs. Ehrlichman gave birth in Santa Fe, New Mexico, to a son. Ehrlichman has five grown children by his first marriage, which ended in 1978 after almost 30 years.

Q *Where is the love retreat that Mick Jagger, leader of the Rolling Stones rock group, has just bought? Did it really cost him $5 million?—Jane Devney, Jersey City, N.J.*

Mick Jagger

A Last year, Jagger purchased the magnificent 17th-century chateau Fourchette, in the Loire Valley of France. It was owned by the Richet family, one of whose members, Charles, won the Nobel Prize in 1913 in physiology and medicine for his research on body sensitivity to alien proteins. Richet's descendants received approximately $600,000 for the property.

Q *Who was Thomas Crapper?—David Ellis, Las Vegas, Nev.*

A Thomas Crapper was an English plumber who invented the flushing toilet that bears his name. He died in London in 1910.

Q *I have been told that most of the new toys in the world are manufactured by a secret company in Chicago which then farms them out for manufacture in Hong Kong. Is this correct?—Charles Pomerantz, North Miami, Fla.*

A Marvin Glass and Associates of Chicago reportedly develops a sizable percentage of the new toys manufactured each year. Because toy inventions are easily pirated, the company keeps a low profile, declines all interviews and contact with the news media. It is located at 815 N. La Salle in Chicago, manufactures no toys but services many toy-makers by supplying ideas for new ones.

Q *I would like to know how much Ron Reagan, the president's son, earns as a dancer with the Joffrey II Ballet? Is it true that his parents also give him a yearly allowance of $50,000?—M.T., Los Angeles, Cal.*

A The Joffrey II dancers are paid $270 a week (union scale), plus $20 per day expenses when on the road. President Reagan's son gets no annual allowance of $50,000 from his parents but does regularly receive "a little help" from them.

Q *I am puzzled about the suicide of Rachel Roberts, fourth wife of actor Rex Harrison. She died at 53 on the eve of the Los Angeles opening of his road-show production of My Fair Lady. The newspapers said she took her life because she had no men in her life after her marriage to Harrison, 1962-71. Didn't she live all those years with a Mexican gardener in Los Angeles?—Elena del Valle, Long Beach, Cal.*

A For nearly 10 years following her divorce from Harrison, actress Rachel Roberts lived with Darren Ramirez, 35, who used to manage a boutique in Beverly Hills. He was most recently employed as a hairdresser and fashion designer in that community. Why Rachel Roberts took her life by swallowing too many sleeping pills remains unknown.

John McEnroe

Q *Almost everywhere he plays tennis, John McEnroe is known as "Superbrat." Doesn't he realize he's a disgrace to his parents, his country and the game itself?—Victor Parenti, Orlando, Fla.*

A McEnroe is on occasion a crybaby whose court manners are dreadful. Apparently he lacks the will or discipline to control his emotions. Certainly he does no credit to the game, which has made him a millionaire.

Frank Sinatra

Q *It has been printed about Frank Sinatra that (1) he has had the Vatican annul his first marriage to Nancy Barbato, the mother of his three children; (2) his fourth marriage, to Barbara Marx, was consecrated last year in New York City in St. Patrick's Cathedral; and (3) he is a member of the Knights of Malta. Is any of this true?— G.T., Los Angeles, Cal.*

A None of it is true, according to officials of the Archdiocese of Los Angeles, St. Patrick's Cathedral, and the Sovereign Military Order of Malta.

Q *There's a rumor that several doctors have come up with a secret medicine which grows hair on bald heads. One is a Dr. Baden. If it's true, when will the medicine go on the market?—Peter D., Hillsdale, N.J.*

A Minoxidil, a drug-manufactured by the Upjohn Co. of Kalamazoo, Michigan, is prescribed by physicians to reduce severe high blood pressure. The drug not only reduces hypertension, in some patients it also produces hirsutism—random hair growth. Unfortunately, it does not limit such growth to bald heads. Some patients who regularly take Minoxidil have hair growing out of their ears, arms, faces and stomachs. To help investigate the properties of the drug, Upjohn is financing investigations by Dr. Howard Baden of the Harvard Medical School and Dr. Norman Orentreich, famed pioneer of hair-transplanting. About 40 inmates of the state prison in Jackson, Michigan, are voluntarily having their bald heads rubbed with Minoxidil lotion. If it proves a cure for male baldness, Upjohn—which is downplaying the research—will market the drug for that use within the time limits made expedient by government regulations and pharmaceutical production schedules.

Q *When Elizabeth Taylor was a child star at MGM, was she one of the few who really loved Louis B. Mayer and called him "Uncle Louie"?—Virginia Lord Graham, Las Vegas, Nev.*

A Taylor detested Mayer, has described him as a "liar, hypocrite, total megalomaniac snake."

Q *How much taller is Lady Diana Spencer than Prince Charles?— Audrey Unger, Seattle, Wash.*

A Charles is five-feet-eleven, and his bride-to-be is five-feet-ten in her bare feet. Most probably she will not wear high heels when in public with the Prince.

Q *In your opinion, who was the greatest soldier-statesman in American history?— Norman Woo, Lahaina, Hawaii.*

A Two of the greatest were George Washington (1732-99), first president of the U.S., com-

George Washington

mander-in-chief of the Continental Army in the American revolution; and Gen. George Catlett Marshall (1880-1958), chief of staff of the U.S. Army and director of allied strategy in World War II, U.S. ambassador to China (1945-47), secretary of state (1947-49) and founder of the European Recovery Program (known as the Marshall Plan), secretary of defense (1950-51), and winner of the Nobel Peace Prize in 1953.

Q *Several years ago, it was announced that Richard Zanuck and David Brown were going to produce a sequel to Gone With the Wind. Is the project still on or dead?—Louise Newton, Springfield, ill.*

A At this writing, it appears abandoned. In 1977 when Zanuck and Brown were producers at Universal, they signed writer Anne Edwards, author of Vivien Leigh and Judy Garland biographies, to write a sequel to *Gone With the Wind*. Edwards wrote a novel entitled Tara, set in the period 1872-82. Scenarist James Goldman adapted the novel for the screen, but MGM, a member of the producing consortium, turned it down.

Q *Was Shirley Temple ever married to Ronald Reagan in the movies?—Caroline Godfrey, Grand Junction, Col.*

A In 1947 Reagan proposed to Shirley Temple in *That Hagen Girl*, one of her first roles as a young adult. He played a lawyer old enough to be her

Globe

Shirley Temple

father, and at a sneak preview when he muttered his key line, "I love you," the audience howled. When the final version was released, that line was edited out. Reagan was then 36, Temple 18.

Q *Before Sen. John F. Kennedy married Jacqueline Bouvier in 1953, was he not hopelessly in love with actress Jean Simmons?—B.D., Goddard, Kan.*

A As a gay young blade, John F. Kennedy mowed down almost every attractive actress in sight. But before his marriage, he was never hopelessly in love with any woman. He certainly tried with Jean Simmons, but in 1950 she was freshly married to actor Stewart Granger and therefore immune to the entreaties of other suitors.

Q *Was Lord Byron, the famous British poet, guilty of incest with his sister? Wasn't he also a homosexual? If so, why is his poetry distributed in all our public libraries?—Thomas Y., Davenport, Iowa.*

A George Gordon Noel Byron (1788-1824) engaged in numerous homosexual, adulterous and heterosexual liaisons. His most notorious affair was one with his half-sister Augusta. Lame from birth and fatherless at three, Byron grew into a handsome, restless wanderer whom women found irresistible. Many of his poems—i.e., *Don Juan* and *Childe Harold*—are recognized classics, which is why they are found in schools and libraries. A man's art cannot be judged on his sex life.

WALTER SCOTT'S
PERSONALITY PARADE®

May 31, 1981

Julie Nixon Eisenhower

Q *Can you tell me what's happened to the untitled biography of her mother that Julie Nixon Eisenhower has been writing for years? We'd all like to read the true story of Pat Nixon.—K.L.T., San Clemente, Cal.*

A Julie's publisher, Simon & Schuster, reports that publication of the biography has been postponed.

Q *If any serious misfortune should befall Secretary of State Alexander Haig, who is most likely to be his replacement?—Thomas M., Alexandria, Va.*

A Former Texas Gov. John Connally, now a senior partner in the prestigious Houston law firm of Vinson & Elkins, reportedly is waiting in the wings, anxious to answer a call that may never come. Don Rumsfeld, secretary of defense in Gerald Ford's cabinet and currently chief of G.D. Searle Pharmaceuticals in Skokie, Illinois, is said to be a likely replacement. Another possibility: George P. Shultz, secretary of the treasury in Richard Nixon's cabinet and now with the Bechtel engineering outfit of San Francisco.

Q *I would like to know if the Johnny Carson TV show is written. If so, how much is written by Carson?—Carol Winkler, Pittsburgh, Pa.*

A Carson collaborates with several writers in the preparation of his monologues and skits. Those are the only written parts of the show.

Q *Why didn't Ginger Rogers show up at the Life Achievement Award dinner that the American Film Institute gave this past April for Fred Astaire at 81? Everyone else was there.—Lee Evans, St. Paul, Minn.*

A Reportedly Ginger Rogers was working in New Orleans at the time. Although Rogers and Astaire starred together in 10 films, theirs has never been a really close or buddy-buddy relationship.

Q *From reading the newspapers, I am under the impression that this country is being run by three presidential advisers—Edwin Meese III, James Baker III and Michael Deaver. When I voted for Ronald Reagan, none of their names were on the ballot. How come?—Louise Davis, Long Beach, Cal.*

A White House Counselor Meese, Chief of Staff Baker, and Deputy Chief of Staff Deaver did not run for elective office in 1980. Ronald Reagan did and was elected. When a citizen votes for a presidential candidate, he indirectly votes for the man's advisers, appointees and policies. Voters should bear that in mind.

Q *Wasn't the source of Abraham Lincoln's great sadness the venereal disease that he caught as a young man and which he spread to his wife and children? I can understand why that fact is omitted from the American history books, but isn't it true?—Rupert F., Dallas, Tex.*

Abraham Lincoln

A William Herndon, Lincoln's law partner who knew him as well as any man, writes in his book *Lincoln: The True Story of a Great Life:* "About the year 1835-36, Mr. Lincoln went to Beardstown and during a devilish passion had connection with a girl and caught the disease. Lincoln told me this . . ."

Eventually Lincoln was supposedly cured of the disease by Dr. Daniel Drake of Cincinnati. But Herndon suspected that Lincoln might not have been cured completely and later infected his wife, Mary Todd, and—through her—three of his sons,

who died early. "Poor boys," Herndon wrote, "they are dead now and gone. I should like to know one thing, and that is: What caused the death of the children? I have an opinion, which I shall never state to anyone." His opinion, of course, was that syphilis was the cause, and Herndon was responsible for first raising the question about the disease.

Q *Has any black man ever been governor of any state in this country?—N.P. Avery, Charlotte, N.C.*

A Not yet, although Tom Bradley, three-time mayor of Los Angeles, may give it a try in California come 1984 if he can achieve the Democratic Party's nomination.

Q *The late Sir Carol Reed, famous English motion picture director of Odd Man Out, The Third Man, Oliver, Our Man in Havana and other films—was he the illegitimate son of Edward VIII and Wallis Warfield Simpson, the duchess of Windsor? I have heard that rumor many times in film circles. Is it true?— Jennifer L., N. Hollywood, Cal.*

A It is not true. Carol Reed was the illegitimate son of the brilliant English actor Sir Herbert Beerbohm Tree (1852-1917). Tree had two families: one with his wife, Maud Holt, by whom he had three daughters; and one with his mistress, Beatrice May Pinney, who took the name Reed and by whom Tree had five sons and a daughter. His fourth son, Carol Reed (1906-76), kept secret the identity of his father.

Q *Before Jane Pauley became a TV commentator, what was her relationship with handsome John Lindsay, former mayor of New York City?—V. Livingston, Pensacola, Fla.*

Jane Pauley

A In 1972 when she was 22, Jane Pauley was a lowly campaign worker for John Lindsay, who had a short-lived hope of running for the presidency on the Democratic ticket. Pauley married Doonesbury cartoonist Garry Trudeau in June 1980.

WALTER SCOTT'S
PERSONALITY PARADE®

June 14, 1981

Billie Jean King

Q *What is the inside story of tennis champion Billie Jean King? Is she an out-and-out lesbian? Will she be driven from the ranks of tennis professionals just as "Big Bill" Tilden suffered in the 1950s for his homosexuality? How widespread is homosexuality among women tennis pros? Does Billie Jean's husband, Larry, plan to divorce her?—D.W., New Orleans, La.*

A Billie Jean King is apparently a bisexual who engaged in a long-term (1972-76) lesbian relationship with Marilyn Barnett, 33, her former hairdresser and secretary. At 37, Billie Jean's playing career is drawing to a close. It is likely that within a year or two, most of her commercial sponsors will drop her, but society is far more tolerant now than it was in Tilden's time (1893-1953), and she won't be driven from women's pro tennis, of which she truly is one of the founders. Among the women pros, probably no more than half a dozen are lesbians. They are fairly well-known and no threat to the game.

In 1965, Billie Jean Moffitt married Larry King, then a pre-law student, and she subsidized his education. Today, King, 36, is a sports promoter who guides his wife's career. At this point, he has no intention of divorcing Billie Jean—claims, in fact, that their marriage is more solid than ever.

Unfortunately, as regards her affair with Marilyn Barnett, Billie Jean forgot that hell hath no fury like a woman scorned. Barnett wants the Malibu house in which she lives and the lifetime support that she claims Billie Jean orally promised her. She has sued under California case law, which accords contract property rights to unmarried cohabiting lovers. Whether such rights apply to homosexual lovers, the courts eventually will decide. Billie Jean is learning the hard way that there is no free lunch.

Q *Months ago, it was announced that Farrah Fawcett and Ryan O'Neal were to get married. Why haven't they?—Linda Juarez, San Antonio, Tex.*

A At this writing, Farrah Fawcett has yet to obtain a divorce from actor Lee Majors. Where Ryan O'Neal is concerned, no woman should count on marriage until he has slipped the ring onto her finger.

Q *What is the correct story involving Robert Benchley and Dorothy Parker? Did she try suicide because she was pregnant by Benchley and he would not marry her? I thought these two famous writers were friends, not lovers.—Vivian K., Jacksonville, Fla.*

A Parker and Benchley were good friends but never lovers. Parker was basically a frustrated, unhappy woman who apparently attempted suicide several times. After her third or fourth attempt, Benchley reportedly sent her the following telegram: "You must quit this foolishness, Dottie, or you will ruin your health." Benchley (1889-1945) was a humorist who served as drama critic for the original *Life* magazine (1920-29) and for *The New Yorker* (1929-40). He also wrote, directed and acted in humorous film shorts at MGM, where Parker was a colleague. She died in 1967 at the age of 74.

Q *John Hinckley, Jr., who shot President Reagan and three other men with his .22 caliber revolver—if he had used a .38, which he had previously bought, isn't it safe to assume that he would have killed all four men?—Howard C., Las Vegas, Nev.*

Ronald Reagan

A It is a reasonable assumption, but too many variable factors are involved to make it "safe to assume."

Q *Don't the Democrats plan to run Robert Redford if the Republicans run Ronald Reagan for the presidency in 1984? Isn't Redford the Democrats' "secret weapon"?—Murray Axelrad, San Mateo, Cal.*

A That's just a gag.

Q *The rumor is very much alive that on her 52nd birthday, Jackie Kennedy Onassis will marry Maurice Tempelsman, a New York diamond dealer. How does the Kennedy family feel about this?—Sara L., Cambridge, Mass.*

Jackie Kennedy Onassis and Maurice Tempelsman

A They know nothing about it. International minerals and diamonds financier Maurice Tempelsman, 53, supposedly one of Jackie's financial advisers and a good family friend, has been photographed escorting her to various Manhattan functions. He is married and does not seem to be her romantic type—but then again, neither did Onassis.

Q *Have you ever heard of the Cemp family of Canada? They're supposed to be the richest, most private family on earth. They're supposed to own everything in Canada that's not nailed down, also half of this country.—Yoshio Yamanaka, Bellingham, Wash.*

A Cemp is an acronym embracing the first-name initials of Charles, Edgar, Minda and Phyllis Bronfman, children of the late Sam Bronfman, Canadian liquor tycoon. Cemp Investments Ltd. is a holding company based in Montreal with assets estimated at $10 billion. Edgar Bronfman, 51, a U.S. citizen who lives in New York and runs the Seagram empire from there, is a billionaire business executive and philanthropist. His sisters and brother are also among the world's wealthiest people, but not as wealthy as he.

WALTER SCOTT'S
PERSONALITY PARADE®
June 21, 1981

Sophia Loren

Q *I have a hard job believing that Sophia Loren owes the Italian government $685 million in back taxes, for which they plan to throw her in jail. What's the story?—Joan Bernstein, Bend, Ore.*

A The Italian government recently claimed that actress Sophia Loren owes 685 million lire ($685,000) in back taxes for the years 1963-74. She was named on a list with other actors and actresses in a campaign to crack down on tax evasion. Last year, Loren—now a French citizen who resides in Paris—was sentenced in absentia to 30 days in jail and fined 12 million lire ($12,000) on charges that her advisers and accountants failed to file a tax return for her in 1963. She was threatened with a jail sentence if she appeared in Italy; but she did appear and was not arrested, although she expressed her willingness to go to jail if she had to

Q *Was there ever a homosexual relationship between Brian Epstein, manager of the Beatles, and the boys in his band? Isn't that why Epstein took his own life?—Fran Henderson, Los Angeles, Cal.*

A Brian Epstein was a homosexual in love with John Lennon, the most talented of the Beatles, but Lennon was not "gay" and did not reciprocate his love.

Frustrated, Epstein directed his sexual energy toward others, none of whom were Beatles. One of these relationships ended in Epstein being blackmailed. Whether Epstein's subsequent death from an overdose of drugs was intentional, accidental or even murder has yet to be established. One of the best accounts of Epstein's relationship with the Beatles appears in *Shout! The Beatles in Their Generation* by Philip Norman.

Q *I recently returned from the Bahamas and was told there that in World War II, when the Duke of Windsor was governor general of the Bahamas, he was so stupidly prejudiced that he issued an order banning black people—who comprise more than 90 percent of the population—from entering Government House through the front door. I was also told he had unsavory Nazi connections with Axel Wenner-Gren, a resident of the Bahamas. Is this factual or hate propaganda?—E.Y., West Palm Beach, Fla.*

A In much of his behavior, the Duke of Windsor was a spoiled, arrogant fool. His wartime years in the Bahamas were a travesty. What you were told about him is, unfortunately, true. He was stupid, insensitive, relatively uneducated for an ex-king, and constantly worried about money (though he had millions). For details of his ridiculous behavior in the Bahamas, read *Edward VIII*, a good biography by Frances Donaldson; or, for more detail, *The King Over the Water* by Michael Pye.

Q *I have heard that in order to punish her husband for his friendship with Carmen Ortega, Dovie Beams and other beauties, Philippine First Lady Imelda Marcos has fallen in love with Steve Psinakis, the Greek boyfriend of her best friend. I have also heard that Imelda and Psinakis have rendezvoused at the Waldorf Astoria in New York. Is this true?—R.T., New York, N.Y.*

A Not much of it is true. The Greek you mention, Steve Psinakis, has been married since 1969 to the former Presy Lopez, who at one time was a good friend of Imelda Marcos. In November 1972, however—two months after he declared martial law—Philippine President Ferdinand Marcos had Presy's brother, Eugenio Lopez, Jr., jailed without a trial. Subsequently the Marcos' Meralco Foundation acquired the Manila Electric Company, owned by the Lopez family. Steve Psinakis has for many years been one of the U.S.-based opposition leaders to the Marcos dictatorship. On

December 19, 1980, Imelda Marcos invited him to her suite on the 37th floor of the Waldorf, told him that her husband planned to lift martial law, and sought to enlist his support, which Psinakis declined. No affair or romance was involved. Jet-setter Imelda has long been reconciled to her husband's romantic indiscretions.

Q *Before actress Candy Bergen married French director Louis Malle, wasn't she involved in a blazing affair with English actor Terence Stamp?—Michelle Hayes, Lafayette, Ind.*

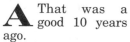

Candy Bergen

A That was a good 10 years ago.

Q *When George Bush was campaigning for the Republican Party's presidential nomination last year, he consistently made fun of Ronald Reagan's economics policy, calling it "voodoo economics." Now he shouts to the high heavens that Reagan's policy is the best, the greatest, the only way to go. What does this say about George Bush?—Hank L. Houston, Tex.*

A It says that Bush is a politician, a team player happy to have been chosen vice president on the Reagan ticket. It says, too, that frequently it is the convert who sings loudest in church.

Q *In his new biography of Ulysses S. Grant, author William McFeely writes that Grant hoped to solve the race problem by taking over the Dominican Republic and "moving the black people of the United States to the Caribbean." Wasn't this originally the plan of President Abraham Lincoln?—Howard Fleming, Denver, Col.*

Ulysses Grant

A Basically it was. On Dec. 3, 1861, Abraham Lincoln urged the Congress to appropriate money for such colonization. Lincoln preferred Liberia or Central America as a home for the blacks.

Joan Crawford

Q *It has been published in the press that Joan Crawford seduced child star Jackie Cooper when he was 17. Was Joan Crawford a sex fiend or something? Or is it not true?—Ann Morgan, Las Vegas, Nev.*

A Jackie Cooper as a teenager was sexually precocious. By age 17, he was a Hollywood bedroom veteran. One evening he visited Joan Crawford in her residence, made a pass and tried to seduce her. Crawford, then in her early 30s, was so amused by the teenager's aggressiveness that she decided to take him on. Strongly sexed herself, she bedded down with young Cooper, thereafter scheduled him for a weekly lesson in sex education. Crawford was no sex fiend, but she liked to demonstrate her sexual prowess over men, regardless of their age. Cooper writes of her nostalgically in his autobiography, *Please Don't Shoot My Dog.*

Q *Who is the Russian who broadcasts each day in a perfect American accent on Radio Moscow's shortwave service to the U.S.?—Ed Green, St. Paul, Minn.*

A The Voice of Moscow, beamed to the U.S. in daily propaganda chats, belongs to Vladimir Pozner, son of a French mother and a Russian father who once worked for MGM in New York City. Young Pozner was educated in the U.S. but in the 1950s returned to the Soviet Union, where he was hired as a reporter by Novosti, the Soviet press agency. He was transferred to the broadcasting division 10 years ago, now has a daily five-minute commentary on Radio Moscow.

Q *Who is this Sissy Spacek who won an Academy Award for* Coal Miner's Daughter? *She looks like a 15-year-old kid. Is she really married to actor Rip Torn?—Annette Sommers, Englewood, N.J.*

A Sissy Spacek, 31 (real name: Mary Elizabeth Spacek), of Quitman, Texas, began playing small roles in such TV series as *The Rookies* before she moved up to acting roles in such feature films as *Prime Cut* and *Badlands.* For her outstanding performance as the psychokinetic teenager in *Carrie,* she was nominated for an Oscar in 1977 but lost out to Faye Dunaway, who won it for her work in *Network.* Spacek's cousin is actor Rip Torn. Her husband is production designer-director Jack Fisk. When Sissy and Jack were married in 1974, she put aside $30 in a secret bank account, "because $30 is how much it costs to file divorce papers in California." Their marriage, however, has been enormously successful, and they remain two of the most un-Hollywood-like people in show business.

Q *I don't understand why Nancy Reagan did not attend the wedding of her stepdaughter Maureen. Her absence and that of her children seemed awfully conspicuous. Did she feel somehow threatened by the presence of Mr. Reagan's first wife, Jane Wyman?—Mimi S. Dawson, Chattanooga, Tenn.*

Ronald Reagan

A Ronald Reagan, as almost everyone knows, has been married twice and has two separate families. The members of Family No. 1 have never been particularly close to the members of Family No. 2. This past April, Nancy Reagan undoubtedly believed that her husband—recovering from a serious gunshot wound in Washington, D.C.—required her presence more than her stepdaughter did in Beverly Hills, California, where at age 40 she was getting married for the third time. Nancy and stepdaughter Maureen are neither bosom pals nor sorority sisters.

If and when the first and second Mrs. Reagan encounter each other at a function, rest assured that each will carry on with aplomb and graciousness. Neither feels threatened by the other.

Q *When George Wallace of Alabama was shot in 1972, wasn't he wearing a bulletproof vest under his shirt?—David Meachum, Birmingham, Ala.*

George Wallace

A He was not. Governor Wallace had decided earlier in the day that it was too hot to wear his bulletproof vest and left it in the trunk of his car.

Q *One of the greatest tragedies of this century, I believe, involved the late J. Robert Oppenheimer. Nine years after he headed the team of U.S. scientists that helped develop the first atomic bomb, Oppenheimer was denied security clearance. Where is Oppenheimer buried? And whatever happened to his wife and children?—T.R., Princeton, N.J.*

A J. Robert Oppenheimer, the brilliant but controversial American physicist who "fathered" the first U.S. atomic bomb, died of cancer at age 62 on February 18, 1967. He was cremated, his ashes flown to the Virgin Islands and scattered on the waters he once sailed. His wife Kitty, a heavy drinker, died of stomach trouble in 1972. His daughter Toni, after an unhappy first marriage, committed suicide in 1977. His son Peter, a contractor in New Mexico at this writing, scrupulously avoids the news media and declines to discuss his parents.

Q *When does ABC plan to telecast the life story of Jacqueline Kennedy Onassis?—Maude Peterson, Salt Lake City, Utah.*

A ABC-TV has no such program in the works. In production for fall viewing, however, is a three-hour biography, tentatively titled *Jacqueline Bouvier Kennedy,* which shows Jackie from age five until the day of her first husband's assassination in 1963. Actress Jaclyn Smith will play Jackie, actor James Franciscus the part of John F. Kennedy.

Anwar Sadat

Q *The truth, please, about Anwar Sadat, assassinated president of Egypt. Wasn't he a terrorist, an opportunist, a revolutionary fanatic, a Hitler supporter and a Nazi spy during World War II? How could Henry Kissinger describe him in* Time *magazine as "a miracle of creation" and "a very great man"?—F.T., Santa Barbara, Cal.*

A Henry Kissinger is a very sincere man who knew Sadat well, and what he wrote about Sadat in his *Time* magazine eulogy is undoubtedly his truthful opinion. History, however, records that in World War II Sadat was an avid Hitler supporter who collaborated with two Nazi spies in Cairo, was captured, court-martialed, dismissed from the Egyptian Army and imprisoned. According to his autobiography, *Revolt on the Nile,* he was a potential terrorist who wanted "to blow up the British Embassy and everybody in it" but was dissuaded by his leader, Gamal Abdel Nasser. In 1946 Sadat began a jail term of almost three years for partaking in the assassination of Egypt's finance minister, Amin Osman Pasha.

Sadat was an opportunist in that his principles were always subject to change. He sided with the Soviet Union and the communist bloc when it suited his purposes, then allied himself with the U.S. when he decided Washington would be more forthcoming. He was more popular in the U.S. than in his own country, where he was never fully trusted by those who knew his history and those who objected to his signing the Camp David accords. Although born poor in a village on the Nile delta on December 25, 1918, he lived the last 10 years of his life with many of the same creature comforts as the wastrel King Farouk he conspired to overthrow in 1952. It is safe to say, however, that Sadat will be remembered as a man who sacrificed his life in the cause of peace.

Q *Is there any automobile manufacturer in the world that equips its passenger cars with airbags?—Joe Gerenspan, Livonia, Mich.*

A Daimler-Benz, manufacturers of Mercedes-Benz automobiles, sell sedans in Europe that come equipped with an airbag for the driver. There is none for the passenger in front. The airbag, which comes as a supplement to the driver's seat belt, is an option costing about $750. It has been available since March in several overseas models.

Q *They say that one of the world's great buildings is now nearing completion in Kuwait. It is supposed to be an architectural wonder. It will house the parliament of Kuwait. Who is the architect?—Willa Farmington, Cape May, N.J.*

A Kuwait's new parliament building was designed by Jorn Utzon, 63, a Danish architect and former furniture and glassware designer who also designed the opera house in Sydney, Australia. It should be finished any day now, ready for occupancy in 1982.

Q *Friends have told me that secret wife auctions are still conducted in Great Britain. If this is so, please tell me where, as I would like to auction off my wife.—F.H., Seattle, Wash.*

A No such auctions are now being conducted. The practice, however, was fairly common in Britain from about 1750 to 1850. Wives were led to the marketplace in halters and made to stand on a chair or table while the husband or auctioneer described their qualities. Adultery was the most frequent reason for wife-selling, and in many cases the wife was sold to her guilty lover. Wife-selling was practiced because divorce was costly in Britain before the Divorce Act of 1857. An excellent source is *Wives for Sale* by Samuel P. Menefee, to be published here in early 1982.

Q *How old was Greta Garbo when she retired from motion pictures, and on what does she live?—Diane Stein, Neptune, N.J.*

A Garbo, born September 18, 1905, retired in 1941 at age 36. She lives on income derived from shrewd investments in California real estate

Greta Garbo

Brooke Shields

Q *Those romances I read about in the gossip columns linking 16-year-old Brooke Shields with John Travolta and Mohammed Khashoggi, son of the millionaire Saudi Arabian playboy, and others— are they true or phony? Isn't Brooke's "serious steady" a member of the faculty at Dwight-Englewood School here in her hometown?—A.S., Englewood Cliffs, N.J.*

A Romances involving Brooke Shields are for the most part phony publicity items. At 16, Shields is too sensible to have a "serious steady." She has never dated a member of her high school faculty, nor would any faculty member presumably be so foolish as to date a 16-year-old student.

Q *When President Reagan's plan to cut Social Security benefits for old people proved unpopular, it was attributed to Martin Anderson, his domestic policy adviser; David Stockman, his budget director; and Richard Schweiker, secretary of health and human services. When a pair of our Navy fliers shot down two Libyan planes and the move proved popular, Reagan was given credit for taking the Libyans on. Who is responsible for making the president appear infallible?—Cal. H., Bridgeport, Conn.*

A His Cabinet and White House staff are understandably dedicated to making Reagan look good, if not infallible.

WALTER SCOTT'S
PERSONALITY PARADE®
January 3, 1982

Ryan O'Neal

Q *Does Ryan O'Neal have any intention of marrying Farrah Fawcett, or is he just stringing her along? How come after 18 months, these two are still not married?—Patricia Rossiter, Ft. Worth, Tex.*

A Fawcett technically still is married to her first husband, actor Lee Majors. Because of property disputes, their divorce case goes to court next February 9. It would surprise no one if Farrah becomes the third Mrs. Ryan O'Neal some time after that.

Q *Does Jimmy Carter hold his beer-guzzling red-neck brother, Billy, responsible for his defeat in the 1980 election? What's happened to Billy? Is he still an alcoholic?—Erika K., Portland, Ore.*

A Billy Carter, 44, now a public relations man in Alabama for Tidwell Industries, insists he hasn't tasted liquor for the past 30 months. He is still friendly with brother Jimmy, who does not hold Billy responsible for his loss to Ronald Reagan.

Q *Arthur J. Goldberg, the former Supreme Court justice, and Arthur J. Goldberg, president of the Parvin Foundation—are they one and the same person or not?—Al Franken, Encino, Cal.*

A They are not. The Arthur J. Goldberg who heads the Parvin Foundation is a retired 81-year-old CPA from Chicago. The distinguished ex-Supreme Court justice of the same name, also from Chicago, is a 73-year-old practicing attorney in Washington, D.C. He served as secretary of labor in the John Kennedy cabinet, was appointed to the Supreme Court and resigned to become our ambassador to the UN. He has no connection with the Los Angeles foundation.

Q *It is said that Johnny Carson will not marry a girl unless her first name is Jo. Is this true? I'd also like to know if Johnny has any children. One never hears about them.—Lita Schroeder, Las Vegas, Nev.*

A It is by pure coincidence that all three of the women Johnny Carson has married have first names beginning with Jo: Jody Wolcott, Joanne Copeland, and Joanna Holland. Carson has three sons who are unpublicized by design: Chris, 31, Ricky, 29, and Cory, 28.

Q *Sally Field, who is so good with Paul Newman in* Absence of Malice—*did they have "a thing" while shooting the film, or is she still one of Burt Reynolds' girls?—Carrie B., Montgomery, Ala.*

A No on-set romance between Field and Newman, though she and Reynolds have drifted apart. At this point, the actress asserts, there is no man in her life. She lives with her mother and two sons—Peter, twelve, and Eli, nine—in her San Fernando Valley, California, home.

Q *What sort of president is Ronald Reagan, who spends $209,000 for new china, serves smoked fillet of mountain trout, duckling a l'orange, rice with raisins, melon with raspberries, and the best California wines for himself and his White House guests at state dinners and then reduces the lunches for American schoolchildren so that instead of getting eight pieces of bread per week, they get only five, and their milk allotment is cut from eight ounces a day to six? I voted for Reagan because I felt he was a warm, compassionate man who loved the common people, of whom he once was one. Was I wrong?—T.U., Canoga Park, Cal.*

A By nature, Reagan is a warm, compassionate man. He believes sincerely that the economics he is practicing is best for all the country. He hopes that by reducing taxes and cutting government expenditures, he will encourage capital investment, which in turn will produce a prosperity whose benefits will trickle down to even the poorest segments of the population. If he is right, he will be reelected; if wrong, we will have a depression.

Marlene Dietrich

Q *Can one believe singer Eddie Fisher when he says that Marlene Dietrich initiated him into the rites of love when she was 55 and he was 25? I believe he makes that observation in his autobiography,* Eddie—My Life, My Loves.— *G.D., Springfield, Mo.*

A Fisher was acquainted with the rites of love before he met Dietrich. She merely furthered his education. "She was the sophisticated older woman," he writes in his revealing memoirs, "and I was the inexperienced boy, just like in one of her own movies, and I was both excited and a little scared. But Marlene knew how to make me feel like a man . . . We began to meet often, and our evenings together always ended in Marlene's apartment . . . She was the most stimulating woman I had ever met." Despite Fisher's exalted opinion of Dietrich, he obeyed his manager, Milton Blackstone, who told him not to be seen in public with the actress at a prize fight because she was too old for him. Fisher in his youth was no practitioner of integrity, independence or courage.

Eddie Fisher

Queen Noor and King Hussein

Q *Did the U.S. taxpayer pick up the tab again for the "ladies of the evening" supplied to Jordan's King Hussein on his recent visit, or is such wooing only to fill gaps between his "queens for the day"?—G. Rodney Crowther III, Washington, D.C.*

A In the past, certain branches of our intelligence community have been known to supply visiting dignitaries with call girls. However, no such hospitality was accorded to King Hussein on his last visit here. Accompanied by his fourth and latest wife, Queen Noor (the former Lisa Halaby of Washington, D.C.), King Hussein was honored with a formal state dinner by President and Mrs. Reagan. The U.S. taxpayer did pick up the tab for that.

Q *From your knowledge and in your opinion, which show business performer is the wealthiest?—Nora Gross, Baltimore, Md.*

A One of the wealthiest, if not *the* wealthiest, surely, is Paul McCartney, 39, the most commercially successful of the Beatles. This son of a Liverpool cotton salesman is worth about $400 million, largely through his music copyright holdings.

Q *Can it possibly be true that actor Sylvester Stallone now asks for and gets $4 million a picture? Other than the Rocky films, has he ever had a hit picture?—Gia Forza, San Francisco, Cal.*

A Sylvester Stallone some weeks ago signed to star in *First Blood* for a salary of $3.5 million. The film concerns the adjustment problems of a Vietnam war veteran. To date, Stallone's success has been confined to *Rocky* and *Rocky II*. *Rocky III* is scheduled for release in June.

Q *Now that Elizabeth Taylor's seventh marriage, to Sen. John Warner of Virginia, apparently hasn't come off, will she become a nun?—Ad Wells, Charlottesville, Va.*

A Liz Taylor will become a nun like Lana Turner—also married seven times—became a nun. Seriously, there is little chance. In addition, Elizabeth Taylor Hilton Wilding Todd Fisher Burton Burton Warner is a convert to Judaism.

Q *I understand Nancy Reagan and Barbara Bush hate one another. Is this true? What is the cause of this personality conflict?—B.K., Mobile, Ala.*

A They don't hate each other, but neither are they close friends. They are cordial and correct in their relations with one another. Moreover, the Bushes make it a point never to upstage the Reagans.

Barbara Bush

Q *Isn't it a fact that the secret secretary of state in the Reagan Cabinet is really Richard Nixon? Isn't it a fact that when Alexander Haig gets in trouble, he calls his old boss for advice?—D.M., Tarzana, Cal.*

A Nixon and Haig have a long history of togetherness. It was Nixon who sent Haig on many missions to Vietnam. It was Nixon who passed over 240 others to make Haig a four-star general. And it was Nixon who chose Haig to replace Bob Haldeman as his chief of staff. It was Haig who helped plan the secret bombings along the Cambodian border in 1969 and who was, in his own words, "aware of the subsequent inaccurate statements that may have been provided to the Congress." It was Haig who first broached the possibili-

ty of a Gerald Ford pardon of Nixon, and it was Nixon who advised Ford to keep Haig on as chief of staff. When Nixon retired to San Clemente, it was Haig who visited him.

But this is not to say that Nixon is "the secret secretary of state." Haig loves power too much to share its rewards. He was amazingly lucky to emerge untarnished from Watergate, and at this stage in his career, Haig is not about to alter his command image by employing Richard Nixon as a sub rosa consultant on foreign affairs. He phones Nixon occasionally for his views, but that's about it. Haig is determined to run his own show.

Q *For the benefit of the thousands of American football fans who groan through Howard Cosell's opinionated, unrelated and ill-founded comments on "Monday Night Football," could you please inform the public as to where we might write seeking relief from this verbose, colorless know-it-all?—Keith Parker, Aiken, S.C.*

A Leonard H. Goldenson is chairman of the board of the American Broadcasting Companies Inc., headquartered in New York City. Roone Arledge is the executive in charge of news and sports. These two are largely responsible for exposing that most loquacious and controversial commentator to the American TV viewing public. Cosell, however, has many supporters who find his brash, arrogant, florid style hilarious, provocative or amusing. Surely, he is not colorless.

Q *Why does Lawrence Welk always end his show dancing with Mary Lou Metzger? He used to dance with others.—Olivia P. Roush, Mifflintown, Pa.*

A Mary Lou, wife of Welk's tuba player, is an excellent dancer and, according to Welk, "the one I feel most comfortable with on the dance floor."

Lawrence Welk

Melissa Sue Anderson

Q *Why would a sweet young thing like Melissa Sue Anderson, who plays the blind girl on TV's* Little House on the Prairie, *want to take Frank Sinatra as a boyfriend? I heard about them on a TV show.—Patti Daniels, Sherman Oaks, Cal.*

A Actress Melissa Sue Anderson, 20, is dating singer Frank Sinatra, Jr., 38, not his father. Frank Sr., 66, has been happily married since 1976 to his fourth wife, the former Barbara Marx.

Q *The rumor around this town is that actress Tatum O'Neal has flipped her lid for Tony Shriver, who is Sen. Ted Kennedy's nephew and the youngest son of Sargent Shriver. Is it serious or just a ski-fling?—Pam Steven, Aspen, Colo.*

A Tatum O'Neal, 18, and Anthony Shriver, 16, went skiing at Aspen a few months ago. Nothing serious—but enough to stimulate the gossips.

Q *When Ronald Reagan retires from the presidency, will he become a "triple-dipper"?—Newton T., Denver, Colo.*

A When Reagan leaves office, he will be eligible for three government pensions: (1) Social Security; (2) his pension as two-term governor of California; and (3) his federal pension, which will include his term of office as U.S. president and as an officer in the armed ser-

vices. Whether he will take all three is, of course, his decision. Certainly he is entitled to them. He currently accepts his California pension of approximately $22,450 per year, although it appears to be in violation of Art. 2, Sec. 1 of the U.S. Constitution, which holds that while a president is in office "he shall not receive within that period any other emolument from the United States, or any of them."

Q *When John Warner, now Republican senator from Virginia, was divorced in 1972 from his wife, the former Catherine Mellon, he reportedly received—indirectly, from the estate of his billionaire father-in-law, Paul Mellon—a settlement worth more than $10 million. When Warner is divorced by film star Elizabeth Taylor, will he receive a like settlement?—D.L., Richmond, Va.*

A No chance, but surely Warner, 55, is a relatively lucky man. His first marriage assured him financial independence for life, and his marriage to Liz Taylor helped him win a seat in the Senate.

Q *I've been seeing Mickey Rooney on TV again. Can you tell me how many wives he's had and how many children?—Ann Ward, Georgetown, S.C.*

A Mickey Rooney, 61, has been married eight times and has fathered 10 children.

Q *I know that John Reed, the American journalist who wrote* Ten Days That Shook the World *and whose life inspired Warren Beatty's film* Reds, *is buried in the Kremlin in Moscow. But where is Edgar Snow, the American journalist who wrote* Red Star Over China, *buried? In the Great Wall of China near Peking?—M.K.J., Gainesville, Fla.*

A After Edgar Snow died of cancer in Switzerland in 1972, his family found a letter with the following instructions: "I love China, I should like part of me to stay there after death, as it always did during life. America fostered and nourished me. I should like part of me to be placed by the Hudson River before it enters the Atlantic to touch Europe and the shores of mankind, of which I have been a part. For I have known good men in almost every land."

Snow was cremated, and some of his ashes were buried in May 1973 on the Peking University campus beneath a marble stone bearing the words: "Edgar

Snow—1905-1972—American Friend of the Chinese People." The remainder of his ashes were buried in May 1974 at Sneden's Landing near Palisades, New York, with only his initials in brass on a burial stone overlooking the Hudson. One of the best sources of information on Snow is the Edgar Snow Memorial Collection at the University of Missouri in Kansas City.

Q *Actor Burt Reynolds recently underwent two operations. Is he suffering from the "Big C"?—Eric Hanks, El Paso, Tex.*

A Burt Reynolds, 46, does not suffer from cancer. Earlier this year, he underwent a second operation for a hernia he developed while filming *The Man Who Loved Cat Dancing* in 1973. In that movie, Reynolds performed his own stunt work—a dangerous task he now leaves to others.

George Washington

Q *George Washington and Andrew Jackson never attended college. Are there any other U.S. presidents who never earned a college degree?—Becky Andrews, Richmond, Va.*

A In addition to Washington and Jackson, you may add the names of Martin Van Buren, Zachary Taylor, Millard Fillmore, Abraham Lincoln, Andrew Johnson, Grover Cleveland and Harry Truman.

Q *I have seen so much in the newspapers about AWACS. What do those initials mean?—Maude Henley, Brunswick, Ga.*

A AWACS is an acronym for Airborne Warning and Control System. Our special aircraft equipped with highly sensitive radar and sophisticated computers have been referred to as AWACS.

WALTER SCOTT'S
PERSONALITY PARADE®

July 18, 1982

Richard Burton

Q *Judith Chisholm, a reporter who maintains that she spent five nights with Richard Burton, says he told her he had made love to Barbra Streisand, Sophia Loren, Claire Bloom, Susan Strasberg and many other screen stars. What do the ladies in question have to say about this kisser-and-teller?—M.F., Las Vegas, Nev.*

A Susan Strasberg, in her book *Bittersweet*, acknowledges her tempestuous love affair with Burton. The others mentioned in the Chisholm account say nothing of Burton's purported allegations.

Q *Have you ever heard of the Reichmann family, supposedly the richest in the world? Do you know where they come from and how they earned their fortune?—M.A., Pittsburgh, Pa.*

A The Reichmanns are Austrian and Hungarian refugees who settled in Toronto in the mid-1950s and proceeded to build the richest real estate empire in North America. The matriarch of the family is Renée Reichmann, whose husband, Sam, died in 1975. She has five sons and a daughter. Three of the sons—Paul, Albert and Ralph—own Olympia & York, among the world's wealthiest private corporations, with assets of $12 billion. The Reichmanns are Orthodox Jews, talmudic scholars who speak half a dozen languages, donate large sums to charity and zealously avoid publicity.

Q *After seeing the J. Robert Oppenheimer story on TV and seeing what a brilliant nuclear physicist he was, I wonder why "Oppie" and his colleagues never told FDR or Truman about the long-lasting effects of radioactivity on the human body.—Jennie Adams, Santa Fe, N.M.*

A Most probably because in the early '40s, when they made the first two nuclear bombs, the physicists involved in the project knew little or nothing about the enduring effects of nuclear radiation.

Q *In his book* Witness to Power, *John Ehrlichman accuses Dan Rather of being lazy, careless in checking his facts, and calls him a reporter who lacks objectivity. How much truth is there in Ehrlichman's charge, or is it just a case of sour grapes?—Nicholas P. Criscuolo, New Haven, Conn.*

A Rather may have weaknesses, but laziness, carelessness and lack of objectivity aren't among them.

Alana Hamilton and Rod Stewart

Q *Rod Stewart, the former grave-digger who became a rock star—was he ever a cocaine addict?—T.F., Los Angeles, Cal.*

A Stewart was never a cocaine addict but, according to his longtime personal assistant, Tony Toon, "Rod liked to 'toot' the drug." Toon recently finished a book, *The Rise and Fall of Rod Stewart*, in which he reveals details of the rock star's hedonistic lifestyle.

Q *Is it true that Elvis Presley's 14-year-old daughter, Lisa, goes to a school owned by the Scientology religious group?—B.Y., Knoxville, Tenn.*

A True.

Q *Many months ago, I read in your publication that in all the years Humphrey Bogart was married to Lauren Bacall, he kept a mistress named Verita Thompson. Is that fact well known in Hollywood, or only by your publication?—Ramon Rodriguez, San Antonio, Tex.*

A It was known by actress Ann Sheridan, who introduced Thompson to Bogart on the Warner Bros. lot; by restaurateur Mike Romanoff, who played chess with Bogart regularly; by Bogart's agent, Sam Jaffe; by Carl Petersen, skipper of the "Santana," the yacht Bogey purchased from actor Dick Powell; and by many others who worked with Bogart on his films and saw him daily with Thompson.

Believing in the strategy that the best defense is an offense, Bogey, when on the road or abroad with Thompson, would introduce her to reporters as "Pete, my executive secretary and mistress." Most of the reporters thought he was kidding and never pursued the lead. In truth, Verita Thompson not only was Bogart's mistress but also the hairstylist in charge of his toupees and the cutting of his two children's hair. Whether "Betty" Bacall ever suspected the relationship between her husband and his employee, only she knows. Understandably, she doesn't care to comment on the subject.

Verita Peterson Thompson lives in Beverly Hills, where her 15-year relationship (1942-57) with Bogart has become an accepted part of screenland lore.

Humphrey Bogart

WALTER SCOTT'S
PERSONALITY PARADE®

October 17, 1982

Margaret Thatcher

Q *I read that Margaret Thatcher, when she came to power as Britain's prime minister in 1979, urged the arms makers to sell to Argentina the munitions that were later used to sink British ships and kill British soldiers in the Falklands. Any truth to that?—D.K., Charlottesville, Va.*

A A few weeks before Argentine forces invaded the Falklands, the British shipped spare parts for the arms they had sold earlier to Argentina. The French Exocet missiles, which damaged the British ships in the war, were made by Aerospatiale, a company run by the brother of France's President Francois Mitterrand. The British previously had contributed parts for the French Super-Etendard planes that fired the Exocets. Since 1979, Britain has sold $300 million in arms to the Argentines and even lent them money to buy two destroyers.

Q *I often wonder why the Ingrid Bergman-Roberto Rossellini marriage broke up—especially after he dumped Anna Magnani for Bergman and she dumped her husband, Dr. Peter Lindstrom, for Rossellini. Do you know?— Heidi Forbes, Eugene, Ore.*

A There were several reasons. Rossellini was insanely jealous and throughout their marriage would not permit Bergman to star in films unless he directed them. After starring in seven Rossellini films—all critical and commercial failures—Bergman disobeyed her husband and flew to Paris, where she acted in Jean Renoir's film *Paris Does Strange Things* and later starred on the stage in *Tea and Sympathy*. "Let's face it," she told Rossellini, "artistically we are no good for each other." Rossellini declined to accept that conclusion. He was also a womanizer, which Bergman found easier to accept than his manic-depressive swings of temperament. If the films they made together had proved successful, most likely their marriage would have endured.

Q *Is it true that President and Mrs. Reagan have individual beauty salons in the White House, paid for with taxpayers' money?—N.F., Little Rock, Ark.*

A Mrs. Reagan has had an upstairs room in the White House outfitted as a beauty salon for her exclusive use. The president gets his hair cut in the White House basement barbershop or in Irving Drucker's barbershop in Beverly Hills when he's visiting California.

Neil Simon and Marsha Mason

Q *What is all this nonsense about actress Marsha Mason leaving her husband, Neil Simon, the world's wealthiest playwright, for actress Joan Hackett?— F.T., Los Angeles, Cal.*

A Just nonsense.

Q *Five years after the death of Elvis Presley, I am interested in why this young man, who had so much to live for, hastened his death by taking drugs. What was the central flaw in his character?— Grace T., Kingston, R.I.*

A Elvis suffered from a lack of self-control and of role models. He knew that his father, Vernon, had been jailed for passing bad checks. He knew that his manager, Tom Parker, was a wheeler-dealer and thus no father-substitute. Having been poverty-stricken in his youth—his family was on welfare—Elvis overcompensated when he came into money, buying in quantity everything he wanted—cars, women and drugs. He remains a classic example of the undisciplined, immature celebrity who submitted in all desires to instantaneous gratification.

The Beatles

Q *Were any of the Beatles ever "gay" or bisexual?—Wendy L., Raleigh, N.C.*

A Their manager, Brian Epstein, was a homosexual in love with John Lennon. No evidence exists, however, that Lennon reciprocated Epstein's love sexually or that any other Beatle was gay or bisexual. Epstein died in 1967 at age 32.

Q *How come the nine-year-old son of Jane Fonda and Tom Hayden goes by the name of Troy Garrity and doesn't use either of his parents' names?—N.M., Birmingham, Mich.*

A Troy was given his paternal grandmother's maiden name because the names Fonda and Hayden were considered controversial and possibly an unnecessary burden for the child to bear.

Q *Angie Dickinson, who was so good in* Police Woman—*was she buddy-buddy with Frank Sinatra and John F. Kennedy?—Dee F., Washington, D.C.*

A In her heyday, when she was in her twenties, Angie Dickinson was romantically linked to Sinatra, Kennedy, David Janssen, many other lotharios.

Imelda Marcos

Q Jet-setter *Imelda Marcos, the iron willed first lady of the Philippines—why do world leaders lend her an ear? What's the source of her power—her beauty?*—F. Austin, Washington, D.C.

A Imelda Marcos, 52, won the Miss Manila beauty contest in 1954, the year she married Ferdinand Marcos, 13 years her senior. He's appointed Imelda and other members of her family to high offices. She is governor of Manila and is expected to somehow succeed her husband, who has chronic respiratory and renal infirmities. Imelda knows of his infidelities and indiscretions and thereby exercises more power than other first ladies. She also lavishes more hospitality on visiting statesmen than most and thus finds it reciprocated when she is abroad. So long as the Marcos family retains the support of the Philippine military and the U.S., Imelda will be received hospitably in most capitals. She is, from many accounts, a ruthlessly ambitious woman.

Q *Has David Niven suffered a stroke, causing a loss of speech?*—Georgia Nichols, Chicago, Ill.

A Niven, 72, reportedly suffered a mild stroke earlier this year, slightly impairing his speech. He may already have recovered.

Q *Why is it that Walter Annenberg—philanthropist, publisher of the* Daily Racing Form *and* TV Guide, *and Nixon's ambassador to Great Britain—refuses to have his picture taken?*—A.T., Rancho Mirage, Cal.

A Annenberg does not refuse to have his picture taken. He has a withered right ear and for years was self-conscious about it, avoiding, when he could, photos taken of him from the right. At 74, he is reconciled to the afflicted ear.

Q *Is it a fact that President Reagan has secretly agreed to continue paying 25 percent of the UN's bills—this when more than 10 million Americans are unemployed and the UN is little more than a debating society?*—T.L., Lackawanna, N.Y.

A At a lunch given for him by UN Secretary-General Javier Pérez de Cuellar in June, Reagan announced that we would continue to pay 25 percent of the UN bills. "American financial support," the president announced, "has not and will not decline."

Paul McCartney

Q *Before he married Linda Eastman, Beatle Paul McCartney's first love was a beautiful actress named Jane Asher. Whatever happened to her?*—Helen Epstein, Ft. Lee, N.J.

A Jane Asher, 36, is a London stage and screen actress. Not too long ago, she married cartoonist Gerald Scarfe, with whom she has a daughter, Kate, eight and a son, Alexander, not yet one.

Q *Can it possibly be that Ingmar Bergman, the great Swedish film director, is one of the most faithful members of the fan club of the* Dallas *TV series? I heard that over the radio.*—Marjorie Walker, Sterling Heights, Mich.

A Bergman has been quoted as saying that the *Dallas* TV series "is the worst thing I have ever seen." He adds: "It is so fascinatingly bad, I try not to miss a single episode. It is bad from the point of view of logic . . . appallingly photographed, badly directed and dreadfully acted by a lot of talentless actors and actresses . . . but it is crazily fascinating."

Winston Churchill

Q *Historians agree that Winston Churchill's father, Lord Randolph Churchill, was a syphilitic. One version is that he picked up the disease while he was at Oxford. He then married Jennie Jerome, and seven months later, in November 1874, Winston was born. Since syphilis is an infectious, transmittable disease, how come Winston and his mother were not syphilisized?*—N.F., Waukesha, Wis.

A It is true that Winston Churchill's father was a syphilitic who died of the disease. When and where he contracted the malady, however, no one is sure. According to Shane Leslie, Jennie Jerome's nephew and Winston's cousin, Lord Randolph Churchill was infected by a chambermaid *after* Winston was born. Once the disease was diagnosed, Randolph no longer engaged in sex relations with his wife. One of the most detailed accounts of Randolph Churchill's affliction appears in *Churchill—Young Man in a Hurry*, 1874-1915, by Ted Morgan.

Q *How could Carlos Hank Gonzalez, mayor of Mexico City, afford to buy a $900,000 estate in New Canaan, Connecticut?*—D.T., San Angelo, Tex.

A Presumably from wise investments.

Lana Turner

Q *Has Lana Turner really had six face-lifts? How old is she anyway? And why, when she comes here, does she attract so many of the gay crowd?—V.D.K., Honolulu, Hawaii.*

A Lana Turner was born in Wallace, Idaho, on February 8, 1920. She has had at least two face-lifts. The gay crowd is extremely loyal to high-camp film stars of yesteryear, of which she is one.

Q *How did Johnny Carson of the Tonight Show beat his rap for drunken driving on the night of February 27 this year?—J.T., St. Louis, Mo.*

A Carson didn't beat the rap. He pleaded no contest to charges of drunken driving, was placed on summary probation, fined $603 and ordered to complete either a course of alcohol treatment or driver's education by next April. He also had his driver's license restricted for 90 days, permitting him to drive only to and from work.

Q *I heard a rumor that the Republicans have hired a private detective, Anthony Ulasewicz, to fly to Monaco to investigate what role Sen. Ted Kennedy played in the death of Princess Grace. Is this true?—E.C., Chula Vista, Calif.*

A No. It's a ghoulish joke, stained with sarcasm. In July 1969, less than a day after the body of Mary Jo Kopechne was extricated from a car driven by Kennedy at Chappaquiddick, Massachusetts, the Nixon White House ordered Ulasewicz to the scene. He posed as a reporter for four days, asking Kennedy embarrassing questions at various press conferences.

Q *The most powerful man in Hollywood is supposed to be someone named Julius Caesar Stein. What does he do?—Milton Jacobs, Berkeley, Calif.*

A Julius Caesar Stein, who preferred to be called Jules, died last year at age 85. Educated as a medical doctor to specialize in ophthalmology, Stein never practiced medicine. Instead, he became a band-booker in Chicago, started his own talent agency and moved to Hollywood, where he bought out Leland Hayward Inc., another talent agency. As president of the Music Corporation of America, Stein shrewdly put together an entertainment conglomerate that enriched him by an estimated $250 million. He also organized and endowed the Jules Stein Eye Institute at the UCLA Medical Center. From 1950 to 1975, Stein was one of the most powerful men in Hollywood. His protégé, Lew Wasserman, 69, has succeeded him in power and philanthropy.

Q *Two questions about the late Ingrid Bergman: (1) Was she a U.S. citizen? (2) When she made For Whom the Bell Tolls in 1943, was she carrying on with her husband, Dr. Peter Lindstrom; her co-star, Gary Cooper; and the novelist Ernest Hemingway?—Ivy C., St. George, Utah.*

A Ingrid Bergman was not a U.S. citizen. She once confided to a reporter that the making of *For Whom the Bell Tolls* was a busy and tempestuous time for her because, she said, "I had to look after my husband, Ernest, and 'Coop' as well."

Q *Over and over, I keep reading in the newspapers of the senior White House official who doesn't mind being quoted but doesn't want his name mentioned. Who is he?—T.B. Sloan, Tucson, Ariz.*

A More often than not, the publicity-shy official is one of the following: Secretary of State George Shultz; Assistant Secretary of State Nicholas A. Veliotes; or William Clark, the president's national security affairs adviser. Years ago, they all learned that it is never good policy to upstage an actor.

Q *What is the real reason NBC decided not to pick up Frank Sinatra's option after making such grand announcements in 1981 that it had signed him for a series of spectaculars?—M.D., Las Vegas, Nev.*

A One possible reason: "Sinatra—The Man and His Music," his first special for NBC under the deal, fared miserably, ranking 48 out of 65 in the Nielsen ratings. At 66, "Ole Blue Eyes" primarily attracts old-timers, which is not the audience that TV advertisers want to attract.

Cindy Williams and Bill Hudson

Q *I understand that pregnant Cindy Williams of the Laverne & Shirley TV series married a guy named Bill Hudson. Is this the same Bill Hudson who married Goldie Hawn three months before their son was born?—T.K., Laguna Hills, Calif.*

A Bill Hudson of the Hudson Brothers singing and comedy group is the same guy.

WALTER SCOTT'S
PERSONALITY PARADE®

December 12, 1982

Alfred Hitchcock

Q *Was Alfred Hitchcock, the great film director, sexually frustrated? Isn't that why he was always so obese? Didn't he try to move in on all of his leading ladies, starting with Madeleine Carroll and ending with Tippi Hedren?—Carla L., Mesa, Ariz.*

A Alfred Hitchcock (1899-1980) was a talented, nervous, basically shy man. There is much evidence that, despite a long marriage with all the exterior trappings of success, Hitchcock lived a life of sexual frustration. Surely he had a fixation on tall, cool, beautiful blondes like Carroll, Hedren, Ingrid Bergman, Grace Kelly, Joan Fontaine, Doris Day and Vera Miles. He found them terribly attractive but used a fatherly approach in directing them. Emotional frustration and sexual repression often lead to obesity, and this may have been true in Hitchcock's case. Whenever he lost off-set control of an actress whose life he sought to dominate—as with Bergman, Miles and Hedren, the latter two of whom he had under personal contract—he'd overeat to compensate for his frustration. In many ways, "Hitch" was a complicated man with a perverse sense of humor who suffered from a Svengali complex.

Q *I'm very much interested in Anthony Andrews, the British actor who starred in the TV series The Pallisers, Danger UXB and Brideshead Revisited. I saw them all on public TV. Do you have any info on Andrews—especially his marital status, or is he gay like so many other British actors?—Wilma G., Irvine, Calif.*

A Anthony Andrews, 34, is one of five children. His father was a musical director for the British Broadcasting Corp.; his mother was a dancer. Andrews was five when his father died. On leaving school—the Royal Masonic in Hertfordshire, where he flunked most of his courses—he became a food caterer, then a chicken salesman. In 1971, he married Georgina Simpson, the potential heiress to a $50 million fortune. Her father owns Simpson's, a fashionable London clothing store. The couple have two children, Joshua, ten, and Jessica, eight. They live in a five-bedroom house in Wimbledon and rent a home in Los Angeles. Andrews definitely is not gay—in fact, he's been rumored to be most friendly with Britain's Princess Anne.

Q *What's your unvarnished opinion of Nancy Reagan? Can you give it?—Lorraine T., Evanston, Ill.*

A The First Lady is a perceptive, wholesomely sexy, intelligent woman, far more beautiful off-camera than on. She simply got in with a social group some of whose members more enjoy the power and privileges of money than the rewards of the life of the mind. Mrs. Reagan is now compensating by working for several worthy social causes.

Q *How many times has film director John Huston been married? "Who's Who" says five. My wife says six and that the sixth is an Indian actress named Zoë. A rather large bet is at stake. Can you help us out?—Victor C., Las Vegas, Nev.*

A Huston, 76, has legally been married five times. The actress your wife refers to is Zoë Sallis, 43, who lives in London with her 20-year-old son, Danny. Both are mentioned briefly in Huston's memoirs, *An Open Book*, which turns out to be not so open. Sallis, who worked in Huston's film *The Bible*, says she lived with him in Mexico two decades ago, but there is no legal evidence that they were married. Danny Sallis insists, however, that Huston is his father. Earlier this year, when *Annie*, the musical film directed by Huston, had its London premiere, Zoë and Danny attended.

Q *When Ronald Reagan was elected California's governor, his rich friends bought him a mansion outside Sacramento. Now I believe they bought him a presidential yacht, the Sequoia, which President Carter had sold because it was too rich for his blood. True?—F.D., Silver Spring, Md.*

A Not exactly. Reagan was allowed to use the California mansion, as he is allowed to use the *Sequoia*, but he owns neither of them. In May 1981, the presidential Yacht Trust purchased the *Sequoia* for $1,065,000 from contributions made by wealthy individuals and patriotic corporations. As of this writing, Reagan has yet to use the yacht, largely because it would foul up the image he seeks to project: a president of all the people and not favoring the rich, who are accustomed to yachts.

APIS / Globe

Princess Grace and Princess Caroline

Q *Where was Princess Caroline when she learned of the serious auto accident of her mother, Princess Grace?—V.B. Purcell, Jacksonville, Fla.*

A Princess Caroline was registered at that time at Forest Mere, a $500-per-week fat farm in Hampshire, England. She was trying to shed some of the weight she had gained on a vacation to Maui with the Argentine tennis star Guillermo Vilas.

Noël Coward

Oscar Wilde

Q *Noël Coward, Sommerset Maugham, Marcel Proust, André Gide, Jean Cocteau and Oscar Wilde: Which of these famous literary figures were heterosexuals?—David W., Sunnyvale, Calif.*

A None. They were all homosexuals of great talent.

Q *I was reading an old movie magazine from 1970 and noted that Frank Sinatra was dating Hope Lange, Diahann Carroll was dating David Frost, Sidney Poitier was dating Joanna Shimkus, Shirley MacLaine was dating Sander Vanocur and Jacqueline Bisset was dating Michael Sarrazin. Did any of these romances last?—Billie Castle, Dallas, Tex.*

A Only one, the romance between actor-director Sidney Poitier and the Canadian actress Joanna Shimkus, which resulted in a happy marriage

Sidney Poitier and Joanna Shimkus

Q *First, what is anorexia? Second, why should a young woman like Princess Diana, who has everything to live for, come down with such a disease? Is it related to cancer, or is she just having a nervous breakdown?—Lily J., Alexandria, Va.*

A Anorexia is the loss or absence of appetite for food. It is not a form of cancer, and Princess Diana is not suffering from it. She is 21, a new mother and not yet acclimated to life in the goldfish bowl. Her mother-in-law, the queen, has asked the British press to go easy on her until she learns how to lead her private life in public—the penalty for marrying into the royal family. Princess Di is not having a nervous breakdown, but she is uptight about being followed by reporters and photographers and reportedly has lost 14 pounds since her marriage.

Q *Now that General and Mrs. Eisenhower and Kay Summersby have all passed on, will we ever learn the truth about the affair between Eisenhower and Summersby, his driver in World War II? What is the true story—or, more accurately, your version of the true story?—Helen L., Midland, Tex.*

A From all accounts, Eisenhower was infatuated with Summersby, his beautiful Irish driver. Like all infatuations, his eventually wore thin. In December 1942, however, Ike tried to have the War Department award Kay the Legion of Merit. General Marshall, his superior, diplomatically scotched the request on the grounds that she was not in the military service. Early in 1944, when Ike tried to get Kay an officer's commission in the Women's Army Corps, Marshall—through the lower echelons—noted that she was a British citizen, not American. Eventually, Kay managed to wangle a commission, but by then Marshall was convinced that the romance had cooled, as Ike was pressuring to have Mamie sent overseas to join him.

The truth about the romance is that, at the beginning, Ike was the lover in pursuit. By war's end, the reverse was true, with Kay trying desperately but unsuccessfully to hold on. Ike decided in 1945, however, that he had too much to lose—his family, reputation, career and future—and he gave Kay up.

Q *How much did it cost the actress Jane Fonda to get her husband elected to the California State Assembly?—Tim Stewart, Mesa, Ariz.*

A About $840,000 in contributions and loans.

Q *I don't know if it's true, but I've been told that a high official of the Reagan administration was kidnapped as a baby and raised by a colony of domestic giraffes in Africa. If true, please identify him.—V.J., Oakland, Calif.*

A The official is David Gergen, a former speechwriter for Richard Nixon who is now assistant to the president for communications. Gergen, however, was never raised by giraffes in Africa; he was reared by humans in Durham, North Carolina, where he grew to be six-feet-six. It is because of his height and lope that Howell Raines of *The New York Times* described him in a 1981 article as a man who looks as if he might have been kidnapped in his youth by kindly giraffes who reared him to adulthood.

Q *Who are Hollywood's longest-married couples?—Kathy Madjerich, Monroeville, Pa.*

A Ray and Gwendolyn Bolger have been married 53 years; Pat and Eloise O'Brien, 51 years; Ray and Muriel Milland, 50 years; Bob and Dolores Hope, nearly 49 years; Robert and Dorothy Mitchum, 42 years; Charlton and Lydia Heston, 38 years; Ricardo and Georgiana Montalban, 38 years.

Gwendolyn and Ray Bolger

Ted Kennedy

Q *What do you think are the real reasons behind Sen. Ted Kennedy taking himself out of the 1984 presidential race?—W. Lerner, Terre Haute, Ind.*

A The senator's three children—Kara, 22, Teddy Jr., 21, and Patrick, 15—need him more than he needs the presidency, especially at this time, when he and their mother have filed for divorce. Another reason is that many voters consider Kennedy "unelectable" in 1984 because of Chappaquiddick, his liberalism, his "rich-kid" image, his divorce and his religion. By 1988, Kennedy will be 56 and will probably have remarried. His children will be on their own. He will have altered his image and will stand a better chance of winning the presidency, if he decides that is what he most wants in life.

Q *After 24 years, is it all over between Robert Redford and his wife, Lola?—R.T., Provo, Utah.*

A No, their marriage is in good shape, despite rumors to the contrary.

Q *Many Germans say the late Albert Speer, Hitler's architect, was a clever, diabolical Nazi who tricked the U.S. into freeing him after 20 years in jail. Is that true?—Hans Ehrlich, Milwaukee, Wis.*

A It's probably true. Speer was a cunning Nazi. Once Hitler committed suicide, Speer decided to fashion for himself the role of a mere apolitical technocrat in the Hitler machine, a decent expert who knew relatively little about Nazi atrocities. In fact, he was involved in the thick of them and probably should have been hanged. Best source is *Albert Speer—The End of the Myth,* by Matthais Schmidt (Scherze-Verlag, Berne and Munich).

Q *How much money did Hollywood movie stars lose on the DeLorean car? Also, how can anyone open a car with gull doors in a normal-size garage?—T.G., Wilmington, Del.*

Sammy Davis Jr.

A Comedian Johnny Carson, a friend of DeLorean, reportedly bought 250,000 shares in the DeLorean Motor Co. at $2 each. Sammy Davis, Jr., bought 75,000 shares at the same price. DeLorean planned to sell the stock to the public at $12.50 a share, but the plan fell through. To open a car with gull-wing doors, one needs a spacious garage

Q *I understand that Vicki Morgan—the mistress of the late Alfred Bloomingdale, who reportedly was a sadist—is writing a book that the White House is trying to kill because it is liberally sprinkled with references to Nancy and Ronald Reagan. Is this correct?—I.P., Pittsburgh, Pa.*

A Vicki Morgan may be writing or contemplates writing her memoirs, but the White House is exerting absolutely no pressure on her. Morgan, however, is finding great difficulty in maintaining the lifestyle to which Alfred Bloomingdale accustomed her. A hefty advance on a possible book may help to keep her financially afloat.

Q *Though her husband, Jules Dassin, is Jewish, Melina Mercouri, the star of* Never On Sunday, *favors the Palestine Liberation Organization. Won't this ruin her marriage?—R.K., Newark, N.H.*

A Melina Mercouri, the Greek minister of culture and film star, doesn't favor the PLO over the Israelis. She feels strongly, however, that the Palestinians are entitled to a homeland. Her marriage is not endangered because of her independent judgments.

Q *I read that Roscoe Hillenkoetter, the first director of our Central Intelligence Agency, died at age 85 in Weekawken, New Jersey I've never heard of this guy. Have you?—Mark Williamson, Renton, Wash.*

A Vice Adm. Roscoe H. Hillenkoetter was President Truman's choice to be our first CIA director.

A graduate of the U.S. Naval Academy, Class of '20, he served as a naval attaché in Spain and Portugal before being sent to Vichy France, where, as naval attaché, he secretly worked with the French underground. After World War II, he was given command of the battleship *Missouri,* which he led on a series of show-the-flag trips.

On May 1, 1947, Truman appointed him head of the newly organized CIA. Three years later, when the Korean war erupted so unexpectedly, the Senate Appropriations Committee asked Hillenkoetter why the U.S. had been caught off-guard. Not long after this grilling, Hillenkoetter asked Truman to return him to sea duty, which Truman did. Hillenkoetter retired in 1957 and landed a job as chief executive officer of the American Banner Lines.

Lana Turner

Q *Lana Turner says she's been celibate since 1969, or is it '79? Can this possibly be true, or is it just publicity?—Kay S., Baltimore, Md.*

A Her former male secretary, who's shared her company, says it's nonsense or a device to raise her self-esteem.

Harrison Ford and Melissa Mathison

Q *Why does actor Harrison Ford of Star Wars, Raiders of the Lost Ark, Blade Runner and other motion pictures keep such a low profile? How old is he? Is he married? Does he have any kids?—Sue Reid, Charleston, S.C.*

A Harrison Ford, 40, married his childhood sweetheart, Mary, and has two sons: Benjamin, 15, and Willard, 13. For four years, he has been living with scriptwriter Melissa Mathison, who penned the fabulously successful films *The Black Stallion* and *E.T.* Ford prefers anonymity to fame, can carry on in public without being recognized

Q *Pepperdine University of Malibu, California, plans to give Nancy Reagan an honorary doctor of laws degree on May 1. What is the degree for—excellence in surfing?—Arthur Little, Torrance, Calif.*

A Mrs. Reagan will receive the honorary doctorate for "distinguished public service on behalf of charitable causes." Her husband received the same sort of Pepperdine honorary degree in 1970. Neither he nor the First Lady excels in surfing.

Q *Daphne du Maurier, who wrote such wonderful novels as Rebecca, My Cousin Rachel and Frenchman's Creek, seems to have disappeared. What's happened to her?—Lois Walker, Fredericks-*

burg, Va.

A Dame Daphne du Maurier, 75, at this writing lives in Cornwall, England. Her literary career is at an end, reportedly owing to mental illness.

Q *Is it true that Gen. Douglas MacArthur hated Gen. George Marshall and Gen. Dwight Eisenhower and did everything to hamstring their miliary careers?— E.K., West Point, N.Y.*

A MacArthur resented Marshall's role on the general staff of the American Expeditionary Force in France in World War I. When MacArthur became U.S. Army chief of staff (1930-35), he ordered Marshall to take over the Illinois National Guard Division in 1933 and denied him promotion to brigadier general. In 1939, when Marshall himself became chief of staff, he gave no indication that MacArthur had ever treated him shabbily and went out of his way to treat the general with great courtesy and fairness—which was not easy, since MacArthur, though brilliant, was also pompous, cocky, vainglorious, demanding and publicity-hungry. MacArthur was envious of Eisenhower, who had served under him in Washington and the Philippines, but he never voiced as much resentment of Ike as he did of General Marshall.

Q *Why does Dan Rather of CBS have a higher rating than Roger Mudd and Tom Brokaw of NBC and Frank Reynolds and Peter Jennings of ABC? All three networks basically offer the same nightly news.—Charlene Carver, N. Las Vegas, Nev.*

A Rather, who inherited the anchorman spot from Walter Cronkite, obviously generates more charisma and rapport than his competitors. Another factor is the popularity of local newscasts, which precede the network news. Generally, viewers don't like to switch channels. CBS affiliates may produce better local newscasts than their rivals.

Q *Was Grace Kelly's marriage to Prince Rainier of Monaco a love marriage or an arranged marriage? I understand that it was arranged—designed to attract American millionaires to Monaco—and that Grace's true love was actor Ray Milland, while Rainier's true love was French actress Gisele Pascal. I also understand that Rainier had the choice of marrying Marilyn Monroe or Grace and chose Grace because she projects a more sedate image.*

Grace Kelly

Your comment, please, as to the truth of the above.—G.E., Bartlesville, Okla.

Prince Rainier

A Grace Kelly and Ray Milland fell in love in 1953 during the production of *Dial M for Murder.* But Milland was married, and Grace did not want to break up the marriage or marry a man who'd been divorced. In the 1950s, Prince Rainier's steady girlfriend was Gisele Pascal, an actress four years his senior whose parents ran a vegetable and fruit stand in Nice. She was a divorcée, however, making her ineligible for marriage to Rainier.

In 1953, Aristotle Onassis purchased large shares of stock in the Société des Bains de Mer et Cercle des Étrangers, which owned the leading gambling casino in Monte Carlo. He hired George Schlee, a friend of Greta Garbo, to attract socially prominent American "high-rollers" to Monaco. Schlee sought the advice of the publishing magnate Gardner Cowles, who suggested that Rainier marry Marilyn Monroe. Cowles arranged a meeting at his Connecticut farm between Marilyn, Schlee and himself. Marilyn was receptive to the idea of marrying a prince but never got to meet Rainier. He proposed to Grace after a three-day courtship in Philadelphia, and she accepted. Their marriage would be more accurately described as "arranged."

Richard Chamberlain

Q *Richard Chamberlain, star of the Dr. Kildare TV series and the Shogun and Thorn Birds mini-series, seems to be a recluse. I have never seen him linked romantically with any female. Can you tell us anything succinct about him?—Eugenia Allen, Kansas City, Kan.*

A George Richard Chamberlain is regarded as an immensely talented actor both in this country and in England. He was born in Los Angeles on March 31, 1935, educated at Beverly Hills High School and Pomona College. Originally he wanted to become a painter but abandoned that as "too lonely a profession" and turned to acting. In the 1960s, he starred for five years in the top-rated *Dr. Kildare* TV series, then departed for England and serious stage work. His *Hamlet* in London was declared superb, and he was cast in many films. At this writing, Chamberlain has been neither married nor coupled seriously with any female. He has an apartment in London and a home in Beverly Hills but shuns the Hollywood social game. He is six-feet-one, weighs 170 pounds, has blue eyes, brown hair, served 16 months in Korea as a U.S. Army clerk.

Q *Luciano Pavarotti vacationed here with a young chick named Madelyn Renee. Is she his daughter, his wife or what?—D.D., Honolulu, Hawaii.*

A Renee, 27, is a soprano who's been the Italian opera star's protégée for five years. She serves as a secretary-friend and traveling companion too.

Q *Was Ronald Reagan ever operated on for cancer?—Mary Ellen Woods, Baltimore, Md.*

A When Reagan was governor of California, the late Dr. Richard Barton of Los Angeles removed an inconsequential malignant growth from his lip.

Q *Who was the first black woman elected to the U.S. Congress, and whatever became of her?—Rachel Lawrence, Spartanburg, S.C.*

A Shirley Chisholm, 58, a Democrat from Brooklyn, New York, was the first black woman elected to Congress and the first to try for the presidency. Chisholm was elected to the House of Representatives in 1968, served seven terms, then retired. At this writing, she teaches politics at Mount Holyoke College in South Hadley, Massachusetts.

Q *I read in the papers and heard on the radio that the comic Groucho Marx was a lecherous old man who made his lady manager, Erin Fleming, walk about in the nude, for which he left her $150,000 in his will. How much of this is accurate, or is it all made up to sell papers?—F.L., Las Vegas, Nev.*

A The late Groucho Marx was a man immoderately given to sexual indulgence. He died in 1977 at 86, having been impotent for the last six years of his life. At times, he was not only lecherous but mean, irascible, cantankerous and demanding as well. Erin Fleming, 50

The Marx Brothers

years his junior, occasionally traipsed about his home in the nude, but she also looked after him in his old age and motivated him to work and take an interest in life. He bequeathed to her $150,000 and a half-interest in one of his companies, a bequest later opposed in court by his children, Arthur, 61, Miriam, 55, and Melinda, 36.

Nikita Krushchev

Joseph Stalin

Q *Russian refugees tell me that of Joseph Stalin, Nikita Khrushchev and Leonid Brezhnev, the Russian people cared most for Khrushchev. Is this acknowledged by Kremlinologists? And if so, why was Khrushchev thrown out of office, reduced*

Leonid Brezhnev

to a nonperson and hardly mentioned in the Soviet encyclopedia?— Shirley Adams, Cambridge, Mass.

A After Khrushchev succeeded Stalin in 1953, he diplomatically criticized the homicidal aspects of Stalin's dictatorship. He also began releasing political prisoners from Soviet labor camps. Roy Medvedev, a Soviet historian whose books may be published abroad but not in the USSR, maintains that Khrushchev's denunciation of Stalin endeared him to the relatives of millions who'd been exiled, imprisoned and executed on Stalin's orders. Khrushchev's rivals accused him of goofing in the 1962 Cuban missile crisis and removed him from office in 1964, downgrading his reputation and confining him to his dacha outside Moscow. A bold, feisty, impetuous man, Khrushchev was silenced by his successors because he knew too much about their past and was apt to talk. Yuri Andropov, current Soviet leader, was a Khrushchev disciple, however, and may yet rehabilitate the old man's reputation.

Reagan and Neal

Q *Did Ronald Reagan and Patricia Neal ever have a fling? Didn't they commiserate with each other when they starred in* The Hasty Heart?—*Louella T.Y., Nashville, Tenn.*

A The Hasty Heart *was filmed in England in 1949. For the length of the production, Reagan and Neal occupied adjoining suites in London's Savoy Hotel. The two had worked together in the film* John Loves Mary, *so they already knew each other. It was during* The Hasty Heart, *however, that they became, in Reagan's words, "fast friends." They commiserated on the abysmal English climate and undoubtedly were drawn together because of their mutual unhappiness. At the time, both Reagan's marriage to Jane Wyman and Neal's love affair with Gary Cooper had soured.*

Q *Armand Hammer, chief of Occidental Petroleum—did he build a swimming pool in Buckingham Palace for Prince Charles and Princess Di as a wedding gift?— Bernadette Davis, Warren, Mich.*

A No. Prince Charles and Princess Di occupy a nine-room apartment in London's Kensington Palace, which has no swimming pool. At their country home in Gloucestershire, however, they do have a swimming pool that was built last summer as a wedding gift from the British army.

Louis Armstrong

Q *Is it true, as Lena Horne remembers, that when she, Ethel Waters, Louis Armstrong and Duke Ellington were making* Cabin in the Sky *at MGM in 1943, they were banned from the commissary because they were black? Did Louis B. Mayer, head of the studio, have in effect a policy of such blatant racial segregation?—G.L., Watts, Calif.*

Duke Ellington

A At lunch on their first day of shooting, the black cast members of *Cabin in the Sky* were told by Frances Edwards, the lady in charge of the MGM commissary, that they were not permitted to eat at the tables in the main dining room but could eat at the counter. Understandably indignant, they protested loudly. Louis B. Mayer, en route to the commissary, heard their protestations. He quickly invited the black performers to lunch with him in his private dining room and promised that the main dining room would no longer be off-limits to anyone working at the studio. He then phoned his brother Gerry, who was studio manager and had invoked the policy. Mayer read Gerry the riot act. From that day on, no performer of any race was banned from a table in the MGM dining room.

Q *Has every Republican president in this century been a member of California's Bohemian Grove cult? Do members really gather in forest groves to prance about in the nude and celebrate pagan rituals? It all sound too fantastic to be true.—R.C.M., Boston, Mass.*

A Bohemian Grove is the name of a 2,700-acre plot of land 65 miles north of San Francisco owned by the Bohemian Club. Every Republican president in this century except Warren G. Harding has been a member of this all-male club, which is composed mostly—but not exclusively—of leading businessmen. Members do not prance about in the nude or perform pagan rituals. They do, however, participate in humorous skits, listen to serious lectures, and engage in the camaraderie stimulated by good food, wine and spirits.

Q *Why is Larry Speakes still referred to as President Reagan's deputy press secretary? Does this mean that Jim Brady still holds the position of press secretary? Is Brady still on full salary?—John R. Eichholtz, Fresno, Calif.*

A James Brady still carries the title of press secretary and remains on full salary of $69,800 a year. The removal of his title, it is felt, might prove detrimental to his recovery from brain wounds he suffered on March 30, 1981, during John Hinckley's attempted assassination of President Reagan. Larry Speakes, who was hired by Brady, is fully content with his title of deputy press secretary. He is recognized as Reagan's principal spokesman.

Q *Why do actresses continue to date Burt Reynolds when they know what he's done to Dinah Shore, Sally Field, Dolly Parton, Tammy Wynette, Loni Anderson and the rest?—Marsha K., Irving, Tex.*

Burt Reynolds

A Hope for matrimony springs eternal in the female breast. That's one reason. A second is that dating Reynolds affords an actress maximum exposure—especially in the news media.

Ronald Reagan

Q *I know there is a tremendously large press corps in Washington. Yet it seems to be the same small group of White House correspondents President Reagan calls upon. There must be hundreds who never get to ask a question. Has Helen Thomas of UPI been specially designated to open and close the press conferences? Is any special system used to pick the others?—Lee Hessel, St. Louis, Mo.*

A Helen Thomas is the senior wire service correspondent covering the White House. As such, she is by custom and tradition the first or second correspondent called upon by the president and the one who closes the press conference by calling out, "Thank you, Mr. President." There is no special system or order in which the president acknowledges the others after he first calls upon the two correspondents who represent United Press International and the Associated Press.

Q *I see that actress Patricia Neal lost her husband to her best friend after 30 years of marriage. Who was her best friend, and has she married Pat's ex-husband, writer Roald Dahl?—Kimberly P., San Fernando, Calif.*

Patricia Neal

A Pat Neal's "best friend" has been reported to be Felicity Crosland, a British divorcée who at this writing has not yet married Roald Dahl, 67.

Q *What are Luci Johnson Nugent and Pat Nugent doing now? Has either remarried? Who has custody of the children?—Anne K., Sacramento, Calif.*

A Luci Johnson, 36, the late President Lyndon Johnson's younger daughter, and Patrick Nugent, 40, were divorced in 1979 after 13 years of marriage. Luci has custody of their four children. Nugent has remarried, to the former Betty Bailey. They reside in Austin, Texas, as does Luci Johnson, who last month announced her engagement to Ian Turpin, 38, an English banker living on Grand Cayman, one of the Cayman islands in the Caribbean. Patrick Nugent is executive director of the Association of Texas Intrastate Natural Gas Pipelines.

Lorne Greene

Q *Canadians Rich Little, Lorne Greene, Anne Murray, Christopher Plummer and Robert Goulet have made millions in the U.S. Have any become U.S. citizens?— William Buck, Honolulu, Hawaii.*

A Goulet, born in Massachusetts, is a U.S. citizen. The others remain Canadian citizens.

Q *In the history of the U.S., has any congressman other than Rep. Gerry Studds of Massachusetts ever had the courage to stand up in Congress and announce to the world that he was a homosexual?—E.M., Detroit, Mich.*

A Studds (D., Mass.) and Rep. Daniel Crane (R., Ill.) have the dubious distinction of being the first two members of the House of Representatives to appear on the floor and acknowledge their improper sexual conduct involving congressional pages. The House ethics committee revealed this summer that Studds "engaged in a sexual relationship in 1973 with a 17-year-old male page (who may have been 16 when the relationship began) and made sexual advances in 1973 to two other male pages, one who was 16 or 17 years old at the time, the other 17 years old." At the same time, the committee revealed that Crane "engaged in a sexual relationship with a 17-year-old female page in 1980." Censured by their colleagues, both men publicly admitted this misconduct, and Crane apologized.

Q *Is it true that Henry Kissinger asked friends and associates not to cooperate with Seymour Hersh when Hersh was preparing his book* The Price of Power—Kissinger in the Nixon White House?—J.T., Compton, Calif.*

A Kissinger himself refused to be interviewed by Hersh, as did several of his friends, who told Hersh of Kissinger's request.

Henry Kissinger

Betty Grable

Q *A question about the marriage of actress Betty Grable and trumpeter Harry James. Since they were divorced and are both deceased, can you possibly tell if it was true that Harry used to slug Betty regularly?—A.T., Watts, Calif.*

A Not true. Betty Grable, one of the pinup beauties of World War II, and Harry James were married from 1943 to 1965. For the most part, their marriage was a happy one. Once in 1950, however, James reportedly accused Grable of fooling around with her leading man, Dan Dailey. In the altercation that followed, she wound up with a black eye.

Q *After Ferdinand Marcos goes, who takes over the Philippines—his wife or the army?—A.S., San Francisco, Calif.*

Imelda Marcos

A Possibly both. Imelda Marcos gets on very well with Gen. Fabian Ver, chief of staff of the armed forces, head of the Philippines' national intelligence agency and a relative of her husband. There is a large segment of the population, however, that resents Imelda Marcos' extravagant lifestyle and may lead in rejecting her as leader of the Philippines.

Q *Please unravel the ball of wax concerning Harry Morgan, the actor who played Colonel Potter, the commanding officer in M*A*S*H.—W. Thomas, Washington, D.C.*

A Harry Morgan, born in Detroit on April 10, 1915, and christened Harry Bratsburg, is self-admittedly one of the luckiest character actors in show business. A child of the Depression, he dropped out of the University of Chicago as a pre-law student and sold office equipment in Washington, D.C. Later, Day Tuttle, the director-owner of the summer stock theater in Mt. Kisco, New York, gave him parts in *The Virginian* and *The Petrified Forest.*"Morgan subsequently moved to New York, became a protégé of sorts of the late actress Frances Farmer and worked in many Broadway dramas. He and his wife, Eileen, hit Hollywood in the 1940s, and Morgan landed a contract with 20th Century-Fox. Over the years, he has appeared in more than 70 films and several successful, residual-paying TV series—*December Bride, Pete and Gladys, Dragnet, The Richard Boone Show* and, of course, *M*A*S*H.* Happily married for 45 years, Morgan is the father of four sons and the grandfather of seven. He owns homes in Los Angeles and Santa Rosa, California, is widely respected in the profession for his talent, modesty and clean living.

Q *Having read Autobiography of a Spy by Mary Bancroft, am I safe in assuming that Allen Dulles, former chief of our CIA,, indulged in affairs with his female agents?— N.F., Austin, Tex.*

Allen Dulles

A You are safe in assuming that in World War II, when Dulles headed our intelligence service in Switzerland, he had an affair with Mary Bancroft.

Q *How much money, if any, does Jerry Lewis make on the telethons he hosts every Labor Day?—Jack Bonner, Fairless Hills, Pa.*

A Comedian Lewis earns nothing personally from his Muscular Dystrophy Association telethons, which have raised more than $300 million in 18 years.

Ava Gardner and Frank Sinatra

Q *I believe it was in 1939 that Ava Gardner and Frank Sinatra had a love child, a son they put up for adoption because they weren't married. Where is their son today?—K.S., Ft. Lauderdale, Fla.*

A Not a word of truth in your premise or question. Frank Sinatra hadn't heard of Ava Gardner in 1939. In that year, he was married to the former Nancy Barbato, who divorced him in 1951 after bearing him three children, Nancy, Frank Jr., and Christina. Despite three marriages—to Mickey Rooney (1942-43), Artie Shaw (1945-46) and Frank Sinatra (1951-57)—Ava Gardner regretfully remained childless—in and out of wedlock.

Q *Is it true that among the upper classes in London, Princess Di is regarded as little more than a healthy, attractive brood mare whose primary job is to propagate—after which, Prince Charles, like so many of his predecessors, will dilly-dally with a series of mistresses?—R.R., Alexandria, Va.*

A Princess Di has already fulfilled her prime purpose in producing a son, Prince William, next in line to his father as heir to the British throne. Di is expected to give birth to more children, who eventually will be charged with carrying out the manifold duties of the royal family. The British people love and admire Di and regard her not as a brood mare but as a role model to emulate in fashion, behavior and taste. As for Prince Charles following in the footsteps of his wayward predecessors, there is no assurance at this time that he will or will not.

WALTER SCOTT'S
PERSONALITY PARADE®

December 25, 1983

Rod Stewart

Q *Has rock singer Rod Stewart bounced his wife, Alana, for a beautiful Danish model named Christina Meyers? I understand that Rod wants to live and raise their two kids in England, but Alana wants to live and rise them in Hollywood. What's the score?—Lana Crowley, Los Angeles, Calif.*

A One needs a computer to keep track of Stewart and his romances. The Rod Stewart Organization recently booked leggy model Christina Meyers on the same London-to-New York Concorde flight as the rock singer. Moreover, Stewart prefers to reside in his million-dollar mansion in Penn, Buckinghamshire, than anywhere in Los Angeles. Insiders say the Rod-Alana marriage is not for long.

Q *Aren't Jennifer Beals of Flashdance and John F. Kennedy, Jr., son of the late president, having a secret romance? Didn't he date her when he was a student at Brown and she at Yale?—Tara R., Baltimore, Md.*

John F. Kennedy, Jr.

A Beals and Kennedy have never met. He is traveling in India, and she is attending classes at Yale.

Q *I have one question, which I'd like you to answer truthfully if you can. Who, in your opinion, controls Ronald Reagan?—Ron J., Washington, D.C.*

A Ever since Ronald Reagan was elected governor of California in 1966, his detractors have pictured him as a puppet tied to the manipulative strings of such multimillionaires as Holmes Tuttle, the California Ford car dealer; the late "Cy" Rubel, head of Union Oil; Henry Salvatori, the geologist who founded Western Geophysical; Leonard Firestone of the rubber company; the late Taft Schreiber, Reagan's agent at MCA; Justin Dart of Dart & Kraft; William French Smith, Reagan's lawyer; Earle Jorgensen of Jorgensen steel; and others of that wealthy stripe. As president, Reagan has been rumored at various times as being controlled by Ed Meese, Michael Deaver and William Clark—three former members of his gubernatorial staff—and by James Baker III, former campaign manager for Gerald Ford and George Bush.

The truth is that no one controls Ronald Reagan but Ronald Reagan. His wife, Nancy, can influence him greatly in his appointment of close advisers, because she is an instinctively shrewd judge of people, and he trusts her judgment in that department. But it is he who calls the shots, sets the philosophy and makes the major decisions in his administration.

Q *Of all the women in pro tennis, who are the most beautiful and glamorous? Please run their photos.—Linda Morton, Hilton Head, S.C.*

A Beauty lies in the eye of the beholder. Two of the most attractive young women on the pro circuit are Andrea Temesvari, 17, of Budapest and Carling Bassett, 16, of Toronto.

Q *What is the real family name of Martin Sheen, the Hollywood star? Isn't it the same as mine?—Linda Estevez, San Antonio, Tex.*

A Martin Sheen's original name was Ramon Estevez. His father was Spanish-born and his mother, who died when he was 11, was of Irish descent. Sheen, 43, and his wife Janet have been married 22 years and live in Malibu, California, with their daughter, Renee, and sons Emilio, Ramon and Carlos.

Q *Is it a fact that, in World War II, General Eisenhower (in charge of U.S. troops) and General Montgomery (in charge of British troops) tried to get each other fired because they were jealous of one another?—H.M., Eugene, Ore.*

A That is not a fact. Eisenhower was not jealous of Field Marshal Montgomery, but Montgomery—hero of the British Eighth Army's magnificent triumph in North Africa—was surely jealous of Eisenhower. Montgomery was so pathologically arrogant, so insufferably conceited, so complaining, that even some of his fellow British officers at the Supreme Allied Headquarters suggested his dismissal from Operation Overlord, the Allied invasion of Europe.

In April 1943, after a long talk with Eisenhower, Montgomery wrote to Gen. Sir Frank Simpson, an old friend in the British War Office, describing Ike as "a nice chap and probably quite good in the political line. But his knowledge of how to make war or how to fight battles is definitely nil. He must be kept right away from that sort of thing—otherwise we shall lose the war." Eisenhower's tolerance of Montgomery's offers and demands to revise the strategy of Overlord and head its command was saintly, under the circumstances.

Dwight Eisenhower

WALTER SCOTT'S
PERSONALITY PARADE®

January 15, 1984

Mary Tyler Moore and Dr. Robert Levine

Q *When Mary Tyler Moore, 46, married Dr. Robert Levine, 30, her fans said that their age difference shouldn't count, that Mary should grab at happiness because she'd known so many tragedies. Mary Tyler Moore is said to be worth $25 million. She was married to Grant Tinker, now head of NBC, for 17 years. She's had a great acting career. She won an Oscar nomination for Ordinary People. What tragedies has she known?—Christy Davis, Brooklyn, N.Y.*

A Mary Tyler Moore (born in Brooklyn on December 29, 1937) is a diabetic. She got married two months after graduating from Immaculate Heart High School and later gave birth to a son, Richard Meeker, Jr. Her first marriage foundered, and Richard—her only child—accidentally shot himself to death in October 1980 at age 24. In 1978, her sister, Elizabeth Ann, died of a drug overdose at age 21. Despite her career success and her marriage of 17 years to Grant Tinker, life hasn't always been wine and roses for Mary Tyler Moore

Q *Is Frank Sinatra the new owner of the Golden Nugget in Las Vegas?—G.A.M., Richmond, Va.*

A He is not. He has, however, signed a three-year, multimillion-dollar performance contract with the Golden Nugget, which includes an option to buy 150,000 shares of Golden Nugget stock at a special price. There is a Golden Nugget casino in Atlantic City, New Jersey, as well as one in Las Vegas.

Q *Whose decision was it to prevent reporters from landing with our armed forces in the invasion of Grenada? No one, it seems, wants to take credit for this move. Why was it made in the first place?—H.H., Culver City, Calif.*

A The decision was made by Gen. John W. Vessey Jr., chairman of the joint chiefs of staff. It was OK'd by President Reagan, the commander in chief, and by Caspar Weinberger, the secretary of defense. Weinberger explained that the government's thoughtful consideration of the reporters' safety, in addition to the need for secrecy, motivated the decision. Possibly more truthful is the explanation of a presidential aide and a member of the National Security Council, who said reporters were banned from the first landings on Grenada because the military had encountered too many problems with the press in Vietnam. "Mr. President," General Vessey is quoted as having said to Reagan, "if I do this, I'm not taking the press with me."

Jill St. John

Q *Can you tell me anything about Jill St. John, who at various times has been paired with Frank Sinatra, Robert Wagner, Henry Kissinger and David Frost? I know she's an actress on the TV program Emerald Point N.A.S., but has she ever acted in a really good picture?—Ann Bigelow, Aspen, Colo.*

A Jill St. John (born Jill Oppenheim in Los Angeles on August 19, 1940) began her show-business career at age four and has been acting on and off ever since. She has been married three times: to Neil Dubin in 1957, Lance Reventlow in 1960 and Jack Jones in 1967. Reventlow, the only child of Barbara Hutton, heiress to the Woolworth fortune, died in a plane crash. St. John lives in Aspen, where she has a successful handknit sweater business. Over the years, she has dated some prominent men—among them widower Robert Wagner—but she has yet to act in a truly memorable picture or to take a fourth husband.

Q *Joan Baez, Willie Nelson, Bob Dylan, Johnny Cash and most of the top guitarists supposedly have a special, secret guitar-maker in Italy who makes their acoustic guitars. Can you identify this gentleman, give his address and tell how much he charges?—Tawny Wells, Detroit, Mich.*

A Those musicians use acoustic guitars crafted by C. F. Martin & Co. of Nazareth, Pennsylvania. Founded in New York City 150 years ago by Christian Frederick Martin, a German immigrant, the family business is today run by his great-grandson, C. F. Martin III, age 89. A new Martin guitar sells for $1,200 and up, vintage models for much more.

Q *Broadcast journalists are so highly paid that one wonders if print journalists, like William Safire and Ellen Goodman, are equally well paid.—Elaine Rafferty, Eau Claire, Wis.*

A Broadcast journalists—particularly TV anchormen like Dan Rather, Tom Brokaw and Peter Jennings—are the highest paid in the business. Print journalists, even the most celebrated, earn much less.

Warren Beatty

Joan Collins

Q *I know this has to be guesswork, but who do you think is the most sexually experienced male movie star in Hollywood? Also, your guess on the sexually experienced female movie star?—Michael P., Newark, N.J.*

A Warren Beatty, 46, and Joan Collins, 50, are veterans in the field. Each practiced on the other long ago.

Frank Sinatra   **Mia Farrow**

Steinberg / Globe

Q *Is it true that Mia Farrow has a reunion with her first husband, Frank Sinatra, at least once a year for old times' sake? How old were Frank and Mia when they were married? And why did their marriage fail?—G.K., Tampa, Fla.*

A Mia Farrow and Frank Sinatra have no annual reunions. Farrow was 20 and Sinatra 50 when they were wed in 1966. They were divorced two years later because of mutual incompatibility.

Q *Do you have any idea what percentage of the U.S. population (235 million) are lesbians or male homosexuals?—Ronald J. Jenkins, Las Vegas, Nev.*

A Dr. Charles Socarides of New York, a scholar on the subject, suggests "2 percent to 3 percent of the adult population of the country." The Kinsey Institute puts the figures at 4 percent for males, 1 percent to 2 percent for females.

Q *Which of our living ex presidents— Richard Nixon, Gerald Ford and Jimmy Carter—is the richest? And what does it cost the taxpayers each year to provide these men with round-the-clock Secret Service protection, office personnel, pensions and all the other perks?—J.V., Youngstown, Ohio.*

A All three are millionaires, but Gerald Ford is probably the wealthiest, with a fortune estimated at $6 million to $7 million. Ford has homes in Rancho Mirage, California, Vail, Colorado, and Los Angeles. He sits on the boards of at least eight corporations, gives 20 to 30 lectures a year at $10,000 and up per lecture, and is partnered in other enterprises with Leonard Firestone, the rubber heir. According to Sen. Lawton Chiles (D., Fla.), it will cost the American taxpayer approximately $14.9 million in 1984 to finance the overhead of the libraries of Presidents Hoover,

Roosevelt, Truman, Eisenhower, Kennedy, Johnson and Ford; $1.2 million more in office allowances for Nixon, Ford and Carter; and an additional $12.7 million for the Secret Service protection for these three living ex-presidents—for a grand total of $28.8 million.

Q *What is the strange voodoo religious sect that singer Michael Jackson belongs to? I thought he was a Baptist.— Jerry Jones, Jackson, Miss.*

A Michael Jackson is a member of the Jehovah's Witnesses, a religious sect founded in this country in 1872 by Charles Taze Russell and known as the Russellites or as the Watch Tower Bible and Tract Society. It espouses a religious doctrine that centers on the second coming of Christ, and each of its Witnesses is considered a minister of God. It is neither strange nor voodoo.

Gloria and Jimmy Stewart

Globe

Q *What is the truth about actor Jimmy Stewart's cancer? Isn't it more serious than his wife, Gloria, makes out?— Ellen T., Evanston, Ill.*

A Gloria Stewart is telling the truth when she discloses that her husband, Jimmy, 75, has been treated for minor facial skin cancer at St. John's Hospital in Santa Monica, California.

Q *Who specifically made the decision to break up the telephone company, when it has provided us with good service at nominal rates since its inception?—John L. Hess, El Cajon, Calif.*

A On January 8, 1982, the U.S. Justice Department, then under William French Smith, agreed to a deal that would break up American Telephone & Telegraph, which had long been a regulated monopoly held by many to be in violation of federal antitrust laws. On August 5, 1983, U.S. District Judge Harold Greene finally approved of the divestiture agreement between AT&T and the Justice Department.

Q *Is Indira Gandhi, daughter of the late Mahatma Gandhi, the most powerful woman politician in the world? Can you give a rundown on her?—R.P., Salt Lake City, Utah.*

A Indira Gandhi, 66, is in no way related to Mahatma Gandhi. A small woman (five-feet-two and weighing 100 pounds), she is the only child of India's first prime minister, Jawaharlal Nehru, a member of the wealthy Brahmin class. Mrs. Gandhi's surname is the result of her parentally disapproved marriage to Feroze Gandhi, a member of the lower Parsi class, who died of a heart attack in 1960.

Indira Gandhi

Ruler and prime minister of India, the world's most populous democracy (750 million people) for 15 of the last 18 years, Indira Gandhi is European-educated, having attended boarding school in Switzerland and Somerville College in Oxford. A fighter for India's independence, she was jailed by the British in 1942, a few months after her honeymoon. Two years following her father's death in 1964, Indira Gandhi became the head of his Congress Party and then prime minister. For a time, she envisioned a high political future for the younger of her two sons, Sanjay, but he was killed in 1980 in a plane crash. Sanjay's widow, Maneka, is bitterly estranged from her mother-in-law and is in fact her political enemy; so Mrs. Gandhi now relies on her elder son and only surviving child, Rajiv, as a general assistant. She is a fascinating, controversial, magnetic personality who frequently describes herself as "one of the sights of India," and she is surely one of the most powerful women politicians in the world.

Mick Jagger and Jerry Hall

Q *I would like to know if Mick Jagger, the Rolling Stone, has made an "honest woman" yet out of model Jerry Hall, who gave birth to his kid some months ago.—Aileen L., Cohasset, Mass.*

A As of this writing, they have not married.

Q *Has actress Victoria Principal of the Dallas television program ever had a "nose job" or "nose bob" or whatever they call it? Has she ever had her bowlegs improved by her boyfriend, Dr. Harry Glassman, the plastic surgeon?—Penny U., Brigham City, Utah.*

A Victoria Principal maintains that she's had neither a nose job nor a leg job. Bernie Cornfeld, the controversial financier who lived with her in London about 13 years ago, reportedly insists that the actress underwent two nose bobs but had nothing done to her legs.

Q *How much in blood and bullion did the failure of our peacekeeping mission in Lebanon cost the U.S. public?— Arthur Gordon, El Paso, Tex.*

A On March 30, President Reagan notified Congress that he had terminated U.S. participation in the multinational peacekeeping mission at a cost of 264 killed, 137 wounded and $59.7 million.

Q *What is the real name of pianist-comedian Victor Borge? How old, and what is his nationality?—Linda Sutter, St. Paul, Minn.*

A Borge (real name: Boerge Rosenbaum) was born in Denmark on January 3, 1909, escaped into Finland when the Nazis invaded Copenhagen in 1940, then caught a ship to the U.S. He became an American citizen in 1948.

Q *I would like to know if actress Mia Farrow, currently the bright flame in Woody Allen's life, is the daughter of Irish immigrants? Where was Mia born?—Charlotte O'Keefe, Milwaukee, Wis.*

A Mia Farrow—born in Los Angeles on February 9, 1946—is the daughter of immigrants. Her mother, actress Maureen O'Sullivan, was born in Ireland. Her father, writer-director John Farrow, was born in Australia.

Liberace

Q *I am puzzled as to why Scott Thorson's suit against Liberace was thrown out of court. Isn't Thorson right in claiming payment for sexual services rendered?—N.T., East Las Vegas, Nev.*

A In 1982, a suit for some $113 million was filed against Liberace by Scott Thorson, the young man he used to live with, who asserted that the pianist had promised to support him in exchange for sexual services. Liberace's lawyers requested a summary adjudication without trial on that one issue. Judge Ricardo Torres of the Los Angeles Superior Court granted the request and ruled that contracts involving sexual services in return for money are equivalent to payment for prostitution and are therefore illegal and unenforceable.

The judge also ruled, however, that Thorson, 24, could pursue his breach-of-

contract suit, in which he alleges that Liberace, 65, promised to pay as much as $30,000 a year for the care of his pets, in addition to paying $70,000 a month and providing luxury living accommodations, autos and other property in exchange for Thorson's services as a confidant, bodyguard, secretary and chauffeur.

Jack Dempsey

Q *Is it true that because of the brain damage incurred by Muhammad Ali, Joe Louis, Jack Dempsey and Gene Tunney, pro boxing will soon be banned in Great Britain, Sweden, Norway and other countries?—D. Reynolds, West Hartford, Conn.*

A Professional boxing was banned in Sweden in 1970 and in Norway in 1983. As of this writing, it has not been banned in Britain, although a recent report by the British Medical Association reveals that brain damage is widespread among professional and amateur boxers in that country. The precise extent to which former heavyweight champions Joe Louis, Jack Dempsey, Gene Tunney and Muhammad Ali suffered brain damage in their fighting careers is not known. It is believed, however, that Dempsey and Tunney suffered relatively little if any brain damage, while Louis suffered a great deal. Of the four champions you list, only Ali—age 42 and retired—survives.

Muhammad Ali

WALTER SCOTT'S
PERSONALITY PARADE®

June 24, 1984

Patti Davis

Q *Is Nancy Reagan heartbroken or crushed because her daughter, actress Patti Davis, 31, is engaged to marry Paul Grilley, a socially unprominent yoga instructor who is only 25?*—T.M., Winston-Salem, N.C.

A Over the years, Nancy Reagan has learned to accept philosophically the judgments, preferences and choices of her two children, Ron and Patti. She was not ecstatically happy when Ron married Doria Palmieri, seven years his senior, in November 1980, and she will probably sound few huzzahs when and if Patti becomes Mrs. Paul Grilley. The First Lady is, however, a supportive parent.

Q *Actress Elizabeth McGovern, who has played in such films as* Ordinary People, Ragtime, Lovesick *and* Racing With the Moon, *has stolen my heart. How old is she? Is there anyone special in her life?*—Rich Gonzales, Fremont, Calif.

A Elizabeth McGovern, 22, an extremely talented young actress from Los Angeles, fell in love with Sean Penn, her co-star in *Racing With the Moon*. After a year of togetherness, however, they reportedly have quarreled—but that was yesterday.

Q *Can you explain why George Washington never signed the Declaration of Independence or the Constitution of the U.S.?*—Shirley T. Merrels, Locust Grove, Va.

A Washington did sign the U.S. Constitution. He was too busy fighting the British to sign the Declaration of Independence, which was adopted by the delegates of the 13 colonies on July 4, 1776.

George Washington

Q *Muammar Qaddafi of Libya is such a pain in the neck to the civilized world with his terrorism, why don't the intelligence services of Great Britain, Israel, France and the U.S. get together and knock this nut off? What are intelligence services for, anyway? Wouldn't this have been a better world if we had assassinated Adolf Hitler? Isn't Qaddafi another version of Hitler?*—V.B.T., Tucson, Ariz.

A Assassinating Qaddafi would be an example of meeting terrorism with terrorism, of condoning in us the behavior we condemn in others. Qaddafi may be another version of Hitler, but who has the right to take another man's life until he is reasonably sure that the other man is intent upon taking his?

Q *If the present Prince Charles of Great Britain died, who would become the next king of the United Kingdom? Would it be his brother, Prince Andrew, or his son, Prince William? If the latter, would Diana, his mother, act as queen until William became of age?*—V.M.H., Pittsburgh, Pa.

A If Prince Charles died, his son, Prince William, would become next in line to inherit the throne. If he became king while still under age, William would rule through a regency consisting of royal elders. Diana, Princess of Wales, can never be the queen of Great Britain. If her husband, Prince Charles, lives to become king, Diana will become queen consort.

Q *How many times has Peter O'Toole, the actor, had his nose bobbed?*—Leo Levitt, Gardena, Calif.

A Peter O'Toole, 50, has had his nose altered at least twice.

Q *How old are Dustin Hoffman and Robert Duvall? How, without sex appeal, have they become such big stars? Surely they are not in the tradition of such leading men as Cary Grant, Clark Gable and Gary Cooper?*—Ethel Campbell, St. Louis, Mo.

A Hoffman, 46, and Duvall, 53, are basically character actors whose extraordinary talent—not their looks—has earned them screen stardom.

Jane Fonda

Q *Is Jane Fonda the richest actress in the world? I read somewhere or heard that she has earned $1 billion on her movies, TV shows, books, video cassettes, workout studios and workout clothes. If this is true, wouldn't that make her Hollywood's first billionaire?*—Ursula W., Goldsboro, N.C.

A Jane Fonda, by virtue of her films and collateral enterprises, is surely one of the world's wealthiest actresses. Nevertheless, despite the success of the films produced by her own company (*Coming Home, The China Syndrome, On Golden Pond and 9 to 5*), in addition to her other profitable ventures, she is far from enjoying billionaire status. She is, however, a multimillionaire who at 46 is probably nearing the apogee of her earnings cycle. A guesstimate of her net worth: $50 million.

Prince

Q *Is Prince, the new black star of the hit movie* Purple Rain, *gay? Where does he live? Is he married? Is he moving in with Michael Jackson? What's his real name? Does he have a girlfriend?—Trish Byrd, Mineola, N.Y.*

A Prince Rogers Nelson (his real name) is 24, single, five feet five, lives in Minneapolis, is not in the slightest gay—in fact, quite the opposite. Reportedly, he has had a lengthy string of girlfriends, among them Apollonia Kotero, who played his lover in the film *Purple Rain;* vocalist Vanity, who used to be with his band; and Sheila Escovedo, another singer. Prince, who writes explicitly sexy lyrics, has no intention of moving in with Michael Jackson in Encino, a suburb of Los Angeles. At this writing, he prefers to maintain his headquarters in Minneapolis, Minnesota, where he was reared and where he attended Central High School.

Q *It is assumed here that James Baker, chief of staff to President Reagan, will resign his post. Who will replace him in a possible second Reagan term? What position would Baker take?—B.L., Houston, Tex.*

A If Baker resigns as chief of staff, the position possibly will be offered to Drew Lewis, who as Reagan's secretary of transportation helped break the air-traffic controllers' strike. In a second Reagan term, Baker probably would be offered the cabinet position of U.S. attorney general should Ed Meese, for any of a number of reasons, not make it to that job.

Q *Does Bjorn Borg plan to play tennis ever again in the U.S.? Did he retire because tennis and a wife were too much to handle? Is his wife a witch who put a spell on him?—Mrs. H. Gustafson, Zephyrhills, Fla.*

A Bjorn Borg, 28, plans to play in various exhibition matches, not only in the U.S. but also in other countries throughout the world. A five-time winner of the Wimbledon title, he retired at age 26, a multimillionaire, because of tennis "burnout" and the sameness of his competitive life. His wife, the former Mariana Simionescu of Romania, is no "witch who put a spell on him." She is a delightful, attractive young woman of 28 who reportedly plans to divorce Borg in Monte Carlo where they maintain a residence. Borg is said to be enamored of Jannike Bjorling, a 17-year-old Swedish beauty with whom he reportedly vacationed in Hawaii. Borg and Simionescu were married in 1980 in a civil ceremony in Bucharest.

Coretta Scott King

Q *One never hears any mention of romance in the life of Coretta Scott King. Has she been in love since the death of her husband? Would she consider remarrying?—Oren M. Spiegler, Pittsburgh, Pa.*

A Since the assassination of her husband in 1968, Coretta Scott King has been busy rearing their four children: Yolanda Denise, born in 1955; Martin Luther King III, born in 1957; Dexter, born in 1961; and Bernice Albertine, born in 1963. She also has been hard at work supporting her husband's causes, particularly the blacks' fight for civil rights and justice in the U.S. According to friends, Mrs. King has had no time for romance and is married to her late husband's humanitarian objective of equal rights. At 57, however, she remains a beautiful, intelligent activist who might one day consider remarrying—provided, of course, there entered into her life a man courageous enough to follow Martin Luther King, Jr., winner of the Nobel Peace Prize in 1964 and, as one of Mrs. King's associates describes him, "a hard act to follow."

Ulysses Grant

Dwight Eisenhower

Q *I know that two generals—Eisenhower and Grant—made U.S. president. Were there any other generals from our military who achieved the presidency of this country?—Gordon L., Salt Lake City, Utah.*

A Yes. In addition to Eisenhower and Grant, there were Washington, Jackson, William H. Harrison, Taylor, Pierce, Johnson, Hayes, Garfield, Arthur, and Benjamin Harrison—to date, a total of 12.

Q *A relation informs me that two girls named Jennifer—Jennifer Grant and Jennifer Brokaw—are students at Stanford University and supposedly have famous fathers they won't discuss. Who are their fathers?—J.S., Redwood Falls, Minn.*

A Jennifer Grant is the daughter of retired screen star Cary Grant, 80. Jennifer Brokaw is the daughter of NBC-TV commentator Tom Brokaw, 44.

WALTER SCOTT'S
PERSONALITY PARADE®

November 11, 1984

Princess Di, Prince Charles and family

Q *Is there a British law that says the heir to the throne will be paid $100,000 a year for every child he has? I understand that's why Prince Charles plans to have half a dozen. Why not, if the poor public has to support them?—P.N., Albermarle, N.C.*

A There's no such law. Prince Charles and Princess Di have never announced how many offspring they plan to have. Once Charles assumes the throne, his children will be voted annual sums by the government. Until then, Charles pays for their support.

Q *How does Ethel Kennedy persevere in the face of so many tragedies? Her husband, Robert, was assassinated. Her son David died from drugs. Another son, Bobby, became a victim of drugs. She has lost so many dear ones on both sides of her family. Where does this gallant woman find the will to go on?—Frances E., Ogden, Utah.*

A Ethel Kennedy finds strength in her own character, in faith in her church and its tenets, and in continued support by her family.

Q *Johnny Carson's three marriages have cost him millions. Has he learned his lesson, or will he marry again?—Alma Clark, Evansville, Ind.*

A Carson, 59, has grown accustomed to marriage. Our guess is that he'll take a fourth bride, only this one will have to sign a prenuptial agreement limiting her financial settlement in the event of divorce.

Q *Please settle once and for all what D-day means. You said, "Day of Decision," while the Army said it "is simply an alliteration, as in H-hour." Doesn't anyone know? Can't the truth be found in the Eisenhower literature?—H.L. Keller, Honolulu, Hawaii.*

A Thomas Wright of Mahanoy Plane, Pennsylvania, sent us a copy of a 1964 letter from Ike's executive assistant, Brig. Gen. Robert Schulz. It reads: "General Eisenhower asked me to respond to your letter. Be advised that any amphibious operation has a 'departure date'; therefore, the shortened term 'D-day' is used." The French, however, insist the D means "disembarkation"; others prefer "debarkation."

Q *Last year, I read that Cary Grant was going to become a father again at the age of 80, that the baby was due in July 1984. I have not read or heard anything more. Did his wife have a miscarriage, or wasn't it true?—Robert Kent, Tucson, Ariz.*

A The story of Mrs. Grant's pregnancy wasn't true.

Joan Crawford

Q *For a long time, I've heard the rumor—and I'm sure you have too—that when Joan Crawford was a big star, she was obsessed with introducing young men, not yet 21, into her wonderful world of sex. Any truth to that?—D.K., Sparks, Nev.*

A Joan Crawford, who died in 1977, was a fiercely independent, highly sexed woman. She was not obsessed, as rumor has it, with "young stud-blood." From time to time, however, she exercised a penchant for teaching the delights of sex to a young man she fancied and awing him with her technique. One such beneficiary of her largesse was the actor Jackie Cooper, a former child star. For six months in 1939, when Cooper was 17 and Crawford was 35 and divorced from actor Franchot Tone, she wowed him on occasion with her instruction.

Ronald Reagan

Q *Is it true that Ronald Reagan has always been a tight man with a buck? A few years ago, it was printed—I believe in The Wall Street Journal—that in 1978 and 1979, when he made a million dollars giving speeches, Reagan even charged the Boy Scouts of America $5,000 as a speech-making fee. Is that true too?—D.W., Williamsport, Pa.*

A Reagan was born into poverty. His father was an itinerant, alcoholic shoe salesman in Illinois. Reagan as a youngster learned quickly and unforgettably the value of a dime. *The Wall Street Journal* of June 30, 1980, in a front-page story on Reagan's financial worth, wrote: "In all, Mr. Reagan received about $1 million for his speeches and commentary during nearly two years of undeclared campaigning before his formal entry into the presidential race last November 13 . . . Mr. Reagan nevertheless accepted two fees for Boy Scout fund-raising appearances in California last year, $2,500 to address a San Gabriel Valley group and $5,000 for a talk in Bakersfield." The newspaper also reported that, according to Michael Deaver, Reagan was "sensitive" about charging for charity affairs and did not charge for about 20 percent of his speeches.

WALTER SCOTT'S
PERSONALITY PARADE®

November 25, 1984

Alfred Hitchcock

Q *Two outstanding Englishmen in the movie world were actor James Mason and director Alfred Hitchcock. Would you happen to know why neither of them was ever knighted by the British crown?—Alice Martindale, Honolulu, Hawaii.*

A In the case of Mason, the fact that he was a pacifist who registered as a conscientious objector in World War II, refusing to fight for king and country, probably was a contributory reason. Another was that—despite his dark good looks, his appealing air of menace and his undeniable acting talent—he failed over a lengthy career to establish himself as a really top-ranking star.

As regards Hitchcock, he departed England for the U.S. with his family on March 1, 1939. The following year, when German bombs rained down on Britain, the nation's press denounced Hitchcock—unfairly, some thought—for remaining in Hollywood, secure and munificently employed, instead of returning to defend his homeland. Later, some Britons in high places frowned upon Hitchcock for becoming a U.S. citizen, which he did on April 20, 1955, a decade after his wife.

Q *Is Jane Seymour, who played in Lassiter with Tom Selleck, descended in any way from Lady Jane Seymour, who was the third queen of Henry VIII?—Trudy Baker, Columbia, S.C.*

A No. Jane Seymour's name was Joyce Frankenberg before she had it changed.

Q *When the Jacksons began their Pepsico Victory Tour, Michael promised to donate his share of the proceeds to charity. Did he say which charities and how much?—Petey James, Atlantic City, N.J.*

A Michael Jackson's one-sixth share of the Pepsico Victory Tour, which ends December 2, will approach a minimum of $3 million. According to his manager, Michael will donate all of it to the United Negro College Fund, the T. J. Martell Foundation for Leukemia and Cancer Research, and Camp Good Times, a camp for young cancer victims and their families in Malibu, California.

Q *Can you identify the only two U.S. senators brave enough to vote in 1964 against the Gulf of Tonkin resolution, which gave Lyndon Johnson a free hand to send 500,000 of our troops to fight the war in Vietnam? Where are these senators now? I would also appreciate knowing which members of the House of Representatives voted against the resolution.—F. Zimmerman, Beloit, Wis.*

Lyndon Johnson

A The Gulf of Tonkin resolution of August 7, 1964, authorizing President Johnson to "take all necessary measures to repel any armed attack against the forces of the United States and to prevent further aggression," was passed in the Senate by a vote of 88 to 2 and in the House by a vote of 416 to 0. The two courageous, dissenting U.S. senators, both now deceased, were Wayne Morse (Independent, Ore.) and Ernest Gruening (D., Alaska).

Q *Is it a fact that the film career of James Dean was limited to only three pictures:* Rebel Without a Cause, East of Eden *and* Giant? *How old was Dean when he died? Is it true that he was kept for a time by the late heiress to the Woolworth fortune, Barbara Hutton?—Don S., Marion, Ind.*

James Dean

A In addition to those three major movies, James Dean played small parts in the early 1950s in four undistinguished films: *Fixed Bayonets, Sailor Beware, Has Anybody Seen My Gal?* and *Trouble Along the Way.* Dean died in a car crash at 24. He was never "kept" by any woman, and rumors that he enjoyed a weekend affair with Barbara Hutton at the Beverly Wilshire Hotel in Beverly Hills have never been substantiated.

Q *Queen Elizabeth II of Great Britain recently visited King Hussein in Jordan. Has she ever visited Jordan's neighbor, Israel?—L.H., Chicago, Ill.*

A Queen Elizabeth over the years has visited several Arab countries. She has not yet visited the State of Israel. It was her country, however, which in 1917 supported the creation of a Jewish homeland in Palestine.

Q *Who is Goldie Hawn's latest lover, and where do they live—in Santa Barbara or La Jolla, California?—Pam T., Santa Rose, Calif.*

A Goldie Hawn and Kurt Russell, her leading man in the disappointing film *Swing Shift,* reside in Pacific Palisades, a western suburb of Los Angeles.

Globe

John F. Kennedy

Q *Could you please tell me if John F. Kennedy accepted his salary when he was president? A friend says he didn't.—Faye Mackey, Mulvane, Kan.*

A Kennedy donated his salary to charity.

Q *Does anyone know the true reasons why Josef Stalin's daughter, Svetlana, recently returned to Moscow and again became a Soviet citizen? Could it be she is, or was, an intelligence agent carefully planted here by the KGB?—D.F., Arlington, Va.*

A Svetlana Alliluyeva Peters, 58, who defected to this country in 1967 and moved to Cambridge, England, in 1982, is the only person at this writing who truly knows why she returned to the Soviet Union. Speculation has it that she was unhappy, homesick and deeply missed the son and daughter she left behind 17 years ago: Moscow cardiologist Josef Alliluyev, now 39, and Yekaterina ("Katya") Zhdanov, 34. She also was eager to meet the grandson and granddaughter in Moscow she had never seen. Reportedly she was disillu-sioned with life in the U.S. and England. Her marriage to William Wesley Peters—an American architect based in Arizona, by whom she has a daughter, Olga, 13—soured after 22 months. They were divorced in 1973.

Though she had earned $1 million from the two books she authored, *Twenty Letters to a Friend* and *Only One Year*, which dealt with her years in Russia and her subsequent defection, Mrs. Peters lost most of that money in a disastrous Wisconsin agricultural investment. In Russia, it is understood, she will qualify for a pension. Given her background and emotional makeup, it is highly improbable that Mrs. Peters ever spied for the KGB, the Soviet security apparatus. It is likely, however, that in the future the KGB will pressure this troubled, four-times-married woman to denounce publicly the two Western countries that gave her sanctuary.

Q *Were there any athletes at the 1984 Olympic Games in Los Angeles who failed to pass the rigorous drug tests? If so, their identities were sure hushed up. Do you know of any? I understand there were quite a few.—C. Cohen, Venice, Calif.*

A Reportedly only a handful of athletes at the Los Angeles Olympic Games failed the dope tests. Among them were a Finnish 10,000-meter runner and a female javelin-thrower from Greece.

Q *Some questions I would like answered about Col. Tom Parker, manager of the late Elvis Presley: Is Parker alive? Was he the all-time "highest roller" in the history of Las Vegas gambling? Did he talk Elvis out of marrying Ann-Margret, the singer-actress?—Selena Henry, Chicago, Ill.*

A Parker, 75 and alive at this writing, was reputedly a "high roller" at the Vegas gaming tables but not in the same league, according to observers of the Vegas scene, with Adnan Khashoggi of Saudi Arabia and many others. As regards Elvis' extensive love life, the colonel rigidly abstained from interfering with it. Where women were concerned, Elvis called his own shots.

Q *I keep hearing that Nancy Reagan has done so much in the areas of drug abuse and children that I would like to know what it is that she has done.—Jean Noble, Bethesda, Md.*

A Ever since 1967, Nancy Reagan has donated her time and support to Fos-ter Grandparents, a program that matches elderly people with handicapped children. She also has traveled throughout the country visiting, encouraging and supporting drug-rehabilitation centers, especially for minors.

Watson / Camera Press / Globe

Amy Irving and Steven Spielberg

Q *When I was young, getting a girl pregnant was reason enough to marry her. Now I read where Steven Spielberg, the director of* Indiana Jones and the Temple of Doom, *has got his girlfriend, Amy Irving, in a family way, but they have no plans to marry. Has marriage gone out of style among movie people?—Dan P., Cedar City, Utah.*

A At this writing, neither Spielberg, 36, nor actress Irving, 31, has publicly disclosed marital plans, which doesn't necessarily mean they have none. In some cases, today's woman does not consider pregnancy out of wedlock to be sufficient reason for marriage. She prefers to marry a man who genuinely loves her, rather than one who does not but who feels obligated to marry her because she's pregnant. Among independent actresses like Ursula Andress, Vanessa Redgrave, Catherine Deneuve and others, it appears that so-called "shotgun marriages" belong to yesterday's mores.

WALTER SCOTT'S
PERSONALITY PARADE®

January 6, 1985

Barbra Streisand

Q *Aren't Barbra Streisand and composer Richard Baskin, heir to the Baskin Robbins ice cream fortune, secretly married?—T.J., Wheaton, Ill.*

A Not at this writing, though they've been enjoying each other's company in Hollywood and London.

Q *I know this sounds crazy, but is it true that a wife of Gen. Douglas MacArthur was once married to a notorious Hollywood sex fiend? A very knowledgeable friend claims it is true, only she can't remember the sex fiend's name.—B.T., Hackensack, N.J.*

A General MacArthur's first wife was the former Mrs. Louise Cromwell Brooks, heiress to a Philadelphia fortune. They were divorced in 1929 after seven years of marriage. A few months later, she married Lionel Atwill, an actor who played "mad doctor" roles in many films. Atwill was an Englishman of perverse and erotic tastes whose home in the Pacific Palisades was the site of weekend sex orgies, the likes of which his wife could not tolerate. She left Atwill in 1939, moved to Washington, D.C., and divorced him in 1943. General MacArthur was married again when he was 57, this time to Jean Faircloth, his widow since 1964.

Q *Novelist James Michener is 77. Since 1947, he has written more than 25 books, among them* Tales of the South Pacific, The Bridges at Toko-Ri, Sayonara, Hawaii, Iberia, Centennial, Chesapeake, *and* Space. *Surely they constitute a creditable body of work. Why, then, has he never won a Nobel Prize in literature? Isn't he in the same literary ballpark as Sinclair Lewis, Pearl S. Buck, Ernest Hemingway, John Steinbeck and Saul Bellow, each an American writer and Nobel Prize-winner?—H.F., Lockhart, Tex.*

A Some literary critics regard James Michener as a popularizer of history, as a government propagandist and as a novelist in the Edna Ferber tradition, catering to the mass and middlebrow audience. Admittedly no stylist or creator of great literature, Michener is a careful researcher who simplifies his findings for a vast audience in a memorable, entertaining and well-structured way. Critics may castigate him because he is no literary elitist, but the public's response to his work is consistently overwhelming. In time, the Nobel nominating committee may judge his output to be the qualitative equal of Buck's or Steinbeck's and worthy of its laureate.

George S. Patton

Q *I'm sure that Gen. George S. Patton, Jr., and Jim Thorpe both competed in the 1912 Olympics, but not against each other in the decathlon and pentathlon. Am I correct?—Keith Roberts, Las Vegas, Nev.*

A You are. According to Rochelle Evans, recordkeeper for the U.S. Olympic Committee, Jim Thorpe competed in the decathlon and pentathlon, "but the pentathlon he participated in was not the same . . . as the modern pentathlon, in which George Patton participated. The modern pentathlon is a largely military sport, consisting of an equestrian event, fencing, running, swimming and shooting. Patton did finish fifth in this competition. He was also on the fencing team but was eliminated in the first round. The pentathlon Jim Thorpe competed in and won is a five-part track and field event."

Q *When I was young, two of the most talented child stars in Hollywood were Judy Garland and Deanna Durbin. Both sang like angels. Judy Garland, after a most unhappy life, died in 1969. What became of Deanna Durbin? We hear absolutely nothing of her.—M. McGraw, State College, Pa.*

A Deanna Durbin, born Edna Mae Durbin on December 4, 1921, in Winnipeg, was one of Hollywood's brightest singing stars from 1936 to 1949. At 28, she retired and went to live in France. There, with third husband Charles David, a French film director 16 years her senior, she settled down in the Paris suburb of Neauphle-le-Chateau, where she still lives in a picturesque two-story farmhouse. She retains her Canadian citizenship, declines all interviews, travels widely and periodically visits her 38-year-old daughter, Jessica, who resides in the south of France. At 63, she apparently is content to be Madame Charles David and, unlike many a superannuated film celebrity, refuses to live in the past.

Q *I know there have been news reports about President Reagan's penchant for nodding off in cabinet meetings and once at a meeting with the Pope in the Vatican. But how about Secretary of State George Shultz? This man, when he speaks, appears to have the dynamism of a hibernating bear in*

Ronald Reagan

midwinter. Has he ever put a foreign dignitary to sleep while conversing in his usual somniferous voice?—J. Edward Hakes, Tallahassee, Fla.

A As a speaker, Shultz is no spellbinder. There is a droning quality to his voice, but to date no one has held that voice responsible for putting the president or any dignitary to sleep.

Clark Gable

Q *Clark Gable married five times and had only one natural child—a son, John, born to wife No. 5, Kay Spreckels. Did Gable have any other children, legitimate or illegitimate?—T.H., Denver, Colo.*

A Reportedly he had a daughter born out of wedlock.

Q *To the victor belong the spoils. What, in your opinion, are the most important spoils Ronald Reagan got when he defeated Walter Mondale on Election Day?—H. Ferguson, Chicago, Ill.*

A One of the most important is control of the federal judiciary appointments. Reagan has the power to appoint—for life—not only the U.S. Supreme Court justices but also all other federal judges. Five of the nine Supreme Court justices are more than 75 years old. It is likely that some will retire or die within the next four years, thus giving Reagan the opportunity to appoint their successors and, through them, to alter in part the philosophy of the court for the balance of the 20th century. In addition, more than 100 vacancies on the federal bench will have to be filled in the near future, providing Reagan with a further opportunity to appoint judges in his own conservative image.

There is, of course, the possibility that Reagan's judicial appointees eventually will differ from him in ideological direction. For example, when Theodore Roosevelt appointed Oliver Wendell Holmes, Jr., to the Supreme Court, he was convinced he knew how Holmes would rule. Holmes turned out to be far more independent than Roosevelt expected. When President Eisenhower appointed Earl Warren as chief justice, he believed Warren was a strict constructionist of the Constitution. Warren proved in his decisions that he was anything but.

Q *Please tell the truth about Mrs. Nancy Reagan. Isn't she suffering from anorexia nervosa? Isn't she down to size two?—K.T., Appleton, Wis.*

A Nancy Reagan, who wears a size four, does not suffer from anorexia nervosa, a disorder characterized by a pathological fear of weight gain. She does, however, suffer from anemia.

Q *How does Mike Wallace of TV's 60 Minutes avoid the mandatory age-65 retirement that CBS enforces on others?—K.L.M., Dallas, Tex.*

A A federal statute permits any person so desiring to work to age 70 before retiring by company rule. Wallace, 66, is such a person.

Aristotle and Jackie Onassis

Q *Before Aristotle Onassis married Jackie Kennedy in 1968, wasn't he involved with Greta Garbo in a torrid, ultrasecret affair?—T.O., Oyster Bay, N.Y.*

A Garbo and Onassis were friends but not lovers. Before Onassis married Jacqueline Kennedy, his lover and mistress was the late opera star Maria Callas.

Audrey Hepburn

Q *Is Audrey Hepburn secretly married to Robert Wolders, the Dutch actor who was married to movie queen Merle Oberon from 1975 to 1979? How many children does Hepburn have, and who is their father? Is it also true that when Oberon died, she left Wolders $10 million? Is Audrey Hepburn's film career finished?—Sara J., Raleigh, N.C.*

A Wolders and Hepburn have been sharing lives since 1981. At this writing, however, each is unmarried. Audrey Hepburn is the mother of two sons, Sean and Luca. Sean was fathered by Hepburn's first husband, actor Mel Ferrer, in 1960. Luca was fathered by her second husband, Dr. Andrea Dotti, in 1970. Oberon reportedly bequeathed a handsome inheritance to her young widower, now 48, but $10 million seems too high. As for Hepburn's film career, it has diminished considerably in quantity and quality. She never was endowed with a high sex-appeal quotient, even in the 1950s and '60s, when in her prime. Now that she's 55, good roles for her age bracket are scarce. Three of her last films, *Robin and Marian, Bloodline* and *They All Laughed,* are easily forgettable. Her name-value at the box office remains highest in Japan but appears to be passé in this country.

Q *Is it on the level that neither Queen Elizabeth II of the United Kingdom nor Danielle Mitterrand, First Lady of France, gives a tinker's damn about clothes but that each wears couturier clothes basically to promote her country's fashion industry?—D.S., Glencoe, Ill.*

A Yes. Queen Elizabeth's clothes have often been criticized by fashion leaders as "dowdy," and Danielle Mitterrand, it is said, wore no designer outfits until her husband was elected president of France, and she felt it her patriotic duty to plug French fashions.

Pearl Buck

Q *Have any women ever won the Nobel Prize for anything? I can't think of any. Can you? My wife says there are at least a dozen winners of her sex. Which of us is right?—Ted A., Portland, Ore.*

A Your wife. At least 20 women have won Nobel Prizes: Mother Teresa, Betty Williams, Mairead Corrigan, Bertha von Suttner, Barbara McClintock, Selma Lagerlof, Sigrid Undset, Pearl Buck, Marie Curie, Irene Joliot-Curie, Maria Goeppert-Mayer, Rosalyn Yalow, Jane Addams, Emily Balch, Gabriela Mistral, Nelly Sachs, Alva Myrdal, Gerty Cori, Grazia Deledda and Dorothy Hodgkin.

Q *I see that Sylvester Stallone's wife, Sasha, has sued him for divorce without naming any rivals for her husband's affection. If the divorce goes through, how much will it cost Stallone—$10, $20, or $30 million bucks?—Glenn R., Brooklyn, N.Y.*

A Sylvester Stallone's wife sued him for divorce in 1978, then changed her mind and later was reconciled with the star of the Rocky movies. Recently, she again filed for divorce on grounds of irreconcilable differences and demanded custody of their two children, Sage, eight, and Seargeoh ("Seth"), six The Stallones were married on December 28, 1974. In the 10 ensuing years, the actor-writer-director has amassed a multimillion-dollar estate that is considered community property. What portion of it Sasha will obtain is not known at this time. A reasonable guess would give her $5 million plus support payments for the two children.

Q *I've read in the papers that Richard Burton, the movie star, left an estate worth more than $4.5 million to his fourth wife, Sally. Can this be true? I thought Burton was flat broke when he died last August.—Cleo L., Geneva, N.Y.*

Richard Burton

A The actor's widow, former BBC-TV production assistant Sally Hay, 36, denies the printed report of her $4.5 million inheritance and classifies it as "pure speculation." Richard Burton was not "flat broke" at the time of his death at age 58, but his estate, according to friends, will not approach $4.5 million.

Ronald Reagan

Q *Ronald Reagan and Walter Mondale both appeared on TV and elsewhere wearing American Legion hats. What active military background, if any, did either of them have?—Arthur Merish, Apollo Beach, Fla.*

A Ronald Reagan served in the U.S. Army Air Corps from 1942 to 1945. Walter Mondale served in the U.S. Army from 1951 to 1953.

Q *Is Harrison Ford—who reached screen stardom by playing in the Star Wars movies and the Steven Spielberg films Raiders and Indiana Jones—the same Harry Ford who went to high school in Park Ridge, Illinois, in the late '50s and to Ripon College in the '60s? If so, how much is he worth?—T.R., Ripon, Wis.*

A He is one and the same. At 42, Ford is probably a multimillionaire.

Q *Would you please explain to me how a public corporation like 20th Century-Fox can appoint to its board of directors, at $50,000 each annually, two men like Henry Kissinger and ex-President Gerald Ford, neither of whom has any expertise in the motion picture business? Why haven't the shareholders complained?—G.G., Huntsville, Ala.*

A Twentieth Century-Fox is not a public corporation. All of its stock is owned by Denver oilman Marvin S. Davis and his family. Davis has the right to appoint anyone he desires, at any fee, to his board of directors. In fiscal 1983, Kissinger and Ford were paid $50,000 each for serving on the board. In fiscal 1984, they were paid $37,500 each. Several weeks ago, Davis removed both men from the 20th Century-Fox board but retained them as consultants; at what fee or salary has not been disclosed. Fox has been a private company since 1981, when Davis and his then partner, Marc Rich, purchased it for about $725 million. Because several of its debt securities are still publicly held, however, the corporation is required to file public reports with the Securities and Exchange Commission.

Q *Has Marlon Brando retired from motion pictures? How old is he, anyway? And who is his present lady love?—Jacqueline L., Paducah, Ky.*

A Brando, 60, has not retired from filmmaking. He was spotted in London not long ago with a 27-year-old Japanese beauty, Yachio Tsubiki. But there is no assurance that she is his latest "lady love."

Marlon Brando

O.J. and Nicole Simpson

Q *I am wondering if O. J. Simpson, the sportscaster, is still going with that beautiful blonde, or have they split?—Melinda Rooney, Oakland, Calif.*

A O. J. Simpson, 37, married Nicole Brown, 25, a curvaceous interior decorator, on February 2.

Q *I've asked you several times to identify the famous Hollywood comedienne who is also a famous lesbian. Once and for all, will you answer the question? If not, why?—R.R., Los Angeles, Calif.*

A Sorry. Disclosure of her name might well damage her career. Surely you would not want to be party to such an uncharitable action.

Q *Hasn't Christopher Reeve quietly settled $5 million on Gae Exton, who lived with him for seven years and bore him two children? Isn't he leaving Gae for Jacqueline Bisset, who made Anna Karenina with him in Hungary? Isn't that the reason for the settlement?—M.K., Grand Rapids, Mich.*

A Reeve, star of the *Superman* movies, has made no financial settlement with Gae. Nor is he leaving her for Jacqueline Bisset. The Reeve-Exton

relationship, although unsanctioned by marriage, seems to be running well on all burners at this point.

Q *Are beards banned in the U.S. Navy? For months I dated a navy lieutenant, and I can assure you he had a beard, because we were very close. Now my kids tell me beards are not allowed in the service. Since when? And who is responsible for this unconstitutional outrage?—Jayne N., Aiea, Hawaii.*

A Effective January 1, the Navy banned beards on men of all ranks. The order was issued by Adm. James D. Watkins, chief of naval operations. In the early 1970s, when Adm. Elmo Zumwalt was chief, he issued an order permitting neatly trimmed beards.

Q *The name, please, of the disease that actor Peter Lawford died from. And why has it been kept such a secret?—N.M., Florence, S.C.*

A Hospital physicians say Lawford died last December 24 of cardiac arrest. Friends say he died of vodka.

Jacqueline Kennedy Onassis

Q *Now that Jacqueline Kennedy Onassis and Sen. Edward Kennedy, her former brother-in-law, are free to marry, is it not possible that one day they will do so? I ask the question because I notice that Jackie accompanied Teddy on his recent trips to South Africa and Great Britain, which leads me to believe that they have been quietly dating. Your comment on this intriguing situation would be most welcome.—C.B., Danvers, Mass.*

A "Possible" is such an elastic, all-encompassing word. Of course, it is "possible" that one day Jackie and Teddy

Edward Kennedy

might marry each other. Jackie, at 55, is only two and a half years older than the senator, and they have much in common, but such a marriage is highly unlikely. It is not true "that Jackie accompanied Teddy on his recent trips to South Africa and Great Britain." The two did meet in London, however, then traveled to North Wales to attend the funeral of Lord Harlech, the former David Ormsby Gore. Harlech, who died in January at age 66, was a close friend of the Kennedy clan and served Great Britain's ambassador to the U.S. during the John F. Kennedy administration. In 1967, he and Jackie toured the temples of Cambodia, generating speculation that they might marry. A year later, however, the former First Lady announced her engagement to multimillionaire Aristotle Onassis. Then, in 1969, Lord Harlech married Pamela Colin, an American journalist on the staff of the British edition of *Vogue* magazine.

Q *What's the real reason Jeane Kirkpatrick was denied a cabinet post by the president? Because she's a Democrat?—Natalie A., Poughkeepsie, N.Y.*

A It has been reported that Kirkpatrick was not a favorite of James Baker, Richard Darman, Michael Deaver and George Shultz, four presidential advisers with a good deal of clout. The fact that she is a Democrat made no difference. It was as a Democrat that she was appointed by Reagan to be chief U.S. delegate to the UN and as a Democrat that she emphatically supported Reagan at the 1984 Republican Convention. Personality, not party affiliation, probably played a role in her failure to garner a cabinet post in the second Reagan administration.

WALTER SCOTT'S
PERSONALITY PARADE®

May 26, 1985

Jane Fonda

Q *Could you tell us if there is anything to the rumor that Sen. Edward Kennedy and Jane Fonda have been preparing secretly to run for president and vice president on the Democratic ticket in 1988?—Rosemarie Talbot, Clearwater, Fla.*

A Senator Kennedy appears to be preparing himself for a run at the Democratic presidential candidacy in 1988, but not with Jane Fonda as his possible running mate. A Kennedy-Fonda ticket, however, surely would enliven politics in 1988.

Q *Was Lord "Dickie" Mountbatten, the last viceroy of India and a member of British royalty, a practicing homosexual, as was rumored? Is that why his wife, Edwina, took as lovers Paul Robeson, the singer, and Jawaharlal Nehru, first prime minister of India?—J.P.O., Brookline, Mass.*

A Lord Louis Mountbatten, assassinated by members of the Irish Republican army in 1979, was tall, handsome, vainglorious, ego-ridden, charming, theatrical, ambitious and hungry for fame, flattery and publicity, but he was not homosexual. His wife, the fabulously wealthy Edwina Ashley Mountbatten,

played around, but not seriously with singer Paul Robeson. More serious were her affairs with Laddie Sanford, an American polo player; Lt. Col. Harold Phillips, a pre-World War II British army social figure; and Jawaharlal Nehru, one of India's great statesmen.

Q *Can you explain why Mary Lou Retton, who won a single gold medal in the Olympics as a gymnast, has done so much better financially—getting TV commercials and paid-for personal appearances—than Valerie Brisco-Hooks, the track star who won three gold medals, in the 200-, 400- and 1,600-meter relay races? Isn't it because Retton is white and Brisco-Hooks is black?—J.L., Brunswick, Ga.*

A Racism might be a factor, but product endorsement contracts generally are offered to athletes and personalities, black or white, who can do their sponsors the most good. Michael Jordan, for example, black co-captain of the U.S. basketball team, was signed after the Olympics to endorse Nike products and Chevrolet automobiles. Promoters are primarily interested in profits, not in prejudice.

Desi Arnaz, Jr.

Q *We read a lot about Lucille Ball's daughter, Lucie—how happy and successful she is—but not much about her son, Desi Arnaz, Jr. Is it true that he's into drugs?—Nicholas H., Stamford, Conn.*

A Desi Arnaz, Jr., 32, has had a drug and drinking problem for years but seems, at this writing, to have beaten it and is en route to good health.

Q *In your opinion, who are American's three most influential women?—Susan Ward, Youngstown, Ohio.*

A Nancy Reagan, wife of President Ronald Reagan; Katharine Graham, chairman of the board of The Washington Post Co.; and Sandra Day O'Connor, associate justice of the U.S. Supreme Court.

Q *Is it a fact that Susan Anspach, the actress, is the proud mother of two children born out of wedlock and that screen star Jack Nicholson is the father of both? Is Anspach some kind of kook? What is her reputation in Hollywood?—M.H., Appleton, Wis.*

A Susan Anspach, 38, who recently appeared in the TV mini-series *Space,* is the mother of two children born outside of marriage. Jack Nicholson, who acted with Anspach in *Five Easy Pieces,* is the father of her son, Caleb, 14. Steve Curry, who worked with her in *Hair,* is the father of her daughter, Catherine, 16. Anspach, no kook, is an immensely talented and independent woman who in her youth wanted children but not necessarily marriage. She lives with her offspring and husband, writer-musician Sherwood Ball, in Santa Monica, California, where she is admired as a loving, conscientious mother and a generous, civic-minded citizen.

Clint Eastwood

Paul Newman

Q *Who are the highest-paid actors in Hollywood? How much do they get?—L. Ferraro, Buffalo, N.Y.*

A Among the highest paid are Sylvester Stallone, Burt Reynolds, Clint Eastwood and Robert Redford. They also are producers and directors. Stallone, in addition, is a writer. He has been offered as much as $12 million to star in a film. The others will not act in a film without sharing in its profits. That also goes for Dustin Hoffman and Paul Newman. All of the aforementioned probably average $3 million to $5 million a film, depending on the individual deals their agents arrange.

Raquel Welch

Q *Please settle an argument. I say Raquel Welch is of Mexican extraction. My husband says that he knew her in San Diego, and that she is 100 percent American. What's the truth?—Norma Henderson, Glendale, Ariz.*

A Raquel Welch was born in Chicago on September 5, 1940. Her mother, Josephine Hall, was born in the U.S.; her late father, Armand Tejade, in Bolivia. Raquel, one of the most publicized of Hollywood's sex goddesses, is 100 percent American.

Q *She was born in Puerto Rico 53 years ago and was so frustrated in her up-and-down relationship with Marlon Brando that she channeled her frustration into hard work and became the only actress to win an Oscar, two Emmys, a Tony and a Grammy. Can you name her?—Dolores Ferrer, Freeport, N.Y.*

A You probably have in mind the versatile and talented Rita Moreno.

Q *President Reagan's physical condition is sure to be meticulously monitored in the future. If one of his exams should show, Heaven forbid, that some malignant cells from his intestines have spread to another part of his body, would*

he resign or try to serve out his second term?—P.T., Detroit, Mich.

A That question is unanswerable at this time. If the circumstance you hypothesize develops, Reagan most probably would remain in office so long as he and his physicians could convince the public and the Congress that he was physically and mentally capable of performing his duties. Reagan is a man who relishes and enjoys his high office, despite all its strains and stresses. He knows, too, how to delegate authority and husband his strength. If he were to leave the presidency before completing his second term, it would be most reluctantly.

Boris Becker

Q *Why has Boris Becker, the 17-year-old German who won the tennis championship at Wimbledon this year, bought a condominium in Monte Carlo? Does he like to gamble? I thought minors were forbidden to gamble in Monte Carlo.—Nancy King, Kaneohe, Hawaii.*

A The principality of Monaco, in which Monte Carlo is situated, exacts no income tax from persons who establish their official residences there. Becker expects to earn a considerable fortune as a tennis star and intends to take advantage of the tax break. He won about $185,000 at Wimbledon.

Q *At a recent cocktail party, I heard it said that if Don Regan, President Reagan's chief of staff, doesn't make the president look good, "Nancy Reagan will*

have him out of there in six months." Does Nancy Reagan really exercise so much power in the government?—E.C.M., Arlington, Va.

A Many political savants contend that, through her husband, Nancy Reagan exercises more power than any other First Lady since Eleanor Roosevelt. Mrs. Reagan makes no government policy decisions but is fiercely protective of her husband and wary of the men and women around him. She believes that she is a more insightful and accurate reader of people's true character than her husband is, and she greatly influences his personnel decisions. If she concludes that Don Regan is not the help to the president that he should be, it would surprise no one to find Regan returning to the world of Wall Street whence he came.

Q *I know that Ronald Reagan as president is paid $200,000 a year in salary, plus expenses. How much does George Bush as vice president get in salary and expenses?—P. Bennett, Lincoln, Neb.*

A Vice President Bush receives a salary of $91,000 a year and $10,000 for expenses, all of which is taxable.

Q *What is the real reason Madonna Louise Ciccone, the rock star, was rejected by the tenants of a fancy apartment house in New York City when she offered to pay more than $1 million for an apartment there? Wasn't it because she posed nude for Playboy magazine?—I.M.P., Spanish Fork, Utah.*

Madonna

A Tenants of the San Remo, a cooperative in Manhattan, do not make public their reasons for accepting or rejecting the offers of potential residents. Dustin Hoffman and Diane Keaton are two of the many celebrities who occupy apartments in the posh Central Park West building. Madonna did not pose in the nude specifically for *Playboy* magazine. In 1979, when she was down on her luck and trying to earn enough money to put together a band, she posed for two art photographers, Lee Friedlander and Martin Schreiber, who later sold the black-and-white photos.

Brooke Shields

Q *I was speaking with a friend about the high morals of Brooke Shields. My friend said Brooke had been arrested in England once on a drug charge. Is this true?—Jeree Crowther, Long Beach, Calif.*

A It is not.

Q *The newspapers and TV stations say that Ronald Reagan worked for the FBI as an informant in the 1940s. How long was Reagan with the FBI, and why has this side of his career never been made public until recently?—P.G., Los Angeles, Calif.*

A Ronald Reagan was never an FBI agent. In the 1940s, however, he was active in the Screen Actors Guild and became most knowledgeable about the attempts of Communist Party members and sympathizers to infiltrate the various unions and gradually take over the film industry. The FBI questioned him from time to time about trends, tactics and personalities, and Reagan cooperated. He was then a liberal Democrat but alert enough to resign from several organizations that he felt were becoming Communist fronts. He has written in detail of these affiliations in his autobiography, *Where's the Rest of Me?* "It was an interesting period in my life," he recalls in

print. "Nor was it without rewards and sacrifices. By the time it was over, I was president of the Screen Actors Guild—and I had lost my wife." The wife Reagan refers to is Jane Wyman, from whom he was divorced in 1948.

Q *In her life story, Martina Navratilova frankly confesses her sexual orientation to women. She writes that she came to "realize my attractions—social, emotional, professional, intellectual, sexual—were toward women." Since Martina was born in Czechoslovakia, can't she be deported from this country on grounds of unnatural sexual affinity or moral turpitude?—Phil R., Brownsville, Tex.*

A Martina Navratilova is an American citizen. On her application for citizenship, she admitted to bisexuality. She did not perjure herself. Citizenship was granted in 1981. It cannot be revoked now on grounds of her sexual preference.

Q *Whatever happened to the book Lana Wood was writing about her famous sister, the late Natalie Wood? Is it true that Lana has always been in love with her former brother-in-law, actor Robert Wagner?—Jenny Sullivan, Huntsville, Ala.*

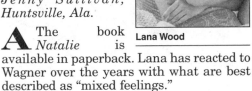

Lana Wood

A The book *Natalie* is available in paperback. Lana has reacted to Wagner over the years with what are best described as "mixed feelings."

Q *How old is Sammy Davis, Jr.? Was he married to Swedish actress May Britt or to Hollywood actress Kim Novak? And does he have any children?—Doris Kaplan, Oak Lawn, Ill.*

A Sammy Davis, Jr., will hit 60 on December 8. He dated Kim Novak in the 1950s—much to the outrage of her employer, Harry Cohn, head of Columbia Pictures—but he never married Kim. Davis did, however, marry May Britt on November 13, 1961. Once under contract to 20th Century-Fox, May abdicated her film career to rear their daughter, Tracey, and two adopted sons, Mark and Jeff. The Britt-Davis marriage was dissolved in 1968, and two years later Sammy married dancer Altovise Gore.

Jackie Kennedy Onassis and Maurice Tempelsman

Q *Is Maurice Tempelsman, the New York City businessman, still the favorite escort of Jackie Kennedy Onassis? Did Tempelsman ever work for the investment banking house of Lazard Frères? And didn't he play some role in negotiating Jackie's prenuptial agreement with Aristotle Onassis, which guaranteed her $25 million in advance?—M.J., Oyster Bay, N.Y.*

A Maurice Tempelsman is one of Jackie Onassis' favorite escorts, one may assume. But Tempelsman never worked for Lazard Frères and had nothing to do with arranging a prenuptial agreement between Jackie and Aristotle Onassis. Those arrangements were undertaken by the late Andre Meyer of Lazard Frères, who served as Jackie's financial adviser. Reportedly Christina Onassis, Aristotle's sole surviving child, settled $26 million on Jackie as her stepmother's share of the Onassis estate.

Q *All the photos I've seen of Mikhail Gorbachev, the new Soviet leader, show him with a large scar on his forehead. Is it a battle scar, a birthmark or what?—B. McNulty, North Las Vegas, Nev.*

Mikhail Gorbachev

A Some physicians suggest it is a birthmark consisting of enlarged capillaries that form a claret-colored patch beneath the skin.

PERSONALITY PARADE®

December 29, 1985

Orson Welles

Q *I'd like to know when Orson Welles attended Brooklyn Technical High School and the date he was graduated.—G. Anderson, Elmont, N.Y.*

A The late Orson Welles never attended Brooklyn Technical High School. He did, however, attend the Todd School in Woodstock, Illinois, from which he was graduated in 1931 at the age of 16.

Q *Is the Rockefeller family going broke? Is that why they sold more than a billion dollars' worth of securities to the public?—L.P., Brewster, N.Y.*

A The Rockefellers aren't going broke. They sold $1.3 billion in their real-estate investment trust—Rockefeller Center Properties in New York—to pay off some short-term debts. This afforded various family members an opportunity to diversify their investments by converting some holdings into cash.

Q *Is it safe to say Mrs. Reagan has had more clout in White House affairs than any other First Lady in this century?—Vinny O'Brien, Fort Wayne, Ind.*

A Nancy Reagan says that she brings her influence to bear on White House matters only when it appears to her that her good-natured, trusting husband is being taken advantage of or poorly served. "If I think that somebody isn't playing straight with him," she explains, "then I get involved." To date, Mrs. Reagan has been held responsible for some key White House personnel changes. It would not be prudent, however, to pinpoint her as the most influential First Lady of the century. Surely she will be remembered as one of the most influential.

Q *Compared to the general public, it seems to me, there's a disproportionate percentage of left-handed people in the entertainment field. Can you verify this observation?—Fred Peterson, Fort Worth, Tex.*

A There are no scientifically acceptable studies that uphold or disprove your observation. Up to 15 percent of the general population, it has been estimated, is left-handed.

Globe

Coretta Scott King

Q *Did Mrs. John F. Kennedy and Mrs. Martin Luther King, Jr., know of their husbands' extramarital affairs? Why haven't these affairs tarnished the reputations of both men?—C. Smith, Dallas, Tex.*

A Mrs. King and the former Mrs. Kennedy are both alert, intelligent, sensitive and perceptive women who were aware of their late husbands' proclivities. Sad to say, the extramarital alliances of both men *have* tarnished their reputations.

Q *Would you please satisfy my curiosity about that marvelous actor,*

George C. Scott? What does the "C" in his name stand for? To whom has he been married? Who is his present wife? What does he mean when he describes himself as a "functional alcoholic"?—Lois G., Davenport, Iowa.

A George Campbell Scott, 58, has been married five times: to Carolyn Hughes, his student in a theater group at Stephens College in Missouri; Pat Reed, an actress; Colleen Dewhurst, an actress to whom he was twice married; and actress Trish Van Devere, his spouse since 1972. Scott reportedly has been afflicted from time to time with a drinking problem. Its chronicity, however, does not prevent him from functioning as an actor on the stage, screen and television.

Q *How valid is the rumor that the British royal family has been tolerant of homosexuals and bisexuals because some of its own members were homosexuals? Didn't that gay playwright, Noël Coward, engage in sexual high jinks with one of the male royals, or was it with more than one?—D.P.D., Washington, D.C.*

Noël Coward

A The late playwright-actor Sir Noël Coward, a self-admitted homosexual, reportedly "engaged in sexual high jinks," to use your expression, with the Duke of Kent, who was killed in an air crash in 1942. Kent—the younger brother of the Prince of Wales, who later became King Edward VIII—was a well-known bisexual whose taste for black women and effeminate white men has been cited in the published diaries of the 1920s and '30s. The British royal family has attracted to its company men of talent, wit and sophistication, among them such bisexuals as Cecil Beaton, Harold Nicolson, Terence Rattigan, Benjamin Britten and others. *Remembered Laughter: The Life of Noël Coward,* by Cole Lesley, *The Noël Coward Diaries, the diaries of Sir Robert Bruce Lockhart* and *Royal Feud,* by Michael Thornton, are among the published works dealing in part with the sexual orientation of the British establishment.

John Wayne

Q *The late John Wayne was such a great and heroic patriot onscreen. Will you please explain then, if you can, how he avoided military service in World War II, when he was only 34 and in prime physical condition?—T. Conroy, Milwaukee, Wis.*

A Wayne already was the father of two boys and two girls when the U.S. went to war in December 1941. He therefore was exempt from the draft. Occasionally he spoke of volunteering to serve in the armed forces but somehow never got around to it.

Q *Who is Tatum O'Neal's mother— Joanna Moore, Leigh Taylor-Young or Farrah Fawcett?—Nell Graham, Dallas, Tex.*

A Tatum O'Neal was born to Joanna Moore, the first of Ryan O'Neal's wives, in 1963.

Q *Whatever happened to the romance between Joan Kennedy, ex-wife of Sen. Edward Kennedy and Dr. Gerald Aronoff, the physician who gave her a facelift? Weren't those two supposed to get married after Joan's divorce came through?—Jane McEwen, New York, N.Y.*

A The Kennedy-Aronoff romance faded. Dr. Aronoff performed no plastic surgery on Joan. Her face reportedly was "lifted" in January 1980 by Dr. Steven Sohn at Hahnemann Hospital in Brighton, Massachusetts, where Mrs. Kennedy registered under her mother's maiden name, Virginia Joan Stead.

Q *Who picked up the postage and labor bills for the mailing and addressing of 125,000 Ronald and Nancy Reagan Christmas cards?—A. Farthing Owens, Woodland, Maine.*

A The Republican National Committee paid for the cards and mailing. Volunteers did the addressing.

Q *What's become of Kate Smith, the famous singer of yesteryear?—Jacquie Shaw, Flagstaff, Ariz.*

A Kate Smith, 78, best known for her rendition of "God Bless America" recently had her right leg amputated at the Raleigh Community Hospital in Raleigh, North Carolina, because of circulatory problems brought on by diabetes.

Q *Is Quincy Jones, one of this country's most outstanding black musicians, married to a woman of his own race? I say he is not. My mother says he is. Would you please identify the present Mrs. Jones?— Roberta Johnson, Corpus Christi, Tex.*

A Quincy Jones, 53—musician-composer-arranger and the producer of the hit film *The Color Purple*—has been happily married since 1974 to Peggy Lipton, 38, the blonde former star of the *Mod Squad* TV series. They have two children: Kidada, twelve, and Rashida, nine.

Q *Who is the well-known governor who beats his wife? If you don't choose to identify him, could you at least give us a hint?—A.T., Jacksonville, Fla.*

A Sorry, we don't know of any such governor in office at this time.

Q *Why have the Hollywood movie studios, even before the era of AIDS, tried so desperately—and, for the most part, so successfully—to keep secret the homosexuality of their male stars? In Europe, homosexual and bisexual actors have not been compelled to lead such ruinous double lives. Your opinion, please.—K.J., Denver, Colo.*

A In this country, homosexuality has long been equated with effeminacy, weakness, wickedness and, most important, the deterioration of the American family. In many cases, Hollywood actors became shining and profitable stars before studio officials even learned of their homosexuality. By then, the studios had invested so much money in these actors that the executives were compelled to protect them from disclosure. Rock Hudson, Montgomery Clift, Tyrone Power, Charles Laughton, James Dean, Ramon Novarro and Sal Mineo were among those homosexuals or bisexuals who eventually were known in the movie colony as "gay deceivers." They joined in the studios' conspiracy of silence because they realized they would never work as actors again if the true nature of their sexuality became public. In Europe, the tolerance of gay artists is far more widespread than it is here.

Rock Hudson

Montgomery Clift

Bing Crosby

Q *I was shocked to learn that the late Bing Crosby was a cowardly monster who beat his boys until their blood ran. His eldest son, Gary, later suffered from alcoholism. How did Bing Crosby manage to deceive his adoring public and hide his shameful crime? Didn't the boys' teachers or the Crosby family doctor become suspicious?—Margaret L. Kempf, Greenbelt, Md.*

A Bing Crosby, who died in 1977, may not have been a particularly good father to his four sons by Dixie Lee Crosby, but he certainly was no "cowardly monster." He believed that sparing the rod would spoil the child. He had a particularly difficult time rearing his first son, Gary, but sent him to the best private schools, including Stanford University, provided him with many professional opportunities and established a handsome trust fund for him, as well as for his other offspring. Bing Crosby was a cool, reserved man whose image as a bright, friendly, cheerful singer-actor was projected and protected by the Paramount Pictures publicity department. He was not a sadistic child-abuser, however, and should not be held responsible for Gary's capitulation to alcoholism. Crosby was a much better father to his second set of children—Mary, Harry and Nathaniel—by his second wife, the actress Kathryn Grant.

Q *Debra Winger, the actress who had a heavy thing going with our Gov. Bob Kerrey, recently married actor Timothy Hutton. How much older is she than Hutton, and how long do you give the Winger-Hutton marriage?—A.S., Lincoln, Neb.*

Bob Kerrey

A Debra Winger was born on May 17, 1955; Timothy Hutton on August 16, 1960. If they can avoid career conflicts—admittedly a difficult task in Hollywood—there is no reason why their marriage can't last, since both are astute, mature people.

Q *Is Rose Kennedy, 95, matriarch of the Kennedy family, really the miser she is made out to be in the press?—D. Ryan, Albany, N.Y.*

A When Mrs. Kennedy was healthy enough to run her household, she was obsessively frugal.

Q *It is my understanding that last year President and Mrs. Reagan were given some $200,000 in gifts by then-President Marcos of the Philippines, King Fahd of Saudi Arabia, Queen Sirikit of Thailand and many others. Where can I obtain a list of who gave what to whom?—L. Davis, Seattle, Wash.*

Ronald Reagan

A If you write to the Superintendent of Documents, U.S. Government Printing Office, Washington, D.C. 20402, enclosing a check to the Superintendent for $1.50 and requesting the March 7, 1986, issue of the *Federal Register,* you will find in it 18 pages of the official gift list, detailing donors and recipients and other salient information.

Q *Oprah Winfrey of WLS-TV in Chicago, who was nominated for an Oscar as Best Supporting Actress for* The Color Purple—*was she really raped by a member of her own family, or was that story leaked to win her sympathy? How was Winfrey chosen for her part of Sophia in the movie? I would appreciate any*

other tidbits about her.—Windy Coleman, Detroit, Mich.

A Oprah Winfrey is 32, five-feet-seven, weighs 190 and works as host of *The Oprah Winfrey Show* (formerly *AM Chicago*), a successful talk show that will be telecast on some 120 stations this fall. She in part owes her role in "Purple" to Quincy Jones, producer of the film, and Steven Spielberg, its director. Jones caught her TV show while lounging about in a Chicago hotel room and suggested to Spielberg that he test her for the Sophia role.

Born in Kosciusko, Mississippi, reared in Milwaukee and Nashville, Winfrey is the product of a broken home. She is the source of information concerning her rape at nine by a cousin and subsequent sexual abuse by a boyfriend of her mother. She attributes much of her success to her father, a Nashville barber and strict disciplinarian who saw to it that she avoided further harm and faithfully attended Tennessee State University, where she earned a degree in speech and drama.

Q *Who are the four U.S. presidents not buried in the U.S.?—Mark Jacobson, Hampton, Va.*

A Nixon, Ford, Carter and Reagan.

Richard Nixon

Joe Kennedy

Q *Well, well, well. I see that Caroline Kennedy, daughter of our assassinated President John F. Kennedy, plans to marry her boyfriend, Edwin Schlossberg, this summer. How much older is Schlossberg than his bride-to-be? Isn't Caroline's grandfather, old Joe Kennedy, turning over in his grave at even the thought of such a marriage, since Schlossberg comes from a Jewish family and Caroline from a Catholic one?—M.M., Chatham, Mass.*

A Caroline Kennedy is 28, her fiancé 41. We cannot contact "old Joe Kennedy" at this time, but we suspect that the late U.S. ambassador to Great Britain, wherever he may be, is thrashing about in fury at the vision of his granddaughter marrying Schlossberg—unless, of course, Schlossberg decides to become a Roman Catholic or agrees that any children from his marriage to Caroline will be reared as Catholics. During World War II, when Kathleen Kennedy, one of Joe and Rose Kennedy's five daughters, married William Hartington, an Englishman and a member of the Church of England (Protestant), her parents disapproved and declined to attend the wedding.

Q *What is the mystery behind Mario Lanza's death? Is it true that the Mafia had him killed? Why hasn't a biography ever been published about him?—Richard Mack, Wheeling, Ill.*

A Mario Lanza (real name: Alfredo Arnold Cocozza) was a mentally disturbed singer-actor who suffered from chronic obesity, alcoholism and drug addiction. Unable to fulfill his contractual commitments in Hollywood, he moved in the late '50s to Rome, where he overate, overspent and overwomanized. Unfortunately, he reportedly gave his word to Lucky Luciano, a Mafia bigwig, that he would perform at a concert in Naples in October 1959. Fearful of appearing but afraid of Luciano's revenge, Lanza checked himself into the Valle Guila Clinic on a weight-loss program. Only 38, he died at the clinic on October 7, 1959—some say of heart failure, others of an embolism. At the time, rumors were rife in Italy that Lanza had reneged on a deal with the Mafioso and had paid with his life. That was the opinion of his wife, Betty, who followed him in death five months later. One fairly truthful biography of the singer is *Lanza: His Tragic Life,* by Raymond Strait and Terry Robinson, who was Lanza's physical trainer and closest friend.

Q *We now have three former U.S. presidents—Nixon, Ford and Carter—living. Have we ever had this situation before?—E.F. Borden, Akron, Ohio.*

A Yes, many times. And once, when Lincoln took office in 1861, we had five living ex-presidents: Van Buren, Tyler, Fillmore, Pierce and Buchanan.

Q *I've read that Robert Redford, Harrison Ford and Kirk Douglas have all had facelifts. Can this be true?—J.D., Washington, D.C.*

Harrison Ford

A It's reported to be true of Kirk Douglas.

Q *To what do you attribute the success of* The Cosby Show? *—Amanda Keeley, Rockville, Md.*

A To Bill Cosby's acting talent and the basic concept of his TV program, which is to treat truthfully and humorously the small, everyday, normal aspects of family life. The writers of *The Cosby Show* make it a point to avoid the trite crisis situations used in most TV sitcoms.

Q *For the fourth time: Who is the member of the Reagan cabinet referred to as "Fathead"? And which of the Washington lobbyists with great access to the White House is known as "The Raging Queen"? Why won't you reply?—K.L., McLean, Va.*

A Sorry, but to answer your two questions would do more harm than good.

Princess Diana, Prince Charles, and family

Q *With Prince Charles flying around the world so much, what would happen if he were killed? Who would become the future king of Great Britain—his brother, Prince Andrew, or his first son, little Prince William? Also, what would Diana's status become? Would she be allowed to remarry?—D.G., San Diego, Calif.*

A If Prince Charles were to die, the next in line to the throne would be Prince William. Diana would remain Princess of Wales and would be allowed to remarry, but it is hardly likely that she would do so without royal permission.

Imelda Marcos

Q *Imelda Marcos, late of the Philippines, had a wardrobe, it turns out, filled with some 3,000 pairs of shoes and 500 black brassieres. How does one describe such a woman? Surely, she must be sick, sick, sick.—Jeremy Marshall, Galveston, Tex.*

A Mrs. Marcos is probably a victim of the "shu-bra syndrome," an affliction caused by the bacillus acquisitivitus.

Q *Why has Steven Spielberg, director of* The Color Purple, *developed into such a controversial Hollywood director? Is he well liked or not well liked by the people he works with? I was under the impression that he was very popular in the motion picture industry. Is he not?—Stephanie Bledsoe, Norfolk, Va.*

Steven Spielberg

A Steven Spielberg, 38, is enormously popular in the screen colony. He is a thoughtful, generous and helpful colleague, especially with young people. His motion pictures have grossed more than $500 million to date. Despite the tremendous box-office success of his films, some critics, both within and without the industry, have judged them to be superficial, sentimental and essentially juvenile. In addition, some of his colleagues—a portion of them no doubt jealous—have accused him of "infantilizing" Hollywood film production. This basically is why Spielberg has yet to win an Oscar for direction and why he is the target of controversy.

Q *I grew up believing that the late Ingrid Bergman was a loyal, wholesome, faithful, beautiful wife and mother until she succumbed to the charms and wiles of Roberto Rossellini. Now I read that while she was married, she had affairs with Spencer Tracy, Gary Cooper, director Victor Fleming, photographer Robert Capa, harmonica player Larry Adler and many others. What is the truth about Bergman?—N.M.P., Bristol, Va.*

A Ingrid Bergman was a lusty, beautiful, self-obsessed, purposeful, goal-oriented actress. Men fell in love with her because she was cheerful, friendly, sympathetic, sexy in a sunny way and endowed with intelligence and a sense of humor. She used her sex appeal to entrap strong men like Gary Cooper and Anthony Quinn to do her bidding, and she proved to be no exemplary wife to any of her husbands—Dr. Petter Lindstrom, Roberto Rossellini and Lars Schmidt. She cheated on all three. Yet she had the ability to generate purity, virtue and honesty. She also was a woman of courage who gallantly fought a terminal disease for 10 years. Bergman was a study in contradictions. A *PARADE* reporter, who knew her well, says: "She tried to go through life doing no harm, but almost always she navigated by the star of self-interest."

Q *Is there a law which says no woman can marry into the British royal family until she first passes a virginity test? Did Sarah Ferguson, 26, fiancée of Prince Andrew, also 26, have to pass such a physical?—Julia F., Jefferson City, Mo.*

A No such law applies to Sarah Ferguson or Prince Andrew, who is fourth in line to the throne.

Q *Why do producers of TV shows like* Meet the Press *and* Face the Nation *invite Caspar Weinberger, the secretary of defense, to appear on their programs when (1) Weinberger is an obvious echo chamber for the administration, (2) Weinberger refuses to answer provocative questions, (3) Weinberger is an expert in the art of filibustering, and (4) Weinberger is obviously smarter than his interrogators and is forthcoming with very little that is newsworthy?—R.G., Springfield, Va.*

A Weinberger has name recognition. Weinberger likes TV and feels at home with the medium. Weinberger is one of the most readily available members of the cabinet. Weinberger has some industrious and knowledgeable men on his public-relations staff, and they do a very good job for him.

John F. Kennedy

Q *How many future U.S. presidents served in the Navy during World War II?—Eddie Maykut, New Britain, Conn.*

Richard Nixon

A Five: John F. Kennedy, Lyndon Johnson, Richard Nixon, Gerald Ford and Jimmy Carter.

WALTER SCOTT'S
PERSONALITY PARADE®

June 1, 1986

Judy Garland

Q *How old is Liza Minnelli? How old was she when her parents split? Who is her current husband? And is it true that the great sorrow of her life is that she is unable to bear children?—Maureen Fitzgerald, Renton, Wash.*

A Liza Minnelli was born March 12, 1946, in Los Angeles. She was five when her parents, singer-actress Judy Garland and film director Vincente Minnelli, were divorced. At this writing, Minnelli is still married to her third husband, Mark Gero. Despite numerous miscarriages, she has not abandoned hope of having offspring. "Mark and I will keep trying," she likes to say, "till I get it right."

Q *Everyone agrees that Libya's No. 1 natural resource is oil. Why then, instead of bombing military and residence targets, didn't President Reagan order our planes to bomb the oil fields, storage deports and refineries on April 14? That would have hurt Qaddafi and Libya where it hurts the most—in the pocket.—J.C., Los Angeles, Calif.*

A Second-guessing is easy. But one possibility which comes quickly to mind is that five U.S. companies—Occidental Petroleum, Conoco, Amerada Hess, Marathon and Grace Petroleum—were then still under contract to operate the oil fields in Libya. Some of their American personnel were given special dispensation by the U.S. Treasury Department to remain there for a while.

Q *How many women agents are there in the FBI? Who was the first?—Mack Miller, Houston, Tex.*

A At this writing, 651 women account for 7.3 percent of the FBI's total force of 8,972 agents. The first woman "special agent" was Jessie Duckstein, appointed on November 6, 1923, by FBI Director William Burns. The first woman "special investigator," however, was Alaska Davidson, appointed on October 11, 1922. Both women worked in the bureau's Washington, D.C., office and both resigned in 1924, the year J. Edgar Hoover took over as director.

Q *Is there any well-known actress who is "the single parent of eight children"? I must have the correct answer, because I'm participating in a quiz.—Dana L., Kennebunkport, Maine.*

A Mia Farrow, 41, is one such parent. She has three sons by her second husband, conductor Andre Previn, and five adopted children—for a total of eight. She and Previn were divorced in 1979.

Q *Please settle this family tiff. My husband says Sally Ride, the first U.S. woman astronaut shot into space, was an ordained Presbyterian minister before becoming an astronaut. I say she was never an minister. Who is right?—M.R., Topeka, Kan.*

A You are, but your husband is not far off the mark. Sally Ride's sister, Karen "Bear" Scott, is a Presbyterian minister in Southern California.

Q *What happened to my favorite movie star, Gregory Peck? Has he retired? If so, why doesn't he run for mayor of Beverly Hills, the way Clint Eastwood ran for mayor of Carmel? I'm sure Greg would win.—Corinne Gatlo, Brawley, Calif.*

A Eldred Gregory Peck, 70, has not retired from acting or producing. He is, in fact, preparing a new screen version of *Dodsworth*, the 1929 novel by Sinclair Lewis. Peck does not live in Beverly Hills, but he has always been a civic-minded participant in the politics of the nation. One day he could possibly, if he so chooses, run for office.

Lyndon Johnson

Franklin Roosevelt

Q *Please answer these two questions if you can: (1) After President Franklin D. Roosevelt died in 1945 and Harry Truman succeeded him, who was vice president of the U.S. from 1945 to 1949? (2) Which U.S. president in this century was elected with the largest percentage of the popular vote?—C.T. Bradbury, Gallup, N.M.*

A We had no vice president from April 12, 1945, to January 20, 1949. Truman served without a vice president until the swearing in of Alben Barkley of Kentucky, with whom he had defeated Thomas Dewey and Earl Warren in the 1948 presidential race. Running against Barry Goldwater for president in 1964, Lyndon Johnson won with 61.05 percent of the vote, breaking the record of 60.79 percent set by FDR in 1936 when he defeated Alfred M. Landon.

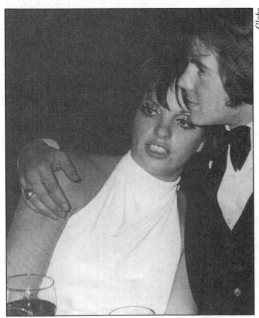

Liza Minnelli

WALTER SCOTT'S

PERSONALITY PARADE®

June 8, 1986

Patti Davis

Ulysses Grant

Q *President Reagan and his wife, Nancy, have two children, Patti and Ron. Patti has had her first novel* Home Front, *published, and her kid brother is a contributing editor to* Playboy *magazine. Do you think either of these two kids could have made it as writers if their surname was Smith or Schwart, and their old man was a dress salesman?—D.G., Charleston, S.C.*

A There is little doubt but what both Reagan offspring have capitalized on their family name or relationship.

Q *Which universities have provided this country with the most presidents? Am I correct in assuming that they are Yale, Harvard and Princeton?—William R., Macon, Ga.*

A Harvard was the undergraduate alma mater of five U.S. presidents: John Adams, John Quincy Adams, Theodore Roosevelt, Franklin D. Roosevelt and John F. Kennedy. The College of William and Mary was the alma mater of three presidents: Thomas Jefferson, James Monroe and John Tyler. Two, James Madison and Woodrow Wilson, were graduated from Princeton when it was still known as the College of New Jersey. And two, Ulysses S. Grant and Dwight D. Eisenhower, were

graduates of the U.S. Military Academy. To date, Yale has been the undergraduate alma mater of only one president, William Howard Taft.

Q *Ever since Edward VIII abdicated his British throne in 1936 for the love of Mrs. Wallis Simpson, it has been rumored that she had some sort of mysterious sexual hold on him which was so pleasurable to him that he could not or would not give her up. Now that she has passed on, was the rumor true?—A.K., Henderson, Nev.*

A For the last 50 years, that particular rumor has been widely circulated in Europe. No evidence is available, however, to substantiate or deny its truth and none is likely to appear. Although beauty lies in the eyes of the beholder, the late Duchess of Windsor was not an especially seductive looking or alluring woman, which is probably why her detractors ascribed to her a potent bedroom technique. To many of them, that seemed the sole reason for which a king would sacrifice his crown.

Q *I recently read about Edwin Wilson, a former CIA agent originally from Nampa, Idaho. He helped supply Libya with plastic explosives and other muni-*

tions. I'd like to find out where Wilson is in jail and for how long.—P.B., Portland, Ore.

A Wilson was convicted of smuggling weapons and of conspiracy to commit murder, and he received sentences totaling 52 years. At this writing, he is confined in the federal penitentiary at Marion, Illinois. He may be eligible for parole consideration around the year 2002.

Q *Do you know of one leading actor or actress in motion pictures, television or on the stage who is willing to come out of the closet and admit to being a gay?—Olive B., Reno, Nev.*

A Not at this time.

Q *Where does Danny Glover come from, Atlanta or New York? He is the hottest black actor of the hour, having worked in* The Color Purple, Silverado, Witness *and* Places in the Heart.—*Wade Bennett, Bronx, N.Y.*

A Glover, 38, is a modest, talented, native San Franciscan who lives in the Haight-Ashbury district of that city with his longtime wife, Asake, a jazz vocalist, and their daughter, Mandisa, 10. Glover attended San Francisco State University, where he graduated from student activism to stage-acting and later to TV and film work.

Ginger Rogers   **Rita Hayworth**

Q *Is it true that Ginger Rogers, 74, and Rita Hayworth, 67—Fred Astaire's former dancing partners—are cousins?—Jov Louras, Greenwich, Conn.*

A Yes. Ginger's aunt married Rita's uncle, making the two screen stars cousins by marriage.

Fred Astaire

Alfred Hitchcock

Grace Kelly

Q *Alfred Hitchcock supposedly said Grace Kelly was not opposed to having affairs with her leading men. Who were the lucky guys?—Laurie S., Scranton, Pa.*

A Ray Milland, Bing Crosby, Clark Gable and William Holden were a few with whom her name was coupled publicly and privately.

Q *Does Johnny Carson have a new lady-love since his third marriage, to Joanna Holland, went south? From his record, he is not a man to go through life without some attractive female companionship.—Claudia H., Lincoln, Neb.*

A You are right. Carson's lady-love is "Alex" Maas, 36, a former secretary.

Q *I am struck by the lifestyle and sensational success of actress Jessica Lange. Ten years ago, she was an unknown in an awful remake of* King Kong. *Since then, she has had two children born out of wedlock—one to the magnificent dancer Mikhail Baryshnikov, another to the actor-playwright Sam Shepard. She also has been in love with Bob Fosse, who directed her in* All That Jazz. *Career-wise, she has won an Oscar for her acting in* Tootsie *and been nominated for two others for her performance in* Frances *and* Sweet Dreams.

In addition, she has become a producer and starred in her own production of Country. *Lange seems to be amazingly versatile and talented. How old is she? Where's she from? What else should we know about her? Is she talented, lucky or both?—Rachel F., Austin, Tex.*

A Jessica Lange—born April 20, 1949, in Cloquet, Minnesota—lived in 18 small towns as a youngster, attended the University of Minnesota for a year or two and fell in love on campus with a filmmaker named Paco Grande, with whom she subsequently spent much time in New York and Paris. They were married in 1970. A dozen years later, Grande, losing his eyesight, filed for divorce and sued Lange for support and legal fees, a large share of which the court ordered her to pay. Trained as a mime in the 1970s in Paris, Lange survived by waitressing and modeling. In 1976, she was signed by Dino De Laurentiis to make her film debut as the blonde victim in *King Kong.* Her photo on the cover of *Time* magazine in the hand of the giant ape brought her instant recognition and publicity. She is both lucky and talented and shows discrimination in her selection of lovers and scripts. She is a lady of character, integrity and independence.

Q *There's a rumor in publishing circles concerning David Stockman, President Reagan's former director of the Office of Management and Budget. Stockman, who got $2 million for his book,* The Triumph of Politics, *is said to have employed a ghostwriter on the project. If true, was the ghostwriter Christopher Buckley, William F. Buckley's son? Did young Buckley get a 50-50 split?—J.Y., Ocean Park, Calif.*

A *The Triumph of Politics* was not ghostwritten; it was authored by David Stockman. Christopher Buckley, however, was paid approximately $75,000 by Stockman and the publishing house of Harper & Row to edit, rewrite, structure and improve the author's draft, as well as to meet the necessary publishing deadlines. In his controversial book, Stockman readily acknowledges Buckley's assistance.

Q *How old are Barbara Stanwyck and Charlton Heston of* The Colbys *TV series? And how come Heston's hairpiece doesn't fit his head?—Phyllis Sterling, Biloxi, Miss.*

A Stanwyck is 79, Heston 62. Some heads are easier to fit with hairpieces than others.

Q *I saw on TV the Smothers Brothers describing Ronald Reagan as a "known heterosexual." How can they get away with such stuff? Isn't there some way the network can be fined for spreading such a dirty lie?—H.G., Prescott, Ariz.*

A It is not a lie. Reagan is a "known heterosexual." Obviously you are confusing heterosexual with homosexual. A heterosexual is one whose sexual attraction is toward a member of the opposite sex. A homosexual is one characterized by a sexual interest in a person of the same sex.

Ronald Reagan

Elizabeth Taylor

Imelda Marcos

Q *Which screen star has the most valuable collection of personal jewelry?—Donna Friedman, Portsmouth, Va.*

A Probably Elizabeth Taylor, 54, who over the years has steadily acquired—through gifts and purchases—some of the most magnificent pieces in the world, especially diamonds.

Q *The Democratic Party will soon control both the U.S. Senate and the House of Representatives. Does that mean President Reagan should be classified a lame duck or a dead duck?—Morton Lewis, Las Vegas, Nev.*

A Ronald Reagan, in our opinion, is more a lame than a dead duck. Like other two-term-presidents with only two years left in the White House, he has moved into a twilight zone of rapidly diminishing political influence and power. Reagan retains, however, an extraordinary amount of Teflonized popularity with legislators and the lay public.

Q *Why is Joan Rivers so controversial? Is there any part of her body that has not been reconstructed by plastic surgeons? Who has had more plastic surgery, Joan or Phyllis Diller?—Lorry Haines, Dallas, Tex.*

A Joan Rivers, 53, is not controversial, but to some her comedy is. They find it nasty, abrasive, distasteful and unladylike. Others consider it witty and hilarious. Joan admittedly has had her face, eyes, nose, stomach and thighs redone. Phyllis Diller, 16 years her senior, says: "I've had so much plastic surgery that the only original parts left are my elbows." Once entertainers take the plastic surgery route to improvement, they find it necessary to repeat the procedures every five to seven years, as their skin loses tone and resilience.

Q *Does Oprah Winfrey, the TV talk-show hostess, have a boyfriend or husband? What is the secret of this woman's amazing success?—Suzanne Earl, Eagle Rock, Calif.*

A Oprah Winfrey's gentleman friend as of this writing is Stedman Graham of Chicago, head of Athletes Against Drugs. Winfrey's success has been attributed to her ability to project sincerity. Many viewers are convinced that she genuinely identifies with them and their problems, because she's black, overweight and has experienced rejection.

Q *How do Ferdinand and Imelda Marcos, who are alleged to be notorious liars, respond to questioners and lawyers who accuse them of plundering the assets of the Philippines?—Manuela R., Kaneohe, Hawaii.*

A In deposition proceedings, Mr. and Mrs. Marcos simply invoke their Fifth Amendment rights and decline to answer questions because they might incriminate themselves. In nonjudicial confrontations, they allegedly lie, deny, evade and play the innocents.

Q *The Second Amendment to our Constitution states: "A well regulated Militia, being necessary to the security of a free State, the right of the people to keep and bear Arms, shall not be infringed." My sister insists that the Second Amendment provides all U.S. citizens with the right to buy and bear arms privately. I maintain that it does not. Has the Supreme Court ruled on this amendment?—A. Winstead, Annapolis. Md.*

A The Supreme Court in two cases, *Presser vs. Illinois* (1886) and *United States vs. Miller* (1939), has held that there is no constitutional right that empowers citizens to bear arms privately.

Q *Recently I saw an example of Nancy Reagan's signature. Some of the letters appeared to be reversed. Does Mrs. Reagan suffer from dyslexia, or is her signature a mark of individualism or fashion?—Doug Walker, Euless, Tex.*

A Nancy Reagan's "manuscript" penmanship is individualistic and representative of the style taught her at The Girls Latin School of Chicago as a teenager. She is not dyslexic.

Q *Has pop star Olivia Newton-John split from her husband, Matt Lattanzi, who is 11 years younger than she is? Who got custody of their daughter?—Morley Richard, Sydney, Australia.*

Olivia Newton-John

A Olivia Newton-John, 38, and her actor-husband, Matt Lattanzi, 27, maintain that they are blissfully happy—especially with their 11-month-old daughter, Chloe. So happy, in fact, that they want another child.

Chris Evert and John Lloyd

Priscilla Presley

Q *After seven years, is the marriage of tennis star Chrissie Evert to John Lloyd over? If it is, whom will she wind up with: singer Adam Faith, actor Malcolm McDowell or actor Warren Beatty?—Maybellene Smith, Indianapolis, Ind.*

A At this writing, Chris Evert Lloyd and her husband, the British tennis pro John Lloyd, are said to have agreed to a trial separation. Obviously, their marriage is rocky. They previously went their separate ways for about six months in 1984, during which Chrissie and Adam Faith, a British show-biz entrepreneur and singer, dated in various cities around the world. Faith, however, is happily reconciled to his wife, and Chrissie—who reportedly has dated actor Judd Nelson and others since her fling with Faith—is seemingly too intelligent to marry on the rebound. It may well be that she will remain married to her tennis until someone or something more exciting comes along.

Q *Priscilla Presley recently announced that she was pregnant by her Brazilian boyfriend, Marco Garibaldi, who is 10 years younger than she is and with whom she has been living. Is Elvis' onetime wife married to Garibaldi, or is she not? And how does Lisa Marie, Priscilla's 18-year-old daughter, feel about her mother's pregnancy?—Jane M., Knoxville, Tenn.*

A Priscilla Presley, 41, is not married to Marco Garibaldi as we go to press, but she may be shortly. Lisa Marie, who was on hand for her mother's announcement of her out-of-wedlock pregnancy, says, "I'm very excited and happy for both my mother and Marco."

Q *Is it possible that if George Bush is elected president in 1988, his first move will be to pull a Gerald Ford and pardon ex-President Ronald Reagan for any of the crimes he may have committed in office?—J.B., National City, Calif.*

A "Possible" is an adjective that offers virtually endless hypotheses. The move you suggest is highly improbable. Ronald Reagan is no Richard Nixon, and George Bush is no Gerald Ford.

Q *The world of fashion seethes with the rumor that Nancy Reagan has dropped her longtime favorite, Jimmy Galanos, for gowns designed by Valentino. True?—Susan G., New York, N.Y.*

A The word in New York fashion circles is that Mrs. Reagan is not dropping Jimmy Galanos but rather including in her wardrobe the creations of Valentino and other designers.

Q *In the 1950s, there was a beautiful brunette at 20th Century-Fox named Debra Paget. What's happened to her?—Eloise McManus, Denver, Colo.*

A In 1962, Debra Paget married L. C. Kung, a Houston oilman of Chinese descent, and retired from the screen at 29. They later divorced.

Q *Big John Connally—former governor of Texas and treasury secretary under Richard Nixon, who wanted him to succeed to the presidency—is supposed to be broke and down on his luck. I thought he was close to being a billionaire and was financially one of the sharpest men in the U.S. What's the story?—F.D., New Orleans, La.*

A Connally and former Lt. Gov. Ben Barnes of Texas are real-estate partners, reportedly $170 million in debt. Connally, also chairman of Chapman Energy in Dallas, has explained: "It's a difficult time for anybody who's in the oil business, the real-estate business or agriculture, and I'm in all three." Connally is a brainy, resourceful man of 69 who may be foundering financially at this writing, but no one should count him out.

Q *When I was in Paris last summer, everyone was raving about the performance as a grandfather given by Yves Montand in the film* Jean de Florette. *At the same time, it was being said of Montand, who had been married for years to the late Simone Signoret, that politically he had crossed from the left to the right and was planning to run as a possible candidate for president of the French Republic. How old is Montand? Does he intend to quit acting for politics? Has he really moved from the far left to the far right?—A.F., New Paltz, N.Y.*

Yves Montand

A Italian-born Yves Montand, 65, is not abandoning the notable career he has fashioned in France as an actor and singer. He has, however, altered what once were considered his pro-Soviet leanings for a more conservative political stance. He says he has no intention of trying to succeed François Mitterrand, current president of France, but he would like his political voice to be heard.

Pope John Paul II

Q Why is it that John Paul II, the most widely traveled pope in history, has not been to Israel, birthplace of Christianity? Surely it cannot be for security or safety reasons, as he has traveled to other "hot spots" and countries where Catholics are not the majority. Israeli officials have said the pope would be allowed to visit and have invited him. Then why the reluctance to go?—Tom Snyder, Arlington, Tex.

A "It may be that Roman Catholic bishops in Israel have not yet invited the pope to make a pastoral visit," explains a spokesman at the Vatican Embassy in Washington. "There also may be other reasons to which we are not privy."

Q Vanna White, hostess on the Wheel of Fortune TV game show—what is the secret of her appeal? All she seems to do is to turn letters on a word-puzzle board. What can you tell us about her?—Laura Schaeffer, Brooklyn, N.Y.

A Vanna White, 29, was reared in North Myrtle Beach, South Carolina, where her dad is in real estate. She tried her luck as a model in Atlanta in 1976, migrated to Hollywood in 1980 and later was signed by Merv Griffin for Wheel of Fortune. Her appeal seems to be based on her normalcy, her looks and the fact that

Vanna White and Billy Hufsey

she arouses no jealousy among females in the audience. For several years, Vanna lived with John Gibson, a TV actor, but he died last May in an aircraft accident. Of late, she has been dating Billy Hufsey of TV's Fame, Vanna is now working on an autobiography in which she'll reveal much. Basically she is a non-Hollywood type who lives in the hills of Hollywood.

Q What can you tell us about Bob Hoskins, who won the Best Actor award at Cannes for playing the cheap crook and driver in the film Mona Lisa? Is he an Englishman or an American? Married? Age?—Jill Greengold, Queens, N.Y.

A Bob Hoskins, 44, who played a screenwriter in Sweet Liberty and the gangster Owney Madden in The Cotton Club, was born in Bury St. Edmunds, 60 miles north of London. The short, squatty son of a bookkeeper and a nursery-school teacher, Hoskins hated school and quit at 15. After working at odd jobs for several years, he joined his dad as an accounting clerk. Then, sitting at the bar in London's Unity Theatre one evening, he was called on to read for the lead in a play, Feather Pluckers. Since he found the business world insufferably dull, Hoskins decided to chance acting. He got the part and an

agent, later married a drama teacher. The marriage lasted six years and produced two children—Alex, now 18, and Sarah, 13. In 1981, Hoskins met another teacher, Linda. They married and have a pair of offspring—Rosa, three, and Jack, one. A playwright as well as a player, Hoskins is regarded as a versatile, gifted, hard-drinking, much-in-demand character actor—in fact, one of England's finest.

Q I see that Vice Adm. John Poindexter, who was chief adviser in the National Security Council, ranked No. 1 among the 900 graduates of the U.S. Naval Academy's Class of 1958. But what were the academic rankings at Annapolis of Lt. Col. Oliver North and his deputy, Lt. Col. Robert Earl? All three officers maintained their constitutional rights in refusing initially to testify before the Senate Intelligence Committee in the Irangate scandal.—C.S., Washington, D.C.

A In 1968, in his class of 836 at the U.S. Naval Academy, Oliver North ranked 468th. Robert Earl ranked 24th out of 890 in 1967 and won a Rhodes Scholarship to Exeter College at Oxford.

Q I understand David Eisenhower has written a big, fat, 1,000-page book on his grandfather, Gen. Dwight Eisenhower. Does he tell anywhere the true story concerning his grandfather's friendship with Kay Summersby, who drove for Ike during World War II?—S.S., Corvallis, Ore.

A In Eisenhower: At War 1943-1945, David Eisenhower writes that Kay Summersby alleged a love affair with Ike but concludes "the truth was known only by them, and both are gone." Beyond that, he has virtually nothing to say about the so-called "Eisenhower-Summersby affair."

Dwight Eisenhower

Madonna

Marilyn Monroe

Q *Is it true that rock star Madonna plans quietly to divorce actor Sean Penn in the weeks to come and devote most of her time to her film career?—Liz Gillespie, Petersburg, Va.*

A According to disk jockey Simon Bates of the British Broadcasting Corp., who interviewed her not too long ago, Madonna is a good Catholic girl who—despite numerous quarrels with her temperamental husband—maintains, "I'm still in love with Sean, and there's no question of my divorcing him . . . I plan to go easy on the music this year and concentrate on three films."

Q *It has been said and written of the late Marilyn Monroe that she was promiscuous, not by nature, but because that was the only way she could survive in her early days in the Hollywood jungle. It also has been said that she engaged in at least one lesbian affair with a writer, a press agent or a drama coach. Are these stories based on fact or fiction?—Jan W., Ann Arbor, Mich.*

A Marilyn Monroe, according to several *PARADE* photographers and at least one reporter who knew her well, used her sexuality to get ahead in Hollywood because she realized early in the game that it was her sole negotiable asset. Few men, in or out of the film industry, were interested in her mind, but she was frequently interested in theirs. She was basically heterosexual but hinted of one lesbian dalliance with a press agent.

Q *Is it true, as printed in* The Chief, *by Lance Morrow of* Time *magazine, that President Kennedy had to have daily sex relations or he would get a bad headache?—C.H., Stanford, Calif.*

A Morrow writes in his book: "Once, John Kennedy told Harold Macmillan that he would get a headache if he did not have sex with a woman at least once a day." Morrow's best memory holds that the late British prime minister picked up that information when he and Kennedy conferred in Bermuda in December 1961. Only Kennedy, of course, knew the truth of his sexual needs.

Q *How did the wife of the late President Lyndon Johnson come to be known as Lady Bird?—Mr. and Mrs. Daniel Bensinger, Grantville, Pa.*

A When the former Claudia Alta Taylor was a tot in Karnack, Texas, a nurse said of her, "She's as pretty as a ladybird." From then on, she was called Lady Bird—a nickname Mrs. Johnson, 74, has retained all through her eventful life.

Q *Does Henry Kissinger own Macy's, the department store chain? That's what I've been told by a friend who is in the retail business.—Nora G., Birmingham, Mich.*

A Kissinger does not own R. H. Macy & Co. According to a 10K report filed with the Securities and Exchange Commission, however, he does own 2,524 preferred shares (or 6.03 percent) of the Macy Acquiring Corp., which last July purchased R. H. Macy in a leveraged buyout. Kissinger also has a seat on the corporation's board of directors.

Q *Diane Sawyer of 60 Minutes and Richard Holbrooke, who was an assistant secretary for East Asian and Pacific affairs under President Carter—weren't they quietly married in Elkton, Maryland, some weeks ago?—Heather R., McLean, Va.*

A At this writing, Sawyer of CBS and Holbrooke, who works for the Shearson Lehman brokerage firm in New York, are not married.

Q *Was Martin Luther King's marriage to Coretta as perfect as I've read, or was it really tough going? How many children did they have, and what is each doing?—Terry Porter, Gary, Ind.*

A The marriage of Martin Luther King, Jr., and Coretta Scott King was not the idyllic coupling some writers have described. It endured from 1953 to 1968, many of those years characterized by almost unbearable stress and strain. The Kings had four children: Yolanda, 31, a producer, lecturer, director and artist; Martin Luther King III, 29, elected last year to a seat on the Fulton County Commission in Atlanta; Dexter, 26, a consultant in Atlanta in the music and real-estate fields; and Bernice, 23, candidate for a law degree and master's degree in theology at Emory University, Atlanta.

Martin Luther King

Coretta King

Prince Charles and sons

Brigitte Nielsen and Sylvester Stallone

Q *In all the articles about Prince Edward, who recently quit the Royal Marines, he is described as "the 22-year-old prince who is fifth in line to the British throne." Who are the four ahead of him?—Rosemary W., Asbury Park, N.J.*

A Prince Charles is first in line to inherit the throne from his mother, Queen Elizabeth II. He is followed in the accession order by his two sons: Prince William, four, and Prince Harry, two. In fourth position is Prince Andrew, and in fifth is Prince Edward—both of them the younger brothers of Prince Charles.

Q *Can you please name the composer and title of the theme music played for the Gallo wine commercial? It is hauntingly beautiful. Is it available in music stores?—A. McGrath, Redondo Beach, Calif.*

A The title of the music is "Hymne," by Vangelis Papathanassiou, best known for his score for the film *Chariots of Fire*. The selection is part of the Vangelis album "Opera Sauvage" (Polydor), available wherever records are sold.

Q *I understand that Sylvester Stallone is so afraid that harm will come to his wife, Brigitte, who towers above him, that he has hired at least three bodyguards to look after her at all times. Is that true?—Kimberley H., Henderson, N.C.*

A Stallone's wife, the former Brigitte Nielsen, seems always to have at least one bodyguard within arm's length—except when she goes to the powder room, and then the guard stands outside. It is Stallone, however, who is accompanied by a minimum of three bodyguards.

Q *I read in the papers that Johnny Carson is about to take a fourth bride in the form of Alex Maas, a shapely blonde he met on the beach near his house. How much support money does Johnny have to pay his third wife, Joanna?—Anna Silverman, Los Angeles, Calif.*

A The former Joanna Holland, to whom the comic was married from 1972 to 1985—reportedly receives $20,000 a month. The divorce settlement also gave her ownership of several properties.

Q *How old is Gloria Vanderbilt, and how many husbands has she had? Was director Stanley Kubrick one of them?—Cheryl D., Sioux City, Iowa.*

A Gloria Vanderbilt, 63, has been married four times—to talent agent Pat di Cicco, orchestra conductor Leopold Stokowski, director Sidney Lumet and writer Wyatt Cooper. Only Lumet, 62—director of such films as *Dog Day Afternoon*, *Network* and *The Morning After*—survives.

Q *Harold Macmillan, the former British prime minister who recently died at 92, had a wife, Dorothy, daughter of the ninth Duke of Devonshire. It was well known in upper-class British circles that she cheated on her husband. Was her lover Winston Churchill?—A.L., Washington, D.C.*

A Her lover was Robert Boothby, a life peer and member of the House of Lords. Lady Dorothy Macmillan died in 1966.

Q *Is it true that Dr. Martin Luther King, Jr., was uncontrollably oversexed? Is that why he had harems in so many cities across the country? And isn't that why a jealous J. Edgar Hoover of the FBI had his phones tapped? Didn't he plan to ruin King's marriage and reputation by distributing those tapes to the press?—Ilena Morales, El Paso, Tex.*

A There is no evidence that Dr. King was "uncontrollably oversexed" or "had harems in so many cities across the country." He was, however, a charismatic personality who attracted women of all races to his hotel rooms—in many of which the FBI had recording equipment. Hoover, a lifelong bachelor, detested King—not only because of the black leader's expansive sex life but also because he felt King was under the influence of Stanley Levison, a lawyer and adviser who allegedly was a Communist. Hoover's assistant, William Sullivan, had tape recordings attesting to King's activities in the bedroom mailed to several reporters and King's associates in the Southern Christian Leadership Conference, but the tactic did not bring King down. A good book on the subject is *Bearing the Cross*, by David J. Garrow.

Q *Is it true that Arnold Schwarzenegger—the body-builder, film star and California real-estate entrepreneur—is a Republican, even though he's married to Maria Shriver, the most successful grandchild of the Joseph P. Kennedy Democratic dynasty?—Susan Kessler, Santa Cruz, Calif.*

Arnold and Maria

A Schwarzenegger makes no secret of the fact that he is a Republican and a staunch supporter of Ronald Reagan.

Desi Arnaz and Lucille Ball

Q *At the services for her first husband, Desi Arnaz, Lucille Ball described him as a great father, a great husband, a great producer, a great businessman and a great entertainer. If he was all that great, why did she divorce him? Was he too young for her?—G. Martinez, North Miami, Fla.*

A Desi Arnaz, who died last year at age 69, was six years younger than Lucille Ball, but the age difference was not the cause of their divorce in 1960. Desi reportedly suffered from a bad case of the roving eye, a strong yen for the grape and an insecure ego. He was also a generous, fun-loving, multitalented man who was incapable of handling a strong, authoritarian wife.

Q *Linda Evans, star of* Dynasty, *is sexy, captivating and simply beautiful. Why then did her husband, John Derek, drop her? How old is Linda? Where was she born? And is Linda Evans her real name?—F. Margulies, Towson, Md.*

A John Derek fell in love in 1973 with 16-year-old Mary Cathleen Collins (now Bo Derek) and fell out of love with his third wife, Linda—who was born in Hartford, Connecticut, on November18, 1942, and christened Linda Evanstad.

George Bush

Q *Does George Bush believe he can be nominated for and win the presidency in 1988 on the basis of his unswerving loyalty to the Ronald Reagan record?—M.A., Kennebunk, Maine.*

A Bush believes he can win on such factors as loyalty to Reagan; his experience in government as a congressman, ambassador and director of the CIA; and his personality and political philosophy.

Ronald Reagan

Q *Lillian Hellman who wrote* The Little Foxes, The Children's Hour, Watch on the Rhine *and other hit plays and books, was well recognized as the lover of writer Dashiell Hammett of* Thin Man *fame. She also was supposedly the lover of a famous publisher. Was he William Randolph Hearst, Henry R. Luce or Marshall Field?—K.H., New Orleans, La.*

A Lillian Hellman (1905-84) was heavily involved for a time in the early '40s with the late Ralph Ingersoll, founder of the newspaper *PM* and publisher of several others. An excellent book on her work, love affairs and turbulent relationships is *Lillian Hellman, the Image, the Woman,* by William Wright.

Q *I would like to know why Barbara Walters is the highest-paid journalist in television.—Melissa Clark, Muscle Shoals, Ala.*

A Barbara Walters is one of the highest-paid TV journalists. The highest is Dan Rather, with an annual salary of $2.5 million to $3 million. Walters earns about half that munificent sum.

Q *I recently saw a TV salute to Clint Eastwood. At the start of the show, he introduced his son and daughter, but there was no mention of their mother. Who is she? Were she and Eastwood ever married?—Cindy Dobbs, Baltimore, Md.*

A Eastwood and the former Maggie Johnson married in 1953, split in 1980. Their son, Kyle, was born in 1968; daughter, Alison, in 1972.

Q *When President Reagan was sworn into office in 1981, he took an oath to uphold the Constitution. Now some say he violated that oath by supporting members of his staff who circumvented the so-called "Boland Amendment" of October 1984, passed by the Congress, banning military aid to the Contras. Where in our Constitution does it say a president must support all the laws passed by Congress?—M.G., Washington, D.C.*

A Art. II, Sec. 3, of the Constitution says: "he [the President] shall take care that the laws be faithfully executed." It does not say "all the laws" or "some of the laws" or "only those laws he favors," but the general interpretation holds that a president must take care to see that all the laws passed by Congress are faithfully executed.

George Burns

Ernest Hemingway

Q *This isn't very important, but perhaps you can settle a family dispute. It concerns George Burns, the comedian who was married to the late Gracie Allen. I maintain that Burns is 91 and was married twice. My boyfriend insists that Burns is 90 and was married only once. What is the right score?—Sybil Haber, Queens, N.Y.*

A George Burns was born Nathan Birhbaum on January 20, 1896, and was married twice. His first wife and vaudeville partner was Hannah Siegal. His second was Gracie Allen, who died in 1964. You are right on both scores.

Q *When Ronald Reagan was a movie star, was he romantically involved with any of the actresses he worked with?—Lay Lanum, Ewing, Ky.*

A Yes, with actress Jane Wyman during the filming of *Brother Rat* in 1938. They were married two years later and divorced in 1948.

Q *How large an estate did Ernest Hemingway's widow, Mary, leave to her black friends and black institutions? Also, who introduced her to Hemingway—novelist Irwin Shaw, photographer Robert Capa or Time magazine's London bureau chief, Walter Graebner?—L.G., Lansing, Mich.*

A Mary Welsh Hemingway—the novelist's fourth and final wife, who died last November 26 at age 78—left an estate of about $3 million. She bequeathed a large share to Meharry Medical School in Nashville, attended mostly by blacks, the United Negro College Fund and the American Museum of Natural History. She also left $200,000 to the Ernest Hemingway Foundation to finance a yearly prize to a previously unpublished fiction-writer. It was Irwin Shaw who introduced Mary Welsh Monks to Hemingway in 1944. Shaw was then a GI in London, Hemingway a war correspondent, Mary a *Time* magazine staffer.

Q *How old is Cybill Shepherd of Moonlighting TV fame, and has she married her chiropodist yet?—C. Whitmore, Hilo, Hawaii.*

A Cybill Shepherd's lover, Bruce Oppenheim, is a chiropractor, not a chiropodist. A chiropractor is one who believes the state of a person's health is determined by the condition of the musculoskeletal and nervous systems and who seeks to restore normal condition, primarily by manipulation of the spinal column. A chiropodist treats disorders of the feet. Shepherd is 37 and reportedly anticipates marriage to her chiropractor any day now.

Q *How tall is the Rev. Jesse Jackson, the black politician? Has Life magazine paid him $1 million for his autobiography? Where did he go to college and from which seminary did he graduate?—Mary Lee Smith, Hickory, N.C.*

A Jesse Jackson, 45, is 6 feet 2 1/2. Simon & Schuster paid him an advance of $350,000 for his autobiography. After graduating from Sterling High School in Greenville, South Carolina, Jackson entered the University of Illinois on a football scholarship in 1959. He soon transferred, however, to North Carolina Agricultural and Technical College in Greensboro, where he graduated in 1964 with a degree in sociology. He then attended the Chicago Theological Seminary but dropped out six months before graduation. Jackson later was ordained a minister at Chicago's Fellowship Baptist Church.

Q *Is Liza Minnelli, daughter of the late Judy Garland and the late film director Vincente Minnelli, involved in a family dispute over her father's will? I thought Liza was his only child, and he left her everything.—D. Anthony, Brooklyn, N.Y.*

A Vincente Minnelli, who died last July at age 83, had two daughters—Liza Minnelli, 41, and Christiane Minnelli Miro, 31, by his second wife, Georgette Magnani. He bequeathed to Liza his Beverly Hills home and personal possessions. He left Christiane, who resides in Mexico, $5,000. Christiane, in the midst of a divorce, reportedly is contesting her father's will on the grounds that he was recovering from a stroke, and was therefore of unsound mind, when the document was drawn.

Q *Is Emilio Estevez, the actor-writer-director and son of actor Martin Sheen, mixed up in a paternity suit? Is he married to Demi Moore, his co-star in Wisdom?—Dana Baker, Seattle, Wash.*

A Carey Salley, a model, is seeking $15,000 a month in child support from Estevez, 24, alleging that he is the father of her son, Taylor, two, and daughter, Paloma, one. Estevez declines to discuss the case but reportedly has been giving Salley more than $3,000 a month. At this writing, he is not married to Demi Moore, but their marriage is expected momentarily and may already have occurred.

David Letterman

Q *Guests on Johnny Carson's and David Letterman's TV talk shows—how much are they paid?—Sandra Reid, Richmond, Va.*

A At this writing, the Carson and Letterman guests are each paid $520 per appearance.

Q *Has Lee Iacocca, the dynamic chairman of Chrysler Motors, divorced his young wife, or have they reconciled?—Stephanie R., Hendersonville, N.C.*

A Last December—after just eight months of marriage—Lee Iacocca, 62, filed for divorce from his 36-year-old wife, Peggy. At press time, however, there was talk that the Iacoccas were back together again or soon would be.

Q *Was Ginger Rogers ever married to a multimillionaire named Michel Bergerac? His name frequently appears in the press in connection with the severance pay of $35 million he received from Revlon.—Hank Lynch, Naples, Fla.*

A Ginger Rogers never was married to Michel Bergerac, former chairman of Revlon. It was his older brother to whom the screen star was married from 1953 to 1957. The actor Jacques Bergerac was Rogers' fourth husband.

Q *I read that Princess Caroline, the eldest child of the late Grace Kelly and Prince Rainier of Monaco, is expecting her third child by husband Stefano Casiraghi. Did Caroline ever succeed in getting the Roman Catholic Church to annul her first marriage, to Philippe Junot? If not, doesn't that make her children illegitimate in the eyes of the church?—Mary Mooney, Boston, Mass.*

A At this writing, the Vatican has not yet ruled on Princess Caroline's application to annul her marriage to Junot. A strict interpretation of church law would probably hold her offspring by Casiraghi to be illegitimate.

Q *Hear, kind sir, this anguished cry for help. I was assigned to write a paper, "The Role of Maria Halpin in U.S. History." Pray tell: Who is or was Maria Halpin?—R.C., Baton Rouge, La.*

A Maria Halpin was an attractive widow who, in the early 1870s, managed the coat section of a department store in Buffalo, New York. One of the men she dated during that time was a lawyer, Grover Cleveland, who later would become president of the U.S. In 1874, she gave birth to a son, Oscar, and named Cleveland as the father. There was much doubt concerning the boy's paternity, but Cleveland accepted the responsibility because he was the only bachelor among the men who had been intimate with the widow and so had less to lose than they. He agreed to support the boy but declined to marry Maria, who then turned to drink.

Cleveland subsequently called upon an old friend, Judge Roswell Burrows, for advice. The judge ordered Mrs. Halpin to a temporary stay in an insane asylum and her son to an orphanage, for which Cleveland paid $5 a week. Upon her release, Maria tried to regain custody of Oscar. She lost her fight in the courts, however, and in 1876 kidnapped the child. The authorities quickly found the boy and returned him to the orphanage. He later was adopted by a prominent New York family and became a physician. Maria remarried. In 1884, when Cleveland ran for president on the Democratic ticket, his opponents chanted: "Ma, ma, where's my pa? Gone to the White House, ha, ha, ha."

Q *Marilyn Monroe's name has been linked with John F. Kennedy and his brother Robert. Who was the Hollywood beauty who was linked romantically with all four Kennedy brothers as well as their father? Wasn't she the late Jayne Mansfield, who was graduated from Bryn Mawr College?—P.W., Ojai, Calif.*

A Some Hollywood beauty may have known or been friendly with all five male Kennedys, but she certainly wasn't the late Jayne Mansfield. Jayne was only 11 years old when Navy pilot Joe Kennedy, Jr., oldest of the four Kennedy brothers, lost his life on August 12, 1944, in World War II. Mansfield, incidentally, was born in Bryn Mawr, Pennsylvania, but never attended the college there. The actress, who died in a car crash in 1967, maintained that she had attended UCLA, the University of Texas and Southern Methodist University but never claimed Bryn Mawr as her alma mater.

John F. Kennedy

Robert Kennedy

Jayne Mansfield

Rita Hayworth

Q *How old was Rita Hayworth when she broke into films? Who were the men in her love life besides those she wed?—Titiana M., Detroit, Mich.*

A Hayworth was 16 when she was hired by the Fox studio in 1935. Between her five marriages, she was romantically involved with Victor Mature, Errol Flynn, Howard Hughes, David Niven and others. Her affair with Mature, she once confided to a reporter, "is one I'll always remember." Ironically, Hayworth came down with Alzheimer's disease, which deprived her of her memory.

Q *After reading about Amy Carter, I'm curious about whether she still is provided Secret Service protection. Yes or no? If yes, how long does it continue?—Barbara Hess, Saginaw, Mich.*

A The Secret Service accorded Amy Carter around-the-clock protection until she reached the age of 16—on October 19, 1983.

Q *I would like to know more about John W. Nields, Jr., who acted as chief House of Representatives counsel during the Iran-Contra hearings. I found him more fascinating to watch than Oliver North.—Sheri Pierce, Seattle, Wash.*

Howard Hughes

A Nields, 44, is a partner in the Washington, D.C., law firm of Howrey and Simon. He was reared in New York City and educated at Andover, Yale and the University of Pennsylvania Law School. He and his wife of 24 years, Gail, 43, live in McLean, Virginia, where they are regarded as one of the best tennis-playing couples in the area. They have three daughters: Nerissa, 20; Katryna, 18; and Abigail, 13. Nields has divided much of his time between work for the government and private law firms. He has served as law clerk to Supreme Court Justice Byron White, as assistant U.S. attorney for the Southern District of New York and as chief counsel in the 1977 Koreagate investigation. He is widely respected as both an expert prosecutor and an able defense attorney. His grandmother was a founder of Bennington College in Vermont.

Q *Has Jesse Jackson, who wants to be the first black man elected president of the U.S., ever held public office? Were there any men who never held elective public office until they won the presidency?—Margaret Weintraub, Reno, Nev.*

A Jesse Jackson has never held elective public office. Neither did Herbert Hoover and Generals Zachary Taylor, Ulysses S. Grant and Dwight D. Eisenhower before they won the presidency.

Q *Queen Elizabeth recently gave her daughter, Princess Anne, the title Princess Royal. What does it mean?—Yolanda Dunn, Aspen, Colo.*

A The title Princess Royal is borne only by the oldest daughter of the British royal family, provided the sovereign sees fit to award it. It was granted to Princess Anne by the queen as a token of recognition for her work with children in Africa, India, Great Britain and the Middle East. Once regarded as rude, arrogant and abrasive, the 37-year-old princess today is held in high light by Britons for her humanitarian endeavors.

Q *I say no black celebrity has ever sought help at the Betty Ford drug-abuse treatment center. My wife says it goes a little further than that. She says black celebrities have sought help, but the Betty Ford Center doesn't treat blacks—celebrities or not. Please provide the answer. If blacks are accepted, would you please name a few of the most recent ones?—Ira Q. McElvin, Westboro, Mass.*

A Michael McFadden, spokesman for the Betty Ford Center at the Eisenhower Medical Center in Rancho Mirage, California, says your wife is wrong—that the Betty Ford Center accepts people of every race, religion and nationality. The center does not publicize any of its patients, however, without their prior permission. "If black celebrities, or celebrities of any color or creed," he explains, "want their presence and progress made public during their treatment, all they need do is to say so upon entering. Otherwise, the center will not violate the hospital-patient privacy relationship."

Q *What's the religion of Boris Becker, the tennis champion from Germany—Catholic, Protestant or Jewish?—Cliff T., Belleville, Ill.*

Boris Becker

A Boris Becker, 19, is a Roman Catholic who practices his faith. Last December, after services at the Vatican, he presented a smiling Pope John Paul II with a tennis racket.

Christina Onassis

Q *Could you please find out which woman of the world has been referred to as "the Greek tanker"?—Ardis J., Avon Park, Fla.*

A In European jet-set circles, Christina Onassis, 37-year-old daughter of the late Greek shipping tycoon Aristotle Onassis, has been known by that title because of her chronic obesity.

Q *Does Ronald Reagan wear bullet-proof garments in public?—G.H., El Paso, Tex.*

A Only when the Secret Service, mindful of local conditions, so advises.

Q *Which one of Ernest Hemingway's granddaughters checked into the Betty Ford Clinic to seek help for drug abuse? Was it Margaux or Mariel?—Laura T., Billings, Mont.*

A It was Margaux Hemingway, 33, who checked into the Betty Ford Clinic last December, determined to defeat alcoholism. Before drink did her in, Margaux was one of the nation's top models, her face adorning the covers of *Vogue* and other magazines. Her attempts at a happy marriage and movie stardom have been disastrous—but, with good health and renewed

beauty, she has some of the attributes necessary for a successful film career.

Dolly Parton

Q *Some sophisticated critics say that Dolly Parton's TV variety program is not so hot because her sincerity and Southern accent are exaggerated. What is your opinion?—Phyllis D., Chattanooga, Tenn.*

A On her TV show, Dolly Parton projects the image of the simple, ingenuous, guileless, unaffected country-western singer—which may be an affectation. More important yet, the TV variety genre seems to have gone out of style with the departure of *The Carol Burnett Show* nearly 10 years ago. Today, we have on television a number of talk shows in which the host interviews a variety of personalities who perform as comics, singers, musicians and celebrities. So who needs the old-fashioned "variety show" format?

Q *Is it a fact that the financial worth of the Rev. Jesse Jackson is a tightly held secret and hardly anyone knows where his money comes from? Do you? If so, please share that hard-to-come-by information.—Arney Johnson, Louisville, Ky.*

A A financial disclosure statement filed by Jackson last October with the Federal Election Commission shows his annual income at more than $250,000. In 1986, he earned $192,000 from Personalities International, a lecture bureau in Chicago. He also earned $33,000 in honoraria for speeches and personal appearances at various churches, universities and conventions. In addition, he received $18,750 from his National Rainbow Coali-

tion. Jackson is the owner of two residences—one in Chicago and one in Washington, D.C.—and recently gave a third to his mother. Estimates of his financial worth, based on little more than hearsay, range from $500,000 to $1 million.

Q *Are William Hurt, the star of Broadcast News, and Marlee Matlin, the deaf actress who worked with him in Children of a Lesser God, still taken with each other, or have they gone their separate ways?—Pat Rose, Pontiac, Mich.*

A The film stars' two-year love affair has diminished to the level where it now can be filed under the heading "Yesterday's Romance."

Q *How many National Security Council advisers has the president appointed to date? Can you name them?—Sam Gordon, East St. Louis, Ill.*

A To date, President Reagan has appointed six NSC chiefs: Richard Allen, William P. Clark, Robert McFarlane, Adm. John Poindexter, Frank Carlucci and now Gen. Colin Powell.

John F. Kennedy

Richard Nixon

Q *May I impose upon you to answer this little bit of trivia: Who was the first president of the United States born in the 20th century, and where and when was he born?—Robert Proctor, Houston, Tex.*

Lyndon Johnson

A John F. Kennedy, born at home (83 Beals St. in Brookline, Massachusetts) on May 29, 1917, was the first U.S. president who'd been born in the 20th century. Lyndon Johnson, Ronald Reagan, Richard Nixon and Gerald Ford, in that order, all were born before Kennedy in this century but came after him in the White House.

WALTER SCOTT'S
PERSONALITY PARADE®

March 27, 1988

Charles A. Lindbergh

Elizabeth Taylor

Q *Who were* Time *magazine's first man and first woman of the year?—Jonathan Lee, Charlottesville, Va.*

A The magazine's first man of the year was Charles A. Lindbergh, in 1927; its first woman of the year was Wallis Warfield Simpson, in 1936.

Q *Each time I see President and Mrs. Reagan depart the White House for Camp David, I notice a crowd of people behind the ropes, waving goodbye to them. Who are these people? Are they tourists who are directed to this event with hopes of getting a glimpse of the Reagans, or are they White House staff and other paid government employees?—V. Milo Hansen, Bellevue, Wash.*

A The people who see the President and Mrs. Reagan off to Camp David consist of White House staff and their invited guests. Occasionally some tourists are allowed.

Q *Some questions about Liz Taylor and her diet book,* Elizabeth Takes Off: *Who wrote it for her? How much of an advance did she get? In her 56 years, what's the most Liz has weighed? Does she lose weight by plastic surgery or genuine dieting? Which of her husbands—she has been married seven times—and nonhusbands has Liz loved most?—Jacie Reed, New Orleans, La.*

A *Elizabeth Takes Off* reportedly was penned by ghostwriter Jane Seovell from tapes by Taylor. According to Chen Sam, who handles her publicity, the actress got an advance of about $750,000. Taylor's weight in the last 40 years has ranged roughly between 115 and 180 pounds, depending on her intake of food and alcohol. She admits to a chin tuck but angrily denies that her hefty weight loss was the result of liposuction or major plastic surgery. She is, after all, a woman of determination and willpower, without which she'd never have survived in the jungles of Hollywood. Of the many men in her life, she loved most the two from whom she learned the most: husband No. 3, Mike Todd, and husband No. 5 and 6, Richard Burton.

Q *I have never seen a motion picture with more extras in it than* The Last Emperor. *How many extras were hired, and how much did the film cost?—Yi Chung, San Francisco, Calif.*

A *The Last Emperor*—filmed in China, directed by Bernardo Bertolucci and with only one big name, Peter O'Toole, in the cast—cost approximately $25 million to produce. Some 19,000 extras were employed in the picture.

Q *Is there any truth to the rumor that Judge Joseph Wapner of TV's People's Court presided over the trial of Charles Manson, who was responsible for the murders of Sharon Tate and others?—Harriette Brent, Aurora, Colo.*

A No. The judge at the Manson trial was Charles H. Older of the California Superior Court.

Q *I am very interested in knowing which was the first country to recognize Israel as a state.—Jack Brauner, Rio Rancho, N.M.*

A The State of Israel came into being at midnight on May 14, 1948. It was first recognized as such 11 hours later, by the United States. Chaim Weizmann and David Ben-Gurion became Israel's first president and prime minister, and the new government was admitted to the United Nations on May 11, 1949.

Q *Is it true that Hugh Hefner, the publisher of* Playboy, *won't date a female over 30? How old is Hefner anyway?—Madeleine N., Atlanta, Ga.*

A Hugh Hefner was born in Chicago on April 9, 1926, which means he is en route to 62. He has dated several women over 30.

Q *Was Ava Gardner ever married to Sammy Davis, Jr.? If so, when were they married and for how many years?—B.J. Helms, Garland, Tex.*

A Ava Gardner was never married to Sammy Davis, Jr. The screen actress was married to Mickey Rooney from 1942 to 1943, to bandleader Artie Shaw from 1945 to 1946 and to Frank Sinatra from 1951 to 1957 (though separated after 1954).

Ava Gardner

Sammy Davis, Jr.

WALTER SCOTT'S
PERSONALITY PARADE ®

May 8, 1988

Patty Hearst

Q *In your March 6 issue, you said President Jimmy Carter pardoned Patty Hearst, who had been sentenced to seven years in jail for participating in armed robbery. I say you were wrong—that President Carter didn't pardon Patty, that he commuted her sentence to time already served—about 23 months. There's a great difference between a pardon and a commutation, is there not?—Laurie Ledbetter, Chapel Hill, N.C.*

A You are right. We goofed. A commutation is the substitution of a lesser punishment for a greater one, a shorter term for a longer one. It can be granted by a president or governor only after conviction, and it does not wipe clean all the legal disabilities of a conviction. A pardon, on the other hand, can be granted at any time—even before a trial—and in the eyes of the law the recipient of a full pardon is as innocent as if he or she had never committed any offense.

Q *I am informed that Debra Murphree, the lady of the night who was hired by TV evangelist Jimmy Swaggart to satisfy his urges, has signed to write a book about her spicy affair with him. What is the title of her book, and what is its publication date?—C.D., Santa Fe, N.M.*

Jimmy Swaggart

A Various publishers and publications have conferred with Murphree on the writing of her memoir. One reportedly subjected her to a lie-detector test as a prelude to a deal. But Murphree has not yet signed to write, or have written for her, the type of book you suggest. She has agreed, however, to pose for a magazine as she posed for Swaggart.

Q *Why would corporations that want to sell their products to the public hire someone like tennis star Jimmy Connors to endorse their wares when Connors, who is 35, hasn't won a leading tennis title in at least three years? As I recall, Jimmy was not the best-mannered competitor in the best of days.—Don C., Hilton Head, S.C.*

A Some corporate executives obviously believe Connors can help popularize and sell their products. His on-court behavior in this country appears to have improved, and he generates a "never-say-die" attitude and a humor that many tennis fans find appealing. Connors has been married for almost 10 years to the former Patti McGuire, one-time *Playboy* magazine centerfold. They have two children—Brett, eight and Aubree Leigh, three—and Connors is far from the hell-raiser he once was.

Q *Why did Melissa Gilbert give actor Rob Lowe the air after six years of their up-and-down affair and then marry the New York playwright and actor Bo Brinkman?—Willie Mae Whitehead, Jacksonville, Fla.*

A Melissa probably concluded that lover-boy Lowe was not ready for a mature commitment.

Q *About* The Tonight Show, *starring Johnny Carson: How much do guests get paid? What is the relationship between Carson and someone named Shirley Wood? What happened to Johnny's brother, Dick, who used to direct* The Tonight Show?—*Cleo Feldman, Brooklyn, N.Y.*

A Guests are paid a minimum of $490. Shirley Wood is a coordinator on *The Tonight Show*, one of the five who discover new guests, update conversation for old guests—provide the program with its lifeblood, figuratively speaking. Wood has been with the show since its inception. She is single and highly regarded by Carson as a friend and colleague. Dick Carson moved on from *The Tonight Show* to direct *The Merv Griffin Show* and currently handles *Wheel of Fortune*, one of the most popular quiz shows on TV. He and Johnny are brotherly and well-wishing.

Q *We know that Vice President George Bush was a Navy fighter pilot and that Sen. Robert Dole was a wounded infantryman in World War II. We also know that Sen. Albert Gore is a veteran of the Vietnam war. But how did the Rev. Jesse Jackson and Gov. Mike Dukakis fulfill their military obligations?—J.F. Rosser, Camp Springs, Md.*

A Jesse Jackson has performed no military service. Michael Dukakis served in the Army from 1955 to 1957, pulled duty in Korea and was honorably discharged as a Specialist 3rd Class.

Robert Dole

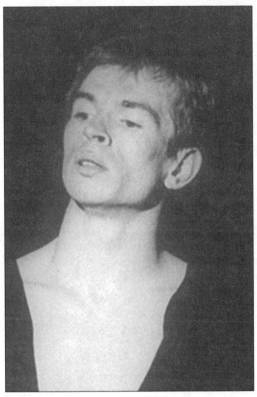

Rudolph Nureyev

Q *Which of these Russian emigres who have made it in the West—writer Aleksandr Solzhenitsyn, cellist Mstislav Rostropovich, dancers Rudolf Nureyev and Mikhail Baryshnikov—would return to live in the Soviet Union if he had the chance? Your opinion, please.—Sara Spiro, Piedmont, Calif.*

A Since all have achieved fame and fortune in the West, there seems to be no reason to return to the Soviet Union except for a visit, if that were permissible. All four, of course, have a deep love of "Mother Russia," but they also love freedom.

Q *Debra Winger and Timothy Hutton, Mary Steenburgen and Malcolm McDowell, Bruce Springsteen and Julianne Phillips—all reportedly are in various stages of splitting from each other. Why can't these young, attractive couples stay married?—Belle Adams, Kinston, N.C.*

A Some of them may stay married, since at this writing none has yet filed for divorce, though some surely will. It is difficult to sustain a show-business marriage in which both husband and wife are talented, ambitious, career-minded, competitive, sensitive and frequently exposed to temptation.

Q *Jane Pauley, co-anchor of the NBC-TV news show* Today, *was awarded the Radcliffe College Alumnae Association medal this past June. Unless I have lost my mind, Jane was not only a sorority sister of mine (Kappa Kappa Gamma) but also attended Indiana University with me. What is she doing with a Radcliffe alumnae medal?—A.S., Indianapolis, Ind.*

A The Radcliffe College Alumnae Association Medal is presented to a distinguished woman—not necessarily a Radcliffe graduate—who has made an outstanding contribution to the community of women. It was established last year to commemorate the alumnae association's 100th anniversary and was then awarded to singer Lena Horne. Jane Pauley is the second recipient of that honor.

Q *Barbra Streisand was truly magnificent in* Nuts. *Her performance as a call girl was super-super in my estimation. Why then did she fail to get even an Oscar nomination for her acting in the film? Could it be that the members of the motion picture academy are prejudiced against her, or can it just be jealousy?—Mandy Fleming, Southern Pines, N.C.*

A In the judgment of academy voters, Streisand's performance in *Nuts* was not as "super-super" as you contend. Streisand, it is said, is not overwhelmingly popular with her fellow workers.

Q *John Wayne, Frank Sinatra and Joe Louis—how many served in the armed forces of the U.S.?—Jimmy Little Turtle, Harrisburg, Pa.*

A Joe Louis (1914-81), one of the foremost heavyweight boxing champions of the century, served in the U.S. Army during World War II. Wayne and Sinatra never served. Wayne had four children and Sinatra a punctured eardrum—circum-

Joe Louis

John Wayne

stances that excused them from military service at the time.

Q *In the movie* Who Framed Roger Rabbit? *whose voice is used by the cartoon character Jessica Rabbit?—Kim Hayes, Michigan City, Ind.*

A The voice of actress Kathleen Turner is used when Jessica speaks, the voice of actress Amy Irving when Jessica sings.

Q *Are singer Linda Ronstadt and movie producer George Lucas engaged or just fooling around? I know that Lucas has previously been married, but how about Ronstadt? Incidentally, are they both diabetics?—R.B.R., Scranton, Pa.*

A At this writing, Ronstadt, 42, and Lucas, 44, are seeing a good deal of each other but are not engaged. To date, Ronstadt has never been married, nor is she a diabetic. Lucas is.

Q *Would you please release the names of the male celebrities with whom the late writer Truman Capote had affairs? I also would like to know if Capote ever had "a thing" with Elizabeth Taylor, who has always been kind to the sick and handicapped.— J.T., Woods Hole, Mass.*

Truman Capote

A Elizabeth Taylor never had an affair with Truman Capote. As for your other question concerning Capote's love life, one of the most complete biographies of the novelist is *Capote*, by Gerald Clarke, published by Simon & Schuster.

Paul McCartney and Linda Eastman

Brigitte Nielsen and Sylvester Stallone

Q *Linda Eastman, who married Beatle Paul McCartney—what was her family name before she married, and where did she go to school?—Gerry Frank, Stamford, Conn.*

A Linda's family name was reportedly Epstein. She was graduated from Scarsdale High School in Scarsdale, New York, and briefly attended Sarah Lawrence College in Bronxville, New York.

Q *President Reagan received blood transfusions following the attempt on his life in 1981. As there was no screening of blood then, doesn't this mean he is a "high-risk" candidate for AIDS? Has he ever been tested for AIDS? Do we have a right to know the results?—Robert B. Andrews, Boston, Mass.*

A Col. John Hutton, Reagan's White House physician, says: "The president was last tested for AIDS and the presence of the HIV virus, said to precede the disease, on December 12, 1986. All the pertinent tests were negative. The president has neither AIDS nor the antibodies indicating exposure to the virus."

Q *When Brigitte Nielsen married Sylvester Stallone, did they really celebrate by having their backsides tattooed as evidence of their great love for each other?—Mary W., Marion, Ill.*

A Not true of Nielsen and Stallone, but reportedly true of Nielsen and the lover who followed Stallone, New York Jets' football player Mark Gastineau.

Q *Is Anne Morrow Lindbergh, widow of the world-famous flyer, still living and writing? If yes, how old is she and where does she live? Did she have four or five children after Charles Lindbergh, Jr., her firstborn, was kidnapped? And who are they?—Elizabeth Norton, Laramie, Wyo.*

A Anne Morrow Lindbergh is 82, still writing and lives in the Connecticut area. Following the kidnapping and death of Charles Lindbergh, Jr., in 1932, she gave birth to Jon (1932), Land (1937), Anne (1940), Scott (1942) and Reeve (1945).

Q *Who is the agent who handles Eddie Murphy's television production company? I understand Mr. Murphy is in the market for a beautiful girl to act in a half-hour sitcom, not necessarily opposite him.—Lana T., Tenafly, N.J.*

A Eddie Murphy Television, which is based on the Paramount Studios lot in Hollywood, is represented by the William Morris Agency. The agency knows nothing at this time of the vacancy or casting search you describe.

Q *While touring Great Britain for several months, I gathered that Prince Charles, who one day will occupy the British throne, is estranged from his father, Prince Philip, the Duke of Edinburgh. Is it a fact that this strained father-son relationship has been kept hidden from the British public?—Arthur Levitan, San Pedro, Calif.*

A Prince Charles, 39, and his father, the Duke of Edinburgh, 67, do not get along too well, but they are not estranged. The duke, no mental heavyweight, is by nature aggressive, competitive, forceful, strong-willed and primarily physical. His eldest child, although a good athlete, is interested in the life of the mind. He is sensitive, literary, musical, responsive, perceptive and insightful. He is more tolerant and understanding than his father, who reportedly bullied him as a boy—something Charles has never forgotten.

It has been rumored in England for years that Prince Charles preferred the companionship of his flamboyant "Uncle Dickie"—Lord Louis Mountbatten, who was assassinated by the Irish Republican army in 1979—to the company of his father, in whose brusque manner he declines to follow. Having frequently encountered the rough side of his old man's tongue, Charles, it is said in court circles, does not invite more of the same. He stays away from the duke, whose favorite child reportedly is his only daughter, Princess Anne, who by reputation is as brash, churlish and impatient as he.

Prince Charles

Andy Warhol

Q *How large an estate did Andy Warhol leave when he died in 1987? How much did his two brothers inherit? What do you think he will be most remembered for?— H. Vincent, Montauk, N.Y.*

A Andy Warhol's estate has been valued at approximately $100 million. His brothers—Paul, 66, and John, 63—each inherited $250,000, according to John. Our guess is that the late artist will be most remembered for: (1) his memorable statement: "In the future, everyone will be famous for 15 minutes"; and (2) endowing the Andy Warhol Foundation for the Visual Arts.

Q *How many legally recognized offspring did Elvis Presley spawn before he died in 1977? And how much did he leave to each of his kids?—Andrea Altman, Virginia Beach, Va.*

Elvis Presley

A Elvis fathered only one lawful child—Lisa Marie, born on February 1, 1968, to Priscilla Beaulieu Presley. Priscilla and Elvis were wed in 1967, divorced in 1973. In his last will and testament, Elvis directed the trustee of his estate "to provide for the health, education, support, comfortable maintenance and welfare of (1) my daughter, Lisa Marie Presley, and any other lawful issue I might have, (2) my grandmother, Minnie Mae Presley, (3) my father, Vernon E. Presley, and (4) such other relatives of mine living at the time of my death who in the absolute discretion of my trustee are in need of emergency assistance . . ." The will also entitles Lisa Marie, on her 25th birthday, to take ownership of all assets in the trust created for her. These consist of Graceland, the Presley home in Memphis, record royalties, licensing fees for use of the Presley name and image, and other properties. When Elvis died, the IRS valued his estate at $15 million. Five years from now, it's expected to be worth $100 million, all of it the property of Lisa Marie, Elvis' sole surviving heir.

Q *It is 10 years since Louise Brown, the world's first test-tube baby, was born in England. Since then, more than 5,000 test-tube babies have been born. Have any been born to well-known actresses? I heard that Joan Collins is a possibility for motherhood by test tube.—Virginia K., Bloomfield Hills, Mich.*

A We are not aware of any well-known actress who has had a baby via the so-called "test-tube method." Joan Collins, 55, has three children, is not a candidate "for motherhood by test tube."

Q *Lt. Gen. Colin Powell, the first black to serve as national security affairs adviser to President Reagan—was he born in the West Indies or the U.S., and was he educated at West Point?—Ed Hill, Chattanooga, Tenn.*

A Lt. Gen. Colin L. Powell, 51—who in January became the sixth man appointed to serve Ronald Reagan as assistant to the president for National Security Affairs—was born in the Bronx in New York City, to Jamaican immigrant parents who worked in the garment trade. Powell did not attend the U.S. Military Academy at West Point. He was educated at the City College of New York, joined the ROTC (Reserve Officers' Training Corps) and was commissioned a second lieutenant in 1958. Later, he pulled two tours of duty in Vietnam, was awarded medals for valor in combat.

Q *It is not well known, but I am told on good authority that Gov. Michael Dukakis, who is running for president, and Sen. Paul Sarbanes of Maryland are cousins who both won Rhodes scholarships to Oxford. Is that information valid or accurate?—Bill Givens, Tempe, Ariz.*

A It is not. Dukakis and Sarbanes are not related. Both men, however, are the sons of Greek immigrant parents. Both were born in 1933, and both were outstanding undergraduates—Sarbanes at Princeton and Dukakis at Swarthmore. It was Sarbanes, however, who won a Rhodes scholarship to Balliol College in Oxford (1954-57), while Dukakis was called up for two years of service in the U.S. Army and sent to Korea. Dukakis and Sarbanes both attended Harvard Law School and were graduated in 1960. Both are married and have three children. Both are members of the Greek Orthodox Church, and both are Democrats.

Rita Wilson and Tom Hanks

Q *How old is Tom Hanks, who, in the movie Big, plays a 13-year-old boy in the body of a 35-year-old man? Also, is he married? What's his salary and next picture?—Gladys Greenwood, Salisbury, Md.*

A Tom Hanks, born 32 years ago in Oakland, California, has been married twice—in 1978 to Samantha Lewes and in 1988 to Rita Wilson. He has two children by his first wife: Elizabeth, 5, and Colin, 10. His current asking price: $5 million and up per picture. His next film: *Punchline*, in which he plays a stand-up comic opposite Sally Field.

WALTER SCOTT'S

PERSONALITY PARADE®

September 18, 1988

Princess Lee Radziwill

Q *Jackie Onassis is still going around with Maurice Tempelsman, the jeweler. But what has happened to her kid sister, Princess Lee Radziwill? Who is she dating?—Yvonne L., Passaic, N.J.*

A Interior decorator Lee Radziwill, 55, has been dating choreographer and director Herbert Ross (*The Turning Point, California Suite*). Widower of ballerina Nora Kaye, Ross, 63, recently finished directing Sally Field, Dolly Parton, Shirley MacLaine and Olympia Dukakis in the

Jackie Onassis and Maurice Tempelsman

film *Steel Magnolias*, shot on location in Natchitoches, Louisiana.

Q *During the Democratic National Convention in July, Gov. Bill Clinton of Arkansas gave a 32-minute speech nominating Michael Dukakis for president. Four of us were watching on TV when one friend, weary of listening to Clinton, blurted out, "Someone should tell Bill Clinton what happened to President William Henry Harrison." What did happen to Harrison?—C.D., Tulsa, Okla.*

A Prior to Ronald Reagan, the oldest man to be elected president was William Henry Harrison (1773-1841). Despite his 68 years, Harrison insisted on delivering his inaugural address outdoors. March 4, 1841, was a cold and blustery day, but Harrison declined to wear a hat, gloves or overcoat. He spoke for one hour and 40 minutes, giving the longest inaugural speech in presidential history. Subsequently, he came down with a cold that developed into pleurisy. On April 4— exactly one month after his inauguration—President Harrison died. He was succeeded by Vice President John Tyler.

Q *Is Liz Taylor by chance a hypochondriac? Every few months, it seems, she's in some hospital recovering from obesity, drug abuse, pneumonia or something.—T. Mills, Lawrence, Kan.*

A In her 56 years, Elizabeth Taylor has been hospitalized for a variety of illnesses. Last month, she spent time in St. John's Hospital in Santa Monica, California, recovering from a compression fracture of a vertebra. As to possible hypochondria, there is no evidence that she is abnormally concerned about her health or obsessed by fears of succumbing to one ailment after another.

Q *On July 17, you wrote that Princess Di had never posed as a centerfold model for a men's magazine. You may be surprised to learn that in a "Playboy" magazine called* The Parody, *Di appears in the foldout, exposing more than her pearly white teeth.—Mike Belk, Indian Trail, N.C.*

A To the many readers who have written us about that nude photo of Diana in *Playboy* magazine, here are the facts: In the winter of 1983, a magazine titled *Playboy—The Parody* was published by Taylor/Shain Inc., which is not the company that publishes *Playboy*. It carried the cover line "Our Reigning Playmate—Lady Di—A Right Royal Spread." Moreover, the

centerfold revealed Di as "Miss Wales," in all her pristine nakedness. What it did not reveal was that the photo was a composite, consisting of Diana's head superimposed on some other young lady's curvaceous body.

Q *On a recent TV talk show, the host and his guests were unanimous in contending that the warmth and friendliness which Oprah Winfrey projects on her talk show are spurious. They said that when the TV cameras are off, Oprah becomes "Miss Iceberg." Truth or sour grapes?—Burns Whitaker, Valparaiso, Ind.*

A In our opinion, a modicum of both. Oprah Winfrey's talk show may lack the chemistry of newness—and Oprah may not generate the warmth and enthusiasm she once did—but "spurious" and "Miss Iceberg" do not accurately reflect her behavior pattern.

Betty Grable

Darryl Zanuck

Q *Did Darryl Zanuck, head of 20th Century-Fox studios, try to force Alice Faye and Betty Grable out of the movies because they refused to succumb to his sexual advances? Isn't that why he secretly destroyed nearly all the master negatives of their films, so that the Betty Grable and Alice Faye motion pictures are not available on video-cassettes?—Jack Biringer, Berkeley, Calif.*

A Darryl Zanuck (1902-79) was a womanizer of insatiable sexual appetite. He made a pass at virtually all the actresses under contract to his studio, including Alice Faye and the late Betty Grable. When rebuffed, however, he took the rejection in stride and moved along to the next possible conquest. He never blacklisted Grable or Faye or destroyed the master negatives of their films. Few of them currently are available on videocassette, but Fox says it does plan to market its older films.

Jane Fonda

Henry Pu Yi

Q *Jane Fonda recently apologized on TV's 20/20 for having visited Hanoi during the Vietnam war. At this year's convention in Louisville, the American Legion refused to accept her apology. What would these war veterans have her do—commit hara-kiri?—Paula Bennett, Norfolk, Va.*

A The American Legion's explanation, in the form of a resolution, declares in part: "We of the American Legion do not believe her [Fonda's] apology was in any way sincere and was only stated on the TV program as a ruse to further her many commercial undertakings."

Q *Do you know when Henry Pu Yi, China's last emperor, died? How many children did he have? Where are they?—Jo Shin, Seattle, Wash.*

A Li Shuxian, 63, the last wife of Henry Pu Yi, says her husband died in 1967 at age 61. She insists that he was impotent throughout his life and fathered no offspring, despite having five or six wives and consorts. "He underwent many hormone treatments," she explained to a reporter from the *Agence France Presse* in Beijing recently, "but he was never able to lead a normal, conjugal life. If he had, we would have had children." According to Li Shuxian, her husband was a friend of Mao Tse-tung and Chou En-lai, the communist leaders, and it was Chou who arranged for her, a nurse, to marry the former emperor a few years after his release from a Chinese prison in 1959. *The Last Emperor—* the Oscar-winning motion picture on Henry Pu Yi's life, which was filmed in the People's Republic of China in 1986-87 by the Italian director Bernardo Bertolucci— is currently the most popular movie in circulation in that country.

Q *I am in my 60s, and when I was a child I heard light-skinned black people called "mulattoes." Now I hardly ever hear that word used anymore to describe people of mixed Negro and Caucasian blood, such as Lena Horne, Whitney Houston, Diana Ross, Michael Jackson and others. How come?—Betty Lange, Pittsburgh, Pa.*

A Several decades ago, persons of mixed Negro and Caucasian blood began proudly and politically to refer to themselves as blacks and not as mulattoes, quadroons or coloreds. It was all part of the civil rights movement and the continuing struggle for equal rights by minorities in this country.

Q *When does Prince Charles of Britain turn 40?—Lucey Hamilton, New Orleans, La.*

A Charles, the Prince of Wales and heir to the British throne, turned 40 last Monday.

Q *When Elvis Presley's daughter got married recently in a Church of Scientology in Hollywood, did she have to?—W.S., Knoxville, Tenn.*

A Not necessarily. Lisa Marie Presley, 20, and her fiancé of two years, musician Danny Keough, 23, were married on October 3. Eight days later, Lisa Marie's mother, Priscilla Presley, announced that the lucky newlyweds were expecting their first child sometime next spring.

Q *Does Bruce Willis, star of the* Moonlighting *TV series, suffer from a receding hairline so badly at 33 that he now has to wear a hairpiece? Why doesn't he go for a hair transplant? I hear those are nifty.—Judy Chambers, Akron, Ohio.*

A Bruce ("Bruno" to his friends) Willis has begun wearing a hairpiece on his TV series. Once an actor wears a hairpiece professionally, he almost always wears one in public, particularly as he grows balder. Eventually Willis may try a transplant.

Ronald Reagan

George Bush

Q *Is it my imagination, or has George Bush suddenly grown taller than Ronald Reagan? In photos prior to Bush's nomination for president, he always appeared much shorter than Reagan. Just curious.—C.D.G., Albuquerque, N.M.*

A Ronald Reagan stands six feet one. George Bush is at least six feet two.

Eddie Murphy

Q *Is it true Eddie Murphy was paying Cher $45,000 a month to rent her home in Palm Springs, California, and decided to buy it for $20 million instead? What's it made of—spun gold? How big is it anyway?—Jan Howard, Hayward, Calif.*

A Eddie Murphy never rented Cher's home in Palm Springs because she had no home there to rent. She did, howev-

Cher

er, own one in Benedict Canyon, north of Beverly Hills, which she recently sold to the comedian for about $5 million. The contemporary-style house is 12,500 square feet, has six bedrooms, seven baths, a pool, spa, gym and atrium. Before he bought Cher's home, Murphy would rent hotel suites or estates when on the West Coast, for which he paid $9,000 to $30,000 per month.

Q *In the tennis-playing family of George Bush, is it true or just presidential propaganda that, despite his 64 years, papa Bush still ranks No. 1?—P. Harding, Sanford, N.C.*

A Bush is a pretty good racket-wielder for a man of his years, but he is not in the same league as his son Marvin, 31, who can spot him four games in each set (maybe five) and win easily.

Q *Did the FBI under J. Edgar Hoover ever try to get the late Rev. Martin Luther King, Jr., to commit suicide by threatening to expose his extramarital sex life? Did the FBI really follow the civil rights leader from hotel to hotel, recording his bedroom exploits?—A.N., Compton, Calif.*

A "Yes" is the answer to both questions. The late J. Edgar Hoover despised Dr. King. He insisted that King, who won the Nobel Peace Prize at age 35, was under Communist influence. In 1963, he pressured U.S. Attorney General Robert Kennedy to approve wiretaps on King's home and office in Atlanta. The FBI then embarked on a rigorous schedule of recording King, who was no angel and in fact had confessed to a friend: "I'm away from home 25 to 27 days a month. [Extramarital sex is] a form of anxiety reduction." In November 1964, an FBI agent sent a package to King at the headquarters of the Southern Christian Leadership Conference. It contained a reel of "sex" tape and an anonymous threatening letter. The package found its way to King's wife, Coretta. She opened it, played the tape and read the letter, which said in part: "King, there is only one thing left for you to do . . . You better take [your life] before your filthy, abnormal, fraudulent self is bared to the nation."

For further details of Dr. King's relationship with the FBI, you may care to read *Bearing the Cross,* the comprehensive, Pulitzer Prize-winning book by David J. Garrow. Another excellent King biography is *Parting the Waters,* by Taylor Branch.

Q *I've been told by several knowledgeable people that the late actor Richard Burton, who suffered from alcoholism, also suffered from epilepsy. True or false?—Rita Bixby, Orlando, Fla.*

A True. Burton's alcoholism was acknowledged, but his periodic epileptic seizures were not.

Q *In Britain, it has long been the right of kings to take some of the best-looking married women in the land as mistresses. Does this tradition apply to Prince Charles? I'm not saying he's fooling around, mind you. I'm just asking if he has the right.—Howard R., West Palm Beach, Fla.*

A There is no such formal British constitutional right empowering the king or heir to the throne to take mistresses, although many have.

Q *Christina Onassis, who died last November 19 at age 37—what exactly did she die of? How much did she leave her ex-husband, Thierry Roussel, and their three-year-old daughter, Athina? If excess weight bothered her, why wasn't*

Christina Onassis

she under constant medical supervision? She sure had enough money to pay for it.—Carmen Clements, Chicago, Ill.

A Christina Onassis died of heart failure, the result of a life of extremes—too many food-gorgings followed by too many diets, too many romances followed by too many disappointments, too many marriages followed by too many divorces. According to the terms of her holographic will, dated October 12, 1988, she bequeathed $1,420,000 a year for life to her fourth husband, Thierry Roussel, 35, whom she divorced in 1987. She left their daughter the bulk of her estate, which is estimated to exceed $500 million and will probably be worth double that when Athina turns 18. Christina Onassis—who was married to an American (Joseph Bolker), a Greek (Alexander Andreadis), a Russian (Sergei Kauzov) and a Frenchman (Roussel)—realized early that her excessive weight was a mental problem, not a physical one, and that constant medical care could not buy what she needed most: a little true love.

WALTER SCOTT'S
PERSONALITY PARADE®

March 5, 1989

Barrett / Globe

Michael J. Fox and Tracy Pollan

Globe

Christopher Reeve

Q *Is Michael J. Fox, formerly of* Family Ties, *en route to becoming a papa? Is he going to star in another TV series? Isn't he too short to become a leading man in feature movies?—Pam Rowland, Baltimore, Md.*

A Fox and his wife, actress Tracy Pollan, expect their first child in midsummer, probably July. The diminutive actor has had enough of TV for a while. Reportedly he would like to confine his talents to acting, directing and producing big-screen motion pictures. At five feet six with lifts in his shoes or when wearing high-heeled boots, Fox is not too short for leading-man roles.

Q *Is it just a coincidence that two actors who played Superman have similar names, or were George Reeves and Christopher Reeve related? Did George Reeves commit suicide because he had difficulty separating himself from his TV role as* Superman?—Frederick B. Muller, Livingston, N.J.

A George Reeves was born in Iowa in 1914. His real name was George Besselo, and he was in no way related to Chris Reeve, born in New York in 1952. Reeves committed suicide in 1959 not only because he found psychological difficulty in separating himself from his role but also because he was being pursued relentlessly by the wife of an MGM executive. It's just a coincidence that two actors named Reeves and Reeve both starred as Superman.

Q *How old is Shirley Temple? How many children does she have, and by how many husbands? What do her children do for a living? Who appointed Shirley as U.S. ambassador to Ghana?—Mira Gaillard, Shreveport, La.*

A Shirley Temple was born April 23, 1928. She has three children: Linda Susan Falaschi, 41, a freelance writer; Charles Alden Black, Jr., 36, who works in the U.S. Department of Commerce; and Lori Alden Black, 34, a freelance photographer and a bass player in a rock band. Linda is the product of Shirley's first marriage, to actor John Agar, from 1945 to 1949; Charles Jr. and Lori are Shirley's children by Charles A. Black, her husband since 1950. Shirley Temple Black was appointed ambassador to Ghana by President Gerald Ford in 1974.

Q *Jasmine Guy, who acts in the TV sitcom* A Different World—*is she black or white? And is she replacing Lisa Bonet?—Ina Rice, Newark, N.J.*

A Jasmine Guy, 24, is the daughter of the Rev. William V. Guy, black pastor of Atlanta's Friendship Baptist Church. Her mother, who divorced Guy after 21 years of marriage, has remarried and teaches high school English in Atlanta; she is white. Lisa Bonet dropped out of *A Different World* to have a baby but will return. She is not being replaced.

Q *What's the inside story of Andreas Papandreou, prime minister of Greece, who used to teach economics at the University of California, and the Olympic Airlines hostess with whom he's infatuated? Where'd they meet?—Olga H., Berkeley, Calif.*

A Andreas Papandreou, 70, apparently met and was attracted to Dimitra "Mimi" Liani, 34, when the tall, buxom, bleached blonde was assigned as his "personal hostess" on a charter flight to India in 1985. The friendship gradually warmed, but Margaret Papandreou, 67, the prime minister's American-born wife, paid it no mind. Having been married since 1951, she was well aware of Andreas' infidelities, including one that reportedly resulted in a daughter born out of wedlock in Sweden. No matter how frequent his suspected liaisons, she was sure he'd return to her. After all, they'd been through much and had four grown children, including a son who is education minister of Greece.

Last fall, however, Mrs. Papandreou was proved wrong. When her husband developed a bad heart and flew to London for major cardiac surgery, he took along not his wife but his mistress. He was convinced, said his apologists, that Margaret cared more for her feminist causes than for him. Prior to his surgery, Papandreou let it be known that if he pulled through, he'd divorce his wife. The operation was a success.

On January 19, Mrs. Papandreou announced: "My personal affair with the prime minister is ended. There remains only the legalization of the separation, which I am trying to get over and done with as quickly as possible." In Athens, where the two have been living together, it's said the prime minister will wed his mistress when expedient. His friends say whimsically that Dimitra won Andreas' heart because she cooks extremely well, and he has loved good cooking since he was 16. But many also predict that his wife will never divorce him.

Irving Berlin

Q *Irving Berlin, the great songwriter who recently lost his wife, Ellin, had several children by her. Is there an Irving Berlin, Jr.? Is he a songwriter like his 100-year-old dad?—Frank Russell, Palm Desert, Calif.*

A Irving Berlin and his late wife, the novelist Ellin Mackay Berlin, had four children: Irving Berlin, Jr., who died in his infancy, and three surviving daughters—Mary Ellin Barrett, Linda Louise Emmet and Elizabeth Irving Peters.

Q *How many times has actress Jane Fonda been married, and was she "expecting" each time? Is it true that her father, the late Henry Fonda, was so opposed to Tom Hayden that he offered Jane $1 million not to marry him? Didn't her father call the political activist "an evil molder of Jane's personality"?—Naomi R., Berkeley, Calif.*

A Jane Fonda has been married twice: to director Roger Vadim from 1965 to 1970, by whom she has a daughter, Vanessa, 20; and to Tom Hayden from 1973 to the present, by whom she has a son, Troy, 15. Jane was "expecting" when she became Mrs. Hayden. It is true that Henry Fonda did not hold Hayden in the highest light as a future son-in-law, but the frugal film star never offered Jane $1 million not to marry him. Nor did he ever accuse Hayden of being "an evil molder of Jane's personality." Fonda utilized that bit of opprobrium to describe Andreas Voutsinas, an aspiring director who was Jane's drama coach early in her career.

Q *George Bush, I'm informed, would like to go down in history as a man who not only was president of the U.S. but also was president of Akaga. Where and what is Akaga? It sounds like one of those secret social societies Bush belonged to at Yale, or a Japanese dessert.—L.F., Beeville, Tex.*

A George Bush, according to one of his intimates, would like to be remembered as president of "A Kinder and Gentler America," whose acronym is AKAGA.

Q *Did Bjorn Borg, the former Swedish tennis star, try to take his life recently, or did he not? He seems to be too emotionally sluggish and apathetic to attempt suicide, especially over a woman.—Louise Anderson, Brooklyn Park, Minn.*

A Borg, 32, the five-time Wimbledon champion, has denied attempting suicide. He has explained that on February 7 in Milan, Italy, he accidentally mixed sleeping pills and liquor to combat an upset stomach, passed out and woke up in a hospital. Stories to the effect that Loredana Berte, the 38-year-old Italian pop singer and love of his life, quarreled with Borg and motivated him to swallow 60 sleeping pills apparently are untrue.

Q *Hawaii is the only state in the union with two U.S. senators of Japanese antecedents—Dan Inouye and Spark Matsunaga. Both were wounded in World War II. Both were heroes. Both are Democrats. Are both issei, nisei, sansei, yonsei or nikkei?—Linda Montgomery, Wellesley, Mass.*

A Sen. Daniel K. Inouye was born September 7, 1924, in Honolulu. Sen. Spark Matsunaga was born October 8, 1918, in Kauai, Hawaii. Both are *nisei,* or second-generation Japanese-Americans, and both are *nikkei,* a term which encompasses Japanese-Americans of any generation. *Issei* refers to first-generation Japanese immigrants (whose American-born children are *nisei*). *Sansei* are third-generation and *yonsei* fourth-generation Japanese-Americans.

Q *Several weeks ago, Liz Taylor was awarded $50,000 by the Onassis Foundation for her campaign against AIDS. What is the Onassis Foundation?—Stan Lombard, Las Vegas, Nev.*

A The Alexander Onassis Foundation was established by Aristotle Onassis in homage to his only son, Alexander, who was killed in a plane crash in 1973 at age 24. In his will, Aristotle Onassis, who died in 1975, wrote: "If my death occurs before I proceed with the establishment of a cultural institution in Vaduz, Liechtenstein, or elsewhere under the name of 'Alexander Onassis Foundation,' its purpose among others [is] to operate, maintain and promote the Nursing, Educational, Literary Works, Religious, Scientific Research, Journalistic and Artistic endeavors, proclaiming International and National Contests, prize awards in money, similar to the plan of the Nobel Institution in Sweden. I entrust and command the undersigned executors of my will to establish such a Cultural Institution."

Anastaselis / Globe

Aristotle Onassis

Elizabeth Taylor

Globe

Shirley Temple

Globe

Myrna Loy

Q *Because Franklin D. Roosevelt was crippled by infantile paralysis, he saw a lot of movies in the White House. My grandfather says FDR's favorite star was Shirley Temple, the child actress who made him forget the cares of the day. Was she really his favorite?—K. Cohen, San Diego, Calif.*

A President Franklin D. Roosevelt saw many movies and admired Shirley Temple, but his favorite screen star was somewhat taller and older than Shirley. She was Myrna Loy, the beautiful, sexy and talented actress who played opposite William Powell in the humorous *Thin Man* series.

Franklin D. Roosevelt

Q *Who is the actress with the Italian accent who played opposite Tom Cruise and Dustin Hoffman in* Rain Man? *Is she currently hitched?—Dan Caldwell, Wilmington, Del.*

A She is Valeria Golino, 22, unmarried as of this writing but reportedly dating Massimo Troisi, 36, an Italian actor.

Q *Could it be that the true cause of the Jane Fonda-Tom Hayden separation is a Tom Hayden midlife crisis? Could it be that Hayden drinks more than Jane thinks he should? Could it be that she is a physical-*

fitness nut who wants him to have the muscles of a Charles Atlas? Could it be that Hayden is tired of being a California assemblyman and would like to be California's state insurance commissioner? Could it be that Jane suffers from a wandering eye? Could it be that Hayden is frustrated and turns to others for tea and sympathy? Could it be that, after nearly 16 years of marriage, Tom and Jane have fallen out of love and spend relatively little time with one another?—K.R., Sacramento, Calif.

A Obviously you are tuned in to the Fonda-Hayden relationship. The causes that you advance for their marital rupture are all valid probabilities.

Q *When Ronald Reagan was president, did he ever take the blame for trading arms for hostages? Did he ever come out and say in plain English, "I was wrong" or "I made a mistake" or "I goofed"?—J.W., Alexandria, Va.*

A There is no record of Reagan admitting error in those words as regards the Iran-Contra hostage mess, but he has said, "Mistakes were made."

Q *In your opinion, who among the following blacks was the greatest baseball player of the century: Willie Mays, Reggie Jackson, Hank Aaron or Jackie Robinson?—Ed Carr, Greensboro, N.C.*

A Our choice is Jackie Robinson (1919-72), not only because he was a great athlete but also because he pioneered the entrance of blacks into major league baseball, demonstrating integrity, resolution and tremendous strength of character. Robinson served as a role model for all who followed.

Q *At a recent get-together, the discussion fell on Enrico Fermi, the Italian physicist, and his contributions to the A-bomb. May we have one of your informative mini-biographies on this genius?—M.O., New Haven, Conn.*

A Enrico Fermi was one of the greatest physicists of the nuclear age. He split the atom (not realizing at first that he'd done so), designed the first atomic piles, directed the first nuclear chain reaction and worked on the atomic-bomb project in Los Alamos, New Mexico. Born in Rome in 1901, son of the chief inspector for Italy's railways, Fermi was a child prodigy of sorts in mathematics and physics. He earned his doctorate at 21, studied physics at the University of Gottingen in Germany, taught math at the University of Florence and in 1926 became a full professor of theoretical physics at the University of Rome, where he soon earned a reputation as a brilliant scientist.

In 1928 he wed Laura Capon, daughter of a Jewish captain in the Italian navy. A year later, Mussolini appointed Fermi to the Royal Academy of Italy, but he showed scant interest in politics and had time for little beyond physics. In 1934 he bombarded various elements with slow neutrons, producing radioactive atoms of elements that he believed lay beyond uranium. Actually, he'd split the atom in a process now known as nuclear fission. For this work, he won the 1938 Nobel Prize in physics and received Mussolini's permission to accept the award in Sweden.

Convinced that Italy's racial laws would tragically affect his wife and two children if they returned, Fermi, a Catholic, instead left Sweden for the U.S. with his family and settled in Leonia, New Jersey. He taught at Columbia University, then moved in 1942 to the University of Chicago, where, as a key scientist in the Manhattan Project, he had the task of producing the first controlled, self-sustaining nuclear chain reaction, which made possible the A-bombs dropped on Japan in 1945 and the later development of nuclear power for peaceful purposes. Fermi died of cancer in 1954; his wife died in 1977. They are survived by a daughter Nella, 58, a financial planner in Chicago, and a son Giulio, 53, a microbiologist in England.

Nicole and O.J. Simpson

Q *O. J. Simpson, the actor and former football star, was charged with beating his beautiful wife, Nicole, after a New Year's party. What disposition was made of the case? Was it quashed?—Marcus Graves, Chicago, Ill.*

A It was not. On May 22, through his attorney, Simpson entered a plea of no contest to one count of spousal battery. The maximum sentence in California for such wife-beating is one year in jail and/or a fine of $1,000. The judge, however, ordered Simpson, 42, to pay a fine of $200 as well as $500 to a shelter for battered women, to perform 120 hours of community service and to continue to obtain psychiatric counseling. Simpson also was placed on probation for two years.

Q *Who is the single most powerful man in Hollywood?—Phyllis Brock, Scottsdale, Ariz.*

Steven Spielberg

A Director-producer Steven Spielberg at this time is not only the most powerful man in Hollywood but also, in our opinion, one of the most talented. In Hollywood, power is equated with money, and to date Spielberg has directed or produced five of the 10 highest-grossing films in history: *E.T., Jaws, Raiders of the Lost Ark, Back to the Future* and *Indiana Jones and the Temple of Doom.* Last year, Spielberg produced *Who Framed Roger Rabbit,* which turned out to be the top seller of 1988, with a domestic gross of $154 million. This year, he directed *Indiana Jones and the Last Crusade,* which will do as well if not better. To date, Spielberg films have grossed more than $2.2 billion worldwide at the box office—to say nothing of the millions derived from videotapes and other revenue-raisers—and this man is only 41 and nowhere near his creative peak. Every major Hollywood studio will pay him anything he wants and agree to almost all of his terms if he'll make a deal with them. The demand for his services and product is unequaled—which is why his power is, too.

Q *When she was a child star under contract to 20th Century-Fox, why did the studio lie about Shirley Temple's age, saying she was younger than she really was?—Cindy Norris, Gary, Ind.*

A The studio "fudged" Temple's age by only one year, insisting in 1934 that she was five when she was really six. Reason: to enhance her box-office image as a wonder-kid.

Q *Geena Davis, who won an Oscar for her role as a dog-trainer in* The Accidental Tourist: *How old? How tall? How married? How good an actress?—Willie Allen, Titusville, Fla.*

A Geena Davis is 31, six feet tall, has been very much married since 1987 to actor Jeff Goldblum, who is six feet four. They've worked together in *Transylvania 6-5000, The Fly* and *Earth Girls Are Easy.* Davis enjoys the reputation of being a talented outré actress of the Diane Keaton school—intelligent, individualistic and kooky.

Q *There's a shortage of Broadway musicals because there's a shortage of great songwriters. What is the longest-running Broadway musical?—Helena Fernandez, Albuquerque, N.M.*

A *A Chorus Line,* which opened on Broadway on July 25, 1975, is the longest-running musical—and show—in Broadway history. As of today, it has chalked up 5,792 performances.

Q *So many people have written books about Elvis Presley, why hasn't Col. Tom Parker, his ex-manager, written one? The colonel, I'm sure, knew Elvis much better than 90 percent of those who've written biographies.—Marsha Watts, Quincy, Fla.*

A Col. Tom Parker can no doubt write a book or have one written on Elvis as seen through his eyes, but he'd like an advance of $1 million to jog his memory. Money has always stimulated the colonel's power of recall.

Herbert Hoover

Q *How many U.S. presidents were Quakers? Did they believe in or pursue the Quaker tenet of pacifism?—Robert Simmons, Oberlin, Ohio.*

A Herbert Hoover was the first Quaker to be elected president, Richard Nixon the second. Neither practiced pacifism. Nixon enlisted in the Navy in World War II, and Hoover explained that, to his way of thinking, war was justifiable morally when all other attempts to arrive at peace had failed.

Richard Nixon

WALTER SCOTT'S
PERSONALITY PARADE®

October 22, 1989

Zsa Zsa Gabor

Brooke Shields

Q *I remember Zsa Zsa Gabor from her appearances on Hollywood Squares and other TV programs designed to attract viewers with double-digit IQs. But did this hunk of Hungarian goulash ever act in any quality films? What's the real poop on Zsa Zsa as to age, talent, husbands, credits? Was she ever the sweetheart of Millard Fillmore, our 13th president?—C.B., Bartlesville, Okla.*

A Zsa Zsa (real name: Sari Gabor) was born in Budapest, Hungary, on February 6, 1919—45 years too late for President Fillmore. Her appetite for husbands apparently is insatiable. She is currently on her eighth, who she insists is a German prince. Three of the best films she worked in were *Lili, Moulin Rouge* and *Public Enemy Number One*. The great love in her life, she has confessed, was the late Porfirio Rubirosa, a playboy diplomat from the Dominican Republic and ex-husband of heiresses Barbara Hutton and Doris Duke. Zsa Zsa's acting talent is limited, but when it comes to self-promotion, she's nonpareil.

Q *Is Brooke Shields by any chance the granddaughter of Frank Shields, a great tennis champ of the 30s? I was a linesman when he played for our Davis Cup team against Mexico, and he was one of the best players in the world, also one of the most handsome.—Joseph Bryan, Arlington, Va.*

A Brooke Shields, 24, is indeed the granddaughter of the late tennis champion Francis X. Shields, from whom she undoubtedly inherited in part her height (six feet) and her good looks.

Q *Does the average male politician in Japan keep a mistress? Did Japan's Emperor Hirohito have one or many? How large was his fortune when he died?—B. Dorfman, Mar Vista, Calif.*

A It is not unusual for Japanese politicians or successful Japanese males to keep mistresses. It may, in fact, be one of the tacit mores of their culture. Prior to World War II, most Japanese marriages were arranged, a custom that permitted married men to play the field with impunity. Hirohito, from many accounts, did not indulge in the sport. When he died in January, he left about $13 million in assets, mostly stocks, bonds and savings accounts.

Q *As a left-handed person, I notice more and more how many actors appear to be left-handed. Is the percentage of left-handed actors larger than the percentage of southpaws in the general population?—Dorothy Ice, Stratford, Conn.*

A Approximately 25 million Americans, or 10 percent, are left-handed. According to demographers, the same percentage holds true for actors.

Q *Who is Dr. Janet Morgan, whose name has been linked to that of Caspar Weinberger, secretary of defense under Ronald Reagan?—R.O., Pacific Grove, Calif.*

A Dr. Janet Morgan, 43, is a well-known, highly regarded Oxford University academic who edited the diaries of the late Richard Crossman, a British cabinet member, and several other works of literary merit. She's now finishing a biography of Lady Edwina Mountbatten, wife of the late Lord Louis Mountbatten, who was the last British viceroy of India. Dr. Morgan has been described as a "good and close friend" of Caspar Weinberger. At this writing, however, she is a house guest of Lord Balfour, director of the Bank of Scotland, whose marriage went south last year.

Q *I see that the president chose Shirley Temple Black to be our ambassador to Czechoslovakia. I happen to be Czech. My question: Does she know how to read or speak the Czech language? If no, why don't we appoint someone who does? I dare you to answer.— J. Masek, Hemet, Calif.*

A Prior to her confirmation as ambassador, Mrs. Black began taking intensive instruction in the Czech language. She is a quick study and undoubtedly will learn how to get along in it.

Q *Aren't there big fights in the Arnold Schwarzenegger-Maria Shriver family because he's a Republican who campaigned for Bush and she's a Democrat whose uncle was Kennedy?—Norm Christiansen, Salt Lake City, Utah.*

Arnold and Maria

A Film star Arnold Schwarzenegger and his wife, TV journalist Maria Shriver, may differ in their political preferences, but this does not cause "big fights" in the family. Incidentally, the couple are expecting their first child next month.

Dan and Marilyn Quayle

Q *Why has President Bush failed to go to Alaska to inspect firsthand the tremendous damage done to the environment by the "Exxon Valdez" oil spillage?—T. Morrison, Anchorage, Alaska.*

A President Bush, it has been said, was tentatively scheduled to fly to Alaska for a look-see in September, but his brain-trusters decided it would be politically inexpedient for him to do so personally. Instead, Vice President Quayle and his wife, Transportation Secretary Samuel K. Skinner and Coast Guard Commandant Paul Yost were sent to view the extent of the uncompleted Exxon cleanup.

Q *While vacationing in Washington, D.C., I called at the National Press Club to have TV reporter Sam Donaldson autograph his book,* Hold On, Mr. President! *They said he wasn't a member. I thought this to be odd, since Sam was assigned to the White House in the Reagan years and must have needed some social activity. Is Sam just frugal, is he anti-social underneath, or is someone at the club lying?—Jack Strasser, Pomona, Calif.*

A Whatever his real reasons, Sam Donaldson is not a member of the National Press Club.

George Bush

Q *Why is Russian roulette called Russian roulette?—Steven Conner, Honolulu, Hawaii.*

A Because drunken Russian officers of the Czarist court popularized the "game," in which a revolver, loaded with a single bullet, is placed to the head, the barrel spun and trigger pulled.

Q *Has Loretta Swit—who played the role of "Hot Lips Houlihan," the nurse in the M*A*S*H TV series—ever been married? I believe she was a few years ago, but we hear so little about her husband and family. Do they have any children?—Barbara Bailey, Huddleston, Va.*

A Loretta Swit married the actor Dennis Holahan on December 21, 1983. She was 46 at the time, had never been married, and Holahan was 41. Unfortunately, their childless marriage failed—largely because, it is said, her acting career was more successful than his. In divorce papers filed last August, Holahan reportedly asked the court to award him $8,000 a month in support payments, $30,000 in attorney fees and an equitable share of the $3 million that he estimates Swit earned during the five years of their marriage. "I am not able to support myself," he explained, "close to the standard of living that [Loretta Swit] and I maintained during the marriage." California is

one of those community-property states in which a husband, as well as a wife, is entitled to 50 percent of the assets earned or acquired during the period they were married. Holahan concedes that he earns about $35,000 a year, which is not enough for him to lead the lifestyle he grew accustomed to in his marital years with the M*A*S*H star. A check of $8,000 a month from her, he suggests, would help bridge the difference.

Q *Are women allowed to vote in national elections in Japan? If they are, how long have they had that right? What requirements must they meet?—Marianne Yamada, Canoga Park, Calif.*

A In 1925, under the terms of the Universal Manhood Suffrage Law, all male citizens of Japan over the age of 25 were given the right to vote. Women were given no such right. In 1945, however, under the Allied occupation, a "New Election Law" was passed enfranchising all Japanese citizens over the age of 20, male and female. It also made such Japanese citizens eligible to run for seats in the Japanese House of Representatives. In 1946, participating in a general election for the first time, Japanese women voted 24 members of their sex into the House of Representatives. Today, that political body has 511 members, of whom six are women. The term of office is four years.

Q *Has actress Jane Fonda had any "breast augmentation" performed by plastic surgeons? I suspect she has, because she certainly looks more busty this year than she did last.—S.T., Greenwich, Conn.*

A Sneak photos of Jane nude from the waist up, taken as she sunbathed in the Caribbean and published in overseas periodicals some months ago, seem to confirm your suspicion.

Q *Long before President John F. Kennedy used the lines in his inaugural address in 1961, who said: "Ask not what your country can do for you; ask what you can do for your country"?—E.T.E., Summerville, S.C.*

John F. Kennedy

A In a speech given on May 30, 1884, Oliver Wendell Holmes Jr. said, ". . . recall what our country has done for each of us and ask ourselves what we can do for our country in return."

WALTER SCOTT'S

PERSONALITY PARADE®

December 17, 1989

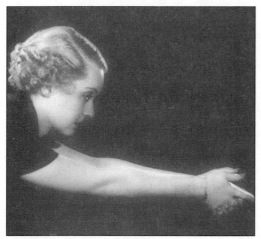

Bette Davis

Q *In her old age, was Bette Davis so broke that she had to advertise in newspapers for an acting job?—Gina Atwood, Myrtle Beach, S.C.*

A The late Bette Davis advertised for work as an actress only once in her career, and that was on September 24, 1962, when she was 54 and co-starring with Joan Crawford in *What Ever Happened to Baby Jane?* Davis took full-page ads in the show-business trade papers *Daily Variety* and *The Hollywood Reporter,* declaring: "Mother of three—10, 11, & 15—divorcée, American, 30 years experience as an actress in motion pictures. Mobile still and more affordable than rumor would have it. Wants steady employment in Hollywood. (Has had Broadway.)" The ads may have been inserted half in jest, but in the 1960s and '70s Davis felt financially compelled to work. She had spent a fortune supporting her mother, sister and three children and helping a variety of husbands. Even so, she left an estate valued at $600,000 to $1 million, consisting mainly of a condominium apartment she owned in West Hollywood. Half of it goes to her adopted son, Michael Woodman Merrill, half to her secretary and companion, Kathryn Sermak. The actress bequeathed nothing to her only natural child, Barbara Davis Hyman, who had criticized her severely in a 1985 book, *My Mother's Keeper.*

Q *Is Sherry Bronfman—one of the most, if not the most, beautiful black women in America—married to Edgar Bronfman, head of the World Jewish Congress and one of the wealthiest billionaires in America?—Donna Jackson, Camden, N.J.*

A Sherry Bronfman, the former actress-model Sherry Brewer, is married to Edgar M. Bronfman, Jr. His father is chairman of the Seagram Co. and a well-known Jewish philanthropist.

Q *LiPeng, the Chinese premier who reportedly ordered the army to shoot at the students in Beijing, says he's opposed to an elite society. Yet he rides around in two Mercedes cars. What sort of hypocrite is he?—C. Quan, Vancouver, Wash.*

A Premier Peng says he has relinquished the use of a Mercedes 280 and a Mercedes 560 in favor of a small Audi. His supporters maintain that he is not a hypocrite but rather an adaptive leader who behaves as a role model, trying to modernize his nation without abandoning "the Chinese way." Peng believes in the adage that rules exist to be bent by those with the power to enforce them.

Q *I've been reading about Linda Wertheimer, Cokie Roberts and Nina Totenberg—the three lady commentators who do such a brilliant job on National Public Radio, covering politics and the courts. To whom are these brainy ladies married, and what do they look like? I mean the ladies, not their husbands.—Bud Robinson, Charlottesville, Va.*

A Linda Wertheimer is married to Fred Wertheimer, head of Common Cause; Cokie Roberts is the wife of Steven Roberts, a writer for *U.S. News & World Report;* Nina Totenberg is married to former Sen. Floyd Haskell (D., Colo.).

Q *Now that the Soviet Union admits that communism doesn't work and is adopting the ways and means of capitalism, will Vladimir Lenin—the father and founder of Soviet Russia and the denouncer of capitalism—still be regarded in his country as a hero-genius and semi-saint? Or will he be downgraded by the people, as has been that other Communist icon, Mao Zedong of China?—Leon Goodman, Washington, D.C.*

A Every nation needs a father or father-substitute to whom it can attribute the glories of its past. Vladimir Lenin (1870-1924) continues to occupy that position in the Soviet Union. His photo still hangs in all schools, factories and public buildings, and his statue stands in virtually every town square in the nation. His corpse, which was embalmed in 1924 under the supervision of the Soviet Immortalization Commission, remains the No. 1

Vladimir Lenin

tourist attraction in Moscow and the ritualist object of Soviet honeymooners and out-of-towners.

It may be, as *perestroika* advances and the Soviets are permitted to research and write honestly, that Lenin eventually will be blamed for the introduction of a faulty economic and governmental system, which led to the horrors of Stalinism. But if Lenin's image is downgraded too quickly, especially in exposé fashion, with whose image will the Communist replace his—Khrushchev's, Gorbachev's? There is no one at this time to play the respected historic father-figure role in the Soviet Union except Lenin. Hence his position appears to remain secure for at least the next few years.

Mikhail Gorbachev

Nikita Krushchev

1990

1991

1992

1993

1994

1995

Amy Irving and Steven Spielberg

Q *It cost Steven Spielberg about $100 million to get out of his marriage to actress Amy Irving. Now that he's free to marry his girlfriend, actress Kate Capshaw, they say he's changed his mind. True or false?—A. Waldman, Newark, N.J.*

A Spielberg has been working long and hard on several films—particularly the recently released *Always*, with Holly Hunter and Richard Dreyfuss. Once the pressure subsides, he may get around to marrying Capshaw, reportedly with child. He is not one, however, who takes marriage lightly.

Q *Which of former President Ronald Reagan's four children are still under Secret Service protection?—M.S., Los Angeles, Calif.*

A None of Mr. Reagan's offspring is guarded by the Secret Service. The only Reagans currently accorded such protection are the ex-president, who turns 79 on February 6, and his wife Nancy, who will be 69 in July. Former presidents and their wives are entitled to Secret Service protection for life, unless they decline it.

Q *Can you think of any Hollywood film star, male or female, who was a Rhodes scholar?—Alma Sheehan, El Paso, Tex.*

A One comes quickly to mind—Kris Kristofferson, 53, from Brownsville, Texas. The actor, songwriter and troubadour was graduated Phi Beta Kappa from Pomona College and awarded a Rhodes scholarship to Oxford, where he did graduate work in English literature in 1957 and 1958. Some of his better films: *A Star Is Born, Blume in Love, Alice Doesn't Live Here Anymore.* Some of the well-known

women coupled with him in print and elsewhere: Janis Joplin, Carly Simon, Barbra Streisand, Jane Fonda, Rita Coolidge.

Q *In November, The Dallas Morning News ran an interview in which President Bush was asked if he was going to keep Dan Quayle on the Republican ticket in 1992. He said: "Absolutely. He is doing a good job . . . I think he has been an outstanding vice president." Why would Bush issue so preemptive and emphatic an endorsement of Quayle so early in the political game?—C.M., Arlington, Tex.*

A President Bush has been highly sensitive and defensive concerning his selection of Dan Quayle as his running mate in 1988. In many quarters back then, Quayle was considered too young (born February 4, 1947), too inexperienced and too unscholarly to occupy the vice presidency. If Bush died early in office, people asked, would Quayle be qualified to lead the country? In any case, Bush, a cautious and prudent man, was judged by several Republican bigwigs to have been imprudent and careless in the appointment. As a result, he may continue to congratulate Quayle to prove to the public how right he was in choosing "handsome young Dan" for eight years of on-the-job training.

Rita Hayworth

Q *Is it true that Rita Hayworth's father used to rape her, then rent her out to motion picture casting directors? Is it because of her sordid youth and her five awful marriages that she died of Alzheimer's disease?—R.G., Gainesville, Fla.*

A Rita's father was the Spanish dancer Eduardo Cansino, who enlisted his daughter (real name: Margarita Carmen

Cansino) as a dancing partner. There is no conclusive evidence, however, that he abused her sexually or insisted that she service various Hollywood executives. Such horrors have been attributed to her first husband, Ed Judson, who reportedly placed her on starvation diets, had her face and figure reshaped, urged her to exchange casting-couch favors for film roles. Such tactics certainly were not true of her other husbands: Orson Welles, Prince Aly Khan, Dick Haymes, and writer-producer James Hill, none of whom was right for Rita.

A *PARADE* writer who knew her fairly well says: "Rita Hayworth was a pleasant, simple, uneducated woman who had the misfortune of being born into the world of show business, where she was unable to contend with the men who found her physically attractive. She

Orson Welles

was no match for Orson Welles, Harry Cohn, Howard Hughes, Aly Khan and all the others—the agents, the producers, the publicity guys and the actors. Her cousin by marriage, Ginger Rogers, had the drive, the fight, the spirit to compete and garner a successful movie career. But she, too, suffered through five unhappy marriages—and, in Rogers' case, each was childless. Had Hayworth married a housepainter in San Diego or a schoolteacher in Dallas, she might have achieved what she really wanted—an average, middle-class life unracked by feelings of inferiority and insecurity. Perhaps there is a correlation between such negative feelings and the presence of Alzheimer's. No one yet knows."

Howard Hughes

Paul Newman

Q *Seeing the movie* Blaze, *based on the love affair of burlesque queen Blaze Starr with former Louisiana Gov. Earl K. Long, I am moved to inquire if Blaze was equally involved with the late John F. Kennedy, former Mayor Frank Rizzo of Philadelphia and other politicians and officials of the 1950s and 1960s.—M.F., Scranton, Pa.*

A Starr, 57, says she knew Kennedy and Rizzo—but not, of course, in the tempestuous way she knew the late Earl Long. Incidentally, the former stripper is entitled to 4 percent of the profits, if there are any, from the film *Blaze,* which stars Paul Newman as Long and Lolita Davidovitch as Starr.

Q *Roseanne Barr announced in December that she was calling off her January 20 marriage to boyfriend Tom Arnold because he was undergoing drug and alcohol rehabilitation. Is that the same reason she wants to quit TV—afraid it will drive her to drugs?—Linda Keller, Anchorage, Alaska.*

A Doing a weekly TV series, especially situation comedy, is a difficult, nerve-racking job under the best of circumstances. ABC's *Roseanne* has been punctuated by the worst of circumstances—acrimony, ultimata and internecine warfare. Roseanne Barr is a feisty, talented, opinionated performer with a host of professional and personal problems. Success on TV has brought her money but not fun or happiness. Hence her desire to escape from the rigors of a medium that she fears will do little for her physical and mental health.

Q *We would like to know who invented Velcro and for what purpose. Was it invented by NASA for use on spacesuits or by a British clothier to prevent his pockets from being picked?—Carol McGough and Anne Tiernan, Hingham, Mass.*

A Velcro was not invented by NASA or a British clothier. It was discovered and developed in 1948 by a Swiss engineer, George deMestral, who was curious as to why cockleburs stuck to his socks and his dog after a walk in the woods. He examined the burs under a microscope and discovered that they consisted of hundreds of tiny hooks, which attached themselves to anything loopy. He invented a method of duplicating the hook-and-loop configuration in nylon and named the product Velcro. The basic patent expired in 1978, and dozens of manufacturers throughout the world currently produce variations. Largest producer in this country is Velcro USA, with headquarters in Manchester, New Hampshire.

Q *After all the ballyhoo,* Prime Time Live, *the TV newsmagazine with Sam Donaldson and Diane Sawyer, turns out to be a disappointment. What went wrong?—David L., Alexandria, Va.*

A The concept of the show is unclear. The chemistry between Donaldson and Sawyer lacks combustion and excitement. Use of the studio audience detracts from the program, which badly needs *perestroika,* or restructuring. *Prime Time Live* reportedly has two years to find a successful formula.

Q *Did Jaclyn Smith, star of the old* Charlie's Angels *TV series, pay her husband $10 million for sole custody of their kids? I can't believe it. Where did she get the loot?—Kevin D., Carver, Minn.*

A To avoid a prolonged and potentially nasty divorce suit, Jaclyn Smith has agreed to pay her third husband, the British cameraman Tony Richmond, about $4 million for sole custody of their son Gaston, seven, and daughter Spencer, three. Daughter of a wealthy Texas dentist, Smith, 41, earned a small fortune doing TV commercials. She earned another fortune starring in *Charlie's Angels* and a third endorsing a line of clothes for Kmart. And she invested her money wisely. Says Tony Richmond: "I'm not selling out my kids, no matter what it looks like. Jaclyn and I wanted a quick settlement. It was heartbreaking to give up custody. I love my children more than anything in the world, but I realized they needed their mother full-time, and I'm just getting what's fair." Incidentally, David Niven, Jr., son of the late British actor, reportedly has been in love with Smith for years.

Elle Macpherson

Q *Is Elle Macpherson, the international model from Australia, divorcing French photographer Gilles Bensimon so she can marry actor Peter Horton of the* thirtysomething *TV series? Isn't Horton married to Michelle Pfeiffer, who recently finished filming* The Russia House *opposite Sean Connery?—Claudia J., Baltimore, Md.*

A Peter Horton was married to Michelle Pfeiffer from 1981 to 1988. Should Elle Macpherson split from Gilles Bensimon, it would surprise few of her admirés if she then wound up with Horton.

Peter Horton

Greer Garson

Q *Can you tell me about Greer Garson, among whose best films was* Mrs. Miniver? *Is she alive?—Barbara Leonard, Scottsdale, Ariz.*

A Greer Garson is today an 81-year-old widow who divides her time between Los Angeles, New Mexico and Texas. She is best remembered for the uxorial and lady-like qualities she displayed in several movies of the 1940s. She won a "Best Actress" Oscar for *Mrs. Miniver* (1942) and attracted many fans for her work in *Random Harvest, Madame Curie, The Valley of Decision* and other films. By the mid-1950s, however, her stardom was rapidly fading. Fortunately, her third and last husband, the wealthy rancher Elijah "Buddy" Fogelson, continued to support her in the comfortable Bel Air style to which she by then had become accustomed. When he died in 1987, Fogelson left her a small fortune, much of which she has donated to various charities. Her first husband, Edward Snelson, was a British military attaché in India; her second, actor Richard Ney, who played her son in Mrs. Miniver, later became a stockbroker.

Q *Is it a fact that blacks who murder whites in this country are more likely to get the death penalty than those*

people who murder blacks?—*C.M. Jones, Tarboro, N.C.*

A According to "Death Penalty Sentencing," a report recently released by the General Accounting Office, an investigative agency of the U.S. Congress, a pattern of racial discrimination exists in the use of the death penalty in this country. The GAO reviewed 28 studies on the subject and found that in 82 percent of them, the race of the victim made a difference in whether the defendant was sentenced to die. There seems to be little doubt in the contention that those who murder whites are much more likely to be sentenced to the death penalty than those who take the lives of blacks.

Q *Why is it that actors like Sylvester Stallone, Jack Nicholson, Arnold Schwarzenegger, Tom Cruise and Paul Newman are paid more than twice what Meryl Streep, Barbra Streisand, Jane Fonda, Sally Field and Shirley MacLaine are paid? Isn't the answer "sexism"?—Libby Arcello, Cicero, Ill.*

A According to Hollywood executives, male stars attract more filmgoers than female stars do.

Q *What kind of job does the Rev. Jesse Jackson have, and what is his source of income? He must be very wealthy or have inherited a large family fortune to dress so well and travel so widely.—Lucille Foster, Farmington, N.M.*

A Jesse Louis Jackson, president of The National Rainbow Coalition Inc., earns money from his lectures, writings and TV appearances. He inherited no family fortune. He recently signed a deal to syndicate his one-hour TV program, Voices of America With Jesse Jackson, which is scheduled to start in September in more than 95 markets.

Q *Doesn't a U.S. senator outrank a state governor in the field of politics? Why, then, is Sen. Pete Wilson of California giving up his seat in the U.S. Senate after one term to run for governor of California?—G. Pappas, Flagstaff, Ariz.*

A Sen. Pete Wilson, a former mayor of San Diego (1971-83), says he has always wanted to be governor of California. In fact, he ran unsuccessfully for the Republican gubernatorial nomination in 1978. Wilson maintains that a major reason he wants to run for governor this year is because, if elected, he can play a leading role in preventing California from being

badly gerrymandered (redistricted) by the Democrats. If not elected, he'll still have four years of his second term to spend in the U.S. Senate. The possibility also exists that, in exchange for running for governor, GOP leaders have promised Wilson a shot at the vice presidency or even a future run for the presidency.

Q *Is it still necessary for a young actress who wants a job in Hollywood to prove her talent on the casting couch? When Marilyn Monroe was under contract to 20th Century-Fox, was she obligated to take care of studio chief Darryl Zanuck in order to hold her job?—B.R., Gulfport, Miss.*

Marilyn Monroe

A A session on the casting couch with a studio executive or some other man of influence is no longer a prerequisite for an acting job in Hollywood. As for Marilyn Monroe and Darryl Zanuck, he was one of the most active lechers of his time—but not where Monroe was concerned. For some strange reason, he found her unappealing. His idea of a sexually irresistible actress was Joan Collins of 30 years ago. He gave Joan a bad time.

Darryl Zanuck

Tom Cruise

Q *Who is Hollywood star Tom Cruise cruising with, now that he has stopped cruising with his first wife, actress Mimi Rogers?—Leonora Kelsey, Albany, N.Y.*

A Cruise, 27, reportedly has been romancing Nicole Kidman, 22, the statuesque Australian redhead who plays opposite him in the new film *Days of Thunder,* which deals with auto racing.

Q *As odd as it may seem, I am often asked, as a historical interpreter, why the second-oldest institution of higher education in this country—the College of William and Mary, here in Williamsburg—isn't considered an Ivy League college. Who originated the name Ivy League?—Karen Schlicht, Williamsburg, Va.*

A The Ivy League consists of eight universities and colleges—Yale, Harvard, Princeton, Dartmouth, Columbia, the University of Pennsylvania, Brown and Cornell—all of which are situated in the Northeast. The College of William and Mary, founded in 1693, is considered a Southern institution. *The Encyclopedia of Word and Phrase Origins* attributes the term "Ivy League" to Caswell Adams, a *New York Herald Tribune* sportswriter who, when asked in the mid-1930s to compare the football teams of Columbia and Princeton with the powerful team of Fordham University, remarked: "Oh. They're just ivy league schools."

Q *Before Gen. Manuel Noriega of Panama took refuge in the papal embassy in Panama City, President George Bush offered a million-dollar reward for information leading to his capture. Has the reward been given to anyone or claimed by anyone legitimately?—H. Fernandez, San Antonio, Tex.*

A Noriega turned himself in on January 3 to the U.S. military authorities, thereby saving our government $1 million. To date, no one has claimed the reward for information leading to his surrender.

Hume Cronyn and Jessica Tandy

Q *Jessica Tandy, who was so wonderful in* Driving Miss Daisy, *is one actress I have not seen much of, despite her age (80) and long career. Is she foreign-born? I would be grateful for a rundown of her background. She must have been a beauty in her youth, and there must have been many men in her life.—Alice H., Wilmington, Del.*

A Jessica Tandy is a London-born, repertory-trained British actress who made her stage debut at 16 and whose leading men included Laurence Olivier and John Gielgud, the latter playing Hamlet to her memorable Ophelia. She made her film debut in 1932, at which time she married Jack Hawkins, one of the most handsome and popular leading men in British films. They had a daughter, Susan, but the marriage ended in a bitter divorce, after which Tandy left for New York. Having established a superb reputation in London, she had little difficulty obtaining work on Broadway. In 1947 she was cast as the neurotic Blanche DuBois in *A Streetcar Named Desire,* which she still rates as the best role of her career.

It was in the early 1940s in New York that Tandy met her second husband, the talented character actor Hume Cronyn, a former member of the Canadian Olympic boxing team and heir to the Labatt ale fortune. They were married in 1942 and by 1945 had produced a son Christopher and a daughter Tandy. Although regarded primarily as stage actors, the couple have worked from time to time in films. They live in Connecticut, and not a molecule of scandal has tainted their good names in 48 years of marriage.

Q *Nadia Comaneci, the 14-year-old darling of the 1976 Montreal Olympics, who won the gold medal in gymnastics for Romania—has she, at 28, become a nasty, money-grubbing, hard-hearted Hannah? Is Walt Disney Productions making a movie of her life? Was she the mistress of Nicu Ceausescu, son of the late Romanian dictator? What is the opinion of her in Romania? I gather it is not favorable.—V. Kirkpatrick, West Hollywood, Calif.*

A Nadia Comaneci is not the cute, sweet little girl she was 14 years ago. Some sportswriters in Bucharest describe her as stupid, selfish, aggressive and conceited. Disney has no plans for a film on her career. In an effort to excuse Nadia's behavior and reputation, her mother explains that Nadia was forced by Nicu Ceausescu to become his sex slave for 11 years. "He raped her at 17 at a party and ruined her whole life," says Stephania Comaneci. Nadia denies her mother's allegations, however, and many Romanians are skeptical.

Nadia Comaneci

Paula Zahn

Q *Paula Zahn, the TV newswoman who replaced Kathleen Sullivan on CBS This Morning: Age? Salary? Married? Children? Does she know her stuff, or is she just another of those morning TV blondes?—Ira Rothblatt, San Marino, Calif.*

A Paula Zahn, 34, knows her stuff—which is why CBS is paying her $1.1 million a year. Born in Naperville, Illinois, a Chicago suburb, she developed into one of those too-good-to-be-true achievers. At Naperville Central High, she was co-valedictorian, Class of 1974, and she captained the girls' swimming and tennis teams. She also entered beauty contests, played the cello and impressed nearly everyone with her versatility, brilliance and personality. At Stephens College in Columbia, Missouri, she majored in communications, was graduated with honors and broke into TV. She subsequently pulled TV stints in Houston, Boston and Los Angeles. In 1987 she married Richard Cohen, a Boston real-estate developer. They have a daughter, Haley Brynne, born last June. CBS is counting on Zahn to beat Joan Lunden of ABC's *Good Morning America* and Deborah Norville of NBC's *Today* in what is called "The Battle of the Breakfast Blondes."

Q *Here are the last 10 U.S. presidents: Franklin Roosevelt, Harry Truman, Dwight Eisenhower, John F. Kennedy, Lyndon Johnson, Richard Nixon, Gerald Ford, Jimmy Carter, Ronald Reagan, George Bush. Which one do you think lived the most adultery-free life?—C. Green, Jacksonville, Fla.*

A Our guess: Harry Truman; runner-up, Jimmy Carter.

Q *Oprah Winfrey's sister, Patricia Lloyd, has given out a story that Oprah had a baby out of wedlock when she was 14. She says the baby was born dead. She also says Oprah was a wild teenager who sneaked men home while her mother was out working. How much of these stories is true? Does Oprah have any comment to make?—Danielle H., Milwaukee, Wis.*

A When confronted by the above allegations, Oprah Winfrey—actress, producer and star of her own TV talk show—issued this statement:

Oprah Winfrey

"It saddens me deeply that a publication would pay large sums of money to a drug-dependent, deeply disturbed individual and then publish her remarks. My heart goes out to my half-sister, who is obviously in a lot of pain. Truth has been the foundation of my adult life, and I have always told the truth about my childhood—which, as I have said many times, was unfortunately very troubled and confusing.

"It is true that when I was 14 years old, I became pregnant. The baby was born prematurely and died shortly after birth. The experience was the most emotional, confusing and traumatic of my young life. I had hoped that this matter could stay private until I was fully able to deal with my own deep emotions and feelings, so that I could share this experience in a way that could best help educate other young girls who are trying to cope with all the ramifications of sexual abuse."

Friends of Oprah Winfrey say that she is a "soft touch" who has paid in the past for some of her half-sister's drug-abuse treatment and who undoubtedly will help her in the future, if a cure is what Patricia Lloyd really wants.

Q *Does anyone know the truth about Cuban dictator Fidel Castro? Does the CIA know, for example, how many children and mistresses he has, where he lives, whether he has large deposits in Swiss banks? If Cuba goes democratic, will Castro remain or go into exile in Spain or the U.S.? Do you have any information of that sort you might share?—Carlos Garcia, Delray Beach, Fla.*

A Relatively few people possess the type of intimate and important information you seek on Fidel Castro. He has at least one son from his marriage in 1948. That son, Fidelito, 40, is a Soviet-trained nuclear physicist who lives outside Havana. Castro also has a daughter, Alina Revuelta—34, beautiful and headstrong—who works in Cuba as a model, an occupation her father considers fatuous but one in which she persists.

In the 31 years he has held power, Castro, a ladies' man, has taken countless mistresses, who—so the legend grows—have produced at least half a dozen of his progeny. To avoid assassination, he reportedly sleeps in various residences with various females or alone every few nights. On the whole, he is well-liked and respected in Cuba. If a national election were held there today, he no doubt would win, even if opposition were allowed. He's admired by Hispanics, albeit grudgingly in some cases, as the only Latin-American *jefe* (chief) in modern times to have defeated a U.S.-backed invasion of his country.

Q *What does this headline mean: "Madonna Dumps Beatty for Jellybean"? Does "Jellybean" have anything to do with Ronald Reagan, who likes to eat them?—Ginny Lewington, Lisbon Falls, Maine.*

Madonna

A It means singer-actress Madonna, 30, has traded in her 52-year-old Romeo, actor Warren Beatty, for Jellybean Benitez, 33, the record-producer she once loved prior to her disappointing marriage to actor Sean Penn.

Michelle Pfeiffer

Q *Who is Michelle Pfeiffer's love of the moment: her husband, actor Peter Horton, or actor Michael Keaton of* Batman, *John Malkovich of* Dangerous Liaisons *or Fisher Stevens of* Twelfth Night?—*Anne Bromley, Chicago, Ill.*

A Michelle Pfeiffer, 32, is divorced from Peter Horton. She developed friendships with Keaton and Malkovich but reportedly is in love with Fisher Stevens, 26.

Q *A friend of mine who worked for Marilyn Monroe says the actress had an ectopic pregnancy by a photographer early in her career. What is an ectopic pregnancy? And who was the photographer?—B.B., North Park, Tex.*

A An ectopic pregnancy is one in which the fertilized egg does not move on to the womb. Instead, it most often remains in the fallopian tube or implants itself in the wall of the abdomen. A pregnancy outside the womb or uterus—the words are synonyms—is known as an ectopic or misplaced pregnancy. Women under 30 with a history of infertility, pelvic infections or abdominal surgery, it is said, are more likely to have ectopic pregnancies. Marilyn Monroe, who suffered a variety of gynecological ills, may well have had one. In her time, she knew several photographers well, was married three times, never carried a pregnancy to term.

Q *Before Richard Gere struck it rich in his last two films—*Internal Affairs *and* Pretty Woman—*his girlfriend for eight years was Sylvia Martins, a Brazilian painter. Who is his current girlfriend? Is Gere a genuine Buddhist, or does he just say he is one for publicity's sake? Are his parents Buddhists?—Mona Styne, Tucson, Ariz.*

A Richard Gere, 40, is a one-woman-at-a-time man. For more than two years now he has been sharing his life with model Cindy Crawford, 23. Gere's parents are Methodists, but he says he has made a serious conversion to Buddhism as practiced in Tibet. The actor was born in Philadelphia but reared in Syracuse, New York.

John F. Kennedy

Nikita Krushchev

Q *Did President John F. Kennedy and Premier Nikita Khrushchev ever discuss secretly a joint space flight to Mars by U.S. and Soviet astronauts? Or is that just one of the stories kicked around in NASA circles?—Russ Whitehead, Galveston, Tex.*

A It's true. In 1961, when Kennedy and Khrushchev held talks in Vienna, they came up with an idea for a joint flight to Mars. Both were enthusiastic about the idea, but when Khrushchev returned to Moscow and broached the suggestion to his associates, the military discouraged it on the grounds that it would reveal to us the latest Soviet rocket developments. It was not until July 1975, when Gerald Ford was president and Leonid Brezhnev was head of the USSR, that U.S. astronauts and Soviet cosmonauts participated in a joint test space project.

Q *Yves Montand, the French actor who partook in a notorious affair with the late Marilyn Monroe when she was married to playwright Arthur Miller, is involved in a scandal in Paris. Could you explain what it's about? Knowing some-* *thing about Montand's career, I'm sure sex or politics, or both, are involved.—Patricia Williams, Vail, Colo.*

A You are correct in your assumption. Yves Montand (real name: Ivo Livi), 68, has been ordered by a court in Paris to take a blood test to determine if he is the father of a 14-year-old girl, Aurora, whose mother filed a paternity suit against him. The court has decided that Montand and Anne Florange, a former actress, engaged in an intimate relationship for several years from 1972 onward, when they filmed *Le Hasard et la Violence* together in the south of France. Florange is demanding $170,000 to cover the costs of supporting the girl.

Montand was born in Italy but discovered in Paris by the legendary singer Edith Piaf, with whom he lived for a time. He was married to the actress Simone Signoret for 34 years—from 1951 until her death in 1985. They had no children, but three years after his wife's death the actor fathered a boy by his young girlfriend, Carole Amiel. As we go to press, Montand has not yet decided to submit to a blood test in the Florange matter. He remains one of the most popular and political entertainers in France.

Yves Montand

Lana Turner

Elizabeth Taylor

Q *An awful lot is written about actresses like Lana Turner and Elizabeth Taylor and how many times they've been married. Now I'd like to know which Hollywood actor has been married the most times. Would you please name his wives?—Lona Briskin, Atlantic City, N.J.*

A Mickey Rooney, who will be 70 in September, has had at least eight wives: Ava Gardner, Betty J. Rase, Martha Vickers, Elaine Mehnkenm, Barbara Thomason, Margie Dane, Carolyn Hockett and Janice Chamberlin.

Q *In your opinion, what is it that has done in multimillionaire Donald Trump?—Franklin Crowley, Las Vegas, Nev.*

A A lust for power, money and fame and an inability to limit self-admiration, self-praise and self-glorification may have affected Donald Trump adversely.

Q *Who are the two members of Congress who have publicly admitted that they are homosexual, and is homosexuality any reason for dismissal from elective office?—R.F., Wilmington, Del.*

A Rep. Gerry E. Studds, 53, and Rep. Barney Frank, 50—both Massachu-setts Democrats—are self-admitted homosexuals, but that is not automatically grounds for congressional expulsion.

Q *Was Peter Graf, father of tennis ace Steffi Graf, recently involved in a paternity blackmail case? It has been discussed all over the tennis circles.—N.L., San Marino, Calif.*

A Peter Graf, 52, was the target of attempted blackmail after a *Playboy* magazine model claimed she had given birth to his baby. The model, Nicole Meissner, 22, reportedly admitted that she had engaged in an affair with Graf during the time he was escorting his famous daughter around the international tennis circuit. Now, the German police are questioning Nicole's boyfriend about cash demands allegedly made by him on Steffi Graf's father after the baby girl was born in January.

The Youth Office in Frankfurt filed a paternity suit against Graf, who continued to deny the allegation. However, Nicole Meissner signed a sworn statement vouching that Graf was not the father of the infant, who was christened Tara Tanita.

According to the German magazine *Quick,* Nicole's boyfriend, Eberhard Thust, a boxing promoter, presumably hoped to profit by the circumstances nevertheless. The prosecutor's office in Frankfurt says that Thust and Meissner were detained June 19 and jailed the next day in connection with an investigation relating to extortion—the alleged attempt to blackmail Graf.

As for Steffi, the world's No. 1 woman tennis player, she maintains: "This story is not true. It is a pity that these magazines and newspapers do not have more respect for my family and private life. There will be consequences."

Q *Before he married the Swedish actress May Britt, didn't Sammy Davis, Jr., insist she convert to Judaism?—Cathy Hutchinson, Media, Pa.*

A No, he did not. Maybritt Wilkens (her original name) converted to Judaism as a surprise for Sammy, and later, when the family was blessed with children—a daughter and two adopted sons—she brought them up in the Jewish faith.

Q *I have a neighbor who says Clark Gable had dentures and, with them, a bad case of bad breath. My neighbor says Vivien Leigh had a hard time getting close to Gable in* Gone With the Wind. *Could you shed some light on this for me?—Howard H. Mullett, Crystal River, Fla.*

Clark Gable

A Gable suffered from halitosis, and Joan Crawford, with whom he had a rapturous and lengthy love affair, was one of the first who so advised him. The cause, however, was not his dentures. His stomach trouble, his sinuses, drinking and smoking all contributed to the problem. Gable made it a point to clean his dentures prior to engaging in "close shots" with Vivien Leigh and other actresses, but this was not particularly efficacious, since it did not attack the root cause.

Vivien Leigh

Barbra Streisand

Q *Wasn't Jon Peters, now one of the chief executives of Columbia Pictures, once the hairdresser and boyfriend of Barbra Streisand? How did this talented, ambitious man get from being a hairdresser to one of the most powerful positions in Hollywood?—Michele Gerhardt, Coronado, Calif.*

A Peters, now 45, was lucky, dynamic, aggressive and determined to get ahead when he arranged to meet Streisand in 1974. She was lonely and available at the time, having gone through actor Elliott Gould, Canadian Prime Minister Pierre Trudeau, actor Ryan O'Neal and several other admirers. Three years younger than Streisand, Peters gave her his complete devotion, which she welcomed. Together they worked on a rock 'n' roll remake of the classic Hollywood story *A Star Is Born,* with Kris Kristofferson as Streisand's co-star. The film was panned when it was released in 1976, but it made money—the goal of the game—and the Streisand-Peters duo was off to the races. Eventually each outgrew the other. The film *Shampoo,* starring Warren Beatty and Julie Christie, is said to mirror much of the Streisand-Peters relationship.

Q *There's a widespread rumor in Havana that Jacqueline Kennedy*

Onassis is pressuring Castro to sign a contract for his memoirs. Could this be true?—Jane O'Connor, Swampscott, Mass.

A It could be, but in publishing circles no credence is given to it. Perhaps one day, if he ever makes it to exile, Fidel Castro may pen his autobiography with Jackie's editorial help.

Q *Rock star Madonna has received heaps of adverse criticism this year for her raunchy personal appearances. I have never seen one of Madonna's concerts. What does she do onstage that is so controversial?—D. McCallister, Denver, Colo.*

A Madonna, dressed in scanty attire, engages in suggestive movements with band members as well as with herself.

Madonna

Q *Was King Hussein of Jordan ever married to a switchboard operator from Ipswich, England, whom he crowned Princess Muna? How many wives has he had, anyway? And does he make them all princesses or queens? Oh! How tall is the little king?—Mike Greenfield, Satellite City, Fla.*

A King Hussein is five feet two, has been married four times in his 54 years. His first wife, Sharifa Dina Abdel Hamid, was an Egyptian cousin known as Princess Dina. Hussein divorced her in 1956 after a year of marriage. In 1961 he married Antoinette Gardiner, a British citizen who had been a switchboard operator and secretary. He made her Princess Muna. Hussein divorced her in 1972 and took as his third wife Alia Baha Eddin Toukan, a Jordanian beauty, whom he made Queen Alia. She was killed in a helicopter accident in 1977. In 1978 Hussein married Elizabeth "Lisa" Halaby, American-born, Princeton-educated daughter of "Jeeb" Halaby, an avi-ation executive and U.S. government official. Hussein made Lisa his Queen Noor.

Q *My history teacher told me Winston Churchill's wife, Clementine, was illegitimate. As a result, she was constantly afraid—because of her background—that one day her famous prime minister of a husband would leave her, although he never did. Is that bit of history true?—H.J., Bremerton, Wash.*

A It's a complicated story. Clementine Churchill's mother was Lady Blanche Ogilvy, the oldest daughter of the 10th Earl of Airlie—an old Scottish family. In 1878 Blanche Ogilvy, 26, married Henry Hozier, 40, who worked for Lloyd's of London. Their marriage was a miserable one, and Hozier insisted that he wanted no children. After five years, since her husband refused to impregnate her, Blanche Hozier set out in search of a man who would. She chose for breeding purposes Capt. George "Bay" Middleton, a superb horseman of the 12th Lancers. It was Middleton who fathered two daughters, Kitty and Clementine, by Blanche Hozier. After Middleton was killed in a hunting accident, Blanche reputedly continued to rotate a pool of 10 lovers. For further details, you may care to read *Churchill: Young Man in a Hurry—1874-1915,* by Ted Morgan. Apparently Clementine Hozier's legal father was not her natural father.

Q *Is it true that copies of Elvis Presley's last electrocardiogram—from August 16, 1977, showing him dead—are on sale in England for $5,000?—Claudey Owens, Bessemer, Ala.*

A Not true. A London auctioneer, Phillips, was scheduled to put Elvis Presley's final electrocardiogram up for bidding, but the item was withdrawn from auction because it was considered to be in bad taste.

Elvis Presley

Barbara Bush

Q *How many wives of U.S. presidents are still living, and what are their birth dates?—Terry Downey, South Bend, Ind.*

A Herewith, in order, the birth dates of the seven living First Ladies, past and present:

Pat Nixon	March 16, 1912
Lady Bird Johnson	Dec. 22, 1912
Betty Ford	April 8, 1918
Nancy Reagan	July 6, 1921
Barbara Bush	June 8, 1925
Rosalynn Carter	Aug. 18, 1927
Jacqueline Kennedy Onassis	July 28, 1929

Q *Has Larry King, the talk-show host, been married more than three times? How old is he? Any children? Where does he live?—Elizabeth K., Rockville, Md.*

A King, 57, has been married three to six times, depending on one's source. He has a daughter, Chaia, 23, and an adopted son, Andy, 35. He lives in Arlington, Virginia, was reared in Brooklyn, New York, under the name Larry Zeiger. King was 10 when his father died, and his youth was no picnic. He's a complex, well-liked, talented interviewer, humorist and raconteur whose listeners and earnings number in the millions. He is obviously addicted to women and, despite protestations, will no doubt marry again.

Q *Why is it that Michael Chang, who won the French Open Championships, and Peter Sampras, who won the U.S. Open Championships, look so clean-cut, neat, trim, tidy and dapper on the tennis court—and someone like Andre Agassi looks so messy, sloppy, unwashed and unkempt?—Nicole Foster, Las Vegas, Nev.*

A Chang and Sampras have a more conservative taste in clothes and personal grooming, which sits well with such sponsors as Du Pont and Reebok. Agassi, on the other hand, bleaches his hair, dresses like an unmade bed and appeals to the poets and free souls among his fans. All three young men are, of course, superb tennis champions.

Q *Has any incumbent U.S. representative, with the exception of Gerald Ford, ever been elected president of the U.S.?—Nicola Ettinger, Chicago, Ill.*

A Gerald Ford was not elected president. He was first appointed vice president under a provision of the 25th Amendment, then sworn in as president when Richard Nixon resigned on August 9, 1974. The only incumbent U.S. representative ever elected president was James A. Garfield, a Republican from Ohio who was elected in 1880.

Q *How old is Paul Newman? How old is his wife, actress Joanne Woodward? How long have they been married? How many children do they have?—Emm Berger, Shreveport, La.*

A Newman was born January 26, 1925. Woodward was born February 27, 1930. They were married in January 1958. It was her first marriage, his second. Newman's first wife was actress Jacqueline Witte, with whom he parented a son, Scott (deceased), and two daughters, Susan and Stephanie. Newman also has fathered three daughters by Joanne Woodward. They are Elinor, Melissa and Clea.

Q *In terms of congressional appropriations, any difference between "a black program" and "a program for blacks"?—E.T., Aberdeen, Md.*

A "A program for blacks" is one legislated primarily to benefit black persons. "A black program" is a secret one, the details and cost of which are so hidden in the budget that neither the public nor most members of Congress can identify or track them. The overall CIA appropriation is an example of "a black program."

Q *Was there ever an intimate liaison between Laurence Olivier, the great English actor, who died in 1989, and Danny Kaye, the great American musical comedian, who died in 1987? I believe Olivier was 82 when he died, and Kaye was 74. In England, the story of their alleged friendship is old hat. In the U.S., however, it's supposed to have been a dark secret, although a novel based on their affair is scheduled to be published shortly. Is it true that Olivier was fond of more than Kaye's sensational Chinese cooking?—H.W., Manhasset, N.Y.*

A In the late 1940s, when Danny Kaye (real name: Daniel Kaminski) became one of the darlings of the Palladium Theatre set in London, Olivier discovered that he liked far more than Kaye's cooking. He liked his wit, his comedy, his companionship, and therefore cultivated his friendship.

Laurence Olivier

WALTER SCOTT'S
PERSONALITY PARADE®

March 17, 1991

Brooke Shields

Q *I was thinking of applying to Princeton University in your country. But I gather that those young women who go there and join one of the various eating clubs—which once were all-male—have to conform to the traditional ritual of drinking, retching and cavorting in the nude. Can this be true? Did my favorite actress, Brooke Shields, attend Princeton, or was it Harvard?—K.T., Sydney, Australia.*

A Brooke Shields, Princeton Class of 1987, was a member of Cap and Gown, one of 12 eating clubs on campus. It was another club—all-male until last month—that previously upheld the tradition you describe.

Q *When does the 13-year-old TV series* Dallas *end, and what happens to "J.R.," played by Larry Hagman? Does he survive so that the series can be revived someday?—M.T., Portsmouth, Va.*

A The two-hour final episode of *Dallas* reportedly is scheduled for showing in May. In this concluding roundup, insiders say, J.R. is knocked off at Southfork.

Q *Do you have any idea who discovered the Saudi Arabian oil fields and when?—Allan P., Tucson, Ariz.*

A The first was discovered in 1938 by a geologist from Stanford University, Max Steineke, Class of 1921. Unfortunately, Steineke died in 1952, and not much is known about him. One helpful book is *Trek of the Oil Finders,* by E. W. Owen, published in 1975 in Tulsa by the American Association of Petroleum Geologists. Another good source is Carol King, historian of Stanford University's School of Earth Sciences.

Q *Last year, Connie Chung, the TV newswoman, announced that, at 44, she was most anxious to have a baby. She said she and her husband, newsman Maury Povich, would concentrate on producing a little one. Have they scored yet?— F. Chu Yun, Seattle, Wash.*

A Not as we go to press, although Povich has offspring from a previous marriage.

Q *Last year,* Life *magazine, after consulting many historians and experts, compiled a list of the 100 most influential Americans of the 20th century. How many actors, athletes and U.S. presidents made the list, and who are they?—Kathy Goode, Milwaukee, Wis.*

Marlon Brando

A Only one actor, Marlon Brando, made the list. Four athletes—Babe Ruth, Muhammad Ali, Jackie Robinson and Billie Jean King—also made it. The 17 men who have served in this century as presidents of the U.S. were discussed separately in the magazine and thus not included on the list.

Arnold Schwarzenegger and Maria Shriver

Q *Is Arnold having another little Schwarzenegger? Didn't he also have a brother who was killed in a weight-lifting accident? Was Schwarzenegger a conscientious objector? How much is he paid per picture?—Karl Reisch, El Paso, Tex.*

A Arnold's wife, Maria Shriver, is again with child. His brother, Meinhard, died in a car crash. Arnold served in the Austrian army; he was never a conscientious objector. He gets about $12 million per picture, plus a hefty slice of the profits.

Q *What's cooking with Barbra Streisand's love life? One rumor has her remarrying actor Elliott Gould at the instigation and encouragement of their son, Jason, 24. Streisand and Gould were married from 1963 to 1969. Another has her contemplating marriage to James Newton Howard, 39, a composer nine years her junior who was formerly married to actress Rosanna Arquette. If you were a betting man, whom would you bet on—Gould or Howard?—Lena Covington, Brooklyn New York.*

A Our money would edge toward Howard, who's under contract to do the music for Barbra's next picture, *The Prince of Tides.* Years ago, when asked about her taste in men, Streisand cleverly replied, "I'll settle for people enjoying my work, and my friends enjoying me."

Muhammad Ali

Cindy and Kevin Costner

Q *Ever since he won an Oscar for his brilliant directorial debut in* Dances With Wolves, *Kevin Costner has been hassled by the European press to acknowledge love stories of yesterday involving his former girlfriends. Should he?—Al Friedman, Mexico City, Mexico.*

A It depends on how "former" his girlfriends are. No harm will accrue to Costner for acknowledging yesterday's wifeless romances. Today, however, he's married to a beautiful girl, Cindy, has three adorable children and must be careful.

Q *I am trying to get some info about Marion Hargrove, author of* See Here, Pvt. Hargrove, *a best-selling book that came out during World War II. I gave Hargrove recruit training at Fort Bragg, North Carolina, in the early 1940s. Also, I have noticed a Dean Hargrove listed in TV credits, and I was wondering if he was any relation to Marion Hargrove. I would appreciate any info on either of them.—Henry D. Ussery, Jr., Gadsden, Ala.*

A Marion and Dean Hargrove are not related, though both worked in Hollywood at one time as writers—Marion at Warner Bros., Dean at Universal. Marion Hargrove, now 71, has retired to Santa Cruz, California. Dean, 52, is still active.

Q *What is the status of the Merv Griffin-Brent Plott affair?—Cyrus W., Miami, Fla.*

A Brent Plott, a Florida gentleman, has filed a breach-of-contract suit seeking half the profits from the TV game shows *Jeopardy* and *Wheel of Fortune,* once owned by Merv Griffin. Plott, 39, says he suffered illness and distress after Griffin severed their nine-year relationship last year. Griffin, 65, calls the lawsuit "a shameless attempt to extort money from me." Plott contends that he was Griffin's secretary, personal adviser and lover, also that he helped the multimillionaire in many of his business deals. Griffin says only that Plott was once his bodyguard and horse trainer.

Q *What is the age and marital status of Nick Nolte, the actor? This guy has had quite a roller-coaster career. Does he drink?—Amy Clayton, Toledo, Ohio.*

A After seven years of all kinds of living, Nick Nolte, 49, and his wife, Rebecca, 30, are seeking a divorce in Los Angeles, where they will amicably share custody of their son, Brawley King Nolte, nearly five. The actor—who was born in Omaha—has been known to bend an elbow.

Q *Of our 50 states, how many have only one member in the House of Representatives, and who are they?—Peter Dyches, Towson, Md.*

A In the 102nd Congress, there are six states that have only one U.S. representative. They are Alaska, with Don Young (R); Delaware, with Thomas Carper (D); South Dakota, with Tim Johnson (D); Vermont, with Bernard Sanders (Independent); and Wyoming, with Craig Thomas (R).

Q *My husband and I would like to send a get-well card to Michael Landon. Would you please let us have an address we can write to?—Virginia Galante, Toms River, N.J.*

A You can reach the actor at Michael Landon Productions, 10202 W. Washington Blvd., Culver City, California, 90232.

Q *Is it true that the grave of rock star Jim Morrison, leader of The Doors, is the most popular attraction in Paris,*

James Dean

where he died in 1971 at 27? Can you also tell me where the following are buried: James Dean, Liberace, Karl Marx and Buddy Holly?—Newton Hemsley, Chicago, Ill.

A The grave of Jim Morrison is the fourth most visited site in the Paris area—after Versailles, the Louvre and the Eiffel Tower. James Dean is buried in Fairmont, Indiana; Liberace rests in Forest Lawn Cemetery, near Hollywood; Karl Marx lies in London, and Buddy Holly in Lubbock, Texas.

Liberace

Jayne Mansfield

Q *I thought actress Jayne Mansfield was decapitated in a car accident in Germany. But people keep telling me she died right here in America. Who's right?—Shirley Ohlinger, Fleetwood, Pa.*

A The blond sex symbol was killed on the outskirts of New Orleans on June 29, 1967, when her car rammed into the rear of a truck. She was 34. Mansfield's chauffeur and lawyer also died, but three of her children—asleep in the backseat—survived.

Q *I've heard rumors that Whitney Houston lip-syncs to a tape whenever she performs "The Star-Spangled Banner." Can this be true?—Scheritha Willis, Elberton, Ga.*

A Whitney Houston, 28, says she never lip-syncs—knowingly. The rumors began in January at Super Bowl XXV in Tampa. Under NFL policy, the designated performer always makes a taped version of the national anthem as a precaution. At game time, officials decided to play Houston's tape on the public-address system to be sure the statuesque singer could be heard over a flyby of four military jets. "Whitney's camp felt very strongly against lip-syncing . . . and she for sure was singing," says Bob Best, pro-

ducer of the pregame show. She only later learned that her mike was not plugged in.

Q *Has actor Mickey Rourke ever been married? If so, to whom?—Joanne Burch, Jamaica, N.Y.*

A Philip Andre "Mickey" Rourke has been married since 1980 to actress Debra Feuer, his co-star in the movie *Homeboy*. Their marriage, however, has been called bizarre—even by Hollywood standards—and the pair reportedly go for long periods without seeing each other. Rourke, 35, once said, "To me, actresses are the most unattractive women on the face of the earth. They're so neurotic and needy. You can't trust them, and they're big babies." His latest "big baby" is Carre Otis, a beauty he met while filming *Wild Orchid*.

Q *I read recently that a German scientist who played an important role in our space program is reapplying for his U.S. citizenship after being expelled as a Nazi war criminal. Who is he? And were there many Nazis who came here after the war to work in our space program?—S.Z., New York, N.Y.*

A Arthur Rudolph was one of 118 Nazi rocket engineers secretly brought to the U.S., where he later designed the Saturn V rocket that launched our astronauts to the moon. In 1984—after the Justice Department charged that, while he was director, thousands of slave laborers had been worked to death at the Nazi factory that made V-2 rockets—Rudolph voluntarily relinquished his U.S. citizenship and returned to Germany rather than face trial as a war criminal. Rudolph, now 84 and seeking to return to this country, has steadfastly maintained his innocence.

Q *What can you tell us about Christiane Amanpour, who was so visible on CNN during the Persian Gulf war?—Lu Vobora, Medford, Ore.*

A Christiane Amanpour, 33, born in London to an Iranian father and English mother, began broadcasting radio news in Britain and later in this country. She joined Cable News Network in 1983 and became an on-air correspondent three years later. After the Gulf war ended, she remained in Iraq, doing reports on the Kurdish refugees. Amanpour says she faced no problems as a woman reporter in that part of the world.

Now, however, she's back at CNN's bureau in romantic Paris, where—as an attractive single woman—she faces dangers of a different nature.

Q *Do George and Barbara Bush ever have a spat?—Luretta Bagby Martin, Tucson, Ariz.*

A No couple can be married 46 years without having a spat, but as yet the neighbors haven't complained about loud domestic disturbances at 1600 Pennsylvania Ave. Washington gossips, however—after feasting on the previous occupants at the White House—may well be complaining about the Bushes.

Q *How much did Jackie Kennedy inherit upon the death of John Kennedy in 1963? How much did she get from Aristotle Onassis? Did she marry Onassis purely for his money? And what's she worth today?—Ellie Knight, Winchester, Va.*

John F. Kennedy

A Though he was one of the richest men ever to occupy the White House, John Kennedy left his widow less than $70,000 in cash and an income of $200,000 a year from a trust fund. She subsequently married the Greek shipping tycoon Aristotle Onassis because he was kind to her two children—and because his billions could buy her privilege, privacy and security. Like JFK, however, her second husband had an appetite for women, and their marriage was on the rocks when Onassis died in 1975—yet Jackie negotiated a tidy $26 million settlement with his heirs. Her current fortune has been estimated at $200 million.

Jackie and Aristotle Onassis

George Bush

Q *How does President Bush get paid? I mean, does some office boy go around and leave a check on his desk?—William L. Collins, Westfield, Ind.*

A Like all federal employees, George Bush, 67, is paid every two weeks. His money goes in via direct deposit. At $200,000 a year, that works out to nearly $7,700 per paycheck—before Uncle Sam grabs his share.

Q *With all the concern about AIDS, I was surprised when two gay characters turned up on the* Roseanne *show. My husband says this proves what he's always suspected—that Roseanne is gay. I don't believe it. Who's right?—J.G., Brookline, Mass.*

A You. Roseanne Barr Arnold's real-life brother and sister are homosexuals, however, and she says, "My show seeks to portray various slices of life, and homosexuals are a reality. I feel it's appropriate to present this slice of life as well." And it doesn't hurt the ratings, either.

Q *I'm upset by Baseball Commissioner Fay Vincent's decision to drop the asterisk next to Roger Maris' name in the record books, indicating that he hit his 61*

homers in a 162-game schedule, while Babe Ruth swatted 60 homers in a season with eight fewer games. What's the reasoning behind this cockamamie ruling?—C.D., Larchmont, N.Y.

A Roger Maris' name does not appear with an asterisk in the current record books. Instead, he and Ruth are listed side by side. Maris, who died in 1985 at the age of 51, has never been fully recognized because he, like Hank Aaron, had the misfortune of surpassing America's greatest sports legend, an achievement some still find unforgivable. When baseball's committee on statistical accuracy meets this fall, there's a bettor's chance it may finally give Maris sole possession of the home-run record.

Q *Watching Mariah Carey's latest music video, I noticed that she keeps her head turned to the left. Is this just a habit, or is it because of that mole she has on the side of her mouth? Also, is she of black ancestry?—Stephanie Kong, San Jose, Calif.*

Mariah Carey

A There's no anatomical explanation for Mariah Carey's head position on her video. That's just the way she likes to look at the camera. The sultry singer, whose second album, "Emotions," is due out this month, was born 21 years ago to an Irish-American mother and a black Venezuelan father. She has had little contact with her father since her parents divorced when she was three years old.

Q *Is Artie Shaw, one of my favorite bandleaders, still active in the music business? Has he written any books?—George R. Vojtko, La Jolla, Calif.*

A Artie Shaw, 81 and living in Los Angeles, quit the music business in 1954. He has had three books published—a novel, an autobiography and a book of short stories—and has almost completed a second novel. Shaw, who was a bandleader for 18 years, maintains, "I was the Elvis of my day." And at least some ladies agreed: Although now divorced, he was married seven times, most notably to the screen goddesses Lana Turner and Ava Gardner.

Q *Every time I pick up the paper, it seems that some movie star and his girlfriend—like Warren Beatty and Annette Bening, Jack Nicholson and Rebecca Broussard—are having a baby without bothering to get married. Don't they know that when their kids grow up, this may pose a problem for them? What do these actors have against marriage anyway?—S.G., Decatur, Ill.*

A Divorce, Hollywood style, can be extremely expensive for wealthy megastars like Beatty and Nicholson. Those two, both 54, are simply hedging their bets by staying single while they have families—and they remain supremely confident that their box-office public will overlook any self-indulgence. Seemingly less important to either man is the baby's last name. Incidentally, Nicholson—whose love child, Lorraine, is now 18 months old—is reported to be the one who sold buddy Beatty on the joys of fatherhood.

Q *Donald and Ivana Trump had a much-publicized prenuptial agreement that said she'd receive "only" $25 million in the event they divorced. How did she come out?—D.B., White Plains, N.Y.*

A Although Ivana failed in her effort to upset that prenuptial agreement, she didn't do all that badly. Ivana, 42, received $14 million in cash, a home in Connecticut, a penthouse apartment in New York City and use of the 118-room Trump mansion in Florida one month a year. She also gets $350,000 a year in alimony and $300,000 annually to support her three children.

Ivana Trump

Prince Charles

Q *Queen Elizabeth has bestowed titles on three of her four children—Charles is the Prince of Wales, Andrew is the Duke of York and Anne is the Princess Royal. Only Edward remains titleless. Do you think the queen will make him the Duke of Windsor, the title created for his uncle, King Edward VIII?—Michael G. Friedel, Bettendorf, Iowa.*

A By tradition, the queen is free to choose whatever titles she deems appropriate for her offspring. Windsor was adopted as the name of the royal family in 1817 and has been used only once as a royal title—for Edward VIII when he gave up the throne for the woman he loved in 1936. It is highly unlikely that the queen would revive painful memories by using that particular title for her son.

Q *I've heard that Michael Jackson's renegade sister, La Toya, is planning a tell-all book, and her family tried to stop her. What secrets are they afraid she'll reveal?—M.S., Sacramento, Calif.*

A La Toya may blow the lid off the family compound in Encino, California, with *La Toya: Growing up in the Jackson Family,* her forthcoming autobiography. "Hate is the other side of

intense love, and my father has skeletons in his closet," says La Toya, 32. "He is afraid of that door being opened widely." The secrets she reveals reportedly include attempted suicides by family members.

Q *Is Mike Tyson the highest-paid athlete in the world?—M.K., Las Vegas, Nev.*

A No, it's his nemesis, the heavyweight champ Evander Holyfield, 28, who earned $60.5 million last year. Tyson, 25, only made $31.5 million. Tyson hopes to get the title back when they fight November 8.

Q *How many U.S. presidents have been southpaws? And how does that compare with the national average?—Doug Naef, Milwaukie, Ore.*

A Of the 40 men who have served as U.S. president, four (10 percent) have been left-handed—James Garfield, Harry Truman, Gerald Ford and George Bush. Lefties make up 10 percent to 15 percent of the rest of us.

Q *First I heard that my favorite singer, Cat Stevens, became a monk and took a vow of silence. Then I heard that he became an atheist. Can both of these stories be true?—Angela Boggs, Sandis, Ohio.*

A Cat Stevens (real name: Stephen Demetri Georgiou), 43, made about $15 million from eight gold albums. "I decided in the '60s," he said, "to become as wealthy as possible so I could live whatever life I wanted." He became a devout Muslim in 1977, changed his name to Yusef Islam and set up an Islamic school and Muslim Aid, a relief organization near London, where he lives with his wife and five children. "I'm not looking for applause now," he says, "I'm looking for real solutions."

Q *How much of the money pledged to the U.S. toward the cost of the war in the Gulf has been received? From whom did we receive it, and who still has to pony up? And how much did the war cost?—William Faison, Pikesville, Md.*

A The total bill may reach $60 billion. To date, the U.S. has received $46.6 billion from a half dozen major contributors. The two countries that benefited the most—Kuwait and Saudi Arabia—have yet to pay in full.

Q *AIDS has spread through all walks of life, yet I can't remember hearing about any actor or actress in X-rated movies who has caught it. Is the adult-movie industry covering up? Any facts on this?—Paula Shurman, Las Vegas, Nev.*

A Spokesmen for the adult-video business, as you suspect, adamantly deny that AIDS has claimed any victims in their industry. However, the death certificate for John Holmes—a bisexual porn star and intravenous drug user—tells a different story. It states that the actor died in 1988 at 43 in Sepulveda, California, of encephalitis as a result of AIDS. No doubt there have been other casualties in the porn trade.

Greta Garbo

Q *When Greta Garbo's purported nephew made a bid to share in her $20 million estate, he claimed the screen star had a drinking problem. That comes as news to me. Is it true?—J.J., Johnstown, Pa.*

A Around the time she died at 84 in April last year, Garbo was ordering up to her Manhattan apartment one bottle of vodka and two bottles of scotch every week. She also smoked—all this while undergoing dialysis three times a week. Even so, the "nephew" failed to prove mental incompetence and got nothing.

Sheryl Berkoff and Rob Lowe

Q *What has actor Rob Lowe been up to since his widely publicized sex-video incident? How badly did that damage his career in the eyes of Hollywood?—David Horowicz, East Meadow, N.Y.*

A Despite his pretty-boy looks and Brat Pack reputation, Rob Lowe, 27, is nobody's fool. He was clever enough not to let his videotaped sex romp with an underage girl in a Georgia hotel room turn him into the laughingstock of Hollywood. Instead, he poked fun at himself by playing a lecher with a penchant for video cameras in *Bad Influence*. Lowe's latest film, *Wayne's World,* pairs him with one of Hollywood's hottest new stars—Lara Flynn Boyle of *Twin Peaks* fame. He also has settled down and married Sheryl Berkoff, a makeup artist.

Q *Abbott and Costello—they were lovably hilarious on the screen in the 1940s, but I understand they didn't get along in private life. True?—John Raleigh, Bergenfield, N.J.*

A It's a sad story. Bud Abbott and Lou Costello were the first screen team to get a percentage of their films' grosses. At the height of their popularity, during World War II, Costello—the short, funny half of the pair—demanded that they split their income 60-40 in his favor. Their relationship, never ideal to begin with, soured after that, and they finally split up in 1956. Costello died of a heart attack three years later, at age 53. Abbott survived until 1974, when he died penniless at age 79.

Q *In 1989, the U.S. Postal Service honored the late Lou Gehrig by issuing a stamp with his name and image. Have any other baseball players been so honored?—Steven Zurlnick, Warwick, N.Y.*

A Three other Hall of Famers, all deceased, also have had their portraits on U.S. postage stamps: Jackie Robinson (1982), George Herman "Babe" Ruth (1983) and Roberto Clemente (1984). Suggestion from one long-suffering fan in Chicago: Put the entire Cubs team on a postage-due stamp.

Q *I'm confused about singer Amy Grant. Where does she stand on her Christianity these days? In her latest record and video, she's obviously involved in a romantic relationship, so I assume she's looking for money, not for God.—Kathy Catlin, Montrose, Colo.*

Amy Grant

A Amy Grant, 30—whose hit single "Baby, Baby" is, as you suggest, a departure from her previous religious material—insists her faith hasn't faltered. "Some feel that if music doesn't have some kind of evangelical content, it doesn't have any value," she says. "I feel differently. I want to be able to turn on the radio and hear fun songs where I'm not being pressured materially, sexually or violence-wise." And, yes, Amy is involved in "a romantic relationship," but it's with musician Gary Chapman, her husband and father of her two children—not the actor in her video.

Q *The book and movie Reversal of Fortune stirred my interest in the von Bulows. Where is this family from originally, and how did they get to America?—Jane Gambone, Allentown, Pa.*

A The central character in Reversal of Fortune was born Claus Cecil Bor-

Claus Von Bulow

berg, the son of a wealthy Dane. His mother was a member of the Danish branch of the Bulows, a noted family that produced a German chancellor and a conductor who married the daughter of composer Franz Liszt. Claus took his mother's maiden name after his parents divorced, later adding the aristocratic "von" while a student at Cambridge. He met the former Martha ("Sunny") Crawford, heiress to a utilities fortune, during a business trip to America in 1965 and married her a year later. Von Bulow, now 65, was convicted in 1982 of trying to murder his wife for her millions, but the conviction was overturned upon appeal in 1985.

Q *With so much media attention focusing on the Martina Navratilova-Judy Nelson palimony case, I've been wondering about the reported romance between Martina and former U.S. Olympic ski team member Cindy Nelson. Is it still going on, and did it cause Martina's breakup with Judy?—Warren Hammer, White Plains, N.Y.*

A Tennis great Martina Navratilova, 35, denies that Cindy Nelson—who won notoriety several years ago by posing for a suntan-oil commercial clad only in a pair of ski boots—had anything to do with her breakup with Judy Nelson after seven years. Says Martina of Cindy, 35, who is no relation to Judy: "I'm very, very close to Cindy. We're very good friends. But she is not the reason I left Judy . . . It just became too intense." Incidentally, at this writing, Martina is still trying to reach an out-of-court settlement with Judy Nelson, 45, the former Miss Texas who was her live-in companion and business partner in several sporting-clothes ventures.

Glenn Close

Q *People are always comparing Glenn Close and Meryl Streep, two of our greatest movie actresses. Streep has received two Oscars. How many has Close won?—M.A., Washington, D.C.*

A Always a bridesmaid, never a bride, Glenn Close, 44, has been nominated five times—for *The World According to Garp, The Big Chill, The Natural, Fatal Attraction* and *Dangerous Liaisons*—but has never won. Her problem is that she's so talented, she makes what she does on the screen look easy, allowing other actresses who chew up the scenery to walk away with the prizes.

Q *Before the Persian Gulf war, there was a considerable outcry from black leaders that black soldiers would be carrying a disproportionate share of the dangers of combat. Did their warnings turn out to be true?—Sid McAllister, Brevard, N.C.*

A The Pentagon reports that 291 Americans lost their lives in the Persian Gulf operation. Of those, 74 percent were white and 18 percent black. That 18 percent is higher than the figure for blacks in the overall American population—12.4 percent—but it is considerably lower than the figures for the Persian Gulf contingent of blacks in the Army (29.8 percent) and the Navy (21.3 percent) and only slightly higher than in the Marines (16.9 percent). Black servicemen and women acquitted themselves with distinction in the Gulf, and the U.S. military gained new stature as an institution of opportunity for all minorities.

Q *Whatever became of Buddy Holly's pregnant widow and child?—Linda Mowry, Florence, Ala.*

A When Buddy Holly died in a plane crash on February 3, 1959, at the age of 22, his wife of six months, Maria Elena, miscarried as a result of her psychological trauma. The young Mrs. Holly, who became immortalized as "the widowed bride" in Don McLean's song "American Pie," later married a Texas businessman and had three children. Now 60, divorced and living near Dallas, Maria Elena says: "I never let Buddy go. I froze in time. I'm still the same person as the day Buddy died. My life went through all these situations, but it was like sleepwalking." Fans of the rocker never let Buddy go, either. His legend has grown—thanks to records, a movie about his brief life and a Broadway musical.

Ted Danson

Q *Does Ted Danson—the macho star of television's long-running sitcom Cheers—wear a toupee?—J. Ryan, Springfield, Ill.*

A Ted Danson, 43, began wearing a hairpiece during the filming of *Cousins* in 1988. Like many men his age, he was self-conscious about his thinning hair. While on vacation in 1990, however, Ted took off the toupee and, off-camera, hasn't worn it since. He still wears one on the show, but in 1990 the actor accepted an Emmy for *Cheers* au naturel.

Q *I understand that before it was cleaned up, "Word to the Badd!"—Jermaine Jackson's song from his new album, "You Said"—contained some pretty scathing words about his brother Michael's attempts to chemically lighten his skin. Would you print the offending lyrics?—A.R., Fort Myers, Fla.*

A "Once you were made, / You changed your shade. / Was your color wrong? / Could not turn back / It's a known fact. / You were too far gone."

Q *I recently bought the novel* Thinner, *by Richard Bachman, because I'm a Stephen King fan and had heard that he wrote it under that pen name. But the back of the book has a photo of someone else. Is all this a product of King's bizarre imagination?—L.J., Moscow, Pa.*

A Yes, it is. The prolific Mr. King wrote five books from 1977 to 1984 under the pen name Richard Bachman. To throw readers off the trail, he used someone else's photo on the jacket of *Thinner*. In an interview, the author later explained that Bachman represented the darker, more violent side of his nature. Richard Bachman finally "died," he said, "of cancer of the pseudonym." Also, Bachman's name did not sell nearly as many books as King's.

Q *I heard Arnold Schwarzenegger took steroids. When and for how long?—S.H., Millburn, N.J.*

A Arnold Schwarzenegger began taking steroids under a doctor's supervision in 1967, for six to eight weeks before each competition. He did so, he says, "because, at 20, all you want to do is be a champion." And, indeed, in 1970 he won three major titles—Mr. Universe, Mr. World and Mr. Olympia—a feat unequaled among bodybuilders. Now 44 and head of the President's Council on Physical Fitness & Sports, however, the muscleman-turned-actor insists he wouldn't do it again, because steroids are unhealthy, and "bodybuilding is what the name implies: to make your body stronger—and healthier."

Arnold Schwarzenegger

WALTER SCOTT'S
PERSONALITY PARADE®

January 5, 1992

Valerie Bertinelli

Q *Did Valerie Bertinelli and Eddie Van Halen have a baby? What's its name? How long have they been married?*—K.M., Glendora, Calif.

A Valerie Bertinelli, 31, who rose to fame on TV's *One Day at a Time*, and rock star Eddie Van Halen, 36, have been married 10 years. They've had their share of troubles, with Eddie being treated for alcohol abuse and Valerie suffering a miscarriage. The marriage has endured, however, and last spring the couple had some good news—a baby boy, Wolfgang, named for the composer Mozart. They said they thought Amadeus "would be hard to go through life with—not that Wolfgang will be so easy."

Q *That attractive and talented Kathleen Sullivan—what has she been up to since she was fired as the co-anchor of CBS This Morning? Is she currently employed?*—Billy Mack, Atlanta, Ga.

A Kathleen Sullivan, 37, who has taken time off to play in celebrity tennis events and climb volcanoes in Hawaii, will be back on the tube next summer. Along with the veteran sportscasters Ahmad Rashad and Don Criqui, Sullivan will be co-host of NBC's pay-per-view Olympic coverage on cable television.

Q *Is it true that Tom Mix, the Western movie star of the 1920s and early '30s, wasn't just some celluloid cowboy but that he really had a fabulous life of adventure?*—D.G., Pelham, Ala.

A Tom Mix was the real McCoy. Born in 1880 in Pennsylvania, he served in the Spanish-American War, China and the Boer War. Later, while a member of the Texas Rangers, Mix was shot and carried three slugs in his body for the rest of his life. At various times, he was a sheriff and deputy marshall in Oklahoma, a cowboy, trick rider and roper. All this gave authority to his performances when he took to making Westerns. Mix starred in more than 170 films over 24 years, many of them with his famous horse, Tony. He retired in 1934 but died in a car crash six years later near Florence, Arizona, at the age of 60.

Q *I was taken aback by the comment by multimillionaire Ted Turner that "Christianity is a religion for losers." Was Turner raised in an agnostic family? Does he recognize any God other than the almighty dollar?*—Christopher James Fagan, State College, Pa.

A After making that comment two years ago, Ted Turner publicly apologized, saying, "I've offended just about every group there is." In his typically candid manner, the Atlanta-based media mogul—who grew up as a Fundamentalist Christian and once planned to be a missionary—explained that he couldn't reconcile the concept of an all-powerful God with so much suffering on earth. The 52-year-old multimillionaire said he rejected the idea of Heaven because "streets of gold and so forth turns me off."

Q *Why did the government sell the presidential yacht Sequoia, and whatever happened to it?*—A.J. Wylie, Camillus, N.Y.

Jimmy Carter

A Jimmy Carter ordered the *Sequoia* sold in 1977 because he considered it an unnecessary luxury. The Presidential Yacht Trust, a group of prominent Washingtonians, bought the vessel in 1981 with the intention of donating it to the government, then sailed it to Norfolk, Virginia,

Franklin D. Roosevelt

for repairs. Last July, however, when the trust was unable to pay its $2.2 million bill, the Norfolk Shipbuilding & Drydock Corp. obtained the *Sequoia* for a mere $50,000. The 104-foot teak yacht has a colorful history: Christened the *Savarona* when it was launched in 1924, it became the official presidential yacht in 1933. Franklin Roosevelt used it to plan wartime strategy, John Kennedy celebrated his last birthday in its rear salon, and Richard Nixon was on board when he told his family he was resigning the presidency.

Richard Nixon

Q *I'm a fan of Patrick Swayze and would like to know where he was born and if he's married. Also, I've seen him smoke on film, but does he smoke offscreen?*—Melodie Tacket, Indianapolis, Ind.

A Patrick Swayze, 39, star of *Dirty Dancing* and *Ghost*, was born in Houston and has been married for 14 years to the actress-dancer Lisa Niemi. "She's still my best friend," he says. "She's 50 percent responsible for my success." Swayze, who quit drinking five years ago, still smokes but says he is trying acupuncture to help him kick the habit.

Magic and Cookie Johnson

Q *I've read so much about Magic Johnson and his positive HIV test, but I'm still disturbed by two questions: What are the chances that his unborn child is also infected? And how did his admission that he had sex with many women affect his relationship with his wife?—Lisa Brown, New Caney, Tex.*

A Earvin (Magic) Johnson and his wife, the former Earletha (Cookie) Kelley, both 32, say they've grown closer since the basketball star's bombshell announcement—just six weeks after their marriage—that he's carrying the AIDS virus. Cookie treats her husband's confession that he had sex with "as many women as I could" as part of his past. She has tested negative twice, which means she and her unborn baby—who shares her blood supply—probably are not infected. However, to be sure, Cookie still must pass another test six months after the last time she and Magic had unprotected sexual intercourse.

Q *What are the religious affiliations of the U.S. Supreme Court justices?—E.R., Seattle, Wash.*

A Chief Justice William Rehnquist is a Lutheran. Bryon White, Sandra Day O'Connor and David Souter are Episcopalians. Antonin Scalia and Anthony Kennedy are Roman Catholics. Harry Blackmun is a Methodist. John Paul Stevens is a nondenominational Protestant. And Clarence Thomas was raised a Catholic but now attends an Episcopal church.

Q *There's been plenty of publicity stemming from Michael Jackson's hypersexual/hyperviolent video "Dangerous." What do his brothers think about the negative reaction? Have they come to his defense?—John Ferri, Fort Lauderdale, Fla.*

A The other Jackson brothers—Jackie, Marion, Tito, Jermaine and Randy—not only have not come to Michael's defense, but they even have formed their own film and TV production company. Says Jackie Jackson, in an obvious knock on Michael's video: "Everything is murder-this and sex-that. We want to help kids grow up the right way." They might start by teaching kids brotherly love.

Q *Is there really a close friendship between the supermodels Linda Evangelista and Christy Turlington? Are both of them married? How tall are they? And how old were they when they got into modeling?—M.H., Jacksonville, Fla.*

A Christy Turlington, 22, is five feet ten, started modeling in Florida at 14. Canadian-born Linda Evangelista, 26, is five feet nine, got her start in Paris at 19. Linda is married to Gerald Marie, 39, who runs the Paris offices of the Elite model agency. Christy is married to actor Roger Wilson, 32, whose initials are tatooed on her right ankle. The women like each other's company because they have lots in common: Both live in Paris and New York, are beautiful, fun-loving, constantly fending off unwanted advances—and rich, each earning more than $1 million a year.

Q *What were the lifetime royalties earned by Dr. Seuss? Was he treated fairly by those publishers who enjoyed the fruits of his extraordinary talent?—Steven Pitzpatrick, Marietta, Ga.*

A Theodore Seuss Geisel, who died last year at 87, enjoyed a warm, 50-year relationship with Random House, which published 200 million copies of his works. The author and illustrator of more than 40 books beloved by children and adults alike, Geisel was a shy and intensely private man who never publicly discussed his phenomenal financial success. A conservative estimate of his lifetime earnings, however, would put the figure at more than $100 million. He is survived by his second wife, Audrey, whom he wed in 1968. Dr. Seuss, who understood children so well, had none of his own.

Q *I've lost track of Tommy Lee Jones. Does he still make movies?—Mary Lou Anderson, Denver, Colo.*

A Tommy Lee Jones, 45, best known for his portrayal of the murderer Gary Gilmore in *The Executioner's Song*, is still making movies. He currently appears in *JFK*, the controversial Oliver Stone film about the assassination of John F. Kennedy—though his fans may not recognize him. The usually macho Jones plays a homosexual and wears frizzy white hair in the role of Clay Shaw, the New Orleans businessman who was charged in 1967 with conspiring to murder the president but later acquitted. Born in San Saba, Texas, the versatile actor was graduated from Harvard in 1969 and made his screen debut the following year in *Love Story*.

Tommy Lee Jones

Marlon Brando

Q *I heard that Marlon Brando is emotionally distraught and having real money problems because of his children. Can you shed some light on his tangled state of affairs?—E.E., Vail, Colo.*

A To pay the mounting legal and medical bills of his son, Christian, and daughter, Cheyenne, the 67-year-old actor is writing his autobiography for about $3 million. He also will earn several million to star as the Grand Inquisitor Torquemada in the movie *Christopher Columbus: The Discovery.* Christian Brando, 33, is serving a 10-year sentence for shooting Cheyenne's lover, Dag Drollet, in Marlon's Hollywood mansion last year. Cheyenne, 22, later gave birth to Drollet's son, then twice attempted suicide. She recently was arrested in France and extradited to Papeete, the French Polynesian capital, to face possible charges of complicity in Drollet's death. Cheyenne is free on $1 million bail and living on her father's private island near Tahiti. By all accounts, Marlon Brando is guilt-ridden over the family tragedy.

Q *The U.S. has given billions to Israel—more than any other country. What has Israel done for us in return?—Michael Paster, Elizabeth, N.J.*

A Supporters of Israel point out that more than 80 percent of the $3 billion a year in aid which we give to Israel is spent on goods made in the U.S. Most of it is military-related equipment, whose manufacture employs thousands of Americans. As our one democratic ally in a region of dictatorships, Israel also provides a steady flow of secret intelligence data on terrorism and other threats to American lives and security.

Q *What has become of the iconoclastic Irish singer Sinead O'Connor? Is she still recording? And how does she get along with other Irish musicians such as Van Morrison and U2?—T.S., Seattle, Wash.*

A The outspoken Ms. O'Connor, 24, lives with her son, Jake, four, in London, where she rarely sees other Irish musicians, such as Van Morrison and the members of U2. She's working on a new record, rehearsing for the role of Joan of Arc in an upcoming movie—and still shaving her head once a week. Recently Sinead lived up to her reputation for biting the hand that feeds her by blasting Hollywood—the film and music capital of the world—as a "filthy, incredibly violent place . . . full of sick people."

Dinah Shore

Q *Did singer Dinah Shore and actor Burt Reynolds ever have any children? How many children does Dinah have? To whom was she married, and when?—Estelle Ayers, St. Albans, W. Va.*

A Dinah's on-again, off-again affair with Burt Reynolds went on for six years, from 1970 to 1976. They never married and didn't have children: Dinah was, after all, in her 50s. Reynolds, now 56, has been married since 1988 to actress Loni Anderson, with whom he adopted a son, Quinton. Still, he remains close friends with Dinah, 74, whom he credits with helping to shape his acting career. The singer was married twice—to cowboy actor George Montgomery from 1943 to 1962 and to tennis pro Maurice Smith from 1963 to 1964. Dinah and Montgomery had a daughter, Melissa Ann, born in 1948, and they adopted a son, John David, in 1954.

George Bush   **Barbara Bush**

Q *After President Bush collapsed at the Tokyo summit, I couldn't help but wonder why Barbara Bush doesn't tell her husband, "Hey, George—you're 67 years old, and it's time you started acting your age!"—C. Evans, Darien, Conn.*

A According to White House insiders, the First Lady has told the president just that. But—as the latest joke in the West Wing goes—the hyperactive George Bush is like the floppy-eared bunny in the Energizer battery commercials: He keeps going and going and going, and just won't stop.

Q *Why did David Duke—the onetime grand wizard of the Ku Klux Klan and member of the American Nazi Party, who is now seeking the Republican presidential nomination—have a face-lift? He looked better before.—F.A.C., Trenton, Fla.*

A David Duke, 41, who is not on the ballot in this Tuesday's New Hampshire presidential primary, insists he has never had a face-lift—only surgery "to remove chin scars and repair a broken nose." When it comes to answering questions about his past, however, the former KKK leader and Nazi may be a little like Pinocchio, another character who had problems with his nose.

PERSONALITY PARADE®

May 17, 1992

McAffe/Globe

John F. Kennedy, Jr.

Q *With all the fuss over the rape charges against William Kennedy Smith, I haven't heard a lot recently about one of the people who publicly came to his support—his cousin, John F. Kennedy, Jr. What does John-John do when he's not working as an assistant district attorney in New York City? And who is he dating?—W. Hartley, Pasadena, Tex.*

A When he's not riding the subways to his frequent court appearances or tooling around Central Park on weekends on his bike, JFK, Jr., 31, is often with his longtime girlfriend, actress Christina Haag, 32, with whom he has appeared onstage

Globe

Madonna

and in an amateur film. He also can be found in Manhattan's trendy restaurants in the company of stars like Daryl Hannah. Madonna also is said to have expressed a romantic interest in the man described as America's most-eligible bachelor—but, when asked to comment, young Kennedy's only reply was, "I wish."

Q *As far as I'm concerned, the real star of the TV series* Brooklyn Bridge *is Gary David Goldberg, creator and producer of the show. How did he get started in TV, and what else has he done that deserves notice?—Albert Ellman, Albany, N.Y.*

A Gary David Goldberg was a late bloomer. Born in Brooklyn, he entered Brandeis University in 1962 but didn't graduate until 13 years and many colleges later. Once in Hollywood, however, he made up for lost time. In less than 10 years, Goldberg graduated from writing for *The Bob Newhart Show* to creating the huge hit *Family Ties.* Now 47 and the father of two, Goldberg has won a pair of Writers Guild awards, a Peabody, two Emmys and practically every other award in the book.

Q *Is it true that Val Kilmer—the star of* The Doors, Top Secret! *and* Thunderheart—*wanted to be a poet in his younger days? Where did he grow up? Is he married? And what has he done recently?—Joanna Bernstein, Pittsburgh, Pa.*

A Val Kilmer, 32, who grew up in California's San Fernando Valley, calls himself "a writer of bad poetry" and has published a collection of his verse, titled *My Edens After Burns.* He is married to British actress Joanne Whalley-Kilmer, 27, and they have a six-month-old daughter, Mercedes. A gifted actor (he was the youngest student in his class at the Juilliard drama school), Kilmer recently starred onstage in a New York Shakespeare Festival production of *'Tis Pity She's a Whore.*

Q *I've heard a rumor that singer Whitney Houston is co-starring in a movie with Kevin Costner. True?—Amy Reed, Atlanta, Ga.*

A Yes. Costner thought Houston, 28, would be perfect for the part of a pop singer in *The Bodyguard,* of which he's both the star and co-producer—and, he says, he waited three years for the singer to say "yes" to her first feature film. "It turned out to be an easy-to-take movie," adds Costner. Moviegoers will get to judge for themselves whether Whitney also is easy to take onscreen, when *The Bodyguard* arrives in theaters next winter.

Q *I recently read that Boris Yeltsin shocked the art world when he said that he knew the exact location of "the fabled Amber Chamber." What is this room, and where did it get its name? Also, what* makes it so valuable, and where do you suppose it is now?—Sarah Blanding, Ninilchik, Alaska.

A The Amber Chamber, as it is called by art historians, was an ornate room in a czarist palace near St. Petersburg. The name comes from its priceless, 18th-century translucent amber wall panels. Snatched from the Soviet Union by Nazi Army officers in 1942, its contents have been missing ever since. During a visit to Germany last year, Russian President Yeltsin stated that the treasure was hidden in a bunker under the city of Weimar. His words were greeted with skepticism, however, since German art experts have been searching for the room for decades with the same obsession that Indiana Jones pursued the Lost Ark—and with far less luck.

Q *I read that John Wayne, who presented himself as a superpatriot on and off the screen, was excused from service after Pearl Harbor even though he was only 34—still the prime of life, in my opinion. How come?—H. Grobe, St. Charles, Mo.*

A During World War II, men between ages 18 and 37 were required to serve in the military. However, deferments could be obtained by those who were physically or mentally unfit, by farmers and by the heads of large households. As the father of four, Wayne requested and received a deferment.

John Wayne

WALTER SCOTT'S
PERSONALITY PARADE®

September 13, 1992

Irving Berlin

Q *Is it true that after Irving Berlin died, a trunk was found in his house containing dozens of unpublished songs? Where is this music today?—Chris Martens, Delran, N.J.*

A During his long lifetime—the composer died in 1989 at age 101—Irving Berlin was known as both a musical genius and a brilliant businessman. He kept scrupulous files to protect his hundreds of copyrights. No trunk was found after his death, but scholars did discover a few unpublished pieces in those files. Since Berlin never failed to publish a song he thought would make money, these discoveries are probably not of the same caliber as "White Christmas" and "God Bless America." They're being studied, but there are no plans to publish at this time.

Q *Bo Derek was so stunningly memorable in the 1979 movie* 10, *then faded so completely from view. Can you explain how this glittering star fell from grace?—Diana Nedwitch, Fairfield, Conn.*

A After Bo (real name: Mary Cathleen Collins) romped through *10* in a skintight bathing suit and cornrow hairstyle, the five-foot-three former model put her career in the hands of her Svengali-like husband, John, a former actor once married to Ursula Andress and Linda Evans. Trouble was, John proceeded to cast his shapely blond wife in one raunchy flop after another. At 35, Bo is no longer in demand in Hollywood, though she recently finished a film in France called *Hot Chocolate*. Bo's 15-year marriage to John, now 66, has fared better than her career.

Q *I find singer k.d. lang's masculine appearance so disconcerting, I must close my eyes to enjoy her music. Is her appearance a big minus, or am I just being a prim old lady?—Harriett Craig, Forsyth, Ga.*

A Arrayed in her boots and butch haircut, the Canadian singer—born Katherine Dawn Lang 30 years ago in Consort, Alberta—no longer tries to hide her lesbianism. This may disturb some fans, such as yourself, but it hasn't hurt k.d.'s popularity any more than her espousal of vegetarianism (she's an active member of the "Meat Stinks" campaign) or her claim that she inhabits the reincarnated body of country music icon Patsy Cline.

Billy Graham

Q *I understand evangelist Billy Graham has a condition similar to Muhammad Ali's. Is it Parkinson's? What is the nature of this ailment? How is it treated or cured?—P.D. Smith, St. Louis, Mo.*

A During a checkup at the Mayo Clinic, Billy Graham, 73, was diagnosed as suffering from Parkinson's disease—a chronic-progressive nervous disorder marked by tremors and rigid muscles. No one knows its cause, and as yet there is no cure—only medication to treat the symptoms. Muhammad Ali, 50, suffers from Pugilistica Dementia, similar to Parkinson's disease. However, physicians believe

Muhammad Ali

the former heavyweight champ's slurred speech and trembling hands are not caused by a nervous disorder but rather are the result of the repeated blows to his head that Ali suffered while in the boxing ring.

Q *I've seen Jennifer Jason Leigh play a prostitute in three movies—*Last Exit to Brooklyn, The Men's Club *and* Miami Blues—*and a druggie in* Rush. *Though I'm a devoted fan of her hard-edged acting style, I know little about this talented woman. Where does she get the inspiration for her shocking roles?—David Jones, Detroit, Mich.*

A Jennifer Jason Leigh's parents, actor Vic Morrow and screenwriter Barbara Turner, divorced when she was two. At 18, Jennifer had herself legally declared an "emancipated minor" and moved out of her home. Two years later, while filming a helicopter scene for *Twilight Zone—The Movie,* her father was killed in a grisly accident. "Being witness to extreme pain is not something foreign to me," says the 30-year-old actress, who plays Bridget Fonda's psychotic roommate in *Single White Female,* her latest film. "And, in a certain way, I'm thankful for it. I can put it into a movie, and express it, and not live it."

Q *I know that President Bush and Gov. Bill Clinton are both left-handed. But is this the first time in our history that the presidential candidates of the two major parties have been lefties?—Wynn Loewenthal, New York, N.Y.*

A Yes. And by the way, if Ross Perot had remained in the race, he would have created a statistically improbable three-way, all-southpaw battle for the White House.

Kathie Lee Gifford

Q *I have this bet with my best friend. I say Kathie Lee Gifford of TV's* Live with Regis and Kathie Lee *is Jewish. My friend says she's not. Who is right?—Norma Manna, Hobe Sound, Fla.*

A Gifford calls herself "a Hebrew Christian." Her father, Aaron Epstein, was Jewish; her mother, Joan, is Christian; and Kathie Lee attended a Methodist Sunday school. When she was 12, however, Kathie Lee and her parents became born-again Christians. Now 39, she's not a regular churchgoer but says nightly prayers with her son, Cody, two. Incidentally, Kathie Lee's parents are still happily married after 40 years.

Q *I haven't heard any news recently about Amy Carter, the only daughter of President Jimmy Carter and his wife, Rosalynn. Has Amy graduated from college yet? Is she married? Does she have a career?—Doris Lindgron, Inglewood, Calif.*

A Amy Lynn Carter dropped out of Brown University in 1987 after two years, during which she was arrested twice at demonstrations against recruiting on campus by the CIA and against apartheid in South Africa. In 1988, Amy enrolled in the Memphis College of Art, from which she was graduated last December with a degree in painting. Now 24 and still single, Amy has yet to decide exactly what she wants to do. She'll probably enter graduate school.

Q *Christopher Walken has been cast as menacing weirdos in a number of movies, including* The Deer Hunter *and* Batman Returns. *What does the actor say about the way he's typecast?—K. Smith, Chicago, Ill.*

A It doesn't seem to bother him. Walken, 49, understands that his looks—pale skin, sunken eyes, lean frame—have ruled him out as a romantic leading man. "I tend to play mostly villains and twisted people, unsavory guys," says the actor, who won an Oscar for *The Deer Hunter* (1978). "If you're not really handsome and not really homely, they give you the villain part. That applies to me." Moviegoers, unfortunately, have seen little of his versatility onscreen. A native New Yorker, Walken is not only a stage-trained actor but also a song-and-dance man who began his career in an off-Broadway show with Liza Minnelli. His next project is the film, *Scam.*

Duchess of York surrounded by the Royal Family

Q *Now that it's clear to the entire world that the Duchess of York—last seen cavorting topless with a Texas millionaire—is guilty of totally outrageous behavior, what's preventing Queen Elizabeth from sending her packing?—Diane Jones, Fort Lauderdale, Fla.*

A The former Sarah Ferguson, 32, holds a couple of trump cards in her negotiations with Buckingham Palace. Fergie's daughters—Princesses Beatrice, four, and Eugenie, two—stand fifth and sixth in line of succession to the throne, and their mother must therefore be treated with royal protocol. The queen also has to worry that Fergie could retaliate by writing a kiss-and-tell book about the other members of the dysfunctional British royal family.

Q *I've heard many stories behind Phil Collins' song "In the Air Tonight." Is it true that it's about how his brother drowned at a party, and the host watched him die?—Adam Burnside, Glyndon, Minn.*

A The 1977 hit was inspired by a painful incident in Phil Collins' life—but not one concerning his brother. After the singer's first wife, Andrea, left him, he poured his heart into "In the Air Tonight." Collins explains: "People ask me, 'Aren't you embarrassed? You're putting your private life out for all to see.' It's like I oughtn't to let people see that I was hurt, that I cry, that I do 'unmanly' things. But I'm not embarrassed by it." Collins, 41, wed the former Jill Tavelman in 1984 and no doubt hopes this marriage doesn't end with another sad song—no matter how many records it might sell.

Q *In the controversial movie* Basic Instinct, *did Michael Douglas and Sharon Stone actually play those nude sex scenes? I contend that most, if not all, of those shots were performed by body doubles. Am I right?—Robert Ryan, Braintree, Mass.*

A The actors in those explicit scenes were the real McCoy. It was a matter of personal pride with Michael Douglas, who just turned 48—practically an old geezer by Hollywood standards—that he was still in such good shape that he didn't need a body double. As for the beautifully packaged Miss Stone, 33, she puts many body doubles to shame.

Michael Douglas and Sharon Stone

Bridget Fonda and Eric Stoltz

Q *As a fan of Bridget Fonda, I thought she was at the top of her form in the film* Single White Female. *There's something I've always wondered, however. Was growing up part of the Fonda family a plus or a minus for Bridget in Hollywood?—Don Parker, Cleveland, Ohio.*

A If there's such a thing as genes for acting, then Bridget Fonda, 28—granddaughter of Henry, daughter of Peter and niece of Jane—certainly inherited them. Bridget, whose parents divorced when she was eight, says she grew up feeling that her family name stood in the way of people taking her seriously as an actress. Now that she has become the most active Fonda in Hollywood, however, Bridget seems less sensitive. In fact, she and her boyfriend, actor Eric Stoltz, 31—former beau of Jennifer Jason Leigh, Bridget's psycho roommate in *Single White Female*—reportedly are talking about having a baby and passing on those Fonda genes to the next generation.

Q *What has happened to reporter Peter Arnett of CNN since the war in the Persian Gulf? I haven't seen him but once in the past year or so. Is he still active?—Peggy Gray, Blountville, Tenn.*

A For the time being, Peter Gregg Arnett, 57, has turned in his microphone for a word processor. Arnett is on a leave of absence from CNN while he writes an autobiography about his more than three decades of covering hot spots all over the globe.

Q *I recently saw Carol Channing on television with John Williams and the Boston Pops. Is it true that Carol carries her own food with her wherever she goes? If so, does she have food allergies or some other dietary restrictions?—Margot M. Engelman, Green Valley, Ariz.*

A Friends of Carol Channing joke that the musical-comedy star is almost as famous for her offstage eating habits as for her public performances. Channing, 71, has suffered for many years from an allergic reaction to chemicals used in food production and preparation. When on tour, she travels everywhere with special organic foods packed in silver Tiffany containers, and additional supplies are shipped to her by airmail—even if she's invited by the Queen of England to dinner at Buckingham Palace.

John Lennon

Q *The late John Lennon once said he wrote the song "Dear Prudence" for Prudence Farrow, who was the Maharishi Mahesh Yogi in India when the Beatles made their celebrated visit in 1968. Does Mia Farrow have a sister Prudence? Did Mia go along on the trip?—R.L. O'Brian, New York N.Y.*

A At 22, Mia (born Maria de Lourdes Villiers Farrow), who was then Mrs. Frank Sinatra, became interested in Eastern mysticism and traveled to India with her younger sister, Prudence, for a two-month course in transcendental meditation. While there, the pair met John, Paul, George and Ringo. Ringo went home after 10 days, complaining that the food was too spicy. Soon after, Mia became fed up with

Mia Farrow

the Maharishi and departed with her sister, who reclusiveness inspired John to write the lyrics, "Dear Prudence, won't you come out to play?"

Q *Can you clear away the smoke and shed some light on why the baseball owners wanted to fire Commissioner Fay Vincent? What was really behind this bitter dispute?—R. Sanders, Biloxi, Miss.*

A Mostly money. At least half of the 26 major league teams say they're in the red, and many of the owners viewed Francis Thomas Vincent, Jr. as a high-handed autocrat who added to their financial woes with his decisions on how to split the proceeds from the new teams in Miami and Denver and his plans to realign the National League. As Eddie Einhorn, co-owner of the Chicago White Sox, likes to say: "There's a game of baseball and a business of baseball."

Q *My generation grew up watching the Star Wars trilogy. We all know that James Earl Jones provided the voice of Darth Vader. But who was actually inside that flowing robe and shiny black helmet?—Dan Scoreby, Midvale, Utah*

A Dave Prowse, 56—a former professional weight-lifter who once billed himself as "Britain's Strongest Man"—stalked through those three Star Wars films as the sinister Darth Vader. He was chosen by director George Lucas, who recalled seeing him as a muscle-bound bodyguard in the 1971 movie *A Clockwork Orange*. Prowse also acted in such films as *Horror of Frankenstein* and *Hammerhead*, and for years he toured Great Britain as "The Green Cross Code Man," talking to kids about road safety. Prowse now owns a gym in London and raises funds for arthritis research.

Jack Nicholson and Rebecca Broussard

Q *I hear that Rebecca Broussard left Jack Nicholson for a younger man. Didn't they have a son just a few months ago? Is it possible the child wasn't really Jack's? What young stud won her away from the actor?—Leta Brehme, Churchville, Pa.*

A Broussard, 28—the mother of Lorraine, two, and Raymond, seven months—got fed up waiting for a proposal and left the 55-year-old actor in September. Some tabloids said the "younger man" was Jonathan Silverman, 26, her co-star in *Blue Champagne,* a film Nicholson co-financed. But more reliable sources identify him as actor Adam Storke, 29. Rebecca's bold move reportedly shocked Jack into asking her to return, with the promise of a wedding ring. As for Raymond's real father, a Nicholson spokesman says flatly: "It's Jack's son."

Q *Why doesn't the National Hockey League do something about the violence during games? It's obscene.—Doug Pollen, New York, N.Y.*

A The NHL does, in fact, have a rule allowing referees to eject a player who commits an illegal hit to his opponent's back. But it's not enough to deter the brutality that mars practically every game.

Two superstars, Wayne Gretzky and Mario Lemieux, have had serious back problems brought on by unwarranted violence, and Mike Bossy retired in 1987 because of a bad back. As usual, it all comes down to economics: Many fans want to keep hockey a blood sport. But, as Lemieux says, "If you eliminate the people who sell tickets, you're not helping the game."

Q *Is Bill Cosby really serious about buying the NBC-TV network from its corporate owner, General Electric? Or is this just another example of an ego-inflated star trying to get some publicity?—Jose Arnaud, Washington, D.C.*

A Cosby, who is worth an estimated $300 million, is dead serious about putting together a consortium of investors to buy the troubled network. The 55-year-old comic is upset by the way African-Americans are portrayed on TV and has been particularly critical of what he describes as NBC's "subversive" interference in the series *Here and Now,* produced by Cosby. The trouble is, even though the peacock network has dropped out of first place in the ratings, GE's asking price is still around $3.5 billion—a hefty sum even by Cosby's standards.

Renee Suran and Saul "Slash" Hudson

Q *How and when did guitarist Slash team up with Axl Rose to form Guns N' Roses? Has Slash kicked his drug habit? Does he have a steady girlfriend?—Maritza Traynor, Valley Stream, N.Y.*

A Slash (real name: Saul Hudson) was born in Britain to an English father and an African-American mother. In the mid-1980s—after his family moved to L.A.—Slash met Axl Rose, with whom he shared a love of rock music and a penchant for obnoxious public behavior. "Not being sexist or anything," Slash once boasted, "it's amazing how much abuse girls will take." Now 27, the guitarist has kicked his heroin habit, and in October he wed Renee Suran, 27, a model. But don't be deceived: Slash and his pal, Axl, remain as nasty as ever.

Q *While watching George Michael's latest video, "Too Funky," on MTV with my children, we had a heated dispute that I hope you can settle: I said that all the "women" prancing down the runway were, in fact, female impersonators. My son said that only some of them were men. Who's right?—Mrs. R. Gonzales, Fort Worth, Tex.*

A Your son is. The 29-year-old rock singer (real name: Georgios Kyriakou Panayiotou) used several female impersonators in his *"Too Funky"* video, including one named Lypsinka. However, Michael also cast some real females, among them the supermodel Linda Evangelista—who may not be too thrilled to hear that you thought she was a man.

Q *You see Isabella Rossellini in films and commercials for beauty products, but you don't hear much about her twin sister, Isotta. What became of this other daughter of Ingrid Bergman and Roberto Rossellini?—Anita Korpisy, Baltimore, Md.*

A Somewhere along the line, Isabella's fraternal twin sister—Isotta Ingrid Frieda Giuliana Rossellini—dropped the Isotta and now goes by Ingrid, her mother's name. At 40, she is a scholar working on her Ph.D. at Columbia University in New York City, where she also has taught Italian. A very private person, Ingrid is now married to an American named Richard Aborn, and they have a daughter, Francesca, two. She also has a son, Tomasso, 13, by her first husband, Alberto Acciatrito.

Isabella Rossellini

Julia Roberts and Jason Patric

Q *From what I hear, Julia Roberts' string of boyfriends—Kiefer Sutherland, Jason Patric and now Daniel Day-Lewis—has led her on a pretty wild chase. Is it true she's gone around the bend? And has she, as whispered, developed some sort of addiction?—David Goldman, San Antonio, Tex.*

A At 25, Julia Roberts is still a very impressionable young lady, and two of the actors you mention—Sutherland and Patric, both 26—may not always have provided the best environment for a serious actress. However, Day-Lewis, 35, an Oscar-winner who is into fitness and health, may have a steadying influence. As for addictions, you won't find any ugly facts about this *Pretty Woman.* The only substances Julia abuses are cigarettes and cappuccino—and lately she has been trying to give them up.

Q *I don't get it with Sade, the sultry soul singer. Every time she makes it with a big new song or album, she disappears off the face of the earth. Is this just my impression, or am I onto something here?—Mike Morman, Ashland, Ky.*

A You are correct. The Nigerian-born singer (real name: Helen Folasade Adu), 33, has gone into seclusion twice in her career—in 1985, after "Promise" topped the charts, and again in 1988, with the release of "Stronger Than Pride." As a result, she has been the target of rumors about drug addiction and nervous breakdowns. The real cause of her disappearances is far less dramatic: Sade (pronounced Shar-day) simply got fed up with the media pressure and wanted a hassle-free life.

Q *Sometimes I wonder if Woody Allen and Mia Farrow are trying to keep their feud alive because the publicity is good for business. How has the sex-and-child-abuse scandal affected their pocketbooks?—Ruth McDonnell, Chicago, Ill.*

A So far, Mia, 47, seems to be making out better financially than Woody, 57. Doubleday reportedly offered more than $3 million for her memoirs, and Mia has been talking to director Mike Nichols about starring in his next movie, *Wolf,* with

Woody Allen

Jack Nicholson. By contrast, the public turned thumbs down on Allen's latest movie, *Husbands and Wives,* which cost $15 million but looks like it will return only about $10 million to TriStar Pictures.

Q *One of my favorite films of the past few years was Bette Midler's For the Boys. I heard that a lawsuit was filed against Midler by Martha Raye, accusing Bette of stealing the idea for the film. Is that accurate?—Kim Riordan, Seymour, Conn.*

A Though the facts in the case are still in dispute, it is true that Martha Raye, 76, filed a $6 million lawsuit last July against Bette Midler, her production company, 20th Century-Fox and the producers of *For the Boys,* alleging that the 1991 movie—a major box-office flop—was ripped off from a written film treatment of Raye's life story. According to the comedienne's lawyers, Fox has admitted that the story was "inspired by Martha Raye's life." The studio, however, would not comment.

Q *Bill Clinton, who comes out of the South, talks like Jimmy Carter and even acts a little like him. In your opinion, is he going to be another Jimmy Carter?—Donna Hartman, Syracuse, N.Y.*

A Bill Clinton is no Jimmy Carter. Unlike the former peanut farmer from Georgia, who was an introvert and a Washington outsider, the president-elect is a genuinely gregarious individual who knows his way around the corridors of power in Washington. What's more, Clinton carefully avoided Carter's mistaken go-it-alone approach to the presidency. He has made a point of establishing a dialogue with the Democratic leadership in Congress, which should stand him in good stead when he begins trying to get his programs passed in the House and Senate.

Q *I'm a fan of TV's Montel Williams, and I understand that he recently remarried. What's his new wife's name? What does she do for a living? And is she a Caucasian or an African-American?—M.J. Crenshaw, Fort Worth, Tex.*

A Williams, 35, wed Grace "Bambi" Moerhle in Las Vegas last June. A onetime chorus girl in burlesque shows who gives her age as "twenty-something," Moerhle has appeared in two films—*In the Loop* and *American Me.* She is Caucasian.

Montel and Bambi Williams

PERSONALITY PARADE®

January 17, 1993

Linda Hamilton and James Cameron

Q *I've been waiting for news about one of my favorite actresses, Linda Hamilton, who rose to prominence in TV's* Beauty and the Beast *and hit it even bigger as the muscular heroine in the* Terminator *films. When is her next movie coming out?—Melissa Ordences, Miami, Fla.*

A After a long career that began in children's theater, Linda Hamilton, 36, has put away her greasepaint—and her barbells—for the time being. With a baby due this month, the actress has been staying at home and spending time with *Terminator* director James Cameron, reportedly the child's father. She also has been looking after her three-year-old son, Dalton, from her marriage to actor Bruce Abbott. "She'll make a decision about her next film" says Hamilton's manager, "after the baby comes."

Q *Is there any truth to the rumor that Susan Dey of* L.A. Law *once lit up the screen in an X-rated movie?—Michelle Clark, Oakland, Calif.*

A There's no substance to that story. Back in the late '70s, however, when Dey was trying to make the transition from her squeaky-clean TV role in *The Partridge Family* to mature feature films, she appeared as a sexpot in *First Love*, with actor William Katt. "I just stopped wearing clothes," she said of that experience. "Every day, we'd go to the studio and go to bed." When it was released in 1977, *First Love* got an R rating—not an X. Incidentally, the actress, now 40, has left *L.A. Law* and stars in a new series, *Love & War.*

Q *Where did Tipper Gore, wife of our next vice president, attend college? Did she ever hold a full-time job? And what issues do you think she will promote while her husband holds high office?—Anne Haulsee, Alexandria, Va.*

A The former Mary Elizabeth Aitcheson (she acquired the nickname "Tipper" when she was a year old), 44, has an undergraduate degree from Boston University and an M.A. from George Peabody College at Vanderbilt, both in psychology.

Tipper Gore

After marrying Albert Gore, Jr., she worked as a photographer for the *Tennessean* in Nashville. The mother of four—Karenna, 19, Kristin, 15, Sarah, 13, and Albert 3rd, 10—Tipper campaigned to have warning labels put on sexually explicit albums. Now that the record industry has volunteered to do so, friends expect Mrs. Gore to devote more time to the homeless and mental-health issues.

Q *How many children did Malcolm X have? Do any take after their father, in the sense that they publicly speak out in favor of policies to reform our society?—Shashika Johnson, New York, N.Y.*

A Malcolm X lived to see the birth of four daughters—Attallah, Qubilah, Ilyasah and Gamilah. Shortly after he was cut down by assassins' bullets in 1965, his widow, Betty Shabazz, gave birth to twin girls, Malaak and Malikah. Of his six daughters, 28-year-old Gamilah is the most outspoken. A rap artist, she had a hit with "America's Living in a War Zone," featuring excerpts from her father's speeches. Her message: "Before you can give money abroad, before you want me to fight in your wars, take care of home base."

Q *About that six-year, $43.75 million deal Barry Bonds recently signed with the San Francisco Giants: If he plays in every game of the regular sea-son, how much will he be paid each time he steps up to the plate?—A.M. Steiner, Milwaukee, Wis.*

A Under the terms of his record-setting contract, the 28-year-old Bonds will receive $7,291,667 a year. Assuming he comes to bat an average of four times in each of the team's 162 scheduled games, the Giants' outfielder will earn $11,253 every time he faces a pitcher.

Q *When and why did singers Kenny Loggins and Jim Messina break up? Weren't they successful as a team? How many big solo albums and No. 1 songs has Loggins had since he went out on his own? Is he married? And how involved is he in environmental issues?—D.C. Morin, Bristol, Conn.*

A Kenneth Clarke Loggins and Jim Messina, both 45, turned out two platinum and five gold albums in their six years together. In 1976, Loggins got married and decided it was time to pursue a solo career. Since then, he has gone platinum with four albums and had one No. 1 song, "Footloose." Last year, unfortunately—after two sons and a daughter—Loggins and his wife, Eva, also went solo. A dedicated environmentalist, the singer-songwriter does benefits for such groups as the National Park Service.

Kenny Loggins

Globe

Kevin Costner

Q *Tell me this about Kevin Costner: He's handsome, but not drop-dead handsome. He's a good actor, but no Spencer Tracy. So what explains his amazing appeal?—Paul Dannen, Chicago, Ill.*

A Not even the high-paid executives who run Hollywood's studios pretend to know the formula for stardom. However, Costner, who turned 38 last week, believes he understands one of the ingredients. "The secret," he says, "is in picking your script. If the writer gets the words down on paper right in the first place, they'll usually come out right when the actor says them on film."

Q *What's the story behind George Stephanopoulos, the Clinton campaign's handsome communications director with a face Bill Clinton described as "angelic funk"?—E. Jackson, Memphis, Tenn.*

A The son and grandson of Greek Orthodox priests, Stephanopoulos, 31, received a master's in theology from Oxford University—where, like President Clinton, he studied as a Rhodes scholar. Before emerging as one of Clinton's most influential advisers, Stephanopoulos served as an aide to House Majority leader Richard Gephardt and in Michael Dukakis' 1988 presidential campaign. By all accounts, the youthful bachelor has an ego to match his brains. He enjoys receiving notes from female admirers after his TV appearances, and he once had his hair styled by Christophe of Beverly Hills—Hillary Clinton's hairdresser.

Q *I'm a big fan of the up-and-coming female rap group TLC and would like to know more about its three talented members, including their ages and ethnic backgrounds. And while you're at it, what does TLC stand for—Tender Loving Care or something else?—Eve aul, Lutz, Fla.*

A TLC is an acronym for the first letters in the nicknames of the three African-American performers—T-Box, Left Eye and Chilli. T-Box (a hip-hop term for "The Boss") is Tionne Watkins, 22, from Des Moines. Left Eye is Lisa Lopes, 21, from Philadelphia. And Chilli is Rozonda Thomas, 22, who is part Puerto Rican and hails from Atlanta, where the group was discovered by Pebbles Reid, a singer well known in her own right.

Herbert Hoover

John F. Kennedy

Q *When he ran for president, Ross Perot promised that, if elected, he would accept no salary. My question is: Has there ever been a president who served in office without pay?—David C. Graham, San Diego, Calif.*

A Herbert Hoover and John F. Kennedy—two men who could hardly have been more different—shared one historic distinction: They were the only presidents who, on record, refused their White House salaries. Hoover donated his pay to charity, and Kennedy would accept no salary.

Q *My brother-in-law, a minister in Florida, says that CNN talk-show host Larry King is an ex-con. Is this true? And what were the charges?—C.D. Marshall, Moore Island, Ind.*

A Larry King, 59, never served time, but in 1971—when he had a talk show on Miami's top-rated radio station—he piled up heavy gambling debts and was charged with "misuse of funds" totaling $5,000. The case never went to trial, because the statute of limitations ran out, but King was fired and forced to declare bankruptcy. Asked today how the experience affected him, King says: "The fact that I paid for it was the best thing that happened to me . . . I'm sympathetic to people with pressure problems."

Q *I recently saw My Wicked, Wicked Ways, based on the life of swashbuckling movie idol Errol Flynn. Whatever became of the children he left behind?—Judy Dos Santos, Kaneohe, Hawaii.*

A Since Errol Flynn's death in 1959 from a heart attack at age 50, biographers have accused him of being everything from a homosexual to a drug addict to a Nazi agent during World War II. Flynn's daughters from his marriage to actress Nora Eddington—Deirdre, 48, a Hollywood stunt woman, and Rory, 45, a former model and photographer—have fought to clear their father's name. Flynn's marriage to another actress, Lili Damita, produced a son, Sean, an actor and photographer who was 29 when he disappeared in war-torn Cambodia in 1970 while on a magazine assignment. Flynn's youngest child, Arnella, 39, had a brief fling as a model before moving to Jamaica to help her mother, actress Patrice Wymore, work the family ranch.

Errol Flynn

Candice Bergen

Q *Candice Bergen of Murphy Brown supports the right of single women to have babies so long as there are—in her words—"commitment, caring and love." What can you tell us about her childhood that might shed light on her point of view?—Paul R. Koval, Santa Maria, Calif.*

A There is a lot of Brown in Bergen. As the child of ventriloquist Edgar Bergen—who was a cool and reserved father—Candice grew up with deep feelings of unworthiness. Perhaps to compensate for that early sense of powerlessness, Bergen learned to become the kind of independent woman who goes after what she wants. Now 46, she has achieved many of those goals through marriage to French film director Louis Malle, 60, with whom she shares a daughter, Chloe, seven—and family values.

Q *James Carville, the brilliant strategist who led the Clinton campaign—what is he up to now? And how did Bill Clinton come to choose him in the first place?—Nettie Grant, Tiltonsville, Ohio.*

A James Carville, Jr., 48—snapped up by the Democrats after masterminding Harris Wofford's come-from-behind Senate win in Pennsylvania—is on retainer for the Democratic National Committee and running campaigns for Gov. Jim Florio in New Jersey and Richard Katz for the mayor of Los Angeles. He's writing a book with his companion, Mary Matalin, who helped run the Bush campaign. He recently helped craft the president's economics speech to the nation, given before both houses of Congress, the cabinet and Supreme Court.

Q *I hear that the British Royal Family is, as they say in Merrie Olde England, down on its uppers. How bad off are they financially?—Howard Fisher, Detroit, Mich.*

A With a fortune estimated at several billion dollars, Queen Elizabeth II isn't exactly hard up. However, the British treasury is. Many of the queen's subjects resent having to pay taxes to support her family's plush lifestyle. But times are changing: The British Ministry of Defense announced that it might scuttle the royal yacht *Britannia*, a 375-foot vessel with a dining room that seats 100. Furthermore, the Queen will begin paying taxes in April. Estimates on the amount she'll pay range from $1.5 million to $3 million a year.

Q *Patti Hansen was once a big-time model. Then she went off and married Keith Richards of the Rolling Stones and totally vanished from sight. Has living with the rock 'n' roll "Prince of Darkness" taken its toll?—Lee Harris, La Mesa, Calif.*

A When Hansen exchanged vows with Richards atop a Mexican hill almost 10 years ago, few people gave their marriage much chance to last. But despite past bouts with heroin, Richards, 49, surprised everyone—including himself—and became a good husband and father. He dotes on their daughters Alexandra, six, and Theodora, eight, and putters around his Connecticut estate with Hansen, 36, who was the January cover model for *Mirabella* magazine. "We're a great couple, me and Patti," explains Richards. "You gotta have a good girl."

Keith Richards and Patti Hansen

Q *Why do middle-aged entertainment people like country music singer Kenny Rogers and his wife, Marianne—who should know better—get divorced after so many years of married life? Aren't these people mature enough to work things out?—Barbara Carter, Dan Diego, Calif.*

A Rogers, 54, and his wife of 15 years—the former *Hee Haw* TV star Marianne Gordon, 47—separated (though Marianne and their son, Cody, 11 are living on their Georgia farm) after three women had charged in a Texas court that Rogers enticed them to leave sexually compromising messages on a private telephone line. Rogers admitted that he did record such messages—but only from women who he said called "voluntarily." Talent for showbiz success differs from talent needed to hold a family together.

Kenny Rogers and Marianne Gordon

Q *During the past year, I have seen several movies featuring the actor Liam Neeson. He seems totally different in each role. Where is he from? Also, why has there been so much buzz about him lately?—Ray LaPierre, Weston, Mass.*

A Neeson, 40, is a 6-foot-4, Irish-born, Irish-trained stage actor who has turned in sensitive-hunk performances in Leonard Nimoy's *The Good Mother* and Woody Allen's *Husbands and Wives*. But he didn't become really well known until his name was linked romantically with Julia Roberts and Barbra Streisand. A bewildered Neeson asks, "Is that what's going to be on my tombstone? 'He dated Julia Roberts and Barbra Streisand'?" Doubtful, unless dating proves fatal!

PERSONALITY PARADE®

July 4, 1993

Johnny Cash

Q *Did singer Roseanne Cash use her famous father, Johnny, to get to the top of the music business?—Lauren Needham, Detroit, Mich.*

A "Roseanne never asked me to help with her career, never asked me for money," says proud papa Johnny Cash, 61. "She did all that on her own." Indeed, Roseanne, 37, has called upon incidents from her own troubled life as creative fodder for her songs. The child of a broken home, she survived a failed marriage to singer-songwriter Rodney Crowell, a bout with drug addiction, extended psychotherapy and rumors of lesbianism. There must be an easier way to get inspiration.

Q *My mother-in-law says Richard Gere was born and raised in Brooklyn, Pennsylvania I say it was Pittston. Who's right? And is it true he broke into films with no acting experience?—Roseanne Robbins, Pittston, Pa.*

A Gere, 43, was born in Philadelphia and raised on a farm near Syracuse, New York. After two years at the University of Massachusetts, he dropped out to work onstage. Gere starred in several Broadway plays before breaking into films in 1975. Explaining his move to Hollywood, the actor said: "A lot of what theater is doing is what it has been doing for centuries—dealing with a logical story, showing feelings, presenting the well-made play. The movies do that better now." He might have added that film stars make a lot more than stage actors, attract gorgeous models like Cindy Crawford and can plug their political causes at the Oscars.

Q *A couple of questions about the pairing of Dan Rather with Connie Chung on the CBS evening news: Did Dan really welcome her aboard as his co-anchor? And is Connie considered a first-class journalist by her colleagues?—Eric Noonan, Detroit, Mich.*

A Although Dan Rather, 61, and Connie Chung, 46, are old friends—and the veteran anchorman has been saying he looks forward to being able to get out of the studio and report more from the field—insiders say their pairing on the tube was a shotgun marriage. The CBS brass were upset that, although the network ranks first in the entertainment ratings, Rather has long trailed ABC's Peter Jennings on the nightly newscast. Rather's bosses finally got up the courage to tell him to make room at the anchor desk for the warm and fuzzy Ms. Chung, who scores high with viewers in popularity polls. As for her journalistic credentials, it is widely held among her colleagues that Connie has more of an eye for the TelePrompTer than a nose for hard news.

Q *Actress Karina Lombard steamed up my glasses during her sex scenes in the movie* Wide Sargasso Sea. *Now I hear that she's just as hot playing opposite Tom Cruise in* The Firm. *Is that really her up there on the big screen, or does she use a body double like Julia Roberts and the rest of them?—Henry Stevens, Chicago, Ill.*

A "No body double for me, thanks," purrs the 24-year-old sex kitten. If further proof is needed, just ask Mrs. Cruise, actress Nicole Kidman. She reportedly was so worried about the steamy beach scenes between her husband and Lombard—a one-time fashion model who is part Lakota Indian—that she insisted on being present on the set of *The Firm* every time Karina slithered into her string bikini.

Q *I have a terrible case of stage fright. Every time I speak in public, my heart pounds and my knees go wobbly. A friend says I'm far from unique—that this problem can strike even veteran performers. One name he mentioned was Barbra Streisand. Is my friend right?—Donna Harrison, Chicago, Ill.*

A Back in 1967, Streisand gave a concert in New York's Central Park despite a death threat she had received shortly before going onstage. "I forgot my words in front of 135,000 people," the singer later revealed. "I went blank." As a result of that experience, Streisand was stricken with stage fright and refused to appear before a live audience for two decades, though she continued to make movies. Today, Streisand—51 years old and reportedly worth $100 million—appears to have regained her old self-confidence. She now makes live appearances on behalf of liberal causes.

Globe

Barbra Streisand

Q *I often see the angelic face of Lucie de la Falaise in ads for Yves St. Laurent. Is that her real name? Is she related to the French designer? What can you tell us about her?—L.L., New York, N.Y.*

A Lucie de la Falaise (her real name), 20, is not related to St. Laurent, 57. But her Anglo-French family goes back a long way with the French fashion genius. Lucie's aunt Loulou—once a denizen of the Andy Warhol crowd—is St. Laurent's closest woman friend and was the inspiration for many of his clothing designs. Her grandmother, Maxime, was an international beauty who worked for *Vogue*. Lucie, the daughter of a furniture designer, takes dancing lessons and paints. And what does her family call this angelic beauty? "Muff."

Yves St. Laurent

Amy Irving and Steven Spielberg

Q *What's happened to my favorite actress, Amy Irving, since she and director Steven Spielberg were divorced? Has she remarried? Does she plan to return to a career in film?—Julie Davis, Lincoln, Neb.*

A When her 3 1/2-year marriage to Steven Spielberg ended in 1989, Amy Irving reportedly came away with a whopping divorce settlement of $100 million—the kind of money that makes an actress think twice before putting on the greasepaint. However, the 39-year-old star has never entirely stopped working. In the past four years, she has made two movies, *Crossing Delancey* and *A Show of Force*, appeared onstage in *The Heidi Chronicles* and served as host of a TV special on the exploitation of child laborers. In addition, Irving has had her hands full with two young sons: Max Spielberg, eight; and Gabriel Davis Barreto, three, her child by the Brazilian director Bruno Barreto, whom she married in 1990.

Q *Whenever I see Quincy Jones, he's with a different woman. Is he married with children?—E. Batie, Aurora, Colo.*

A Producer-composer-publisher Quincy Jones, 60, has been married three times and dated several beautiful women. For the last two years, he has been involved in a well-publicized relationship with the actress Nastassja Kinski, 33. In February, the couple had a daughter named Kenya Julia Miambi Sarah Jones—his seventh child, her third. Since then, Jones and Kinski reportedly have come close to calling it quits many times. When last

heard from, they were still living together. It seems only a matter of time, however, before Jones feels free to escort a new lady.

Q *What's the real story behind the strange choice of David Gergen—who was always associated with Republican presidents—as Bill Clinton's director of communications and counselor to the president? Is Gergen so brilliant that he can save a mistake-prone Democrat like Clinton from future blunders?—Howard Jones, Washington, D.C.*

A President Clinton has told friends that he blames the early disasters of his administration on poor White House communications. He hired David Gergen, editor-at-large of *U.S. News & World Report*, with one purpose in mind; to improve relations with the press corps. As a savvy Washington insider who knows how reporters value access to their sources, Gergen, 51, has invited selected journalists to the White House for lunches and dinners with the president. Though flattered, the journalists likely will continue to report the news—both favorable and critical—irrespective of the spin prescribed by "Dr. Gergen."

Q *What can you tell me about the late actor Leslie Howard? Have any books been written about him?—Angie Jones, Tuscaloosa, Ala.*

A Born Leslie Stainer in London in 1893, the son of Hungarian immigrants, Howard became an actor when a doctor suggested it as therapy for the shell shock he suffered in World War I. Howard made his first film in 1917 and earned Oscar nominations for *Berkeley Square* (1933) and *Pygmalion* (1938), but he is best known for his role as Ashley Wilkes in *Gone With the Wind*. Howard died in 1943 when the Nazis shot down his plane on a flight from Portugal, apparently believing Winston Churchill was on board. A good book on the actor is *A Quite Remarkable Father*, written in 1959 by his daughter, Leslie Ruth Howard.

Q *Jon Bon Jovi is back, and I'd like to know if he's still married. At his recent live performances, he wasn't wearing a wedding band. Is there trouble at home?—Lisa Kingsmill, Corvallis, Ore.*

A All those tabloid tales about the torrid romance between Cher and

Bon Jovi's lead guitarist, Richie Sambora, seem to have inspired stories about the band's leader, Jon Bon Jovi (real name: John Bongiovi), 31. But that's all they are —stories. Jon is still married to his childhood sweetheart, the former Dorothea Hurley, 30. Their first child, Stephanie Rose Bon Jovi, was born last May in Red Bank, New Jersey.

Q *I keep reading stories about how the dinosaurs in* Jurassic Park *have made mincemeat out of Arnold Schwarzenegger's* Last Action Hero *at the box office. Does this setback for Arnold mean his star is fading?—Howard Steiger, New York, N.Y.*

A "There's a gravitational law that goes beyond Newton," notes former box-office champ Sylvester Stallone. "No one stays on top. There has to be a fall." Arnold Schwarzenegger, who turns 46 next Friday, is the reign-

Sylvester Stallone

ing box-office champ and top-paid actor in Hollywood, guaranteed $15 million a picture. If *Last Action Hero* loses a bundle, as expected, look for heads to roll among the Columbia Pictures executives who greenlighted and supervised the $80 million project. Arnold's head, however, will not be among them. He, like the *Terminator*, will be back.

Arnold Schwarzenegger and Maria Shriver

Q *I've heard that Elvis Presley was one of the last big spenders. How much money did he leave when he died? And did it all go to his daughter, Lisa Marie?—Henry Frost, Los Angeles, Calif.*

A Nobody knows exactly how many millions Elvis earned during his career, but when he died in 1977 at age 42, the singer was down to his last $5 million. The money was left in trust to Lisa Marie, then nine, the only child of Elvis and his ex-wife, Priscilla. Thanks to wise investments by Priscilla, the Presley estate is now worth as much as $100 million—all of which was inherited by Lisa Marie on February 1, 1993, her 25th birthday.

Lisa Marie Presley

Alpha / Globe

Elvis Presley

Q *Harrison Ford stars in a remake of The Fugitive, but my all-time favorite is the man who made the original role such a big hit on TV—David Janssen. What is Janssen doing these days, and who's he married to?—Kimberlin Laks, Daytona Beach, Fla.*

A Sorry, but your favorite actor isn't doing anything these days. David Janssen died at age 48 on February. 13, 1980, under circumstances never adequately explained. Following a massive heart attack that may have been induced by an overdose of drugs, Janssen's body was discovered by his second wife, the former Dani Greco, in their Malibu home. Some believe there was a cover-up, and mystery still follows the star of *The Fugitive*, who lived in the fast lane and was a womanizer of leg-

endary proportions—even by Hollywood standards. Janssen's conquests included such stunning actresses as Angie Dickinson, Terry Moore, Joan Collins and Stephanie Powers.

Q *How many homes across America participate directly in the Nielsen TV ratings? Are the ratings accurate? And why are they important?—John Selinka, Atlanta, Ga.*

A Nielsen Media Research of New York, one of two companies that rank the popularity of TV programs (the other is Arbitron), uses 4,000 homes selected to mirror the latest U.S. Census data. Most network executives dispute the company's results, charging that they do not accurately reflect children, "channel surfers," bar patrons and split-screen watchers. Naturally, Nielsen defends its figures, which are used by advertisers to decide how to spend their money on TV—no small matter, as last year's total was nearly $23 billion. The fact is that the Nielsen ratings may be flawed, but so far no one has come up with a better system.

Q *What can you tell us about the recording artist RuPaul, who performs the hit song "Supermodel"? Age? Height? And how did he/she get into the cross-dressing game?—M.S., San Diego, Calif.*

A Born in New Orleans, RuPaul Andre Charles was reared in San Diego and Atlanta. Inspired by Diana Ross and other performers, he broke into the New York drag-queen club scene nine years ago. RuPaul insists he's 28 (though friends say he's older), six feet five (though that may include the spike heels) and just an average red-blooded American male (though other males might argue with that assessment). "So many children can't go home, because their families won't accept them" RuPaul says in defense of his chosen way of life. "Hopefully, by my coming out and being who I am, I can shed some light on what the lifestyle is like, which is just like anybody else's."

Q *People say that the Clintons, Bill and Hillary, have a good sense of humor and that this helps them cope with tough times. Can you tell us one of their favorite jokes?—Hedda Brown, Detroit, Mich.*

A James Carville—the witty "Ragin' Cajun" who, as chief political strategist, is credited with guiding the Arkansas governor into the White House—recalls the

following exchange, which got a laugh from the Clintons: The new president was being criticized for trying to give his wife a government job. "Heck, if I weren't married to Hillary, she'd be first in line for any of these appointments," declared the president. To which Carville replied, "Heck, if you weren't married to Hillary, you wouldn't be making any of these appointments!"

Q *With the death of Rudolf Nureyev, Mikhail Baryshnikov remains unchallenged as the greatest living male dancer of his time. But very little is ever written about his private life. Why doesn't he dance ballet anymore? How many children does he have? Is he married?—S.B., San Diego, Calif.*

A At 45, Mikhail Baryshnikov is old enough to be the father of some of today's leading dancers. Nonetheless, thanks to his discipline and training, the Russian-born star is still able to perform brilliantly—as he demonstrated most recently on a national tour with the choreographer Twyla Tharp. "Misha" has never married. However, he has three children: Alexandra, twelve, by the actress Jessica Lange; and Peter, three, and Anna, one, by dancer Lisa Rinehart.

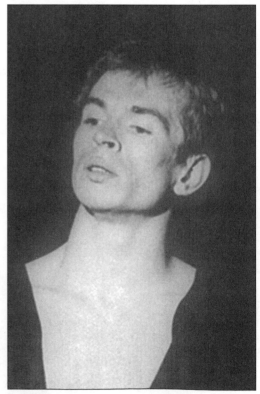

Rudolf Nureyev

WALTER SCOTT'S
PERSONALITY PARADE®

September 19, 1993

Sean Connery

Q *I recently returned from a vacation in Europe, where rumors were rife about Sean Connery. As best I could make out, the reports said Connery was suffering from a fatal illness. Is there any truth to this alarming talk?—Herbert Ackerman, Atlanta, Ga.*

A Stories about Sean Connery dying of cancer began in Europe when word leaked out that the 63-year-old Scottish actor was seeing a doctor for a serious condition called dysplasia, an abnormal cell growth, in his throat. Properly treated, however, dysplasia is not considered life-threatening. Connery does not comment, but his wife, Micheline, 62, swears the superstar is "fit as a fiddle." You can take her word for it.

Q *I read that supermodel Christy Turlington just broke up with her "boyfriend" of six years. But I thought she was married to a real-estate agent and that the tattoo on her ankle had his initials. What's the real story?—Lucille Gannon, Brooklyn, N.Y.*

A Turlington, 24, has never been married. However, she did recently end a six-year relationship with Roger Wilson, an actor-screenwriter in his 30s, whose initials are tattooed on her right ankle. The

daughter of an El Salvadoran mother and an American father, Turlington currently is not dating anyone because, her spokesman says, "Christy is busy modeling 300 days a year."

Q *My husband and I happened to catch an old movie the other night called* The Big Clock. *Imagine our surprise when we discovered that this film had almost the exact same plot as one of our favorite recent movies—Kevin Costner's* No Way Out. *This couldn't just be a coincidence, could it?—Amanda Croushore, Annandale, Va.*

A It's no coincidence. The 1987 Costner film was a remake of the 1948 thriller starring Ray Milland, Charles Laughton and Maureen O'Sullivan, which in turn was based on a 1946 novel by Kenneth Fearing titled *The Big Clock*. For all

Kevin Costner

their similarities, however, the golden oldie doesn't contain anything like the window-steaming scene between Costner and actress Sean Young in the backseat of a limousine, which made *No Way Out* a cult classic.

Q *Angie Dickinson—now there's a glamorous star from the past whom I can still get excited about. Is she working as an actress? Married? Children? And what about all those affairs she had with famous men?—Gerald A. Black, Pomona, Calif.*

A The twice-divorced Dickinson (real name: Angeline Brown) has a daughter, Nikki, 26, from her marriage to songwriter Burt Bacharach. Now single and 61, the long-stemmed actress always has gotten more publicity out of her reported liaisons with famous men like John Kennedy and Frank Sinatra than from any innate acting ability. She readily admits loving the public eye, saying: "I don't miss being on television, I miss being 'important.' " She has a small role in the new film *Even Cowgirls Get the Blues*, which will be out this fall.

Q *I'm a big fan of Wilson Phillips, and I heard the group might be breaking up. Any truth to this? If so, can you tell me the cause and what the ladies are planning to do?—E. Barthlow, Columbus, Ind.*

A The truth is that Wilson Phillips' last album, "Shadows and Light," was a big disappointment, and the trio canceled a tour because tickets didn't sell as well as expected. Wendy Wilson, 23, and big sister Carnie, 24, are planning to record a Christmas album and possibly another disc without Chynna Phillips, 25. Wendy also is considering a career in writing. Chynna is thinking seriously of returning to acting. And Carnie, who wants to act and do voice-overs, says: "I'll admit it's a high-stress job. I'm 24, and I feel like I'm 40." Despite their individual aspirations, the singers' record company denies rumors of a breakup and insists the three will perform together next year.

Q *Wherever I look, I see that stars like Barbra Streisand, Robert Redford and Michael J. Fox are directing movies. Since when does being an actor qualify you to sit behind the camera? What's this new trend all about anyway?—H. Baker, Milwaukee, Wis.*

A Actors have been sitting behind the camera since silent days, when Chaplin and some other stars decided to direct as well. A trend has developed in recent years, however, because of the fierce competition among Hollywood studios to win the allegiance of big box-office stars. By allowing the Streisands, Redfords and Foxes to direct, studio executives hope to sign them to star in movies as well. Incidentally, Streisand, 51, did an impressive job as director of *Prince of Tides*. Redford, 56, won an Oscar in 1981 for his directing debut, *Ordinary People*, and got good reviews last year for *A River Runs Through It*. It remains to be seen how Fox, 32, does next year when the actor gets his first chance to direct for the big screen with the comedy *30 Wishes*. Fox has directed some episodes of TV's *Brooklyn Bridge* and a short film shown on David Letterman's show.

Charlie Chaplin

Michael J. Fox

WALTER SCOTT'S
PERSONALITY PARADE®

January 16, 1994

Jordy Lemoine

Q *Somebody recently told me about Jordy, a French kid who's burning up the record charts all over Europe. What can you tell me about him? Is he really only 5?—Elizabeth Hackworth, Yorktown, Va.*

A Jordy Lemoine, who turned six on January 14, has sold more than three million copies worldwide of his disco/pop hit *"Dur Dur D'Etre Bebe!"* (titled "It's Tough To Be a Baby!" in America). The son of a French record-producer father and a deejay mother, Jordy literally was born into the business. He now lives part of the year in the U.S., where his parents plan to exploit his popularity with a line of Jordy clothing, school supplies and, naturally, more records. No wonder this busy boy sings, "It's tough to be a baby."

Q *One of my favorite female singers of all time was Karen Carpenter. Whatever happened to her brother, Richard? Did he ever write a book about Karen and the Carpenters?—Janet Hart, Tampa, Fla.*

A Richard Carpenter retired from the spotlight after his sister—who struggled for years against anorexia nervosa, a serious eating disorder—died of a heart attack in 1983 at age 32. A decade later, he's living in California off the income generated by the Carpenters, the most popular brother-and-sister act since Fred and Adele Astaire. In their heyday, the Carpenters sold 60 million albums and had 16 consecutive Top 20 songs. Now 47, Richard hasn't written a book yet, but he does devote himself to preserving the Carpenters' legacy by reissuing their hits in anthologies, such as the recent "Yesterday Once More."

Q *A few questions about Rosie Perez: Where is she from? How old? How was she discovered? Who is she dating?—Giovanni Williams, Sebastopol, Calif.*

A Perez was born out of wedlock in the Bushwick section of Brooklyn, New York. She has 10 brothers and sisters—some full, some half. The actress tells reporters she's "under 25," but she also admits lying about her age. Some relatives have displayed a birth certificate that would make her 29. Perez says she was dancing in an L.A. nightclub when director Spike Lee tried hitting on her. "He says he wasn't, but he was," she insists. Nevertheless, Lee cast her in his 1989 film *Do the Right Thing*, in which she made her screen debut as Tina. Perez, who just finished filming *Cop Gives Waitress $2 Million Tip*, is seriously dating the rapper K7.

Q *Would you tell us what's at the root of the dispute between Axl Rose and his ex-girlfriend, model Stephanie Seymour? Why don't these two settle their dispute in private?—Danielle Evans, Dallas, Tex.*

A It's a tangled story. Rose, 31, demanded that Seymour, 24, return $100,000 worth of jewelry, including an engagement ring, and other gifts. The pugnacious rock singer also said his former fiancée threatened to release a photo of herself with a black eye, so he covered his flanks by filing a suit charging that Seymour attacked him with a kitchen chair at a 1992 Christmas party in his Malibu home. The slim Victoria's Secret model denied the whole affair—including their engagement. Rose later dropped his demands that Seymour return the jewelry

Axl Rose and Stephanie Seymour

and gifts. Now they say the items will be sold, with the proceeds going to charity. Clearly, these two are interested in only one thing: winning all the publicity they can get.

Q *Sean Penn was incredible as the stoned lawyer in* Carlito's Way. *Where has he been hiding? Will we be seeing more of him again on the screen? Does he still carry the torch for Madonna?—Dorothy Whiteley, Hixson, Tenn.*

A Penn, 33—perhaps most famous for punching out photographers and others during his 3 1/2-year marriage to Madonna—currently is mourning the loss of his Malibu home, which burned down in California's recent fires. But he isn't pining for Madonna or his past life. Though he agreed to act in *Carlito's Way* because he couldn't pass up the opportunity to work with Al Pacino and director Brian DePalma, Penn intends to devote himself exclusively to directing. His first effort, *The Indian Runner,* was a critical if not commercial success in 1991. He's now directing his second film, *Crossing Guard,* starring Jack Nicholson and Robin Wright, Penn's live-in girlfriend.

Sean Penn and Robin Wright

Q *I've heard that a small army of 500 people is being paid to work on the president's controversial health-care plan. How much do they cost us taxpayers? And what does Mrs. Clinton get for leading this effort?—Elise T. Bowman, Chaptico, Md.*

A The White House says the Health Care Task Force employs 10 to 15 people full-time. It is true that hundreds have worked on the Clinton health plan, but many were unpaid volunteers or loaners from other government agencies. There is no way to estimate their total cost to taxpayers. Even if their salaries, travel and other expenses amounted to millions, however, it would be only a tiny fraction of America's 1993 health expenditure, estimated at $903 billion. As for Hillary Rodham Clinton, federal law prohibits the president's wife from receiving any financial compensation.

Keanu Reeves

Q *As a fan of film star Keanu Reeves, I've made it my business to know a lot about him—including the fact that his first name is Hawaiian and that many critics don't think he can act worth a darn. What I don't know is: Is it true that Keanu is part of a rock band that has toured America and overseas?—Daria Smith, Bloomington, Ind.*

A When Keanu Reeves isn't working in films like Bertolucci's *Little Buddha*, which opens this spring, the 29-year-old actor plays bass guitar in a Los Angeles rock band called Dogstar. "It's just a hobby," says Reeves' publicist. "The band is like a release for him—he thinks he can get up onstage and just have fun, but of course everyone recognizes him." Dogstar, which consists of a bunch of Reeves' old friends, has played around California but never has gone on the road for an extended tour. The actor has another hobby, however, that does take him out on the road. He rides a classic 1972 Norton 850 Commando motorcycle.

Q *On TV, I've noticed on several occasions that President Clinton attends Sunday church services without his spouse and daughter. Is that for security reasons? Do Mrs. Clinton and Chelsea attend different services? What are the religious affiliations of the First Family?—M.J. Drahl, Hackettstown, N.J.*

A President Clinton was raised a Baptist and continues to be a member of that denomination. Hillary Clinton considers herself a Methodist. They generally attend church services together with 13-year-old Chelsea. Photographers often focus exclusively on the president as he leaves church, however, giving the misleading impression that his wife and daughter are not in attendance.

Q *One of my favorite actors is Christopher Walken, who recently has played wonderfully villainous creepy characters in movies like* True Romance *and* Wayne's World II. *Am I right that he once had an affair with actress Susan Sarandon, Tim Robbins' live-in lover, and that Walken is as temperamental in real life as he appears to be on the screen?—Linda Strauss, Oakland, Calif.*

Thon and Walken

A Sorry to disappoint you, but you're wrong on both counts. Those rumors about Walken, 50, having a steamy affair with Sarandon, 47—his co-star in a 1982 PBS film directed by Jonathan Demme, *Who Am I This Time?*—are totally unfounded. On the contrary, the actor has been happily married for 24 years to the former Georgianne Thon, a dancer and casting director. They have no children. As for being temperamental, Walken, who won an Oscar as Best Supporting Actor for the 1978 film *The Deer Hunter*, is considered by his colleagues to be one of the easiest professionals to work with in all of Hollywood.

Q *Leona Helmsley, the "Queen of Mean"—is she still in prison? And what about her husband, Harry? How does he put up with her?—Robert Larson, Gordon, Wis.*

A After a month behind bars in 1992 in Lexington, Kentucky, Mrs. Helmsley spent 17 months in a Connecticut prison for evading federal taxes. ("Only the little people pay them," she said.) Leona, 73, then did a short stretch at a halfway house in New York City before being released late last year under the supervision of a probation officer. Her long-suffering husband, whose real-estate empire is worth about $5 billion, said he was "thrilled" to have Leona home. At 84, however, Harry's health is failing, and perhaps he only remembers the good times.

Q *I thought of myself as a true basketball fan until Larry Bird retired last year. Now I find that I'm losing interest. I'd like to know why he retired and how much money he gave up by leaving the game.—Ronda Gillespie, Flora Vista, N.M.*

A Bird, 37, retired after 13 years and three world championships with the Boston Celtics because of severe back problems that required bone-fusion surgery on his lower spine. When he walked off the court for the last time on August 8, 1992, after playing with our Olympic "Dream Team," Bird still had two years to go on a three-year, $10 million contract with the Celtics. Precise figures are not publicly available, but it's safe to say Bird will continue to cash in on his legendary status in the years to come—making millions as a consultant to Celtics Executive Vice President Dave Gavitt and as a spokesman for such products as Converse footwear, Spalding sporting goods and McDonald's.

Q *It's hard to keep up with all the new talk shows. I just started watching* The Bertice Berry Show *and became an instant convert. Where did Berry come from all of a sudden?—Laura Carter, Lynchburg, Pa.*

Bertice Berry

A You're right about the glut of TV talk shows. The dreadlocked, boisterous Bertice Berry, 33, has a more colorful background than most of the mob trying to ride the Phil-and-Oprah gravy train. The sixth of seven children of a poor single mother in Wilmington, Delaware, Berry earned a Ph.D. in sociology and became a popular professor at Kent State. She later went on the college lecture circuit by day and, encouraged by her students, tried the comedy clubs at night. Berry eventually was interviewed on the Oprah Winfrey show, where a TV producer, Steve Clemens, spotted her and suggested that Berry become a talk-show host herself. The idea was sold to 20th Television, which put her syndicated show on the air last September. People compare her to Oprah, Berry says, "because we're African-American women with thighs larger than Barbie's."

Snoop Doggy Dogg

Q *There are three things I'd like to know about Snoop Doggy Dogg, the accused murderer whose album "Doggystyle" hit the top of the charts: Where did he get his Southern accent? How tall is he? And, in his song "Deep Cover," what is the meaning of this phrase: "I'm lettin' my gat pop/'Cuz it's 1-8-7 on an undercover cop"?—Doris Pinkus, New York, N.Y.*

A Snoop Doggy Dogg (real name: Calvin Broadus), 22, was born in Long Beach, California, but picked up a Southern twang from his Mississippi-born parents. He is not only the hottest of the so-called "gangsta rappers" these days but also, at 6 feet 4, probably the tallest. In the lines you quote, "1-8-7" is Los Angeles police slang for homicide, so the phrase means that the narrator—Snoop himself—is boasting about shooting an undercover cop to death. Unconscionable lyrics like these lead some critics to predict that it will soon be "1-8-7 on gangsta rap." Snoop and two others were indicted by a grand jury and pleaded not guilty to charges that they shot a man to death last summer in an L.A. park. A pretrial hearing is scheduled for March 11.

Q *President Clinton was elected with only 43 percent of the popular vote, but he obviously got a majority in the Electoral College. Has a candidate ever won a plurality of the popular votes but actually lost in the Electoral College?—Walter Gaskins, Phoenix, Ariz.*

A There have been three cases where a candidate won the popular vote but not the White House: Andrew Jackson lost out to John Quincy Adams in 1824. (Jackson even won a plurality in the Electoral College—but not the required majority, since the vote was split among four candidates. The decision then went to the House of Representatives, which chose Adams.)

Samuel J. Tilden lost out to Rutherford B. Hayes in 1876. And Grover Cleveland lost out to Benjamin Harrison in 1888.

Q *I've heard that Hollywood's definition of a blockbuster is any movie that makes more than $100 million. How many of these big winners were there in 1993?—Rita Thompson, Rochester, N.Y.*

A Tom Sherak, executive vice president of 20th Century-Fox, says Hollywood defines a blockbuster as a film that takes in $100 million or more in U.S. ticket sales. Of the 408 movies distributed by Hollywood studios last year, seven broke the blockbuster barrier: *Jurassic Park* ($337.8 million in U.S. tickets sales), *The Fugitive* ($179.3 million), *The Firm* ($158.3 million), *Sleepless in Seattle* ($126.5 million), *Aladdin* ($117.9 million), *Indecent Proposal* ($106.6 million) and *In the Line of Fire* ($102 million).

Q *I've followed John Malkovich ever since his film debut in* The Killing Fields. *Still, nothing prepared me for his incredible performance as the assassin in* In the Line of Fire. *What can you tell me about his private life that might help explain his art as an actor?—Krissy Weidmer, West Palm Beach, Fla.*

Michelle Pfeiffer

A A huge talent like Malkovich's can never be explained away. The actor is a rugged individualist who often works without a toupee and steadfastly refuses to have his teeth fixed to win leading-man roles. Malkovich says he got his dark side from his dad, who had "a major temper." Unlike many screen stars, he's not "politically correct"—he favors capital punishment and blames the homeless for their own plight. Malkovich, 40, was married from 1982 to 1988 to actress Glenne Headly, 38, and had an affair with Michelle Pfeiffer, 36, his co-star in the 1988 film *Dangerous Liaisons*. He has lived for several years with Nicoletta Peyran, an Italian-born scholar of Asian culture. They have a daughter, Amandine, three, and a son, Loewy, one.

Q *I've been following the up-and-coming tennis star Mary Pierce. Is it true that, after years of being coached by her father, they have had a falling out? If so, will this*

affect her performance on the court?—Evan Davis, Fort Meyers, Fla.

A Jim Pierce often was heard yelling at his daughter from the players' box and even threw a bag at her after she lost a tennis match in Italy two years ago. Last spring, after repeated outbursts against officials and players during Mary's matches, the volatile Mr. Pierce, 57, was ejected from the French Open and subsequently barred from future tournaments by the Women's Tennis Association. In addition, Mary—who is now ranked No. 12 worldwide and trains with Nick Bollettieri in Bradenton, Florida—obtained a legal restraining order forbidding her father from interfering in her life. Since then, 18-year-old Mary has played some of the best tennis of her young career, including upsets of Martina Navratilova and Gabriela Sabatini, and earned nearly $350,000. Jim Pierce reportedly has said he's through trying to control his daughter's tennis game, and the two met in Florida at Christmas.

Q *What's the real story behind the decision by the powers-that-be at* Beverly Hills, 90210 *to dump Shannen Doherty from the show? So she's a temperamental star. So she's late sometimes. Is that any reason to get rid of a first-rate actress?—Stuart Fisher, New York, N.Y.*

A Many actors are habitually tardy, but Doherty reportedly was late a total of 23 hours during the last TV season, costing thousands in production losses, The "90210" cast—including Luke Perry and Jason Priestley—also complained about her tardiness. Despite all that, producer Aaron Spelling and his staff asked the 22-year-old star to meet with them to discuss a new contract. On the appointed day, however, Shannen was late again and was kicked off the show. She now says she quit and accuses her former co-stars of tardiness.

Shannen Doherty

PERSONALITY PARADE®

July 3, 1994

Abraham Lincoln

Richard Nixon

Ronald Reagan

Q *Until Richard Nixon passed away recently, was it the first time in U.S. history that our country had five former presidents alive at the same time?—Bob Reardon, North Adams, Mass.*

A No. When Abraham Lincoln took office in March 1861, there also were five living former presidents: Martin Van Buren, John Tyler, Millard Fillmore, Franklin Pierce and James Buchanan. Ten months later, membership in that exclusive club fell to four, with the death of Tyler. It took 131 years for the phenomenon to occur again—when Bill Clinton entered the White House, and the roster of living former presidents included Richard Nixon, Gerald Ford, Jimmy Carter, Ronald Reagan and George Bush.

Q *I'd really appreciate some facts about the young movie actor who starred in* School Ties, *played the cave man in* Encino Man *and was so memorable in* With Honors. *How old? Who's he dating? What's next?—K.M., Pinellas Park, Fla.*

A The actor you're referring to is 25-year-old, six-foot-two Brendan Fraser, who has won good notices from film critics even though the quality of his movies hasn't been all that good. Born to Canadian parents, Fraser studied acting in Seattle, then moved to Los Angeles, where he quickly landed film roles. The actor lives in a rented loft in West Los Angeles, avoids the club scene and currently is dating a young woman whose name he prefers to keep out of the press. Fraser's next film is *Airheads*, due out in August, in which he's the leader of a rock group that takes over a radio station.

Q *Can you update me on those stories about people who died in hospital emergency rooms and whose bodies emitted a gas or an odor that made the hospital staff ill? I'm not looking for plagues or anything, but I would like to know one thing: What could cause such an odor of death?—Kathy Morgan, Austin, Tex.*

A California health officials still are baffled by the strange case of Gloria Ramirez, a 31-year-old mother of two, who may have emitted toxic fumes while she lay dying in the emergency room of Riverside General Hospital on February 10. Six hospital employees fell sick—one seriously—while treating Ramirez, and some of them later reported that an ammonialike smell came from her blood. A lengthy autopsy so far has failed to turn up any conclusive evidence. The woman's family charges that she has been unfairly characterized as a "toxic monster." John Duncan, a spokesman for the State Department of Industrial Relations, said that it is continuing to investigate the causes.

Q *I think Melissa Etheridge is one of the great female rockers of our time. What was the most important musical influence on her career? And is it true that she's dating Lou Diamond Phillips' former girlfriend?—C.S., Cincinnati, Ohio.*

A When Melissa Etheridge was growing up in Leavenworth, Kansas, she found inspiration on the AM-radio rock stations and from her father's extensive record collection. As for her sexual orientation, the 32-year-old singer is openly gay, but she tries to appeal to the largest possible audience. "I've had to compromise and say, 'I love you,' instead of 'I love her,' because that limits the song," explains Etheridge. "That 'straight' woman in Poughkeepsie is listening to my record and thinking about her boyfriend. But I've always wanted to be truthful, so I'm not going to sing, 'I love him.' " Etheridge's longtime lover is Julie Cypher, 30, a music-video director who was divorced from the actor Lou Diamond Phillips in 1991 after four years of marriage. Etheridge and Cypher live in Los Angeles.

Q *After rereading Richard Bach's* The Bridge Across Forever, *written with Leslie Parrish back in 1984, I'm wondering whatever became of Bach and his soulmate.—S.B.G., Corvallis, Ore.*

A Richard Bach, 58, author of *Jonathan Livingston Seagull*, lives on an island off of Oregon with Leslie Parrish-Bach, 59, an actress best known for the film *The Manchurian Candidate*. From their home, they respond: "We continue our gentle adventure together. Our vows to disappear and our promises never to write another book have held for years . . . but sometimes they waiver. " The two wrote One in 1988.

Q *Whatever happened to the whale in last year's film* Free Willy? *I've heard that he was seriously injured. Is he still in captivity? How has the film studio shown its responsibility toward this poor animal?—Jane M. Johnson, West Cornwall, Conn.*

A Confined to a small dolphin tank in a Mexico City amusement park, Keiko—the 21-foot, 7,000-pound orca whale that played Willy—is in declining health. His dorsal fin has collapsed, his bottom teeth are worn down from gnawing on the sides of his tank, and he has a chronic skin infection. Warner Bros.—now shooting a sequel, *Free Willy 2*, again starring young Jason James Richter but with a different whale—has spent $500,000 on Keiko's care. But the studio seems powerless to rescue the whale from his owners. Michael Jackson, who wrote and performed the theme song of *Free Willy*, also was trying to rescue Keiko. The singer wanted to move the whale to his Neverland Ranch in California, but he had to put those plans on hold to concentrate on fighting the child-molestation charges against him. Some marine biologists warn that, unless Keiko is released to the wild within four years, he will die. Others contend that, after a life in captivity, the whale will be unable to survive in the wild.

WALTER SCOTT'S
PERSONALITY PARADE®

September 25, 1994

Q *I was really impressed by Cameron Diaz in* The Mask. *In addition to being very pretty, she has a natural acting talent and a strong presence on film. What can you tell us about her background and her plans for the future?—Frank Bonilla, Riverside, Ill.*

Carrey and Diaz

A A native of Long Beach, California, Diaz had been modeling for five years when she picked up *The Mask* script from her agent's desk. Coaxed into auditioning for a part, she landed the female lead—a lounge floozy who falls for Jim Carrey. Though she has resumed modeling, Diaz was bitten by the acting bug and is busy pursuing a film career. Perhaps to avoid typecasting, the vivacious 22-year-old is considering a role as a victim of Lou Gehrig's disease. With her exotic looks (a mixture of Native American and Cuban), Diaz should make it in Hollywood. But if things don't work out, she can always go back to her first love: zoology.

Q *We always hear conflicting reports about Mickey Rourke and Carré Otis. Are they still married? Living together? Or what?—T.N., Dallas, Tex.*

A Otis recently announced a return to modeling—a sign that the roller-coaster romance is over. The pair first made headlines when Rourke picked Guess? jeans model to co-star in his steamy 1990 film *Wild Orchid*. Carré subsequently quit modeling, acquired a set of tattoos, accidentally shot herself while handling a gun on the set of one of Mickey's movies and married her man in June 1992. When his screen career took a nosedive and he began making a fool of himself in the boxing ring, some reports said the marriage was on the rocks. Last month, the conflicting reports turned to reports of conflict: Rourke, 41, was charged with slapping and kicking Otis, 24. She apparently has had it up to her tattoos with her scrappy husband—in fact, it's said Otis had those tattoos surgically removed.

Q *Sen. Alfonse D'Amato has taken a holier-then-thou attitude toward the president and White-water and Mrs. Clinton and her commodity investments. But doesn't he have his own problems with the appearance of impropriety?—Ella Zeitz, West Palm Beach, Fla.*

A The problems of Alfonse D'Amato (R., N.Y.), 56, go beyond mere appearance. The Senate Ethics Committee reprimanded him in 1991 for conducting his office in an "improper and inappropriate manner" after his brother, Armand, used the senator's stationery to lobby for a defense contractor who paid Armand $120,000 between 1986 and 1988. D'Amato denied any knowledge of Armand's actions and never was charged with breaking the law. More recently, it was revealed that, like Mrs. Clinton, D'Amato made a killing in investments—$37,000 in one day in 1993—when a stock he owned went public. At this writing (again, like the First Lady), there's no evidence he broke any law.

Q *I've been following the fine work of Harvey Keitel for 20 years. I'm sorry to hear that, while his career is soaring since* The Piano, *he's having lots of personal problems. Can you explain why there's so much upset in his private life?—J.G., Bethlehem, Pa.*

A It's a sordid story. Keitel, 55, is locked in a bitter fight with his ex-lover, actress Lorraine Bracco, 39, for custody of their eight-year-old daughter, Stella. Keitel sued after learning that Bracco's current husband, actor Edward James Olmos, 47, had been accused of fondling Stella's 14-year-old babysitter during a trip the family took to Florida last year. Olmos insists the girl fabricated the tale about him after being spurned by his 17-year-old son. Nonetheless, Keitel continues to fight for full custody of Stella, arguing that she should be removed from the reach of an accused child-molester. Bracco says Keitel is "motivated by jealousy and hate," and Olmos calls him "vicious and disturbed." The only one who hasn't been heard from is little Stella, the victim of all this "adult" bickering.

Lorraine Bracco and Edward James Olmos

Q *Something has been puzzling me: Why has David Letterman yet to make any reference to O. J. Simpson? In the past, he has found time to joke about Tonya Harding, Erik and Lyle Menendez, Amy Fisher and Lorena Bobbitt. Is there some reason O. J. is missing for Dave's hit list?—Ann Irwin, Wheat Ridge, Colo.*

A When Howard Stern appeared on Letterman's show shortly after the Simpson case became a national obsession, the shock-jock tried to tell a few O. J. jokes but floundered badly when he got no help from host. "Double homicide does not crack me up," Letterman later explained—though that hadn't kept him from making comments about the Menendez double-murder trial. His reticence regarding the Simpson case is puzzling, given Letterman's reputation for the outrageous and the fact that his rival, Jay Leno, has done O. J. jokes. Maybe Madonna had it right when, during her controversial guest appearance in March, she accused the new Dave of playing it safer than the old late-night Letterman.

David Letterman

Q *What accounts for the insights into politics provided so effortlessly by Cokie Roberts, one of the panelists on* This Week With David Brinkley? *Has she written any books? Does she have any political aspiration?—Brenda Schueler, Westport, Wash.*

A When it comes to politics, Mary Martha Corinne Morrison Claiborne Boggs Roberts is to the manner born: She's the daughter of Rep. Hale Boggs (D., La.), whose plane disappeared in 1972, and his wife, Lindy, who took over his House seat and held it until 1990. Her brother, Tommy, is a Washington lobbyist; and her sister, Barbara, was mayor of Princeton, New Jersey, until her death in 1990. Cokie, 50, has been married for 27 years to journalist Steven V. Roberts, 51, and has two children—Lee, 26, and Rebecca, 24. She hasn't written any books and laughs at the notion of political office, saying: "I don't expect anyone wants me to run!"

Q *I keep hearing reports that Kevin Costner is going to retire from Hollywood to regain some privacy for himself and his family. It would be a shame if we lost him from the big screen. Is there any foundation to the rumors?—Mary E. Moore, Salinas, Calif.*

Kevin Costner

A Kevin Costner, 39, has no intention of giving up his triple-threat career as actor, director and producer. He reportedly is earning $14 million for his role in the futuristic adventure film *Waterworld*, scheduled for release next year. It is true, however, that he was stung by the failure of *Wyatt Earp*, this summer's biggest box-office bomb, and that he wants to take a break from acting for a year. Some published reports suggest that it was his wife, Cindy, 39, who insisted that the actor focus on family duties and their three children rather than work. A sabbatical also may quiet other rumors, not related to retirement: At times during their 16 years of marriage, the Costners have had to weather gossip about the stability of their union.

Q *What is the real story on Melba Moore? I heard she is broke and that Freddie Jackson won't have anything to do with her. If he hadn't been discovered by her, he would still be singing in small nightclubs.—Arnitta Baxter, Carmel, Ind.*

A Regarding her financial status, it's true that Melba Moore, 49, applied for welfare benefits last December—with a camera crew from a tabloid TV show in tow—but it's completely untrue that singer Freddie Jackson has abandoned his friend. "They have a great personal relationship," says a spokesman for Jackson. Moore's recent troubles stem from her bitter 1993 divorce from Charles Huggins, who also was her manager. She has publicly accused Huggins of cheating her out of her share of their management company. He, in turn, has accused Moore of violating a nondisclosure clause in their divorce settlement and has filed a multimillion-dollar libel suit against her and the publications that reported her accusations. While the courts try to sort out all the acrimony, the singer-actress, who won a Tony Award in 1970 for the musical *Purlie*, has returned to the stage in a road-show revival of *Anything Goes*.

Q *Is Rose Fitzgerald Kennedy, the mother of our slain president, still mentally alert? How does she pass her days? And can you tell us if Rose was made aware of Jackie's death?—J.J., Salem, Ore.*

A The matriarch of the Kennedy clan turned 104 in July and is extremely frail. Laurence Leamer, author of the recently published book *The Kennedy Women*, reports that Mrs. Kennedy is unable to speak and manages to communicate only by nodding. However, she still enjoys Irish songs, visits from family and friends, and watching documentaries about her famous offspring (specially edited, with all the tragic episodes carefully excised). Rose never got along that well with Jackie, but Leamer says she nonetheless was spared the news on May 19 when her daughter-in-law died of cancer at age 64. During the funeral on May 23, however, CNN reported that Mrs. Kennedy was watching on TV.

Q *I caught Alicia Silverstone in the movie* The Crush. *When can I look forward to seeing this beautiful actress again? While you're at it, fill us in on her background.—G.D., Virginia Beach, Va.*

A Her debut last year as a sexually obsessed teen in *The Crush* was trounced by critics and ignored by moviegoers, but Silverstone has gone on to achieve small-screen stardom as the voluptuous vixen in Aerosmith's last three music videos. Born to English parents and raised in San Francisco, Alicia, 17, studied ballet before switching full-time to acting. She receives many offers to play jailbait roles. Last month, Alicia starred in *The Cool and the Crazy* on Showtime cable TV. She soon will pad her brief resume with three film projects: *The Babysitter*, with George Segal; *The Hideaway*, with Jeff Goldblum; and *True Crime*, with Kevin Dillon.

Q *Tom Hanks won the Oscar as Best Actor for 1993 for* Philadelphia. *Now he looks like a shoo-in to be nominated for* Forrest Gump. *Has the Oscar ever been awarded to the same actor in two consecutive years?—Norma Vasquez, Perris, Calif.*

Tom Hanks

A Two actors have earned back-to-back Oscars: Spencer Tracy won Best Actor for *Captains Courageous* (1937) and *Boys Town* (1938); and Jason Robards, Jr. won Best Supporting Actor for *All the President's Men* (1976) and *Julia* (1977). Two actresses also have scored twice in a row: Luise Rainer won for *The Great Ziegfeld* (1936) and *The Good Earth* (1937); and Katharine Hepburn won for *Guess Who's Coming to Dinner* (1967) and *The Lion in Winter* (1968), when she shared the award with Barbra Streisand for *Funny Girl*. The Great Kate also won for *Morning Glory* (1933) and *On Golden Pond* (1981), making her the only performer with four Oscars.

Katharine Hepburn

Q *I understand that Phil Collins and his wife, Jill, are divorcing after 10 years of marriage. Why?—Cathy Timmerman, East Dubuque, Ill.*

A "I am not in love with my partner anymore" is the way Collins, 43, explains his split from the former Jill Tavelman, 38, mother of his five-year-old daughter, Lily. Still, the Genesis drummer and singer could have found a gentler way to inform his wife about his waning ardor than by sending her a fax demanding a divorce. Some think Collins is going through a midlife crisis. He recently announced that he'd had an affair with Lavinia Lang, whom he called "The pivotal woman in my teenage years." The two were engaged more than 20 years ago, but nothing is likely to come of the rock star's rekindled love for his old flame, since (1) Lang, 43, strongly denies having any affair with Collins, and (2) her husband, Bret Hudson, a TV producer and the father of their two children, says he and Lavinia "plan to be together for the rest of our lives."

Elvis Presley

Lisa Marie Presley and Michael Jackson

Globe

Q *Given all the bad publicity he got as a result of the child-molestation charges, I can understand why Michael Jackson wanted to marry Lisa Marie Presley. What I can't quite grasp is why she wanted to marry him. Can you help?—R.G., New Bedford, Mass.*

A Not even their closest friends pretend to understand the strange chemistry between the King of Pop and the daughter of the late King of Rock (does that make her the Princess?). Privately, however, some friends suggest a connection between Lisa Marie's childhood and her motive for marrying Michael. They say the only offspring of Elvis Presley would have a natural affinity for someone like her father, who was not only the most popular entertainer of his era but also a sexually immature man with childlike hobbies and tastes. That description, they hardly need to point out, fits Michael Jackson to a tee. It's also clear that Lisa Marie, 26, didn't have to worry that Michael 35, was marrying her for her money—and vice versa.

Q *I've been fascinated by Brad Pitt ever since Thelma & Louise. Can you tell us why he hasn't become a bigger star?—S.B., Baton Rouge, La.*

A His memorable roles in *Thelma & Louise* and *A River Runs Through It* proved Pitt has what it takes to be a major movie star: a combination of Robert Redford looks and James Dean talent. But he has been careless with his career—confusing movie-goers with too many different kinds of roles, including a grungy serial killer in *Kalifornia*. Nevertheless, Hollywood is suddenly abuzz with talk that Pitt's performance in the eagerly awaited *Interview with the Vampire* is so powerful, he may end up stealing the movie from Tom Cruise. He'll follow that film with *Legends of the Fall*, co-starring Anthony Hopkins and Aidan Quinn. One sign that, at 30, Pitt's star may be rising: His asking price has doubled to $3.5 million, according to David Geffen, producer of *Vampire*.

Q *I seem to remember hearing that Ella Fitzgerald was quite ill and that some surgery had been required. What was the nature of her operation? And how is she now?—Gordon Reeder, Culver, City, Calif.*

A The jazz world's "First Lady of Song" had both legs amputated below the knee because of complications from diabetes. The surgery took place in 1993 but was not revealed until last April. Sadly, Ella has had health problems for years, including cataract surgery in 1971 and a quintuple coronary bypass in 1986. She lives in Beverly Hills, frail but still an indomitable spirit at 76.

Q *Now that Nirvana's Kurt Cobain is gone, I understand Dave Grohl and Krist Novoselic plan to continue the band. Is this true? If so, what is the status of Nirvana?—Jennifer Bayer, Kalamazoo, Mich.*

A After Cobain took his life with a shotgun last April, drummer Grohl and bass player Novoselic tried to put together an album of the grunge trio's live recordings. They've abandoned their efforts for now, however, because the death of singer-guitarist Cobain is "still obviously a little tender for them," says their spokesman. Instead, the two decided to put out an album recorded during Nirvana's "Unplugged" special on MTV, plus two songs not aired on the show. It will be released next month by DGC Records. As for the group, a spokesman says sadly, "There is no more Nirvana." Grohl, 25, and Novoselic, 28, have called it quits.

Q *Why was Amy Locane let go from Melrose Place? And does she regret not being on that hit TV show anymore?—M.T., Syracuse, N.Y.*

A After its less-than-successful debut on Fox in 1992, the producers decided that what *Melrose Place* needed to appeal to post-college viewers was more sex. "Hotter" characters were introduced in 1993—including, most noticeably, Heather Locklear as Amanda, the show's new bad girl. It also was decided that Amy Locane's character, the aspiring actress Sandy Harling, had run its course after 13 episodes. Even though *Melrose Place* went on to become a huge hit, Locane says she has no regrets about her departure. Making movies has always been a top priority for the 22-year-old actress, who already had the films *School Ties*, *Lost Angels* and *Cry-Baby* under her trim belt before joining the "Melrose" cast. Since leaving the series, the blue-eyed blonde has appeared as Jessica Lange's daughter in *Blue Sky* (a film shot back in 1991) and as Brendan Fraser's girlfriend in *Airheads*.

Q *I'd like to know if any of the top decision-makers in TV are women. Who is the highest-ranking female executive in television today, and what is her position?—Marcia Ross, San Diego, Calif.*

A When it comes to the four major TV networks, it's still a man's world at the top. One bright exception: Lucie Salhany, 48, who was chairman of Fox Broadcasting for about 17 months—until she left to become head of the fledgling United/Paramount network, which is scheduled to start up in January. Women fare better in the up-and-coming world of cable TV, where more than a dozen hold important positions. Among the most powerful people on the production side of TV, three are women: Linda Bloodworth-Thomason, 46 (creator of Delta Burke's new show, *Women of the House*); Diane English, 45 (*Murphy Brown*); and Marcy Carsey, 49 (*Roseanne*).

WALTER SCOTT'S

PERSONALITY PARADE®

December 4, 1994

Q *For some time now, I have been attempting to locate John Lennon's grave. No one seems to know where it is. Can you help me out?—B.R., Columbia City, Ind.*

John Lennon

A After the 40-year-old former Beatle was fatally shot in front of his Manhattan apartment on December 8, 1980, Lennon's widow, Yoko Ono, decided to have his remains cremated. Although the ashes of the British-born rock star are said to be in the U.S., Ono has refused to reveal where they're kept. "She didn't want to create an environment that would be like Elvis' or Jim Morrison's grave," said one of Ono's publicists. But she did finance a public memorial where Lennon's fans can pay their respects— Strawberry Fields, a 2.5-acre site in Central Park, not far from the spot where he was shot. It features a marble mosaic with the word "Imagine," the title of one of Lennon's finest songs.

Q *Barbra Streisand is my favorite entertainer. However, I've heard that her mother lives a meager existence while Barbra enjoys great wealth. Is this true?— Jane Austin, Clayton, N.M.*

A The story you've heard appeared in *Her Name Is Barbra*, an unauthorized biography by Randall Riese. He wrote that the entertainer keeps her mother in a rundown condo and sends $1,000 a month in support. In response, Streisand—who reportedly is worth more than $100 million—says simply that "the book contains gross inaccuracies." In fact, Barbra's mother, Diana Kind, lives in a Beverly Hills apartment described as "spacious, lovely and well-decorated" by a close friend, who adds that the 85-year-old widow "wants for nothing, including a full-time housekeeper/companion." Barbra's half-sister, Roslyn Kind, stays with their mother when in town. Streisand, 52, only recently began to speak openly about her strained relationship with her mother. She says her mother failed to praise her while she was growing up in Brooklyn, which left her with a huge inferiority complex. "We get along better now," Streisand told an interviewer. "We're able to say, 'I love you.'" Her father, Emanuel Streisand, died in 1943, and her mother married Louis Kind in 1949.

Q *Any truth to the rumor that Robert Plant and Jimmy Page are planning to revive Led Zeppelin and go on tour?— Marc Bohn, Alexandria, Va.*

A Aging rockers Plant, 46, and Page, 50, insist that the days of Led Zeppelin ended when drummer John Bonham choked to death in 1980 after a drinking binge. Plant and Page reunited for an MTV "Unplugged" special that aired this fall and are scheduling a world tour for February, but the third surviving member of the band—bassist John Paul Jones, 48—says the two didn't even tell him of their plans. "Maybe I might have joined them, and maybe I wouldn't," he adds. "But I think it was a bit discourteous of them not to say anything at all."

Q *Gene Kelly recently had a stroke, and I'm sure that his many millions of fans would like to know how he is doing. Also, is this his first or second stroke?— M.P., Bakersfield, Calif.*

A The 81-year-old performer—best known for his acrobatic dancing in *Singin' in the Rain* and other film musicals of the 1940s and '50s—was released from UCLA Medical Center in September after treatment for a stroke. That stroke, on July 23, was Kelly's first. He had been hospitalized only two months before, however, for a case of cellulitis, a bacterial infection, in his right leg. Age and illness have left him in frail condition, though a spokesman does say that Kelly is "coming along nicely." The film star lives in Beverly Hills with his third wife, the former Patricia Word, 40, in an identical copy of his previous home on that site, which was destroyed in a Christmas tree fire in 1983.

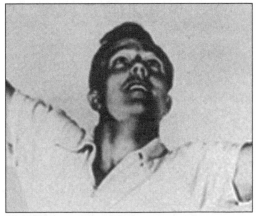

Gene Kelly

Q *I've heard of the Medal of Freedom and the Presidential Medal of Freedom. What's the difference? Who awards them? And for what service are they awarded?—Joe Fletcher, Sacramento, Calif.*

A The Medal of Freedom was established by President Truman in 1945 to honor American and foreign civilians who had "performed a meritorious act or service" outside the U.S. that aided this country in wartime on or after December 7, 1941. After 1952, it

Margaret Thatcher

was presented for acts "during any period of national emergency." It could be awarded by the secretary of state or various military officials. In 1963, it was replaced by the Presidential Medal of Freedom as our highest nonmilitary award. The medal is now given annually by the president to people recommended to him for their contribution to (1) the security or national interests of the U.S., (2) world peace or (3) cultural or other significant public and private endeavors. To date, more than 300 persons—from Margaret Thatcher to Lucille Ball—have received the Presidential Medal of Freedom.

Q *What can you tell us about the talented comic Adam Sandler, who appears on* Saturday Night Live? *Who was the greatest influence on his career? And what can we expect from him in the future?—Chau Nguyen, Bowling Green, Ohio.*

A The 27-year-old comic, who grew up in Manchester, New Jersey, has emerged as one of the most popular members of *Saturday Night Live*, which was raked over the coals by critics last season for being especially unfunny. Having survived an overhaul of the 19-year-old show this summer, Sandler has settled in for his fifth season on "SNL" while branching out into records and movies. He has a hit comedy album called "They're All Gonna Laugh at You," and he starred as a brainless rock musician in the summer film *Airheads*. This month, Sandler will appear with Steve Martin, Juliette Lewis and Madeline Kahn in *Mixed Nuts*, directed by Nora Ephron. Sandler says the greatest influence on his career was the comic Rodney Dangerfield—to whom he gives a lot of respect.

Q *It has been well documented that all three major candidates for President in 1992—Bill Clinton, George Bush and H. Ross Perot—were left-handed. How many lefties actually have been elected to the highest office in the land? And am I correct that none of those left-handed presidents ever served a second term?—W.R. Pfortner, Valatie, N.Y.*

George Bush

A You are correct. Only five of the 41 men who served as president were southpaws: James Garfield, Harry Truman, Gerald Ford, George Bush and Bill Clinton. Garfield was shot by an assassin at age 49 and died on Sept. 19, 1881—less than a year into his first term in office. Truman, who completed three years of Franklin Roosevelt's fourth term plus four years of his own, chose not to run for a second full term in 1952. Ford, who ascended to the presidency upon the resignation of Richard Nixon, lost his bid for a full term to Jimmy Carter. And Bush became a one-term president when he was defeated at the (left) hand of Bill Clinton, who now appears to have an uphill battle if he hopes to avoid the southpaw curse in 1996.

Q *After fine performances in such films as* Boyz N the Hood *and* Malcolm X, *Angela Bassett scored a breakthrough as Tina Turner in* What's Love Got to Do with It. *I just saw the video. Did she go through any special training or preparations for that role? And what will she do next?—J.W.D., York, Pa.*

A Angela Bassett, 35, recently finished filming *Strange Days*, a thriller scheduled for release next fall, in which she plays Ralph Fiennes' lover. The actress—who earned two drama degrees from Yale and spent years on the New York stage—prepared for the rigorous Turner role by whipping herself into physical shape. She worked out with free weights and went on a month-long diet of skinless chicken breasts, broccoli and brown rice. During filming in 1993, she fractured a hand. She also had to soak her feet in ice between takes of "Proud Mary," the most demanding musical number in the movie. "I felt like someone was beating me with a piano toward the end," says Bassett. But it did earn her an Oscar nomination as best actress.

Q *I'd be interested in hearing how Kevin Costner is doing after the painful separation from his wife. Has he begun to get over it? And is there another lady in his life?—Barbara Adams, Ypsilanti, Mich.*

A Friends say Costner, 39, is still devastated by the upheaval in his personal life. He and his college-sweetheart wife, Cindy, 38, had struggled to save their marriage amid the stress of frequent separations and constant rumors of Kevin's womanizing. Their separation last October followed reports of his affair with Michelle Amaral, 35, a Hawaiian hula dancer and mother of three, on the set of Costner's latest film, the financially troubled *Waterworld*. Amaral and her husband have denied the reports. In the final analysis, however, it wasn't any watery affair that sank Kevin's marriage to Cindy, who stands to come away with an $80 million divorce settlement. It was the job. In the past, the actor often invited his wife and children (Annie, ten, Lily, eight, and Joe,

Kevin Costner

seven) to join him on location. But it apparently became harder to juggle family and filmmaking. When Cindy reportedly pressured him to take a sabbatical, Costner—a workaholic who has expressed concern that he only has a few good years left to play romantic leading roles—chose his work over his wife.

Q *I'm a longtime admirer of Frank Zappa and his family. I recently heard that the rights to all of his music were sold. If it's true, to whom and for how much? And why?—Dave Konstantin, San Diego, Calif.*

A In 1993, shortly before his death from cancer at age 52, Zappa arranged to sell the rights to his recordings. Ryko, a Massachusetts-based record label, acquired the Zappa catalog—more than 60 discs—as part of a $44 million expansion last October. "It was Frank's expressed desire to have them sold," says Rob Simonds of Ryko. "He didn't want his wife burdened with the record business." But Gail Zappa still holds the publishing rights to her husband's songs. Incidentally, Frank Zappa—one of rock's great experimental artists—was equally creative at naming his children. His sons are Dweezil,

25, and Ahmet Rodin, 20; his daughters are Moon Unit, 27, and Diva, 15.

Q *With the success of* Interview with the Vampire, *will we see other Anne Rice books made into movies?—Michael Jordan, Madison Heights, Va.*

A It's a pretty safe bet that we'll be seeing more Anne Rice novels on the big screen. David Geffen, who produced *Interview*, owns the rights to *The Vampire Lestat* and *The Witching Hour*; and Carolco Pictures owns the rights to *The Mummy*. All are in the early stages of development. If *The Vampire Lestat* gets the go-ahead, the 53-year-old author would like to write the script. "I'm being told 'no,'" she says, "but I'm knocking on the door repeatedly." As for *The Mummy*, Rice has been taking a survey on who should star. Her answering machine asks callers: "Do you think Antonio Banderas could play the mummy?" The Spanish heartthrob helped to make a hit out of *Interview*, in which he plays the vampire Armand.

Q *In my opinion,* The Tonight Show *has become a poor imitation of David Letterman's* Late Show. *Is Letterman still holding his own against Jay Leno's challenge?—Susan Kay, Las Vegas, Nev.*

A Despite Leno's redesigned set, closer camera angles and surprise guests, Letterman still leads with an average Nielsen rating of 5.6 vs. 4.7. But *The Tonight Show* has been making progress since the season began in September, closing the gap to as little as .1 in some weeks. Veteran TV experts say Leno's rise is largely due to the strength of NBC's prime-time lineup—especially on Thursday nights, with *ER* providing a big lead-in. Most viewers would agree with you that Dave is still the freshest face on late-night TV.

David Letterman

INDEX